Pro Spring MVC:

With Web Flow

Marten Deinum
Koen Serneels

**with Colin Yates, Seth Ladd,
and Christophe Vanfleteren**

**Foreword by Erwin Vervaet,
Spring Web Flow project founder**

Pro Spring MVC

ISBN-13 (pbk): 978-1-4302-4155-3

ISBN-13 (electronic): 978-1-4302-4156-0

Trademarked names, logos, an d images may app ear in this book. Rather than us e a trademark s ymbol with every occurrence of a trademarked name, logo, or image we use the names, logos, and images only in an editorial fashion and to the benefit of the trademark owner, with no intention of infringement of the trademark.

The use in this publication of trade names, tr ademarks, service marks, and similar terms, ev en if th ey are not identified as such, is not to be ta ken as an expression of opinion as to whether or not they are subject to proprietary rights.

While the advice and information in this book are believed to be true and accurate at the date of publication, neither the authors nor the editors nor the publisher can accept any legal responsibility for any errors or o missions that may be made. The publisher makes no warranty, express or implied, with respect to the material contained herein.

President and Publisher: Paul Manning
Lead Editor: Steve Anglin
Technical Reviewers: Manuel Jordan
Editorial Board: Steve Anglin, Ewan Buckingham, Gary Cornell, Louise Corrigan, Morgan Ertel, Jonathan
    Gennick, Jonathan Hassell, Robert Hutchin son, Michelle Lowman, James Markham, Matthew Moodie, Jeff
    Olson, Jeffrey Pepper, Douglas Pundick, Ben Renow-Clarke, Dominic Shakeshaft, Gwenan Spearing, Matt
    Wade, Tom Welsh
Coordinating Editor: Jennifer L. Blackwell and Stephen Moles
Copy Editors: Patrick Meader and James Compton
Compositor: Bytheway Publishing Services
Indexer: SPi Global
Artist: SPi Global
Cover Designer: Anna Ishchenko

Distributed to the book trade worldwide by Springer Scie nce+Business Media New York, 233 Spring Street, 6th Floor, New York, NY 10 013. Phone 1-800-SPRINGER, fax (201) 348-4505, e-mail orders-ny@springer-sbm.com, or vi sit www.springeronline.com.

For information on translations, please e-mail rights@apress.com, or visit www.apress.com.

Apress and friends of ED book s may be purchased in bulk f or academic, corporate, or promo tional use. eBoo k versions and licenses are also available for most ti tles. For more information, reference our Special Bulk Sales–eBook Licensing web page at www.apress.com/bulk-sales.

Any source code or other supplementary materials referenced by the author i n this text is av ailable to re aders at www.apress.com. For detailed inf ormation about how to lo cate your book's source code, go to www.apress.com/source-code.

To my wife for your love and endless support.

–Marten Deinum

To Sonja Korte, die große liebe meines lebens, thank you for your patience and support. You almost made me believe in automatically refilling coffee mugs. To mum and dad, for always being there for me and buying an 80386 instead of that 8bit NES.

–Koen Serneels

Contents at a Glance

▓ Foreword.. xvi

▓ About the Authors.. xviii

▓ About the Technical Reviewer xx

▓ Acknowledgments xxi

▓ Introduction xxiii

▓ Chapter 1: Configuring a Spring Development Environment 1

▓ Chapter 2: Spring Framework Fundamentals 25

▓ Chapter 3: Web Application Architecture... 51

▓ Chapter 4: Spring MVC Architecture.. 65

▓ Chapter 5: Implementing Controllers... 107

▓ Chapter 6: Implementing Controllers — Advanced 177

▓ Chapter 7: REST and AJAX... 215

▓ Chapter 8: Resolving and Implementing Views 237

▓ Chapter 9: Testing Spring MVC Applications 273

▓ Chapter 10: Spring Web Flow 321

▓ Chapter 11: Building Applications with Spring Web Flow 373

▓ Chapter 12: Advanced Spring Web Flow.. 429

▓ Chapter 13: Spring Security... 477

▓ Appendix: Cloud Foundry: Deploying to the Cloud 535

▓ Index 555

Contents

Foreword... xvi

About the Authors.. xviii

About the Technical Reviewer xx

Acknowledgments xxi

Introduction xxiii

Chapter 1: Configuring a Spring Development Environment 1

Prerequisites...1

    Java Development Kit...2

    Servlet Container 2

    Integrated Development Environment 2

The Sample Application 2

    A Bookstore Sample Application 3

    The Build System..4

    Building the Sample Application...6

    Deploying the Sample Application..8

SpringSource Tool Suite (STS)..10

    Configuring STS for Gradle projects 10

    Importing the Sample into STS...12

    Running the Application on the SpringSource vFabric tc Server............................17

    Editing the Application...19

Summary 22

■ Chapter 2: Spring Framework Fundamentals 25

The Spring Framework 25

Dependency Injection 29

ApplicationContexts 34

Resource Loading 38

Component-Scanning 40

Scopes 41

Profiles 41

Enabling Features 44

Aspect-Oriented Programming 45

Web Applications 47

Summary 50

■ Chapter 3: Web Application Architecture 51

The MVC Pattern 51

Application Layering 53

Separation of Concerns 56

Spring MVC Application Layers 56

The Domain Layer 56

The User Interface Layer 57

The Web Layer 58

The Service Layer 59

The Data Access Layer 62

More Roads to Rome 63

Summary 64

■ Chapter 4: Spring MVC Architecture 65

DispatcherServlet Request Processing Workflow 65

The Workflow 66

The Request Processing Summary 73

The DispatcherServlet 74

Bootstrapping the DispatcherServlet 74

Configuring the DispatcherServlet 78

The Spring MVC Components 88

HandlerMapping 88

HandlerAdapter 94

MultipartResolver 96

LocaleResolver 97

ThemeResolver 99

HandlerExceptionResolver 101

RequestToViewNameTranslator 102

ViewResolver 103

FlashMapManager 104

Summary 105

Chapter 5: Implementing Controllers..107

Introducing Controllers 107

Interface-based Controllers 108

Annotation-based Controllers 110

Configuring View Controllers 111

Request-Handling Methods 112

Supported Method Argument Types 115

Supported Method Argument Annotations 118

Supported Method Return Values 123

Writing Annotation-based Controllers.. 125

A Simple Login Controller 125

Book Search Page 130

Book Detail Page 133

Data Binding 136

    Customizing Data Binding 137

    Per Controller Customization 139

    ModelAttributes 141

    Type Conversion 148

    Validating Model Attributes 162

Internationalization 170

    Message Source 170

    LocaleResolver 172

    LocaleChangeInterceptor.. 172

Summary 176

Chapter 6: Implementing Controllers — Advanced 177

Using Scoped Beans... 177

    Adding Something to the Cart 178

    Implementing the Checkout 183

Crosscutting Concerns.. 185

    Interceptors 186

    Exception Handling... 197

    SimpleMappingExceptionResolver 201

Extending Spring @MVC 205

    Extending RequestMappingHandlerMapping 205

    Extending the RequestMappingHandlerAdapter... 207

    Using the RequestDataValueProcessor 212

Summary 213

Chapter 7: REST and AJAX.. 215

Representational State Transfer (REST) 215

    Identifying Resources... 215

Working with Resources 216

Asynchronous JavaScript and XML (AJAX) 220

Adding AJAX to Our Application 221

Combining AJAX and REST 226

Progressive Enhancement 227

Handling File Uploads 228

Configuration 228

Request Handling Method for File Upload 231

Exception Handling 235

Summary 235

Chapter 8: Resolving and Implementing Views 237

View Resolvers and Views 237

View Resolvers 238

BeanNameViewResolver 239

XmlViewResolver 240

ResourceBundleViewResolver 241

UrlBasedViewResolver 243

InternalResourceViewResolver 245

XsltViewResolver 245

ContentNegotiatingViewResolver 246

Implementing Your Own ViewResolver 247

View Technologies 248

Java Server Pages 249

JavaServer Faces 249

Tiles 250

Velocity and FreeMarker 254

PDF 263

Excel 265

XML and JSON 268

JasperReports 270

Summary 272

Chapter 9: Testing Spring MVC Applications 273

Introducing Testing 273

Why Should I Bother Writing Tests? 273

Promoting Testing Within Your Project 276

Different Types of Testing 277

Setting Up a Basic Unit Test 280

Testing Code Coverage 284

Using Spring's Test Support 286

Setting Up Our Integration Test 286

Testing the JpaBookRepository 292

Using Mock Objects 294

What Are Mock Objects? 295

Testing the AccountService 296

Testing Your MVC Logic 301

Using Spring Mock Objects 302

Introducing Spring MVC Test 305

Automated Front-End Testing 309

Front-End Testing Using Selenium 310

Writing a Selenium Test 312

Using the Selenium IDE 314

Running the Front-End Tests via Gradle 318

Summary 319

Chapter 10: Spring Web Flow 321

Why Web Flow 321

The Flow Concept 322

Fine-Grained Scoping 323

Automatic State Management 326

Request Synchronization 327

Post Redirect Get (PRG) 330

Controlled Navigation 331

When to Avoid Web Flow 332

The Basic Ingredients of a Flow 332

Flow 333

The View State 338

State Transitions 341

The Evaluate Action 342

Expressions 343

Configuration 345

Dependencies 346

Web Flow Configuration 346

Gluing Spring MVC and Spring Web Flow 350

Building Your First Flow 353

Creating the Home Page 355

Implementing the Create Order Flow 356

Overview 371

Summary 372

Chapter 11: Building Applications with Spring Web Flow 373

Important Web Flow Concepts 373

Flow Definition 373

Different Web Flow Scopes 374

Implicit Objects 379

Enhancing the Bookstore 381

Selecting the Category 381

Selecting Books and Delivery Options 387

Form Validation Using JSR 303 Annotations 388

Setting Variables and Accessing Scopes 400

Flow Variables 401

Accessing Scoped Variables from Views 402

Programmatically Accessing Scopes 402

Controlling Action Execution 404

<on-start> 404

<on-end> 404

<on-entry> 404

<on-exit> 405

<on-render> 405

Controlling Action Execution: Sub-elements 405

Global Transitions 406

Subflows 406

Further Enhancing the Bookstore 408

Implementing Authentication as a Subflow 410

Decision State 416

Action State 417

Working with Outcome Events 419

Overview 420

Subflow Input/Output Mapping 421

Creating the Order Process as a Subflow 423

End State 425

Summary 427

Chapter 12: Advanced Spring Web Flow 429

Inheritance 429

Flow Inheritance 430

State Inheritance 434

Web Flow Configuration Customizations 434

Execution and Conversation Snapshots 435

Changing the Expression Parser 436

Web Flow 1 Migration 437

Exception Handling 439

The On Exception Transition 439

Custom Exception Handler 440

Explicit Form Binding 443

Web Flow AJAX Support 445

Configuring Web Flow for AJAX 447

Preparing the View 447

Adjusting the Flow 453

Adding AJAX to the View with Spring JS and JQuery 454

Flow Execution Listeners 459

Writing Flow Execution Listeners 459

Flow Execution Listener Methods 460

Flow Managed Persistence Context 463

From Database to View 463

Prolonging the Persistence Context 465

Applying Flow Managed Persistence Context 466

Reworking the Orders Overview 468

Summary 475

Chapter 13: Spring Security 477

Introducing Security 478
What Is Application Security? 478
General Security Principles 478
What We Will Cover 479

Preparing the Example Application 480

Securing Our Bookstore 482
Adding the Right Dependencies 482
Enabling Spring Security 484
Defining Which Resources to Secure 489
Configuring Access to Resources 490
Configuring Authentication 494
Putting It All Together 497
The Complete Security Configuration 503

Going to the Database 504

Securing Our Flows, the Right Way 506
Adding Access Attributes to Your Flows 507
Configuring the SecurityFlowExecutionListener 508

Transport Security 510

Localization 516

Role-Based Access Control 517

Authorizing Access 523
Using Tag Libraries in Our Pages 523
Using Annotations in Our Code 531

Summary 533

Appendix: Cloud Foundry: Deploying to the Cloud 535

Cloud Computing 535

xiv

Cloud Foundry 536

Deploying Our Application 537

    Installing the Cloud Foundry Plug-in 537

    Making Some Adjustments 538

    Deploying 544

    Configuring the Services 547

    How Does It Work? 551

    Other Configuration Options 551

    Deploying Locally 552

Debugging with Cloud Foundry 552

Summary 554

Index 555

Foreword

I still remember first learning about the Spring framework back in 2004. I had been using J2EE and Struts heavily, and had struggled with many difficulties in effectively using those technologies while building Java enterprise applications. Instead of trying to do away with J2EE altogether, Spring tried to make using J2EE drastically simpler and more productive by offering a large collection of best practice implementations and an inversion of control container gluing it all together. An exciting proposition indeed!

While in general Spring did not try to reinvent the wheel by providing solutions competing with existing parts of J2EE or other established frameworks (notably Hibernate), there was one important exception to this rule: web application development. Spring shipped with its own web framework, Spring MVC, a fully functional web application framework that can serve as a direct alternative to something like Struts. At the time, I saw further opportunity to enhance Spring-based web application development by adding a page flow component to Spring MVC called Spring Web Flow. Spring MVC and Spring Web Flow are the prime subjects of this book.

The design of Spring MVC benefited from the lessons learned working with earlier frameworks. Flexibility and long-term productivity were core design goals. Well-designed Spring MVC applications can grow and change while remaining manageable and maintainable. Still, all was not good. Many found the initial learning curve when adopting Spring, and more specifically Spring MVC, too steep. New frameworks such as Ruby on Rails popped up and focused on short term-productivity and making it very easy to get up-and-running. The Spring developer community recognized this shortcoming, and the recent 3.0 and 3.1 releases of Spring MVC have largely addressed it: extensive use of convention-over-configuration and annotations have made the framework easier to use than ever, as this book will demonstrate! It is a real testament to the flexibility and design quality of Spring MVC that all of this has been possible while remaining 100% backward-compatible. You now have a framework offering the best of both worlds: easy to get started with while the fundamental principles underpinning it all pay dividends in the long term. Spring Web Flow is currently undergoing a similar evolution.

Since 2004, Spring MVC and Spring Web Flow have seen a steady and continued increase in popularity. They are now mature and well established Java development frameworks. If you build a Java web application on top of these frameworks, you can rest assured that you are building on a very solid foundation!

In this book, Marten and Koen take a practical approach to introducing Spring MVC and Spring Web Flow. Of course, they help you in setting up a productive development environment and guide you while getting started developing with Spring MVC and Web Flow. But they don't stop there. I really appreciate how they did not simply cover the technical details, but took the time to explain many of the underlying concepts, bringing a deeper understanding to you, the reader. Furthermore, the book also covers other important topics such as enforcing security constraints and making sure your web applications are well tested. After having read this book you should be well prepared to develop real-life web application based on Spring technologies.

I'm excited to see that to this day people are still benefiting from Spring and the small component I added to it back in 2004. I highly recommend this book for all those eager to learn about Spring MVC and Spring Web Flow, and I applaud the excellent job the authors have done in helping developers learn about these exciting Spring technologies.

Erwin Vervaet
Spring Web Flow project founder

About the Authors

Marten Deinum is a Java/software consultant working for Conspect. He has developed and architected software, primarily in Java, for small and large companies. He is an enthusiastic open source user and longtime fan, user and advocate of the Spring Framework. He has held a number of positions including Software Engineer, Development Lead, Coach, and also as a Java and Spring Trainer. When not working or answering questions on the Spring Framework Forums, he can be found in the water training for the triathlon or under the water diving or guiding other people around.

Koen Serneels is a Senior JAVA software engineer with several IBM, Cisco, and Oracle certifications. For more than 10 years he has developed enterprise solutions using Java(EE), Spring, Spring MVC, Web Flow, JSF, and Hibernate. He holds a keen interest in system architecture and integration, data modeling, relational databases, security and networks. Beginning his career with the Belgian federal government, Koen developed highly transactional Java-based applications with legacy integration. Currently, he is employed by Hewlett-Packard and is a Java software consultant and technical lead for the Flemish government in Belgium. He also teaches a graduate course on "Software Development with Java" at the Groep T Engineering School in Leuven, Belgium.

Colin Yates is a J2EE principal architect who specializes in web-based development. He has been a freelance consultant for the past three years and has worked in a number of environments, both structured and chaotic. Since graduating with a software engineering degree in 1997, he has held a number of positions, including development lead, principal systems engineer, mentor, and professional trainer. His principal skill set includes mentoring others, architecting complex problems into manageable solutions, and optimizing development processes.

Colin was first introduced to the Spring Framework in January 2003 by his mentors, Peter Den Haan and David Hewitt, and he has never looked back.

Seth Ladd is a software engineer and professional Spring Framework trainer and mentor specializing in object-oriented and testable web applications. He started his own company building websites at age 17, but now enjoys having a real job. Currently working for Camber Corporation, Seth has built and deployed systems for NEC, Rochester Institute of Technology, Brivo Systems, and National Information Consortium. He has architected and developed enterprise applications in Java and C for both the server and remotely connected embedded devices. He enjoys speaking and teaching, and is a frequent presenter at local Java user groups and at corporate developer conferences. Seth is very thankful for living and working in Kailua, Hawaii, with his wife.

Christophe Vanfleteren is a software engineer who has been working with Java technologies since 2001. Working for EDS / HP, he has mostly worked on projects for the Flemish government in Belgium, including some large-scale, event-driven applications like the one tracking the Flemish elections in 2006 and the Flemish fiscal platform, which collects several different taxes from 6 million people. He is able to work all the way up the stack, from heavy transactional code all the way to JavaScript-based front-ends. Since 2010, Christophe has been an independent contractor.

About the Technical Reviewer

 **Manuel Jordan Elera** is an autodidactic developer and researcher who enjoys learning new technologies for his own experiments and creating new integrations.

Manuel won the 2010 Springy Award – Community Champion. In his little free time, he reads the Bible and composes music on his guitar. Manuel is a Senior Member in the Spring Community Forums, where he is known as dr_pompeii.

Manuel is the Technical Reviewer for these books (All published by Apress):

Pro SpringSource dm Server, by Gary Mak, Daniel Rubio (2009)

Spring Enterprise Recipes, by Gary Mak, Josh Long (2009)

Spring Recipes, by Gary Mak, Daniel Rubio, Josh Long (Second Edition, (2010)

Pro Spring Integration, by Dr. Mark Liu, Mario Gray, Andy Chan, Josh Long (2011)

Pro Spring Batch, by Michael T. Minella (2011)

Pro Spring 3, by Clarence Ho, Rob Harrop (2012)

Read and contact him through his blog at http://manueljordan.wordpress.com/ and follow him on his Twitter account, @dr_pompeii.

Acknowledgments

One thing I quickly learned during this endeavor is that writing a book is not something you do alone. I would like to thank the whole team at Apress for their support; without you this book would have never seen the light of day. I also learned that writing a book is harder than I ever expected. Nevertheless, it was quite an experience. I thank Manuel Jordan for introducing me to the people at Apress, which started this endeavor.

I owe a big thanks to Koen Serneels for helping me out writing this book and sitting it out all the way, you wrote more than you, initially, signed up for. Thanks for helping me out Koen!

Another big thanks goes to Chris Nelson for keeping all of us focused and for his advice on the book; it was a pleasure working with you. The same thanks go to the coordinating editors, Stephen Moles and Jennifer Blackwell, who in addition to the focus on quality tried to keep everything within the schedule (sorry for slipping past the initial date).

This book would never have seen the light without the comments and suggestions given by Manuel Jordan and Erwin Vervaet. Although at times the comments drove me to desperation, without your comments and suggestions this book would never have become what it is now. So thanks for the comments and suggestions and keeping a clear vision.

The appendix was written entirely by Christophe Vanfleteren, who took on this task with great dedication and determination. He did an excellent job of making our application deploy on Cloud Foundry and writing down the steps it took. Thanks, Christophe, for fulfilling this task.

Thanks also to my family and friends for the times they missed out on me, and to my dive-buddies for all the dives and trips I missed in the last months.

Last but definitely not least I thank my wife, Djoke Deinum, for her endless support, love and dedication, despite the long evenings, sacrificed weekends and holidays to finish the book. Without your support I probably long ago would have abandoned the endeavor.

Marten Deinum

I thank Erwin Vervaet for giving me the chance to coauthor this book and for being a great colleague and mentor over the last years. With Erwin on your side there are no problems, only solutions. Thank you Erwin.

Thanks to Marten Deinum for having me as coauthor and Chris Nelson, Manuel Jordan, Jennifer Blackwell and Stephen Moles for their endless dedication and advice. Without you guys this project would never have reached this paper version; thank you all. After all these months of hard work I realize that writing a book is even harder than writing good software. In fact, writing a book is comparable to a software project without the luxury of automated testing.

Christophe Vanfleteren did an excellent job investigating Cloud Foundry and helping us out writing the appendix. I had the pleasure to work together with Christophe before, and he is by far one of the most talented developers I have worked with in my career. Thank you Christophe for your time and dedication.

Special thanks to everyone who keeps Spring alive, by developing for it or by using it. I have been using Spring since 2004, and to this day it still keeps me amazed. I have used many frameworks, but Spring remains a top-notch framework with its superior code base, agility, liveness, good design and completeness. It is my believe that Spring has many years to go and will be able to serve us on a daily basis to make our work easier, faster and help us create quality projects.

I thank my girlfriend, Sonja Korte, for bearing with me and forgiving me sacrificing our holidays and nearly all evenings and weekends over the last 4 months, and my family and friends for missing out on me.

Last but not least, I want to thank you for reading this book. I'm also a reader of many IT books, so I know what is good and what isn't. I really hope we have succeeded at bringing the good stuff into practice and offer you a top-quality book with exiting technology that will make your daily job easier.

Koen Serneels

Introduction

Welcome to the first edition of *Pro Spring MVC with Web Flow*, the first Pro Spring book focused entirely on web development using the Spring Framework 3.1 ecosystem.

What This Book Will Teach You

This book will teach you everything you need to know in order to get started building enterprise-quality web applications using version 3.1 of the Spring Framework. Topics include but are not limited to:

- The building blocks of the Spring MVC components
- Configuring your development environment
- Providing a web front end to a Spring based application
- A pragmatic approach to testing the web front end
- Deploying to a local web server and to a remote cloud-based deployment platform
- An introduction to Spring Web Flow
- How to build applications with Spring Web Flow

After reading this book you will be familiar with the Spring MVC toolkit and capable of building your own web application from scratch or providing a new web interface to an existing application.

All too often trivial examples are used to demonstrate the power of a framework; it is only when you start using the framework in real situations that its limitations appear. The intention of this book is to show how Spring MVC answers those hard questions (as well as the easy questions!) that web developers are faced with, like managing state in non-trivial multi-page use cases, for example, or providing multiple views of the same resource for different consumers.

And because the real-world problems this book tackles are hard, sometimes the answers Spring MVC provides are not as easy as one would like. This book will not shy away from highlighting those issues or providing pragmatic advice on how to do the right thing.

Who Is This Book For?

This book is for those who are familiar with Spring and want to gain an in-depth understanding of Spring MVC. While it is primarily aimed at those new to Spring MVC, there is information here that will take even expert MVCers by surprise!

The typical reader will be a web developer who has some understanding of the core Spring framework (after reading *Pro Spring* for example) and wants to investigate Spring MVC in more detail.

If you are unfamiliar with Spring, then by all means continue reading; particularly Chapter 2. However if you find that is insufficient then you might find the Spring Reference Guide[1] or *Pro Spring 3* (Apress, 2012).

The original Spring book, *Expert One-on-One J2EE Design and Development* (Wrox, 2002)[2], by Rod Johnson (the "father" of the Spring framework), is fairly old now but still relevant and full of wisdom.

How to Read This Book

This book will take the reader through the thought process of designing, implementing, and deploying a Java web application. The order of the chapters follows the chronological order defined by the development lifecycle. During these chapters we use a sample application to illustrate the topics discussed in the chapter.

Each chapter will address a real-world problem by introducing a new concept or capability which is then used to upgrade the sample application.

Note There is a never-ending dilemma that authors face: should we show the answers first and then the questions, or show the questions and then the answers? The first approach risks overloading the reader, while the second approach can be frustrating and slow for those already familiar with the subject matter. The authors believel that the pace of this book is sufficient for those unfamiliar with Spring MVC; more experienced readers may want to skip certain chapters. For example, if you already have a development environment configured and are familiar with Spring then you can skim Chapter 1 to get hold of the sample application and then jump straight to Chapter 3.

The Application Example

While the example cannot be a true enterprise application (because we need to keep this book under 10K pages ;)), it is realistic enough to highlight the typical design challenges that are faced in real-world projects.

The example in question is the site for a web-enabled bookstore. It offers users the following capabilities:

- An anonymous user can browse the site.

- A logged-in user can submit an order for one or more books.

---

[1] http://static.springsource.org/spring/docs/current/spring-framework-reference/html/

[2] http://www.wrox.com/WileyCDA/WroxTitle/productCd-0764543857.html

- A logged-in user can see his previous orders.

- An author can manage the books.

- An administrator can manage the categories

Throughout the rest of this book, each chapter adds a new aspect to the sample application. The simplest way of capturing this in the example was to have a new project for each chapter.

The Sample Code

We need to explain a little about the coding and referencing style used throughout the book. You'll find that some of the code listings are complete and can be taken directly from the book to the development environment. In others we omit some imports or methods that are mentioned in earlier listings; we've marked those with `// Imports omitted` or `// Methods omitted`. Most include a reference to the code listing in which the methods or imports can be found. This approach was needed for readability, as some code listings contain only a few new lines and others would span multiple pages.

Another thing to mention is that we did not include the fully qualified package names for common classes like `java.lang.String` or `java.util.HashMap` (most of the `java.util` packages aren't included), as a Java developer in general knows where to find those classes. Also, we only mention the fully qualified classname on the first significant reference (after the main heading); for example, the package first identified as `org.springframework.web.servlet.DispatcherServlet` will in subsequent references be called simply `DispatcherServlet`. This is again for readability, but we also feel the need to show you the location of the class and believe this was an acceptable approach.

How This Is Book Structured

The book consists of a series of chapters, each explaining a part of the framework or how to use a certain technology. The first four chapters are quite theoretical and are used to explain some of the more general concepts and how they apply or work within Spring MVC (the same goes for the start of the Spring Web Flow part of the book; Chapter 10 is also more or less theoretical).

After that introduction to the concepts behind Spring MVC, the remaining chapters follow a more practical and hands-on approach as we start to develop an application.

The chapters are:

- Chapter 1, "Configuring a Spring Development Environment." This chapter presents the prerequisites for your development environment, which you can use to develop the sample application. The structure and purpose of the sample application (an online bookstore) are also explained in this chapter.

- Chapter 2, "Spring Framework Fundamentals," provides a broad overview of the fundamental building blocks of the Spring framework. It introduces the concepts of Dependency Injection (DI) and Inversion of Control (IoC). This chapter is particularly recommended if you are unfamiliar with Spring.

- Chapter 3, "Web Application Architecture." In this chapter we take you on a slight detour to explain web application architecture. We will explain the different layers that (generally) make a web application and we will explain the Model View Controller triad.

- Chapter 4, "Spring MVC Architecture." This chapter is the first "down and dirty" chapter dealing with Spring MVC. It defines exactly what MVC is, how web applications are typically structured, or layered, and it dives into the powerhouse of the Spring MVC engine: the wonderful `DispatcherServlet`.

- Chapter 5, "Implementing Controllers." At this point, you're probably ready to say, "Show me the code!" In this chapter we will take the knowledge from the previous chapters and start writing controllers; we'll also get more insight into the internals of Spring @MVC. At the end we will have the start of the sample application. Exciting!

- Chapter 6, "Implementing Controllers – Advanced." Every application requires the same behavior in a number of different places, as well as behavior that isn't really part of your core application but needs to be stuck in somewhere. This chapter will introduce Aspect Oriented Programming (AOP) and how Spring MVC easily solves some common web problems. We will also explore the internals of Spring MVC a bit more and explain how to extend the existing infrastructure and how to tailor it to our needs.

- Chapter 7, "REST and AJAX." Now that our bookstore is taking off, we want to add some nifty behavior to our application and we also want to expose our controllers as REST web services so that others might be able to integrate with us. For this we are going to explore REST and AJAX and apply those techniques to our application.

- Chapter 8, "Resolving and Implementing Views." Chapter 8 digs a bit deeper into how views are resolved within Spring MVC and builds on the information you've learned so far. In this chapter you will get to revisit the `ViewResolver` infrastructure and start to see the power of the MVC architecture shine through when you re-use the same infrastructure to provide different renditions of the same model.

- Chapter 9, "Testing Spring MVC Applications." Now that the craving to get something done has been somewhat satisfied and we've written some code, it is time to look at testing. This chapter explains *how* to test Spring MVC applications but also crucially *what* to test. This chapter will include a good discussion of different strategies for testing, including how to ensure you are testing only what you need to test. You will also be given the chance to test-drive the HTML as well!

- Chapter 10, "Spring Web Flow." Up to now all of the page interactions have been pretty simple; each use-case was one or two pages. Now the manager wants to introduce some nontrivial use-cases. Chapter 10 introduces Spring Web Flow— a companion partner to Spring MVC that provides some pretty nifty features for managing web conversations with clients.

- Chapter 11, "Building Applications with Spring Web Flow." Following the previous chapter's introduction to Spring Web Flow and the problems it helps to solve, Chapter 11 explores in practice how to build an application with Spring Web Flow.

- Chapter 12, "Advanced Spring Web Flow," builds on the information gained in Chapter 11 and demonstrates how you can dig a little deeper into Spring Web Flow and find some real gems.

- Chapter 13, "Spring Security," shows how to keep the scruffy hackers out of our web-application through the use of another well-established tool in the Spring toolbox, Spring Security.

- Appendix A, "Cloud Foundry—Deploying to the Cloud." In this appendix we explain the steps needed to deploy the application to the cloud, especially to Cloud Foundry, as that integrates seamlessly with our chosen development environment.

A Thousand-Mile View of the Spring Ecosystem

So before going any further let's take the first peek at Spring MVC and where it fits into the existing Spring ecosystem.

The first piece of good news is that Spring MVC *is* Spring. You configure Spring MVC using the existing powerful Spring container. Beans defined in Spring MVC are just like any other beans.

The following image from `http://static.springsource.org/spring/docs/3.1.0.M2/spring-framework-reference/html/overview.html` is very helpful:

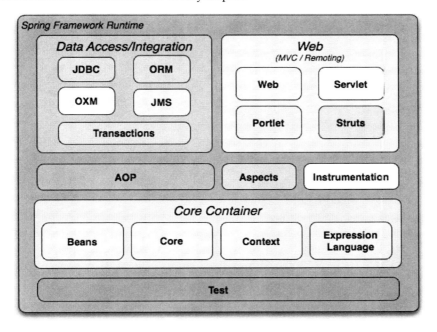

As you can see— Spring MVC is powered by the rest of Spring!

Onward!

Now that you have an idea about the style and purpose of this book let's waste no more time in getting you set up with a development environment. We'll see you in Chapter 1.

Contacting the Authors

Marten Deinum can be contacted at `marten@deinum.biz` for queries and suggestions for this book. His blog can be found at `http://mdeinum.wordpress.com`. Feel free to contact him if you have found a mistake, want to ask a question, or want to discuss anything else related to the book.

Koen Serneels can be contacted at `koen.serneels@error.be` for anything related to this book. If you have suggestions, remarks, or questions, or have found something to be inaccurate, feel free to drop him a message. His blog can be found at `http://www.error.be`.

CHAPTER 1

Configuring a Spring Development Environment

Before you can really start your journey into Spring MVC, you need to make sure you have your development environment set up right. This chapter will begin by walking you through that process. Next, it will provide some details about the sample bookstore application that ships with this book. But before going into either the details of the development environment or the sample application, this chapter will provide an overview of the prerequisites for your environment in general.

The sample application that ships with the book is used to explain the concepts of Spring MVC and MVC in general. It is not intended to be a full-blown, ready-to-use production application; nor is it to be used as a Java or full Spring Framework application. The main intent of the app is to help explain and express the Spring MVC concepts used throughout the book.

Prerequisites

To build the sample application, you need to have a Java Development Kit (JDK) installed; and for (standalone) deployment, you need a servlet container that supports version 3.0 of the Servlet Specification (we chose to use Tomcat 7). To make development easier, you will need to use an integrated development environment (IDE); for this book, we, the authors, chose to use the SpringSource Tool Suite (STS). Table 1-1 lists the products and versions used while writing this book. Development on the selected products still continues, so it might be that there is a newer version available at the time you read this. However, there is nothing in the code that shouldn't work on or with newer versions of the software.

Table 1-1. Software Versions and Download Sites

Product	Version	Download
JDK	1.6.0 Update 31	www.oracle.com/technetwork/java/javase/cownloads/index.html
Tomcat	7.0.26	http://tomcat.apache.org/download-70.cgi
SpringSource Tool Suite	2.9.0	www.springsource.com/developer/sts

Java Development Kit

The first ingredient is the Java Development Kit. JDK7 was recently released; however, it seems that JDK6 is still much more widely used, particularly in the enterprise. There are no known issues with running the sample application with JDK7, so those who want to "live on the edge" are free to do so. Those who want the smoothest ride possible should choose JDK6.

■ **Note** You may already have the Java Runtime Edition installed; however, you still need the Java Development Edition (JDK). The JRE is only for running Java applications, whereas the JDK is for compiling Java code.

Servlet Container

To run a Java web application, you need a web container. The sample application is using Servlet 3.0 features; and as such, you need a Servlet 3.0 capable web container. Tomcat (`http://tomcat.apache.org/`) is an excellent candidate and widely used in production systems. There is nothing Tomcat-specific in the sample file, so feel free to use Jetty, JBoss, Glassfish, or any other modern web container or application server.

■ **Tip** STS includes its own version of Tomcat called *tc-server* (`www.vmware.com/products/vfabric-tcserver/`). This is an excellent product built on top of Tomcat, and it offers value for both developer and production environments.

Integrated Development Environment

Although Spring itself doesn't require a particular development environment (over and above the Java Development Kit), becoming familiar with a good IDE is highly recommended.

Given Spring's ubiquity in Enterprise Java development, excellent support for it can be found in the major IDEs like Eclipse (`www.eclipse.org`) and IntelliJ IDEA (`www.jetbrains.com/idea/`). SpringSource has also invested significant effort into providing its own distribution based upon Eclipse called the SpringSource Tool Suite (STS). And while the "vanilla" version Eclipse is excellent, STS provides additional levels of polish when it comes to developing Spring-based applications.

The Sample Application

This section delves into the sample application you will build throughout the book. For example, you will learn about the build system selected and used for the sample application. Next, you will learn how to import the sample application into STS and take your first steps in deploying the first part of the application.

The main intent of the sample application is to show the features and possibilities of Spring MVC. Although Spring MVC is part of the Spring Framework, this application is not intended to provide full, in-depth coverage on all the features of the Spring Framework. If you want to read and learn more about the Spring Framework, we suggest checking out *Pro Spring 3* (Apress, *2012*).

A Bookstore Sample Application

The sample application that will be built and used throughout this book is a simple bookstore. You will learn how to add functionality for searching, displaying, and buying books. To buy books, the user of the app needs to have an account with the app's associated bookstore, so there is also going to be some account registration and a login page. The sample application will remain more or less the same throughout the book. In the Spring Web Flow chapters, however, you'll see some important differences that exist mainly to illustrate some of the Spring Web Flow functionality.

You can find the code for the sample application with the source code for this book. Go ahead and download and extract it. Note that the top-level directory contains a number of folders entitled chapterX-bookstore. As you progress through this book, you will continually be adding new functionality to the sample application. In some cases, you will be revisiting code from previous chapters. For simplicity and clarity, the authors decided to separate each chapter's progression into a separate project; to see the relevant code for Chapter X, simply load the project in the chapterX-bookstore folder.

In addition to the directories for each chapter, you can also find two projects that are shared between all the book's chapters (see Figure 1-1). These projects are called bookstore-shared and bookstore-web-resources, and they are shared with all projects. One project contains the shared business layer, while the other has the images, stylesheets, and other, similar files.

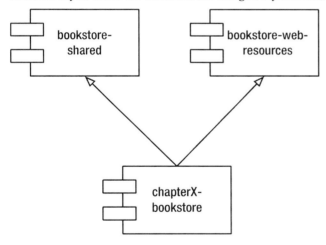

Figure 1-1. An overview of the bookstore components

■ **Note** The project in chapterX-bookstore contains the solution for Chapter X.

While this approach does have the downside of requiring you to load many projects into STS (one per chapter), it also means that you can see exactly how the application progresses—if you want to solve the problems in Chapter 7 yourself, then copy the Chapter 6 project and start working, using Chapter 7 as a reference point if you get stuck.

For convenience, the root directory of the sample application for the relevant chapter (i.e., chapter1- bookstore for this chapter) will be referred to as SAMPLE_ROOT. The SAMPLE_ROOT will obviously be different for each chapter.

The authors tried to create a realistic but simple sample application; to that end, we tried to use the technologies of today. For example, we use JPA 2.0 for the persistence layer, relying on Hibernate 4.1 for our specific implementation. For the web pages, the primary technology used is Java Server Pages (JSPs). A thorough tutorial on JSPs is outside the scope of this book; however, there are many good books on this topic available, such as *Pro JSP 2* (Apress, 2005). You can also find a wealth of other resources for this technology, including Oracle's own tutorial at http://download.oracle.com/javaee/5/tutorial/doc/bnagx.html.

■ **Note** The observant reader probably noticed the JEE5 bit in the tutorial URL. The JEE6 version of the tutorial covers JSF but not JSP; hence, the reference to the JEE5 tutorial.

The Build System

The topic of how to build applications has been subject to decades of arguments, fanaticism, and downright stupidity. We could have taken the easy way out and avoided this discussion by building and deploying entirely with the SpringSource Tool Suite (STS), which we will discuss later in this chapter. However, the authors felt that was a disservice to you. STS is sufficient for managing a developer's workflow, but it isn't quite sufficient for the operational management aspects. Typically, an application is built using one mechanism (the IDE), while an entirely different mechanism is used to deploy it to production. This is often a source of frustration, and it leads to the wonderful "works on my machine" syndrome.

With this in mind, our strong opinion is that it is the developer's responsibility to ensure that an application works in an environment as close to production as possible, *including the build mechanism itself!* You will see how sophisticated build tools make that possible. The build tool you are going to use in this book is Gradle (http://gradle.org). This is a fairly new but up-and-coming *project-automation* tool (project automation is a fancy term for *build tool*) that has a strong pedigree and has already established a very good reputation. A full discussion on build tools is outside the scope of this book; however, suffice it to say that Gradle combines the power of Maven's "configuration over convention" approach with the succinctness of Groovy.

■ **Note** The Gradle project won the 2010 Springy Award for Most Innovative Product/Project[1] and was a finalist in the 2011 JAX Innovation Awards election.

---

[1] http://www.springsource.org/node/2871

The Gradle infrastructure is driven by a `build.gradle` script (this is somewhat equivalent to Maven's `pom.xml`) and an optional `settings.gradle` file; both can be found in the `SAMPLE_ROOT` directory.

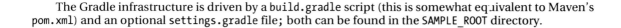 **Tip** If you prefer to use Maven, please note that Gradle is perfectly capable of generating Maven POMs (project object models). For more information, read "Maven POM generation" at
`http://gradle.org/maven_plugin.html`.

Dependency Management

Java's strength is its ecosystem. The wealth of high quality libraries is the currency used to pay for the language's verbosity and pain. However, its greatest strength is, as ever, its greatest weakness: it isn't unusual for small-to-medium projects to have a dependency graph of more than 50 libraries. This proliferation of libraries is made worse by the correct use of modularization!

The problem with the dependencies is that the dependencies also have dependencies, which also have dependencies, which also... Well, you probably get the point. There are direct dependencies (dependencies for the project) and transitive dependencies (dependencies needed by the direct dependencies). However, that isn't the only problem because there is also something that could be called *versioning hell*. If there are multiple dependencies and these dependencies have a dependency on both library x and on different versions of that library, this presents an additional challenge. But, wait, there's more! You don't want to sit at your computer and Google for all the missing (transitive) dependencies, download them, redeploy your application, and *then* notice you have still another missing dependency (or maybe the wrong version of a dependency).

Dependency management helps you out here. For example, it helps you with downloading and discovering what you need, and it tries to resolve all of the versioning conflicts. In this case, you can let the computer do the hard work for you, and you can focus at the task at hand, which is solving the business problem—selling books, in this book's example (not searching for dependencies late into the night).

Note Gradle's dependency management infrastructure is compatible with the somewhat industry-standard Maven repositories—and it has excellent support for resolving dependencies.

The Gradle Build File

Gradle is more than a dependency-management tool, as already mentioned. It is also a build tool; and, as such, it can do a lot for you. For example, if you open the `build.gradle` file, you'll see the dependencies needed by all the subprojects. Gradle can also help you build (compile, test, and create a war archive) your application, and the Groovy language can be used to easily modify or influence the way you build your application. To help build the application, there is a plugin that can deploy the application to an embedded Tomcat instance. This instance can, in turn, be used to run the integration tests (see Chapter 9).

These functions are just the beginning of what Gradle can provide. If you are interested in more complex builds, try reading the Gradle reference guide[2] or taking a look at the Gradle build[3] as used by the Spring Framework[4] (yes, even SpringSource uses Gradle).

Building the Sample Application

To build the sample, cd into the SAMPLE_ROOT directory and execute the gradlew script. Assuming you are on Unix system, this will look something like Figure 1-2.

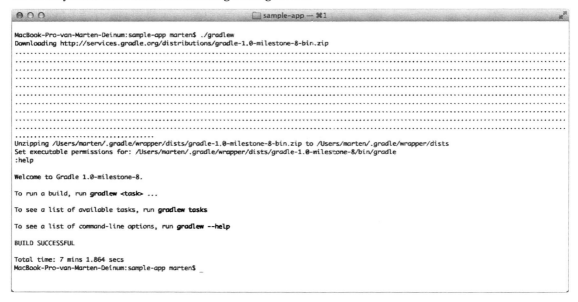

Figure 1-2. The initial build output

You will notice the first thing that the gradlew script does is download the Gradle distribution itself! This is why there is no "install gradle" step—it is self-installing.

■ **Note** We recommend checking the gradlew script into source control. The Continuous Integration (CI) server and (as well as other developers) all use this script. Upgrading to a new version of Gradle is as simple as updating the gradlew script which, when executed, will silently upgrade itself.

---

[2] http://www.gradle.org/docs/current/userguide/userguide.html
[3] https://github.com/SpringSource/spring-build-gradle
[4] https://github.com/SpringSource/spring-framework

Note Speaking of upgrades; at the time of writing, v1.0 hadn't been released, so the code in this book relies on the latest milestone: milestone 9. Your output might differ slightly.

After Gradle has downloaded itself, you should build the sample application by executing `../gradlew build` (see Figure 1-3).

Figure 1-3. Building ample application output

Notice how Gradle downloaded the sample dependencies and went through the lifecycle of compiling, testing, and packaging the sample application. Similar to Maven, Gradle contains a local cache of JARs (a `.gradle` directory in your home folder). Subsequent executions are much faster because no network access is required (see `http://gradle.org/documentation` for more information).

■ **Tip** For a list of all tasks that can be executed, type `gradlew tasks`.

Assuming everything went well, the output should be a `chapter1-bookstore-1.0.0.war` file in the `build/libs` directory.

Deploying the Sample Application

The next step is to deploy the application to a web container. Tomcat (`http://tomcat.apache.org/`) is an excellent candidate, so you could download and install that. As noted previously, there is nothing Tomcat-specific in the sample file, so feel free to use Jetty, JBoss, Glassfish, or any other modern web container.

■ **Note** With a view toward reducing the number of new things you must learn—if you're more familiar with another web container, then it probably makes sense to stick with what you know for now.

Now copy the WAR file from `SAMPLE_ROOT/build/libs/chapter1-bookstore-1.0.0.war` to `TOMCAT_ROOT/webapps`. If Tomcat hasn't started, then start it by executing `TOMCAT_ROOT/bin/startup.sh` run (or `.bat` for Windows).

Now open up your favorite web browser and navigate to `http://localhost:8080/chapter1-bookstore-1.0.0`. If everything went well, you should see the screen in Figure 1-4.

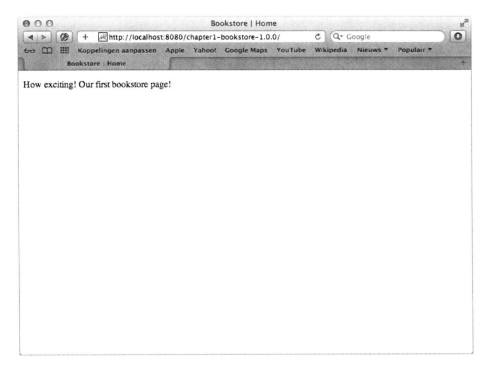

Figure 1-4. The bookstore's home page

What! Is that the best you can do? That screen looks awful! Of course, you can do better :).

However, the point of this sample app is to start *really* simple and build up, so there is no extraneous *fluff* getting in the way of the details. Don't worry; the application will get **much** better as you go.

■ **Note** `chapter1-bookstore-1.0.0` isn't the best name; for one, it doesn't exactly roll off the tongue. The default naming strategy in Tomcat is to set the *context path* to be the name of the WAR file. For example, if the name of the WAR file were `bookstore.war`, then the context path would be `/bookstore`.

Congratulations! You have accomplished the critical, but often overlooked step of ensuring that your application can be built and works outside your IDE. The next step is to install STS and actually look at the sample that you have just so excellently deployed.

Before doing so, make sure to press `Control-C` to shutdown Tomcat.

SpringSource Tool Suite (STS)

As we explained earlier, Spring doesn't require a specific development environment, but we do recommend that you consider a good IDE. Leading IDEs like Eclipse and IntelliJ IDEA are excellent choices, but the SpringSource Tool Suite (STS), based on Eclipse, provides additional benefits for developing Spring-based applications. We use STS in this book.

Configuring STS for Gradle projects

To install Gradle support, click Install Extensions. The first time you do this, STS will download a list of extensions, which can take a few seconds. Eventually, the Install Extensions page will be ready (see Figure 1-5).

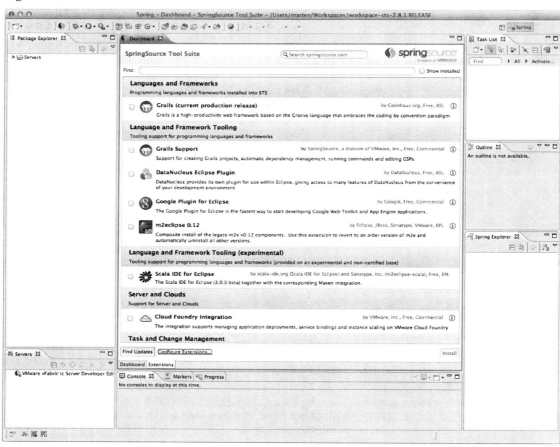

Figure 1-5. The Extensions tab in STS

Next, search for "gradle"; Figure 1-6 shows the results.

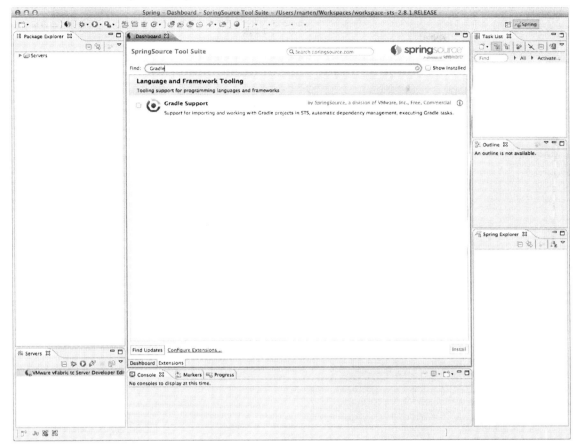

Figure 1-6. *The "gradle" search results*

Now select the check box next to Gradle Support and click Install on the bottom right. Review the prompt and click Next to open the Install dialog (see Figure 1-7).

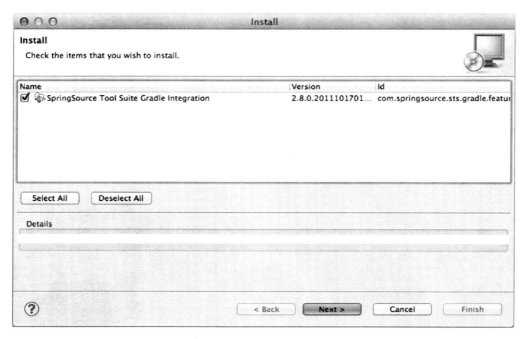

Figure 1-7. The Install dialog

Click Next to get to the Install Details dialog and click Next again to get to the license. Finally, read the license agreements (who reads these?) and click Finish. The Gradle plugin should now start downloading and installing. Once it finishes, you will be asked to restart—click Yes. As mentioned previously, typical Java applications can have large dependency graphs. Gradle has already dealt with this, and it would be painful to have to manually resolve the dependencies in order to register them with STS. Luckily, STS actually understands Gradle projects (just as it understands Maven projects).

Importing the Sample into STS

Now that STS knows how to navigate a Gradle project, the next step is to import the project into STS. To do this, select File ➤ Import (i.e. choose the Import option from the File menu). This opens the Import dialog. Choose Gradle ➤ Gradle Project (see Figure 1-8). Finally, click Next (see Figure 1-9).

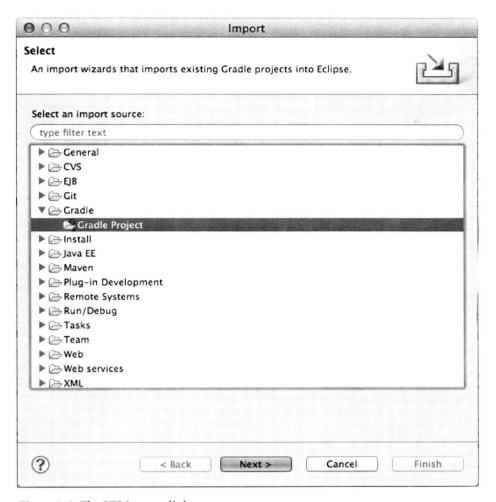

Figure 1-8. The STS Import dialog

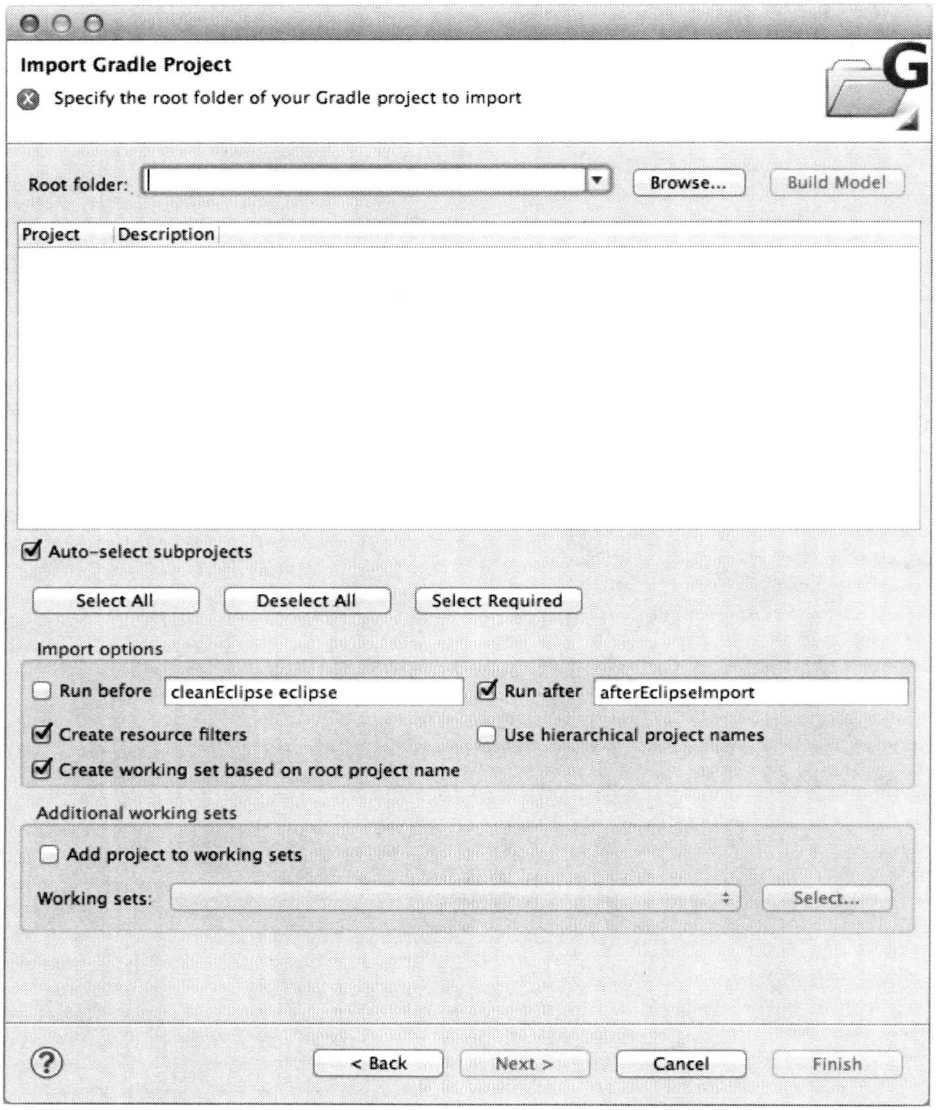

Figure 1-9. The Import Gradle Project dialog

Now click Browse and navigate to the directory containing the sample projects. Next, click Build Model.

■ **Note** STS will download its own version of Gradle and, if you skipped the previous step of building the sample application via the command line, STS will also download the application's dependencies. This may take a few minutes.

Once Gradle has built its internal representation of the structure of your project (i.e. the project and any subprojects), it will allow you to choose which projects to import (see Figure 1-10).

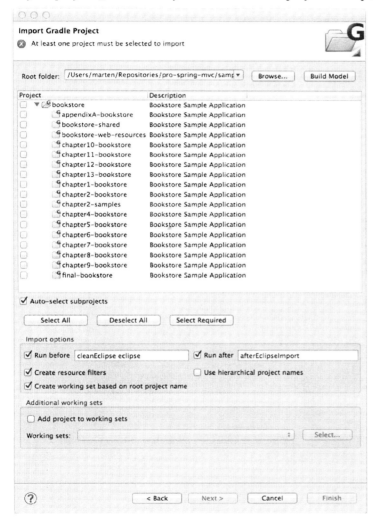

Figure 1-10. Gradle projects that can be imported.

You can either select the root bookstore project or click Select All to import all projects. Afterwards, click Finish to instruct STS to actually import your project. This might take a while as STS is downloading all missing dependencies and will compile all projects. However, the projects should eventually appear in STS (see Figure 1-11).

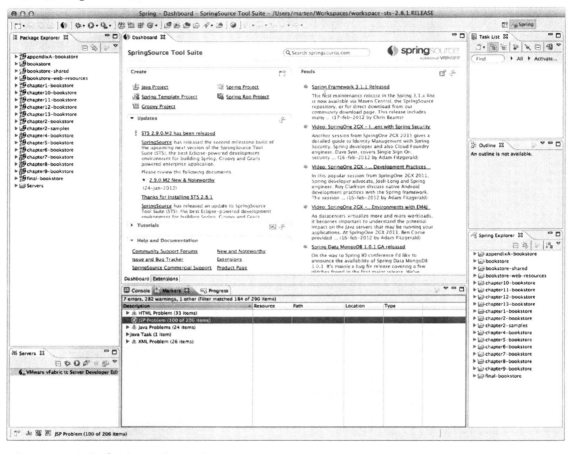

Figure 1-11. *STS after importing projects*

■ **Tip** We suggest that you close the projects you aren't currently working on. To do this, select the projects to close, right-click, and then select the menu option, Close Project. You can reopen a project by double-clicking it.

Running the Application on the SpringSource vFabric tc Server

Before you can run the application, you must tell STS which web container to run the application on. You have two choices: use the Tomcat installation you downloaded earlier or use the prebuilt VMware vFabric tc Server.

■ **Note** Registering Tomcat is as simple as right-clicking the Servers section at the bottom right, choosing New ➤ Server, expanding the menu to Apache/Tomcat v7.0 Server, clicking Next, browsing to the installation root of Tomcat, clicking Open, and then clicking OK.

To run the application on the server, right-click the project and choose Run As ➤ Run on Server (see Figure 1-12).

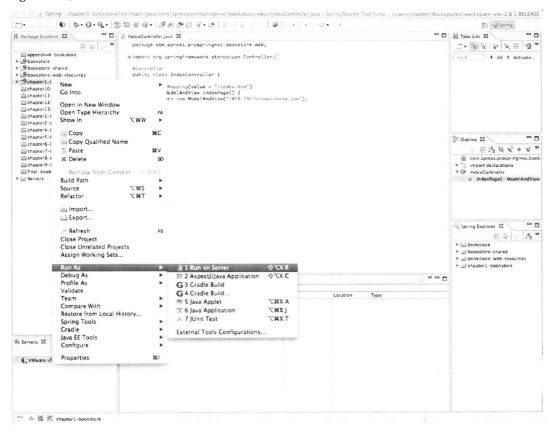

Figure 1-12. *Selecting the Run on Server menu option*

Choosing Run on Server should open the Run On Server dialog (see Figure 1-13).

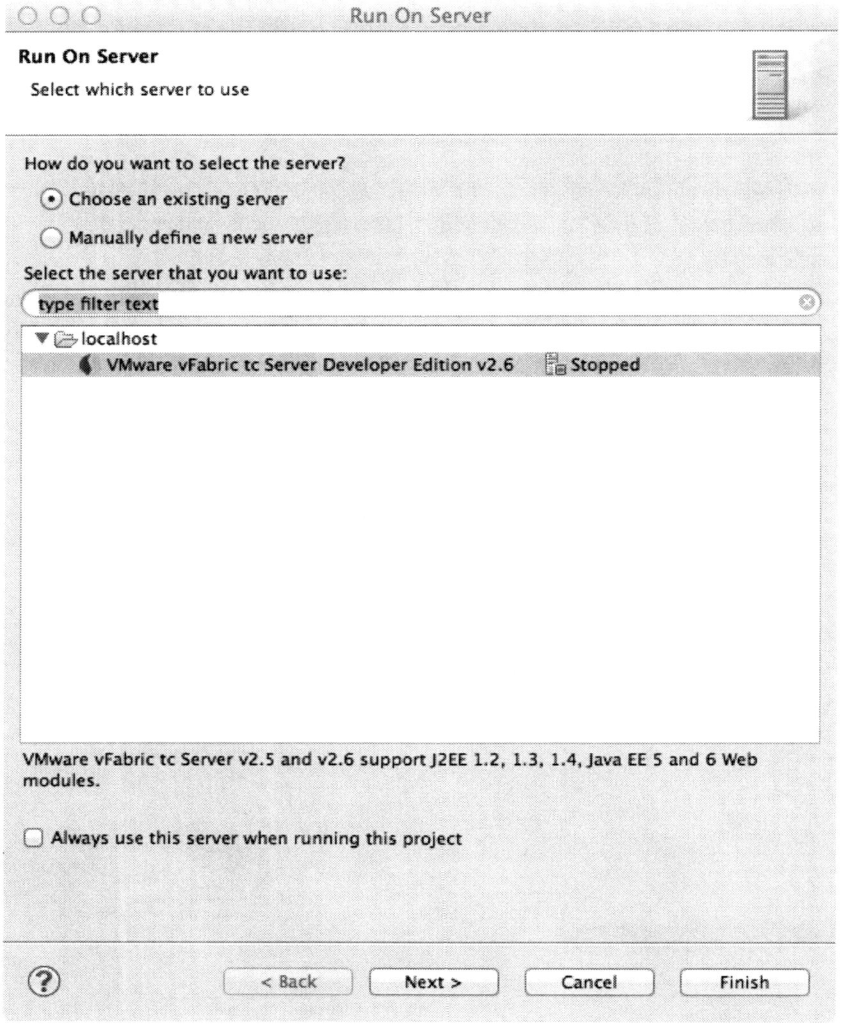

Figure 1-13. *The Run On Server dialog*

Choose the VMware vFabric tc Server Developer Edition v2.6 entry (or Tomcat, which will be shown if you decide to use that). Next, ensure that "Always use this server when running this project" is selected and click Finish. The application should then be built and deployed onto the tc Server. Once it starts, the Welcome page should load (see Figure 1-14).

■ **Note** You may notice that tc Server takes considerably longer to start than vanilla Tomcat as it initializes various sub-components.

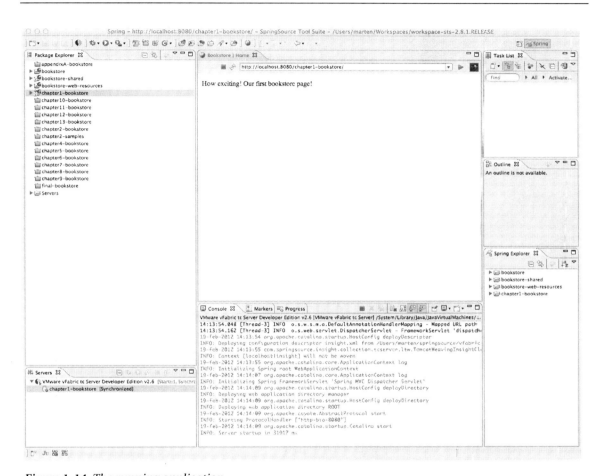

Figure 1-14. The running application

Editing the Application

Congratulations on getting this far! Was it worth it? The authors think so. To demonstrate the power of STS, let's do some editing. Don't worry about the details at this point; they will be explained in detail later. For now, you should just focus on using STS.

Open IndexController (use Control-Shift-T and then type **IndexController** or use the tree to navigate to it) and navigate to Line 12 (see Figure 1-15).

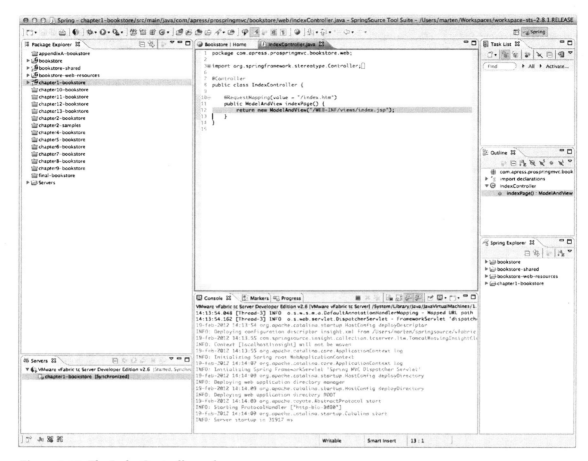

Figure 1-15. *The IndexController code*

Now replace (or modify) the code on the IndexController tab, as shown in Listing 1-1.

Listing 1-1. *The IndexController with the Model Attribute*

```
package com.apress.prospringmvc.bookstore.web;

import org.springframework.stereotype.Controller;
import org.springframework.web.bind.annotation.RequestMapping;
import org.springframework.web.servlet.ModelAndView;

@Controller
public class IndexController {
```

```
@RequestMapping(value = "/index.htm")
public ModelAndView indexPage() {
    ModelAndView mav = new ModelAndView("/WEB-INF/views/index.jsp");
    mav.addObject("theModelKey", "Spring says HI!");
    return mav;
}
}
```

Next, open up `index.jsp` by using Control-Shift-R to open resources and then typing **index.jsp** (see Figure 1-16).

Figure 1-16. *The contents of index.jsp*

Under the paragraph line (<p>), enter **
<p>The model says ${theModelKey}</p>**. Next, save the changes and pay attention to the fact that the new changes are reloaded automatically in the Console tab. Refresh the web page by clicking the double-arrow icon on the web page (the fourth icon in from the left) to view the changes (see Figure 1-17).

21

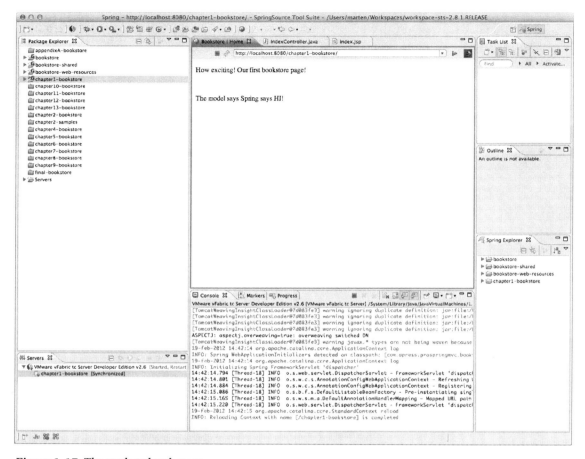

Figure 1-17. *The updated web page*

Excellent! No redeployments are necessary here because STS automatically deployed the changes you made.

Summary

In this chapter, you learned the prerequisites for building and running the sample bookstore application. You also learned about the supporting technologies used by the sample application (i.e., Hibernate/JPA 2.0 and JSPs).

Next, you learned about Gradle, the build system used to develop the sample application; you also learned how it will help you in your project.

To write and debug code for this book, it is best to use an IDE (integrated development environment). The authors chose to use STS (SpringSource Tool Suite), installed the Gradle plugin, and then used that plugin to import and build the sample project. The project was then deployed to the embedded tc Server instance.

You also wrote your first Java code for your MVC application, slightly modifying the basic code for this chapter and using that to explore the automatic redeploy features of the embedded server.

In the next chapter, you will improve on this application as you get a better understanding of the inner workings of Spring MVC.

CHAPTER 2

Spring Framework Fundamentals

The Spring Framework evolved from the code written for *Expert One-on-One J2EE Design and Development* by Rod Johnson (Wrox, 2002). The framework combines best practices for Java Enterprise Edition (JEE) development from the industry and integration with the best-of-breed third-party frameworks. It also provides easy extension points to write your own integration if you need one that doesn't yet exist. The framework was designed with developer productivity in mind, and it makes it easier to work with the existing, sometimes cumbersome Java and JEE APIs.

Before we start our journey into Spring MVC and Spring Web Flow, we will provide a quick refresher course on Spring Core (formerly known as the Spring Framework). Spring is now a longtime de-facto standard for Java enterprise software development. It introduced many of us to concepts such as *dependency injection, aspect-oriented programming* (AOP), and programming with *plain-old-Java-objects* (POJOs).

In this chapter, we will cover dependency injection and AOP. Specifically, we will cover how the Spring Framework helps us implement dependency injection and how to use programming to our advantage. To be able to do the things mentioned here, we will explore the Inversion of Control (IoC) container; the *application context*.

We will only touch on the necessary basics of the Spring Framework here. If you want more in-depth information about it, we suggest the excellent Spring Reference guide (`www.springsource.org`) or books such as *Pro Spring 3* (Apress, 2012) or *Spring Recipes, 2nd Edition* (Apress, 2011).

Let's begin by taking a quick look at the Spring Framework and the modules that comprise it.

■ **Tip** You can find the sample code for this chapter in the `chapter2-samples` project. Different parts of the sample contain a class with a `main` method, which you can run to execute the code.

The Spring Framework

In the introduction, we mentioned that the Spring Framework evolved from code written for the book *Expert One-on-One J2EE Design and Development* by Rod Johnson. This book was written to explain some of the complexities in JEE and how to overcome them. And while many of the complexities and problems in JEE have been solved in the newer JEE specifications (especially since JEE 6), the Spring Framework remains very popular.

It remains popular due to its simple (not simplistic!) approach to building applications. It also offers a consistent programming model for different kinds of technologies, be they for data access or messaging infrastructure. The framework allows developers to target discrete problems and build solutions specifically for them.

The framework consists of several modules (see Figure 2-1) that work together and build on each other. We can pretty much cherry pick the modules we want to use.

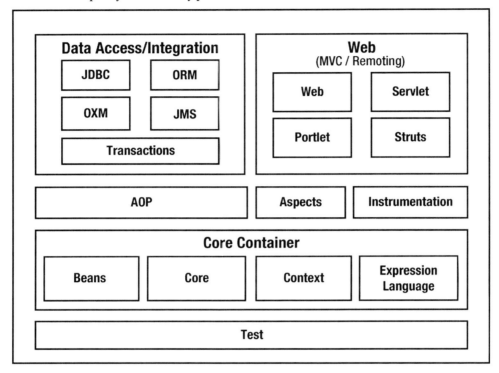

Figure 2-1. Overview of the Spring Framework

All of the modules from Figure 2-1 are represented as jar files that we can include on the classpath if we need a specific technology. In Table 2-1, we list all the modules coming with Spring 3.1 and give a brief description of the content of each module, as well as any artifact names that might be used for dependency management. The name of the actual jar file might differ, depending on how one obtains the module. The downloadable distribution contains jars in this form: `org.springframework.[module-name]-[version].jar`. Jars that come from the maven repositories use this form: `spring-[artifact].jar`. See table 2-1.

Table 2-1. The Spring Framework Module Overview

Module	Artifact	Description
AOP	`spring-aop`	The proxy-based AOP framework for Spring.
	`spring-asm`	Repacked ASM to prevent conflicts with third-party library dependencies from ASM.
Aspects	`spring-aspects`	AspectJ-based aspects for Spring.
Beans	`spring-beans`	Spring's core bean factory support.
Context	`spring-context`	Application context runtime implementations. Also contains scheduling and remoting support classes.
Context	`spring-context-support`	Support classes for integrating third-party libraries with Spring.
Core	`spring-core`	Core utilities.
Expression Language	`spring-expression`	Classes for the Spring Expression Language (SpEL).
Instrumentation	`spring-instrument`	Instrumentation classes to be used with a Java agent.
Instrumentation	`spring-instrument-tomcat`	Instrumentation classes specific to Apache Tomcat.
JDBC	`spring-jdbc`	JDBC support package that includes datasource setup classes and JDBC access support.
JMS	`spring-jms`	JMS support package that includes synchronous JMS access and message listener containers.
ORM	`spring-orm`	ORM support package that includes support for Hibernate, JPA, JDO, and iBATIS.
OXM	`spring-oxm`	XML support package that includes support for object-to-XML mapping. Also includes support for JAXB, JiBX, XStream, and Castor.
Struts	`spring-struts`	Support package for integrating Spring with Struts 1.x applications.
Test	`spring-test`	Testing support classes.

Module	Artifact	Description
Transactions	`spring-tx`	Transaction infrastructure classes. Includes JCA integration and DAO support classes.
Web	`spring-web`	Core web package for use in any web environment.
Servlet	`spring-webmvc`	Spring MVC support package for use in a Servlet environment. Includes support for common view technologies.
Portlet	`spring-webmv-portlet`	Spring MVC support package for use in a Portlet environment.

Most of the modules have a dependency on some other module in the Spring Framework. The core module is an exception to this rule. Figure 2-2 gives an overview of the commonly used modules and their dependencies on other modules. Notice that the `instrumentation`, `aspect`, and `test` modules are missing from the figure; this is because their dependencies depend on the project and what other modules are used. The Spring Framework has only one required dependency: `commons-logging`, a logging abstraction framework. The other dependencies differ based on the needs of the project.

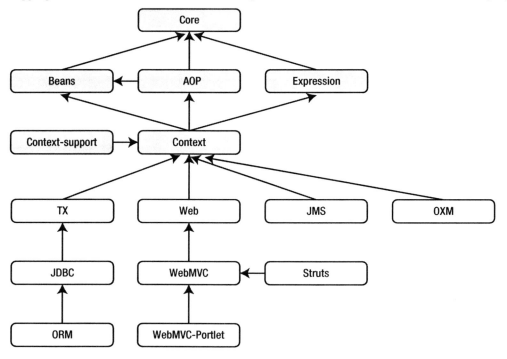

Figure 2-2. *The Spring Framework Module dependencies*

Dependency Injection

The concept of dependency injection (DI), objects are given their dependencies at construction time, is one of the foundations of the Spring Framework. You have also probably heard of *Inversion of Control* (IoC)[1]. IoC is a broader, more general concept that can be addressed in different ways. IoC lets developers decouple and focus on what is important for a given part of an enterprise application, but without having to think about what other parts of the system do. Programming to interfaces is one way to think about decoupling.

Almost every enterprise application consists of multiple components that need to work together. In the early days of Java enterprise development, we simply put all the logic of constructing those objects (and the objects those objects needed) in the constructor (see Listing 2-1). At first sight, there is nothing wrong with that approach; however, as time progressed, object construction became slow, and objects had a lot of knowledge they shouldn't have had (see the Single Responsibility Principle[2]). Those classes became hard to maintain, and they were also quite hard to unit and/or integration test.

Listing 2-1. A MoneyTransferService implementation with hardcoded dependencies

```java
package com.apress.prospringmvc.moneytransfer.simple;

import java.math.BigDecimal;

import com.apress.prospringmvc.moneytransfer.domain.Account;
import com.apress.prospringmvc.moneytransfer.domain.MoneyTransferTransaction;
import com.apress.prospringmvc.moneytransfer.domain.Transaction;
import com.apress.prospringmvc.moneytransfer.repository.AccountRepository;
import com.apress.prospringmvc.moneytransfer.repository.MapBasedAccountRepository;
import com.apress.prospringmvc.moneytransfer.repository.MapBasedTransactionRepository;
import com.apress.prospringmvc.moneytransfer.repository.TransactionRepository;
import com.apress.prospringmvc.moneytransfer.service.MoneyTransferService;

public class SimpleMoneyTransferServiceImpl implements MoneyTransferService {

    private AccountRepository accountRepository = new MapBasedAccountRepository();
    private TransactionRepository transactionRepository = new MapBasedTransactionRepository();

    public SimpleMoneyTransferServiceImpl() {
        super();
        ((MapBasedAccountRepository) this.accountRepository).initialize();

    }

    @Override
    public Transaction transfer(String source, String target, BigDecimal amount) {
        Account src = this.accountRepository.find(source);
        Account dst = this.accountRepository.find(target);
```

---

[1] http://www.martinfowler.com/articles/injection.html
[2] http://www.objectmentor.com/resources/articles/srp.pdf

```
            src.credit(amount);
            dst.debit(amount);

            MoneyTransferTransaction transaction = new MoneyTransferTransaction(src, dst, amount);
            this.transactionRepository.store(transaction);
            return transaction;
        }
}
```

The class from Listing 2-1 programs to interfaces, but it still needs to know about the concrete implementation of an interface simply to do object construction. Applying IoC by decoupling the construction logic (collaborating objects) makes the application easier to maintain and increases testability. There are seven ways to decouple this dependency construction logic:

1. Factory pattern

2. Service locator pattern

3. Dependency injection

    a. Constructor based

    b. Setter based

    c. Interface based

    d. Annotation driven

4. Contextualized lookup

When using the factory pattern, service locator pattern, or contextualized lookup, the class that needs the dependencies still has some knowledge about how to obtain the dependencies. This can make things easier to maintain, but it can still be hard to test. Listing 2-2 shows a contextualized lookup from JNDI (Java Naming and Directory Interface). The constructor code would need to know how to do the lookup and handle exceptions.

Listing 2-2. MoneyTransferService implemenation with contextualized lookup

```
package com.apress.prospringmvc.moneytransfer.jndi;

import javax.naming.InitialContext;
import javax.naming.NamingException;

//other import statements ommited.
public class JndiMoneyTransferServiceImpl implements MoneyTransferService {

    private AccountRepository accountRepository;
    private TransactionRepository transactionRepository;

    public JndiMoneyTransferServiceImpl() {
        try {
            InitialContext context = new InitialContext();
            this.accountRepository = (AccountRepository) context.lookup("accountRepository");
            this.transactionRepository = (TransactionRepository) context.lookup↵
("transactionRepository");
```

```
        } catch (NamingException e) {
            throw new IllegalStateException(e);
        }
    }

    //transfer method omitted, same as listing 2-1
}
```

The immediately preceding code isn't particularly clean; for example, imagine if there were multiple dependencies from different contexts. The code would quickly become messy and increasingly hard, if not impossible, to unit test (see Chapter 9 for more information on testing).

To solve the problem of the construction/lookup logic in the constructor of an object, we can use dependency injection. We simply pass the object the dependencies it needs to do its work. This makes our code clean, decoupled, and easy to test (see Listing 2-3). Dependency injection is a process where objects specify the dependencies they work with. The IoC container uses that specification; when it constructs an object, it also injects its dependencies. This way our code is cleaner, and we no longer burden our class with construction logic. It is easier to maintain and also easier to unit and/or integration test. Testing is easier because we could inject a stub or mock object to verify the behavior of our object.

Listing 2-3. A MoneyTransferService implementation with constructor-based dependency injection

```
package com.apress.prospringmvc.moneytransfer.constructor;

// import statements ommitted

public class MoneyTransferServiceImpl implements MoneyTransferService {

    private AccountRepository accountRepository;
    private TransactionRepository transactionRepository;

    public MoneyTransferServiceImpl(AccountRepository accountRepository,
                                    TransactionRepository transactionRepository) {
        super();
        this.accountRepository = accountRepository;
        this.transactionRepository = transactionRepository;
    }
 //transfer method omitted, same as listing 2-1
}
```

As the name implies, constructor-based dependency injection uses the constructor to inject the dependencies in the object. Listing 2-3 uses constructor-based dependency injection. It has a constructor that takes two objects as arguments: com.apress.prospringmvc.moneytransfer.repository .AccountRepository and com.apress.prospringmvc.moneytransfer.repository.TransactionRepository. When we construct an instance of com.apress.prospringmvc.moneytransfer.constructor .MoneyTransferServiceImpl, we need to hand it the needed dependencies.

Setter-based dependency injection uses a *setter* method to inject the dependency. The JavaBeans specification defines both setter and getter methods. If we have a method named setAccountService, then we set a property with the name, accountService. The property name is created using the name of the method, minus the "set" and with the first letter lowercased (the full specification can be found in the JavaBeans specification[3]). Listing 2-4 shows an example of setter-based dependency injection.

Listing 2-4. *A MoneyTransferService implementation with setter-based dependency injection*

```
package com.apress.prospringmvc.moneytransfer.setter;

// imports ommited

public class MoneyTransferServiceImpl implements MoneyTransferService {

    private AccountRepository accountRepository;
    private TransactionRepository transactionRepository;

    public void setAccountRepository(AccountRepository accountRepository) {
        this.accountRepository = accountRepository;
    }

    public void setTransactionRepository(TransactionRepository transactionRepository) {
        this.transactionRepository = transactionRepository;
    }
//transfer method omitted, same as listing 2-1
}
```

Finally, there is annotation-based dependency injection (see Listing 2-5). For this to work, we do not need to specify a constructor argument or a setter method to set the dependencies. We begin by defining a class-level field that can hold the dependency. Next, we put an annotation on that field to express our intent to have that dependency injected into our object. Spring accepts several different annotations: @Autowired, @Resource, and @Inject. All these annotations more or less work in the same way. It isn't within the scope of this book to explain the differences among these annotations in depth, so we suggest the Spring Reference Guide or *Pro Spring 3* (Apress, 2012) if you want to learn more. The main difference among them is that the @Autowired annotation is from the Spring Framework, whereas @Resource and @Inject are Java standard annotations.

---

[3] http://download.oracle.com/otn-pub/jcp/7224-javabeans-1.01-fr-spec-oth-JSpec/beans.101.pdf

Listing 2-5. A MoneyTransferService implementation with annotation-based dependency injection

```
package com.apress.prospringmvc.moneytransfer.annotation;

import org.springframework.beans.factory.annotation.Autowired;

//other imports ommitted

public class MoneyTransferServiceImpl implements MoneyTransferService {

    @Autowired
    private AccountRepository accountRepository;

    @Autowired
    private TransactionRepository transactionRepository;

    //transfer method ommitted, same as listing 2.1
}
```

> **Note** @Autowired and @Inject can be placed on methods and constructors to express dependency injection configuration, even in cases where there are multiple arguments!

Note that interface-based dependency injection isn't supported by the Spring Framework. This means that we need to specify which concrete implementation to inject for a certain interface.

> **Note** Google Guice[4] supports interface-based injection out of the box.

To sum things up, we want to use dependency injection for the following reasons:

1. Cleaner code

2. Decoupled code

3. Easier code testing

The first two reasons make our code easier to maintain. The fact that the code is easier to test should allow us to write unit tests to verify the behavior of our objects—and thus, our application.

After seeing three different approaches to dependency injection, you may wonder which one we should use. That is more or less a philosophical discussion, but here's a rule of thumb we can use: if a

---

[4] http://code.google.com/p/google-guice/

dependency is mandatory for the object to function correctly, we should use constructor- or annotation-based dependency injection. If we use annotation-based dependency injection and the dependency wouldn't be injected, we would get an exception at the startup of our application. This is because, by default, the dependencies are mandatory when using annotation-based dependency injection. In light of recent developments and additions to Java and JEE, the authors of this book believe that the annotation-based approach is the best way to go. The addition of the `javax.annotation.Resouce` annotation to Java and JSR-330 (Dependency Injection for Java) indicates quite clearly that that is the future envisioned by the Java Community Process (JCP).

In this book, we will use a Java-based configuration approach wherever possible. If a Java-based configuration option isn't possible or available, we will fall back to an XML-based configuration. This is the case when we cover web flow. At the time of writing, web flow hasn't been updated so it can benefit from a Java-based configuration approach.

ApplicationContexts

To be able to do dependency injection in Spring, we need an *application context*. In Spring, this is an instance of the `org.springframework.context.ApplicationContext` interface. The application context is responsible for managing the beans defined in it. It also enables more elaborate things like applying AOP to the beans defined in it.

The `ApplicationContext` interface can be configured in different ways. The most well-known way is to use one or more XML files; however, we could also use a properties file or Java classes. We could even mix-and-match different configuration approaches. In general, it is best to stick with a single approach. Doing so makes it easier to understand and figure out what your configuration is. This also removes the need to hunt down Java, XML, and properties files.

Spring provides several different `ApplicationContext` implementations (see Figure 2-3). Each of these implementations provides the same features, but differs in how it loads the application context configuration. Figure 2-3 also shows us the `org.springframework.web.context.WebApplicationContext` interface, which is a specialized version of the `ApplicationContext` interface used in web environments.

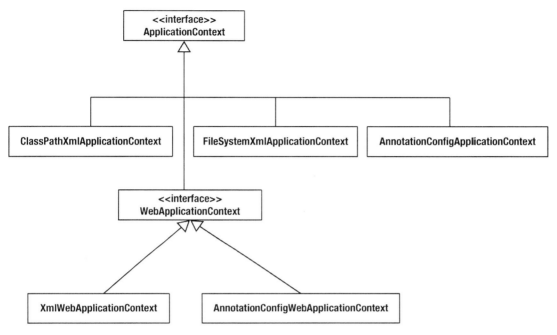

Figure 2-3. Various ApplicationContext implementations (simplified)

As mentioned previously, the different implementations have different configuration mechanisms (i.e., XML or Java). Table 2-2 shows the default configuration options and indicates the resource loading location.

Table 2-2. An ApplicationContext Overview

Implementation	Location	File type
org.springframework.context.support.ClassPathXmlApplicationContext	Classpath	XML
org.springframework.context.support.FileSystemXmlApplicationContext	File system	XML
org.springframework.context.annotation.AnnotationConfigApplicationContext	Classpath	Java
org.springframework.web.context.support.XmlWebApplicationContext	Web Application Root	XML
org.springframework.web.context.support.AnnotationConfigWebApplicationContext	Web Application Classpath	Java

Let's take a look at a Java-based configuration file, the
`com.apress.prospringmvc.moneytransfer.annotation.ApplicationContextConfiguration` class (see Listing 2-6). There are two annotations used in the class: `org.springframework.context.annotation.Configuration` and `org.springframework.context.annotation.Bean`. The first stereotypes our class as a configuration file, while the second indicates that the result of the method is to be used as a factory to create a bean. The name of the bean is, by default, the method name. In Listing 2-6, we have three beans. They are named `accountRepository`, `transactionRepository`, and `moneyTransferService`. We could also explicitly specify a bean name by setting the `name` attribute on the `Bean` annotation.

Listing 2-6. The ApplicationContextConfiguration configuration file

```
package com.apress.prospringmvc.moneytransfer.annotation;

import org.springframework.context.annotation.Bean;
import org.springframework.context.annotation.Configuration;

import com.apress.prospringmvc.moneytransfer.repository.AccountRepository;
import com.apress.prospringmvc.moneytransfer.repository.MapBasedAccountRepository;
import com.apress.prospringmvc.moneytransfer.repository.MapBasedTransactionRepository;
import com.apress.prospringmvc.moneytransfer.repository.TransactionRepository;
import com.apress.prospringmvc.moneytransfer.service.MoneyTransferService;

@Configuration
public class ApplicationContextConfiguration {

    @Bean
    public AccountRepository accountRepository() {
        return new MapBasedAccountRepository();
    }

    @Bean
    public TransactionRepository transactionRepository() {
        return new MapBasedTransactionRepository();
    }

    @Bean
    public MoneyTransferService moneyTransferService() {
        return new MoneyTransferServiceImpl();
    }
}
```

■ **Caution** Configuration classes can be `abstract`; however, they cannot be `final`. To parse the class, Spring will create a dynamic subclass of the configuration class.

Having a class with only the `Configuration` annotation isn't enough. We also need something to bootstrap our application context. We use this to basically launch our application. In the sample project, this is the responsibility of the MoneyTransferSpring class (see Listing 2-7). This class bootstraps our configuration by creating an instance of org.springframework.context.annotation .AnnotationConfigApplicationContext and passes it the class containing our configuration (see Listing 2-6). The process is similar for an XML-based approach, which loads the XML file from the classpath. The result for both is the same. We included both approaches to highlight the differences between the XML- and Java-based configurations; however, nothing changes in the resulting application or its execution.

Listing 2-7. The MoneyTransferSpring class

```
package com.apress.prospringmvc.moneytransfer.annotation;

import java.math.BigDecimal;

import org.slf4j.Logger;
import org.slf4j.LoggerFactory;
import org.springframework.context.ApplicationContext;
import org.springframework.context.annotation.AnnotationConfigApplicationContext;
import org.springframework.context.support.ClassPathXmlApplicationContext;

import com.apress.prospringmvc.ApplicationContextLogger;
import com.apress.prospringmvc.moneytransfer.domain.Transaction;
import com.apress.prospringmvc.moneytransfer.service.MoneyTransferService;

public class MoneyTransferSpring {

    private static final Logger logger = LoggerFactory.getLogger(MoneyTransferSpring.class);

public static void main(String[] args) {

        ApplicationContext ctx1 = new AnnotationConfigApplicationContext↵
(ApplicationContextConfiguration.class);
        transfer(ctx1);

        ApplicationContext ctx2 = new ClassPathXmlApplicationContext(
                "/com/apress/prospringmvc/moneytransfer/annotation/applicatior-context.xml");
        transfer(ctx2);

        ApplicationContextLogger.log(ctx1);
        ApplicationContextLogger.log(ctx2);
    }

    private static void transfer(ApplicationContext ctx) {
        MoneyTransferService service = ctx.getBean("moneyTransferService",↵
MoneyTransferService.class);
        Transaction transaction = service.transfer("123456", "654321", new↵
BigDecimal("250.00"));
        logger.info("Money Transfered: {}", transaction);
    }
}
```

Finally, note that application contexts can be in a hierarchy. We can have an application context that serves as a parent for another context (see Figure 2-4). An application context can only have a single parent, but it can have multiple children. Child contexts can access beans defined in the parent context; however, parent beans cannot access beans in the child contexts. For example, if we enable transactions in the parent context, this won't apply to child contexts (see the "Enabling Features" section later in this chapter).

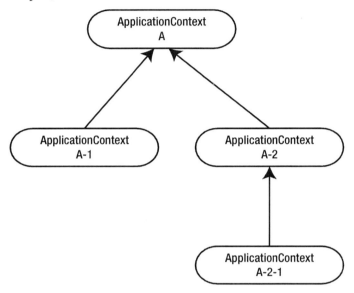

Figure 2-4. The ApplicationContext Hierarchy

This feature allows us to separate our application beans (e.g., services, repositories, and infrastructure) from our web beans (e.g., request handlers and views). It can be quite useful to have this separation. For example, assume that multiple servlets need to reuse the same application beans. Instead of recreating them for each servlet, we can simply reuse the already existing instances. This can be the case when there is one servlet handling the web UI and another that is handling the web services.

Resource Loading

Table 2-2 provided an overview of the different ApplicationContext implementations and the default resource loading mechanisms. However, this doesn't mean that we are restricted to loading resources only from the default locations. We also have the option to load resources from specific locations by including the proper prefix (see Table 2-3).

Table 2-3. A Prefixes Overview

Prefix	Location
classpath:	Root of the classpath
file:	File system
http:	Web application root

Listing 2-7 shows bootstrapping code that uses an application context implementation that loads from the classpath by default. We could also have used an implementation that loads from the file system by default, but loads from the classpath when the proper prefix is used (see Listing 2-8).

Listing 2-8. Using prefixes to load resources in MoneyTransferSpringFileSystem

```
package com.apress.prospringmvc.moneytransfer.annotation;

import org.springframework.context.support.FileSystemXmlApplicationContext;

// Other imports ommitted see listing 2-7

public class MoneyTransferSpringFileSystem {

    private static final Logger logger = LoggerFactory.getLogger
(MoneyTransferSpringFileSystem.class);

public static void main(String[] args) {

        ApplicationContext ctx1 = new AnnotationConfigApplicationContext(
                            ApplicationContextConfiguration.class);
        transfer(ctx1);

        ApplicationContext ctx2 = new FileSystemXmlApplicationContext(
                "classpath:/com/apress/prospringmvc/moneytransfer/annotation
/application-context.xml");
        transfer(ctx2);

        ApplicationContextLogger.log(ctx1);
        ApplicationContextLogger.log(ctx2);
    }
  // transfer method ommitted see listing 2-7
}
```

In addition to being able to specify where to load files from, we can also use ant-style regular expressions to specify which files to load. An ant-style regular expression is a resource location containing ** and/or * characters. A * character indicates "on the current level" or "a single level," whereas ** characters indicate "this and all sub levels." Table 2-4 shows some examples. This technique will only work when dealing with file resources on the classpath or file system; it will not work for web resources or package names.

Table 2-4. Ant-Style Regular Expressions

Expression	Description
`classpath:/META-INF/spring/*.xml`	Will load all files with the XML file extensions from the classpath in the `META-INF/spring` directory.
`file:/var/conf/**/*.properties`	Will load all files with the properties file extension from the `/var/conf` directory and all subdirectories.

Component-Scanning

Spring also has something called *component-scanning*. In short, this feature enables Spring to scan your classpath for classes that are annotated with `org.springframework.stereotype.Component` (or one of the specialized annotations like `org.springframework.stereotype.Service`, `org.springframework.stereotype.Repository`, `org.springframework.stereotype.Controller`, or `org.springframework.context.annotation.Configuration`). If we want to enable component-scanning, we need to instruct the application context to do so. The `org.springframework.context.annotation.ComponentScan` annotation enables us to accomplish that. This annotation needs to be put on our configuration class to enable component-scanning. Listing 2-9 shows the modified configuration class.

Listing 2-9. Implementing component-scanning with ApplicationContextConfiguration

```
package com.apress.prospringmvc.moneytransfer.scanning;

import org.springframework.context.annotation.ComponentScan;
import org.springframework.context.annotation.Configuration;

@Configuration
@ComponentScan(basePackages = {
        "com.apress.prospringmvc.moneytransfer.scanning",
        "com.apress.prospringmvc.moneytransfer.repository" })
public class ApplicationContextConfiguration {}
```

A look at Listing 2-9 reveals that the class has no more content. There are just two annotations. One annotation indicates that this class is used for configuration, while the other enables component-scanning. The component-scan annotation is configured with a package to scan.

▨ **Caution** It is considered bad practice to scan the whole classpath by not specifying a package or to use too broad a package (like *com.apress*). This can lead to scanning a large part or even all classes, which will severely impact the startup time of your application.

If we're using component-scanning and a class with the `Configuration` annotation is found, then it will be used to add more beans to the context. In general, these are beans that cannot be automatically created, like datasources or JMS configuration.

Scopes

By default, all beans in a Spring application context are *singletons*. As the name implies, there is a single instance of a bean, and it is used for the whole application. This doesn't typically present a problem because our services and repositories don't hold state; they simply execute a certain operation and (optionally) return a value.

However, a singleton would be problematic if we wanted to keep state inside our bean. We are developing a web application that we hope will attract thousands of users. If we have a single instance of a bean and all those users operate on the same instance, then the users will see and modify each other's data or data from several users combined. Obviously, this is not something we want. Fortunately, Spring provides several scopes for beans that we can use to our advantage (see Table 2-5).

Table 2-5. *An Overview of Scopes*

Prefix	Description
singleton	The default scope. A single instance of a bean is created and shared throughout the application.
prototype	Each time a certain bean is needed, a fresh instance of the bean is returned.
thread	The bean is created when needed and bound to the current executing thread. If the thread dies, the bean is destroyed.
request	The bean is created when needed and bound to the lifetime of the incoming `javax.servlet.ServletRequest`. If the request is over, the bean instance is destroyed.
session	The bean is created when needed and stored in `javax.servlet.HttpSession`. When the session is destroyed, so is the bean instance.
globalSession	The bean is created when needed and stored in the globally available session (which is available in Portlet environments). If no such session is available, the scope reverts to the session scope functionality.
application	This scope is very similar to the singleton scope; however, beans with this scope are also registered in `javax.servlet.ServletContext`.

Profiles

Spring introduced the concept of profiles in version 3.1. Profiles make it easy to create different configurations of our application for different environments. For instance, we can create separate profiles for our local environment, for testing, and for our deployment to CloudFoundry. Each of these environments requires some environment-specific configuration or beans. One can think of database configuration; messaging solutions; and for testing environments, stubs of certain beans.

To enable a profile, we need to tell the application context which profiles are active. To activate certain profiles, we need to set a system property called `spring.profiles.active` (in a web environment, this can be a servlet initialization parameter or web context parameter). This is a comma-separated string containing the names of the active profiles. If we now add some (in this case static inner) classes (see Listing 2-10) with the `org.springframework.context.annotation.Configuration` and `org.springframework.context.annotation.Profile` annotations, then only the classes that match one of the active profiles will be processed. All other classes will be ignored.

Listing 2-10. ApplicationContextConfiguration with profiles

```
package com.apress.prospringmvc.moneytransfer.annotation.profiles;

import org.springframework.context.annotation.Bean;
import org.springframework.context.annotation.Configuration;
import org.springframework.context.annotation.Profile;

import com.apress.prospringmvc.moneytransfer.annotation.MoneyTransferServiceImpl;
import com.apress.prospringmvc.moneytransfer.repository.AccountRepository;
import com.apress.prospringmvc.moneytransfer.repository.MapBasedAccountRepository;
import com.apress.prospringmvc.moneytransfer.repository.MapBasedTransactionRepository;
import com.apress.prospringmvc.moneytransfer.repository.TransactionRepository;
import com.apress.prospringmvc.moneytransfer.service.MoneyTransferService;

@Configuration
public class ApplicationContextConfiguration {

    @Bean
    public AccountRepository accountRepository() {
        return new MapBasedAccountRepository();
    }

    @Bean
    public MoneyTransferService moneyTransferService() {
        return new MoneyTransferServiceImpl();
    }

    @Configuration
    @Profile(value = "test")
    public static class TestContextConfiguration {
        @Bean
        public TransactionRepository transactionRepository() {
            return new StubTransactionRepository();
        }
    }

    @Configuration
    @Profile(value = "local")
    public static class LocalContextConfiguration {

        @Bean
        public TransactionRepository transactionRepository() {
```

```
        return new MapBasedTransactionRepository();
    }
  }
}
```

Listing 2-11 shows some example bootstrap code. In general, we will not be setting the active profiles from our bootstrap code. Instead, we will set up our environment using a combination of system variables. This enables us to leave our application unchanged, but still have the flexibility to change our runtime configuration.

Listing 2-11. MoneyTransferSpring with profiles

```
package com.apress.prospringmvc.moneytransfer.annotation.profiles;

import java.math.BigDecimal;

import org.slf4j.Logger;
import org.slf4j.LoggerFactory;
import org.springframework.context.ApplicationContext;
import org.springframework.context.annotation.AnnotationConfigApplicationContext;
import org.springframework.context.support.ClassPathXmlApplicationContext;

import com.apress.prospringmvc.ApplicationContextLogger;
import com.apress.prospringmvc.moneytransfer.domain.Transaction;
import com.apress.prospringmvc.moneytransfer.service.MoneyTransferService;

public class MoneyTransferSpring {

    private static final Logger logger = LoggerFactory.getLogger(MoneyTransferSpring.class);

    public static void main(String[] args) {

        System.setProperty("spring.profiles.active", "test");

        AnnotationConfigApplicationContext ctx1 = new AnnotationConfigApplicationContext(
                ApplicationContextConfiguration.class);
        transfer(ctx1);
        ApplicationContextLogger.log(ctx1);

        ApplicationContext ctx2 = new ClassPathXmlApplicationContext(
                "/com/apress/prospringmvc/moneytransfer/annotation/profiles↵
/application-context.xml");
        transfer(ctx2);

        ApplicationContextLogger.log(ctx2);

        System.setProperty("spring.profiles.active", "local");
        AnnotationConfigApplicationContext ctx3 = new AnnotationConfigApplicationContext(
                ApplicationContextConfiguration.class);
        transfer(ctx3);
        ApplicationContextLogger.log(ctx3);
```

```
        ApplicationContext ctx4 = new ClassPathXmlApplicationContext(
                "/com/apress/prospringmvc/moneytransfer/annotation/profiles↩
/application-context.xml");
        transfer(ctx4);
        ApplicationContextLogger.log(ctx4);

    }

    private static void transfer(ApplicationContext ctx) {
        MoneyTransferService service = ctx.getBean("moneyTransferService",↩
MoneyTransferService.class);
        Transaction transaction = service.transfer("123456", "654321", new↩
BigDecimal("250.00"));
        logger.info("Money Transfered: {}", transaction);
    }
}
```

You might wonder why we should use profiles, anyway. One reason is that it allows for flexible configurations. This means that our entire configuration is under version control and in the same source code, instead of being spread out over different servers, workstations, and so on. Of course, we can still load additional files containing some properties (like usernames and passwords). This can prove useful if a company's security policy won't allow us to put these properties into version control. We are going to use profiles extensively when we cover testing and deploying to the cloud because the two tasks require different configurations for the datasource.

Enabling Features

The Spring Framework gives us a lot more flexibility than just dependency injection; it also provides a lot of different features we can enable. We can enable these features using annotations (see Table 2-6). Note that we won't use all of the annotations mentioned in this table; however, our sample application will use transactions, and we will use some AOP. The largest part of this book is about the features provided by the org.springframework.web.servlet.config.annotation.EnableWebMvc annotation.

Table 2-6. An Overview of the Features Enabled by Annotations

Annotation	Description
org.springframework.context.annotation.EnableAspectJAutoProxy	Enables support for handling beans stereotyped as org.aspectj.lang.annotation.Aspect.
org.springframework.scheduling.annotation.EnableAsync	Enables support for handling bean methods with the org.springframework.scheduling.annotation.Async or javax.ejb.Asynchronous annotations.
org.springframework.cache.annotation.EnableCaching	Enables support for bean methods with the org.springframework.cache.annotation.Cacheable annotation.

Annotation	Description
`org.springframework.context.annotation` `.EnableLoadTimeWeaving`	Enables support for load-time weaving. By default, Spring uses a proxy-based approach to AOP; however, this annotation enables us to switch to load-time weaving. It is also required by some JPA providers.
`org.springframework.scheduling.annotation` `.EnableScheduling`	Enables support for annotation-driven scheduling, letting us parse bean methods annotated with the `org.springframework.scheduling.annotation.Scheduled` annotation.
`org.springframework.beans.factory.aspectj` `.EnableSpringConfigured`	Enables support for applying dependency injection to non-Spring managed beans. In general, such beans are annotated with the `org.springframework.beans.factory` `.annotation.Configurable` annotation. This feature requires load-time or compile-time weaving because it needs to modify class files.
`org.springframework.transaction.annotation` `.EnableTransactionManagement`	Enables annotation-driven transaction support, using `org.springframework.transaction.annotation.Transact` `ional` or `javax.ejb.TransactionAttribute` to drive transactions.
`org.springframework.web.servlet.config` `.annotation.EnableWebMvc`	Enables support for the powerful and flexible annotation-driven controllers with request handling methods. This feature detects beans with the `org.springframework.stereotype.Controller` annotation and binds methods with the `org.springframework.web.bind.annotation` `.RequestMapping` annotations to URLs.

■ **Note** For more information on these features, we recommend that you examine the Java documentation of the different annotations, as well as the dedicated reference guide chapters.

Aspect-Oriented Programming

To enable the features listed in Table 2-4, Spring uses aspect-oriented programming (AOP). AOP is another way of thinking about the structure of software. It enables you to modularize things like transaction management or performance logging, features that span multiple types and objects (crosscutting concerns). In AOP, there are a couple important concepts to keep in mind (see Table 2-7).

Table 2-7. *Core AOP Concepts*

Concept	Description
Aspect	The modularization of a crosscutting concern. In general, this is a Java class with the `org.aspectj.lang.annotation.Aspect` annotation.
Join Point	A point during the execution of a program. This can be the execution of a method, the assignment of a field, or the handling of an exception. In Spring, a join point is always the execution of a method!
Advice	The specific action taken by an aspect at a particular join point. There are several types of advice: *before, after, after throwing, after returning,* and *around.* In Spring, an advice is called an *interceptor* because we are intercepting method invocations.
Pointcut	A predicate that matches join points. The advice is associated with a pointcut expression and runs at any join point matching the pointcut. Spring uses the AspectJ expression language by default. Join points can be written using the `org.aspectj.lang.annotation.Pointcut` annotation.

Now let's take a look at transaction management and how Spring uses AOP to apply transactions around methods. The transaction advice, or interceptor, is `org.springframework.transaction.interceptor.TransactionInterceptor`. This advice is placed around methods with the `org.springframework.transaction.annotation.Transactional` annotation. To do this, Spring creates a wrapper around the actual object, which is known as a *proxy* (see Figure 2-5). A proxy acts like an enclosing object, but it allows (dynamic) behavior to be added (in this case the transactionality of the method).

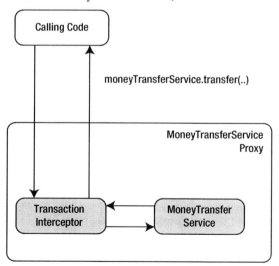

Figure 2-5. *A proxy method invocation*

The `org.springframework.transaction.annotation.EnableTransactionManagement` annotation will register the beans containing the pointcut (acting on the `org.springframework.transaction.annotation.Transactional` annotation). At this point, the interceptor is ready for us to use. The other annotations for enabling features work in a similar way; they register beans to enable the desired feature, including AOP (and thus proxy creation) for most features.

Web Applications

So how does all the aforementioned technology apply to a web application? For example, how do application contexts play a role? And what about all the other things mentioned?

When developing a web application, we have our actual business logic (e.g., our services, repositories, and infrastructure information), and we have our web-based beans. These things should be separated, so we need to have multiple application contexts and have a relationship between them.

We also need code that bootstraps our application, or else nothing will happen. In this chapter's examples, we used a class `MoneyTransferSpring` with a main method to start the application context. This is not something we can do in a web environment. Spring ships with two components that can bootstrap an application: `org.springframework.web.servlet.DispatcherServlet` and `org.springframework.web.context.ContextLoaderListener`. Both components will bootstrap and configure an application context.

Let's take a look at the class that configures `DispatcherServlet`. This is the `com.apress.prospringmvc.bookstore.web.BookstoreWebApplicationInitializer` class (see Listing 2-12). This class is detected by our Servlet 3.0 container, and it's used to initialize our application (see Chapter 3 for more information on this topic). We create the `DispatcherServlet` and pass it `org.springframework.web.context.support.AnnotationConfigWebApplicationContext`. Next, we map the servlet to everything (the "/") and tell it to load on startup.

Listing 2-12. The BookstoreWebApplicationInitializer class

```
package com.apress.prospringmvc.bookstore.web;

import javax.servlet.ServletContext;
import javax.servlet.ServletException;
import javax.servlet.ServletRegistration;

import org.springframework.web.WebApplicationInitializer;
import org.springframework.web.context.WebApplicationContext;
import org.springframework.web.context.support.AnnotationConfigWebApplicationContext;
import org.springframework.web.servlet.DispatcherServlet;

import com.apress.prospringmvc.bookstore.web.config.WebMvcContextConfiguration;

public class BookstoreWebApplicationInitializer implements WebApplicationInitializer {

    @Override
    public void onStartup(final ServletContext servletContext) throws ServletException {
        registerDispatcherServlet(servletContext);
    }

    private void registerDispatcherServlet(final ServletContext servletContext) {
        WebApplicationContext dispatcherContext = createContext↵
```

```
(WebMvcContextConfiguration.class);
        DispatcherServlet dispatcherServlet = new DispatcherServlet(dispatcherContext);
        ServletRegistration.Dynamic dispatcher = servletContext.addServlet↵
("dispatcher", dispatcherServlet);
        dispatcher.setLoadOnStartup(1);
        dispatcher.addMapping("/");
    }

private WebApplicationContext createContext(final Class<?>... annotatedClasses) {
        AnnotationConfigWebApplicationContext context = new↵
 AnnotationConfigWebApplicationContext();
        context.register(annotatedClasses);
        context.getEnvironment().setActiveProfiles("local");
        return context;
    }
}
```

Let's make things a bit more interesting by adding a ContextLoaderListener class, so that we can have a parent context and a child context (see Listing 2-13). The newly registered listener will use com.apress.prospringmvc.bookstore.config.InfrastructureContextConfiguration (see Listing 2-14) to determine which beans to load. The already configured DispatcherServlet automatically detects the application context loaded by ContextLoaderListener.

Listing 2-13. The modifcation for the BookstoreWebApplicationInitializer class

```
package com.apress.prospringmvc.bookstore.web;

import org.springframework.web.context.ContextLoaderListener;
import com.apress.prospringmvc.bookstore.config.InfrastructureContextConfiguration;

// other imports ommitted see listing 2-12

public class BookstoreWebApplicationInitializer implements WebApplicationInitializer {

    @Override
    public void onStartup(final ServletContext servletContext) throws ServletException {
        registerListener(servletContext);
        registerDispatcherServlet(servletContext);
    }

// registerDispatcherServlet method ommitted see Listing 2-12

    private void registerListener(final ServletContext servletContext) {
        AnnotationConfigWebApplicationContext rootContext =↵
 createContext(InfrastructureContextConfiguration.class);
        servletContext.addListener(new ContextLoaderListener(rootContext));
    }

private AnnotationConfigWebApplicationContext createContext(final Class<?>...↵
 annotatedClasses) {
        AnnotationConfigWebApplicationContext context = new↵
 AnnotationConfigWebApplicationContext();
```

```
        context.getEnvironment().setActiveProfiles("local");
        context.register(annotatedClasses);
        return context;
    }

}
```

Listing 2-14 is our main application context. It contains the configuration for our services and repositories. This listing also shows our JPA entity manager, including its annotation-based transaction support.

Listing 2-14. The InfrastructureContextConfiguration source file

```
package com.apress.prospringmvc.bookstore.config;

import javax.persistence.EntityManagerFactory;
import javax.sql.DataSource;

import org.springframework.beans.factory.FactoryBean;
import org.springframework.beans.factory.annotation.Autowired;
import org.springframework.context.annotation.Bean;
import org.springframework.context.annotation.ComponentScan;
import org.springframework.context.annotation.Configuration;
import org.springframework.jdbc.datasource.embedded.EmbeddedDatabaseBuilder;
import org.springframework.jdbc.datasource.embedded.EmbeddedDatabaseType;
import org.springframework.orm.jpa.JpaTransactionManager;
import org.springframework.orm.jpa.JpaVendorAdapter;
import org.springframework.orm.jpa.LocalContainerEntityManagerFactoryBean;
import org.springframework.orm.jpa.vendor.HibernateJpaVendorAdapter;
import org.springframework.transaction.PlatformTransactionManager;
import org.springframework.transaction.annotation.EnableTransactionManagement;

@Configuration
@EnableTransactionManagement
@ComponentScan(basePackages = {
        "com.apress.prospringmvc.bookstore.service",
        "com.apress.prospringmvc.bookstore.repository",
        "com.apress.prospringmvc.bookstore.domain.support" })
public class InfrastructureContextConfiguration {

    @Autowired
    private DataSource dataSource;

    @Autowired
    private EntityManagerFactory entityManagerFactory;

    @Bean
    public FactoryBean<EntityManagerFactory> entityManagerFactory() {
        LocalContainerEntityManagerFactoryBean emfb;
        emfb = new LocalContainerEntityManagerFactoryBean();
        emfb.setDataSource(this.dataSource);
        emfb.setJpaVendorAdapter(jpaVendorAdapter());
```

```
        return emfb;
    }

    @Bean
    public JpaVendorAdapter jpaVendorAdapter() {
        return new HibernateJpaVendorAdapter();
    }

    @Bean
    public PlatformTransactionManager transactionManager() {
        JpaTransactionManager txManager = new JpaTransactionManager();
        txManager.setEntityManagerFactory(this.entityManagerFactory);
        txManager.setDataSource(this.dataSource);
        return txManager;
    }

    @Bean
    public DataSource dataSource() {
        EmbeddedDatabaseBuilder builder = new EmbeddedDatabaseBuilder();
        builder.setType(EmbeddedDatabaseType.H2);
        return builder.build();
    }
}
```

Summary

In this chapter, we covered the bare basics of Spring Core. We reviewed the concept of dependency injection and briefly covered three different versions of dependency injection. We also covered constructor-based, setter-based, and annotation-based dependency injection.

Next, we stepped into the Spring world and examined org.springframework.context.ApplicationContexts, including the role they play in our application. We also explained the different types of application contexts (e.g., XML or Java based) and the resource loading in each of them. In our web environment, we use a specialized version of an application context in an implementation of the org.springframework.web.context.WebApplicationContext interface. We also covered how, by default, beans in an application context are singleton scoped. Fortunately, Spring provides us with additional scopes, such as request, session, globalSession, prototype, application, and thread.

To be able to use different configurations in different environments, Spring also includes profiles. We briefly explained both how to enable profiles and how to use them. We will use profiles in our sample application when we test it (see Chapter 9) and when we deploy it to Cloud Foundry (see Appendix A).

We also delved into the way several enabling annotations are required for Spring to enable certain features. These annotations register additional beans in the application context that enable the desired feature. Most of these features rely on AOP to be enabled (e.g., to do declarative transaction management). Spring creates proxies to apply AOP to beans registered in our application contexts.

In the next chapter, we will look at the architecture of an MVC web application, the different layers, and what roles they play in our application.

CHAPTER 3

Web Application Architecture

Before we start our journey into the internals of Spring MVC, we first need to understand the different layers of a web application. And we'll begin that discussion with a brief introduction of the MVC pattern in general, including what it is and why should we use it. We will also cover some of the interfaces and classes provided by the Spring Framework to express the different parts of the MVC pattern.

After reviewing the MVC Pattern, we will go through the different layers in a web application and see what role each layer plays in the application. We will also explore how the Spring Framework can help us out in the different layers and how we can use it to our advantage.

The MVC Pattern

The Model View Controller pattern (MVC pattern) was first described by Trygve Reenskaug when he was working on Smalltalk at Xerox. At that time, the pattern was aimed at desktop applications. This pattern divides the presentation layer into different kinds of components. Each component has its own responsibilities. The view uses the model to render itself. Based on a user action, the view triggers the controller, which in turn updates the model. The model then notifies the view to (re)render itself (see Figure 3-1).

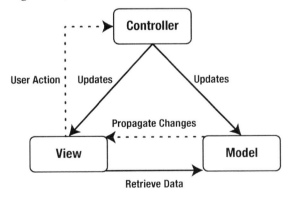

Figure 3-1. The MVC pattern

The MVC pattern is all about separation of concerns. As we mentioned previously, each component has its own role (see Table 3-1). Separation of concerns is important in the presentation layer because it helps us keep the different components clean. This way, we don't burden the actual view with business logic, navigation logic, and model data. Following this approach keeps everything nicely separated, which makes it easier to maintain and test our application.

Table 3-1. *MVC in Short*

Component	Description
Model	The model is the data needed by the view so that it can be rendered. It might be an order placed or a list of books requested by a user.
View	The view is the actual implementation, and it uses the model to render itself in a web application. This could be a JSP or JSF page, but it could also be a PDF or XML representation of a page.
Controller	The controller is the component that is responsible for responding to the action the user takes, such as form submission or clicking a link. The controller updates the model and takes other actions needed, such as invoking a service method to place an order.

The classic implementation of the MVC pattern (as shown in Figure 3-1) involves the user triggering an action. This prompts the controller to update the model, which in turn pushes the changes back to the view. The view then updates itself with the updated data from the model. This is the ideal implementation of an MVC pattern, and it works very well in desktop applications based on Swing, for example. However, this approach is not feasible in a web environment due to the nature of the HTTP protocol. For a web application, the user typically initiates action by issuing a request. This prompts the app to update and render the view, which is sent back to the user. This means that we need a slightly different approach in a web environment. Instead of pushing the changes to the view, we need to pull the changes from the server.

This approach seems quite workable, but it isn't as straightforward to apply in a web application as one might think. The Web (or HTTP) is stateless by design, so keeping a model around can be quite difficult. For the Web, the MVC pattern is implemented as a *Model 2* architecture (see Figure 3-2)[1]. The difference between the original pattern (*Model 1* was shown in Figure 3-1) and the modified pattern is that it incorporates a *front controller* that dispatches the incoming requests to other controllers. These controllers handle the incoming request, return the model, and select the view.

---

[1] http://java.sun.com/blueprints/guidelines/designing_enterprise_applications_2e/web-tier/web-tier5.html

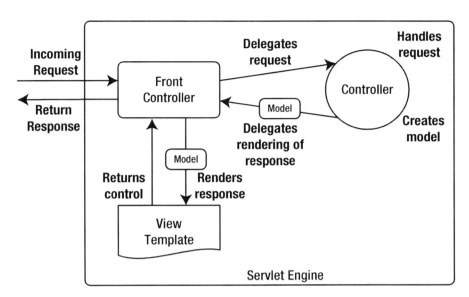

Figure 3-2. The Model 2 MVC pattern

The front controller is the component that handles the incoming requests. First, it delegates the request to a suitable controller. When that controller has finished processing and updating the model, the front controller will determine which view to render based on the outcome. In most cases, this front controller is implemented as a `javax.servlet.Servlet` servlet (e.g., `ActionServlet` in struts or `FacesServlet` in JSF). In Spring MVC, this front controller is `org.springframework.web.servlet.DispatcherServlet`.

Application Layering

In the introduction, we mentioned that an application consists of several layers (see Figure 4-3). We like to think of a layer as an area of concern for the application. Therefore, we also use layering to achieve separation of concerns. For example, the view shouldn't be burdened with business or data access logic because these are all different concerns and typically located in different layers.

Layers should be thought of as conceptual boundaries, but they don't have to be physically isolated from each other (in another virtual machine). For a web application, the layers typically run inside the same virtual machine. Rod Johnson's book, *Expert One-on-One J2EE Design and Development* (Wrox, 2002), has a good discussion on application distribution and scaling.

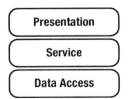

Figure 3-3. Typical application layering

Figure 3-3 is a highly generalized view of the layers of a Spring MVC application. This layering can be seen in many applications. The data access is at the bottom of the application, the presentation is on top, and the services (the actual business logic) are in the middle. In this chapter, we will take a look at this architecture and how everything is organized. Table 3-2 provides a brief description of the different layers.

Table 3-2. *A Brief Overview of Layers*

Layer	Description
Presentation	This is most likely to be a web-based solution. The presentation layer should be as thin as possible. It should also be possible to provide alternative presentation layers like a web front-end or maybe even a web service façade. This should all operate on a well-designed service layer.
Service	The entry point to the actual system containing the business logic. It provides a coarse-grained interface that enables use of the system. This is also the layer that should be the transactional boundary of the system (and probably security, too). This layer shouldn't know anything (or as little as possible) about persistence or the view technology used.
Data Access	An interface-based layer that provides access to the underlying data access technology, but without exposing it to the upper layers. This layer abstracts the actual persistence framework (e.g., JDBC, JDO, or JPA). Note that this layer should not contain business logic.

Communication between the layers is from top to bottom. The service layer can access the data access layer, but the data access layer cannot access the service layer. If you see these kinds of circular dependencies creep into your application, take a few steps back and reconsider your design. Circular dependencies (or bottom to top dependencies) are almost always a sign of bad design and lead to increased complexity and a harder-to-maintain application.

▓ **Note** Sometimes, one might also encounter the term, *tier*. Many people use tier and layer interchangeably; however, separating the two helps when discussing the application architecture or its deployment. We like to use *layer* to indicate a conceptual layer in the application, whereas a *tier* indicates the physical separation of the layers on different machines at deployment time. Thinking in *layers* helps the software developer, whereas thinking in *tiers* helps the system administrator.

Although Figure 3-3 gives a general overview of the layers for a web application, we could break it down a little further. In a typical web application, we can identify five conceptual layers (see Figure 3-4). We can split the presentation layer into a web and user interface layer, but the application also includes a domain layer (see the "Spring MVC Application Layers" section later in this chapter). Typically, the domain layer cuts across all layers because it is used everywhere from the data access layer to the user interface.

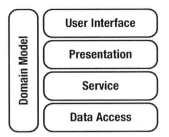

Figure 3-4. *Web MVC application layers*

■ **Note** The layered architecture isn't the only application architecture out there; however, it is the most frequently encountered architecture for web applications.

If we look at the sample application, the architecture shown in Figure 3-4 is made explicit in the package structure. The packages can be found in the *bookstore-shared* project (see Figure 3-5). The main packages include the following:

- `com.apress.prospringmvc.bookstore.domain`: the domain layer

- `com.apress.prospringmvc.bookstore.service`: the service layer

- `com.apress.prospringmvc.bookstore.repository`: the data access layer

The other packages are supporting packages for the web layer and the `com.apress.prospringmvc.bookstore.config` package contains the configuration classes for the root application context. The user interface and web layer we over the course of this book, and these layers will be in the `com.apress.prospringmvc.bookstore.web` package and in Java Server Pages where needed for the user interface.

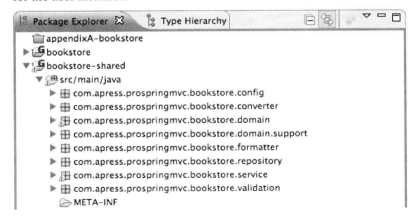

Figure 3-5. *The Bookstore packages overview*

Separation of Concerns

As we mentioned in Chapter 2, it is important to have a clear separation of concerns. If we look at the architecture from Figure 3-4, the separation of concerns is present in the layers. Separating the concerns into different layers helps us achieve a clean design, as well as a flexible and testable application.

Creating or detecting layers can be hard. A rule of thumb is that, if a layer has too many dependencies with other layers, we might want to introduce another layer that incorporates all the dependencies. On the other hand, if we see a single layer throughout different layers, we might want to reconsider this layer and make it an aspect of the application. In this case, we can use the AOP functionality from the Spring Framework to apply these aspects at runtime (see Chapter 2).

Coupling layers—for example, the service layer will need to talk to the data access layer—is done by defining clear interfaces. Defining interfaces and programming to interfaces reduces the actual coupling to concrete implementations. This reduced coupling and reduced complexity results in an easier-to-test and easier-to-maintain application. Another benefit of using interfaces is that Spring can use JDK Dynamic Proxies[2] to create proxies and apply AOP.

■ **Note** Spring can also apply AOP on class-based proxies; however, this requires the `cglib` library (`http://cglib.sourceforge.net`) on the classpath.

The point is this: layering in an application leads to a more maintainable and testable application. A clear separation of concerns also leads to good application architecture.

Spring MVC Application Layers

You might wonder how all the layers fit into a Spring MVC application, as well as how all the different layers help us build our Spring MVC application. In this section, we will take a look at the five layers depicted in Figure 3-4. We will pay particular attention to the roles the different layers play and what should be in each.

The Domain Layer

The domain is the most important layer in an application. It is the code representation of the business problem we are solving, and it contains the business rules of our domain. These rules might check whether we have sufficient funds to transfer money from our account or ensure that fields are unique (e.g., usernames in our system).

A popular technique to determine the domain model is to use the nouns in use case descriptions as domain objects (e.g., `Account` or `Transaction`). These objects contain both state (e.g., the `username` for the `Account`) and behavior (e.g., a `credit` method on the `Account`). These methods are typically more fine-grained then the methods in the service layer. For example, in the money transfer sample in Chapter 2, the `com.apress.prospringmvc.moneytransfer.domain.Account` object has a `debit` and `credit` method. The

---

[2] `http://docs.oracle.com/javase/6/docs/technotes/guides/reflection/proxy.html`

credit method contains some business logic for checking whether we have sufficient money in our account to transfer the money.

In Chapter 2, the implementations of the com.apress.prospringmvc.moneytransfer.service.MoneyTransferService used these supporting methods to implement a use case (in the sample, it transferred money from one account to another account). This is not to be confused with an anemic domain model[3], in which our domain objects only hold state and have no behavior.

In general, your domain model will not need dependencies injected; however, it is still possible to do this. For example, it's possible to use the Spring Framework and AspectJ to enable dependency injection in our domain objects. In that circumstance, we would give our domain classes the org.springframework.beans.factory.annotation.Configurable annotation. Next, we would need to set up load-time weaving or compile-time weaving, and we would have our dependencies injected. For more detailed information on the subject, please see the Spring Reference Guide[4].

■ **Note** This is the setup used in Spring ROO[5]. It uses a *rich domain model*, as advocated by Eric Evans[6].

The User Interface Layer

The user interface layer presents the application to the user. This layer renders the response generated by the server into the type requested by the user's client. For instance, a web browser will probably request an HTML document, a web service may want an XML document, and another client could request a PDF or Excel document.

We separated the presentation layer into a user interface and web layer because, notwithstanding the wide range of different view technologies, we wanted to reuse as much code as possible. Our goal is to reimplement only the user interface. There are many different view technologies out there, including JSP(X), JSF, Velocity, and Freemarker, to name a few. In an ideal world, we would be able to switch our user interface without changing the backend of our application.

Spring MVC helps us in isolating the user interface from the rest of the system. In Spring, the view is represented by an interface: org.springframework.web.servlet.View. This interface is responsible for transforming the result of the action from the user (the model) into the type of response the user requested. The View interface is generic, and it has no dependencies on a particular view technology. For each supported view technology, there is an implementation provided either by the Spring Framework itself or by the view technologies themselves. Out of the box, Spring supports the following view technologies:

- JSP
- PDF
- Excel

[3] http://martinfowler.com/bliki/AnemicDomainModel.html
[4] http://static.springsource.org/spring/docs/3.1.x/spring-framework-reference/html/aop.html#aop-atconfigurable
[5] http://www.springsource.org/spring-roo
[6] http://domaindrivendesign.org/

- Freemarker

- Velocity

- JasperReports

- Tiles 2

- XML (marshaling, XSLT or plain)

- JSON

The user interface in general has a dependency on the domain layer. Sometimes, it is convenient to directly expose and render the domain model. This can be especially useful when we start to use forms in our application. For example, this would let us work directly with the domain objects instead of an additional layer of indirection. Some argue that this creates an unnecessary or unwanted coupling between layers. However, the creation of another layer for the sole purpose of decoupling the domain from the view leads to unnecessary complexity and duplication. In any case, it is important to keep in mind that Spring MVC doesn't requires us to directly expose the domain model to the view—whether we do so is entirely up to us.

The Web Layer

The web layer has two responsibilities. The first responsibility is to guide the user through the web application. The second is to be the integration layer between the service layer and HTTP.

Navigating the user through the website can be as simple as mapping a URL to views or a full-blown page flow solution like Spring Web Flow. The navigation is typically bound to the web layer only, and there isn't any navigation logic in the domain or service layer.

As an integration layer, the web layer should be as thin as possible. It should be the layer that converts the incoming HTTP request to something that can be handled by the service layer, and then transforms the result (if any) from the server into a response for the user interface. The web layer should not contain any business logic—that is the sole purpose of the service layer.

The web layer also consists of cookies, HTTP headers, and possibly an HTTP session. It is the responsibility of the web layer to manage all these things consistently and transparently. The different HTTP elements should never creep into our service layer. If they do, the whole service layer (and thus our application) becomes tied to the web environment. Doing this makes it harder to maintain and test the application. Keeping the service layer clean also allows us to reuse the same services for different channels. For example, it enables us to add a web service or JMS-driven solution. The web layer should be thought of as a client or proxy that connects to the service layer and exposes it to the end users.

In the early days of Java web development, servlets or Java Server Pages mainly implemented this layer. The servlets had the responsibility of processing and transforming the request into something the service layer could understand. More often than not, the servlets wrote the desired HTML directly back to the client. This kind of implementation quickly became hard to maintain and test. After a couple of years, the Model 2 MVC pattern emerged, and we finally had advanced MVC capabilities for the Web.

Frameworks like Spring MVC, Struts, JSF, and Tapestry provide different implementations for this pattern, and they all work quite differently. However, we can identify two main types of web layer implementations: request/response frameworks (e.g., struts and Spring MVC) and component-based frameworks (e.g., JSF and Tapestry). The request/response frameworks operate on `javax.servlet.ServletRequest` and `javax.servlet.ServletResponse` objects. Thus, the fact that they operate on the Servlet API isn't really hidden from the user. The component-based frameworks offer a completely different programming model. They try to hide the Servlet API from the programmer and offer a component-based programming model. Using a component-based framework feels a lot like working with a Swing desktop application.

Both approaches have their advantages and disadvantages. Spring MVC is quite powerful, and it strikes a good balance between the two. It can hide the fact that one works with the Servlet API; however, when needed, it is quite easy to access that API (among other things).

The web layer depends on the domain layer and service layer. In most cases, you want to transform the incoming request into a domain object and call a method on the service layer to do something with that domain object (e.g., update a customer or create an order). Spring MVC makes it easy to map incoming requests to objects, and we can use dependency injection to access the service layer.

In Spring MVC, the web layer is represented by the `org.springframework.web.servlet.mvc.Controller` interface or classes with the `org.springframework.stereotype.Controller` annotation. The interface-based approach is historic, and it has been part of the Spring Framework since its inception; however, it is now considered dated. Regardless, it remains useful for simple use cases, and Spring provides some convenient implementations out of the box. The new annotation-based approach is more powerful and flexible than the original interface-based approach. The main focus in this book is on the annotation-based approach.

After the execution of a controller, the infrastructure (see Chapter 4 for more information on this topic) expects that there is an instance of the `org.springframework.web.servlet.ModelAndView` class. This class incorporates the model (in the form of `org.springframework.ui.ModelMap`) and the view to render. This view can be an actual `org.springframework.web.servlet.View` implementation or the name of a view.

■ **Caution** Don't use the `Controller` annotation on a class with the `Controller` interface. These are handled differently, and mixing both strategies can lead to surprising and unwanted results!

The Service Layer

The service layer is a very important layer in the architecture of an application. It can be considered the heart of our application because it exposes the functionality (the use cases) of the system to the user. It does this by providing a coarse-grained API (as mentioned in Table 3-2). Listing 3-1 describes a coarse-grained service interface.

Listing 3-1. A coarse-grained service interface

```
package com.apress.prospringmvc.bookstore.service;

import com.apress.prospringmvc.bookstore.domain.Account;

public interface AccountService {

    Account save(Account account);

    Account login(String username, String password) throws AuthenticationException;

    Account getAccount(String username);
```

```
}
```

This listing is considered coarse grained because it takes a simple method call from the client to complete a single use case. This is in contrast to the code in Listing 3-2 (fine-grained service methods), which requires a couple of calls to perform a use case.

Listing 3-2. A fine-grained service interface

```
package com.apress.prospringmvc.bookstore.service;

import com.apress.prospringmvc.bookstore.domain.Account;

public interface AccountService {

    Account save(Account account);

    Account getAccount(String username);

    void checkPassword(Account account, String password);

    void updateLastLogin(Account account);

}
```

If at all possible, we should not call a sequence of methods to execute a system function. In fact, we should shield the user from data access and POJO interaction as much as possible. In an ideal world, a coarse-grained function should represent a single unit of work that either succeeds or fails. The user can use different clients (e.g., web application, web service, or desktop application); however, these clients should execute the same business logic. Hence, the service layer should be our single point of entry for the actual system (i.e., the business logic).

The added benefit of having a single point of entry and coarse-grained methods on the service layer is that we can simply apply transactions and security at this layer. We don't have to burden the different clients of our application with the security and transactional requirements. It is now part of the core of the system and generally applied through the use of AOP.

In a web-based environment, we probably have multiple users operating on the services at the same time. The service must be stateless, so it is a good practice to make the service a singleton. In the domain model, state should be kept as much as possible. Keeping the service layer stateless provides an additional benefit: it also makes the layer thread safe.

Keeping the service layer to a single point of entry, keeping the layer stateless, and applying transactions and security on that layer enable us to use other features of the Spring Framework to expose the service layer to different clients. For example, we could use configuration to easily expose our service layer over RMI or JMS. For more information on the remoting support of the Spring Framework, we suggest *Pro Spring 3* (Apress, 2012) or the online Spring Reference Guide (www.springsource.org/documentation).

In our bookstore sample application, the com.apress.prospringmvc.bookstore.service.BookstoreService interface (see Listing 3-3) serves as the interface for our service layer (there are a couple of other interfaces, but this is the most important one). This interface contains several coarse-grained methods. In most cases, it takes a single method call to execute a single use case (e.g., createOrder).

Listing 3-3. *The BookstoreService interface*

```
package com.apress.prospringmvc.bookstore.service;

import java.util.List;

import com.apress.prospringmvc.bookstore.domain.Account;
import com.apress.prospringmvc.bookstore.domain.Book;
import com.apress.prospringmvc.bookstore.domain.BookSearchCriteria;
import com.apress.prospringmvc.bookstore.domain.Cart;
import com.apress.prospringmvc.bookstore.domain.Category;
import com.apress.prospringmvc.bookstore.domain.Order;

public interface BookstoreService {

    List<Book> findBooksByCategory(Category category);

    Book findBook(long id);

    Order findOrder(long id);

    List<Book> findRandomBooks();

    List<Order> findOrdersForAccount(Account account);

    Order store(Order order);

    List<Book> findBooks(BookSearchCriteria bookSearchCriteria);

    Order createOrder(Cart cart, Account account);

    List<Category> findAllCategories();
}
```

As Listing 3-3 demonstrates, the service layer depends on the domain layer to execute the business logic. However, it also has a dependency on the data access layer to store and retrieve data from our underlying data store. The service layer can serve as the glue between one or more domain objects to execute a business function. The service layer should coordinate which domain objects it needs and how they interact together.

The Spring Framework has no interfaces that help us implement our service layer; however, this shouldn't come as a surprise. The service layer is what makes our application; in fact, it is specialized for our application. Nevertheless, the Spring Framework can help us with our architecture and programming model. We can use dependency injection and apply aspects to drive our transactions. All of this has a positive influence on our programming model.

The Data Access Layer

The data access layer is responsible for interfacing with the underlying persistence mechanism. This layer knows how to store and retrieve objects from the datastore. It does this in such a way that the service layer doesn't know which underlying datastore is used. (The datastore could be a database, but it could also consist of flat files on the file system.)

There are several reasons for creating a separate data access layer. First, we don't want to burden the service layer with knowledge of the kind of datastore (or datastores) we use; we want to handle persistency in a transparent way. In our sample application, we use an in-memory database and JPA (Java Persistence API) to store our data. Now imagine that, instead of coming from the database, our com.apress.prospringmvc.bookstore.domain.Account comes from an Active Directory Service. We could simply create a new implementation of the interface that knows how to deal with Active Directory—all without changing our service layer. In theory, we could swap out implementations quite easily; for example, we could switch from JDBC to Hibernate without having to change the service layer. It is quite unlikely that this will happen, but it is nice to have this ability.

The most important reason for this approach is that it simplifies testing our application. In general, data access is slow, so it is important that we keep our tests running as fast as possible. A separate data access layer makes it quite easy to create a stub or mock implementation of our data access layer.

The Spring Framework has great support for data access layers. For example, it provides a consistent and transparent way to work with a variety of different data access frameworks (e.g., JDBC, JPA, Hibernate, iBATIS, and JDO). Each of these technologies Spring provides extensive support for the following abilities:

- Transaction Management

- Resource Handling

- Exception Translation

The transaction management is transparent for each technology it supports. There is a transaction manager that handles the transactions, and it even has support for JTA (Java Transaction API), which enables distributed or global transactions. This excellent transaction support means that the transaction manager can also manage the resources for us. We no longer have to worry that a database connection or file handle might be closed; this is all handled for us. The supported implementations can be found in the org.springframework.jdbc and org.springframework.orm packages.

■ **Tip** The Spring Data project (www.springsource.org/spring-data) provides even deeper integration with several technologies. For several use cases, it can even eliminate the need to write our own implementation of a data access object (DAO) or repository.

The Spring Framework includes another powerful feature as part of its data access support: exception translation. Spring provides extensive exception translation support for all its supported technologies. This feature transforms technology-specific exceptions into a subclass of org.springframework.dao.DataAccessException. For database-driven technologies, it can even take into account the database vendor, version, and error codes received from the database. The exception hierarchy extends from RuntimeException; and as such, it doesn't have to be caught because it isn't a checked exception. For more information on data access support, please see *Pro Spring 3* (Apress, 2012) or the online Spring Reference Guide (`www.springsource.org/documentation`).

Listing 3-4 shows how a data access object or repository might look. Note that the interface doesn't reference or mention any data access technology we use (we use JPA for the sample application). Also, the service layer doesn't care how or where the data is persisted; it simply wants to know how to store or retrieve it.

Listing 3-4. A sample AccountRepository

```
package com.apress.prospringmvc.bookstore.repository;

import com.apress.prospringmvc.bookstore.domain.Account;

public interface AccountRepository {

    Account findByUsername(String username);

    Account findById(long id);

    Account save(Account account);
}
```

More Roads to Rome

As noted previously, the architecture discussed here isn't the only application architecture out there. Which architecture is best for a given application depends on the size of the application, the experience of the development team, and the lifetime of the application. The larger a team or the longer an application lives, the more important a clean architecture with separate layers becomes.

A web application that starts with a single static page probably doesn't require any architecture. However, as the application grows, it becomes increasingly important that we don't try to put everything in that single page because that would make it very difficult to maintain or understand the app, let alone test it.

As an application grows in size and age, we need to refactor its design and keep in mind that each layer or component should have a single responsibility. If we detect some concern that should be in a different layer or touches multiple components, then we should convert it into an aspect (crosscutting concern) of the application and use AOP to apply this aspect to the code.

When deciding how to structure our layers, we should try to identify a clear API (exposed through Java interfaces) for our system. Thinking of an API for our system makes us think about our design, as well as a useful and useable API. In general, if an API is hard to use, it is also hard to test and maintain. Therefore, a clean API is important. In addition, using interfaces between the different layers allows for the separate layers to be built and tested in isolation. This can be a great advantage in larger development teams (or in teams that consists of multiple smaller teams). It allows us to focus on the function we're working with, not on the underlying or higher level components.

When designing and building an application, it's also important to use good OO practices and patterns to solve problems. For example, we should use polymorphism and inheritance to our advantage, and we should use AOP to apply system-wide concerns. The Spring Framework can also help us wire our application together at runtime. Taken as a whole, the features and approaches described in this chapter can help us to keep our code clean and to achieve the best architecture for our applications.

Summary

In this chapter, we covered the MVC pattern, including its origins and what problems it solves. We also briefly discussed the three components of the MVC pattern: the model, view, and controller. Next, we touched on the Model 2 MVC pattern and how using a front controller distinguishes it from the Model 1 MVC pattern. In Spring MVC, this front controller is `org.springframework.web.servlet.DispatcherServlet`.

Next, we briefly covered web application architecture in general. We identified the five different layers generally available in a web application: domain, user interface, web, service, and data access. All of these layers play an important role in our application, and we discussed both what these roles are and how they fit together. We also covered how Spring can help us out in the different layers of an application.

The main take away from this chapter is that the various layers and components in the MVC pattern can help us separate the different concerns. Each layer should have a single responsibility, be it business logic or the glue between the HTTP world and the service layer. Separation of concerns helps us both achieve a clean architecture and create maintainable code. Finally, clean layering makes it easier to test our application.

In the next chapter, we will drill down on the Spring MVC. Specifically, we will explore the `DispatcherServlet` servlet, including how it works and how to configure it. We will also take a closer look at how the different components described in this chapter work in a Spring MVC application.

CHAPTER 4

Spring MVC Architecture

In this chapter, you will dive into the internals of Spring MVC, taking a close look at the `org.springframework.web.servlet.DispatcherServlet`. You will begin by learning how an incoming request is handled by the servlet, as well as how to identify which components play a role in the request handling. After these components have been identified, you will go deeper into the roles and functions of the different components and the different implementations of those components. You will also learn how to configure the `org.springframework.web.servlet.DispatcherServlet,` in part by examining the default configuration.

DispatcherServlet Request Processing Workflow

In the previous chapter, you learned about the important role the front controller plays in a Model 2 MVC pattern. The front controller takes care of dispatching incoming requests to the correct handler and prepares the response, so that it can be rendered into something that the user would like to see. The role of front controller in Spring MVC is played by the `org.springframework.web.servlet` `.DispatcherServlet`. This servlet uses several components to fulfill its role. All these components are expressed as interfaces, for which one or more implementations are available. The next section will explore the general role these components play in the request processing workflow. Another upcoming section will cover the different implementations of the interfaces.

 Note We purposely used the term *handler*. The `DispatcherServlet` is very flexible and customizable, and it can handle more types of handlers than just `org.springframework.web.servlet.mvc.Contrcller` implementations or `org.springframework.stereotype.Controller` annotated classes.

The Workflow

A high-level overview of the request processing workflow is illustrated in Figure 4-1.

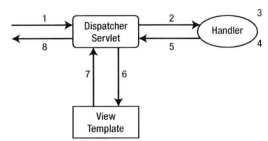

1. The incoming request
2. Dispatching the request to the handler
3. Handling the request
4. Preparing the model and selecting the view
5. Returning org.springframework.web.servlet.ModelAndView
6. Rendering the org.springframework.web.servlet.View with the model
7. Returning control to the servlet
8. Returning the response to the client

Figure 4-1. *The request processing workflow*

In the previous chapters, you learned about the importance of separation of concerns. Within the Spring Framework, the same rules have been applied. A lot of supporting components have been designed as interfaces with extensibility as well as separation of concerns in mind. Although the high level overview in Figure 4-1 is correct, there is more happening behind the scenes. Figure 4-2 shows a more complete view of the request processing workflow.

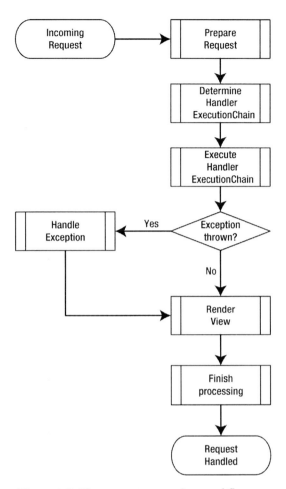

Figure 4-2. *The request processing workflow*

Figure 4-2 provides a global overview of the request processing workflow inside the DispatcherServlet. The following sections will zoom in on the different steps in this flow.

Prepare a Request

Before the DispatcherServlet will start dispatching and handling the request, it first does some preparation and preprocessing of the request. The servlet starts by determining and exposing the current java.util.Locale for the current request using the org.springframework.web.servlet .LocaleResolver. Next, it prepares and exposes the current request in org.springframework.web .context.request.RequestContextHolder. This gives the framework code easy access to the current request, instead of passing it around.

Next, the servlet will construct a so-called `org.springframework.web.servlet.FlashMap`. It does this by calling the `org.springframework.web.servlet.FlashMapManager`, which will try to resolve the input `FlashMap`. This map contains attributes that were explicitly stored in the previous request. In general, this is used when a redirect is made to go to the next page. This topic will be discussed in depth in Chapter 5.

Next, the incoming request is checked for whether it is a multipart HTTP request (this is used when doing file uploads). If so, the request is wrapped in an `org.springframework.web.multipart` `.MultipartHttpServletRequest` by passing it through an `org.springframework.web.multipart` `.MultipartResolver`. After this, the request is ready to be dispatched to the correct handler. Figure 4-3 shows a flow diagram of the first part of the request processing workflow.

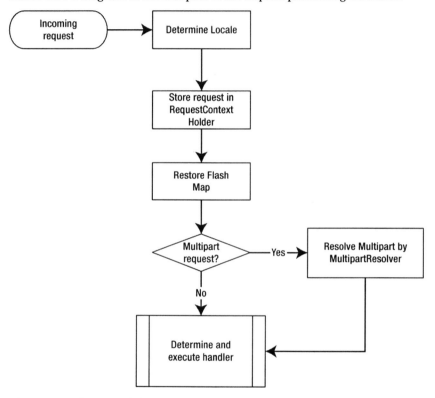

Figure 4-3. The start of the request processing flow

Determine the HandlerExecutionChain

A couple of components are involved in dispatching the request (see Figure 4-4). When a request is ready for dispatching, the `DispatcherServlet` will consult one or more `org.springframework.web.servlet` `.HandlerMapping` implementations to determine which handler can handle the request. If no handler is found, an HTTP 404 response is send back to the client. The `HandlerMapping` returns an `org.springframework.web.servlet.HandlerExecutionChain` (you will learn more about this in the next section). When the handler has been determined, the servlet will attempt to find an `org.springframework`

`.web.servlet.HandlerAdapter` to actually execute the found handler. If no suitable `HandlerAdapter` can be found, a `javax.servlet.ServletException` is thrown.

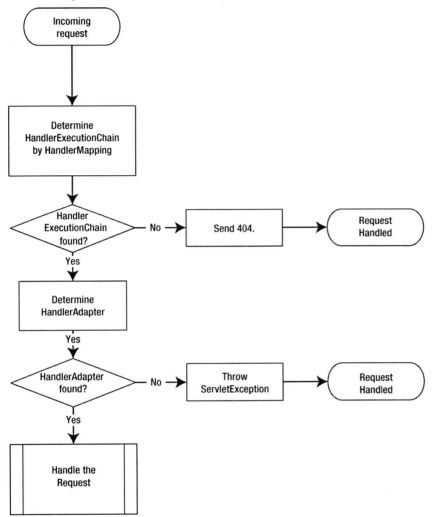

Figure 4-4. *Dispatching the request*

Execute the HandlerExecutionChain

To handle the request, the `DispatcherServlet` uses the `HandlerExecutionChain` to determine what to execute. This class holds a reference to the actual handler that needs to be invoked; however, it also (optionally) references `org.springframework.web.servlet.HandlerInterceptor` implementations that are executed before (`preHandle` method) and after (`postHandle` method) the execution of the handler. These interceptors can be used to apply crosscutting functionality (see Chapter 6 for more information about this topic). If the code executes successfully, the interceptors are called again; and finally, when needed, the view is rendered (see Figure 4-5).

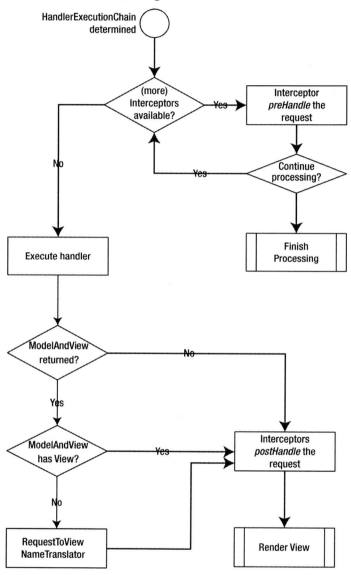

Figure 4-5. Handling the request

The execution of the handler is delegated to the selected HandlerAdapter that was determined in the previous step. It knows how to execute the selected handler and how to translate the response into an org.springframework.web.servlet.ModelAndView. If there is no view in the returned ModelAndView, an org.springframework.web.servlet.RequestToViewNameTranslator is consulted to generate a view name based on the incoming request.

Handle Exceptions

When an exception is thrown during the handling of the request, the DispatcherServlet will consult the configured org.springframework.web.servlet.HandlerExceptionResolvers to handle the thrown exception. The resolver can translate the exception to a view to show the user. For instance, if there is an exception related to database errors, you could show a page indicating the database is down. If the exception isn't resolved, it is rethrown and handled by the servlet container, which generally results in an HTTP 500 response code (internal server error). Figure 4-6 shows this part of the request processing workflow.

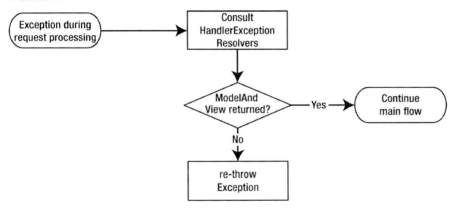

Figure 4-6. Exception handling

Render a View

If a view has been selected during the request processing workflow, the DispatcherServlet first checks whether it is a view reference (this is the case if the view is a java.lang.String). If so, the configured org.springframework.web.servlet.ViewResolvers are consulted to resolve the view reference to an actual org.springframework.web.servlet.View implementation. If there is no view and one cannot be resolved, a javax.servlet.ServletException is thrown. Figure 4-7 shows the view rendering process.

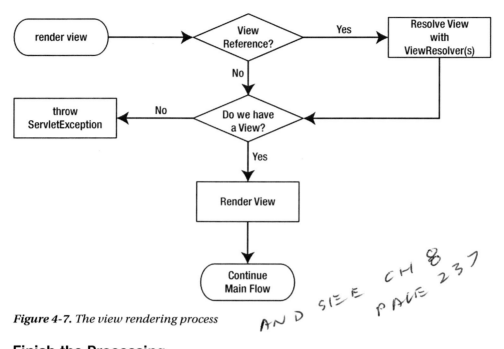

Figure 4-7. The view rendering process

AND SEE CH 8 PAGE 237

Finish the Processing

Each incoming request passes through this step of the request processing flow, regardless of whether there are exceptions. If an HandlerExecutionChain is available, then the afterCompletion method of the interceptors is called. Only the interceptors where the preHandle method was successfully invoked will have their afterCompletion method called. Next, these interceptors are executed in the reverse order that their preHandle method was called. This mimics the behavior seen in servlet filters, where the first filter called is also the last one to be called.

Finally, the DispatcherServlet uses the event mechanism in the Spring Framework to fire an org.springframework.web.context.support.RequestHandledEvent (see Figure 4-8). You could create and configure an org.springframework.context.ApplicationListener to receive and log these events.

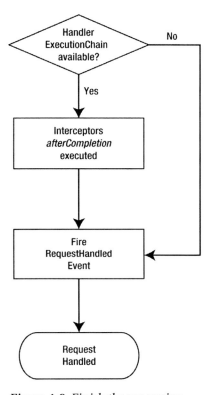

Figure 4-8. *Finish the processing*

The Request Processing Summary

The DispatcherServlet is a key component in processing requests with Spring MVC. It is also highly flexible and configurable. This flexibility comes from the fact that the servlet uses a lot of different components to fulfill its role, and these components are expressed as interfaces. Table 4-1 gives an overview of all the main component types involved in the request processing workflow.

Table 4-1. *The DispatcherServlet Components Used in Request Processing Workflow*

Component type	Description
org.springframework.web.multipart. MultipartResolver	Strategy interface to handle multipart file uploads
org.springframework.web.servlet. LocaleResolver	Strategy for locale resolution and modification
org.springframework.web.servlet. ThemeResolver	Strategy for theming resolution and modification

Component type	Description
org.springframework.web.servlet. HandlerMapping	Strategy to map incoming requests to handler objects
org.springframework.web.servlet. HandlerAdapter	Strategy for the handler object type to execute the handler
org.springframework.web.servlet. HandlerExceptionResolver	Strategy to handle exceptions thrown during handler execution
org.springframework.web.servlet. RequestToViewNameTranslator	Strategy to determine a view name when the handler returns none
org.springframework.web.servlet. ViewResolver	Strategy to translate the view name to an actual view implementation
org.springframework.web.servlet. FlashMapManager	Strategy to simulate flash scope

In the upcoming sections, you will see how to configure the DispatcherServlet. You will also take a closer look at different implementations of the various components.

The DispatcherServlet

Like any servlet, the org.springframework.web.servlet.DispatcherServlet needs to be configured so that the web container can bootstrap and map the servlet. This way, it will be able to handle requests. Configuring the DispatcherServlet is a two-way process. First, you need to tell the container to load a servlet and map it to one or more Urlpatterns.

After bootstrapping, the servlet uses the created org.springframework.web.context .WebApplicationContext to configure itself. The servlet will try to detect the needed components from this application context and if not found, it will use some kind of default (in most cases).

Bootstrapping the DispatcherServlet

The Servlet 3.0 specification introduced several options for configuring and registering a servlet:

- Option 1: Use a web.xml (see Listing 4-1).

- Option 2: Use a web-fragment.xml (see Listing 4-2).

- Option 3: Us a javax.servlet.ServletContainerInitializer (see Listing 4-3).

- Option 4: The sample application uses Spring 3.1, so you can get a fourth option by implementing the org.springframework.web.WebApplicationInitializer interface.

The dispatcher servlet needs a WebApplicationContext that should contain all the beans that enable the dispatcher servlet to configure itself. By default, the dispatcher servlet will create an org.springframework.web.context.support.XmlWebApplicationContext. All samples in the upcoming sections load the org.springframework.web.servlet.DispatcherServlet and map it to all incoming requests (/*). All these configurations lead to the same runtime setup of the servlet. Only the mechanism by which you do that is different. The remainder of the book will use Option 4 to configure the sample application.

░ **Note** The org.springframework.web.context.WebApplicationContext is a specialized extension of the org.springframework.context.ApplicationContext that is needed in web environments (see Chapter 2 for more information).

The sample application that you are building throughout the book will use Option 4 as much as possible to configure the environment and application. Nevertheless, you will learn the basic setup for all four options of configuring the servlet.

Using web.xml

The web.xml file has been around since the inception of the servlet specification. It is an XML file that contains all the configuration you need to bootstrap the servlet, listeners, and/or filters. Listing 4-1 shows the minimal web.xml required to bootstrap the DispatcherServlet. The web.xml file must be in the WEB-INF directory of the web application (this is dictated by the servlet specification).

Listing 4-1. The web.xml configuration (Servlet 3.0)

```
<web-app version="3.0"
        xmlns="http://java.sun.com/xml/ns/javaee"
        xmlns:xsi="http://www.w3.org/2001/XMLSchema-instance"
        xsi:schemaLocation=http://java.sun.com/xml/ns/javaee
                           http://java.sun.com/xml/ns/javaee/web-app_3_0.xsd
        metadata-complete="true">

    <servlet>
        <servlet-name>bookstore</servlet-name>
        <servlet-class>
            org.springframework.web.servlet.DispatcherServlet
        </servlet-class>
        <load-on-startup>1</load-on-startup>
    </servlet>

    <servlet-mapping>
        <servlet-name>bookstore</servlet-name>
        <url-pattern>/*</url-pattern>
    </servlet-mapping>
</web-app>
```

■ **Note** By default, the dispatcher servlet loads a file named [servletname]-servlet.xml from the WEB-INF directory.

The metadata-complete attribute in the web-app element instructs the servlet container to not scan the classpath for javax.servlet.ServletContainerInitializer implementations; neither will it scan for web-fragment.xml files. Adding this attribute to your web.xml can increase startup times considerably because it will scan the classpath, which can take quite some time in a large application.

Using web-fragment.xml

The web-fragment.xml feature has been available since the 3.0 version of the servlet specification, and it allows for a more modularized configuration of the web application. The web-fragment.xml has to be in the META-INF directory of a jar file. It isn't detected in the META-INF of the web application; it has to be in a jar file. The web-fragment.xml can contain the same elements as the web.xml (see Listing 4-2).

The benefit of this approach is that each module, packaged as a jar files can contribute to the configuration of the web application. This can also be considered a drawback because now you have scattered your configuration over your code base, which could be troublesome in larger projects.

Listing 4-2. The web-fragment.xml configuration (Servlet 3.0)

```
<web-fragment version="3.0"
  xmlns="http://java.sun.com/xml/ns/javaee"
  xmlns:xsi="http://www.w3.org/2001/XMLSchema-instance"
  xsi:schemaLocation="http://java.sun.com/xml/ns/javaee
                      http://java.sun.com/xml/ns/javaee/web-fragment_3_0.xsd">

    <servlet>
        <servlet-name>bookstore</servlet-name>
        <servlet-class>
            org.springframework.web.servlet.DispatcherServlet
        </servlet-class>
        <load-on-startup>1</load-on-startup>
    </servlet>

    <servlet-mapping>
        <servlet-name>bookstore</servlet-name>
        <url-pattern>/*</url-pattern>
    </servlet-mapping>
</web-fragment>
```

Using ServletContainerInitializer

Another feature introduced in the 3.0 version of the servlet specification is the option to use a Java-based approach to configuring your web environment (see Listing 4-3). A Servlet 3.0-compatible container will scan the classpath for classes that implement the javax.servlet.ServletContainerInitializer interface, and it will invoke the onStartup method on those classes. By adding a javax.servlet .annotation.HandlesTypes annotation on these classes, you can also be handed classes that you need to

further configure your web application (this is the mechanism that allows the fourth option to use an
org.springframework.web.WebApplicationInitializer).

Like web.fragments, a ServletContainerInitializer allows for a modularized configuration of your
web application, but now in a Java-based way. Using Java gives you all the added benefits of using the
Java language instead of XML. At this point, you have strong typing, can influence the construction of
your servlet, and have an easier way of configuring your servlets (in an XML file, this is done by adding
init-param and/or context-param elements in the XML file).

Listing 4-3. A Java-based configuration

```
package com.apress.prospringmvc.bookstore.web;

import java.util.Set;

// javax.servlet imports omitted.

import org.springframework.web.servlet.DispatcherServlet;

public class BookstoreServletContainerInitializer
implements ServletContainerInitializer {

  @Override
  public void onStartup(Set<Class<?>> classes, ServletContext servletContext)
  throws ServletException {
      ServletRegistration.Dynamic registration;
      registration = servletContext.addServlet("dispatcher", DispatcherServlet.class);
      registration.setLoadOnStartup(1);
      registration.addMapping("/*");
  }
}
```

Using WebApplicationInitializer

Now it's time to look at Option 4 for configuring your application while using Spring. Spring already
provides a ServletContainerInitializer implementation, the org.springframework.web
.SpringServletContainerInitializer that makes life a little easier (see Listing 4-4). The implementation
provided by the Spring Framework will detect and instantiate all instances of org.springframework.web
.WebApplicationInitializer and call the onStartup method of those instances.

Listing 4-4. The WebApplicationInitializer configuration

```
package com.apress.prospringmvc.bookstore.web;

// javax.servlet imports omitted

import org.springframework.web.WebApplicationInitializer;
import org.springframework.web.servlet.DispatcherServlet;

public class BookstoreWebApplicationInitializer implements WebApplicationInitializer {
```

```
    @Override
    public void onStartup(ServletContext servletContext) throws ServletException {
        ServletRegistration.Dynamic   registration
        registration = servletContext.addServlet("dispatcher",↵
DispatcherServlet.class);
        registration.addMapping("/*");
        registration.setLoadOnStartup(1);
    }
}
```

■ **Caution** Using this feature can severely impact the startup time of your application! First, the servlet container needs to scan the classpath for all `javax.servlet.ServletContainerInitializer` implementations. Second, the classpath is scanned for `org.springframework.web.WebApplicationInitializer` implementations. This scanning can take some time in large applications.

Configuring the DispatcherServlet

Configuring the `org.springframework.web.servlet.DispatcherServlet` is a two step process. The first step is to configure the behavior of the servlet by setting properties directly on the dispatcher servlet (the declaration).The second step is to configure the components in the application context (initialization).

The dispatcher servlet comes with a lot of default settings for components. This saves you from doing a lot of configuration for basic behavior, and you can override and extend the configuration however you want. In addition to the default configuration for the dispatcher servlet, there is also a default for Spring @MVC, which can be enabled by using the `org.springframework.web.servlet.config` `.annotation.EnableWebMvc` annotation (see the "Enabling Features" section in Chapter 2).

Dispatcher Servlet Properties

The dispatcher servlet has a number of properties that can be set. All these properties have a setter method, and all can be either set programmatically or set when using XML configuration by including a servlet initialization parameter. Table 4-2 lists and describes the properties available on the dispatcher servlet.

Table 4-2. The DispatcherServlet's Properties

Property	Default	Description
cleanupAfterInclude	true	Indicates whether to clean up the request attributes after an include request. In general, the default suffices, and this property should only be set to false in special cases.

Property	Default	Description
contextAttribute	null	Stores the application context for this servlet. This is useful if the application context is created by some means other than the servlet itself.
contextClass	org.springframework. web.context.support. XmlWebApplication Context	Configures the type of org.springframework.web. context.WebApplicationContext to be constructed by the servlet (it needs a default constructor). Will be configured using the given contextConfig Location. This isn't needed if you pass in an application context by using the constructor.
contextConfigLocation	[servlet-name]-servlet.xml	Indicates the location of the configuration files for the specified application context class.
contextId	null	Provides the Id of the application context. For example, this is used when the context is logged or sent to System.out.
contextInitializers contextInitializerClasses	null	Use the optional org.springframework.context. ApplicationContextInitializer classes to do some initialization logic for the application context, such as activating a certain profile.
detectAllHandlerAdapters	true	Detects all org.springframework.web.servlet.HandlerAdapte rs that can be detected from the application context. When set to false, a single one is detected by using the name, handlerAdapter.
detectAllHandlerException Resolvers	true	Detects all org.springframework.web. servlet.HandlerExceptionResolvers from the application context. When set to false, a single one is detected by using the name, handlerExceptionResolver.
detectAllHandlerMappings	true	Detects all org.springframework.web. servlet.HandlerMappings from the application context. When set to false, a single one is detected by using the name, handlerMapping.
detectAllViewResolvers	true	Detects all org.springframework.web. servlet.ViewResolvers from the application context. When set to false, a single one is detected by using the name, viewResolver.

Property	Default	Description
dispatchOptionsRequest	false	Indicates whether to handle HTTP OPTIONS requests. The default is false; when set to true, you can also handle HTTP OPTIONS requests.
dispatchTraceRequest	false	Indicates whether to handle HTTP TRACE requests. The default is false; when set to true, you can also handle HTTP TRACE requests.
environment	org.springframework.web.context.support.StandardServletEnvironment	Configures the org.springframework.core.env.Environment to use for this servlet. The environment specifies which profile is active and can hold properties specific for this environment.
namespace	[servletname]-servlet	Use this namespace to configure the application context.
publishContext	true	Indicates whether the servlet's application context is being published to the javax.servlet.ServletContext. For production, it is recommended that you set this to false.
publishEvents	true	Indicates whether to fire after request processing an org.springframework.web.context.support.ServletRequestHandledEvent. You can use an org.springframework.context.ApplicationListener to receive these events.
threadContextInheritable	false	Indicates whether to expose the LocaleContext and RequestAttributes to child threads created from the request handling thread.

The Application Context

The org.springframework.web.servlet.DispatcherServlet needs an org.springframework.web.context.WebApplicationContext to configure itself with the needed components. You can either let the servlet construct one itself or use the constructor to pass an application context. In an XML-based configuration file, the first option is used (because there is no way to construct an application context). In a Java-based configuration, the second option is used.

In the sample application, the com.apress.prospringmvc.bookstore.web.BookstoreWebApplicationInitializer is the class that bootstraps the application. To enable Java-based configuration, you need to instruct the servlet to use a Java-based application context (the default is an XML-based one), as well as pass it the configuration classes. You will use the org.springframework.web.context.support.AnnotationConfigWebApplicationContext class to set up the application and to configure the servlet. The changes are highlighted in bold in Listing 4-5.

Listing 4-5. The BookstoreWebApplicationInitializer with ApplicationContext

```
package com.apress.prospringmvc.bookstore.web;

// javax.servlet imports omitted.

import org.springframework.web.WebApplicationInitializer;
import org.springframework.web.context.WebApplicationContext;
import org.springframework.web.context.support
        .AnnotationConfigWebApplicationContext;
import org.springframework.web.servlet.DispatcherServlet;

import com.apress.prospringmvc.bookstore.web.config.WebMvcContextConfiguration;

public class BookstoreWebApplicationInitializer↵
 implements WebApplicationInitializer {

  @Override
  public void onStartup(final ServletContext servletContext)
  throws ServletException {
      registerDispatcherServlet(servletContext);
    }

  private void registerDispatcherServlet(final ServletContext servletContext) {
      WebApplicationContext dispatcherContext = createContext↵
(WebMvcContextConfiguration.class);
      DispatcherServlet dispatcherServlet = new DispatcherServlet(dispatcherContext);
      ServletRegistration.Dynamic dispatcher;
      dispatcher = servletContext.addServlet("dispatcher", dispatcherServlet);
      dispatcher.setLoadOnStartup(1);
      dispatcher.addMapping("/");
  }

  private WebApplicationContext createContext(final Class<?>... annotatedClasses) {
      AnnotationConfigWebApplicationContext context
      context = new AnnotationConfigWebApplicationContext();
      context.register(annotatedClasses);
      return context;
  }
}
```

Listing 4-5 shows how to construct the org.springframework.web.servlet.DispatcherServlet and pass it an application context. This is the most basic way of configuring the servlet.

Chapter 2 covered the notion of profiles. To select a profile, you could include a servlet-initialization parameter (see Chapter 2); however, to be more dynamic, you could use a org.springframework.context.ApplicationContextInitializer. Such initializers are used to initialize an application context just before it loads all the beans.

This is useful in a web application when you want to configure or set the profile(s) you want to use (again, see Chapter 2 for more information). For instance, you might have a custom system property you need to set. Alternatively, you might detect the profile by reading a certain file on the file system or even select a profile based on the operation system. You have an almost unlimited number of options.

In Appendix A, you will learn how to deploy your application to CloudFoundry. There is also an API for CloudFoundry that contains an ApplicationContextInitializer. This implementation detects that it is running on the cloud and activates a profile named cloud (see Listing 4-6).

Listing 4-6. *The CloudApplicationContextInitializer*

```java
package org.cloudfoundry.reconfiguration.spring;

// Other imports omitted

import org.cloudfoundry.runtime.env.CloudEnvironment;
import org.springframework.context.ApplicationContextInitializer;
import org.springframework.context.ConfigurableApplicationContext;
import org.springframework.core.Ordered;
import org.springframework.core.env.ConfigurableEnvironment;
import org.springframework.core.env.EnumerablePropertySource;
import org.springframework.core.env.PropertiesPropertySource;
import org.springframework.core.env.PropertySource;

public final class CloudApplicationContextInitializer
implements ApplicationContextInitializer<ConfigurableApplicationContext>,
        Ordered {

    private static final Log logger =
            LogFactory.getLog(CloudApplicationContextInitializer.class);

    private static final int DEFAULT_ORDER = 0;

    private ConfigurableEnvironment springEnvironment;
    private CloudEnvironment cloudFoundryEnvironment;

    public CloudApplicationContextInitializer() {
        cloudFoundryEnvironment = new CloudEnvironment();
    }

    @Override
    public void initialize(ConfigurableApplicationContext applicationContext) {
        if (!cloudFoundryEnvironment.isCloudFoundry()) {
            logger.info("Not running on Cloud Foundry.")
            return;
        }
        try {
            logger.info("Initializing Spring Environment for Cloud Foundry");
            springEnvironment = applicationContext.getEnvironment();
            addPropertySource(buildPropertySource());
            addActiveProfile("cloud");
        } catch (Throwable t) {
            // be safe
            logger.error("Unexpected exception on initialization: "
                    + t.getMessage(), t);
        }
    }
}
```

```
    // Other methods omitted
}
```

Component Resolution

When the servlet is configured, it will receive an initialization request from the servlet container. When the servlet initializes, it uses the logic, as depicted in Figure 4-9, to detect the components needed. Some components are detected by type, whereas others are detected by name. For the components detectable by type, you can specify (see Table 4-2) that you don't want to do this. In this case, the component will be detected by a well-known name. Table 4-3 lists the different components involved in request processing and the bean name used to detect it. The table also indicates whether the dispatcher servlet detects multiple instances automatically (when yes can be disabled, then a single bean is detected by the name, as specified in the table).

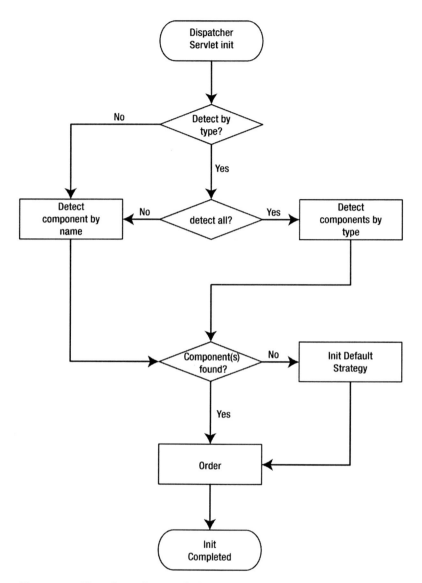

Figure 4-9. *The DispatcherServlet's discovery of components*

Table 4-3. Components and Their Names

Component	Default Bean Name	Detect Multiple
org.springframework.web.multipart. MultipartResolver	multipartResolver	No
org.springframework.web.servlet. LocaleResolver	localeResolver	No
org.springframework.web.servlet. ThemeResolver	themeResolver	No
org.springframework.web.servlet. HandlerMapping	handlerMapping	Yes
org.springframework.web.servlet. HandlerAdapter	handlerAdapter	Yes
org.springframework.web.servlet. HandlerExceptionResolver	handlerExceptionResolver	Yes
org.springframework.web.servlet. RequestToViewNameTranslator	requestToViewNameTranslator	No
org.springframework.web.servlet. ViewResolver	viewResolver	Yes
org.springframework.web.servlet. FlashMapManager	flashMapManager	No

The Dispatcher Servlet's Default Configuration

You might feel a bit overwhelmed by all the components involved in the handling of a request. You might even wonder if you need to configure all of them explicitly. Luckily, Spring MVC has some sensible defaults that, in a lot of cases, are enough—or at least enough to get started. As you can see in Table 4-4, the dispatcher servlet has quite a few default settings. You can find more information on the different implementations in the next section.

Table 4-4. The DispatcherServlet's Default Components

Component	Default implementation(s)
MultipartResolver	No default, explicit configuration is required.
LocaleResolver	org.springframework.web.servlet.i18n. AcceptHeaderLocaleResolver

Component	Default implementation(s)
ThemeResolver	`org.springframework.web.servlet.theme.` `FixedThemeResolver`
HandlerMapping	`org.springframework.web.servlet.handler.` `BeanNameUrlHandlerMapping`
	`org.springframework.web.servlet.mvc.annotation.` `DefaultAnnotationHandlerMapping`
HandlerAdapter	`org.springframework.web.servlet.mvc.` `HttpRequestHandlerAdapter`
	`org.springframework.web.servlet.mvc.` `SimpleControllerHandlerAdapter`
	`org.springframework.web.servlet.mvc.annotation.` `AnnotationMethodHandlerAdapter`
HandlerExceptionResolver	`org.springframework.web.servlet.mvc.annotation.` `AnnotationMethodHandlerExceptionResolver`
	`org.springframework.web.servlet.mvc.annotation.` `ResponseStatusExceptionResolver`
	`org.springframework.web.servlet.mvc.support.` `DefaultHandlerExceptionResolver`
RequestToViewNameTranslator	`org.springframework.web.servlet.view.` `DefaultRequestToViewNameTranslator`
ViewResolver	`org.springframework.web.servlet.view.` `InternalResourceViewResolver`
FlashMapManager	`org.springframework.web.servlet.support.` `SessionFlashMapManager`

The Spring @MVC Defaults

Chapter 2 covered Spring's @Enable annotations. One of those annotations is `org.springframework`
`.web.servlet.config.annotation.EnableWebMvc`. This annotation enables the powerful and flexible
annotation-based request handling components, and it overrides some of the defaults from the
dispatcher servlet. The actual configuration can be found in the `org.springframework.web.servlet`
`.config.annotation.WebMvcConfigurationSupport` class. This is the configuration that is registered when
the annotation is used. Table 4-5 shows the default configuration when @MVC is enabled and highlights
the differences between @MVC and the dispatcher servlet.

Table 4-5. Spring's @MVC Default Components

Component	Default implementation(s)
MultipartResolver	No default, explicit configuration required.
LocaleResolver	org.springframework.web.servlet.i18n. AcceptHeaderLocaleResolver
ThemeResolver	org.springframework.web.servlet.theme. FixedThemeResolver
HandlerMapping	org.springframework.web.servlet.handler. BeanNameUrlHandlerMapping
	org.springframework.web.servlet.mvc.method.annotation. RequestMappingHandlerMapping
HandlerAdapter	org.springframework.web.servlet.mvc. HttpRequestHandlerAdapter
	org.springframework.web.servlet.mvc. SimpleControllerHandlerAdapter
	org.springframework.web.servlet.mvc.method.annotation. RequestMappingHandlerAdapter
HandlerExceptionResolver	**org.springframework.web.servlet.mvc.method.annotation. ExceptionHandlerExceptionResolver**
	org.springframework.web.servlet.mvc.annotation. ResponseStatusExceptionResolver
	org.springframework.web.servlet.mvc.support. DefaultHandlerExceptionResolver
RequestToViewNameTranslator	org.springframework.web.servlet.view. DefaultRequestToViewNameTranslator
ViewResolver	org.springframework.web.servlet.view. InternalResourceViewResolver
FlashMapManager	org.springframework.web.servlet.support. SessionFlashMapManager

The differences might not seem that big, but the new components registered provide significantly different initial defaults compared to those provided by the dispatcher servlet. The essential difference is this: Spring's @MVC components enable you to write more flexible request handling methods (see Chapters 5 and 6).

The Spring MVC Components

In the previous sections, you learned about the request processing workflow and the components used in it. You also learned how to configure the org.springframework.web.servlet.DispatcherServlet. In this section, you will take a closer look at all the components involved in the request processing workflow. For example, you will explore the APIs of the different components and see which implementations ship with the Spring Framework.

HandlerMapping

The HandlerMapping's responsibility is to determine which handler to dispatch the incoming request to. A criterion that you could use to map the incoming request is the URL; however, implementations (see Figure 4-10) are free to choose what criteria to use to determine the mapping.

The API for the org.springframework.web.servlet.HandlerMapping consists of a single method (see Listing 4-7). This method is called by the DispatcherServlet to determine the org.springframework.web .servlet.HandlerExecutionChain. It is possible to have more than one handler mapping configured. The servlet will call the different handler mappings in sequence until one of them doesn't return null.

Listing 4-7. The HandlerMapping API

```
package org.springframework.web.servlet;

import javax.servlet.http.HttpServletRequest;
public interface HandlerMapping {

    HandlerExecutionChain getHandler(HttpServletRequest request)
    throws Exception;

}
```

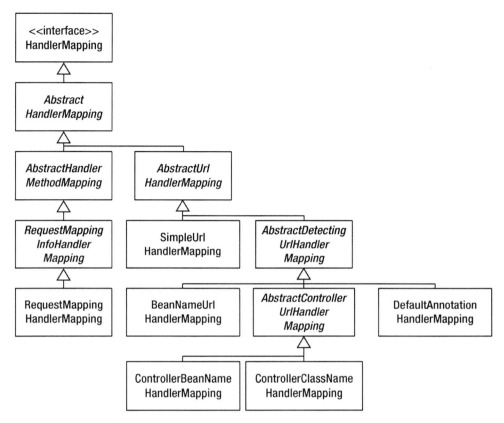

Figure 4-10. HandlerMapping implementations

Out of the box, Spring MVC provides six different implementations. Most of them are based on URL mappings. Two of the implementations offer a more sophisticated mapping strategy, which you'll learn about momentarily. However before looking at the different implementations, it might help to take a closer look at a URL and which parts are important.

A request URL consists of several parts. Let's take a look at the http://www.example.org/bookstore/app/home URL and dissect that. A URL consists for four parts (see Figure 4-11):

1. The hostname of the server

2. The name of the application (none, if it is the root application)

3. The name of the servlet mapping (in the sample app, it is mapped to /)

4. The path inside the servlet

Figure 4-11. *URL mapping*

By default, all the provided handler-mapping implementations use the path relative to the servlet context inside the servlet (the servlet context relative path) to resolve handlers. Setting the alwaysUseFullPath property to true can change this behavior. The servlet mapping is then included, which would (for the example at hand) lead to */app/home* being used to resolve a request handler; otherwise, */home* would be used.

A final feature shared among all implementations is that a default handler can be configured. This is done by setting the defaultHandler property. When no handler can be found for an incoming request, it will always be mapped to the default handler. This is optional, and it should be used with caution, especially when chaining multiple handler mappings. Only the last handler mapping should specify a default handler, or else the chain breaks.

BeanNameUrlHandlerMapping

The org.springframework.web.servlet.handler.BeanNameUrlHandlerMapping is one of the default strategies used by the dispatcher servlet. This implementation treats any bean with a name that starts with a / as a potential request handler. A bean can have multiple names, and names can also contain a wildcard, expressed as an *.

This implementation uses ant-style regular expressions to match the URL of the incoming request to the name of a bean. It follows this algorithm:

1. Attempt exact match; if found, exit.

2. Search all registered paths for a match; the most specific one will win.

3. If no matches are found, return the handler mapped to /* or to the default handler (if configured).

■ **Note** The name of the bean is not the same as the id. Id is defined by the XML specification, and it cannot contain special characters such as /. This means you need to use the name of the bean. You can provide the name for a bean by setting the name attribute on the org.springframework.context.annotation.Bean annotation. A bean can have multiple names, and names can be written like an ant-style regular expression.

Listing 4-8 shows how to use a bean name and map it to the /index.htm url. In the sample application, you could now use http://localhost:8080/chapter4-bookstore/index.htm to call this controller.

Listing 4-8. The BeanNameUrlHandlerMapping sample configuration

```
package com.apress.prospringmvc.bookstore.web.config;

import java.util.Properties;

import org.springframework.context.annotation.Bean;
import org.springframework.context.annotation.Configuration;

import com.apress.prospringmvc.bookstore.web.IndexController;

@Configuration
public class WebMvcContextConfiguration {

    @Bean(name = { "/index.htm" })
    public IndexController indexController() {
        return new IndexController();
    }
}
```

SimpleUrlHandlerMapping

This implementation requires explicit configuration, as opposed to the org.springframework.web
.servlet.handler.BeanNameUrlHandlerMapping, and it doesn't autodetect mappings. Listing 4-9 shows a
sample configuration. Again, you map the controller to the /index.htm.

Listing 4-9. The SimpleUrlHandlerMapping sample configuration

```
package com.apress.prospringmvc.bookstore.web.config;

// Other imports omitted see Listing 4-8

import org.springframework.web.servlet.HandlerMapping;
import org.springframework.web.servlet.handler.SimpleUrlHandlerMapping;

@Configuration
public class WebMvcContextConfiguration {

    @Bean
    public IndexController indexController() {
        return new IndexController();
    }

    @Bean
    public HandlerMapping simpleUrlHandlerMapping() {
        SimpleUrlHandlerMapping urlMapping = new SimpleUrlHandlerMapping();
        Properties mappings = new Properties();
        mappings.put("/index.htm", "indexController");
        urlMapping.setMappings(mappings);
        return urlMapping;
```

```
      }
}
```

You need to explicitly configure the SimpleUrlHandlerMapping and pass it the mappings (see the code in bold). You map the /index.htm URL to the controller named indexController. If you have a lot of controllers, this configuration grows considerably. The advantage of this approach is that you have all your mapping in a single location.

ControllerBeanNameHandlerMapping

This implementation works similarly to the org.springframework.web.servlet.handler .BeanNameUrlHandlerMapping, with one big difference: it doesn't require the bean name to start with a /. This mapping detects all controllers in the application context, takes their names, and prefixes them with a /. Optionally, it can also apply a suffix to the generated URL mapping. Listing 4-10 shows how to map the controller to /index.htm using this handler mapping.

Listing 4-10. The ControllerBeanNameHandlerMapping sample configuration

```
package com.apress.prospringmvc.bookstore.web.config;

// Other imports omitted see Listing 4-8

import org.springframework.web.servlet.HandlerMapping;
import org.springframework.web.servlet.mvc.support.ControllerBeanNameHandlerMapping;

@Configuration
public class WebMvcContextConfiguration {

   @Bean(name = "index")
   public IndexController indexController() {
       return new IndexController();
   }

   @Bean
   public HandlerMapping controllerBeanNameHandlerMapping() {
       ControllerBeanNameHandlerMapping mapping;
       mapping = new ControllerBeanNameHandlerMapping();
       mapping.setUrlSuffix(".htm");
       return mapping;
   }
}
```

ControllerClassNameHandlerMapping

This implementation detects all controllers in the application context, and it uses the simple name of the class to create URL mappings. For the com.apress.prospringmvc.bookstore.web.IndexController, it would create a URL of /index. It takes the simple name of the class, strips the controller part, and makes the remainder lowercase (unless configured otherwise). Listing 4-11 shows a sample configuration of this implementation, and it will map the controller to the /index URL. This mapping implementation doesn't support suffixes (e.g., .htm).

Listing 4-11. The ControllerClassNameHandlerMapping sample configuration

```
package com.apress.prospringmvc.bookstore.web.config;

// Other imports omitted see Listing 4-8

import org.springframework.web.servlet.HandlerMapping;
import org.springframework.web.servlet.mvc.support.ControllerClassNameHandlerMapping;


@Configuration
public class WebMvcContextConfiguration {

    @Bean
    public IndexController indexController() {
        return new IndexController();
    }

    @Bean
    public HandlerMapping controllerClassNameHandlerMapping() {
        return new ControllerClassNameHandlerMapping();
    }
}
```

This mapping implementation can be very convenient if you have some naming conventions in your controllers, and they are directly mapped to URLs. This approach can save a lot of configuration.

DefaultAnnotationHandlerMapping and RequestMappingHandlerMapping

The DefaultAnnotationHandlerMapping and RequestMappingHandlerMapping implementations are the more sophisticated implementations. Both are very powerful, and both use annotations to detect mappings. Also, both detect the org.springframework.web.bind.annotation.RequestMapping annotation on request-handling beans in the application context. This annotation can be on either the class and/or the method level. To map the com.apress.prospringmvc.bookstore.web.IndexController to /index.htm you need to add the annotation. Listing 4-12 is the controller, and Listing 4-13 shows the sample configuration.

Listing 4-12. The IndexController with RequestMapping

```
package com.apress.prospringmvc.bookstore.web;

import org.springframework.stereotype.Controller;
import org.springframework.web.bind.annotation.RequestMapping;
import org.springframework.web.servlet.ModelAndView;

@Controller
public class IndexController {

    @RequestMapping(value = "/index.htm")
    public ModelAndView indexPage() {
        return new ModelAndView("/WEB-INF/views/index.jsp");
```

```
    }
}
```

Listing 4-13. An annotation-based sample configuration

```
package com.apress.prospringmvc.bookstore.web.config;

// Other imports omitted see Listing 4-8

@Configuration
public class WebMvcContextConfiguration {

    @Bean
    public IndexController indexController() {
        return new IndexController();
    }
}
```

The DefaultAnnotationHandlerMapping is one of the default mappings registered by the dispatcher servlet. If you want to use the RequestMappingHandlerMapping, you need to explicitly configure it or use the org.springframework.web.servlet.config.annotation.EnableWebMvc annotation. The RequestMappingHandlerMapping implementation is more powerful and flexible than the default, registered one, and it allows for more flexible configuration and mapping methods. The extensibility and flexibility of this approach are covered in Chapter 6.

HandlerAdapter

The org.springframework.web.servlet.HandlerAdapter is the glue between the dispatcher servlet and the selected handler. It removes the actual execution logic from the dispatcher servlet, which makes the dispatcher servlet infinitely extensible. Consider this component the glue between the servlet and the actual handler implementation. Listing 4-14 shows the HandlerAdapter API.

Listing 4-14. The HandlerAdapter API

```
package org.springframework.web.servlet;

import javax.servlet.http.HttpServletRequest;
import javax.servlet.http.HttpServletResponse;

public interface HandlerAdapter {

    boolean supports(Object handler);

    ModelAndView handle(HttpServletRequest request,
                        HttpServletResponse response,
                        Object handler) throws Exception;

    long getLastModified(HttpServletRequest request, Object handler);

}
```

As Listing 4-14 shows, the API consists of several methods. The `supports` method is called on each handler in the context by the dispatcher servlet, and this is done to determine which `HandlerAdapter` can execute the selected handler. If the handler adapter can execute the handler, the `handle` method is called to actually execute the selected handler. The execution of the handler can lead to an `org.springframework.web.servlet.ModelAndView` being returned. However, some implementations always return `null`, indicating the response has already been sent to the client.

If the incoming request is a `GET` or `HEAD` request, the `getLastModified` method is called to determine the time when the underlying resource was last modified (`-1` means the content is always regenerated). The result is sent back to the client as a `Last-Modified` request header and compared with the `If-Modified-Since` request header. If there was a modification, the content will be regenerated and resent to the client; otherwise, an HTTP Response Code 304 (Not Modified) will be sent back to the client. This is particularly useful when the dispatcher servlet serves static resources, which will save bandwidth.

Out of the box, Spring MVC provides five implementations of the `HandlerAdapter` (see Figure 4-12).

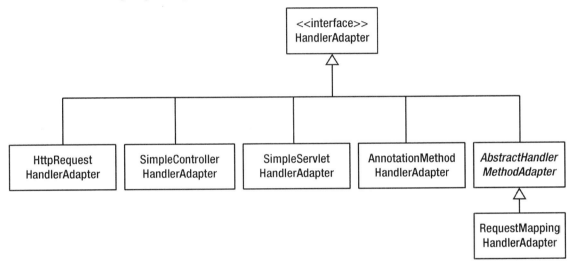

Figure 4-12. HandlerAdapter implementations

HttpRequestHandlerAdapter

The `org.springframework.web.servlet.mvc.HttpRequestHandlerAdapter` knows how to execute `org.springframework.web.HttpRequestHandler` instances. This handler adapter is mostly used by Spring Remoting to support some of the HTTP remoting options. However, there are two implementations of the `org.springframework.web.HttpRequestHandler` interface that you will also use. One serves static resources, and the other forwards incoming requests to the default servlet of the servlet container (see Chapter 5 for more information on this implementation).

SimpleControllerHandlerAdapter

The `org.springframework.web.servlet.mvc.SimpleControllerHandlerAdapter` knows how to execute `org.springframework.web.servlet.mvc.Controller` implementations. It returns the `org.springframework.web.servlet.ModelAndView` returned from the `handleRequest` method of the controller instance.

SimpleServletHandlerAdapter

It can be convenient to configure `javax.servlet.Servlet` instances in the application context and put them behind the dispatcher servlet. To be able to execute those servlets, you need the `org.springframework.web.servlet.handler.SimpleServletHandlerAdapter`. It knows how to execute the `javax.servlet.Servlet`, and it always return `null` because it expects the servlet to handle the response itself.

AnnotationMethodHandlerAdapter

The `org.springframework.web.servlet.mvc.annotation.AnnotationMethodHandlerAdapter` is used to execute methods annotated with `org.springframework.web.bind.annotation.RequestMapping`. It converts method arguments and gives easy access to the request parameters. The return value of the method is converted or added to the `org.springframework.web.servlet.ModelAndView` internally created by this handler adapter. This whole mapping and converting process is quite rigid; however, there are some extension points that enable customizing or adding your own type handling.

RequestMappingHandlerAdapter

The `org.springframework.web.servlet.mvc.method.annotation.RequestMappingHandlerAdapter` is used to execute methods annotated with `org.springframework.web.bind.annotation.RequestMapping`. It will convert method arguments and give easy access to the request parameters. The return value of the method is converted or added to the `org.springframework.web.servlet.ModelAndView` internally created by this handler adapter. The whole binding and converting process is quite configurable and flexible. A lot of the lessons learned from the `org.springframework.web.servlet.mvc.annotation` `.AnnotationMethodHandlerAdapter` have been incorporated in here; the possibilities are explained in Chapters 5 and 6.

MultipartResolver

The `org.springframework.web.multipart.MultipartResolver` strategy interface is used to determine whether an incoming request is a multipart file request (used for file uploads); and if so, it wraps the incoming request in an `org.springframework.web.multipart.MultipartHttpServletRequest`. The wrapped request can then be used to get easy access to the underlying multipart files from the form. File uploading is explained in Chapter 7. Listing 4-15 shows `MultipartResolver` API.

Listing 4-15. *The MultipartResolver API*

```
package org.springframework.web.multipart;

import javax.servlet.http.HttpServletRequest;

public interface MultipartResolver {

    boolean isMultipart(HttpServletRequest request);

    MultipartHttpServletRequest resolveMultipart(HttpServletRequest request)
    throws MultipartException;
```

```
    void cleanupMultipart(MultipartHttpServletRequest request);
}
```

The three methods of the org.springframework.web.multipart.MultipartResolver are called during the preparation and cleanup of the request. The isMultipart method is invoked to determine whether an incoming request is actually a multipart request. If it is, then the resolveMultipart method is called, and this wraps the original request in a MultipartHttpServletRequest. Finally, when the request has been handled, the cleanupMultipart method is invoked to clean up any used resources. Figure 4-13 shows the two out-of-the-box implementations of the MultipartResolver.

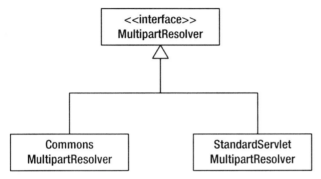

Figure 4-13. The MultipartResolver implementations

CommonsMultipartResolver

The org.springframework.web.multipart.commons.CommonsMultipartResolver uses the Commons fileupload library[1] to handle multipart files. It enables easy configuration of several aspects of the Commons fileupload library.

StandardServletMultipartResolver

The Servlet 3.0 specification introduced a standard way of handling multipart forms. The org.springframework.web.multipart.support.StandardServletMultipartResolver merely serves as a wrapper around this standard approach, so that it is exposed in a transparent way.

LocaleResolver

The org.springframework.web.servlet.LocaleResolver strategy interface is used to determine which java.util.Locale to use to render the page. In most cases, this is used to resolve validation messages or labels in the application. The different implementations are shown in Figure 4-14 and described in the following subsections.

---

[1] http://commons.apache.org/fileupload/

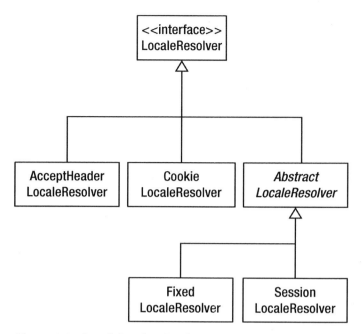

Figure 4-14. *LocaleResolver implementations*

Listing 4-16 shows the API for the org.springframework.web.servlet.LocaleResolver.

Listing 4-16. *The LocaleResolver API*

```
package org.springframework.web.servlet;

import java.util.Locale;

import javax.servlet.http.HttpServletRequest;
import javax.servlet.http.HttpServletResponse;

public interface LocaleResolver {

    Locale resolveLocale(HttpServletRequest request);
    void setLocale(HttpServletRequest request,
                HttpServletResponse response,
                Locale locale);

}
```

The API consists of two methods that each play a role in storing and retrieving the current java.util.Locale. The setLocale method is called when you want to change the current locale. If the implementation doesn't support this, a java.lang.UnsupportedOperationException is thrown. The resolveLocale method is used by the Spring Framework—usually internally—to resolve the current locale.

AcceptHeaderLocaleResolver

The `org.springframework.web.servlet.i18n.AcceptHeaderLocaleResolver` simply delegates to the `getLocale` method of the current `javax.servlet.HttpServletRequest`. It uses the `Accept-Language` HTTP Header to determine the language. The client sets this header value; this resolver doesn't support changing the locale.

CookieLocaleResolver

As its name implies, the `org.springframework.web.servlet.i18n.CookieLocaleResolver` uses a `javax.servlet.http.Cookie` to store the locale to use. This is particularly useful in cases where you want an application to be as stateless as possible. The actual value is stored on the client side, and it is sent to you with each request. This resolver allows the locale to be changed (you can find more information on this in Chapter 6). This resolver also allows you to configure the name of the cookie and a default locale to use. If no value can be determined for the current request (i.e., there is neither a cookie nor a default locale), then this resolver falls back to the locale of the request (see `AcceptHeaderLocaleResolver`).

FixedLocaleResolver

The `org.springframework.web.servlet.i18n.FixedLocaleResolver` is the most basic implementation of an `org.springframework.web.servlet.LocaleResolver`. It allows you to configure a locale to use throughout the whole application. This configuration is fixed; as such, it cannot be changed.

SessionLocaleResolver

The `org.springframework.web.servlet.i18n.SessionLocaleResolver` implementation uses the `javax.servlet.http.HttpSession` to store the value of the locale. The name of the attribute, as well as a default locale, can be configured. If no value can be determined for the current request (i.e., there is neither a value stored in the session nor a default locale), then it falls back to the locale of the request (see `AcceptHeaderLocaleResolver`). This resolver also lets you change the locale (see Chapter 6 for more information).

ThemeResolver

The `org.springframework.web.servlet.ThemeResolver` strategy interface is used to determine which theme to use to render the page. There are several implementations; these are shown in Figure 4-15 and explained in the following subsections. How to apply theming is explained in Chapter 8. If no theme name can be resolved, then this resolver uses the hardcoded default theme.

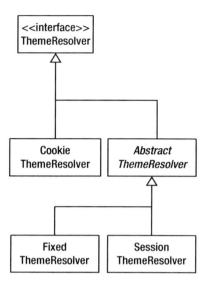

Figure 4-15. ThemeResolver implementations

Listing 4-17 shows the API for the org.springframework.web.servlet.ThemeResolver, which is quite similar to the org.springframework.web.servlet.LocaleResolver API.

Listing 4-17. The ThemeResolver API

```
package org.springframework.web.servlet;

import javax.servlet.http.HttpServletRequest;
import javax.servlet.http.HttpServletResponse;

public interface ThemeResolver {
    String resolveThemeName(HttpServletRequest request);

    void setThemeName(HttpServletRequest request,
                      HttpServletResponse response,
                      String themeName);

}
```

You call the setThemeName method when you want to change the current theme. If changing theme is not supported, it throws a java.lang.UnsupportedOperationException. The Spring Framework invokes the resolveThemeName method when it needs to resolve the current theme. This is mainly done by using the theme jsp tag.

CookieThemeResolver

As its name implies, the `org.springframework.web.servlet.theme.CookieThemeResolver` uses a `javax.servlet.http.Cookie` to store the theme to use. This is particularly useful where you want your application to be as stateless as possible. The actual value is stored on the client side and will be sent to you with each request. This resolver allows the theme to be changed; you can find more information on this in Chapters 6 and 8. This resolver also allows you to configure the name of the cookie and a theme locale to use.

FixedThemeResolver

The `org.springframework.web.servlet.theme.FixedThemeResolver` is the most basic implementation of an `org.springframework.web.servlet.ThemeResolver`. It allows you to configure a theme to use throughout the whole application. This configuration is fixed; as such, it cannot be changed.

SessionThemeResolver

The `org.springframework.web.servlet.theme.SessionThemeResolver` uses the `javax.servlet.http.HttpSession` to store the value of the theme. The name of the attribute, as well as a default theme, can be configured.

HandlerExceptionResolver

In most cases, you want to control how you handle an exception that occurs during the handling of a request. You can use a HandlerExceptionResolver for this. The API (see Listing 4-18) consists of a single method that is called on the `org.springframework.web.servlet.HandlerExceptionResolvers` detected by the dispatcher servlet. The resolver can choose to handle the exception itself or to return an `org.springframework.web.servlet.ModelAndView` that contains a view to render and a model (generally containing the exception thrown).

Listing 4-18. The HandlerExceptionResolver API

```
package org.springframework.web.servlet;

import javax.servlet.http.HttpServletRequest;
import javax.servlet.http.HttpServletResponse;

public interface HandlerExceptionResolver {

    ModelAndView resolveException(HttpServletRequest request,
                                  HttpServletResponse response,
                                  Object handler,
                                  Exception ex);

}
```

Figure 4-16 shows the different implementations provided by the Spring Framework. Each works in a slightly different way, just as each is configured differently (see Chapter 6 for more information).

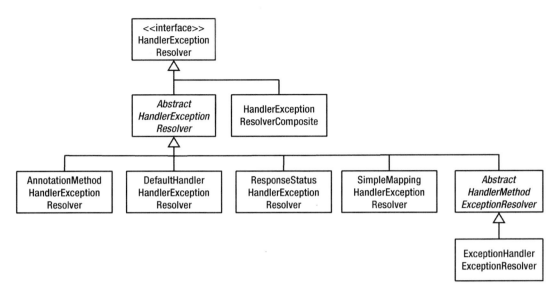

Figure 4-16. *The HandlerExceptionResolver implementations*

The `org.springframework.web.servlet.handler.HandlerExceptionResolverComposite` is an implementation used internally by Spring MVC. It is used to chain several `org.springframework` `.web.servlet.HandlerExceptionResolver` implementations together. This resolver does not provide an actual implementation or added functionality; instead, it merely acts as a wrapper around multiple implementations (when multiple implementations are configured).

RequestToViewNameTranslator

When a handler returns no view implementation or view name and did not send a response itself to the client, then the `org.springframework.web.servlet.RequestToViewNameTranslator` tries to determine a view name from the incoming request. The default implementation (see Figure 4-17), `org.springframework.web.servlet.view.DefaultRequestToViewNameTranslator`, simply takes the URL, strips the suffix and context path, and then uses the remainder as the view name (i.e., `http://localhost:8080/bookstore/admin/index.html` becomes `admin/index`). You can find more information about views in Chapter 8.

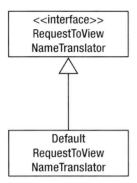

Figure 4-17. *The RequstToViewNameTranslator hierarchy*

The RequestToViewNameTranslator API is shown in Listing 4-19.

Listing 4-19. *The RequestToViewNameTranslator API*

```
package org.springframework.web.servlet;

import javax.servlet.http.HttpServletRequest;

public interface RequestToViewNameTranslator {

    String getViewName(HttpServletRequest request) throws Exception;

}
```

ViewResolver

Spring MVC provides a very flexible view resolving mechanism. It simply takes the view name returned from the handler and tries to resolve it to an actual view implementation (if no concrete org.springframework.web.servlet.View is returned). The actual implementation could be a JSP, but it could just as easily be an Excel spreadsheet or PDF file. For more information on view resolving, refer to Chapter 8.

This API (see Listing 4-20) is pretty simple and consists of a single method. This method takes the view name and currently selected locale (see also the LocaleResolver). This can be used to resolve to an actual View implementation. When there are multiple org.springframework.web.servlet.ViewResolvers configured, the dispatcher servlet calls them in turn until one of them returns a View to render.

Listing 4-20. *The ViewResolver API*

```
package org.springframework.web.servlet;

import java.util.Locale;

public interface ViewResolver {

    View resolveViewName(String viewName, Locale locale) throws Exception;
```

}

The ViewResolver implementations are shown in Figure 4-18. Out of the box, Spring provides several implementations (see Chapter 8 for more information).

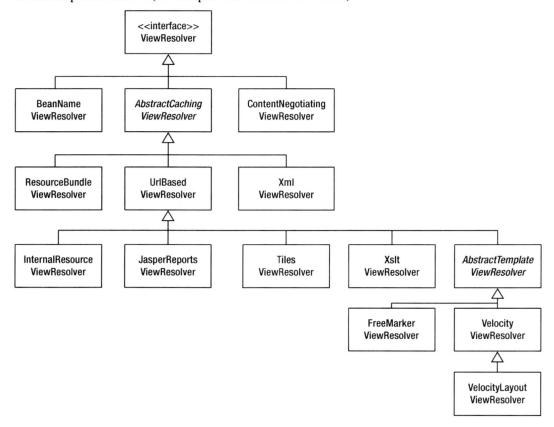

Figure 4-18. The ViewResolver implementations

FlashMapManager

The org.springframework.web.servlet.FlashMapManager is used to enable a flash "scope" in Spring MVC applications. You can use this mechanism to put attributes in a flash map that are then retrieved after a redirect (the flash map survives a request/response cycle). The flash map is cleared after the view is rendered. Spring provides a single implementation, org.springframework.web.servlet.support .SessionFlashMapManager (see Figure 4-19).

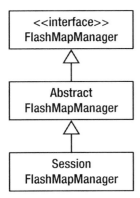

Figure 4-19. *The FlashMapManager hierarchy*

Listing 4-21 shows the API of the FlashMapManager.

■ **Note** The flash "scope" mentioned here has no relation to the "flashscope" used in Spring Web Flow.

Listing 4-21. *The FlashMapManager API*

```
package org.springframework.web.servlet;

import javax.servlet.http.HttpServletRequest;
import javax.servlet.http.HttpServletResponse;

public interface FlashMapManager {

    FlashMap retrieveAndUpdate(HttpServletRequest request,
                              HttpServletResponse response);

    void saveOutputFlashMap(FlashMap flashMap,
                           HttpServletRequest request,
                           HttpServletResponse response);
}
```

Summary

This chapter started by looking at the request processing workflow, identifying which components play a role in this. The DispatcherServlet can be considered the main component in Spring MVC, and it plays the most crucial role, that of the front controller. The MVC pattern in Spring MVC is quite explicit; you have a Model, a View, and also a Controller (handler). The controller processes the request, fills the model, and selects the view to render.

While processing a request, the `DispatcherServlet` uses a lot of different components to play its role. The most important components are the `HandlerMapping` and `HandlerAdapter`; these components are the core components used to map and handle requests, respectively. To apply crosscutting concerns, you can use an `HandlerInterceptor`. After handling a request, a view needs to be rendered. A handler can return an `View` or the name of a view to render. In the latter situation, this name is passed to an `ViewResolver` to resolve to an actual view implementation.

There is also basic support for flash-scoped variables. To make this possible, there is the notion of an `FlashMapManager`. Sometimes, the request processing doesn't progress the way you'd like it to. For example, you might encounter exceptions. To handle those, you can use the `HandlerExceptionResolver`. The final components that play a role here are the `LocaleResolver` and `ThemeResolver`. Together, these enable internationalization and theming in your application.

This chapter also touched on the fact that the dispatcher servlet includes some components that are configured by default and contrasted those defaults against those of the Spring @MVC, which can be enabled by using the `EnableWebMvc` annotation. We also explored the different default components of the two approaches.

Upcoming chapters will explain how to build controllers to handle requests and take a closer look at how to configure Spring MVC.

CHAPTER 5

Implementing Controllers

Controllers play a crucial role in a web application: they execute the actual request, prepare the model, and select a view to render. In conjunction with the dispatcher servlet, controllers also play a crucial role in the request processing workflow. The controller is the glue between the core application and the web interface to the application. In this chapter, we will take a look at the two different controller approaches and cover the out-of-the-box implementations provided with the Spring Framework.

This chapter will also take a look at the supporting components for request processing. For example, we will cover form submission and how to apply internationalization (I18N).

Introducing Controllers

The controller is the component that is responsible for responding to the action the user takes. This action could be a form submission, clicking a link, or simply accessing a page. The controller selects or updates the data needed for the view. It also select the name of the view to render or can render the view itself. With Spring MVC, we have two options when writing controllers. We can either implement an interface or put an annotation on the class. The interface is org.springframework.web.servlet.mvc.Controller, and the annotation is org.springframework.stereotype.Controller. The main focus of this book is the annotation-based approach (aka Spring @MVC) for writing controllers. However, we feel that we still need to mention the interface-based approach.

Although both approaches work for implementing a controller, there are two major differences between them. The first difference is about flexibility, and the second is about mapping URLs to controllers. Annotation-based controllers allow for very flexible method signatures, whereas the interface-based approach has a predefined method on the interface that we must implement. Getting access to other interesting collaborators is harder (but not impossible!).

For the interface-based approach, we must do explicit external mapping of URLs to these controllers; in general, this approach is combined with an org.springframework.web.servlet.handler.SimpleUrlHandlerMapping, so that all the URLs are in a single location. Having all of the URLs in a single location is one advantage the interface-based approach has over the annotation-based approach. The annotation-based approach has its mappings scattered throughout the codebase, which makes it harder to see which URL is mapped to which request-handling method. The advantage of annotation-based controllers is that, when you open a controller, you can see which URLs it is mapped to.

In this section, we will show how to write both types of controllers, as well as how to configure basic view controllers.

Interface-based Controllers

To write an interface-based controller, we need to create a class that implements the `Controller` interface. Listing 5-1 shows the API for that interface. When implementing this interface, we must implement the `handleRequest` method. This method needs to return an `org.springframework.web` `.servlet.ModelAndView` object or `null` when the controller handles the response itself.

Listing 5-1. *The Controller Interface*

```
package org.springframework.web.servlet.mvc;

import javax.servlet.http.HttpServletRequest;
import javax.servlet.http.HttpServletResponse;

import org.springframework.web.servlet.ModelAndView;

public interface Controller {
    ModelAndView handleRequest(HttpServletRequest request,
                            HttpServletResponse response) throws Exception;
}
```

Let's take a look at a small sample. If we take the `com.apress.prospringmvc.bookstore.web` `.IndexController` and create an interface-based controller out of it, it would look something like what you see in Listing 5-2. We implement the `handleRequest` method and return an instance of `ModelAndView` with a view name.

Listing 5-2. *An Interface-based IndexController*

```
package com.apress.prospringmvc.bookstore.web;
// javax.servlet imports omitted
import org.springframework.web.servlet.ModelAndView;
import org.springframework.web.servlet.mvc.Controller;

public class IndexController implements Controller {

    @Override
    public ModelAndView handleRequest(HttpServletRequest request,
                            HttpServletResponse response)
    throws Exception {
        return new ModelAndView("index");
    }
}
```

In addition to writing this controller, we would need to configure an instance of `org.springframework.web.servlet.HandlerMapping` to map `/index.htm` to this controller (see Chapter 3 for more information). We would also need to make sure that there is an `org.springframework.web` `.servlet.mvc.SimpleControllerHandlerAdapter` registered to execute the interface-based controllers (this is registered by default).

The sample given here is quite straightforward. Now image a controller that has some page flow. In that case, we would need to check whether the request is a `GET` or `POST` request; based on that, we would need to execute different controller logic. With large controllers, this can become quite cumbersome.

Table 5-1 shows the `Controller` implementations that ship with the framework. Many of these are deprecated (as of Spring 3.0) or can be considered deprecated in favor of the newer annotation-based controllers. Check the descriptions of each controller for deprecation notes.

Table 5-1. *A List of Existing Controller Implementations*

Controller implementation	Description
`UrlFilenameViewController`	A controller implementation that takes the path of a URL and transforms that into a view name. It can be configured to append a prefix and/or suffix to the view name.
`ParameterizableViewController`	A controller that returns a configured view name.
`ServletForwardingController`	A controller implementation that forwards the request to a named servlet. The named servlet can be a servlet without any mapping. This is useful if you want to use the Spring MVC infrastructure for dispatching requests and to apply interceptors.
`ServletWrappingController`	A controller implementation that wraps and manages a servlet implementation. This is useful if you want to use the Spring MVC infrastructure to dispatch requests and apply interceptors.
`MultiActionController`	A configurable controller that allows different methods to be invoked, depending on the incoming requests. Subclasses need to add the methods that can be invoked. This approach enables slightly more flexible method signatures than the normal interface. *Note: This can be considered deprecated as of Spring 3.0 in favor of annotation-based controllers.*
`SimpleFormController`	A controller implementation that has a simple workflow built in. The first request (typically a `GET` request) renders the form to be filled in, while the second request (`POST`) translates the form to an object, performs validation, and executes the submit action. *Note: This controller is deprecated as of Spring 3.0 in favor of annotation-based controllers.*
`CancellableFormController`	A controller that is basically the same as the `SimpleFormController`; however, this controller includes an option to cancel the current form editing and execute an action when the cancellation occurs. *Note: This controller is deprecated as of Spring 3.0 in favor of annotation-based controllers.*

Controller implementation	Description
`AbstractWizardFormController`	A controller implementation used to implement simple page flow via wizard style pages. This controller allows the use of multiple pages to fill the model and will only execute a submission on the last page. *Note: This controller is deprecated as of Spring 3.0 in favor of annotation-based controllers and Spring Web Flow.*

Note: All of the controllers listed in Table 5-1 reside in the `org.springframework.web.servlet.mvc` package or its `multiaction` subpackage.

Annotation-based Controllers

To write an annotation-based controller, we need to write a class and put the `Controller` annotation on that class. Also, we need to add an `org.springframework.web.bind.annotation.RequestMapping` annotation to the class, a method, or both. Listing 5-3 shows an annotation-based approach to our `IndexController`.

Listing 5-3. *An Annotation-based IndexController*

```
package com.apress.prospringmvc.bookstore.web;

import org.springframework.stereotype.Controller;
import org.springframework.web.bind.annotation.RequestMapping;
import org.springframework.web.servlet.ModelAndView;

@Controller
public class IndexController {

    @RequestMapping(value = "/index.htm")
    public ModelAndView indexPage() {
        return new ModelAndView("index");
    }
}
```

The controller contains a method with the `RequestMapping` annotation, and it specifies that it should be mapped to the `/index.htm` URL, which is the request-handling method. The method has no required parameters, and we can return anything we want; for now, we want to return a `ModelAndView`.

The mapping is in the controller definition, and we need an instance of a `HandlerMapping` to interpret these mappings. There are two implementations that can help us out here: the `org.springframework.web.servlet.mvc.annotation.DefaultAnnotationHandlerMapping` and the `org.springframework.web.servlet.mvc.method.annotation.RequestMappingHandlerMapping`. The first is one of the defaults registered by the `org.springframework.web.servlet.DispatcherServlet`. The second is one of the defaults registered by Spring @MVC (which we enabled with the `org.springframework.web.servlet.config.EnableWebMvc` annotation). We are going to use the Spring @MVC default because it is both more powerful and flexible than the `DefaultAnnotationHandlerMapping`. We will see that power and flexibility throughout the book.

Configuring View Controllers

The two controller samples we have written so far are called *view controllers*. They don't select data; rather, they only select the view name to render. If we had a large application with more of these views, it would become quite cumbersome to maintain and write these. Spring MVC can help us out here, enabling us simply to add an org.springframework.web.servlet.mvc.ParameterizableViewController to our configuration and to configure it accordingly. We would need to configure an instance to return index as a view name and map it to the /index.htm URL. Listing 5-4 shows what needs to be added to make this work.

Listing 5-4. A ParameterizableViewController Configuration

```
package com.apress.prospringmvc.bookstore.web.config;

import org.springframework.web.servlet.mvc.ParameterizableViewController;
import org.springframework.web.servlet.config.annotation.WebMvcConfigurerAdapter;

// Other imports ommitted

@Configuration
@EnableWebMvc
@ComponentScan(basePackages = { "com.apress.prospringmvc.bookstore.web" })
public class WebMvcContextConfiguration extends WebMvcConfigurerAdapter {

    // Other methods ommitted

    @Bean(name = "/index.htm")
    public Controller index() {
        ParameterizableViewController index;
        index = new ParameterizableViewController();
        index.setViewName("index");
        return index;
    }
}
```

So how does it work? We create the controller, set the view name to return, and then explicitly give it the name of /index.htm (see the highlighted parts). The explicit naming makes it possible for the org.springframework.web.servlet.handler.BeanNameUrlHandlerMapping to pick up our controller and map it to the URL. However, if this were to grow significantly larger, then we would need to create quite a few of these methods. Again, Spring MVC is here to help us. Because we have enabled the new Spring MVC configuration, we can utilize it to our advantage. We can override the addViewControllers method (one of the methods of the org.springframework.web.servlet.config.annotation .WebMvcConfigurerAdapter) and simply register our view names to certain URLs. In Listing 5-5 shows how to do this.

111

Listing 5-5. A ViewController Configuration

```
package com.apress.prospringmvc.bookstore.web.config;

import org.springframework.web.servlet.config.annotation.ViewControllerRegistry;
import org.springframework.web.servlet.config.annotation.WebMvcConfigurerAdapter;

// Other imports ommitted

@Configuration
@EnableWebMvc
@ComponentScan(basePackages = { "com.apress.prospringmvc.bookstore.web" })
public class WebMvcContextConfiguration extends WebMvcConfigurerAdapter {

  // Other methods ommitted
    @Override
    public void addViewControllers(final ViewControllerRegistry registry) {
        registry.addViewController("/index.htm").setViewName("index");
    }
}
```

The result is the same. A ParameterizableViewController is created and mapped to the /index.htm URL (see Figure 5-1). However, the second approach is easier and less cumbersome to use than the first one.

Figure 5-1. The index page

Request-Handling Methods

Writing request-handling methods can be a challenge. For example, how should you map a method to an incoming request? Several things could be a factor here, including the URL, the method used (e.g.,

GET or POST[1]), the availability of parameters or HTTP headers[2], or even the request content type or the content type (e.g., XML, JSON, or HTML) to be produced. All these can influence which method is selected to handle the request.

The first step in writing a request-handling method is to put an org.springframework.web.bind .annotation.RequestMapping annotation on the method. This mapping is detected by the org.springframework.web.servlet.mvc.method.annotation.RequestMappingHandlerMapping to create the mapping of incoming URLs to the correct method (see the "Spring MVC Components" section in Chapter 4 for more information on handler mapping). Next, we need to specify which web request we want to execute the specified handler.

The annotation can be put on both the type (the controller) and the method level. We can use the one on the type level to do some coarse-grained mapping (e.g., the URL), and then use the annotation on the method level to further specify when to execute the method (e.g., a GET or POST request).

Table 5-2 shows which attributes we can set on the RequestMapping annotation and how they influence the mapping.

Table 5-2. The RequestMapping Attributes

Attribute	Description
value	Specifies to which URL or URLs this controller reacts, such as /order.htm. We can also use ant-style expressions to specify the URLs.
method	Binds the method on specific HTTP methods. Supported methods include GET, POST, PUT, DELETE, HEAD, OPTIONS, and TRACE. By default, OPTIONS and TRACE are handled by the org.springframework.web.servlet.DispatcherServlet. To have those methods also passed onto controllers, we need to set the dispatchOptionsRequest or dispatchTraceRequest to true respectively on the servlet.
params	Narrows on the existence or absence of request parameters. Supported expressions include the following:

	param-name=param-value	The specified param must have a certain value
	param-name!=param-value	The specified param must not have a certain value.
	!param-name	The specified param must be absent from the request.

---

[1] http://www.w3.org/Protocols/rfc2616/rfc2616-sec9.html
[2] http://www.w3.org/Protocols/rfc2616/rfc2616-sec14.html

Attribute	Description	
headers	Narrows on the existence or absence of HTTP request headers.[3] Supported expressions include the following:	
	`header-name=header-value`	The specified header must have a certain value.
	`header-name!=header-value`	The specified header must not have a certain value.
	`!header-name`	The specified header must be absent from the request header.
	The value in the expression can also contain a wildcard (*) in the case of `Content-Type` or `Accept` headers (i.e., `content-type="text/*"` will match all text-based content types).	
consumes	Specifies the consumable media types of the mapped request. We use this to narrow the primary mapping. For instance, `text/xml` will map all request for the content-type of text or XML, but we could also specify `text/*` to match all textual content types. We can also negate it: `!text/xml` will match all content types except text or XML. This parameter is recommended over the use of the `headers` parameter to specify a `Content-Type` header because it is more explicit.	
produces	Specifies the producible media types this request-handling method accepts. It is used to narrow the primary mapping. The same rules that apply to the `consumes` parameter also apply to this parameter. This parameter is recommended over the use of the `headers` parameter to specify an `Accept` header because it is more explicit.	

In Table 5-3, there are a couple of sample mappings that also show the effect of class- and method-level matching. As already mentioned, the `RequestMapping` annotation on the class applies to *all* methods in the controller. This mechanism can be used to do coarse-grained mapping on the class level and finer-grained mapping on the method level.

Table 5-3. Sample Mappings

Class LEVEL	Method LEVEL	Description
	`@RequestMapping (value="/order.htm")`	Maps to all requests on the order.htm URL.
`@RequestMapping ("/order.htm")`	`@RequestMapping (method=RequestMethod.GET)`	Maps to all GET requests to the order.html URL.

---

[3] http://www.w3.org/Protocols/rfc2616/rfc2616-sec14.html

Class	Method	Description
`@RequestMapping` `("/order.*")`	`@RequestMapping` `(method={RequestMethod.PUT,` `RequestMethod.POST})`	Maps to all PUT and POST requests to the order.* URL. * means any suffix or extension such as .htm, .doc, .xls, and so on.
`@RequestMapping` `(value="/customer.htm",` `consumes="application/json")`	`@RequestMapping` `(produces="application/xml")`	Maps to all requests that post JSON and accept XML as a response.
`@RequestMapping` `(value="/order.htm")`	`@RequestMapping` `(params="add-line",` `method=RequestMethod.POST)`	Maps to all POST requests to the order.htm URL that include an add-line parameter.
`@RequestMapping` `(value="/order.htm")`	`@RequestMapping` `(headers="!VIA")`	Maps to all requests to the order.htm URL that don't include a VIA HTTP Header.

Supported Method Argument Types

A request-handling method can have various method arguments and return values. Most arguments mentioned in Table 5-4 can be used in arbitrary order. However, there is a single exception to that rule: the `org.springframework.validation.BindingResult` argument. That argument has to follow a model object that we use to bind request parameters to.

Table 5-4. The Supported Method Argument Types

Argument Type	Description
`javax.servlet.ServletRequest`	The request object that triggered this method.
`javax.servlet.http.` `HttpServletRequest`	The HTTP request object that triggered this method.
`org.springframework.web.multipart.` `MultipartRequest`	The request object that triggered this method only works for multipart requests. This wrapper allows for easy access to the uploaded files(s). Only exposes methods for multipart file access.
`org.springframework.web.multipart.` `MultipartHttpServletRequest`	The `MultipartHttpServletRequest` exposes both the `HttpServletRequest` and `MultipartRequest` methods.
`javax.servlet.ServletResponse`	The response associated with the request. This is useful if we need to write the response ourselves.

Argument Type	Description
javax.servlet.http.HttpServletResponse	The response associated with the request. This is useful if we need to write the response ourselves.
javax.servlet.http.HttpSession	The underlying HttpSession. If no session exists, one will be initiated. This argument is therefore never null.
org.springframework.web.context.request.WebRequest	Allows for more generic access to request and session attributes without ties to an underlying native API (e.g., Servlet, Portlet, or JSF).
org.springframework.web.context.request.NativeWebRequest	WebRequest extension that has accessor methods for the underlying request and response.
java.util.Locale	The currently selected locale as determined by the configured org.springframework.web.servlet.LocaleResolver.
java.io.InputStream	The stream as exposed by the getInputStream method on the ServletRequest
java.io.Reader	The reader as exposed by the getReader method on the ServletRequest.
java.io.OutputStream	The responses stream as exposed by the getOutputStream method on the ServletResponse. This can be used to write a response directly to the user.
java.io.Writer	The responses writer as exposed by the getWriter method on the ServletResponse. This can be used to write a response directly to the user.
javax.security.Principal	The currently authenticated user (can be null).
java.util.Map	The implicit model belonging to this controller/request.
org.springframework.ui.Model	The implicit model belonging to this controller/request. Model implementations have methods to add objects to the model for added convenience. When adding objects allows method chaining as each method returns the Model.
org.springframework.ui.ModelMap	The implicit model belonging to this controller/request. The ModelMap is a Map implementation that includes some methods to add objects to the model for added convenience.

Argument Type	Description
org.springframework.web.multipart.MultipartFile	Binds the uploaded file(s) to a method parameter (multiple files are only supported by the multipart support of Spring). This works only when the request is a multipart form submission. The name of the request attribute to use is either taken from an optional org.springframework.web.bind.annotation.RequestPart annotation or derived from the name of the argument (the latter works only if that information is available in the class).
javax.servlet.http.Part	Binds the uploaded file(s) to a method parameter (multiple files are only supported by the multipart support of Spring). This works only when the request is a multipart form submission. The name of the request attribute to use is either taken from an optional org.springframework.web.bind.annotation.RequestPart annotation or derived from the name of the argument (the latter works only if that information is available in the class).
org.springframework.web.servlet.mvc.support.RedirectAttributes	Enables specification of the exact list of attributes in case we want to issue a redirect. This can also be used to add flash attributes. This argument is used instead of the implicit model in the case of a redirect.
org.springframework.validation.Errors	The binding and validation results for a *preceding* model object.
org.springframework.validation.BindingResult	The binding and validation results for a *preceding* model object. Has accessor methods for the model and underlying infrastructure for type conversion. (For most usecases this isn't needed, use Errors instead).
org.springframework.web.bind.support.SessionStatus	A handler used to mark handling as complete, which will trigger the cleanup of session attributes that have been indicated by org.springframework.web.bind.annotation.SessionAttributes. See the "Using SessionAttributes" section later in this chapter for more information.
org.springframework.web.util.UriComponentsBuilder	A URI builder for preparing a URL relative to the current request URL.
org.springframework.http.HttpEntity<?>	Represents an HTTP request or response entity. It consists of headers and a body of the request or response.
Command or Form objects	Binds request parameters to bean properties using type conversion. These objects will be exposed as model attributes.

RedirectAttributes

The org.springframework.web.servlet.mvc.support.RedirectAttributes deserve a little more explanation than what is shown in Table 5-4. With RedirectAttributes, it is possible to declare exactly which attributes are needed for the redirect. By default, all model attributes are exposed when doing a redirect. Because a redirect always leads to a GET request, all primitive model attributes (or collections/arrays of primitives) will be encoded as request parameters. However, with the annotated controllers, there are also objects in the model (like the path variables and other implicit values) that don't need to be exposed and that are outside of our control.

The RedirectAttributes can help us out here. When this is used as a method argument and a redirect is being issued, only the attributes added to the RedirectAttributes instance are going to be added to the URL.

In addition to specifying attributes encoded in the URL, it is also possible to specify so called flash attributes. *Flash attributes* are attributes that are stored before the redirect and retrieved and made available as model attributes after the redirect. This is done by using the configured org.springframework.web.servlet.FlashMapManager. The use of flash attributes is useful for objects that cannot be encoded (non-primitive objects) or to keep URLs clean.

UriComponentsBuilder

The UriComponentsBuilder provides a mechanism for building and encoding URIs. It can take a URL pattern and replace or extend variables. This can be done for relative or absolute URLs. This mechanism is particularly useful when creating URLs, as opposed to cases where we need to think about encoding parameters or doing string concatenation ourselves. This component handles all these things in a consistent manner for us. The code in Listing 5-6 creates the /book/detail/42 URL.

Listing 5-6. *The UriComponentsBuilder Sample Code*

```
UriComponentsBuilder.fromPath("/book/detail/{bookId}");
.build();
.expand("42")
.encode()
```

The sample given is quite simple; however, it is possible to specify more variables (e.g., bookId) and replace them (e.g., specify the port or host). There is also the ServletUriComponentsBuilder subclass, which we can use to operate on the current request. For example, we might use it to replace, not only path variables, but also request parameters.

Supported Method Argument Annotations

In addition to explicitly supported types (as mentioned in the previous section), there are also a couple of annotations that we can use to annotate our method arguments (see Table 5-5). Some of these can also be used with the method argument types mentioned in Table 5-4. In that case, they are used to specify what the name of the attribute in the request, cookie, header, or response must be, as well as whether the parameter is required.

All the parameter values are converted to the argument type by using type conversion. The type-conversion system uses an org.springframework.core.convert.converter.Converter or PropertyEditor to convert from a String type to the actual type.

Table 5-5. The Supported Method Argument Annotations

Argument Type	Description
RequestParam	Binds the argument to a single request parameter or to all request parameters.
RequestHeader	Binds the argument to a single request header or all request headers.[4]
RequestBody	Gets the request body for arguments with this annotation. The value is converted using an org.springframework.http.converter.HttpMessageConverter.
RequestPart	Binds the argument to the part of a multipart form submission.
ModelAttribute	Binds and validates arguments with this annotation. The parameters from the incoming request are bound to the given object.
PathVariable	Binds the method parameter to a path variable as specified in the URL mapping (the value attribute of the RequestMapping annotation).
CookieValue	Binds the method parameter to a javax.servlet.http.Cookie.

Note: All annotations live in the org.springframework.web.bind.annotation package.

All these different method argument types and annotations allow us to write very flexible request-handling methods. However, we could extend this mechanism by extending the framework. Resolving those method argument types is done by various implementations of the org.springframework .web.method.support.HandlerMethodArgumentResolver. Listing 5-7 shows that interface. If we want, we can create our own implementation of this interface and register it with the framework. You can find more information on this in Chapter 7.

Listing 5-7. The HandlerMethodArgumentResolver Interface

```
package org.springframework.web.method.support;

import org.springframework.core.MethodParameter;
import org.springframework.web.bind.WebDataBinder;
import org.springframework.web.bind.support.WebDataBinderFactory;
import org.springframework.web.context.request.NativeWebRequest;

public interface HandlerMethodArgumentResolver {

    boolean supportsParameter(MethodParameter parameter);
```

---

[4] http://en.wikipedia.org/wiki/List_of_HTTP_header_fields

119

```
Object resolveArgument(MethodParameter parameter,
                       ModelAndViewContainer mavContainer,
                       NativeWebRequest webRequest,
                       WebDataBinderFactory binderFactory)
                       throws Exception;
}
```

Let's take a closer look at all the different annotation types we can use. All these annotations have a few attributes that we can set and that have default values or may be required.

All of the annotations mentioned in Table 5-5 have a value attribute. This value attribute refers to the name of the object to use (what it applies to depends on the annotation). If this value isn't filled, then the fallback is to use the name of the method argument. This fallback is only usable if the classes are compiled with debug information.[5] An exception to this rule occurs when using the ModelAttribute annotation. Instead of the name of the method argument, it infers the name from the type of argument, using the simple classname as the argument name. If the type is an array or collection, it makes this plural by adding List. If we were to use our com.apress.prospringmvc.bookstore.domain.Book as an argument, then the name would be book; if it were an array or collection, then it would become bookList.

RequestParam

The RequestParam annotation can be placed on any argument in a request-handling method. When present, it is used to retrieve a parameter from the request. When put on a Map, there is some special handling, depending on whether the name attribute is set. If the name is set, the value is retrieved and converted into a Map. For conversion (see the "Data Binding" section in this chapter for more information), if no name is given, all request parameters are added to the map as key/value pairs.

Table 5-6. *The RequestParam Attributes*

Attribute	Default Value	Description
required	true	Indicates whether the parameter is required. If it is required and the parameter is missing, then an org.springframework.web.bind.MissingServletRequestParameterException is thrown.
defaultValue	null	Indicates the default value to use when the parameter is missing from the request. Setting a default value is implicitly setting required to false. The value can either be a hardcoded value or a SpEL expression.
value	Empty string	Indicates the name of the parameter to look up from the request. If no name is specified, then the name is derived from the method argument name. If no name can be found, a java.lang.IllegalArgumentException is thrown.

---

[5] http://docs.oracle.com/javase/6/docs/technotes/tools/windows/javac.html

RequestHeader

The RequestHeader annotation can be placed on any method argument. It is used to bind a method argument to a request header. When placed on a Map, all available request headers are put in the map as key/value pairs. If it is placed on another type of argument, then the value is converted into the type by using a org.springframework.core.convert.converter.Converter or PropertyEditor (see the "Data Binding" section for more information).

Table 5-7. *The RequestHeader Attributes*

Attribute	Default Value	Description
required	true	Indicates whether the parameter is required. If it is required and the parameter is missing, an org.springframework.web.bind .ServletRequestBindingException is thrown. When set to false, null is used as the value; alternatively, the defaultValue is used when specified.
defaultValue	null	Indicates the default value to use when the parameter is missing from the request. Setting a default value is implicitly setting required to false. The value can either be a hardcoded value or a SpEL expression.
value	Empty string	Indicates the name of the request header to bind to. If no name is specified, then the name is derived from the method argument name. If no name can be found, a java.lang.IllegalArgumentException is thrown.

RequestBody

The RequestBody annotation is used to mark a method parameter we want to bind to the body of the web request. The body is converted into the method parameter type by locating and calling an org.springframework.http.converter.HttpMessageConverter. This converter is selected based on the requests content-type. If no converter is found, an org.springframework.web.HttpMediaTypeNotSupportedException is thrown. By default, this leads to a response with code 415 (SC_UNSUPPORTED_MEDIA_TYPE) being send to the client.

Optionally, method parameters can also be annotated with javax.validation.Valid or org.springframework.validation.annotation.Validated to enforce validation for the created object. You can find more information on validation in the "Validation of Model Attributes" section later in this chapter.

RequestPart

When the RequestPart annotation is put on a method argument of the type javax.servlet.http.Part, org.springframework.web.multipart.MultipartFile (or on a collection or array of the latter,) then we will get the content of that file (or group of files) injected. If it is put on any other argument type, the content is passed through an org.springframework.http.converter.HttpMessageConverter for the content type detected on the file. If no suitable converter is found, then an org.springframework.web.HttpMediaTypeNotSupportedException is thrown.

Table 5-8. The RequestPart Attributes

Attribute	Default Value	Description
required	true	Indicates whether the parameter is required. If it is required and the parameter is missing, an org.springframework.web.bind .ServletRequestBindingException is thrown. When set to false, null is used as a value; alternatively, the defaultValue is used when specified.
value	Empty string	The name of the request header to bind to. If no name is specified the name is derived from the method argument name. If no name is found, a java.lang.IllegalArgumentException is thrown.

ModelAttribute

The ModelAttribute annotation can be placed on method arguments, as well as on methods. When placed on a method argument, it is used to bind this argument to a model object. When placed on a method, that method is used to construct a model object, and this method will be called before request-handling methods are called. These kinds of methods can be used to create an object to be edited in a form or to supply data needed by a form to render itself. (For more information, see the "Data Binding" section.)

Table 5-9. The ModelAttribute Attributes

Attribute	Default Value	Description
value	Empty string	The name of the model attribute to bind to. If no name is specified the name is derived from the method argument type.

PathVariable

The PathVariable annotation can be used in conjunction with path variables. Path variables can be used in a URL pattern to bind the URL to a variable. Path variables are denoted as {*name*}in our URL mapping. If we were to use a URL mapping of /book/{isbn}/image, then isbn would be available as a path variable.

Table 5-10. The PathVariable Attribute

Attribute	Default Value	Description
value	Empty string	The name of the path variable to bind to. If no name is specified, then the name is derived from the method argument name. If no name is found, a java.lang.IllegalArgumentException is thrown.

CookieValue

This CookieValue annotation can be placed on any argument in the request-handling method. When present, it is used to retrieve a cookie. When placed on an argument of type javax.servlet.http.Cookie, we get the complete cookie. Otherwise, the value of the cookie is converted into the argument type.

Table 5-11. The CookieValue Attributes

Attribute	Default Value	Description
required	true	Indicates whether the parameter is required. If it is required and the parameter is missing, an org.springframework.web.bind .ServletRequestBindingException is thrown. When set to false, null is used as a value; alternatively, the defaultValue is used when specified.
defaultValue	null	Indicates the default value to use when the parameter is missing from the request. Setting a default value is implicitly setting required to false. The value can either be a hardcoded value or a SpEL expression.
value	Empty string	Indicates the name of the cookie to bind to. If no name is specified, the name is derived from the method argument name. If no name is found, a java.lang.IllegalArgumentException is thrown.

Supported Method Return Values

In addition to all the different method argument types, a request handling method can also have one of several different return values. Table 5-12 lists the default supported and handling of method return values for request handling methods.

Table 5-12. The Supported Method Return Values

Argument Type	Description
org.springframework.web.servlet .ModelAndView	When a ModelAndView is returned, this is used as-is. It should contain the full model to use and the name of a view to render (the latter is optional).
org.springframework.ui.Model	Indicates that this method returned a model. Objects in this model are added to the controller's implicit model and made available for view rendering. The name of the view is determined by the org.springframework.web.servlet .RequestToViewNameTranslator.
java.util.Map org.springframework.ui.ModelMap	The elements in the map are added to the controller's implicit model and made available for view rendering. The name of the view is determined by the org.springframework.web.servlet .RequestToViewNameTranslator.

Argument Type	Description
`org.springframework.web.servlet` `.View`	The actual view to render.
`java.lang.String`	Used as the name of the view to render. If annotated with `ModelAttribute`, it is added to the model.
`java.lang.Void`	The model is already prepared by the controller, and the name of the view is determined by the `org.springframework.web.servlet` `.RequestToViewNameTranslator`

`org.springframework.http` `.HttpEntity<?>`
 	
`org.springframework.http` `.ResponseEntity<?>`
	Specifies the headers and entity body to return to the user. The entity body is converted and sent to the response stream through an `org.springframework.http.converter.HttpMessageConverter`. Optionally, the `HttpEntity` can also set a status code to send to the user.

Any other return type	All other return types are used as model attributes. The name is either derived from the return type or the name specified in the `org.springframework.web.bind.annotation.ModelAttribute`.

When an arbitrary object is returned and there is no `ModelAttribute` annotation present, the framework tries to determine a name to use as the name for the object in the model. It basically takes the simple name of the class (the classname without the package) and lowercases the first letter. For example, the name of our `com.apress.prospringmvc.bookstore.domain.Book` becomes `book`. When the return type is a collection or array, it becomes the simple name of the class, suffixed with `List`. Thus a collection of `Book` objects becomes `bookList`.

This same logic is applied when we use a `Model` or `ModelMap` to add objects without an explicit name. This also has the advantage of using the specific objects, instead of a plain `Map` to gain access to the underlying implicit model.

Although the list of supported return values is already quite extensive, we can use the flexibility and extensibility of the framework to create our own handler. The method's return values are handled by an implementation of the `org.springframework.web.method.support.HandlerMethodReturnValueHandler` interface (see Listing 5-8).

Listing 5-8. The HandlerMethodReturnValueHandler Interface

```
package org.springframework.web.method.support;

import org.springframework.core.MethodParameter;
import org.springframework.web.context.request.NativeWebRequest;

public interface HandlerMethodReturnValueHandler {

    boolean supportsReturnType(MethodParameter returnType);
```

```
void handleReturnValue(Object returnValue,
                       MethodParameter returnType,
                       ModelAndViewContainer mavContainer,
                       NativeWebRequest webRequest) throws Exception;
}
```

Writing Annotation-based Controllers

Let's take some of the theory we've developed thus far and apply it to our controllers. For example, all the menu options we have on our page lead to a 404 error, which indicates that the page cannot be found.

In this section, we are going to add some controllers and views to our application. We will start by creating a simple login controller operating with the request and request parameters. Next, we will add a book search page that uses an object. And finally, we will conclude by building a controller that retrieves and shows the details of a book.

A Simple Login Controller

Before we can start writing our controller, we need to have a login page. In the WEB-INF/views directory, we create a file named login.jsp. The resulting structure should look like the one shown in Figure 5-2.

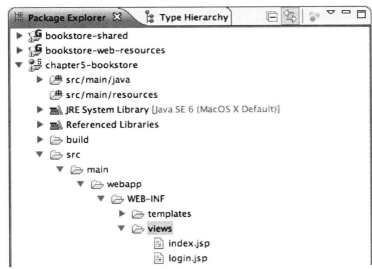

Figure 5-2. The directory structure after adding login.jsp

The login page needs some content, as shown in Listing 5-9.

Listing 5-9. The login page, Login.jsp

```
<%@taglib prefix="c" uri="http://java.sun.com/jsp/jstl/core"%>
<%@taglib prefix="spring" uri="http://www.springframework.org/tags" %>

<c:if test="${exception ne null}">
    <div class="error">${exception.message}</div>
</c:if>
<form action="<c:url value="/login"/>" method="post">
    <fieldset>
        <legend>Login</legend>
        <table>
        <tr>
            <td>Username</td>
            <td>
                <input type="text" id="username" name="username"
                        placeholder="Usename"/></td>
        </tr>
        <tr>
            <td>Password</td>
            <td>
                <input type="password" id="password" name="password"
                        placeholder="Password"/></td>
        </tr>
        <tr><td colspan="2" align="center">
            <button id="login">Login</button>
        </td></tr>
        </table>
    </fieldset>
</form>
```

In addition to the page, we need to have a controller and map it to /login. Let's create the
com.apress.prospringmvc.bookstore.web.controller.LoginController and start by having it render our
page (see Listing 5-10).

Listing 5-10. The Initial LoginController

```
package com.apress.prospringmvc.bookstore.web.controller;

import org.springframework.stereotype.Controller;
import org.springframework.web.bind.annotation.RequestMapping;
import org.springframework.web.bind.annotation.RequestMethod;

@Controller
@RequestMapping(value = "/login")
public class LoginController {

    @RequestMapping(method = RequestMethod.GET)
    public String login() {
        return "login";
    }
```

}

After the application has been redeployed and we click the Login button, we should see a page like the one shown in Figure 5-3.

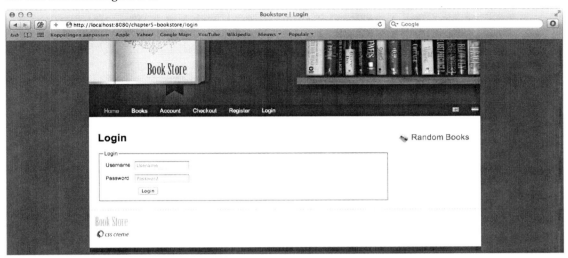

Figure 5-3. The login page

If we now enter the username and password (jd/secret) and press the Login button, we are greeted with an error page (error code 405) that indicates that the method (POST) is not supported. This is correct because our controller doesn't yet have a method that handles a POST request. So, let's add a method to our controller that actually handles our login. Listing 5-11 shows the modified controller.

Listing 5-11. The Modified LoginController

```
package com.apress.prospringmvc.bookstore.web.controller;

// Other imports omitted, see Listing 5-10

import org.springframework.beans.factory.annotation.Autowired;

import com.apress.prospringmvc.bookstore.domain.Account;
import com.apress.prospringmvc.bookstore.service.AccountService;
import com.apress.prospringmvc.bookstore.service.AuthenticationException;

@Controller
@RequestMapping(value = "/login")
public class LoginController {

    public static final String ACCOUNT_ATTRIBUTE = "account";

    @Autowired
    private AccountService accountService;
```

```
@RequestMapping(method = RequestMethod.GET)
public String login() {
    return "login";
}

@RequestMapping(method = RequestMethod.POST)
public String handleLogin(HttpServletRequest request, HttpSession session)
throws AuthenticationException {
    try {
        String username = request.getParameter("username");
        String password = request.getParameter("password");
        Account account = this.accountService.login(username, password);
        session.setAttribute(ACCOUNT_ATTRIBUTE, account);
        return "redirect:/index.htm";
    } catch (AuthenticationException ae) {
        request.setAttribute("exception", ae);
        return "login";
    }
}
}
```

Before we move on, let's drill down on how the handleLogin method works. The username and password parameters are retrieved from the request, and these are used to call the login method on the AccountService. If the correct credentials are supplied, we get an Account instance for the user (which we store in the session), and then we redirect to the index page. If the credentials are not correct, the service throws an AuthenticationException, which, for now, is handled by the controller. The exception is stored as a request attribute, and we return the user to the login page.

Although the current controller does its work, we are still operating directly on the HttpServletRequest. This is a quite cumbersome (but sometimes necessary) approach; however, we would generally want to avoid this and use the flexible method signatures to make our controllers simpler. With that in mind, let's modify the controller and limit our use of directly accessing the request (see Listing 5-12).

Listing 5-12. *The LoginController with RequestParam*

```
package com.apress.prospringmvc.bookstore.web.controller;

import org.springframework.web.bind.annotation.RequestParam;

// Other imports omitted, see Listing 5-11

@Controller
@RequestMapping(value = "/login")
public class LoginController {

    // Other methods omitted

    @RequestMapping(method = RequestMethod.POST)
    public String handleLogin(@RequestParam String username,
                              @RequestParam String password,
                              HttpServletRequest request,
```

```
                                       HttpSession session)
          throws AuthenticationException {
       try {
           Account account = this.accountService.login(username, password);
           session.setAttribute(ACCOUNT_ATTRIBUTE, account);
           return "redirect:/index.htm";
       } catch (AuthenticationException ae) {
           request.setAttribute("exception", ae);
           return "login";
       }
    }
  }
}
```

Using the RequestParam annotation simplified our controller. However, our exception handling dictates that we still need access to the request. This will change in the next chapter when we implement exception handling.

There is still one drawback with this approach, and that is our lack of support for the Back button in a browser. If we go back a page, we will get a nice popup asking if we want to resubmit the form. It is a common approach to do a redirect after a POST[6] request; that way, we can work around the double submission problem. In Spring, we can address this by using RedirectAttributes. Listing 5-13 highlights the final modifications to our controller in bold.

Listing 5-13. The LoginController with RedirectAttributes

```
package com.apress.prospringmvc.bookstore.web.controller;

// Other imports omitted, see Listing 5-11

import org.springframework.web.servlet.mvc.support.RedirectAttributes;

@Controller
@RequestMapping(value = "/login")
public class LoginController {

    // Other methods omitted

    @RequestMapping(method = RequestMethod.POST)
    public String handleLogin(@RequestParam String username,↵
                              @RequestParam String password,↵
                              RedirectAttributes redirect,↵
                              HttpSession session) ↵
    throws AuthenticationException {
        try {
            Account account = this.accountService.login(username, password);
            session.setAttribute(ACCOUNT_ATTRIBUTE, account);
            return "redirect:/index.htm";
        } catch (AuthenticationException ae) {
            redirect.addFlashAttribute("exception", ae);
```

---

[6] www.theserverside.com/news/1365146/Redirect-After-Post

```
        return "redirect:/login";
    }
}
}
```

When the application is redeployed and we log in, typing in the wrong username/password combination will still raise an error message; however, when we press the Back button, the popup request for a form submission is gone.

Until now, everything we have done is quite low level. Our solutions include working with the request and/or response directly or through a bit of abstraction with the org.springframework.web .bind.annotation.RequestParam. However, we work in an object-oriented programming language, and where possible, we want to work with objects. We will explore this in the next section.

Book Search Page

We have a bookstore, and we want to sell books. At the moment, however, there is nothing in our web application that allows the user to search for or even see a list of books. Let's address this by creating a book search page, so that the users of our application can search for books.

First, we create a directory book in the /WEB-INF/views directory. In that directory, we create a file called search.jsp. This file is our search form, and it will also display the results of the search. The code for this can be seen in Listing 5-14.

Listing 5-14. The Search Page Form

```
<%@ taglib prefix="c" uri="http://java.sun.com/jsp/jstl/core"%>

<form method="GET" action="<c:url value="/book/search"/>">
    <fieldset>
        <legend>Search Criteria</legend>
        <table>
            <tr>
                <td><label for="title">Title</label></td>
                <td><input id="title" name="title" /></td>
            </tr>
        </table>
    </fieldset>
    <button id="search">Search</button>
</form>

<c:if test="${not empty bookList}">
    <table>
        <tr><th>Title</th><th>Description</th><th>Price</th></tr>
        <c:forEach items="${bookList}" var="book">
            <tr>
                <td>${book.title}</td>
                <td>${book.description}</td>
                <td>${book.price}</td>
            </tr>
        </c:forEach>
    </table>
</c:if>
```

The page consists of a form with a field to fill in a (partial) title that will be used to search for books. When there are results, we will show a table to the user containing the results. Now that we have a page, we also need a controller that can handle the requests. Listing 5-15 shows the initial com.apress.prospringmvc.bookstore.web.controller.BookSearchController.

Listing 5-15. The BookSearchController with Search

```java
package com.apress.prospringmvc.bookstore.web.controller;

import org.springframework.beans.factory.annotation.Autowired;
import org.springframework.stereotype.Controller;
import org.springframework.ui.Model;
import org.springframework.web.bind.annotation.RequestMapping;
import org.springframework.web.bind.annotation.RequestMethod;

import com.apress.prospringmvc.bookstore.domain.BookSearchCriteria;
import com.apress.prospringmvc.bookstore.service.BookstoreService;

import javax.servlet.http.HttpServletRequest

@Controller
public class BookSearchController {

    @Autowired
    private BookstoreService bookstoreService;

    @RequestMapping(value = "/book/search", method = RequestMethod.GET)
    public String list(Model model, HttpServletRequest request) {
        BookSearchCriteria criteria = new BookSearchCriteria();
        criteria.setTitle(request.getParameter("title");
        model.addAttribute(this.bookstoreService.findBooks(criteria));
        return "book/search";
    }
}
```

The controller will react on the URL; retrieve the title parameter from the request (this is the name of the field in our page, as shown in Listing 5-13); and finally, proceed with a search. The results of the search are put in the model. Initially it will display all the books; however, as soon as a title is entered, it will limit the results based on that title (see Figure 5-4).

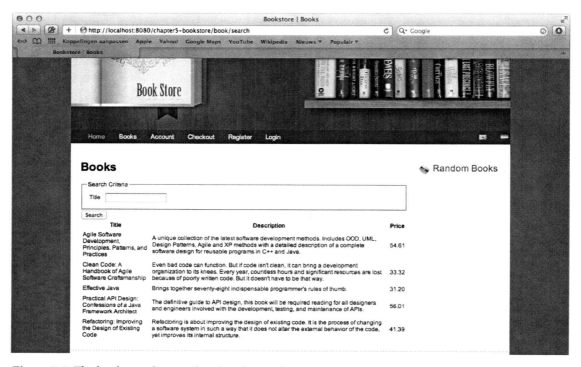

Figure 5-4. The book search page showing the results

As mentioned earlier, working with the HttpServletRequest directly isn't necessary in most cases. Let's make our search method a little simpler by putting the com.apress.prospringmvc.bookstore.domain.BookSearchCriteria in the list of method arguments (see Listing 5-16).

Listing 5-16. The BookSearchController with BookSearchCriteria as a Method Argument

```
package com.apress.prospringmvc.bookstore.web.controller;

import org.springframework.web.bind.annotation.RequestParam;

// Other imports omitted, see listing 5-15

@Controller
public class BookSearchController {

    @Autowired
    private BookstoreService bookstoreService;

    @RequestMapping(value = "/book/search", method = RequestMethod.GET)
    public String list(Model model, BookSearchCriteria criteria) {
        model.addAttribute(this.bookstoreService.findBooks(criteria));
        return "book/search";
```

```
        }
}
```

With Spring MVC, this is what we call *data binding*. To enable data binding, we needed to modify our `com.apress.prospring.bookstore.web.controller.BookSearchController` so it uses a method argument, instead of working with the request directly (see Listing 5-14). Alternatively, it could use `RequestParam` to retrieve the parameters and set them on the object. This will force Spring to use data binding on the `criteria` method argument. Doing so will map all request parameters with the same name as one of our object's properties to that object (i.e., the request parameter `title` will be mapped to the property `title`). Using data binding will greatly simplify our controller (you can find more in-depth information on this in the "Data Binding" section of this chapter).

We can do even better! Instead of returning a `String`, we could return something else. For example, let's modify our controller to return a collection of books. This collection is added to the model with the name `bookList`, as explained earlier in this chapter. Listing 5-16 shows this controller, but where do we select the view to render? It isn't explicitly specified. In Chapter 4, we mentioned that the `org.springframework.web.servlet.RequestToViewNameTranslator` kicks in if there is no explicitly mentioned view to render. We see that mechanism working here. It takes the URL (`http://[server]:[port]/chapter5-bookstore/book/search`); strips the server, port, and application name; removes the suffix (if any); and then uses the remaining `book/search` as the name of the view to render (exactly what we have been returning).

Listing 5-17. The BookSearchController Alternate Version

```
package com.apress.prospringmvc.bookstore.web.controller;

// Other imports omitted, see listing 5-15

@Controller
public class BookSearchController {

    @Autowired
    private BookstoreService bookstoreService;

    @RequestMapping(value = "/book/search", method = RequestMethod.GET)
    public Collection<Book> list(BookSearchCriteria criteria ) {
        return this.bookstoreService.findBooks(criteria);
    }
}
```

Book Detail Page

Now let's put some more functionality into our search page. For example, let's make the title of a book a link that navigates to a book's details page that shows an image of and some information about the book. We'll start by modifying our `search.jsp` and adding links (see Listing 5-18).

Listing 5-18. The Modified Search Page

```
<%@ taglib prefix="c" uri="http://java.sun.com/jsp/jstl/core"%>

<form method="POST" action="<c:url value="/book/search"/>">
    <fieldset>
        <legend>Search Criteria</legend>
        <table>
            <tr>
                <td><label for="title">Title</label></td>
                <td><input id="title" name="title"/></td>
            </tr>
        </table>
    </fieldset>
    <button id="search">Search</button>
</form>

<c:if test="${not empty bookList}">
    <table>
        <tr><th>Title</th><th>Description</th><th>Price</th></tr>
        <c:forEach items="${bookList}" var="book">
            <tr>
                <td><a href="<c:url value="/book/detail/${book.id}"/>">${book.title}</a></td>
                <td>${book.description}</td>
                <td>${book.price}</td>
            </tr>
        </c:forEach>
    </table>
</c:if>
```

The highlighted line is the only change we need to make to this page. At this point, we have generated a URL based on the id of the book, so we should get a URL like /book/detail/4 that shows us the details of the book with id 4. Let's create a controller to react to this URL and extract the id from the URL (see Listing 5-19).

Listing 5-19. The BookDetailController

```
package com.apress.prospringmvc.bookstore.web.controller;

import org.springframework.beans.factory.annotation.Autowired;
import org.springframework.stereotype.Controller;
import org.springframework.ui.Model;
import org.springframework.web.bind.annotation.PathVariable;
import org.springframework.web.bind.annotation.RequestMapping;

import com.apress.prospringmvc.bookstore.domain.Book;
import com.apress.prospringmvc.bookstore.service.BookstoreService;

@Controller
public class BookDetailController {
```

```
    @Autowired
    private BookstoreService bookstoreService;

    @RequestMapping(value = "/book/detail/{bookId}")
    public String details(@PathVariable("bookId") long bookId, Model model) {
        Book book = this.bookstoreService.findBook(bookId);
        model.addAttribute(book);
        return "book/detail";
    }
}
```

The highlighted code is what makes the extraction of the id possible. This is the `org.springframework.web.bind.annotation.PathVariable` in action. The URL mapping contains the `{bookId}` part, which tells Spring MVC to bind that part of the URL to a path variable called `bookId`. We can then use the annotation to retrieve the path variable again. In addition to the controller, we also need a JSP to show the details. The code in Listing 5-20 creates a `detail.jsp` in the book directory.

Listing 5-20. *The Book's Details Page*

```
<%@ taglib prefix="c" uri="http://java.sun.com/jsp/jstl/core"%>

<c:url value="/resources/images/books/${book.isbn}/book_front_cover.png" var="bookImage"/>
<img src="${bookImage}" align="left" alt="${book.title}" width="250"/>

<table>
    <tr><td>Title</td><td>${book.title}</td></tr>
    <tr><td>Description</td><td>${book.description}</td></tr>
    <tr><td>Author</td><td>${book.author}</td></tr>
    <tr><td>Year</td><td>${book.year}</td></tr>
    <tr><td>ISBN</td><td>${book.isbn}</td></tr>
    <tr><td>Price</td><td>${book.price}</td></tr>
</table>
```

If we click one of the links from the search page after redeployment, we should be greeted with a details page that shows an image of and some information about the book (see Figure 5-5).

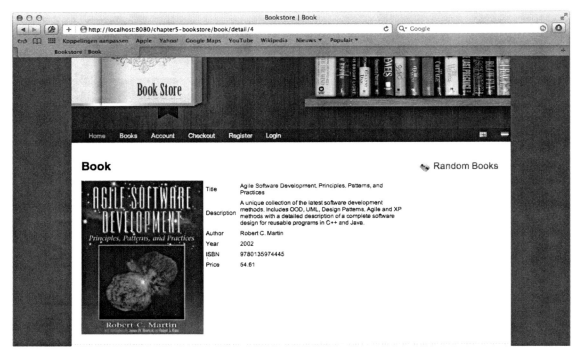

Figure 5-5. The book's details page

Data Binding

In this section, we will explore the benefits and possibilities of using data binding, including how we can configure and extend it. However, we'll begin by explaining the basics of data binding. Listing 5-21 shows our com.apress.prospringmvc.bookstore.domain.BookSearchCriteria JavaBean. It is a simple object with two properties: title and category.

Listing 5-21. The BookSearchCriteria JavaBean

```
package com.apress.prospringmvc.bookstore.domain;

public class BookSearchCriteria {

    private String title;
    private Category category;

    public String getTitle() {
        return this.title;
    }

    public void setTitle(String title) {
        this.title = title;
```

```
    }

    public void setCategory(Category category) {
        this.category = category;
    }

    public Category getCategory() {
        return this.category;
    }
}
```

Assume we receive the following request: `http://localhost:8080/chapter5-bookstore/book/search?title=Agile`. In this case, the `title` property receives the value of `Agile`. Behind the scenes, Spring calls the `setTitle` method on our JavaBean, which we specified as a method argument in the `list` method on our controller. If there were a parameter named `category` in the request, then Spring would call the `setCategory` method; however, it would first try to convert the parameter (which is always a `String`) into a `com.apress.prospring.bookstore.domain.Category` JavaBean.

However, data binding isn't limited to simple setter methods. We can also bind to nested properties and even to indexed collections like maps, arrays, and lists. Nested binding happens when the parameter name contains a *dot* (.); for instance, `address.street=Somewhere` leads to `getAddress().setStreet("Somewhere")`.

To bind to indexed collections, we must use a notation with square brackets in which we enclose the index. When using a map, this index doesn't have to be a numeric. For instance, `list[2].name` would bind a name property on the third element in the list. Similarly, `map['foo'].name` would bind the name property to the value under the key `foo` in the map.

Customizing Data Binding

We have two options for customizing the behavior of data binding: globally or per controller. Of course, we can mix both strategies together by performing a global setup, and then fine-tuning it per controller.

Global Customization

To customize data binding globally, we need to create a class that implements the `org.springframework.web.bind.support.WebBindingInitializer` interface. Spring MVC provides a configurable implementation of this interface, the `org.springframework.web.bind.support.ConfigurableWebBindingInitializer`. An instance of the interface must be registered with the handler mapping implementation, so that it can be used. After an instance of `org.springframework.web.bind.WebDataBinder` is created, the `initBinder` method of the `org.springframework.web.bind.support.WebBindingInitializer` is called.

The provided implementation allows us to set a couple of properties. When a property is not set, it uses the defaults as specified by the `org.springframework.web.bind.WebDataBinder`. If we were to want to specify more properties, it would be quite easy to extend the default implementation and add the desired behavior. It is possible to set the same properties here as in the controller (see Table 5-13).

Table 5-13. The ConfigurableWebBindingInitializer Properties

Attribute	Description
autoGrowNestedPaths	If set to true, a path containing a null value will be populated with a default object value instead of resulting in an exception. Moreover, this default value will be used for further traversal of the expression. This property also controls auto growing of collections when an out-of-bounds index is accessed. The default value is true.
bindingErrorProcessor	Sets the org.springframework.validation.BindingErrorProcessor implementation to use.
conversionService	Sets the instance of an org.springframework.core.convert .ConversionService to use.
directFieldAccess	When set to true, we don't need to write getters/setters to access the fields. The default is false.
messageCodesResolver	Sets the org.springframework.validation.MessageCodesResolver to use.
propertyEditorRegistrar propertyEditorRegistrars	Registers one or more org.springframework.beans .PropertyEditorRegistrars. This is useful when we have old-style PropertyEditors that we want to use for type conversion.
validator	Sets the instance of org.springframework.validation.Validator to use.

When we want to extend the configuration provided by Spring @MVC, we need to do some extending and overriding. This is because the default configuration already configures a org.springframework.web.bind.support.ConfigurableWebBindingInitializer; however, it doesn't expose it as a bean. Instead, we need to extend org.springframework.web.servlet.config.annotation .WebMvcConfigurationSupport and override the requestMappingHandlerAdapter method (see Listing 5-22).

Listing 5-22. Reusing the ConfigurableWebBindingInitializer

```
public class WebMvcContextConfiguration extends WebMvcConfigurationSupport {
    @Override
    @Bean
    public RequestMappingHandlerAdapter requestMappingHandlerAdapter() {
        RequestMappingHandlerAdapter adapter = super.requestMappingHandlerAdapter();
        ConfigurableWebBindingInitializer webBindingInitializer; ↵
        webBindingInitializer = (ConfigurableWebBindingInitializer) ↵
adapter.getWebBindingInitializer();
        webBindingInitializer.setDirectFieldAccess(true);
        //Do other re-configuration
        return adapter;
    }
```

}

Per Controller Customization

For the per controller option, we must implement a method in the controller and put the `org` `.springframework.web.bind.annotation.InitBinder` annotation on that method. The method must have no return value (void) and at least an `org.springframework.web.bind.WebDataBinder` as a method argument. The method *can* have the same arguments as a request-handling method. However, it *cannot* have a method argument with the `org.springframework.web.bind.annotation.ModelAttribute` annotation. This is because the model is available after binding; and in this method, we are going to configure how we bind.

The `org.springframework.web.bind.annotation.InitBinder` annotation has a single attribute named value that can take the model attribute names or request parameter names this init-binder method is going to apply to. The default is to apply to all model attributes and request parameters.

To customize binding, we need to configure our `org.springframework.web.bind.WebDataBinder`. This object has several configuration options (setter methods) that we can use, as shown in Table 5-14.

Table 5-14. WebDataBinder Properties

Attribute	Description
allowedFields	Specifies the fields that are allowed to be used for binding. This is a so-called white list; only fields included in this list will be used for binding. Field names can also contain an * for matching field names with a certain pattern. By default, all fields are allowed. See the `disallowedFields` attribute for information on excluding fields from binding.
autoGrowCollectionLimit	Sets the maximum size to auto grow a collection when binding. This setting can be used to prevent out of memory errors when binding on large collections. By default, it is set to 256.
autoGrowNestedPaths	If set to true, populates a path containing a null value with a default object value instead of raising an exception. This default object value will in turn be used for further traversal of the expression. This property also controls auto growing of collections when an out-of-bounds index is being accessed. By default, it is set to true.
bindEmptyMultipartFiles	By default, replaces the already bound multipart files with an empty multipart file holder if the user resubmits a multipart form without choosing a different file. If this isn't desired and you want null instead, then turn this property off.
bindingErrorProcessor	Sets the `org.springframework.validation.BindingErrorProcessor` implementation to use. Spring provides an `org.springframework` `.validation.DefaultBindingErrorProcessor` as a default implementation.
conversionService	Sets the `org.springframework.core.convert.ConversionService` to use.

Attribute	Description
disallowedFields	Specifies the fields that aren't allowed to be used for binding. This is a blacklist of request parameter names to ignore during binding. In general, it is wise to put fields like the id and version fields in there. Like allowedFields, this property can contain an * for matching field names with a certain pattern.
extractOldValueForEditor	Specifies whether to extract the old values for editors and converters. By default, the old values are kept in the binding result. If this isn't desired, set this property to false. It is also useful to set this to false if you have getters that have side effects (e.g., they set other properties or default values).
fieldDefaultPrefix	Specifies the prefix to identify parameters that contain default values for empty fields. The default value is !.
fieldMarkerPrefix	Specifies the prefix to identify parameters that mark fields that aren't submitted. Generally, this is useful with checkboxes. A checkbox that isn't checked isn't submitted as part of the request. Note that this mechanism still lets us receive a value. The default marker is _ (underscore).
ignoreInvalidFields	If set to true, ignores invalid fields. Should we ignore bind parameters that have corresponding fields in our model object, but which aren't accessible? Generally this happens with a nested path, when part of that path resolves to null. The default is false (i.e., it will *not* ignore these fields).
ignoreUnknownFields	Indicates whether to ignore parameters that aren't represented as parameters on our model objects. When set to false, all the parameters that are submitted must be represented on our model objects. The default is true.
messageCodesResolver	Sets the org.springframework.validation.MessageCodesResolver to use. Spring provides the org.springframework.validation.DefaultMessageCodesResolver as the default implementation.
requiredFields	Sets the fields that are required. When a required field is not set, this leads to a bind error.
validator	Sets the org.springframework.validation.Validator implementation to use.

In addition to setting these properties, we can also tell the org.springframework.web.bind.WebDataBinder to use bean property access (the default) or direct field access. This can be done by calling the initBeanPropertyAccess or initDirectFieldAccess method to set property access or direct field access, respectively. The advantage of direct field access is that we don't have to write getter/setters for each field we want to use for binding. Listing 5-23 shows an example init-binder method.

Listing 5-23. An Example init-binder Method

```
package com.apress.prospringmvc.bookstore.web.controller;

//Imports omitted

@Controller
@RequestMapping(value = "/customer")
public class RegistrationController {

    // Other methods omitted

    @InitBinder
    public void initBinder(WebDataBinder binder) {
        binder.initDirectFieldAccess();
        binder.setDisallowedFields("id");
        binder.setRequiredFields("username", "password", "emailAddress");
    }

}
```

ModelAttributes

To fully utilize data binding, we have to use model attributes. Furthermore, we should use one of these model attributes as the object our form fields are bound to. In our com.apress.prospringmvc .bookstore.web.controller.BookSearchController, we added an object as a method argument, and Spring used that as the object to bind the request parameters to. However, it is possible to have more control over our objects and how we create objects. For this, we can use the org.springframework.web.bind.annotation.ModelAttribute annotation. This annotation can be put both on a method and on method arguments.

Using ModelAttribute on Methods

We can use the ModelAttribute annotation on methods to create an object to be used in our form (e.g., when editing or updating) or to get reference data (i.e., data that is needed to render the form like a list of categories). Let's modify our controller to add a list of categories to the model and an instance of a com.apress.prospring.bookstore.domain.BookSearchCriteria object (see Listing 5-24).

■ **Caution** When a ModelAttribute annotation is put on a method, this method will be called before the request-handling method is called!

Listing 5-24. The BookSearchController with ModelAttribute Methods

```
package com.apress.prospringmvc.bookstore.web.controller;

// Other imports omitted.

import org.springframework.web.bind.annotation.ModelAttribute;

@Controller
public class BookSearchController {

    @Autowired
    private BookstoreService bookstoreService;

    @ModelAttribute
    public BookSearchCriteria criteria() {
        return new BookSearchCriteria();
    }

    @ModelAttribute("categories")
    public List<Category> getCategories() {
        return this.bookstoreService.findAllCategories();
    }

    @RequestMapping(value = "/book/search", method = { RequestMethod.GET })
    public Collection<Book> list(BookSearchCriteria criteria) {
        return this.bookstoreService.findBooks(criteria);
    }
}
```

Methods annotated with `ModelAttribute` have the same flexibility in method argument types as the request-handling methods. Of course, they shouldn't operate on the response and cannot have `ModelAttribute` annotation method arguments. We could also have the method return void; however, we would then need to include an `org.springframework.ui.Model`, `org.springframework.ui.ModelMap` or `Map` as a method argument and explicitly add its value to the model.

The annotation can also be placed on request-handling methods, indicating that the return value of the method is to be used as a model attribute. The name of the view is then derived from the request that uses the configured `org.springframework.web.servlet.RequestToViewNameTranslator`.

Using ModelAttribute on Method Arguments

When using the annotation on a method argument, the argument is looked up from the model. If it isn't found, an instance of the argument type is created using the default constructor. Listing 5-25 shows our `com.apress.prospring.bookstore.web.controller.BookSearchController` with the annotation.

Listing 5-25. The BookSearchController with ModelAttribute Annotation on a Method Argument

```
package com.apress.prospringmvc.bookstore.web.controller;

// Imports omitted see listing 5-22

@Controller
public class BookSearchController {

    // Methods omitted see listing 5-22

    @RequestMapping(value = "/book/search", method = { RequestMethod.GET })
    public Collection<Book> list(@ModelAttribute("bookSearchCriteria") BookSearchCriteria
 criteria) {
        return this.bookstoreService.findBooks(criteria);
    }
}
```

Using SessionAttributes

It can be beneficial to store a model attribute in the session between requests. For example, imagine we need to edit a customer record. The first request gets the customer from the database. It is then edited in the application, and the changes are submitted back and applied to the customer. If we don't store the customer in the session, then the customer record must be retrieved again from the database. This can be inconvenient.

In Spring @MVC, you can tell the framework to store certain model attributes in the session. For this, you can use the org.springframework.web.bind.annotation.SessionAttributes annotation (see Table 5-15). You should use this annotation to store model attributes in the session, so they survive multiple HTTP requests. However, you should not use this annotation to store something in the session, and then use the javax.servlet.http.HttpSession to retrieve it. The session attributes are also only usable from within the same controller, so you should not use them as a transport to move objects between controllers. If you need something like that, we suggest that you use Spring Web Flow (see Chapters 10-12).

Table 5-15. The SessionAttributes Attributes

Argument Name	Description
value	The names of the model attributes that should be stored in the session.
types	The fully qualified classnames (types) of model attributes that should be stored in the session. All attributes in the model of this type will be stored in the session, regardless of their attribute name.

When using the org.springframework.web.bind.annotation.SessionAttributes annotation to store model attributes in the session, we also need to tell the framework when to remove those attributes. For this, we need to use the org.springframework.web.bind.support.SessionStatus interface (see Listing

5-26). When we finish using the attributes, we need to call the setComplete method on the interface. To access that interface, we can simply include it as a method argument (see Table 5-4).

Listing 5-26. *The SessionStatus Interface*

```
package org.springframework.web.bind.support;

public interface SessionStatus {

    void setComplete();

    boolean isComplete();

}
```

Form Tag Library

To be able to use all the data binding features provided by the framework, we also need to use the tag library to write forms. Spring MVC ships with two tag libraries. The first is a general-purpose library (see Table 5-16), and the second is a library used to simplify writing forms in our pages (see Table 5-17). We can use the general-purpose library to write our forms (this was how it worked with the Spring Framework before 2.0). This is a very powerful approach, but it is also quite cumbersome (albeit it can still be used as a fallback in those corner cases where the form tag library isn't sufficient).

Table 5-16. *The Spring Tag Library*

Tag Name	Description
htmlEscape	Sets the default HTML escape value for the current page. If set, this tag overrides the value set in the defaultHtmlEscape context-parameter.
escapeBody	Escapes the enclosed body.
message	Displays a message with the given code and for the selected locale. (See the section about internationalization (I18N) later in this chapter for more information.)
theme	Uses the variable from the currently selected theme. (See Chapter 9 for more information.)
hasBindErrors	Shows or hides part of the page (or element) based on whether an model attribute has bind (or validation) errors.
nestedPath	Selects a nested path to be used by the bind tag's path. For example, it can be used to bind customer.address to street instead of to customer.address.street.
bind	Binds an attribute of the model (attribute) to the enclosed input element.

Tag Name	Description
transform	Transforms the bound attribute using Spring's type-conversion system. This tag must be used inside a `spring:bind` tag.
url	Similar to the jstl core URL tag. It is enhanced so the URL can contain URL template parameters.
param	Specifies a parameter and value to be assigned to the URL. This tag is used inside an `url` tag.
eval	Evaluates a SpEL expression and prints the result or assigns it to a variable.

Table 5-17. The Form Tag Library

Tag Name	Description
form	Renders an HTML form tag and exposes the binding path to the other form tags.
input	Renders an input element with the default type of `text`. The type of the input element can be can be (optionally) specified (like `email`, `date` etc.) . Note that you can't use `radiobutton` or `checkbox` for those types.
password	Renders an input element of type `password`.
hidden	Renders an input element of type `hidden`.
select	Renders an HTML select element. The `option` and/or `options` tag are used to specify the options to render.
option	Renders a single HTML option element inside a select element.
options	Renders a collection of HTML option elements inside a select element.
radiobutton	Renders an HTML input element of the type `radio button`.
radiobuttons	Renders multiple HTML input elements of the type `radio button`.
checkbox	Renders an HTML input element of the type `checkbox`.
checkboxes	Renders multiple HTML input elements of the type `checkbox`.
textarea	Renders an HTML Textarea element.
errors	Displays binding and/or validation errors to the user. It can be used to either specify the path for field-specific error messages or to specify an * to display all error messages.

145

Tag Name	Description
label	Renders a HTML Label and associate it with an input element.
button	Renders an HTML Button element.

When using the form tag library, we need to specify which model attribute property we want to bind the form element to. We do this by specifying the `path` attribute on our form element. There are several properties we can set on the various form tags, but Table 5-18 shows the main properties. For the form tags that use a collection of items (e.g., select, checkboxes, and radiobuttons), there are a few additional shared attributes (see Table 5-19).

Table 5-18. *The Shared Form Tag Attributes*

Tag Name	Description
path	The (nested) attribute of our model attribute to bind to.
readonly	Indicates if this form element is readonly.
disabled	Indicates if this form element is disabled.
cssClass	The CSS class used to render this element.
cssErrorClass	The CSS class used to render this element in the event of bind or validation errors.
id	The explicit id of this element. This can be useful when used with JavaScript because it enables us to always know the name of an element.

Table 5-19. *The Shared Form Tag Attributes for Collection-based Tags*

Tag Name	Description
items	The collection of model attributes to render.
itemValue	The value of a single element to render (e.g., the id of a book).
itemLabel	The label of a single element to render (e.g., the name of a book).
multiple	Indicates if this form element allows multiple selections (cannot be used on radiobuttons because those are always single-select).

We can apply this logic to our order JSP page. The page would still have the same functionality, but it would fully utilize the data binding functionality from Spring MVC (see Listing 5-27). In this case, we simply need to replace the normal input element tags with the form element tags, and then supply the path to bind to. Of course, we also need to add the `taglib` declaration to the top of the JSP.

Listing 5-27. The Order JSP with Form Tags

```
<%@ taglib prefix="c" uri="http://java.sun.com/jsp/jstl/core"%>
<%@ taglib prefix="form" uri="http://www.springframework.org/tags/form" %>
<form:form method="GET" modelAttribute="bookSearchCriteria">
    <fieldset>
        <legend>Search Criteria</legend>
        <table>
            <tr>
                <td><form:label path="title">Title</form:label></td>
                <td><form:input path="title"/></td>
            </tr>
        </table>
    </fieldset>
    <button id="search">Search</button>
</form:form>

<c:if test="${not empty bookList}">
    <table>
        <tr><th>Title</th><th>Description</th><th>Price</th></tr>
        <c:forEach items="${bookList}" var="book">
            <tr>
                <td><a href="<c:url value="/book/detail/${book.id}"/>">${book.title}</a></td>
                <td>${book.description}</td>
                <td>${book.price}</td>
            </tr>
        </c:forEach>
    </table>
</c:if>
```

If we redeploy and issue a new search at this point, we see that our title field keeps the previously entered value (see Figure 5-6). This is due to our use of data binding in combination with the form tags.

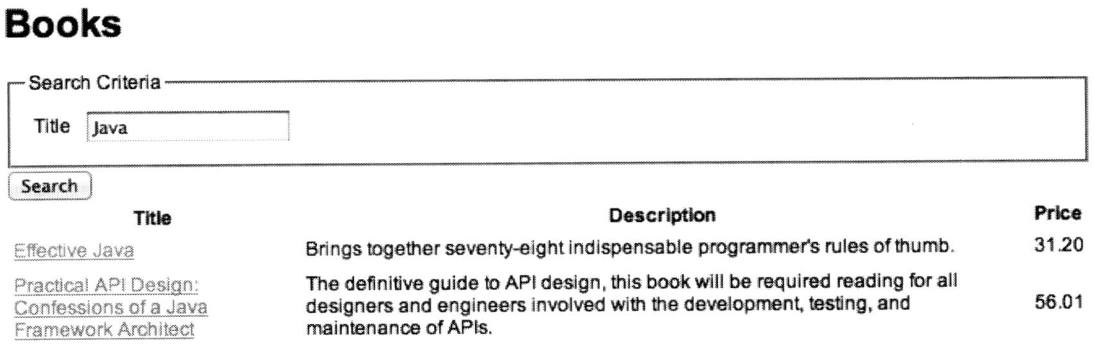

Books

Figure 5-6. The Title field remains filled

Now it's time to make things a bit more interesting by adding a dropdown box (a HTML select) to select a category to search for in addition to the title. We already have the categories in our model (see Listing 5-23). We simply want to add a dropdown and bind it to the id field of the category (see Listing

5-28). We add a select tag and tell it which model attribute contains the items to render. We also specify the value and label to show for the each of the items. The value is bound to the model attribute used for the form.

Listing 5-28. The Search Page with a Category

```
<%@ taglib prefix="c" uri="http://java.sun.com/jsp/jstl/core"%>
<%@ taglib prefix="form" uri="http://www.springframework.org/tags/form" %>
<form:form method="GET" modelAttribute="bookSearchCriteria">
  <fieldset>
    <legend>Search Criteria</legend>
    <table>
      <tr>
        <td><form:label path="title">Title</form:label></td>
        <td><form:input path="title"/></td>
      </tr>
      <tr>
        <td><form:label path="category.id">Category</form:label></td>
        <td>
          <form:select path="category.id" items="${categories}" itemValue="id"↵
  itemLabel="name"/>
        </td>
      </tr>
    </table>
  </fieldset>
  <button id="search">Search</button>
</form:form>

// Result table omitted
```

Type Conversion

An important part of data binding is type conversion. When we receive a request, the only thing we have are String instances. However, in the real world we use a lot of different object types, not just text representations. Therefore, we want to convert those String instances into something we can use, which is where type conversion comes in. In Spring MVC, there are three ways to do type conversion:

- Property Editors
- Converters
- Formatters

Property editors are the old-style of doing type conversion, whereas converters and formatters are the new way of doing type conversion. Converters and formatters are more flexible; as such, they are also more powerful than property editors. In addition, relying on property editors also pulls in the whole java.beans package, including all its support classes, which we just don't need in a web environment.

Property Editors

Support for property editors has been part of the Spring Framework since its inception. To use this kind of type conversion, we create a PropertyEditor implementation (typically by subclassing PropertyEditorSupport). Property editors take a String and convert it into a strongly typed object—and vice versa. Spring provides several implementations for accomplishing this out of the box (see Table 5-20).

Table 5-20. *Spring's Default Property Editors*

Class	Explanation
ByteArrayPropertyEditor	An editor for byte arrays that converts Strings to their corresponding byte representations.
CharsetEditor	An editor for java.nio.charset.Charset that expects the same name syntax as the name method of the java.nio.charset.Charset.
ClassEditor ClassArrayEditor	An editor that parses Strings representing classes into actual classes and vice versa. When a class is not found, a java.lang.IllegalArgumentException is thrown.
CurrencyEditor	An editor for Currency that translates currency codes into Currency objects. It also exposes the currency code as the text representation of a Currency object.
CustomBooleanEditor	A customizable property editor for Boolean properties.
CustomCollectionEditor	A property editor for collections that converts any source Collection into a given target Collection type.
CustomMapEditor	Property editor for Map that converts any source Map into a given target Map type.
CustomDateEditor	A customizable property editor for Date that supports a custom DateFormat. This is *not* registered by default, and it must be user registered as needed with the appropriate format.
CustomNumberEditor	A customizable property editor for any Number subclass like Integer, Long, Float, and so on. It is registered by default, but can be overridden by registering a custom instance of it as a custom editor.
FileEditor	An editor capable of resolving Strings to java.io.File objects. It is registered by default.

Class	Explanation
InputStreamEditor	A one-way property editor capable of taking a text string and producing a java.io.InputStream, so that InputStream properties may be directly set as Strings. Note that the default usage will not close the InputStream for you! It is registered by default.
LocaleEditor	An editor capable of resolving to Locale objects and vice versa (the String format is [language]_[country]_[variant], which is the same behavior the toString() method of Locale provides). It is registered by default.
PatternEditor	An editor capable of resolving Strings to JDK 1.5 Pattern objects and vice versa.
PropertiesEditor	An editor capable of converting Strings (formatted using the format as defined in the Javadoc for the Properties class) to Properties objects. It is registered by default.
StringTrimmerEditor	A property editor that trims Strings. Optionally, it allows transforming an empty String into a null value. It is *not* registered by default; it must be registered by the user as needed.
TimeZoneEditor	An editor for Timezone that translates timezone IDs into TimeZone objects. Note that it does not expose a text representation for TimeZone objects.
URIEditor	An editor for java.net.URI that directly populates a URI property instead of using a String property as a bridge. By default, this editor will encode String into URIs.
URLEditor	An editor capable of resolving a String representation of a URL into an actual java.net.URL object. It is registered by default.

Note: All these property editors can be found in the org.springframework.beans.propertyeditors package.

Converters

The converter API in Spring 3 is a general purpose type-conversion system. Within a Spring container, this system is used as an alternative to property editors to convert bean property value strings into the required property type. We can also use this API to our advantage in our application whenever we need to do type conversion. The converter system is a strongly typed conversion system and uses generics to enforce this.

There are four different interfaces that can be used to implement a converter, all of which can be found in the org.springframework.core.convert.converter package:

- Converter
- ConverterFactory
- GenericConverter

- `ConditionalGenericConverter`

Let's explore the four different APIs.

Listing 5-29 shows the Converter API, which is very straightforward. It has a single convert method that takes a source argument and transforms it into a target. The source and target types are expressed by the S and T generic type arguments.

Listing 5-29. The Converter API

```
package org.springframework.core.convert.converter;

public interface Converter<S, T> {

    T convert(S source);
}
```

Listing 5-30 shows the ConverterFactory API that is useful when you need to have conversion logic for an entire class hierarchy. For this, we can parameterize S to be type we are converting from (the source), and we parameterize R as the base type we want to convert to. We can then create the appropriate converter inside the implementation of this factory.

Listing 5-30. The ConverterFactory API

```
package org.springframework.core.convert.converter;

public interface ConverterFactory<S, R> {

    <T extends R> Converter<S, T> getConverter(Class<T> targetType);
}
```

When we require more sophisticated conversion logic, we can use the org.springframework.core .convert.converter.GenericConverter (see Listing 5-31). It is more flexible, but less strongly typed than the previous converter types. It supports converting between multiple source and target types. During a conversion, we have access to the source and target type descriptions, which can be useful for complex conversion logic. This also allows for type conversion to be driven by annotation (i.e., we can parse the annotation at runtime to determine what needs to be done).

Listing 5-31. The GenericConverter API

```
package org.springframework.core.convert.converter;

import org.springframework.core.convert.TypeDescriptor;
import org.springframework.util.Assert;

import java.util.Set;

public interface GenericConverter {

    Set<ConvertiblePair> getConvertibleTypes();

    Object convert(Object source,
                   TypeDescriptor sourceType,
```

151

```
                              TypeDescriptor targetType);

}
```

An example of this type of conversion logic would be a converter that converts from an array to a collection. A converter would first inspect the type of element being converted, so that we could apply additional conversion logic to different elements.

Listing 5-32 shows a specialized version of the GenericConverter that allows us to specify a condition for when it should execute. For example, we could create a converter that uses one of the BigDecimals valueOf methods to convert a value, but this would only be useful if we could actually invoke that method with the given sourceType.

Listing 5-32. *The ConditionalGenericConverter API*

```
package org.springframework.core.convert.converter;

import org.springframework.core.convert.TypeDescriptor;

    boolean matches(TypeDescriptor sourceType, TypeDescriptor targetType);

}
```

The converters are executed behind the org.springframework.core.convert.ConversionService interface (see Listing 5-33); typical implementations of this interface also implement the org.springframework.core.convert.converter.ConverterRegistry interface, which enables the easy registration of additional converters. When using Spring @MVC, there is a preconfigured instance of the org.springframework.format.support.DefaultFormattingConversionService (which also allows for executing and registering formatters).

Listing 5-33. *The ConversionService API*

```
package org.springframework.core.convert;

public interface ConversionService {

    boolean canConvert(Class<?> sourceType, Class<?> targetType);

    boolean canConvert(TypeDescriptor sourceType, TypeDescriptor targetType);

    <T> T convert(Object source, Class<T> targetType);

    Object convert(Object source, TypeDescriptor sourceType, TypeDescriptor targetType);
}
```

Formatters

The Converter API is a general purpose type-conversion system. It is strongly typed and can convert from any object type to another object type (if there is a converter available). However, this is not something we need in our web environment because we only deal with String objects there. On the other hand, we probably want to represent our objects as String to the client, and we might even want to do so in a localized way. This is where the Formatter API comes in (see Listing 5-34). It provides a simple and robust mechanism to convert from a String to a strongly typed object. It is an alternative to property editors, but it is also lighter (e.g., it doesn't depend on the java.beans package) and more flexible (e.g, it has access to the Locale for localized content).

Listing 5-34. The Formatter API

```
package org.springframework.format;

public interface Formatter<T> extends Printer<T>, Parser<T> {
}

import java.util.Locale

public interface Printer<T> {
    String print(T object, Locale locale);
}

import java.util.Locale
import java.text.ParseException;

public interface Parser<T> {
    T parse(String text, Locale locale) throws ParseException;
}
```

To create a formatter, we need to implement the org.springframework.format.Formatter interface and specify the type T as the type we want to convert. For example, imagine we had a formatter that could convert Date instances to text, and vice-versa. We would specify T as Date and use the Locale to determine the specific date format to use for performing the conversion (see Listing 5-35).

Listing 5-35. The Sample DateFormatter

```
package com.apress.prospringmvc.bookstore.formatter;

// java.text and java.util imports omitted

import org.springframework.format.Formatter;
import org.springframework.util.StringUtils;

public class DateFormatter implements Formatter<Date> {

    private String format;

    @Override
    public String print(Date object, Locale locale) {
        return getDateFormat(locale).format(object);
    }

    @Override
    public Date parse(String text, Locale locale) throws ParseException {
        return getDateFormat(locale).parse(text);
    }
```

```
    private DateFormat getDateFormat(Locale locale) {
        if (StringUtils.hasText(this.format)) {
            return new SimpleDateFormat(this.format, locale);
        } else {
            return SimpleDateFormat.getDateInstance(SimpleDateFormat.MEDIUM, locale);
        }
    }

    public void setFormat(String format) {
        this.format = format;
    }
}
```

Formatters can also be driven by annotations instead of by field type. If we want to bind a formatter to an annotation, we have to implement the org.springframework.format.AnnotationFormatterFactory (see Listing 5-36).

Listing 5-36. The AnnotationFormatterFactory

```
package org.springframework.format;

public interface AnnotationFormatterFactory<A extends Annotation> {

    Set<Class<?>> getFieldTypes();

    Printer<?> getPrinter(A annotation, Class<?> fieldType);

    Parser<?> getParser(A annotation, Class<?> fieldType);
}
```

We need to parameterize A with the annotation type we want to associate with it. The getPrinter and getParser methods should return an org.springframework.format.Printer and org.springframework.format.Parser, respectively. We can then use these to convert from or to the annotation type. Let's imagine we have a com.apress.prospringmvc.bookstore.formatter.DateFormat annotation that we can use to set the format for a date field. We could then implement the factory shown in Listing 5-37.

Listing 5-37. The DateFormatAnnotationFormatterFactory

```
package com.apress.prospringmvc.bookstore.formatter;

import java.util.Date;
import java.util.HashSet;
import java.util.Set;

import org.springframework.format.AnnotationFormatterFactory;
import org.springframework.format.Parser;
import org.springframework.format.Printer;

public class DateFormatAnnotationFormatterFactory implements←
 AnnotationFormatterFactory<DateFormat> {
```

```java
    @Override
    public Set<Class<?>> getFieldTypes() {
        Set<Class<?>> types = new HashSet<Class<?>>(1);
        types.add(Date.class);
        return types;
    }

    @Override
    public Printer<?> getPrinter(DateFormat annotation, Class<?> fieldType) {
        return createFormatter(annotation);
    }

    @Override
    public Parser<?> getParser(DateFormat annotation, Class<?> fieldType) {
        return createFormatter(annotation);
    }

    private DateFormatter createFormatter(DateFormat annotation) {
        DateFormatter formatter = new DateFormatter();
        formatter.setFormat(annotation.format());
        return formatter;
    }
}
```

Configuring Type Conversion

If we want to use an org.springframework.core.convert.converter.Converter or an
org.springframework.format.Formatter in Spring MVC, then we need to add some configuration. The
org.springframework.web.servlet.config.annotation.WebMvcConfigurerAdapter has a method for this.
The addFormatters method can be overridden to register additional converters and/or formatters. This
method has an org.springframework.format.FormatterRegistry (see Listing 5-38) as an argument, and it
can be used to register the additional converters and/or formatters (the FormatterRegistry extends the
org.springframework.core.convert.converter.ConverterRegistry, which offers the same functionality
for Converter implementations).

Listing 5-38. The FormatterRegistry Interface

```java
package org.springframework.format;

import java.lang.annotation.Annotation;

import org.springframework.core.convert.converter.ConverterRegistry;

public interface FormatterRegistry extends ConverterRegistry {

    void addFormatter(Formatter<?> formatter);
    void addFormatterForFieldType(Class<?> fieldType, Formatter<?> formatter);
    void addFormatterForFieldType(Class<?> fieldType, Printer<?> printer, Parser<?> parser);
    void addFormatterForFieldAnnotation(AnnotationFormatterFactory<? extends Annotation>↵
  annotationFormatterFactory);
```

```
}
```

To convert from a String to a com.apress.prospringmvc.bookstore.domain.Category, we will implement an org.springframework.core.convert.converter.GenericConverter (see Listing 5-39) and register it in our configuration (see Listing 5-40). The com.apress.prospringmvc.bookstore.converter .StringToEntityConverter takes a String as its source and transforms it into a configurable entity type. It then uses a javax.persistence.EntityManager to load the record from the database.

Listing 5-39. The StringToEntityConverter

```java
package com.apress.prospringmvc.bookstore.converter;

import java.util.HashSet;
import java.util.Set;

import javax.persistence.EntityManager;
import javax.persistence.PersistenceContext;

import org.apache.commons.lang3.StringUtils;
import org.apache.commons.lang3.reflect.FieldUtils;
import org.springframework.core.convert.TypeDescriptor;
import org.springframework.core.convert.converter.GenericConverter;

public class StringToEntityConverter implements GenericConverter {

    private static final String ID_FIELD = "id";

    private final Class<?> clazz;

    @PersistenceContext
    private EntityManager em;

    public StringToEntityConverter(Class<?> clazz) {
        super();
        this.clazz = clazz;
    }

    @Override
    public Set<ConvertiblePair> getConvertibleTypes() {
        Set<ConvertiblePair> types = new HashSet<GenericConverter.ConvertiblePair>();
        types.add(new ConvertiblePair(String.class, this.clazz));
        types.add(new ConvertiblePair(this.clazz, String.class));
        return types;
    }

    @Override
    public Object convert(Object source, TypeDescriptor sourceType,
                          TypeDescriptor  targetType) {
        if (String.class.equals(sourceType.getType())) {
            if (StringUtils.isBlank((String) source)) {
                return null;
```

```
        }
        Long id = Long.parseLong((String) source);
        return this.em.find(this.clazz, id);
    } else if (this.clazz.equals(sourceType.getType())) {
        try {
            if (source == null) {
                return "";
            } else {
                return FieldUtils.readField(source, ID_FIELD, true).toString();
            }
        } catch (IllegalAccessException e) {
        }
    }
    throw new IllegalArgumentException("Cannot convert " + source + " into a suitable↵
type!");
    }
}
```

Listing 5-40. The CategoryConverter Configuration

```
package com.apress.prospringmvc.bookstore.web.config;

... [import ommitted]

@Configuration
@EnableWebMvc
@ComponentScan(basePackages = { "com.apress.prospringmvc.bookstore.web" })
public class WebMvcContextConfiguration extends WebMvcConfigurerAdapter {

    …

    @Bean
    public StringToEntityConverter categoryConverter() {
        return new StringToEntityConverter(Category.class);
    }

    @Override
    public void addFormatters(final FormatterRegistry registry) {
        registry.addConverter(categoryConverter());
        registry.addFormatter(new DateFormatter("dd-MM-yyyy"));
    }
    …
}
```

In addition to the category conversion, we also need to do date conversions. Therefore, Listing 5-38 also includes an org.springframework.format.datetime.DateFormatter with a pattern for converting dates.

Using Type Conversion

Now that we have covered type conversion, let's see it in action. We will create the user registration page that allows us to enter the details for the `com.apress.prospringmvc.bookstore.domain.Account` object. First, we need a web page under `WEB-INF/views`. Next, we need to create a `customer` directory and place a `register.jsp` file in it. The content is included only in part of Listing 5-41 because there is a lot of repetition in this page for all the different fields.

Listing 5-41. The Registration Page

```
<%@ taglib prefix="c" uri="http://java.sun.com/jsp/jstl/core"%>
<%@ taglib prefix="spring" uri="http://www.springframework.org/tags" %>
<%@ taglib prefix="form" uri="http://www.springframework.org/tags/form" %>

<form:form method="POST" modelAttribute="account">
    <fieldset>
        <legend>Personal</legend>
        <table>
            <tr>
                <td>
                    <form:label path="firstName" cssErrorClass="error">
                        Firstname
                    </form:label>
                </td>
                <td><form:input path="firstName" /></td>
                <td><form:errors path="firstName"/></td>
            </tr>
            // Other Account fields omitted
        </table>
    <fieldset>
        <legend>Userinfo</legend>
        <table>
            <tr>
                <td><form:label path="username" cssErrorClass="error">
                        Username
                    </form:label></td>
                <td><form:input path="username"/></td>
                <td><form:errors path="username"/></td>
            </tr>
            // Password and emailAddress field omitted.
        </table>
    </fieldset>
    <button id="save">Save</button>
</form:form>
```

We also need a controller for this, so we will create the `com.apress.prospringmvc.bookstore.web` `.controller.RegistrationController`. In this controller, we will use a couple of data binding features. First, we will disallow the submission of an `id` field (to prevent someone from editing another user). Second, we will preselect the user's country based on the current `Locale`. Listing 5-42 shows our controller.

Listing 5-42. The RegistrationController

```java
package com.apress.prospringmvc.bookstore.web.controller;

import java.util.Locale;
import java.util.Map;
import java.util.TreeMap;

import org.springframework.beans.factory.annotation.Autowired;
import org.springframework.stereotype.Controller;
import org.springframework.validation.BindingResult;
import org.springframework.web.bind.WebDataBinder;
import org.springframework.web.bind.annotation.InitBinder;
import org.springframework.web.bind.annotation.ModelAttribute;
import org.springframework.web.bind.annotation.RequestMapping;
import org.springframework.web.bind.annotation.RequestMethod;

import com.apress.prospringmvc.bookstore.domain.Account;
import com.apress.prospringmvc.bookstore.service.AccountService;

@Controller
@RequestMapping("/customer/register")
public class RegistrationController {

    @Autowired
    private AccountService accountService;

    @ModelAttribute("countries")
    public Map<String, String> countries(Locale currentLocale) {
        Map<String, String> countries = new TreeMap<String, String>();
        for (Locale locale : Locale.getAvailableLocales()) {
            countries.put(locale.getCountry(), locale.getDisplayCountry(currentLocale));
        }
        return countries;
    }

    @InitBinder
    public void initBinder(WebDataBinder binder) {
        binder.setDisallowedFields("id");
        binder.setRequiredFields("username","password","emailAddress");
    }

    @RequestMapping(method = RequestMethod.GET)
    @ModelAttribute
    public Account register(Locale currentLocale) {
        Account account = new Account();
        account.getAddress().setCountry(currentLocale.getCountry());
        return account;
    }

    @RequestMapping(method = { RequestMethod.POST, RequestMethod.PUT })
```

```
public String handleRegistration(@ModelAttribute Account account, BindingResult result) {
    if (result.hasErrors()) {
        return "customer/register";
    }
    this.accountService.save(account);
    return "redirect:/customer/account/" + account.getId();
}
}
```

The controller has a lot going on. For example, the initBinder method configures our binding. It disallows the setting of the id property and sets some required fields. We also have a method that prepares our model by adding all the available countries in the JDK to the model. Finally, we have two request-handling methods, one for a GET request (the initial request when we enter our page) and one for POST/PUT requests when we submit our form. Notice the org.springframework.validation.BindingResult attribute next to the model attribute. This is what we can use to detect errors; and based on that, we can redisplay the original page. Also remember that the error tags in the JSP those are used to display error messages for fields or objects (we'll cover this in more depth in the upcoming sections). When the application is redeployed and we click the Register link, we should see the page shown in Figure 5-7.

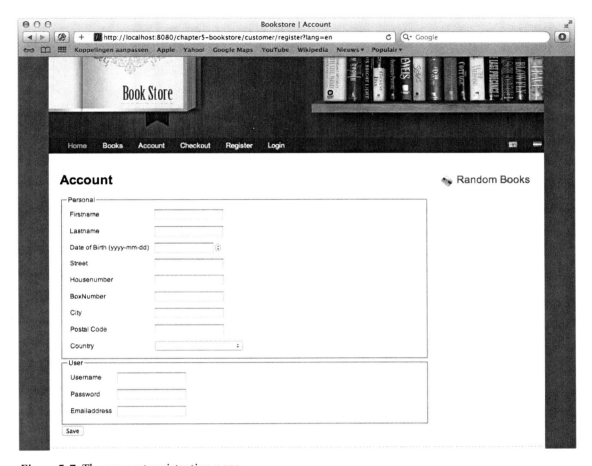

Figure 5-7. *The account registration page*

If we now enter an invalid date; leave the username, password and e-mail address fields blank; and then submit the form; the same page redisplays with some error messages (see Figure 5-8).

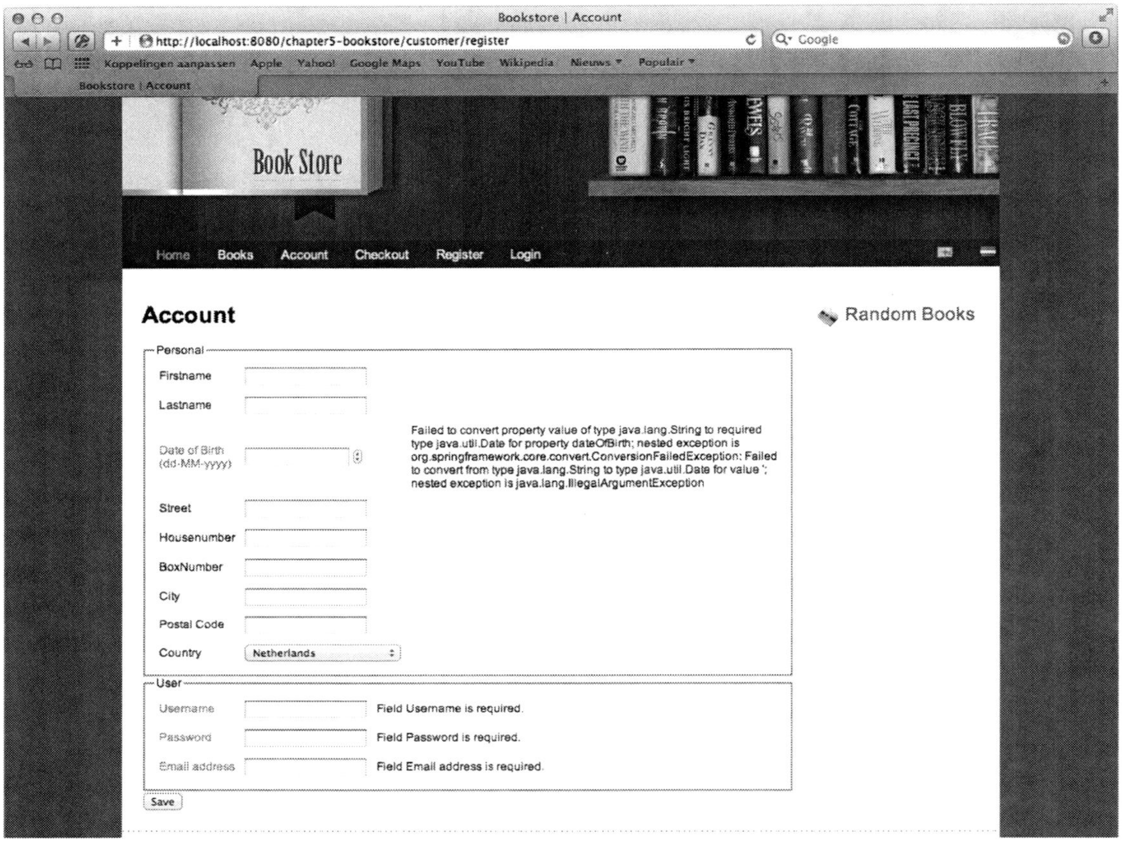

Figure 5-8. *The account registration page showing some errors*

The error messages are created by the data binding facilities in Spring MVC. Later in this chapter, we will see how we can influence the messages displayed. For now, let's leave them intact. If we fill in proper information and click Save, we are redirected to an account page (for which we already have provided the basic controller and implementation).

Validating Model Attributes

We've already mentioned validation a couple of times. We've also referred to the org.springframework.validation package a couple of times. Validating our model attributes is quite easy to accomplish with the validation abstraction from the Spring Framework. Validation isn't bound to the web; it is about validating objects. Therefore, validation can also be used outside the web layer; in fact, it can be used anywhere.

The main abstraction for validation is the org.springframework.validation.Validator interface. This interface has two callback methods. The supports method is used to determine if the validator instance can validate the object. The validate method is used to actually validate the object (see Listing 5-43).

Listing 5-43. The Validator Interface

```
package org.springframework.validation;

public interface Validator {

    boolean supports(Class<?> clazz);

    void validate(Object target, Errors errors);
}
```

The supports method is called to see if a validator can validate the current object type If that returns true, the framework will call the validate method with the object to validate and an instance of an implementation of the org.springframework.validation.Errors interface. When doing binding, this will be an implementation of the org.springframework.validation.BindingResult. When doing validation, it is a good idea to include an Errors or BindingResult (the latter extends Errors) method attribute. This way, we can handle situations where there is a bind or validation error. If this is not the case, an org.springframework.validation.BindException will be thrown.

When using Spring @MVC, we have two options for triggering validation. The first is to inject the validator into our controller and to call the validate method on the validator ourselves. The second is to add the javax.validation.Valid (JSR-303) or org.springframework.validation.annotation.Validated annotation to our method attribute. The annotation from the Spring Framework is more powerful than the one from the javax.validation package. The Spring annotation enables us to specify *hints*; when combined with a JSR-303 validator (e.g., hibernate-validation), can be used to specify validation groups.

Validation and bind errors lead to message codes that are registered with the Errors instance. In general, simply showing an error code to the user isn't very informative, so the code has to be resolved to a message. This is where the org.springframework.context.MessageSource comes into play. The error codes are passed as message codes to the configured message source and used to retrieve the message. If we don't configure a message source, we will be greeted with a nice stacktrace indicating that a message for code x cannot be found. So, before we proceed, let's configure the MessageSource shown in Listing 5-44.

Listing 5-44. The MessageSource Configuration

```
package com.apress.prospringmvc.bookstore.web.config;

import org.springframework.context.support.ResourceBundleMessageSource;
// Other imports omitted

@Configuration
@EnableWebMvc
@ComponentScan(basePackages = { "com.apress.prospringmvc.bookstore.web" })
public class WebMvcContextConfiguration extends WebMvcConfigurerAdapter {

@Bean
    public MessageSource messageSource() {
        ResourceBundleMessageSource messageSource;
        messageSource = new ResourceBundleMessageSource();
```

```
        messageSource.setBasename("messages");
        messageSource.setUseCodeAsDefaultMessage(true);
        return messageSource;
    }
    // Other methods omitted
}
```

We configure a message source, and then configure it to load a resource bundle with basename messages (we'll learn more about this in the "Internationalization" section later in this chapter). When a message is not found, we return the code as the message. This is especially useful during development because we can quickly see which message codes are missing from our resource bundles.

Let's implement validation for our com.apress.prospringmvc.bookstore.domain.Account class. We want to validate whether an account is valid; and for that, we need a username, password and a valid e-mail address. To be able to handle shipping, we also need an address, city, and country. Without this information, the account isn't valid. Now let's see how we can use the validation framework to our advantage.

Implementing Our Own Validator

We'll begin by implementing our own validator. In this case, we will create a com.apress.prospringmvc.bookstore.validation.AccountValidator (see Listing 5-45) and use an init-binder method to configure it.

Listing 5-45. *The AccountValidator Implementation*

```java
package com.apress.prospringmvc.bookstore.validation;

import java.util.regex.Pattern;

import org.springframework.validation.Errors;
import org.springframework.validation.ValidationUtils;
import org.springframework.validation.Validator;

import com.apress.prospringmvc.bookstore.domain.Account;

public class AccountValidator implements Validator {

    private static final String EMAIL_PATTERN =
    "^[_A-Za-z0-9-]+(\\.[_A-Za-z0-9-]+)*@"
    +"[A-Za-z0-9]+(\\.[A-Za-z0-9]+)*(\\.[A-Za-z]{2,})$";

    @Override
    public boolean supports(Class<?> clazz) {
        return (Account.class).isAssignableFrom(clazz);
    }

    @Override
    public void validate(Object target, Errors errors) {
        ValidationUtils.rejectIfEmpty(errors, "username",
                                "required", new Object[] {"Username"});
        ValidationUtils.rejectIfEmpty(errors, "password",
```

```
                                "required", new Object[] {"Password"});
        ValidationUtils.rejectIfEmpty(errors, "emailAddress",
                                "required", new Object[] {"Email Address"});
        ValidationUtils.rejectIfEmpty(errors, "address.street",
                                "required", new Object[] {"Street"});
        ValidationUtils.rejectIfEmpty(errors, "address.city",
                                "required", new Object[] {"City"});
        ValidationUtils.rejectIfEmpty(errors, "address.country",
                                "required", new Object[] {"Country"});

        if (!errors.hasFieldErrors("emailAddress")) {
            Account account = (Account) target;
            String email = account.getEmailAddress();
            if (!emai.matches(EMAIL_PATTERN)) {
                errors.rejectValue("emailAddress", "invalid");
            }
        }
    }
}
```

■ **Note** Specifying `requiredFields` on the `org.springframework.web.bind.WebDataBinder` would result in the same validation logic as with the `ValidationUtils.rejectIfEmptyOrWhiteSpace`. In our case, however, we have all the validation logic in one place, rather than having it spread over two places.

This validator implementation will check if the fields are not null and non-empty. If the field is empty, it will register an error for the given field. The error is a collection of message codes, and this collection of message codes is determined by an `org.springframework.validation`
`.MessageCodesResolver` implementation. The default implementation, `org.springframework.validation`
`.DefaultMessageCodesResolver`, will resolve to four different codes (see Table 5-21). The order in the table is also the order in which the error codes are resolved to a proper message.

Table 5-21. The Error Codes for Field Errors

Pattern	Example
code + object name + field	required.newOrder.name
code + field	required.name
code + field type	required.java.lang.String
code	required

165

The final part of this validation is that we need to configure our validator and tell the controller to validate our model attribute on submission. In Listing 5-46, we show the modified order controller. We only want to trigger validation on the final submission of our form.

Listing 5-46. The RegistrationController with Validation

```
package com.apress.prospringmvc.bookstore.web.controller;

import com.apress.prospringmvc.bookstore.domain.AccountValidator;

import javax.validation.Valid;
// Other imports omitted

@Controller
@RequestMapping("/customer/register")
public class RegistrationController {

    @InitBinder
    public void initBinder(WebDataBinder binder) {
        binder.setDisallowedFields("id");
        binder.setValidator(new AccountValidator());
    }

    @RequestMapping(method = { RequestMethod.POST, RequestMethod.PUT })
    public String handleRegistration(@Valid @ModelAttribute Account account, BindingResult↵
result) {
        if (result.hasErrors()) {
            return "customer/register";
        }
        this.accountService.save(account);
        return "redirect:/customer/account/" + account.getId();
    }

    // Other methods omitted
}
```

If we submit illegal values after redeployment, we will be greeted with some error codes, as shown in Figure 5-9.

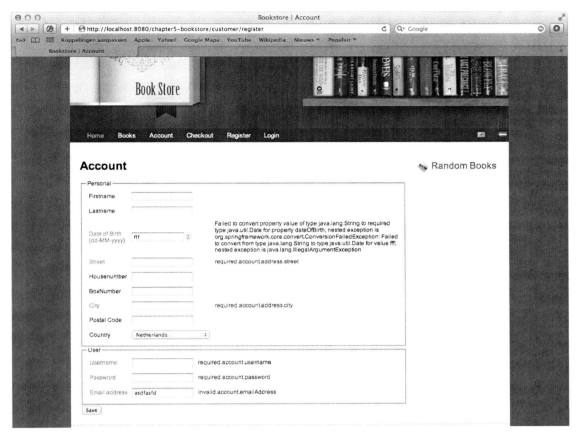

Figure 5-9. The registration page with error codes

Using JSR-303 Validation

Instead of implementing our own validator, we could also the JSR-303 annotations to add validation. For this, we would only need to annotate our com.apress.prospringmvc.bookstore.domain.Account object with JSR-303 annotations (see Listing 5-47) and then leave the javax.validation.Valid annotation in place. When using these annotations, the error code used is slightly different than the one used in our custom validator (see Table 5-22). However, the registration page doesn't need to change, so it remains the same as before. In our init-binder method, we do not need to set the validator because a JSR-303 capable validator is automatically detected (the sample project uses the one from Hibernate).

Listing 5-47. An Account with JSR-303 Annotations

```
package com.apress.prospringmvc.bookstore.domain;

import java.io.Serializable;
import java.util.ArrayList;
import java.util.Date;
import java.util.List;

import javax.persistence.CascadeType;
import javax.persistence.Embedded;
import javax.persistence.Entity;
import javax.persistence.GeneratedValue;
import javax.persistence.GenerationType;
import javax.persistence.Id;
import javax.persistence.ManyToMany;
import javax.validation.Valid;

import org.hibernate.validator.constraints.Email;
import org.hibernate.validator.constraints.NotEmpty;

@Entity
public class Account implements Serializable {

    @Id
    @GeneratedValue(strategy = GenerationType.AUTO)
    private Long id;

    private String firstName;
    private String lastName;

    private Date dateOfBirth;

    @Embedded
    @Valid
    private Address address = new Address();

    @NotEmpty
    @Email
    private String emailAddress;
    @NotEmpty
    private String username;
    @NotEmpty
    private String password;

    // getters and setters omitted
}
```

░ **Note** The NotEmpty and Email annotations come from the org.hibernate.validator.constraints package; thus this package is not a standard JSR-303 annotation, but an extension to it.

Table 5-22. *The Error Codes for Field Errors with JSR-303 Annotations*

Pattern	Example
annotation name + object name + field	NotEmpty.newOrder.name
annotation name + field	NotEmpty.name
annotation name + field type	NotEmpty.java.lang.String
annotation name	NotEmpty

When using JSR-303 annotations, if we submit the form with invalid values, we get a result like the one shown in Figure 5-10. As we can see, there are messages displayed instead of codes. How is that possible? There are some default messages shipped with the validator implementation we use. We can override these if we want by specifying one of the codes from Table 5-22 in our resource bundle (see the next section).

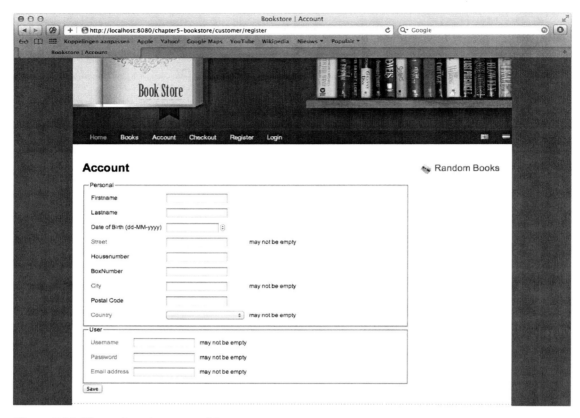

Figure 5-10. *The registration page with error messages*

Internationalization

For internationalization to work, we need to configure different components to be able to resolve messages based on the language (locale) of the user. For example, there is the org.springframework.context.MessageSource, which lets us resolve messages based on message codes and locale. To be able to resolve the locale, we also need an org.springframework.web.servlet .LocaleResolver. Finally, to be able to change the locale, we also need to configure an org.springframework.web.servlet.i18n.LocaleChangeInterceptor (the next chapter will cover interceptors in more depth).

Message Source

The message source is the component that actually resolves our message based on a code and the locale. Spring provides a couple of implementations of the org.springframework.context.MessageSource interface. Two of those implementations are implementations that we can use, while the other implementations simply delegate to another message source.

The two implementations provided by the Spring Framework are in the org.springframework.context.support package. Table 5-23 briefly describes both of them.

Table 5-23. A MessageSource Overview

Class	Description
ResourceBundleMessageSource	Uses the ResourceBundle facility available on the JVM. It can only load resources from the classpath.
ReloadableResourceBundleMessageSource	Works in a similar way as the ResourceBundleMessageSource but adds reloading and caching capabilities. It allows for the resources to be anywhere on the file system it uses the resource loading mechanism in Spring.

We configure both beans more or less the same way. One thing we need is a bean named messageSource. Which implementation we choose doesn't really matter. For example, we could even create our own implementation that uses a database to load the messages.

The configuration in Listing 5-48 configures an org.springframework.context.support .ReloadableResourceBundleMessageSource that loads a file named messages.properties from the classpath. It will also try to load the messages_[locale].properties for the Locale we are currently using to resolve the messages.

Listing 5-48. The MessageSource Configuration in WebMvcContext

```
package com.apress.prospringmvc.bookstore.web.config;

import org.springframework.context.support.ReloadableResourceBundleMessageSource;

// Other imports omitted

@Configuration
@EnableWebMvc
@ComponentScan(basePackages = { "com.apress.prospringmvc.bookstore.web" })
public class WebMvcContextConfiguration extends WebMvcConfigurerAdapter {

    @Bean
    public MessageSource messageSource() {
        ReloadableResourceBundleMessageSource messageSource;
        messageSource = new ReloadableResourceBundleMessageSource();
        messageSource.setBasename("classpath:/messages");
        messageSource.setUseCodeAsDefaultMessage(true);
        return messageSource;
    }
}
```

The following snippets show two properties files (actually resource bundles) that are loaded. The messages in the messages.properties (see Listing 5-49) file are treated as the defaults, and they can be overridden in the language-specific messages_nl.properties file (see Listing 5-50).

Listing 5-49. The messages.properties Snippet

```
home.title=Welcome

invalid.account.emailaddress=Invalid email address.
required=Field {0} is required.
```

Listing 5-50. The messages_nl.properties

```
home.title=Welkom

invalid.account.emailaddress=Ongeldig emailadres.
required=Veld {0} is verplicht.
```

LocaleResolver

For the message source to do its work correctly, we also need to configure an `org.springframework.web`
`.servlet.LocaleResolver` (this can be found this in the `org.springframework.web.servlet.i18n`
package). Several different implementations ship with Spring that can make our lives easier. The locale
resolver is a strategy that is used to detect which `Locale` to use. The different implementations each use a
different way of resolving the locale (see Table 5-24).

Table 5-24. The LocaleResolver Overview

Class	Description
FixedLocaleResolver	Always resolves to a fixed locale. All the users of our website use the same locale, so changing the locale isn't supported.
SessionLocaleResolver	Resolves (and stores) the locale in the user's `HttpSession`. The attribute used to store the locale can be configured, as well as the default locale to use if no locale is present. The drawback to this is that the locale isn't stored between visits, so it must be set at least once on the user's session.
AcceptHeaderLocaleResolver	Uses the `http accept` header to resolve the locale to use. In general, this is the locale of the operating system of the user, so changing the locale isn't supported. It is also the default `LocalResolver` used by the `DispatcherServlet`.
CookieLocaleResolver	Uses a cookie to store the user's locale. The advantage of this resolver is that the locale is kept on the client's machine, so it will be available on subsequent visits to the website. The cookie name and timeout can be configured, as well as the default locale.

LocaleChangeInterceptor

If we want our users to be able to change the locale, we need to configure an `org.springframework.web`
`.servlet.i18n.LocaleChangeInterceptor` (see Listing 5-51). This interceptor inspects the current

incoming requests and checks whether there is a parameter named `locale` on the request. If this is present, the interceptor uses the earlier configured locale resolver to change the current user's `Locale`. The parameter name can be configured.

Listing 5-51. The Full Internationalization Configuration

```
package com.apress.prospringmvc.bookstore.web.config;

import org.springframework.context.MessageSource;
import org.springframework.context.support.ReloadableResourceBundleMessageSource;
import org.springframework.web.servlet.HandlerInterceptor;
import org.springframework.web.servlet.LocaleResolver;
import org.springframework.web.servlet.config.annotation.InterceptorRegistry;
import org.springframework.web.servlet.config.annotation.ResourceHandlerRegistry;
import org.springframework.web.servlet.i18n.CookieLocaleResolver;
import org.springframework.web.servlet.i18n.LocaleChangeInterceptor;

// Other imports omitted

@Configuration
@EnableWebMvc
@ComponentScan(basePackages = { "com.apress.prospringmvc.bookstore.web" })
public class WebMvcContextConfiguration extends WebMvcConfigurerAdapter {

    @Override
    public void addInterceptors(InterceptorRegistry registry) {
        registry.addInterceptor(localeChangeInterceptor());
    }

    @Bean
    public HandlerInterceptor localeChangeInterceptor() {
        LocaleChangeInterceptor localeChangeInterceptor;
        localeChangeInterceptor = new LocaleChangeInterceptor();
        localeChangeInterceptor.setParamName("lang");
        return localeChangeInterceptor;
    }

    @Bean
    public LocaleResolver localeResolver() {
        return new CookieLocaleResolver();
    }

    @Bean
    public MessageSource messageSource() {
        ReloadableResourceBundleMessageSource messageSource;
        messageSource = new ReloadableResourceBundleMessageSource();
        messageSource.setBasename("classpath:/messages");
        messageSource.setUseCodeAsDefaultMessage(true);
        return messageSource;
    }
}
```

> ■ **Note** In general, it is a good idea to have the LocaleChangeInterceptor as one of the first interceptors. If something goes wrong, we want to inform the user in the correct language.

If we redeploy our application, we should get localized error messages if we switch the language (of course, this works only if we add the appropriate error codes to the resource bundles). However, using the MessageSource for error messages isn't its only use; we can also use MessageSource to retrieve our labels, titles, error messages, and so on from our resource bundles. We can use the message tag for that. Listing 5-52 shows a modified book search page, which uses the message tag to fill the labels, titles, and headers. If we switch the language, we should get localized messages (see Figures 5-11 and 5-12).

Listing 5-52. *The Book Search Page with the Message Tag*

```
<%@ taglib prefix="c" uri="http://java.sun.com/jsp/jstl/core"%>
<%@ taglib prefix="spring" uri="http://www.springframework.org/tags" %>
<%@ taglib prefix="form" uri="http://www.springframework.org/tags/form" %>

<form:form method="GET" modelAttribute="bookSearchCriteria">
    <fieldset>
        <legend><spring:message code="book.searchcriteria"/></legend>
        <table>
            <tr>
                <td><form:label path="title">
                    <spring:message code="book.title" />
                </form:label></td>
                <td><form:input path="title" /></td>
            </tr>
            <tr>
                <td><form:label path="category">
                    <spring:message code="book.category" />
                </form:label></td>
                <td>
                <form:select path="category" items="${categories}"
                            itemValue="id" itemLabel="name"/>
                </td>
            </tr>
        </table>
    </fieldset>
    <button id="search"><spring:message code="button.search"/></button>
</form:form>

<c:if test="${not empty bookList}">
    <table>
        <tr>
            <th><spring:message code="book.title"/></th>
            <th><spring:message code="book.description"/></th>
            <th><spring:message code="book.price" /></th>
        </tr>
        <c:forEach items="${bookList}" var="book">
```

```
        <tr>
            <td>
    <a href="<c:url value="/book/detail/${book.id}"/>">${book.title}</a>
            </td>
            <td>${book.description}</td>
            <td>${book.price}</td>
        </tr>
    </c:forEach>
    </table>
</c:if>
```

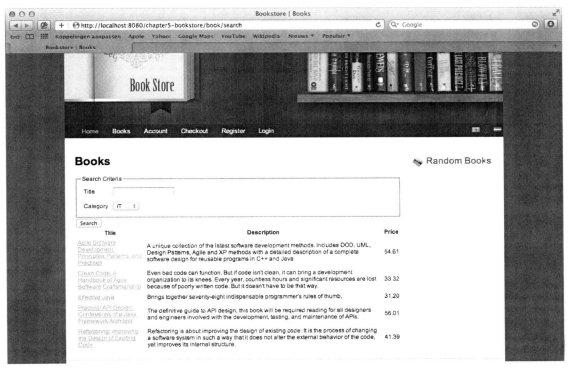

Figure 5-11. The book search page in English

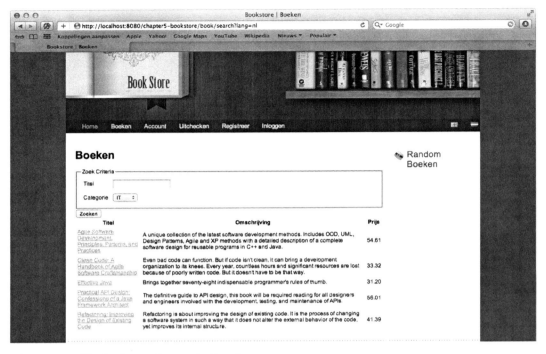

Figure 5-12. The book search page in Dutch

Summary

This chapter covered all things we need to write controllers and handle forms. We began by exploring the RequestMapping annotation and how that can be used to map requests to a method to handle a request. We also explored flexible method signatures and covered which method argument types and return values are supported out of the box.

Next, we dove into the deep end and started writing controllers and modifying our existing code. We also introduced form objects and covered how to bind the properties to fields. And we explained data binding and explored Spring's type-conversion system and how that is used to convert from and to certain objects. We also wrote our own implementation of a Converter to convert from text to a Category object.

In addition to type conversion, we also explored validation. There are two ways of doing validation: we can create our own implementation of a Validator interface, or we can use the JSR-303 annotations on the objects we want to validate. Enabling validation is done with either the Valid or the Validated annotation.

To make it easier to bind certain fields to attributes of a form object, there is the Spring Form Tag library, which helps us to write HTML forms. This library also helps us to display bind and validation errors to the user.

Finally we covered how to implement internationalization on our web pages and how to convert the validation and error codes to proper messages to show to the end user.

In the next chapter, we are going to explore some more advanced features of Spring MVC. Along the way, we will see how we can further extend and customize the existing infrastructure.

CHAPTER 6

Implementing Controllers — Advanced

In this chapter, we are going to take a look at some of the more advanced parts of Spring MVC, and then see how we can tap into the framework itself to extend it to suit our needs.

We'll begin by examining scoped beans and how we can use them to our advantage. Next, we'll explore how we can add generic functionality (so-called crosscutting concerns) to our application. For this, we are going to take a look at interceptors, including how to create them and how to wire them into our application.

No matter how robust or well-thought out our application is, there is going to be a time when our application doesn't behave as expected (e.g., maybe someone will trip over the wire to our database server), and this will result in exceptions in our application. In general, we want to prevent the user from seeing the often cryptic stack traces; and for this, we are going to explore the exception-handling facilities in Spring MVC.

After we cover all these topics, we are going to dive into the internals of Spring @MVC and explore a couple of APIs we can extend; we'll then use these extended APIs to augment the functionality of the framework.

Using Scoped Beans

In Chapter 2, we noted the different scopes for beans that are supported by the Spring Framework. Table 6-1 lists them again. In this section, we are going to use scopes to our advantage. Specifically, we will walk through a practical example that leverages a scoped bean to create an online shopping cart (com.apress.prospringmvc.bookstore.domain.Cart).

Table 6-1. An Overview of Scopes

Prefix	Description
singleton	The default scope. A single instance of a bean is created and shared throughout the application. The lifecycle of the bean is tied to the application context it is constructed in.
prototype	Each time a certain bean is needed, a fresh instance of the bean is returned.
thread	The bean is created when needed and bound to the current executing thread. If the thread dies, the bean is destroyed.

Prefix	Description
request	The bean is created when needed and bound to the lifetime of the incoming `javax.servlet.ServletRequest`. If the request is over, the bean instance is destroyed.
session	The bean is created when needed and stored in the `javax.servlet.http.HttpSession`. When the session is destroyed, so is the bean instance.
globalSession	The bean is created when needed and stored in the globally available session (which is available in Portlet environments). If a global session is not available, it falls back to the `session` scope functionality.
application	This scope is very similar to the `singleton` scope. The major difference is that beans with this scope are also registered in the `javax.servlet.ServletContext`.

We've already worked with the `singleton` scope—that is the default for bean creation in the Spring Framework. The `org.springframework.context.annotation.Scope` annotation is used to specify the scope of a bean; its properties are listed in Table 6-2.

This annotation can be used as a type-level or method-level annotation. When you use Scope as a type-level annotation, all beans of this type will have the scope specified by the annotation. When you use it as a method-level annotation, beans created by this annotated method will have the scope specified by the annotation. You must put it on a method annotated with the `org.springframework.context.annotation.Bean` annotation.

Table 6-2. *The Scope Annotation Properties*

Property	Description
value	The name of the scope to use (see Table 6-1). Defaults to `singleton`.
proxyMode	Indicates whether scoped proxies should be created and by which proxy mechanism. This property defaults to `NO`.

Adding Something to the Cart

In this section, we are going to take the first step in actually enabling site visitors to buy books from our bookstore. Specifically, we are going to implement logic that lets us add books to our shopping cart. For this, we first need to define a session-scoped `Cart` bean.

Listing 6-1 shows how to define a bean (our shopping cart) with `session` scope. This bean can be injected into other beans, just like any other bean in the framework. Spring will handle the complexity of managing the lifecycle of the bean. The lifecycle of the bean depends on the scope of the bean (see Table 6-1). For example, a `singleton`-scoped bean (the default) is tied to the lifecycle of the application context, whereas a session-scoped bean is tied to the lifecycle of the `javax.servlet.http.HttpSession` object.

Listing 6-1. Cart Session Scoped Bean

```
package com.apress.prospringmvc.bookstore.web.config;

//Other imports omitted

import org.springframework.context.annotation.Scope;
import org.springframework.context.annotation.ScopedProxyMode;
import com.apress.prospringmvc.bookstore.domain.Cart;


@Configuration
@EnableWebMvc
@ComponentScan(basePackages = { "com.apress.prospringmvc.bookstore.web" })
public class WebMvcContextConfiguration extends WebMvcConfigurerAdapter {

    //Other methods omitted
    @Bean
    @Scope(value = "session", proxyMode = ScopedProxyMode.TARGET_CLASS)
    public Cart cart() {
        return new Cart();
    }

}
```

In this case, we have a bean declaration with the annotation, and we are using session scope. We want to use class-based proxies (com.apress.prospringmvc.bookstore.domain.Cart doesn't implement an interface, so we need class-based proxies). We can now simply have this bean injected into other beans and use it like any other bean. Let's create a controller that uses this bean, the com.apress .prospringmvc.bookstore.web.controller.CartController (see Listing 6-2).

░ **Note** To be able to use class-based proxies, Spring requires an additional library called CGLIB.[1]

---

[1] http://cglib.sourceforge.net/

Listing 6-2. The CartController Bean

```java
package com.apress.prospringmvc.bookstore.web.controller;

import org.slf4j.Logger;
import org.slf4j.LoggerFactory;
import org.springframework.beans.factory.annotation.Autowired;
import org.springframework.stereotype.Controller;
import org.springframework.web.bind.annotation.PathVariable;
import org.springframework.web.bind.annotation.RequestHeader;
import org.springframework.web.bind.annotation.RequestMapping;

import com.apress.prospringmvc.bookstore.domain.Book;
import com.apress.prospringmvc.bookstore.domain.Cart;
import com.apress.prospringmvc.bookstore.service.BookstoreService;

@Controller
public class CartController {

    private Logger logger = LoggerFactory.getLogger(CartController.class);

    @Autowired
    private Cart cart;

    @Autowired
    private BookstoreService bookstoreService;

    @RequestMapping("/cart/add/{bookId}")
    public String addToCart(@PathVariable("bookId") long bookId,
                            @RequestHeader("referer") String referer) {
        Book book = this.bookstoreService.findBook(bookId);
        this.cart.addBook(book);
        this.logger.info("Cart: {}", this.cart);
        return "redirect:" + referer;
    }

}
```

In this case, we simply autowire the session-scoped bean cart, just as we would for any other bean. The addToCart method contains the logic for adding a book to the cart. After the book has been added, we redirect to the page from which we came (the referer request header).

This controller is mapped to the URL, /cart/add/{bookId}; however, currently nothing is going to invoke our controller because we have nothing pointing to that URL. Let's modify our book search page and add a link, so that we can add a book to our shopping cart (see Listing 6-3). The parts highlighted with bold show the changes.

Listing 6-3. *The Book Search Page with an Add to Cart Link*

```
<%@ taglib prefix="c" uri="http://java.sun.com/jsp/jstl/core"%>
<%@ taglib prefix="spring" uri="http://www.springframework.org/tags" %>
<%@ taglib prefix="form" uri="http://www.springframework.org/tags/form" %>

// Search Form Omitted

<c:if test="${not empty bookList}">
    <table>
        <tr>
            <th><spring:message code="book.title"/></th>
            <th><spring:message code="book.description"/></th>
            <th><spring:message code="book.price" /></th>
            <th></th>
        </tr>
        <c:forEach items="${bookList}" var="book">
            <tr>
                <td>
                    <a href="<c:url value="/book/detail/${book.id}"/>">
                        ${book.title}
                    </a>
                </td>
                <td>${book.description}</td>
                <td>${book.price}</td>
                <td>
                    <a href="<c:url value="/cart/add/${book.id}"/>">
                        <spring:message code="book.addtocart"/>
                    </a>
                </td>
            </tr>
        </c:forEach>
    </table>
</c:if>
```

After redeploying our application, we should have an Add to Cart link on the Books page (see Figure 6-1). If we click that link, we should stay on the Books page. We did add something to our shopping cart, however. If we switch to our logging output (see Figure 6-2), we can see that there is actually something in the shopping cart.

Bookstore | Books
http://localhost:8080/chapter6-bookstore/book/search
Book Store
Home Books Account Checkout Register Login
Books
Random Books
Search Criteria
Title
Category IT
Search
Title Description Price
Agile Software Development, Principles, Patterns, and Practices
A unique collection of the latest software development methods. Includes OOD, UML, Design Patterns, Agile and XP methods with a detailed description of a complete software design for reusable programs in C++ and Java.
54.61
Add to Cart
Clean Code: A Handbook of Agile Software Craftsmanship
Even bad code can function. But if code isn't clean, it can bring a development organization to its knees. Every year, countless hours and significant resources are lost because of poorly written code. But it doesn't have to be that way.
33.32
Effective Java
Brings together seventy-eight indispensable programmer's rules of thumb.
31.20
Practical API Design: Confessions of a Java Framework Architect
The definitive guide to API design, this book will be required reading for all designers and engineers involved with the development, testing, and maintenance of APIs.
56.01
Refactoring: Improving the Design of Existing Code
Refactoring is about improving the design of existing code. It is the process of changing a software system in such a way that it does not alter the external behavior of the code, yet improves its internal structure.
41.39

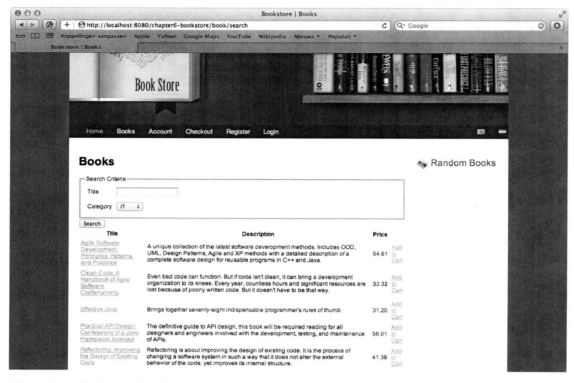

Figure 6-1. A book search with an Add to Cart link

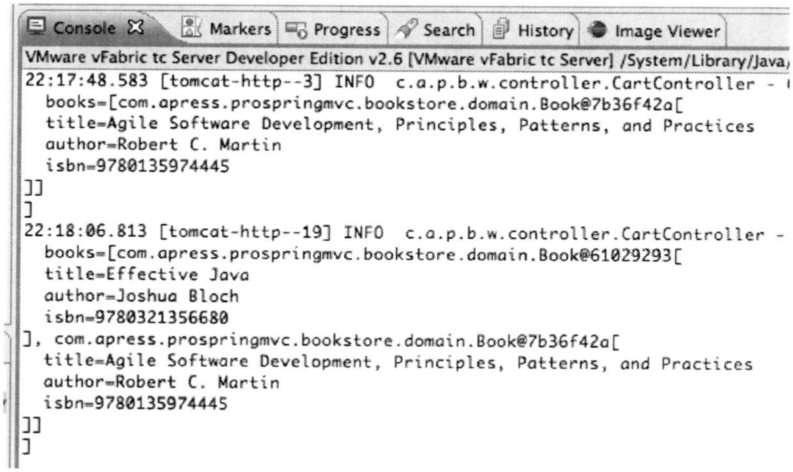

Console Markers Progress Search History Image Viewer
VMware vFabric tc Server Developer Edition v2.6 [VMware vFabric tc Server] /System/Library/Java/
22:17:48.583 [tomcat-http--3] INFO c.a.p.b.w.controller.CartController -
books=[com.apress.prospringmvc.bookstore.domain.Book@7b36f42a[
title=Agile Software Development, Principles, Patterns, and Practices
author=Robert C. Martin
isbn=9780135974445
]]
]
22:18:06.813 [tomcat-http--19] INFO c.a.p.b.w.controller.CartController -
books=[com.apress.prospringmvc.bookstore.domain.Book@61029293[
title=Effective Java
author=Joshua Bloch
isbn=9780321356680
], com.apress.prospringmvc.bookstore.domain.Book@7b36f42a[
title=Agile Software Development, Principles, Patterns, and Practices
author=Robert C. Martin
isbn=9780135974445
]]
]

Figure 6-2. Cart logging that shows the books added to the cart

Implementing the Checkout

To finalize the ordering process, we will give our customers an opportunity to check out their cart. This will create an actual com.apress.prospringmvc.bookstore.domain.Order object and entry in the database. The checkout is a combination of a lot of things we covered in the previous chapter and the previous section. The controller is the com.apress.prospringmvc.bookstore.web.controller .CheckoutController (see Listing 6-4), and it contains a lot of logic. The checkout.jsp file is the JSP that contains our screen; it can be found in /WEB-INF/views/cart.

Listing 6-4. The CheckoutController

```
package com.apress.prospringmvc.bookstore.web.controller;

//Other imports omitted
import com.apress.prospringmvc.bookstore.validation.OrderValidator;

@Controller
@SessionAttributes(types = { Order.class })
@RequestMapping("/cart/checkout")
public class CheckoutController {

    private final Logger logger;
    logger  = LoggerFactory.getLogger(CheckoutController.class);

    @Autowired
    private Cart cart;

    @Autowired
    private BookstoreService bookstoreService;

    @ModelAttribute("countries")
    public Map<String, String> countries(Locale currentLocale) {
        Map<String, String> countries = new TreeMap<String, String>();
        for (Locale locale : Locale.getAvailableLocales()) {
            countries.put(
                        locale.getCountry(),
                        locale.getDisplayCountry(currentLocale));
        }
        return countries;
    }

    @RequestMapping(method = RequestMethod.GET)
    public void show(HttpSession session, Model model) {
        Account account = (Account)
        session.getAttribute(LoginController.ACCOUNT_ATTRIBUTE);
        Order order = this.bookstoreService.createOrder(this.cart, account);
        model.addAttribute(order);
    }

    @RequestMapping(method = RequestMethod.POST, params = "order")
    public String checkout(SessionStatus status,
```

```
                          @Validated @ModelAttribute Order order,
                          BindingResult errors) {
        if (errors.hasErrors()) {
            return "cart/checkout";
        } else {
            this.bookstoreService.store(order);
            status.setComplete(); //remove order from session
            this.cart.clear(); // clear the cart
            return "redirect:/index.htm";
        }
    }

    @RequestMapping(method = RequestMethod.POST, params = "update")
    public String update(@ModelAttribute Order order) {
        order.updateOrderDetails();
        return "cart/checkout";
    }

    @InitBinder
    public void initBinder(WebDataBinder binder) {
        binder.setValidator(new OrderValidator());
    }

}
```

The first method called on the controller when we click checkout is the show method, it takes our cart and uses the Account stored in the session to create an order and add that to the model. The order is stored in the session in between requests; this due to the use of SessionAttributes. When this is done, the checkout page is rendered (see Figure 6-3).

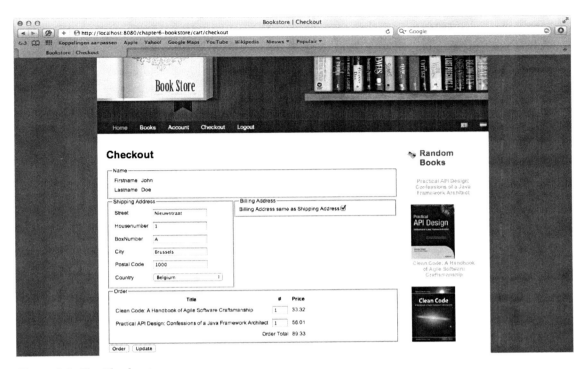

Figure 6-3. The Checkout page

When the form is filled in, the customer can do two things: he can press the Order button or the Update button. When the Update button is pressed, the update method is called. This submits the form and then updates the order (and recalculates the total price). When the Order button is pressed, the order is submitted and then validated by the com.apress.prospringmvc.bookstore.validation .OrderValidator. In any errors occur, the page is redisplayed and error messages are shown to the customer. The interesting part occurs when there are no errors. First, the order is stored in the database. When we are finished with the order, we need to remove it from the session, which we accomplish by calling the setComplete method on the org.springframework.web.bind.support.SessionStatus object (see the Chapter 5 section, "Supported Method Argument Types"). Finally, before redirecting to the index page again, we need to clear the shopping cart. We do this so that the customer can add new books to the cart. Because we cannot simply replace the session-scoped object, we need to call a method to clear it. If we were to replace the cart with a fresh instance we would basically destroy the scoped proxy object.

Crosscutting Concerns

When developing an enterprise application, we are often faced or challenged with crosscutting concerns. These are concerns that affect many objects and actions. Examples of crosscutting concerns include transaction management and security, but also actions such as exposing generic data for each incoming web request.

In general, these concerns are hard to implement in our codebase by using traditional object-oriented approaches. If we were to implement them in traditional ways, it would lead to code duplication and hard-to-maintain code. For our general objects, we can use aspect-oriented programming (AOP) to address these crosscutting concerns; however when it comes to applying it to requests, we need a slightly different approach.

Spring MVC gives us two ways of implementing crosscutting concerns. The first approach uses *interceptors* to implement generic logic, while the second relies on exception handling. In this section, we are going to take a look at both techniques of applying crosscutting concerns in our web application.

Interceptors

Interceptors are to request handlers what filters are to servlets. According to the servlet specification,[2] a filter is a reusable piece of code that can transform the content of HTTP requests, responses, and header information. Filters modify or adapt the requests for a resource, and modify or adapt responses from a resource. Examples of filtering include authentication, auditing, and encryption.

Filters and interceptors both implement common functionality (crosscutting concerns) to apply to all (or a selection) of incoming HTTP requests. Filters are more powerful than interceptors because they can replace (or wrap) the incoming request/response, whereas this cannot be done by an interceptor. The interceptor, on the other hand, has more lifecycle methods than the filter (see Table 6-3).

Table 6-3. *Interceptor Callbacks*

Method	Description
preHandle	Called before the handler is invoked.
postHandle	Called when the handler method has been successfully invoked and just before the view is rendered. This can be used to place shared objects in the model.
afterCompletion	Called when the request processing is done, after view rendering. This method is always called on interceptors where the preHandle method has been called successfully, even when there was an error during request processing. This can be used to clean up resources.

Spring MVC has two different interceptor strategies:

- org.springframework.web.servlet.HandlerInterceptor (see Listing 6-5)

- org.springframework.web.context.request.WebRequestInterceptor (see Listing 6-6)

---

[2] See Servlet Specification 3.0, chapter 6.

Listing 6-5. The HandlerInterceptor Interface

```
package org.springframework.web.servlet;

import javax.servlet.http.HttpServletRequest;
import javax.servlet.http.HttpServletResponse;

public interface HandlerInterceptor {

  boolean preHandle(HttpServletRequest request,
                    HttpServletResponse response,
                    Object handler) throws Exception;

  void postHandle(HttpServletRequest request, HttpServletResponse response,
                  Object handler, ModelAndView modelAndView) throws Exception;

  void afterCompletion(HttpServletRequest request,
                       HttpServletResponse response,
                       Object handler,
                       Exception ex) throws Exception;
}
```

Listing 6-6. The WebRequestInterceptor Interface

```
package org.springframework.web.context.request;

import org.springframework.ui.ModelMap;

public interface WebRequestInterceptor {

  void preHandle(WebRequest request) throws Exception;

  void postHandle(WebRequest request, ModelMap model) throws Exception;

  void afterCompletion(WebRequest request, Exception ex) throws Exception;
}
```

As is often the case within the Spring Framework, both strategies are expressed as interfaces for which we could provide an implementation. The main difference between the strategies is that the WebRequestInterceptor is independent from the underlying technology. It can be used in a JSF or Servlet environment without changing the implementation. The HandlerInterceptor is only usable in a Servlet environment. An advantage of the HandlerInterceptor is that we can use it to prevent the handler from being called. We do this by returning false from the preHandle method.

Configuring Interceptors

To use an interceptor, we need to configure it in our configuration. Configuring an interceptor consists of two steps:

1. We need to configure the interceptor itself.

2. We need to connect it to our handlers.

Connecting an interceptor to our handlers can be done in two ways. It is possible to use both approaches together, but we don't recommend this. First, we can explicitly add the interceptors to our handler mappings in our configuration. Second, we can use the `org.springframework.web.servlet` `.config.annotation.InterceptorRegistry` to add interceptors.

In general, it is preferable to use the `InterceptorRegistry` to add the interceptors, simply because that is a very convenient way to add them. It is also very easy to limit which URLs the interceptors are matched to (as we will explain in the section about the `InterceptorRegistry`.)

Explicitly Configuring a HandlerMapping with Interceptors

To register the interceptors with the handler mapping, we first need to get the handler mappings involved. To do this, we need to either explicitly add them or extend the Spring base classes to get a reference to them (see Listing 6-7). Next, we simply add all interceptors to the instances. When using multiple handler mappings, this can be quite cumbersome, especially if we want to apply the interceptor only to certain URLs.

Listing 6-7. A Sample of Explicit HandlerMapping Configuration with Interceptors

```
package com.apress.prospringmvc.bookstore.web.config;

import org.springframework.context.annotation.ComponentScan;
import org.springframework.context.annotation.Configuration;
import org.springframework.web.servlet.config.annotation.EnableWebMvc;
import org.springframework.web.servlet.config.annotation.WebMvcConfigurationSupport;
import org.springframework.web.servlet.mvc.method.annotation.RequestMappingHandlerMapping;


@Configuration
@EnableWebMvc
@ComponentScan(basePackages = { "com.apress.prospringmvc.bookstore.web" })
public class WebMvcContextConfiguration extends WebMvcConfigurationSupport {

    @Override
    public RequestMappingHandlerMapping requestMappingHandlerMapping() {
        RequestMappingHandlerMapping handlerMapping;
        handlerMapping = super.requestMappingHandlerMapping();
        handlerMapping.setInterceptors(getAllInterceptors());
        return handlerMapping
    }
}
```

Using the InterceptorRegistry

A more powerful and flexible way to register interceptors is to use the `org.springframework.web` `.servlet.config.annotation.InterceptorRegistry`. The interceptors added to this registry are added to all configured handler mappings. Additionally, mapping to certain URLs is very easy to accomplish with this approach. To get access to the registry, we need to implement the `org.springframework.web` `.servlet.config.annotation.WebMvcConfigurer` interface on the configuration class that configures our web resources. This interface has several callback methods that are called during the configuration of Spring @MVC.

Tip The framework provides an `org.springframework.web.servlet.config.annotation` `.WebMvcConfigurerAdapter` that we can extend. This saves us from implementing all methods from the `org.springframework.web.servlet.config.annotation.WebMvcConfigurer` interface.

We could also extend the `org.springframework.web.servlet.config.annotation` `.WebMvcConfigurationSupport`, so that we can simply add to the default configuration. We could then omit the `org.springframework.web.servlet.config.annotation.EnableWebMvc` annotation.

The `InterceptorRegistry` has two methods (one for each interceptor type) that we can use to add interceptors (see Listing 6-8). Both methods return an instance of `org.springframework.web` `.servlet.config.annotation.InterceptorRegistration` that we can use to fine-tune the mapping of the interceptor. We can use ant-style path patterns[3] to configure a fine-grained mapping for the registered interceptor. If we don't supply a pattern, the interceptor will be applied to all incoming requests.

Listing 6-8. *The InterceptorRegistry Interface*

```
package org.springframework.web.servlet.config.annotation;

import java.util.ArrayList;
import java.util.List;

import org.springframework.web.context.request.WebRequestInterceptor;
import org.springframework.web.servlet.HandlerInterceptor;
import org.springframework.web.servlet.handler.WebRequestHandlerInterceptorAdapter;


public class InterceptorRegistry {
```

---

[3] See Chapter 3 for information about ant-style expressions.

```
    public InterceptorRegistration addInterceptor(
            HandlerInterceptor interceptor) { .. }

    public InterceptorRegistration addWebRequestInterceptor(
            WebRequestInterceptor interceptor) { .. }
}
```

Listing 6-9 shows our current configuration. At this point, we have configured an interceptor to change the locale, and this interceptor is being applied to all incoming requests (we didn't specify a URL pattern to match against). Next, we configure the interceptor and use the addInterceptor method to add it to the registry. The framework will take care of the additional details for registering the interceptors with the configured handler mappings.

Listing 6-9. *Using the InterceptorRegistry to Add Interceptors*

```
package com.apress.prospringmvc.bookstore.web.config;

//Other imports omitted

import org.springframework.web.servlet.HandlerInterceptor;
import org.springframework.web.servlet.config.annotation.InterceptorRegistry;

@Configuration
@EnableWebMvc
@ComponentScan(basePackages = { "com.apress.prospringmvc.bookstore.web" })
public class WebMvcContextConfiguration extends WebMvcConfigurerAdapter {

    @Override
    public void addInterceptors(InterceptorRegistry registry) {
        registry.addInterceptor(localeChangeInterceptor());
    }

    @Bean
    public HandlerInterceptor localeChangeInterceptor() {
        LocaleChangeInterceptor localeChangeInterceptor;
        localeChangeInterceptor = new LocaleChangeInterceptor();
        localeChangeInterceptor.setParamName("lang");
        return localeChangeInterceptor;
    }
    //… Other methods omitted

}
```

Listing 6-10 shows a snippet of code in which we change the mapping from all URLs to only URLs starting with /customer.

Listing 6-10. Limiting an Interceptor to Certain URLs

```
package com.apress.prospringmvc.bookstore.web.config;
//Imports omitted
@Configuration
@EnableWebMvc
@ComponentScan(basePackages = { "com.apress.prospringmvc.bookstore.web" })
public class WebMvcContextConfiguration extends WebMvcConfigurerAdapter {

    @Override
    public void addInterceptors(InterceptorRegistry registry) {
        InterceptorRegistration registration;
        registration = registry.addInterceptor(localeChangeInterceptor());
        registation.addPathPatterns("/customers/**");
    }
    //Other methods omitted
}
```

Implementing an Interceptor

Thus far, we have covered different types of interceptors and how to register them, so that they can be used. Now let's implement interceptors for our store. We are going to implement two different interceptors. The first will add some commonly used data to our model, so that we can show it to the user. The second will address a security need: we want the account and checkout page to be accessible only by registered users.

Implement a WebRequestInterceptor

In this section, we are going to implement an org.springframework.web.context.request .WebRequestInterceptor. If we look at our web page in Figure 6-4, we can see a section called Random Books. This section on our web page has remained empty thus far. Now we are going to create an interceptor that will add some random books to the model. For this, we are going to implement the postHandle method (see Listing 6-11).

░ **Note** In a real web shop, we would probably call this section "New Books" or "Suggested Books."

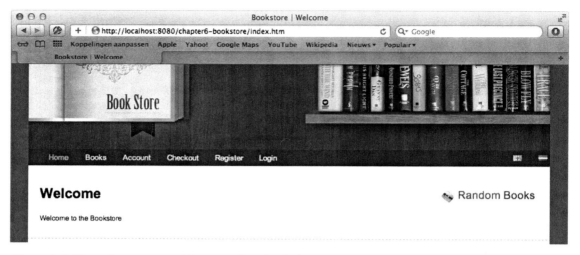

Figure 6-4. The welcome page without random books listed

Listing 6-11. The CommonDataInterceptor

```
package com.apress.prospringmvc.bookstore.web.interceptor;

import org.springframework.beans.factory.annotation.Autowired;
import org.springframework.ui.ModelMap;
import org.springframework.web.context.request.WebRequest;
import org.springframework.web.context.request.WebRequestInterceptor;

import com.apress.prospringmvc.bookstore.service.BookstoreService;

public class CommonDataInterceptor implements WebRequestInterceptor {

    @Autowired
    private BookstoreService bookstoreService;

    @Override
    public void preHandle(WebRequest request) throws Exception {
    }

    @Override
    public void postHandle(WebRequest request, ModelMap model)
    throws Exception {
        if (model != null) {
            model.addAttribute("randomBooks", this.bookstoreService.findRandomBooks());
        }
    }

    @Override
    public void afterCompletion(WebRequest request, Exception ex)
```

```
    throws Exception {
    }

}
```

The postHandle method adds some random books to the model, but only when this model is available. This is why our code includes a null check. The model can be null when we are going to do AJAX or write the response ourselves.

To have our interceptor applied to incoming request, we need to register it. The interceptor needs to be called for every incoming request, so it doesn't require much additional configuration (see the highlighted line in Listing 6-12).

Listing 6-12. The CommondDataInterceptor Configuration

```
package com.apress.prospringmvc.bookstore.web.config;

import org.springframework.web.context.request.WebRequestInterceptor;
import org.springframework.web.servlet.config.annotation.InterceptorRegistry;
com.apress.prospringmvc.bookstore.web.interceptor.CommonDataInterceptor;

// Other imports omitted

@Configuration
@EnableWebMvc
@ComponentScan(basePackages = { "com.apress.prospringmvc.bookstore.web" })
public class WebMvcContextConfiguration extends WebMvcConfigurerAdapter {

    @Override
    public void addInterceptors(InterceptorRegistry registry) {
        registry.addInterceptor(localeChangeInterceptor());
        registry.addWebRequestInterceptor(commonDataInterceptor());
    }

    @Bean
    public WebRequestInterceptor commonDataInterceptor() {
        return new CommonDataInterceptor();
    }
    // Other methods omitted
}
```

Now when we redeploy our application and access a page, we should see random books displayed in the Random Books section on our page (see Figure 6-5). (The logic used in our template for selecting the random books is shown in Listing 6-13.)

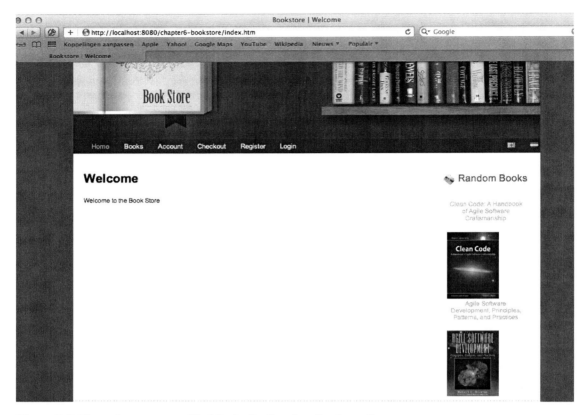

Figure 6-5. *The welcome page with titles in the Random Books section*

Listing 6-13. *The Random Books Section from the Template*

```
<div class="right_box">

<div class="title">
  <span class="title_icon">
    <img src="<c:url value="/resources/images/bullet4.gif"/>" alt="" title="" />
  </span>
  <spring:message code="main.title.randombooks"/>
</div>
<c:forEach items="${randomBooks}" var="book">
  <div class="new_prod_box">
    <c:url value="/book/detail/${book.id}" var="bookUrl" />
    <a href="${bookUrl}">${book.title}</a>
    <div class="new_prod_img">
      <c:url value="/resources/images/books/${book.isbn}/book_front_cover.png"↩
var="bookImage"/>
      <a href="${bookUrl}">
```

```
        <img src="${bookImage}" alt="${book.title}" title="${book.title}"↵
  class="thumb" border="0" width="100px"/>
      </a>
    </div>
  </div>
</c:forEach>
</div>
```

Implementing a HandlerInterceptor

Currently, our account pages aren't secure. For example, someone could simply change the id in the URL to see the content of another account. Let's use the interceptor approach to apply security to our pages. We are going to create an interceptor that checks whether we are already logged in (our account is available in the HTTP session). If not, it will throw a com.apress.prospringmvc.bookstore.service .AuthenticationException (see Listing 6-14). We will also store the original URL in a session attribute; that way, we can redirect the user to the URL he wants to visit after he logs in.

Listing 6-14. The SecurityHandlerInterceptor

```
package com.apress.prospringmvc.bookstore.web.interceptor;
// javax.servlet imports omitted
import org.springframework.web.servlet.HandlerInterceptor;
import org.springframework.web.servlet.handler.HandlerInterceptorAdapter;
import org.springframework.web.util.WebUtils;

import com.apress.prospringmvc.bookstore.domain.Account;
import com.apress.prospringmvc.bookstore.service.AuthenticationException;
import com.apress.prospringmvc.bookstore.web.controller.LoginController;

public class SecurityHandlerInterceptor extends HandlerInterceptorAdapter {

    @Override
    public boolean preHandle(HttpServletRequest request,
                             HttpServletResponse response,
                             Object handler) throws Exception {
        Account account= (Account) WebUtils.getSessionAttribute(
                         request, LoginController.ACCOUNT_ATTRIBUTE);
        if (account == null) {
            //Retrieve and store the original URL.
            String url = request.getRequestURL().toString();
            WebUtils.setSessionAttribute(
                     request, LoginController.REQUESTED_URL, url);
            throw new AuthenticationException(
                 "Authentication required.", "authentication.required");
        }
        return true;
    }

}
```

For this interceptor, our configuration is a bit more complex because we want to map it to certain URLs (see the highlighted part in Listing 6-15).

Listing 6-15. *SecurityHandlerInterceptor Configuration*

```
package com.apress.prospringmvc.bookstore.web.config;

import com.apress.prospringmvc.bookstore.web.interceptor.SecurityHandlerInterceptor;

//Other imports omitted

@Configuration
@EnableWebMvc
@ComponentScan(basePackages = { "com.apress.prospringmvc.bookstore.web" })
public class WebMvcContextConfiguration extends WebMvcConfigurerAdapter {

    @Override
    public void addInterceptors(InterceptorRegistry registry) {
        registry.addInterceptor(localeChangeInterceptor());
        registry.addWebRequestInterceptor(commonDataInterceptor());
        registry.addInterceptor(new SecurityHandlerInterceptor()).
                addPathPatterns("/customer/account*", "/cart/checkout");
    }

    // Other methods omitted
}
```

Finally, we also need to make a modification to our `com.apress.prospringmvc.bookstore.web` `.controller.AccountController`. Currently, we expect an id as part of the URL. However, instead of retrieving the account from the database, we are going to restore it from the session. Listing 6-16 shows the necessary modifications.

Listing 6-16. *The AccountController*

```
package com.apress.prospringmvc.bookstore.web.controller;

// Imports omitted

@Controller
@RequestMapping("/customer/account")
@SessionAttributes(types = Account.class)
public class AccountController {

    //Fields and other methods omitted

    @RequestMapping(method = RequestMethod.GET)
    public String index(Model model, HttpSession session) {
        Account account = (Account) session.getAttribute(LoginController.ACCOUNT_ATTRIBUTE);
        model.addAttribute(account);
        model.addAttribute("orders", this.orderRepository.findByAccount(account));
        return "customer/account";
    }
```

```
@RequestMapping(method = { RequestMethod.POST, RequestMethod.PUT })
public String update(@ModelAttribute Account account) {
    this.accountRepository.save(account);
    return "redirect:/customer/account";
}
}
```

When we redeploy our application and click Account in the menu bar, we will be greeted with an error page (see Figure 6-6). We use the default exception-handling mechanism to send an error code back to the client, so that the browser can act upon it. In the next section, we are going to cover exception handling in more detail.

Figure 6-6. A 403 error page after clicking a secured link

While we have protected our resources, it would be nicer if we could show the login page to the user with a message that she needs to log in to see the requested page. This is what we are going to do in the next section.

Exception Handling

As mentioned in Chapter 4, when an exception occurs during request processing, Spring will try to handle the exception. To give us a generic way of handling exceptions, Spring uses yet another strategy that can be utilized by implementing the org.springframework.web.servlet.HandlerExceptionResolver interface.

The org.springframework.web.servlet.HandlerExceptionResolver provides a callback method for the dispatcher servlet (see Listing 6-17). This method is called when an exception occurs during the request processing workflow. The method can return an org.springframework.web.servlet .ModelAndView, or it can choose to handle the Exception itself.

Listing 6-17. The HandlerExceptionResolver Interface

```
package org.springframeowork.web.servlet;

import javax.servlet.http.HttpServletRequest;
import javax.servlet.http.HttpServletResponse;

public interface HandlerExceptionResolver {

  ModelAndView resolveException(HttpServletRequest request,
                                HttpServletResponse response,
                                Object handler,
                                Exception ex);
}
```

By default, the dispatcher servlet looks for all beans in the application context of the type
`org.springframework.web.servlet.HandlerExceptionResolver` (see the "Configuring the
DispatcherServlet" section in Chapter 4). When multiple resolvers are detected, the dispatcher servlet
will consult each of them until a viewname is returned or the response is written. If the exception cannot
be handled, then the exception is rethrown, so that the servlet container can handle it. The servlet
container will use the error-pages configuration from its configuration or simply propagate the
exception to the user. (In most cases, you will get an error 500 with a stacktrace on screen.)

Spring MVC comes with several implementations of the `org.springframework.web.servlet`
`.HandlerExceptionResolver` interface, as we can see in Figure 6-6. Note that each of these
implementations works differently. Table 6-4 gives a short overview on how the different
implementations work.

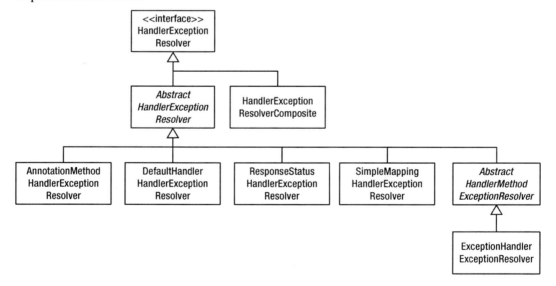

Figure 6-7. The HandlerExceptionResolver hierarchy

Table 6-4. The HandlerExceptionResolver Implementations

HandlerExceptionResolver	Description
AnnotationMethodHandler ExceptionResolver ExceptionHandler ExceptionResolver	Searches the current controller for methods annotated with @ExceptionHandler and selects the best exception-handling method to handle the exception. It then invokes the selected method.
DefaultHandler ExceptionResolver	Translates well-known exceptions to a proper response for the client. Returns an empty ModelAndView and sends the appropriate HTTP Response Code to the client.
ResponseStatus ExceptionResolver	Looks for the org.springframework.web.bind.annotation.ResponseStatus annotation on the exception and uses that to send a response to the client.
SimpleMapping ExceptionResolver	Maps exceptions to view names by the exception class name or part (substring) of that class name. This implementation can be configured either globally or for certain controllers.
HandlerExceptionResolver Composite	Used internally by the @MVC configuration to chain exception resolvers. It can only be used by the framework.

As the class diagram in Figure 6-7 illustrates, all usable implementations for resolving exceptions extend the org.springframework.web.servlet.handler.AbstractHandlerExceptionResolver. This is a convenient superclass that provides common features and configuration options to all implementations. Table 6-5 lists and briefly describes its common properties.

Table 6-5. Common HandlerExceptionResolver Properties

Property	Description
mappedHandlerClasses	A set of handler classes for which the HandlerExceptionResolver should handle exceptions. Exceptions propagated from handlers of a type not in the set will not be handled by this HandlerExceptionResolver.
mappedHandlers	Similar to mappedHandlerClasses, but instead of classes it contains actual handlers (controllers, in this case).
preventResponseCaching	Enables us to prevent caching for the views resolved by this HandlerExceptionResolver. The default value is false, which allows browsers to cache the error pages.
warnLogCategory	Sets the category used for logging the exceptions (the log level is WARN). The default is no category, which translates to no logging.

All attributes are defined on the AbstractHandlerExceptionResolver.

The DefaultHandlerExceptionResolver

The DefaultHandlerExceptionResolver implementation will always return an empty ModelAndView and sends an HTTP response code to the client. In Table 6-6, we can see the exception to the HTTP response code and description mapping.

Table 6-6. Exception HTTP Response Code Mapping

Exception	HTTP Code	Description
NoSuchRequestHandlingMethodException	404	Not Found
HttpRequestMethodNotSupportedException	405	Method not Allowed
HttpMediaTypeNotSupportedException	415	Unsupported Media Type
HttpMediaTypeNotAcceptableException	406	Not Acceptable
ConversionNotSupportedException HttpMessageNotWritableException	500	Internal Server Error
MissingServletRequestParameterException ServletRequestBindingException TypeMismatchException HttpMessageNotReadableException MethodArgumentNotValidException MissingServletRequestPartException	400	Bad Request

ResponseStatusExceptionResolver

The ResponseStatusExceptionResolver checks if the thrown exception is annotated with an org.springframework.web.bind.annotation.ResponseStatus annotation (see Listing 6-18). If that is the case, it will handle the exception, send the HTTP response code from the annotation to the client, and then return an empty ModelAndView indicating the exception was handled. If that annotation isn't present, it simply returns null to indicate that the exception wasn't handled.

Listing 6-18. Handling an AuthenticationException

```
package com.apress.prospringmvc.bookstore.service;

import org.springframework.http.HttpStatus;
import org.springframework.web.bind.annotation.ResponseStatus;

@ResponseStatus(value = HttpStatus.FORBIDDEN)
public class AuthenticationException extends Exception {

    private String code;
```

```
public AuthenticationException(String message, String code) {
    super(message);
    this.code = code;
}

public String getCode() {
    return this.code;
}
}
```

When we throw this exception, the org.springframework.web.servlet.mvc.annotation
.ResponseStatusExceptionResolver will detect that it has been annotated with the
org.springframework.web.servlet.bind.annotation.ResponseStatus. This annotation has two
properties we can use to specify information (see Table 6-7).

Table 6-7. ResponseStatus Properties

Property	Description
value	Sends the HTTP response code to send to the client. This is required.
reason	Sends the reason to the client. This is optional. It can also be used to provide additional information.

■ **Note** This is the mechanism we use to have the framework handle our
com.apress.prospringmvc.bookstore.service.AuthenticationException.

SimpleMappingExceptionResolver

The SimpleMappingExceptionResolver can be configured to translate certain exceptions to a view. For
example, we can map (partial) exception class names to a view. We say partial here because matching is
done based on the name of the class and not on its concrete type. The matching is done with a simple
substring mechanism; as such, wildcards (ant-style regular expressions) aren't supported.

Listing 6-19 shows the configuration for a SimpleMappingExceptionResolver. It is configured to map
an AuthenticationException to the view with the name login. We also set a HTTP response code to send
with the login view.

Listing 6-19. A SimpleMappingExceptionResolver Configuration

```
package com.apress.prospringmvc.bookstore.web.config;

import org.springframework.web.servlet.HandlerExceptionResolver;
import org.springframework.web.servlet.handler.SimpleMappingExceptionResolver;

// Imports omitted
```

```
@Configuration
@EnableWebMvc
@ComponentScan(basePackages = { "com.apress.prospringmvc.bookstore.web" })
public class WebMvcContextConfiguration extends WebMvcConfigurerAdapter {

    @Override
    public void configureHandlerExceptionResolvers(
                    List<HandlerExceptionResolver> exceptionResolvers) {
        exceptionResolvers.add(simpleMappingExceptionResolver());
    }

    @Bean
    public SimpleMappingExceptionResolver simpleMappingExceptionResolver() {
        SimpleMappingExceptionResolver exceptionResolver;
        exceptionResolver = new SimpleMappingExceptionResolver();
        Properties mappings = new Properties();
        mappings.setProperty("AuthenticationException", "login");

        Properties statusCodes = new Properties();
        mappings.setProperty(
                    "login",
                    String.valueOf(HttpServletResponse.SC_UNAUTHORIZED));

        exceptionResolver.setExceptionMappings(mappings);
        exceptionResolver.setStatusCodes(statusCodes);
        return exceptionResolver;
    }
    // Other methods omitted
}
```

The matching is done based on the class name, rather than the concrete type. If the class name of the exception thrown matches the specified pattern, then the corresponding view name will be used. The pattern doesn't support wildcards; it is merely a substring that matches the class name. We need to choose the pattern carefully. For instance, Exception will match almost all exceptions thrown (because most exceptions have Exception as part of their class name). Similarly, DataAccessException will more or less match all of Spring's exceptions for data access.

We need to make one final adjustment; namely, we need to modify our com.apress.prospringmvc .bookstore.web.controller.LoginController. At the moment, there is exception handling inside the controller; however, this can be removed because the AuthenticationException will be handled by our just configured HandlerExceptionResolver (see Listing 6-20 for the improved controller).

Listing 6-20. *The Improved Login Controller*

```
package com.apress.prospringmvc.bookstore.web.controller;
// Imports omitted

@Controller
@RequestMapping(value = "/login")
public class LoginController {

    public static final String ACCOUNT_ATTRIBUTE = "account";
    public static final String REQUESTED_URL = "REQUESTED_URL";
```

```
@Autowired
private AccountService accountService;

@RequestMapping(method = RequestMethod.GET)
public void login() {}

@RequestMapping(method = RequestMethod.POST)
public String handleLogin(@RequestParam String username,
                          @RequestParam String password,
                          HttpSession session)
throws AuthenticationException {
    Account account = this.accountService.login(username, password);
    session.setAttribute(ACCOUNT_ATTRIBUTE, account);
    String url = (String) session.getAttribute(REQUESTED_URL);
    session.removeAttribute(REQUESTED_URL); // Remove the attribute
    if (StringUtils.hasText(url) && !url.contains("login")) {
        return "redirect:" + url;
    } else {
        return "redirect:/index.htm";
    }
}

}
```

If we click Account on the menu bar after redeployment, we will be greeted with a login page (see Figure 6-8).

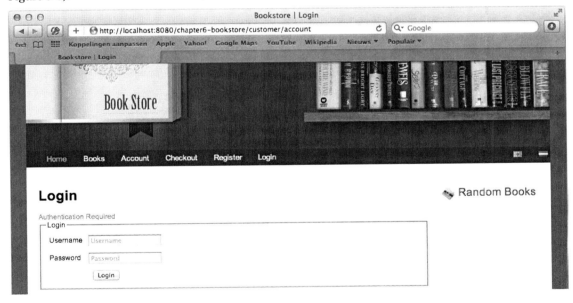

Figure 6-8. The Login page

ExceptionHandlerExceptionResolver and AnnotationMethodHandlerExceptionResolver

Both the AnnotationMethodHandlerExceptionResolver and ExceptionHandlerExceptionResolver will look in the current controller for methods annotated with org.springframework.web.bind.annotations .ExceptionHandler. This is also a drawback because this pair of exception resolvers only operates on methods in the currently assigned controller. If you use this technique, it isn't possible to define an exception handler for the whole application.

Exception-handling methods are very much like controller methods (as explained in Chapter 5); they can use the same method parameters and the same return values. An exception-handling method uses the same underlying infrastructure to detect the return types and method-argument types. However, there is one addition to these methods that we can also pass in the thrown exception; namely, we can specify an argument of type Exception (or a subclass).

The method in Listing 6-21 will handle all exceptions thrown in the controller it is defined in. It will cause an error code 500 to be sent back to the client, along with the given reason. This is the most basic exception-handling method we can write. As mentioned previously, we can use multiple parameters in the method signature. This goes for the method arguments, as well as the method return types. (See Tables 5-3 and 5-4 in the preceding chapter for an overview.)

Listing 6-21. A Basic Exception-handling Method Sample

```
@ExceptionHandler()
@ResponseStatus(
    value=HttpStatus.INTERNAL_SERVER_ERROR,
    reason="Exception while handling request.")
public void handleException() {}
```

Listing 6-22 shows a more elaborate example. When an org.springframework.dao .DataAccessException occurs, it fills the model with as much information as possible. After that, the view named db-error will be rendered.

Listing 6-22. An Advanced Exception-handling Method Sample

```
@ExceptionHandler
public ModelAndView handleIOException(DataAccessException ex,
                                      Principal principal,
                                      WebRequest request) {
    ModelAndView mav = new ModelAndView("db-error");
    mav.addObject("username", principal.getName());
    mav.addAllObjects(request.getParameterMap());

    for(Iterator<String> names = request.getHeaderNames(); names.hasNext(); ) {
        String name =  names.next();
        String[] value = request.getHeaderValues(name);
        mav.addObject(name, value);
    }
    return mav;
}
```

Extending Spring @MVC

In previous chapters, we explained how Spring MVC works and how we can write controllers. However, there might come a time when the support from the framework out-of-the-box isn't sufficient, and we will want to change or add to the behavior of the framework. In general, the Spring Framework is quite flexible due to the way it is built. It uses a lot of strategies and delegation, and this is also something we can use to extend or modify the behavior of the framework. In this section, we will dive into the internals of request mapping, request handling, and form rendering. Finally, we will cover how to extend these features.

Extending RequestMappingHandlerMapping

To map incoming requests to controller methods, Spring uses a handler mapping. For our use case, we have been using the org.springframework.web.servlet.mvc.method.annotation .RequestMappingHandlerMapping, and we already have mentioned a couple times that it is quite flexible. To match the requests based on methods with the org.springframework.web.bind.annotation .RequestMapping annotation, the handler mapping consults several org.springframework.web.servlet .mvc.condition.RequestCondition implementations (see Figure 6-8).

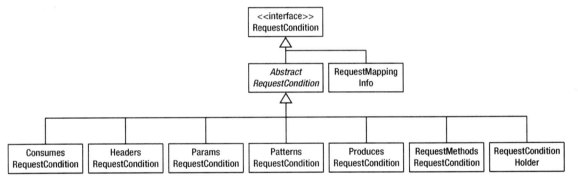

Figure 6-9. The RequestCondition Class Diagram

As the diagram illustrates, there is an implementation for each of the attributes (i.e., consumes, headers, methods, params, produces, and value; for more details, see Table 5-2) of the org.springframework.web.bind.annotation.RequestMapping annotation. The RequestConditionHolder and RequestMappingInfo are two implementations used internally by the framework.

To create an implementation, we need two things. First, we need an implementation of the interface (see Listing 6-23 for the API). Second, we need to extend the org.springframework.web.servlet .method.annotation.RequestMappingHandlerMapping. This class contains two callback methods that act as factory methods for our custom request method (see Listing 6-24). The getCustomTypeCondition method is called to create an instance to match the type-level condition, while the getCustomMethodCondition method is used for method-level conditions.

Listing 6-23. The RequestCondition API

```
package org.springframework.web.servlet.mvc.condition;

import javax.servlet.http.HttpServletRequest;

import org.springframework.web.bind.annotation.RequestMapping;

public interface RequestCondition<T> {

    T combine(T other);

    T getMatchingCondition(HttpServletRequest request);

    int compareTo(T other, HttpServletRequest request);
}
```

Listing 6-24. The RequestMappingHandlerMapping

```
package org.springframework.web.servlet.mvc.method.annotation;

import java.lang.reflect.Method;

import org.springframework.core.annotation.AnnotationUtils;
import org.springframework.stereotype.Controller;
import org.springframework.web.bind.annotation.RequestMapping;
import org.springframework.web.servlet.mvc.condition.ConsumesRequestCondition;
import org.springframework.web.servlet.mvc.condition.HeadersRequestCondition;
import org.springframework.web.servlet.mvc.condition.ParamsRequestCondition;
import org.springframework.web.servlet.mvc.condition.PatternsRequestCondition;
import org.springframework.web.servlet.mvc.condition.ProducesRequestCondition;
import org.springframework.web.servlet.mvc.condition.RequestCondition;
import org.springframework.web.servlet.mvc.condition.RequestMethodsRequestCondition;
import org.springframework.web.servlet.mvc.method.RequestMappingInfo;
import org.springframework.web.servlet.mvc.method.RequestMappingInfoHandlerMapping;

public class RequestMappingHandlerMapping
extends RequestMappingInfoHandlerMapping {

    // Other methods omitted.

    protected RequestCondition<?> getCustomMethodCondition(Method method) {
        return null;
    }

    protected RequestCondition<?> getCustomTypeCondition(Class<?> handlerType) {
        return null;
    }
}
```

Extending the RequestMappingHandlerAdapter

Like the RequestMappingHandlerMapping, the RequestMappingHandlerAdapter uses a couple of different strategies to do its work. To determine what to inject into a method argument, the adapter consults several org.springframework.web.method.support.HandlerMethodArgumentResolver implementations. For the return types, it consults the registered org.springframework.web.method.support .HandlerMethodReturnValueHandler implementations.

HandlerMethodArgumentResolver

The HandlerMethodArgumentResolver is used by the RequestMappingHandlerAdapter to determine what to use for a method argument. There is more or a less an implementation for each of the supported method-argument types or annotations (see the Chapter 5 section, "Supported Method Argument Types"). The API is quite simple, as we can see in Listing 6-25.

Listing 6-25. The HandlerMethodArgumentResolver API

```
package org.springframework.web.method.support;

import org.springframework.core.MethodParameter;
import org.springframework.web.bind.WebDataBinder;
import org.springframework.web.bind.support.WebDataBinderFactory;
import org.springframework.web.context.request.NativeWebRequest;

public interface HandlerMethodArgumentResolver {

    boolean supportsParameter(MethodParameter parameter);

    Object resolveArgument(MethodParameter parameter,
                           ModelAndViewContainer mavContainer,
                           NativeWebRequest webRequest,
                           WebDataBinderFactory binderFactory)
        throws Exception;

}
```

The supportsParameter method is called on each registered HandlerMethodArgumentResolver. The one that returns true will be used to detect or create the actual value to use for that method argument. We do this by calling the resolveArgument method.

HandlerMethodReturnValueHandler

The HandlerMethodReturnValueHandler is similar to the HandlerMethodArgumentResolver, but with one important difference. As its name implies, HandlerMethodReturnValueHandler works for method return values. There is an implementation for each of the supported return values or annotations (see the Chapter 5 section, "Supported Return Values"). This API is also quite simple, as we can see in Listing 6-26.

Listing 6-26. The HandlerMethodReturnValueHandler

```
package org.springframework.web.method.support;

import org.springframework.core.MethodParameter;
import org.springframework.web.context.request.NativeWebRequest;

public interface HandlerMethodReturnValueHandler {

    boolean supportsReturnType(MethodParameter returnType);

    void handleReturnValue(Object returnValue,
                           MethodParameter returnType,
                           ModelAndViewContainer mavContainer,
                           NativeWebRequest webRequest)
    throws Exception;

}
```

The supportsReturnType method for each registered HandlerMethodReturnValueHandler will be called with the return type of the method. The one that returns true will be used to actually handle the return value. This is accomplished by calling the handleReturnValue method.

Implementing Your Own

We can use the strategies used by the RequestMappingHandlerAdapter to our advantage. For example, we want an easy way to store and retrieve objects in the javax.servlet.http.HttpSession. For this, we first need an annotation to mark a method argument or return type as something we want to retrieve or put in the HttpSession. Listing 6-27 describes the annotation we will use.

Listing 6-27. The SessionAttribute Annotation

```
package com.apress.prospringmvc.bookstore.web.method.support;

import java.lang.annotation.Documented;
import java.lang.annotation.ElementType;
import java.lang.annotation.Retention;
import java.lang.annotation.RetentionPolicy;
import java.lang.annotation.Target;

@Target({ ElementType.PARAMETER, ElementType.METHOD })
@Retention(RetentionPolicy.RUNTIME)
@Documented
public @interface SessionAttribute {

    String value() default "";

    boolean required() default true;

    boolean exposeAsModelAttribute() default false;
```

}

However, all by itself adding an annotation isn't much help because we still need a class that uses that annotation. Because we want to be able to retrieve from and store in the HttpSession, we will create a class that implements both the HandlerMethodReturnValueHandler and HandlerMethodArgumentResolver interfaces (see Listing 6-28).

Listing 6-28. The SessionAttributeProcessor

```
package com.apress.prospringmvc.bookstore.web.method.support;

import org.springframework.core.MethodParameter;
import org.springframework.web.bind.MissingServletRequestParameterException;
import org.springframework.web.bind.support.WebDataBinderFactory;
import org.springframework.web.context.request.NativeWebRequest;
import org.springframework.web.context.request.WebRequest;
import org.springframework.web.method.support.HandlerMethodArgumentResolver;
import org.springframework.web.method.support.HandlerMethodReturnValueHandler;
import org.springframework.web.method.support.ModelAndViewContainer;

public class SessionAttributeProcessor implements↩
HandlerMethodReturnValueHandler, HandlerMethodArgumentResolver {

    @Override
    public boolean supportsReturnType(MethodParameter returnType) {
        return returnType.getMethodAnnotation(SessionAttribute.class) != null;
    }

    @Override
    public void handleReturnValue(Object returnValue,
                                  MethodParameter returnType,
                                  ModelAndViewContainer mavContainer,
                                  NativeWebRequest webRequest)
    throws Exception {

        SessionAttribute annotation;
        annotation = returnType.getMethodAnnotation(SessionAttribute.class);
        webRequest.setAttribute(annotation.value(), returnValue,↩
WebRequest.SCOPE_SESSION);
        exposeModelAttribute(annotation, returnValue, mavContainer);
    }

    @Override
    public boolean supportsParameter(MethodParameter parameter) {
        return parameter.hasParameterAnnotation(SessionAttribute.class);
    }

    private void exposeModelAttribute(SessionAttribute annotation,
                                      Object value,
                                      ModelAndViewContainer mavContainer) {
        if (annotation.exposeAsModelAttribute()) {
            mavContainer.addAttribute(annotation.value(), value);
```

```
        }
    }

    @Override
    public Object resolveArgument(MethodParameter parameter,
                                  ModelAndViewContainer mavContainer,
                                  NativeWebRequest webRequest,
                                  WebDataBinderFactory binderFactory)
    throws Exception {

        SessionAttribute annotation;
        annotation = parameter.getParameterAnnotation(SessionAttribute.class);

        Object value = webRequest.getAttribute(
                    annotation.value(), WebRequest.SCOPE_SESSION);
        if (value == null && annotation.required()) {
            throw new MissingServletRequestParameterException(
                    annotation.value(),
                    parameter.getParameterType().getName());
        }
        exposeModelAttribute(annotation, value, mavContainer);
        return value;
    }
}
```

Before we can use the processor, we need to configure it. For this, we need to modify our configuration class. Specifically, we need to add the processor as a bean and make the environment aware of the bean's existence (see Listing 6-29).

Listing 6-29. The Modified WebMvcContextConfiguration

```
package com.apress.prospringmvc.bookstore.web.config;

com.apress.prospringmvc.bookstore.web.method.support.SessionAttributeProcessor;

// Other imports omitted

@Configuration
@EnableWebMvc
@ComponentScan(basePackages = { "com.apress.prospringmvc.bookstore.web" })
public class WebMvcContextConfiguration extends WebMvcConfigurerAdapter {

    @Bean
    public SessionAttributeProcessor sessionAttributeProcessor() {
        return new SessionAttributeProcessor();
    }

    @Override
    public void addArgumentResolvers(
                    List<HandlerMethodArgumentResolver> argumentResolvers) {
        argumentResolvers.add(sessionAttributeProcessor());
    }
```

```
    @Override
    public void addReturnValueHandlers(
            List<HandlerMethodReturnValueHandler> returnValueHandlers) {
        returnValueHandlers.add(sessionAttributeProcessor());
    }
    // Other methods omitted
}
```

Now that we have configured our processor, we are finally ready to use it. Let's begin by modifying the controllers for accounts, as shown in Listing 6-30. We removed the need for directly accessing the session and the need for adding the account to the model, this is now all handled by the processor. Bold font reflects the changes; it is simply an annotation on a method argument. At this point, we no longer need direct access to the HTTP session.

Listing 6-30. The Modified AccountController

```
package com.apress.prospringmvc.bookstore.web.controller;

// Imports omitted

@Controller
@RequestMapping("/customer/account")
@SessionAttributes(types = Account.class)
public class AccountController {

    @RequestMapping(method = RequestMethod.GET)
    public String index(
            Model model,
            @SessionAttribute(value =↵
LoginController.ACCOUNT_ATTRIBUTE, exposeAsModelAttribute = true) Account account) {
        model.addAttribute("orders", this.orderRepository.findByAccount(account));
        return "customer/account";
    }
    // Other methods omitted
}
```

If we now relaunch the application and click Account (after logging in), we are greeted by our Account page (see Figure 6-10).

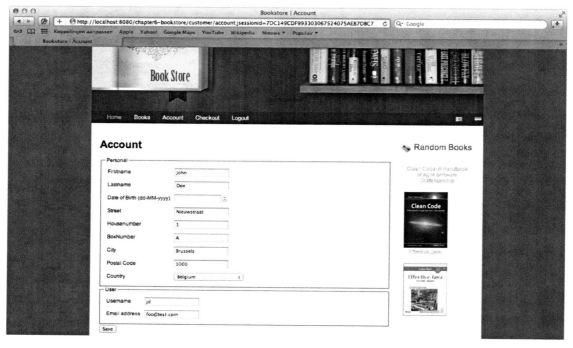

Figure 6-10. The Account page

Using the RequestDataValueProcessor

The org.springframework.web.servlet.support.RequestDataValueProcessor is an optional component that we can use to inspect or modify request parameter values before they are rendered or before a redirect is issued.

We can use this component as part of a solution[4] to provide data integrity, confidentiality, and protection against cross-site request forgery (CSRF).[5] We can also use it to automatically add hidden fields to all forms and URLs.

The RequestDataValueProcessor API consists of four methods (see Listing 6-31).

---

[4] http://www.hdiv.org
[5] http://www.owasp.org

Listing 6-31. The RequestDataValueProcessor API

```
package org.springframework.web.servlet.support;

import java.util.Map;

import javax.servlet.http.HttpServletRequest;

public interface RequestDataValueProcessor {

    String processAction(HttpServletRequest request, String action);

    String processFormFieldValue(HttpServletRequest request, String name,
                                String value, String type);

    Map<String, String> getExtraHiddenFields(HttpServletRequest request);

    String processUrl(HttpServletRequest request, String url);
}
```

We can use this interface to do some interesting things. For example, we might create a checksum over the not editable fields (like id) in the controller (or an interceptor), and then review this checksum to see whether any fields have been tampered with.

The processUrl method is used by the Url tag; and on a redirect, we could use it to encode or add extra parameters to the URL to secure our URLs (for instance, we could add a checksum to check the validity of our parameters).

There is no default instance provided by the framework. Therefore, an implementation needs to be tailored for our application (the HDIV website has a plugin to protect a site from a whole range of vulnerabilities). To configure a RequestDataValueProcessor, we need to add it to the application context and then register it with the name, requestDataValueProcessor. This is the name the framework uses to detect the registered instance.

Summary

In this chapter, we covered some more advanced techniques that we can use to build web applications. For example, we started by looking at scoped beans and how we can use them to our advantage. To that end, we implemented a shopping cart in our sample application.

At times we find ourselves in need of the ability to reuse code or to execute code across a large amount of classes or URLs. These so-called crosscutting concerns can be addressed by using aspect oriented programming; however, in a web application, this isn't always a good fit. In Spring MVC, we can use interceptors and an advanced exception-handling strategy to address those crosscutting concerns. For example, we can use interceptors to execute a piece of code for a large number of controllers. When configuring these interceptors, we can specify whether to map to all controllers or only to certain controllers based on the URL.

Although we all try to build our applications to be as robust as possible, there is always a chance that things will go wrong. When things do go wrong, we want to be able to handle the problems gracefully. For example, we might want to show the user an error page or login page when we need the user's credentials. For this, we took an in-depth look at the exception-handling strategies inside Spring MVC.

We followed this by diving deeper into the infrastructure classes of Spring MVC and examined how to extend the framework, if the need arises. We also explained how to expand the request matching by specifying an additional request condition. Next, we explained (and showed) how to write a processor to handle method-argument types and return values for request-handling methods.

Finally, we ended the chapter with a brief introduction to the request data value processor, covering how to use this to protect against CSFR and provide data integrity.

REST and AJAX

Until now we have been building quite a classic web application: we send a request to the server, the server processes the request, and we render the result and show it to the client. Over the last decade, however the way we build web applications has changed considerably. Now we have JavaScript and JSON/XML, which allow for AJAX-based web applications and also push more and more behavior push to the client, including validation, rendering parts of the screen, and so on.

In this chapter we start with REST[1] (Representational State Transfer), a concept or architectural style that has influenced how we as developers think of web resources and how we should handle them. We next discuss AJAX and consider it in combination with REST.

The second part of this chapter covers file uploads. You will see how to do file uploading with the Spring Framework and how to handle the task in our controllers. However before we get into this let's take a look at REST.

Representational State Transfer (REST)

This section briefly explains the topic of REST. The concept essentially has two parts: first the resources and how we identify them, and then the way we operate or work with these resources. REST was described in 2000 by Roy Thomas Fielding in a paper called '*Architectural Styles and the Design of Network-based Software Architectures*'.[2] It describes how to work with resources using the HTTP protocol and the features offered by this protocol.

Identifying Resources

In Chapter 4 we briefly discussed the parts a URL (Unique Resource Locator) consists of. For REST this doesn't really change; however, the URL is important as it points to a unique resource. Table 7-1 gives a couple of samples of resource locations.

---

[1] www.ics.uci.edu/~fielding/pubs/dissertation/rest_arch_style.htm
[2] www.ics.uci.edu/~fielding/pubs/dissertation/top.htm

Table 7-1. *Resource Locators*

URL	Description
http://www.example.com/book	A list of books to search
http://www.example.com/book/9781430241553	The details of the book with ISBN 978-1-4302-4155-3

In REST it is all about a *representation* of a resource, and hence the URL/URI is important. It gives us the location of an actual resource (web page, image on the web page, mp3 file, or whatever). What we see in our web browser isn't the actual resource but a representation of that resource. The next section explains how we can use this resource location to work with (modify, delete, and so on) that resource.

Working with Resources

The HTTP protocol specifies several methods (HTTP methods[3]) to work with information from our application. Table 7-2 gives an overview of the methods.

Table 7-2. *Available HTTP Methods*

Method	Description
GET	Retrieves a representation of a resource (for example, a book) from the given location.
HEAD	Similar to GET; however, the actual representation is not returned, but only the headers belonging to that resource. Useful to identify if something has changed and if a GET request needs to be send.
PUT	Stores a representation of a resource (book) on the server. Used to update or create a new resource. If a user issues the same PUT request multiple times, the result should always be the same.
POST	Similar to PUT with the difference that the server is in control of creating resources or initiating actions. A POST is useful for creating new resources (such as a user) or for triggering an action (in our example, create a new book). Issuing the same request multiple times does not produce the same result (that is, the book would be created twice).
DELETE	Deletes the addressed resource (in this case, delete the book).
OPTIONS	Determines the options associated with this resource or the capabilities of the server. (For example, the supported HTTP methods, whether security is enabled, any versions, and so on).

---

[3] www.w3.org/Protocols/rfc2616/rfc2616-sec9.html

Method	Description
TRACE	Intended for testing and debugging purposes. The server should do nothing more than reflect the request data back to the client.

The TRACE and OPTIONS methods aren't actually used in REST but are mentioned here for completeness.

In the previous section, "Identifying Resources," we mentioned how a URL points to a resource. If we combine REST with the resources from Table 7-1, we could actually work with them, as outlined in Table 7-3.

Table 7-3. REST with Resources

URL	Method	Description
http://www.example.com/book	GET	Get a list of books to search.
http://www.example.com/book	PUT	Update a list of books.
http://www.example.com/book	POST	Create a new list of books.
http://www.example.com/book	DELETE	Delete all the books.
http://www.example.com/book/9781430241553	GET	Get a representation of the book with ISBN 978-1-4302-4155-3.
http://www.example.com/book/9781430241553	PUT	Update the book with ISBN 978-1-4302-4155-3.
http://www.example.com/book/9781430241553	POST	Create the book with ISBN 978-1-4302-4155-3.
http://www.example.com/book/9781430241553	DELETE	Delete the book with ISBN 978-1-4302-4155-3.

The list of HTTP methods is larger than most web browsers support. In general, they only support the GET and POST methods, and not the other methods identified. To be able to use the different methods in a classic web application, we need to use a workaround; for this Spring MVC has the HiddenHttpMethodFilter.

HiddenHttpMethodFilter

The org.springframework.web.filter.HiddenHttpMethodFilter will transform a POST request to another specified type of request. It uses a request parameter to determine which method to use for the incoming request. By default it uses a request parameter with the name _method; however, this name can be configured. A POST request can be "transformed" to a PUT or DELETE by making sure the request parameter is there; the request will then be wrapped in a HttpMethodRequestWrapper (which is an inner class for the filter). A GET request is processed as is and will not be transformed into another type of request. This is because a GET request, unlike the other types, has all parameters encoded in the URL. By contrast the POST and PUT requests have them encoded in the request body.

Let's configure the HiddenHttpMethodFilter for our web application. Open com.apress .prospringmvc.bookstore.web.BookstoreWebApplicationInitializer and let's add a method that adds our filter. Listing 7-1 shows the modification needed.

Listing 7-1. BookstoreWebApplicationInitializer with HiddenHttpMethodFilter

```
package com.apress.prospringmvc.bookstore.web;

import java.util.EnumSet;

// javax.servlet imports omitted

import org.springframework.web.WebApplicationInitializer;
import org.springframework.web.filter.HiddenHttpMethodFilter;

public class BookstoreWebApplicationInitializer implements WebApplicationInitializer {

    private static final String DISPATCHER_SERVLET_NAME = "dispatcher";

    @Override
    public void onStartup(ServletContext servletContext) throws ServletException {
        registerListener(servletContext);
        registerDispatcherServlet(servletContext);
        registerHiddenHttpMethodFilter(servletContext);
    }

    private void registerHiddenHttpMethodFilter(ServletContext servletContext) {
        FilterRegistration.Dynamic registration;
        registration = servletContext.addFilter("hiddenHttpMethodFilter",
                            HiddenHttpMethodFilter.class);
        registration.addMappingForServletNames(
                EnumSet.of(DispatcherType.REQUEST, DispatcherType.FORWARD),
                false,
                DISPATCHER_SERVLET_NAME);
    }
    // Other methods omitted
}
```

Now that we have configured the filter, we need to modify our account page. Open up the account.jsp file and make sure there is a hidden field with the name _method and the value PUT. Listing 7-2 shows the start of the page; as you can see, the opening of the form has this hidden field defined.

Listing 7-2. Account.jsp Heading

```
<%@ taglib prefix="c" uri="http://java.sun.com/jsp/jstl/core"%>
<%@ taglib prefix="spring" uri="http://www.springframework.org/tags" %>
<%@ taglib prefix="form" uri="http://www.springframework.org/tags/form" %>

<form:form method="POST" modelAttribute="account" id="accountForm">
    <input type="hidden" name="_method" value="PUT" />
    <fieldset>
        <legend><spring:message code="account.personal"/></legend>

// Remainder of page omitted
```

When the page is submitted, the HiddenHttpMethodFilter will do its work and transform our POST request into a PUT request. The controller was already written with this in mind; see Listing 7-3 for the update method. Here we reused the same method for both POST and PUT, but we could have handled them separately.

Listing 7-3. AccountController Update Method

```
package com.apress.prospringmvc.bookstore.web.controller;

//Imports omitted

@Controller
@RequestMapping("/customer/account")
@SessionAttributes(types = Account.class)
public class AccountController {

    @RequestMapping(method = { RequestMethod.POST, RequestMethod.PUT })
    public String update(@ModelAttribute Account account) {
        this.accountRepository.save(account);
        return "redirect:/customer/account";
    }
    // Other methods omitted
}
```

The use of the filter is still a workaround to make REST possible with browsers and normal forms, which can be useful if we choose to use progressive enhancement or graceful degradation for our website. Progressive enhancement means adding rich behavior to a basic page and first making sure our basic page works as we want it to. Graceful degradation is the other way around—we develop a rich website and try to make sure the whole site still works even if certain features aren't available.

Asynchronous JavaScript and XML (AJAX)

The term AJAX was coined[4] by Jesse James Garrett[5] in 2005. AJAX by itself isn't a technology, it is a collection of technologies working together to create a rich user experience for our web application. AJAX incorporates the following technologies:

- Standards-based presentation by using HTML and CSS

- Dynamic display and interaction by using the Document Object Model (DOM)

- Data interchange and manipulation (using XML or JSON)

- Asynchronous data retrieval using the XMLHttpRequest

- JavaScript to bring all this together

Although the acronym stands for Asynchronous JavaScript and XML, it is often used with JavaScript Object Notation (JSON) to pass data between the client and server.

As AJAX has already been in use for a couple of years, there are quite a lot of JavaScript frameworks out there that make it easier to create a rich user experience. For Spring MVC, it doesn't matter which JavaScript library you choose, and it is beyond the scope of the book to discuss the abundance of JavaScript libraries out there. For our example we use jQuery,[6] as at the moment of writing it is one of the most widely used libraries out there. To be able to use jQuery, we need to load the JavaScript file containing this library. For this we modify the template.jsp file to include jQuery (see Listing 7-4).

Listing 7-4. Modified template.jsp Header

```
<!DOCTYPE HTML>
<%@ taglib prefix="c" uri="http://java.sun.com/jsp/jstl/core"%>
<%@ taglib prefix="spring" uri="http://www.springframework.org/tags" %>
<%@ taglib prefix="tiles" uri="http://tiles.apache.org/tags-tiles" %>

<html>
<head>
    <meta charset="utf-8">
    <c:set var="titleKey">
        <tiles:getAsString name="title" />
    </c:set>
    <title>Bookstore | <spring:message code="${titleKey}" text="Your Home in Books"/></title>
    <link rel="stylesheet" type="text/css" href="<c:url value="/resources/css/style.css"/>" >
    <script src="<c:url value="/resources/jquery/jquery-1.7.1.min.js"/>"></script>
</head>
//Body Omitted
</html>
```

This adds the jQuery JavaScript library to all of our pages; however, by itself it doesn't do much. We still need to add logic to our page. In the next sections we are going to add AJAX behavior to our sample

---

[4] http://www.adaptivepath.com/ideas/ajax-new-approach-web-applications
[5] http://www.jjg.net
[6] http://www.jquery.org

application. We will start with a simple form submit and along the way explore the features that Spring MVC offers to work with AJAX and how it helps us building REST applications.

Adding AJAX to Our Application

Thanks to the flexibility of Spring MVC, it is quite easy to add AJAX behavior to our application and integrate it nicely with Spring MVC. In this section we will see how we can change our form submit into an AJAX-based form submit (with and without the use of JSON). However a form submit isn't the only possible use for AJAX; it merely serves our sample application, it is also quite possible to create auto-completion fields, automatic field/form validation, and so on.

AJAX Form Submit with HTML Result

Let's take a look at our book search page and transform that into a more dynamic web page. We will start by changing the normal form submit into an AJAX form submit. Open the `search.jsp` file and add the script as shown in Listing 7-5 right after the form or at the bottom of the page.

Listing 7-5. Book Search Page with AJAX Form Submit

```
<script>
$('#bookSearchForm').submit(function(evt){
    evt.preventDefault();
    formData = $('#bookSearchForm').serialize();
    $.ajax({
        url: $('#bookSearchForm').action,
        type: 'GET',
        data: formData
    });
});
</script>
```

This script replaces the actual form submit. It first prevents the actual submit from happening, and then builds an AJAX request that will pass the data to the server. If we now redeploy our application, navigate to our book search page, and press Submit, it looks like nothing happens. At least we don't see anything change on the screen. If we debug our application, we can see the request arrive at the server and the search being issued. So why isn't the result being rendered?

At the beginning of this section, we mentioned that AJAX is a collection of technologies, and one of those is asynchronous data retrieval using the `XMLHttpRequest`. This is also where our current problem lies. We send a request to the server but we haven't included anything to handle the response from the server. Listing 7-6 shows the modified script (see the highlighted part) to actually render the returned page.

Listing 7-6. Book Search Page with Success Handler

```
<script>
$('#bookSearchForm').submit(function(evt){
    evt.preventDefault();
    formData = $('#bookSearchForm').serialize();
    $.ajax({
        url: $('#bookSearchForm').action,
        type: 'GET',
        data: formData,
        success: function(html) {
            resultTable = $('#bookSearchResults', html);
            $('#bookSearchResults').html(resultTable);
        }
    });
});
</script>
```

We added the success handler for this script and what it does is render the result we receive from the server. The result is the whole page as it would normally be rendered. We select the table with the results and we replace the current table on screen with the detected table. If the application is redeployed and a search is issued, the page would work again.

AJAX Form Submit with JSON Result

The previous section showed a basic AJAX form submit from which we got back HTML. Although this approach works, it is not very efficient. We send data to the server and we get the full page as we would normally render back. It would be better if we could simply return the data we need to render and process that on the client. For this we need to change a little in our JavaScript but we also need to extend our server side. We need an additional method to return JSON-encoded data to the client (see Listing 7-7).

Listing 7-7. BookSearch Controller with JSON Producing Method

```
package com.apress.prospringmvc.bookstore.web.controller;

import org.springframework.http.MediaType;
import org.springframework.web.bind.annotation.ResponseBody;

// Other imports omitted

@Controller
public class BookSearchController {

    // Other methods omitted

    @RequestMapping(value = "/book/search",
                    method = ( RequestMethod.GET ),
                    produces = MediaType.APPLICATION_JSON_VALUE )
    public @ResponseBody Collection<Book> listJSON(
```

```
    @ModelAttribute("bookSearchCriteria") BookSearchCriteria criteria) {
        return this.bookstoreService.findBooks(criteria);
    }
}
```

The method does the same as the original list method on the same controller; however, there are two important differences, which are highlighted. The first is that this method is invoked whenever an incoming request has specified that it wants to receive JSON (by setting the Accept headers as explained in Chapter 4). Second we use the org.springframework.web.bind.annotation.ResponseBody annotation to instruct Spring MVC to use the returned value as the body of the response (see the section "Supported Method Argument Annotations" in Chapter 5). The returned value is converted by using an org.springframework.httpconverter.HttpMessageConverter.

■ **Tip** Spring MVC automatically registers the org.springframework.http.converter.json .MappingJacksonHttpMessageConverter when the Jackson Java JSON-processor[7] is found on the classpath.

In addition to the controller, we also need to modify our JavaScript a little, to specify that we want to receive JSON from the server. Because we'll receive JSON, we also need to use JSON to replace the content of our result table. In Listing 7-8 you can see the result for the search.jsp file.

Listing 7-8. Book Search Page with JSON Success Handler

```
<script>
$('#bookSearchForm').submit(function(evt){
    evt.preventDefault();
    formData = $('#bookSearchForm').serialize();
    $.ajax({
        url: $('#bookSearchForm').action,
        type: 'GET',
        dataType: 'json',
        data: formData,
        success: function(data) {
            var content = '';
            var books = data;
            var baseDetailUrl = <c:url value="/book/detail/"/>;
            var baseAddCartUrl = <c:url value="/cart/add/" />;
            for (var i = 0; i<books.length; i++) {
                content += '<tr>';
                content += '<td><a href="'
                        + baseDetailUrl + books[i].id+'">'
                        + books[i].title+'</a></td>';
                content += '<td>'+books[i].description+'</td>';
                content += '<td>'+books[i].price+'</td>';
                content += '<td><a href="'+ baseAddCartUrl +books[i].id+'">
```

---

[7] http://jackson.codehaus.org/

```
                         <spring:message code="book.addtocart"/>
                         </a></td></tr>';
                }
            $('#bookSearchResults tbody').html(content);
        }
    });
});
</script>
```

When the application is redeployed and a search is issued, our new method will be invoked and JSON will be returned to the client. The client will use the JSON objects to create a new table body, and when the body is created it will replace the current table body.

Sending and Receiving JSON

It is possible to send JSON to the server as well as to receive JSON from the server. . The advantage of sending JSON is that it is quite compact and therefore faster to send and process (both client and server side) than XML. A drawback can be that you need some hand-coding to prepare the JSON for sending to the server, especially when reusing existing objects (as we can see in our sample).

To make this possible, we need to modify our client-side JavaScript and also make some changes to our request handling method. The controller needs to know that we aren't using a normal model attribute but instead want to use JSON for our BookSearchCriteria. To enable this, we are going to annotate our method argument with RequestBody; it is analogous to ResponseBody, but for incoming requests. Listing 7-9 highlights the changes that need to be made to the controller.

Listing 7-9. BookSearchController with RequestBody Annotation

```
package com.apress.prospringmvc.bookstore.web.controller;

import org.springframework.web.bind.annotation.RequestBody;

//Other imports omitted

@Controller
public class BookSearchController {

// Other methods omitted

@RequestMapping(value = "/book/search",
                method = { RequestMethod.POST },
                produces = MediaType.APPLICATION_JSON_VALUE)
    public @ResponseBody Collection<Book> listJSON(
                                @RequestBody BookSearchCriteria criteria) {
        return this.bookstoreService.findBooks(criteria);
    }
}
```

Notice the change from a GET request to a POST request; this is needed because we are using the RequestBody annotation. As the name of the annotation implies, it operates on the body of a request, but a GET request in general encodes the data in the URL instead of the body.

■ **Note** When using the `RequestBody` and `ResponseBody` annotations, Spring MVC doesn't use the type conversion system to convert from an `id` to an actual object (like our category). That's because in REST, everything to represent/build the resource should be part of the request.

Having modified our controller, we also need to modify our JavaScript again. We need to convert the data from the form into a JSON string that we can send to the server. Listing 7-10 shows what needs to be changed.

Listing 7-10. Book Search Page with JSON Form Submit

```
<script>
$('#bookSearchForm').submit(function(evt){
    evt.preventDefault();
    var title = $('#title').val();
    var category = $('#category').val();
    var json = { "title" : title, "category" : { "id" : category}};

    $.ajax({
        url: $('#bookSearchForm').action,
        type: 'POST',
        dataType: 'json',
        contentType: 'application/json',
        data: JSON.stringify(json),
        success: function(books) {
            var content = '';
            var baseDetailUrl = '<c:url value="/book/detail/"/>';
            var baseAddCartUrl = '<c:url value="/cart/add/" />';
            for (var i = 0; i<books.length; i++) {
                content += '<tr>';
                content += '<td><a href="'+ baseDetailUrl + books[i].id+'">'
                        +books[i].title+'</a></td>';
                content += '<td>'+books[i].description+'</td>';
                content += '<td>'+books[i].price+'</td>';
                content += '<td><a href="'+ baseAddCartUrl +books[i].id+'">
                        <spring:message code="book.addtocart"/>
                        </a></td></tr>';
            }
            $('#bookSearchResults tbody').html(content);
        }
    });
});
</script>
```

The first highlighted block is the conversion of our form data into a JSON object. The second highlighted line is the type. We need to change it to POST. This is needed because the content is the body of the request, and a GET request doesn't have a body but encodes everything into the URL. The last highlighted line is the conversion of the JSON object into a JSON string which can be sent to the server. Everything else remains the same.

If the application is redeployed and we issue a search, the search results will be shown to the user again.

▒ **Note** jQuery has a plugin architecture, and there are a couple of plugins out there that make form-to-JSON conversion easier. We choose not to use a plugin, as that would focus too much on the plugin.

Combining AJAX and REST

We briefly covered REST and we also touched on the subject of AJAX, but we covered each topic separately. However, it is also very easy to combine the two. In the REST section, we changed the account update form into a form that was issued with a PUT request, but this was a simulation using POST. With the JavaScript library we use, it is actually possible to create a real PUT request instead of a POST request that is being used as a PUT request.

To be able to issue and handle PUT requests, we need to do two things: the form must be submitted by AJAX as a PUT request, and we need to prepare the server to be able to handle PUT requests. There are some differences between the POST and PUT requests. A major difference is that a POST request must have the form data available (this is required by the specification), but for the PUT request that is not the case. Spring provides a org.springframework.web.filter.HttpPutFormContentFilter, which can help us here.

The filter kicks in when a PUT request with a content-type of application/x-www-form-urlencoded is detected. It parses the body of the incoming request (delegated to an org.springframework.http .converter.xml.XmlAwareFormHttpMessageConverter), and the result is a map of parameters that can be used just like normal form parameters. Listing 7-11 shows how to register the filter.

Listing 7-11. Register HttpPutFormContentFilter

```
package com.apress.prospringmvc.bookstore.web;

import org.springframework.web.filter.HttpPutFormContentFilter;
// Other imports omitted.

public class BookstoreWebApplicationInitializer implements WebApplicationInitializer {

    private static final String DISPATCHER_SERVLET_NAME = "dispatcher";

    @Override
    public void onStartup(ServletContext servletContext)
    throws ServletException {
        registerListener(servletContext);
        registerDispatcherServlet(servletContext);
        registerHttPutFormContentFilter(servletContext);
        registerHiddenHttpMethodFilter(servletContext);

    }

    private void registerHttPutFormContentFilter(
            ServletContext servletContext) {
        FilterRegistration.Dynamic registration;
```

```
        registration = servletContext.addFilter(
                        "httpPutFormContentFilter",
                        HttpPutFormContentFilter.class);
        registration.addMappingForServletNames(
            EnumSet.of(DispatcherType.REQUEST, DispatcherType.FORWARD),
            false,
            DISPATCHER_SERVLET_NAME);
    }
    // Other methods omitted
}
```

Next we also need to add some JavaScript to our `account.jsp` file. It is quite similar to the script we first added to our book search page, with one major difference—we now use a PUT instead of a GET. See Listing 7-12 for the JavaScript that is added right after the form or at the end of the page. The controller method (see Listing 7-3) remains the same, as it still is a PUT request for the controller.

Listing 7-12. Account Page PUT Ajax Form Submit

```
<script>
$('#accountForm').submit(function(evt){
    evt.preventDefault();
    formData = $('#accountForm').serialize();
    $.ajax({
        url: $('#accountForm').action,
        type: 'PUT',
        data: formData
    });
});
</script>
```

Progressive Enhancement

The way we have been applying the AJAX features is a technique called *progressive enhancement*. It means that one builds a simple web page that functions as is, and then add dynamic and rich behavior to the page with JavaScript.

The opposite approach is also possible; this technique is called *graceful degradation*, which means that we start with a page with all the behavior we want and depending on the features offered by the browser we scale down on the rich behavior used.

The trend nowadays is to use progressive enhancement because, in general, it is easier to build and maintain. It also has the advantage that we can enhance based on the capabilities of the device that connects to our application (an iPhone has different features than a Windows 7 PC with Internet Explorer 9).

Handling File Uploads

HTTP file uploading or form based file upload in HTML is defined RFC 1867.[8] After adding an HTML input field with type file to the form and setting the encoding to multipart/form-data, the browser can send text and/or binary files to the server as part of a POST request.

To be able to handle file uploads we first need to register an org.springframework.web.multipart .MultipartResolver. Out of the box, Spring provides two ways of handling file uploads. The first is the multipart support as described in the Servlet 3.0 specification, and the second is by using the features offered by the Commons FileUpload[9] project from Apache.

The Spring Framework provides two implementations: the org.springframework.web.multipart .support.StandardServletMultipartResolver and the org.springframework.web.multipart.commons.CommonsMultipartResolver. The first implementation can only be used in a Servlet 3.0 environment with multipart enabled on the servlet, and the second uses commons-fileupload.

For the actual handling of file uploads we need to modify the controller. These modifications are mostly independent from the file uploading technology used. Spring provides several abstractions to handle file uploads. We can write a request-handling method that takes an argument of the type org.springframework.web.multipart.MultipartFile (or collection); we could also use a org.springframework.web.multipart.MultipartHttpServletRequest and retrieve the files ourselves. When we are in a Servlet 3.0 environment and also use the multipart parsing support, we can also use the javax.servlet.http.Part interface to get the file.

The final way to indicate to do something with a file upload is to annotate the method argument with org.springframework.web.bind.annotation.RequestPart (see Chapter 4). When put on anything else as described above, Spring uses the type conversion system to transform the content of the file.

We will first discuss the configuration for the two different strategies. After that, we will look at how to handle file uploads inside a controller.

Configuration

The first step in enabling file uploads is to configure our environment. As Spring provides two different technologies out of the box, each of these requires a different set of configuration items. We will look at the Servlet 3.0 multipart support and afterward at commons-fileupload.

Which one to choose depends on the requirements. If the application is strictly to run in a Servlet 3.0 environment, use the standard multipart support as specified by the Servlet specification. If the application needs to run in older containers also, choose the commons-fileupload support.

---

[8] http://www.ietf.org/rfc/rfc1867.txt
[9] http://commons.apache.org/fileupload/

Configuring Servlet 3.0 File Uploading

The first step in multipart parsing on the org.springframework.web.servlet.DispatcherServlet we need to add, depending on our configuration, a multipart-config section to XML configuration or include a javax.servlet.MultipartConfigElement in our org.springframework.web.WebApplicationInitializer implementation (see Listing 7-13).

Listing 7-13. BookstoreWebApplicationInitializer with MultipartConfigElement

```java
package com.apress.prospringmvc.bookstore.web;

import javax.servlet.MultipartConfigElement;

//Other imports omitted

public class BookstoreWebApplicationInitializer implements WebApplicationInitializer {

    private static final String DISPATCHER_SERVLET_NAME = "dispatcher";

    private static final long MAX_FILE_UPLOAD_SIZE = 1024 * 1024 * 5;
    private static final int FILE_SIZE_THRESHOLD = 1024 * 1024;
    private static final long MAX_REQUEST_SIZE = -1L;

    private void registerDispatcherServlet(ServletContext servletContext) {
        AnnotationConfigWebApplicationContext dispatcherContext;
        dispatcherContext = createContext(WebMvcContextConfiguration.class);
        ServletRegistration.Dynamic dispatcher;
        dispatcher = servletContext.addServlet(DISPATCHER_SERVLET_NAME,
                new DispatcherServlet(dispatcherContext));
        dispatcher.setLoadOnStartup(1);
        dispatcher.addMapping("/");

        dispatcher.setMultipartConfig(
            new MultipartConfigElement(null,
              MAX_FILE_UPLOAD_SIZE, MAX_REQUEST_SIZE, FILE_SIZE_THRESHOLD));
    }
    // Other methods omitted
}
```

When the servlet is configured for multipart parsing, we then need to add the StandardServletMultipartResolver to our configuration (Listing 7-14). There is no more configuration to be done for the multipart resolver; that is already done with the MultipartConfigElement.

Listing 7-14. WebMvcContextConfiguration with StandardServletMultipartResolver

```
package com.apress.prospringmvc.bookstore.web.config;


import org.springframework.web.multipart.MultipartResolver;
import org.springframework.web.multipart.support.StandardServletMultipartResolver;

// Other imports omitted

@Configuration
@EnableWebMvc
@ComponentScan(basePackages = { "com.apress.prospringmvc.bookstore.web" })
public class WebMvcContextConfiguration extends WebMvcConfigurerAdapter {

    // Other methods omitted

    @Bean
    public MultipartResolver multipartResolver() {
        return new StandardServletMultipartResolver();
    }
}
```

Configuring Apache Commons File Uploading

In older servlet containers or for a more portable way of file uploading, we can use the commons file upload support in Spring MVC. This requires only the registration of a CommonsMultipartResolver to enable file uploads (Listing 7-15). We don't have the multipart parsing on the servlet anymore, and so we need to do configuration for max file size and the like on the multipart resolver.

Listing 7-15. WebMvcContextConfiguration with a CommonsMultipartResolver

```
package com.apress.prospringmvc.bookstore.web.config;

import org.springframework.web.multipart.MultipartResolver;
import org.springframework.web.multipart.commons.CommonsMultipartResolver;

// Other imports omitted

@Configuration
@EnableWebMvc
@ComponentScan(basePackages = { "com.apress.prospringmvc.bookstore.web" })
public class WebMvcContextConfiguration extends WebMvcConfigurerAdapter {

    private static final long MAX_FILE_UPLOAD_SIZE = 1024 * 1024 * 5; //5 Mb file limit
    private static final int FILE_SIZE_THRESHOLD = 1024 * 1024; // After 1Mb start↵
writing files to disk

    // Other methods omitted
```

```
    @Bean
    public MultipartResolver multipartResolver() {
        CommonsMultipartResolver multipartResolver = new CommonsMultipartResolver();
        multipartResolver.setMaxInMemorySize(FILE_SIZE_THRESHOLD);
        multipartResolver.setMaxUploadSize(MAX_FILE_UPLOAD_SIZE);
        return multipartResolver;
    }
}
```

Request Handling Method for File Upload

In addition to configuring the upload, we also need a page with a form that can submit a file. For this we need to create a form that has its encoding set to multipart/form-data (Listing 7-16). This form doesn't change if we change the different techniques available; it is only the way the uploads are handled that changes. When adding an input element with the type file, it is important to give it a name, especially if we do a single file upload. This name is also needed to retrieve the file from the request.

Listing 7-16. Upload Order Form for Account Page

```
<form id="orderForm" action="<c:url value="/order/upload"/>" method="POST"↵
 enctype="multipart/form-data">
    <fieldset>
        <legend>Upload order</legend>
        <input type="file" placeholder="Select File" id="order" name="order"/>
        <button id="upload"><spring:message code="button.upload"/></button>
    </fieldset>
</form>
```

We add this form to the account.jsp file right after the already existing form. When we now render the account page, it will look like Figure 7-1.

Figure 7-1. Account Page with File Upload

In the following sections we will explore the different ways of handling file uploads in a controller. Most of the methods are portable between the two different file upload technologies; however, the last one is only available when using the Servlet 3.0 multipart support. Each of the different request handling methods has the same output when a file is uploaded; it will print the name of the uploaded file and the size of the file, as shown in Figure 7-2.

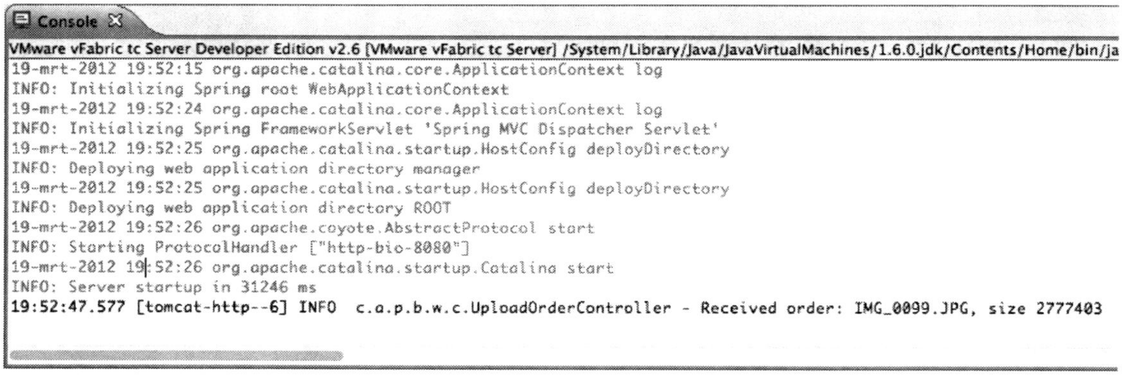

Figure 7-2. Sample File Upload Output

Writing a Request Handling Method with Multipart File

When writing a request handling method, if we want to do file upload and use the multipart file abstraction from Spring, we need to create a method, annotate it, and make sure it has a `MultipartFile` as a method argument. When there are multiple files uploaded with the same name, we can also receive a collection of files instead of a single element. Listing 7-17 shows a controller with a method that can handle file uploads using this technique.

Listing 7-17. UploadOrderController with MultipartFile

```
package com.apress.prospringmvc.bookstore.web.controller;

// Other imports omitted
import org.springframework.web.multipart.MultipartFile;

@Controller
public class UploadOrderController {

    private Logger logger;
    logger = LoggerFactory.getLogger(UploadOrderController.class);

    @RequestMapping(value = "/order/upload", method = RequestMethod.POST)
    public String handleUpload(MultipartFile order) {
        logFile(order.getOriginalFilename(), order.getSize());
        return "redirect:/customer/account";
    }

    private void logFile(String name, long size) {
        this.logger.info("Received order: {}, size {}", name, size);
    }
}
```

Using MultipartHttpServletRequest to Handle File Uploads

Instead of accessing the file(s) directly, it is also possible to use `MultipartHttpServletRequest` to get access to the multipart files (Listing 7-18). This interface defines some methods to get access to the files. The methods that are exposed to get access to the multipart files are defined in the super interface `org.springframework.web.multipart.MultipartRequest`.

Listing 7-18. UploadOrderController with MultipartHttpServletRequest

```
package com.apress.prospringmvc.bookstore.web.controller;

// Other imports omitted
import org.springframework.web.multipart.MultipartFile;
import org.springframework.web.multipart.MultipartHttpServletRequest;

@Controller
public class UploadOrderController {

    private Logger logger;
    logger = LoggerFactory.getLogger(UploadOrderController.class);

    @RequestMapping(value = "/order/upload", method = RequestMethod.POST)
    public String handleUpload(MultipartHttpServletRequest request) {
        Map<String, MultipartFile> files = request.getFileMap();
        for (MultipartFile file : files.values()) {
            logFile(file.getOriginalFilename(), file.getSize());
        }
        return "redirect:/customer/account";
    }

    private void logFile(String name, long size) {
        this.logger.info("Received order: {}, size {}", name, size);
    }
}
```

Using a Form Object to Handle Upload

Instead of handling the upload directly, we could also make it part of a form object (model attribute). This can be convenient if the upload is part of a form that includes more fields (like our customer account page, which includes a picture). To be able to do this we need to create a class that can be used as the form object, with an attribute of type `MultipartFile` (Listing 7-19).

Listing 7-19. UploadOrderForm

```
package com.apress.prospringmvc.bookstore.web;

import org.springframework.web.multipart.MultipartFile;

public class UploadOrderForm {
```

```
    private MultipartFile order;

    public MultipartFile getOrder() {
        return this.order;
    }

    public void setOrder(final MultipartFile order) {
        this.order = order;
    }
}
```

We need to modify the controller to take the form as a method argument (see Listing 7-20).

Listing 7-20. *UploadOrderController with UploadOrderForm*

```
package com.apress.prospringmvc.bookstore.web.controller;

// Other imports omitted
import com.apress.prospringmvc.bookstore.web.UploadOrderForm;

@Controller
public class UploadOrderController {

    private Logger logger;
    logger = LoggerFactory.getLogger(UploadOrderController.class);

    @RequestMapping(value = "/order/upload", method = RequestMethod.POST)
    public String handleUpload(UploadOrderForm form) {
        logFile(form.getOrder().getOriginalFilename(), form.getOrder().getSize());
        return "redirect:/customer/account";
    }

    private void logFile(String name, long size) {
        this.logger.info("Received order: {}, size {}", name, size);
    }
}
```

Writing a Request Handling Method Using Servlet 3.0

In a strict Servlet 3.0 environment, we can use the standard interface javax.servlet.http.Part to get access to the uploaded file. We simply create a method that takes the Part as an argument (see Listing 7-21) We need to create a method, annotate it, and give it a method argument. This technique only works in a Servlet 3.0 environment and is in that regard less portable than using the MultipartFile argument.

Listing 7-21. *UploadOrderController with Part*

```
package com.apress.prospringmvc.bookstore.web.controller;

// Other imports omitted
import javax.servlet.http.Part;
```

```
@Controller
public class UploadOrderController {

    private Logger logger;
    logger = LoggerFactory.getLogger(UploadOrderController.class);

    @RequestMapping(value = "/order/upload", method = RequestMethod.POST)
    public String handleUpload(final Part order) {
        logFile(order.getName(), order.getSize());
        return "redirect:/customer/account";
    }

    private void logFile(String name, long size) {
        this.logger.info("Received order: {}, size {}", name, size);
    }
}
```

Exception Handling

Uploading a file can also fail. The file could be too large to handle (larger than the configured maximum file size), or our disks could be full. There are many reasons it might fail. If possible, we want to handle the errors and show a nice error page to the users. We can use the exception handling (as explained in Chapter 6) to handle the exception for us and show a nice error page. When an exception occurs, the multipart support will throw an `org.springframework.web.multipart.MultipartException`, and we can use this exception to show an error page.

▪ **Note** The `CommonsMultipartResolver` throws a more specific `MaxUploadSizeExceededException` in this particular case, else it will throw a `MultipartException`.

Summary

This chapter covered Representation State Transfer (REST), as explained by Roy Thomas Fielding, and you saw how we can configure Spring MVC to facilitate the different methods as used by REST. We discussed the configuration of the `HiddenHttpMethodFilter` and the use-case for this filter.

Next we briefly explained Asynchronous JavaScript and XML (AJAX) and how we can use that on the client and have controllers react to those requests. Although AJAX was originally about XML, nowadays it is about JSON; and we explored the JSON features offered by Spring MVC by using the `RequestBody` and `ResponseBody` annotation.

It is also very useful to combine AJAX and REST and it allows for creating a REST-based API for our application. However to allow for easy processing of PUT requests we need to configure the `HttpPutFormContentFilter`, which makes the PUT body content available as request parameters.

The final part of this chapter looked at uploading files to our application. For this purpose we looked at the configuration needed for Servlet 3.0 multipart support and commons-fileupload support and then explored the different ways of writing a controller that can handle file uploads.

CHAPTER 8

Resolving and Implementing Views

So far we have mainly used Java Server Pages (JSP) as our view technology; however, Spring MVC provides a very powerful and flexible mechanism to resolve and implement views. We looked briefly at the view resolving mechanism in Chapter 4; in this chapter we will take a closer look at the different ViewResolver implementations and see how we can create and use our own implementation.

We will also see which view technologies are supported by Spring MVC out-of-the-box, and we will create some custom implementations. Before we dive into the internals, however, let's recap the view rendering process and API.

View Resolvers and Views   *PAGE 71-72*   *? PAGE 103~104*

In Chapter 4 we discussed the request processing workflow of the dispatcher servlet. Resolving and rendering a view is part of that process. In Figure 8-1 you can see the view rendering process (see the section "Render View" in Chapter 4 for a description).

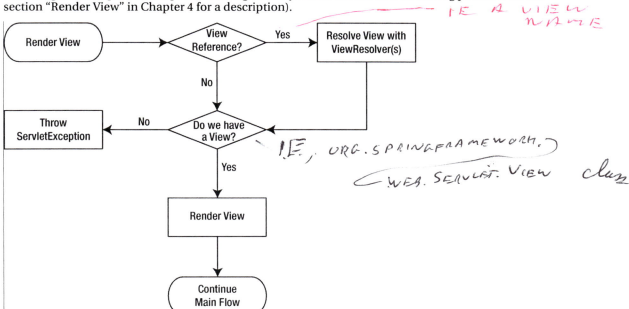

IE A VIEW NAME

I.E., ORG.SPRINGFRAMEWORK. WEB.SERVLET.VIEW class

Figure 8-1. View rendering process

The controller can return an `org.springframework.web.servlet.View` implementation or a reference to a view (view name). In the latter case the `ViewResolvers` configured are consulted to translate the reference into a concrete implementation. When an implementation is available it will be instructed to render; otherwise, a `javax.servlet.ServletException` is thrown.

The `ViewResolver` (see Listing 8-1) has only a single method that is used to resolve to a `View`.

Listing 8-1. *ViewResolver API*

```
package org.springframework.web.servlet;

import java.util.Locale;

public interface ViewResolver {

    View resolveViewName(String viewName, Locale locale) throws Exception;

}
```

When a view has been selected, the dispatcher servlet will call the render method (see Listing 8-2) on the view instance. The getContentType method is used to determine the type of content. This value is used to set the content type on the response; it is also used by the `org.springframework.web.servlet` `.view.ContentNegotiatingViewResolver` to determine the best matching view (see the upcoming section about this view resolver for more information).

Listing 8-2. *View API*

```
package org.springframework.web.servlet;

import java.util.Map;

import javax.servlet.http.HttpServletRequest;
import javax.servlet.http.HttpServletResponse;

public interface View {

    String getContentType();

    void render(Map<String, ?> model,
            HttpServletRequest request,
            HttpServletResponse response) throws Exception;

}
```

View Resolvers

In Chapter 4 we showed the hierarchy for the different `ViewResolver` implementations. Let's take a closer look at the generic usable implementations, how they work, and how they can be configured. Figure 8-2 shows the different implementations again. The implementations specific to particular view technologies are explained in the "View Technologies" section. [

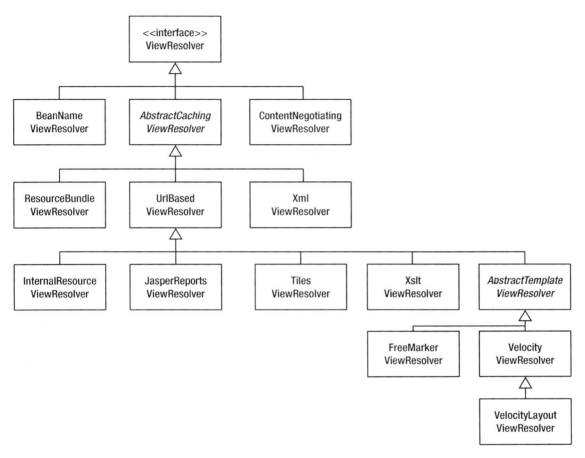

Figure 8-2. *ViewResolver hierarchy*

BeanNameViewResolver

The `org.springframework.web.servlet.view.BeanNameViewResolver` is the most basic implementation available and one of the default ones configured. It takes the name of the view and looks in the `org.springframework.context.ApplicationContext` to see if there is a `View` with that name. If there is, the resolver will return it; otherwise, it returns `null`. This view resolver is useful in small(er) applications; however, it has one big drawback in that each view needs to be configured in the application context. It has a single property that can be configured, and that is the order in which it is being called (see Table 8-1).

Table 8-1. BeanNameViewResolver Properties

Property	Purpose
order	The order in which this view resolver is called in the chain, the higher the number the lower the order in the chain.

In Listing 8-3, you can see how and what we would need to configure to have our index page served and resolved by this view resolver. We have explicitly configured the BeanNameViewResolver; this is only needed if the defaults of the dispatcher servlet don't suffice. We also need to add a View instance, and as we are using a JSP with JSTL support, we are returning an org.springframework.web.servlet.view .JstlView.

Listing 8-3. BeanNameViewResolver configuration

```
package com.apress.prospringmvc.bookstore.web.config;

// Other imports omitted
import org.springframework.web.servlet.view.BeanNameViewResolver;
import org.springframework.web.servlet.view.JstlView;

@Configuration
public class ViewConfiguration {

    @Bean
    public ViewResolver viewResolver() {
        BeanNameViewResolver viewResolver = new BeanNameViewResolver();
        viewResolver.setOrder(1);
        return viewResolver;
    }

    @Bean
    public View index() {
        JstlView view = new JstlView();
        view.setUrl("/WEB-INF/views/index.jsp");
        return view;
    }
}
```

XmlViewResolver

The org.springframework.web.servlet.view.XmlViewResolver is very similar to the BeanNameViewResolver with the difference that it requires an additional Spring XML configuration file to hold all the views. By default it will load the file named /WEB-INF/views.xml; however, this can be configured. Table 8-2 shows the available properties.

Table 8-2. XmlViewResolver Properties

Property	Purpose
location	The location of the XML file defining the view beans. Defaults to /WEB-INF/views.xml.
order	The order in which this view resolver is called in the chain. The higher the number, the lower the order in the chain.

Listing 8-4 shows the configuration for the XmlViewResolver. Listing 8-5 shows the /WEB-INF/views.xml file used to configure the view for the index page.

Listing 8-4. XmlViewResolver configuration

```
package com.apress.prospringmvc.bookstore.web.config;

//Other imports omitted
import org.springframework.web.servlet.view.XmlViewResolver;

@Configuration
public class ViewConfiguration {

    @Bean
    public ViewResolver viewResolver() {
        XmlViewResolver viewResolver = new XmlViewResolver();
        viewResolver.setOrder(1);
        return viewResolver;
    }
}
```

Listing 8-5. Sample views.xml

```
<?xml version="1.0" encoding="UTF-8"?>
<beans xmlns="http://www.springframework.org/schema/beans"
    xmlns:xsi="http://www.w3.org/2001/XMLSchema-instance"
    xsi:schemaLocation="http://www.springframework.org/schema/beans
        http://www.springframework.org/schema/beans/spring-beans.xsd">

    <bean id="index" class="org.springframework.web.servlet.view.JstlView">
        <property name="url" value="/WEB-INF/views/index.jsp"/>
    </bean>
</beans>
```

ResourceBundleViewResolver

Very similar to the XmlViewResolver, this implementation uses a properties file instead of an XML file to hold the view configuration. The advantage of the org.springframework.web.servlet.view.ResourceBundleViewResolver is that we could have different views for different languages. This is

241

because it uses the standard resource bundle mechanism in Java to load the configuration files. Table 8-3 lists the properties for this implementation.

Table 8-3. *ResourceBundleViewResolver Properties*

Property	Purpose
basename basenames	The location of the resource bundles defining the view beans. Defaults to views.properties on the classpath.
cache	If a view is resolved, should it be cached for a faster lookup in the future? The default is true.
cacheUnresolved	Should unresolved views be cached? That is, if a view has resolved to null, should it be put into the cache? The default is true.
defaultParentView	Specifies the name of the default parent view. Can be used to configure shared properties and have them applied automatically.
localesToInitialize	The locales to initialize on startup. By default this is null, allowing for lazy initialization of views.
order	The order in which this view resolver is called in the chain. The higher the number, the lower the order in the chain.

Listing 8-6 shows the sample configuration for the ResourceBundleViewResolver. In Listing 8-7, we see the views.properties file in use.

Listing 8-6. *ResourceBundleViewResolver configuration*

```
package com.apress.prospringmvc.bookstore.web.config;

// Other imports omitted
import org.springframework.web.servlet.view.ResourceBundleViewResolver;

@Configuration
public class ViewConfiguration {

    @Bean
    public ViewResolver viewResolver() {
        ResourceBunldeViewResolver viewResolver;
        viewResolver = new ResourceBundleViewResolver();
        viewResolver.setOrder(1);
        return viewResolver;
    }
}
```

Listing 8-7. Sample views.properties

```
index.(class)=org.springframework.web.servlet.view.JstlView
index.url=/WEB-INF/views/index.jsp
```

UrlBasedViewResolver

The `org.springframework.web.servlet.view.UrlBasedViewResolver` expects the view name to map directly to a URL. It can optionally modify the URL by adding a prefix and/or suffix to the view name. In general this class serves as a base class to the different view technologies like JSP and template-based view technologies (see section "View Technologies" later in this chapter). In Table 8-4 we can see the properties for this type of view resolver.

Table 8-4. UrlBasedViewResolver Properties

Property	Purpose
attributes	Sets some static attributes to be included in each view resolved by this view resolver.
attributesMap	Displays attributes. This allows you to set them in a map.
cache	If a view is resolved, should it be cached for a faster lookup in the future? The default is `true`.
cacheUnresolved	Should unresolved views be cached? That is, if a view has resolved to null, should it be put into the cache? The default is `true`.
contentType	Sets the content type[1] (`text/html`, `application/json` and so on) for all views resolved by this view resolver, except for view implementations that determine or return the content-type themselves and ignore this property (like JSPs).
exposePathVariables	Should the path variables (see Chapter 5) be added to the model or not? In general the views decide for themselves; setting this property can override that behavior.
order	The order in which this view resolver is called in the chain. The higher the number, the lower the order in the chain.
prefix	The prefix to add to the view name to generate a URL.

[1] `http://www.iana.org/assignments/media-types/index.html`

Property	Purpose
redirectContextRelative	Should a redirect URL starting with a / be interpreted as relative to the servlet context or not? The default is true. When this property is set to false, the URL will be resolved relative to the current URL.
redirectHttp10Compatible	Should the redirect be HTTP 1.0 compatible? When true, an HTTP status code 302 is used to issue a redirect; otherwise, an HTTP status code 303 is used to redirect.
requestContextAttribute	Sets the name of the org.springframework.web.servlet.support .RequestContext attribute for all views. The default is null, which means you are not exposing the RequestContext. Exposing a RequestContext can be useful when using standard JSP tags like useBean or for technologies that don't have access to the request, like Velocity.
suffix	The suffix to add to the view name to generate a URL.
viewClass	The type of view to create; this needs to be a subclass of org.springframework.web.servlet.view.AbstractUrlBasedView. This property is required.
viewNames	The names of the views that can be handled by this view resolver. Names can include the * wildcard for matching names. The default is null, indicating to resolve all views.

In Listing 8-8 we see a sample configuration for this view resolver. We need to specify the view class (required,) and in general it is also necessary to add a prefix and/or suffix to generate a URL pointing to the actual view implementation. The advantage is that we can use a naming convention for our views and we don't have to specify our views explicitly in the configuration (as we did with the BeanNameViewResolver, for instance).

Listing 8-8. UrlBasedViewResolver configuration

```
package com.apress.prospringmvc.bookstore.web.config;

// Other imports omitted
import org.springframework.web.servlet.view.JstlView;
import org.springframework.web.servlet.view.UrlBasedViewResolver;

@Configuration
public class ViewConfiguration {

    @Bean
    public ViewResolver viewResolver() {
        UrlBasedViewResolver viewResolver = new UrlBasedViewResolver();
        viewResolver.setOrder(1);
        viewResolver.setPrefix("/WEB-INF/views/");
        viewResolver.setSuffix(".jsp");
```

```
        viewResolver.setViewClass(JstlView.class);
        return viewResolver;
    }
}
```

InternalResourceViewResolver

This extension of the `UrlBasedViewResolver` is a convenience subclass that preconfigures the view class and adds some additional support to include beans in the model so that they are available in the view for rendering. Listing 8-9 shows a sample configuration for the `org.springframework.web.servlet.view` `.InternalResourceViewResolver`. The result is essentially the same as in Listing 8-8.

Listing 8-9. InternalResourceViewResolver configuration

```
package com.apress.prospringmvc.bookstore.web.config;

// Other imports omitted
import org.springframework.web.servlet.view.InternalResourceViewResolver;

@Configuration
public class ViewConfiguration {

    @Bean
    public ViewResolver viewResolver() {
        InternalResourceViewResolver viewResolver;
        viewResolver = new InternalResourceViewResolver();
        viewResolver.setOrder(1);
        viewResolver.setPrefix("/WEB-INF/views/");
        viewResolver.setSuffix(".jsp");
        return viewResolver;
    }
}
```

XsltViewResolver

The `org.springframework.web.servlet.web.view.xslt.XsltViewResolver` can be used to resolve the view name to an XSLT stylesheet to transform the model into something to show to the user. To work with this view resolver and views we need an XSLT template for transforming our model to a view. The returned view, an instance of `org.springframework.web.servlet.view.xslt.XsltView`, will detect which model object to render. It supports the following types:

- `javax.xml.transform.Source`

- `org.w3c.dom.Document`

- `org.w3c.dom.Node`

- `java.io.Reader`

- `java.io.InputStream`

- `org.springframework.core.io.Resource`

The `org.springframework.web.servlet.view.xslt.XsltView` will take the supported type and use the XSLT stylesheet to transform it into what we want it to be. Although this mechanism can be powerful, it is the author's belief that this isn't something to be used to create a view layer for a web application. It in general is easier to return XML (or JSON) from the controller and directly process that on the client with JavaScript.

ContentNegotiatingViewResolver

The `org.springframework.web.servlet.view.ContentNegotiatingViewResolver` is a very special view resolver: it can resolve views by name and content-type. It works by first determining which content-type is requested, which it does by checking the file extension, checking the Accept header, or checking a request parameter (this is configurable; see Table 8-5). After the content-type is determined, the resolver consults all configured view resolvers to collect the candidate views by name. Finally, it selects the best matching view by checking if the requested content-type is supported. Table 8-5 shows the configurable properties of the view resolver.

Table 8-5. *ContentNegotiatingViewResolver Properties*

Property	Purpose
defaultContentType	Sets the default content-type to use when it cannot be determined. The default is `null`.
defaultViews	Sets the default views to consult. Used when no specific view can be found. Very useful when using a marshaling view or to return JSON.
favorParameter	Should we favor the request parameter over the Accept header to determine the content type? The default is `false`.
favorPathExtension	Should we favor the path extension over the Accept header to determine the content type? The default is `true`.
ignoreAcceptHeader	Should we ignore the Accept header and use either the path extension or the request parameter to determine the content-type?. The default is `false`.
mediaTypes	Configures the media types to content-type mapping. This property is optional; when not specified it will fall back to the Java Activation Framework (JAF) (if available) to determine filetypes.
parameterName	The name of the request parameter to check for the content-type. The default is `format`.
useJaf	Should we use the Java Activation Framework? The default is detected `true` if JAF is available.
useNotAcceptableStatusCode	When no suitable view can be found, should we send a HTTP response code of 406 to the client? The default is `false`.

Property	Purpose
viewResolvers	List of view resolvers to consult. By default it detects all view resolvers in the application context.

■ **Note** When multiple view resolvers are used, the ContentNegotiatingViewResolver must have the highest order to function correctly. This is already set by default, but if you change the order keep this in mind.

Implementing Your Own ViewResolver

This section explains how to implement our own view resolver. We will create a simple implementation that resolves the view name from a map of configured views.

Implementing your own view is quite easy to do; you just create a class and let it implement the ViewResolver interface (see Listing 8-1) and provide the necessary implementation. Listing 8-10 shows our com.apress.prospringmvc.bookstore.web.view.SimpleConfigurableViewResolver.

Listing 8-10. SimpleConfigurableViewResolver

```
package com.apress.prospringmvc.bookstore.web.view;

// Other imports omitted
import org.springframework.web.servlet.View;
import org.springframework.web.servlet.ViewResolver;

public class SimpleConfigurableViewResolver implements ViewResolver {

    private Map<String, ? extends View> views = new HashMap<String, View>();

    @Override
    public View resolveViewName(String viewName, Locale locale)
    throws Exception {
        return this.views.get(viewName);
    }

    public void setViews(Map<String, ? extends View> views) {
        this.views = views;
    }
}
```

(handwritten annotations: table with columns "VIEW NAME" and "VIEW CLASS"; "// LOOKUP VIEW CLASS BASED ON VIEW NAME"; "// ESTABLISH THE MAPPING")

We are going to use this implementation in the next section when we need to add views for PDF and Excel.

View Technologies

Spring MVC supports many different technologies, and if there isn't support, you can probably add it yourself by implementing org.springframework.web.servlet.View or by extending one of the provided View classes. In this section we will discuss several view technologies and see how Spring MVC supports them. For some there is extensive support; for others very little. Figure 8-3 shows the View class hierarchy, where we can see some of the supported view technologies. For some of the technologies we need to specify a specific a ViewResolver to work, others work hand-in-hand with the already configured view resolvers.

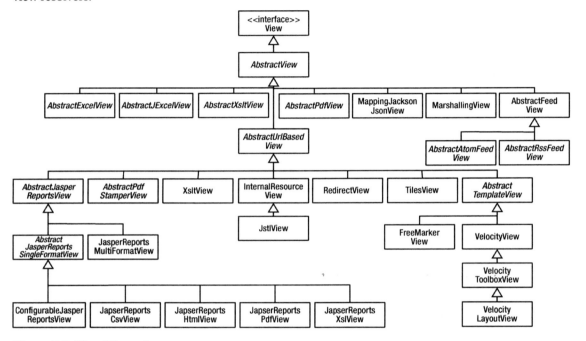

Figure 8-3. *View Hierarchy*

The next part of this section briefly covers some of the supported view technologies. It will show the support classes and how to set up Spring to work with the specified technology. It does not provide in-depth coverage of all the different supported view technologies; there are books available for most of the technologies mentioned here.

■ **Note** The TilesViewResolver has order 2 in most listings in this section. This is to make sure it is executed at the right moment, especially when using the ContentNegotiatingViewResolver, which should execute before (which is the default) the TilesViewResolver.

Java Server Pages

Until now we have been using Java Server Pages for our application. Spring has excellent support for it, including its own tag library (see Chapters 5 and 6). Spring has support and integration classes and in general it is the tool used with the `org.springframework.web.servlet.view` `.InternalResourceViewResolver` to enable JSTL support and integrate with the default formatting and functions library from Sun.

JavaServer Faces

JavaServer Faces (JSF) has very little support in Spring MVC in general. If you want to use JSF, it is suggested to use Spring Web Flow with JSF as the view layer; that approach provides for a rich environment. The Spring support for JSF is simply that we can reuse our beans from the application context. We do this by defining a customized `javax.faces.el.VariableResolver` (JSF 1.1) or `javax.el.ELResolver` (JSF 1.2+) to gain access to the spring beans in the JSF environment.

The easiest way to integrate Spring into a JSF environment is by configuring `org.springframework.web.jsf.DelegatingVariableResolver`, which will do lookups on the default resolver of the JSF implementation used. If a name cannot be resolved, the resolver will then delegate to the look up to the root application context. This allows for reuse of services and other general components within JSF. Listing 8-11 shows the configuration for the JSF part of the application. This can be found in `faces-context.xml`.

Listing 8-11. DelegatingVariableResolver sample configuration (faces-context.xml)

```
<faces-config>
    <application>
        <variable-resolver>
        org.springframework.web.jsf.DelegatingVariableResolver
        </variable-resolver>
    </application>
</faces-config>
```

There is also the `org.springframework.web.jsf.SpringBeanVariableResolver`, which works in a similar way; however, it first consults the root application context and afterwards the default resolver of the JSF implementation. This is useful when using scoped beans from the application context in JSF.

For a JSF 1.2+ environment, we could also configure the `org.springframework.web.jsf.el` `.SpringBeanFacesELResolver`, which does a lookup first in the root application context and then in the default resolver from the used JSF implementation. Listing 8-12 shows a sample configuration for this bean.

Listing 8-12. SpringBeanFacesELResolver sample configuration (faces-context.xml)

```
<faces-config>
    <application>
        <el-resolver>
        org.springframework.web.jsf.el.SpringBeanFacesELResolver
        </el-resolver>
    </application>
</faces-config>
```

If we have some custom JSF components and need access to the current application context, we can use org.springframework.web.jsf.FacesContextUtils. This utility class provides two convenience methods to gain access to the application context and retrieve beans from it, which in turn can be used from the custom component.

Tiles

Apache Tiles[2] is a powerful page composition framework that allows you to compose your page of different page components (the *tiles*). These page components can be reused and configured in different page layouts. Originally it was designed as a JSP composition framework; however, it can also be used to compose Velocity and Freemarker-based views.

To get started with Tiles we must configure and bootstrap the engine for it. Next we also need to configure the view resolver to be able to return Tiles-based views, and finally we need to specify our page composition and add the different templates (tiles).

There is the org.springframework.web.servlet.view.tiles2.TilesConfigurer that we need to add to our configuration. Next to that we need the special org.springframework.web.servlet.view.tiles2 .TilesViewResolver. Finally, we also need to specify our page compositions and add the templates.

Configuring Tiles

Before we can start using the tiles support we need to bootstrap Tiles. For this Spring provides the org.springframework.web.servlet.view.tiles2.TilesConfigurer class. Next we also need to configure a view resolver to work with tiles for this we can use org.springframework.web.servlet.view.tiles2 .TilesViewResolver. Listing 8-13 shows the most basic configuration for tiles.

Listing 8-13. ViewConfiguration for Tiles

```
package com.apress.prospringmvc.bookstore.web.config;

// Other imports omitted
import org.springframework.web.servlet.view.tiles2.TilesConfigurer;
import org.springframework.web.servlet.view.tiles2.TilesViewResolver;

@Configuration
public class ViewConfiguration {

    @Bean
    public TilesConfigurer tilesConfigurer() {
        return new TilesConfigurer();
    }

    @Bean
    public TilesViewResolver tilesViewResolver() {
        TilesViewResolver tilesViewResolver = new TilesViewResolver();
        tilesViewResolver.setOrder(2);
        return tilesViewResolver;
```

---

[2] http://tiles.apache.org/

```
    }
}
```

The `TilesConfigurer` by default loads a file called `tiles.xml` from the WEB-INF directory; this file contains the page definitions. Before we take a look at the definition file, let's look at the properties of the configurer in Table 8-6.

Table 8-6. *TilesConfigurer Properties*

Property	Purpose
checkRefresh	Should we check the Tiles definitions for changes? The default is `false`; setting it to `true` impacts performance but can be quite useful during development.
completeAutoload	When set to `true` (the default is `false`), initialization of Tiles is completely left to Tiles itself. It renders the other properties of this configurer class useless.
definitions	The list of files containing the definitions. The default refers to /WEB-INF/`tiles.xml`.
definitionsFactoryClass	Sets the `org.apache.tiles.definition.DefinitionsFactory` implementation class to use to create the Tiles definitions. By default uses the `org.apache.tiles.definition.UrlDefinitionsFactory` class.
prepareFactoryClass	Sets the `org.apache.tiles.preparer.PreparerFactory` implementation class to use. By default uses the `org.apache.tiles.preparer` `.BasicPreparerFactory` class.
tilesInitializer	Sets the custom initializer to initialize Tiles. When setting a custom implementation, the initializer should initialize Tiles completely, as setting this property renders the other properties on this class useless.
tilesProperties	Additional Tiles properties to set. Works only on Tiles 2.1.
useMutableTilesContainer	Should we use a mutable tiles container? The default is `false`.
validateDefinitions	Specifies whether we should validate the definitions xml file. The default is `true`.

The `TilesViewResolver` has no additional properties to set; it has the same set of properties as the `UrlBasedViewResolver`. It is a convenience subclass that automatically configures the correct view type to return. For Tiles, we need to create instances of the `org.springframework.web.servlet.view.tiles2` `.TilesView`.

Configuring and Creating Templates

Tiles requires one or more files to define our pages; these are called the *definitions files*. The default file loaded by the TilesConfigurer is the /WEB-INF/tiles.xml (see Listing 8-14).

Listing 8-14. *Tiles Definitions*

```
<?xml version="1.0" encoding="UTF-8" ?>
<!DOCTYPE tiles-definitions PUBLIC
    "-//Apache Software Foundation//DTD Tiles Configuration 2.1//EN"
    "http://tiles.apache.org/dtds/tiles-config_2_1.dtd">

<tiles-definitions>

    <definition name="template" template="/WEB-INF/templates/template.jsp">
        <put-attribute name="header" value="/WEB-INF/templates/header.jsp"/>
        <put-attribute name="footer" value="/WEB-INF/templates/footer.jsp"/>
    </definition>

    <definition name="*" extends="template">
        <put-attribute name="title" value="{1}.title" />
        <put-attribute name="body" value="/WEB-INF/views/{1}.jsp" />
    </definition>

    <definition name="*/*" extends="template">
        <put-attribute name="title" value="{1}.{2}/title" />
        <put-attribute name="body" value="/WEB-INF/views/{1}/{2}.jsp" />
    </definition>

</tiles-definitions>
```

We have created three definitions: the definition with the name template is the general layout configuration, the other definitions extend this general layout (and could override the predefined attributes). We can add more definitions when needed. For Spring to select the correct definition, our definition name has to match the name of the view (or a * wildcard as we did in our sample). Our template page (template.jsp) consists of three tiles (header, footer and body), and we need a property title that contains a message key so that we can use our message source (see the Chapter 5 discussion of internationalization) to resolve the actual title. Listing 8-15 shows our template.jsp, which is used for the general layout. Listing 8-16 shows our index.jsp, which is used as the body for the welcome page. Figure 8-4 shows the resulting page.[Au: OK? CE]

Listing 8-15. *Template JSP*

```
<!DOCTYPE HTML>
<%@ taglib prefix="c" uri="http://java.sun.com/jsp/jstl/core"%>
<%@ taglib prefix="spring" uri="http://www.springframework.org/tags" %>
<%@ taglib prefix="tiles" uri="http://tiles.apache.org/tags-tiles" %>

<html>
<head>
    <meta charset="utf-8">
    <c:set var="titleKey">
```

```
        <tiles:getAsString name="title" />
    </c:set>
    <title>
        Bookstore | <spring:message code="${titleKey}" text="Your Home in Books"/>
    </title>
    <link rel="stylesheet" type="text/css" href="<c:url value="/resources/css/style.css"/>" >
</head>
<body>
    <div id="wrap">
        <tiles:insertAttribute name="header"/>
        <div class="center_content">
        <div class="left_content">
            <h1><spring:message code="${titleKey}" text="${titleKey}" /></h1>
            <tiles:insertAttribute name="body" />
        </div><!--end of left content-->

        <div class="right_content">

            <div class="right_box">

                <div class="title"><span class="title_icon"><img src="<c:url
value="/resources/images/bullet4.gif"/>" alt="" title="" /></span><spring:message
code="main.title.randombooks"/></div>
                    <c:forEach items="${randomBooks}" var="book">
                        <div class="new_prod_box">
                            <c:url value="/book/${book.id}" var="bookUrl" />
                            <a href="${bookUrl}">${book.title}</a>
                            <div class="new_prod_img">
                            <c:url value="/book/${book.isbn}/image" var="bookImage"/>
                            <a href="${bookUrl}"><img src="${bookImage}" alt="${book.title}"
title="${book.title}" class="thumb" border="0" width="100px"/></a>
                            </div>
                        </div>
                    </c:forEach>
            </div>

        </div><!--end of right content-->
        <div class="clear"></div>
        </div><!--end of center content-->

        <tiles:insertAttribute name="footer" />
    </div>
</body>
</html>
```

░ **Tip** The highlighted code sets a variable based on the content of the title attribute from our ⸻iles.xml. That way, we can specify a key on the configuration and use the Spring message tag to resolve the actual value.

Listing 8-16. *Index JSP used as content*

```
<p>Welcome to the Book Store</p>
```

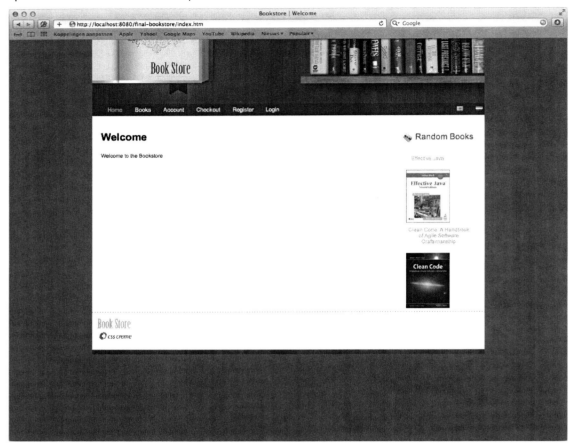

Figure 8-4. *Resulting Welcome Page*

Velocity and FreeMarker

Both Velocity[3] and FreeMarker[4] are templating frameworks for and written in Java. You can use them, among others, to create templates for HTML pages. They are text-based templating engines and both are widely used in applications for all kind of templating solutions.

---

[3] http://velocity.apache.org
[4] http://www.freemarker.org

Velocity and FreeMarker templates aren't compiled into Java code as JSPs are. They are interpreted at runtime by their templating engines; this is much like the XSLT processing we discussed earlier. One might think that this interpretation instead of compilation could lead to performance degradation of our application, but this is often not true. Both engines have extensive caching of interpreted templates, which make them quite fast.

Another advantage of using a templating approach over JSP is that in the latter case you might be tempted to put Java code in your JSPs. Putting Java code in your pages, although possible, is not an approach that one should take. It generally leads to pages that are hard to maintain and modify.

The disadvantage is that we need to add some extra configuration to our application. We first need to configure the templating engine of our choice, and next we need to configure view resolving for that templating engine.

Configuring the Template Engine

The Spring Framework extensively supports both Velocity and FreeMarker, and there are some helper classes to make configuring the engines easier. For Velocity there is the org.springframework.web .servlet.view.velocity.VelocityConfigurer (Table 8-7) and for FreeMarker there is the org.springframework.web.servlet.view.freemarker.FreeMarkerConfigurer (Table 8-8). Each is used to configure the respective templating engine.

Table 8-7. VelocityConfigurer Properties

Property	Purpose
configLocation	The location of the configuration file containing the velocity engine settings.
overrideLogging	Should the internal Velocity logging be redirected to commons-logging (the Spring default)? The default is true.
preferFileSystemAccess	Should we prefer file system access for loading the Velocity templates? The default is true, set to false if your templates aren't on the file system but, for example, on the classpath in a jar file.
resourceLoaderPath	Sets the path to the Velocity templates; this can be a comma-separated list of paths. It is allowed to mix different resource paths (see "Resource Loading" in Chapter 2).
velocityProperties velocityPropertiesMap	Directly sets the properties for the templating engine. Can be used to override properties from the configuration file or to fully configure the template engine, using either Properties or a Map.

Table 8-8. FreeMarkerConfigurer Properties

Property	Purpose
configLocation	The location of the configuration file containing the velocity engine settings.
defaultEncoding	Sets the encoding for the FreeMarker configuration file. The default is to use the platform encoding.
freemarkerSettings	Directly sets the properties for the templating engine. Can be used to override properties from the configuration file or to fully configure the template engine.
freemarkerVariables	Sets the map of well-known FreeMarker objects. These objects will be passed as variables to the FreeMarker configuration.
postTemplateLoaders	Specifies freemarker.cache.TemplateLoader to load templates. These will be registered after the default template loaders.
preferFileSystemAccess	Should we prefer file system access for loading the FreeMarker templates? The default is true; set this to false if your templates aren't on the file system but for instance on the classpath in a jar file.
preTemplateLoaders	Specifies freemarker.cache.TemplateLoader to load templates. These will be registered before the default template loaders.
templateLoaderPath templateLoaderPaths	Sets the path to the FreeMarker templates; this can be a comma-separated list of paths. It is allowed to mix different resource paths (see "Resource Loading" in Chapter 2).

The most important properties in these tables are the ones that set the location from which to load the templates. For Velocity this is the resourceLoaderPath and for FreeMarker the templateLoaderPath. It is a best practice to make them inaccessible for web clients, which can be done by putting them inside the WEB-INF directory.

■ **Note** There are also org.springframework.beans.factory.FactoryBeans to configure the respective templating engines. These are for bootstrapping the engines for use as non-web templates, like email.

In addition to setting up the different engines, we also need to configure a view resolver to resolve to correct view implementations. Spring ships with the org.springframework.web.servlet.view.velocity .VelocityViewResolver or org.springframework.web.servlet.view.velocity .VelocityLayoutViewResolver. For FreeMarker there is the org.springframework.web.servlet.view .freemarker.FreemarkerViewResolver. It isn't required to use these specialized view resolvers; an extensively configured InternalResourceViewResolver would also do. However, using these specialized view resolvers makes our life easier. Listings 8-17 and 8-18 show sample Velocity and FreeMarker configurations.

Listing 8-17. *Velocity Configuration*

```
package com.apress.prospringmvc.bookstore.web.config;

// Other imports omitted
import org.springframework.web.servlet.view.velocity.VelocityConfigurer;
import org.springframework.web.servlet.view.velocity.VelocityViewResolver;

@Configuration
public class ViewConfiguration {

    @Bean
    public VelocityConfigurer velocityConfigurer() {
        VelocityConfigurer velocityConfigurer = new VelocityConfigurer();
        velocityConfigurer.setResourceLoaderPath("WEB-INF/velocity");
        return velocityConfigurer;
    }

    @Bean
    public ViewResolver velocityViewResolver() {
        VelocityViewResolver viewResolver = new VelocityViewResolver();
        viewResolver.setSuffix(".vm");
        return viewResolver;
    }
}
```

Listing 8-18. *FreeMarker Configuration*

```
package com.apress.prospringmvc.bookstore.web.config;

// Other imports omitted
import org.springframework.web.servlet.view.freemarker.FreeMarkerConfigurer;
import org.springframework.web.servlet.view.freemarker.FreeMarkerViewResolver;

@Configuration
public class ViewConfiguration {

    @Bean
    public FreeMarkerConfigurer freeMarkerConfigurer() {
        FreeMarkerConfigurer freeMarkerConfigurer;
        freeMarkerConfigurer = new FreeMarkerConfigurer();
        freeMarkerConfigurer.setTemplateLoaderPath("WEB-INF/freemarker");
        return freeMarkerConfigurer;
    }

    @Bean
    public ViewResolver freeMarkerViewResolver() {
        FreeMarkerViewResolver viewResolver = new FreeMarkerViewResolver();
```

```
        viewResolver.setSuffix(".ftl");
        return viewResolver;
    }
}
```

When a controller now returns index as the view name, for Velocity a template would be loaded from WEB-INF/velocity/index.vm, and for FreeMarker it would become WEB-INF/freemarker/index.ftl. The resourceLoaderPath/templateLoaderPath is prefixed to the view name. Both the view resolvers also allow for setting an additional prefix (inherited from the UrlBasedViewResolver). Table 8-9 describes the different properties for the view resolvers.

Table 8-9. Additional Properties for the View Resolvers

Property	Purpose
allowRequestOverride	Should request attributes override model attributes when we merge the model? When set to true, request attributes can override model attributes when they are stored under the same name. The default is false, which would lead to an exception when an attribute with the same name is encountered.
allowSessionOverride	Should session attributes override model attributes when we merge the model? When set to true, session attributes can override model attributes when they are stored under the same name. The default is false, which would lead to an exception when an attribute with the same name is encountered.
exposeRequestAttributes	Should all request attributes be put in the model? The default is false.
exposeSessionAttributes	Should all session attributes be put in the model? The default is false.
exposeSpringMacroHelpers	Should the macros (see Table 8-10 in the next section) be exposed so that they are available for rendering? The default is true.
dateToolAttribute *	The name for the DateTool helper object. It will be exposed in the model under that name.
numberToolAttribute *	The name for the NumberTool helper object. It will be exposed in the model under that name.
toolboxConfigLocation *	The configuration for the optional toolbox library. Will create an org.springframework.web.servlet.view.velocity.VelocityToolboxView to render the view.

*The properties marked with * are for Velocity only.*

The Templating Language

Now that we have configured our environment, we also need to write a template that shows the page to us. Both templating languages are very similar. Listings 8-19 and 8-20 show the book search page written for Velocity and FreeMarker, respectively.

Listing 8-19. Velocity Template

```
<!DOCTYPE HTML>
<html>
<head>
<title>Booksearch</title>
</head>
<body>
<h1>#springMessage("book.title")</h1>

<p>

    <form method="POST">
        <fieldset>
            <legend>#springMessage("book.searchcriteria")</legend>
            <table>
                <tr><td>#springMessage("book.title")</td><td>#springFormInput↲
("searchCriteria.title" "")</td></tr>
                <tr><td>#springMessage("book.category")</td><td>#springFormSingleSelect↲
("searchCriteria.category" $categories "")</td></tr>
            </table>
        </fieldset>
        <button id="search">#springMessage("button.search")</button>
    </form>

    #if ($bookList.empty eq false)
        <table>
            <tr><th>#springMessage("book.title")</th><th>#springMessage↲
("book.description")</th><th>#springMessage("book.price")</th></tr>
            #foreach($book in $bookList)
                <tr><td>${book.title}</td><td>${book.description}</td><td>$↲
{book.price}</td><td><a href="#springUrl("/cart/add/${book.id}")">#springMessage↲
("book.addtocart")</a></td></tr>
            #end
        </table>
    #end
</p>

</body>
</html>
```

Listing 8-20. FreeMarker Template

```
<#ftl>
<#import "/spring.ftl" as spring />
<!DOCTYPE HTML>
<html>
<head>
<title>Booksearch</title>
</head>
<body>
<h1><@spring.message code="book.title" /></h1>

<p>

    <form method="POST">
        <fieldset>
            <legend><@spring.message code="book.searchcriteria" /></legend>
            <table>
                <tr><td><@spring.message code="book.title" /></td><td><@spring.formInput↩
 "searchCriteria.title" /></td></tr>
                <tr><td><@spring.message code="book.category"↩
 /></td><td><@spring.formSingleSelect "searchCriteria.category", categories, "" /></td></tr>
            </table>
        </fieldset>
        <button id="search"><@spring.message code="book.search" /></button>
    </form>

    <#if bookList?has_content>
        <table>
            <tr><th><@spring.message code="book.title"/></th><th><@spring.message↩
code="book.description"/></th><th><@spring.message code="book.price" /></th></tr>
            <#list bookList as book>
                <tr><td>${book.title}</td><td>${book.description}</td><td>$↩
{book.price}</td><td><a href="<@spring.url "/cart/add/${book.id}"/>"><@spring.message↩
 code="book.addtocart"/></a></tr>
            </#list>
        </table>
    </#if>
</p>

</body>
</html>
```

Looking at the templates, we can see that they are similar to the JSPs we wrote in the previous chapters. The Velocity (Listing 8-19) and FreeMarker (Listing 8-20) templates also have tag libraries available (in the listings bound to Spring). Both libraries offer more or less the same support as the Spring Form Tag library for JSP. Table 8-10 provides an overview of the different tags, or better macro libraries, for both Velocity and FreeMarker.

Table 8-10. Macros Available for Velocity and FreeMarker

Macro	Velocity	FreeMarker
message (output a string from a resource bundle based on the code parameter)	`#springMessage($code)`	`<@spring.message code/>`
messageText (output a string from a resource bundle based on the code parameter, falling back to the value of the default parameter)	`#springMessageText($code $text)`	`<@spring.messageText code, text/>`
url (prefix a relative URL with the application's context root)	`#springUrl($relativeUrl)`	`<@spring.url relativeUrl/>`
formInput (standard input field for gathering user input)	`#springFormInput ($path $attributes)`	`<@spring.formInput path, attributes, fieldType/>`
formHiddenInput * (hidden input field for submitting non-user input)	`#springFormHiddenInput ($path $attributes)`	`<@spring.formHiddenInput path, attributes/>`
formPasswordInput * (standard input field for gathering passwords. Note that no value will ever be populated in fields of this type)	`#springFormPasswordInput ($path $attributes)`	`<@spring.formPasswordInput path, attributes/>`
formTextarea (large text field for gathering long, freeform text input)	`#springFormTextarea ($path $attributes)`	`<@spring.formTextarea path, attributes/>`
formSingleSelect (drop down box of options allowing a single required value to be selected)	`#springFormSingleSelect ($path $options $attributes)`	`<@spring.formSingleSelect path, options, attributes/>`
formMultiSelect (a list box of options allowing the user to select 0 or more values)	`#springFormMultiSelect ($path $options $attributes)`	`<@spring.formMultiSelect path, options, attributes/>`
formRadioButtons (a set of radio buttons allowing a single selection to be made from the available choices)	`#springFormRadioButtons ($path $options $separator $attributes)`	`<@spring.formRadioButtons path, options separator, attributes/>`
formCheckboxes (a set of checkboxes allowing 0 or more values to be selected)	`#springFormCheckboxes ($path $options $separator $attributes)`	`<@spring.formCheckboxes path, options, separator, attributes/>`
formCheckbox (a single checkbox)	`#springFormCheckbox ($path $attributes)`	`<@spring.formCheckbox path, attributes/>`

| showErrors | #springShowErrors ($separator $classOrStyle) | <@spring.showErrors separator, classOrStyle/> |

The parameters to any of the macros listed have consistent meanings:

- **path:** the name of the field to bind to (that is, "searchCriteria.title").

- **options:** a map containing all the available values that can be selected from in the input field. The keys to the map represent the values that will be POSTed back from the form and bound to the command object. The values belonging to the key are used as the labels to show to the user. Usually such a map is supplied as reference data by the controller. Any Map implementation can be used, depending on required behavior.

- **separator:** where multiple options are available as discrete elements (radio buttons or checkboxes), the sequence of characters used to separate each one in the list (for example, <br>).

- **attributes:** an additional string of arbitrary tags or text to be included within the HTML tag itself. This string is echoed literally by the macro. For example, in a textarea field you may supply attributes as 'rows="5" cols="60"' or you could pass style information such as 'style="border:1px solid silver"'.

- **classOrStyle:** for the showErrors macro, the name of the CSS class that the span tag wrapping each error will use. If no information is supplied (or the value is empty), the errors will be wrapped in <b></b> tags.

▨ **Tip** The two macros marked (*) in the table exist for FreeMarker; however, they are not actually required, as you can use the normal formInput macro specifying hidden or password as the value for the fieldType parameter.

The difference between the FreeMarker and Velocity macros is that with FreeMarker you can, as in JSP, specify which library to use. This isn't possible with Velocity macros, because they are global and are included (and accessible) on every page. For FreeMarker we need to specify the library by using the import directive (see top of Listing 8-20).

Dates and Numbers

Velocity has several useful tools available for formatting dates and numbers. Spring can also integrate with those tools so that they can use the current selected locale. To enable this support we need to set the dateToolAttribute and/or the numberToolAttribute. Setting these properties will expose the tools to the model so that they can be used in the view template.

PDF

Spring uses the iText library[5] to add PDF support. To enable this we need to write our own view implementation and for that we need to extend org.springframework.web.servlet.view .document.AbstractPdfView. When we extend this class we must implement the buildPdfDocument method.

We are going to create a PDF that gives an overview of one of our orders on our account page. Listing 8-21 shows the view implementation.

Listing 8-21. View Implementation to Create a PDF

```java
package com.apress.prospringmvc.bookstore.web.view;

// Other imports omitted
import org.springframework.web.servlet.view.document.AbstractPdfView;

import com.apress.prospringmvc.bookstore.domain.Order;
import com.apress.prospringmvc.bookstore.domain.OrderDetail;
import com.lowagie.text.Document;
import com.lowagie.text.Paragraph;
import com.lowagie.text.Table;
import com.lowagie.text.pdf.PdfWriter;

public class OrderPdfView extends AbstractPdfView {

    @Override
    protected void buildPdfDocument(Map<String, Object> model,
                                    Document document,
                                    PdfWriter writer,
                                    HttpServletRequest request,
                                    HttpServletResponse response)
    throws Exception {

        Order order = (Order) model.get("order");

        document.addTitle("Order :" + order.getId());
        document.add(new Paragraph("Order date: " + order.getOrderDate()));
        document.add(new Paragraph("Delivery date: " + order.getDeliveryDate()));

        Table orderDetails = new Table(4);
        orderDetails.addCell("Title");
        orderDetails.addCell("Price");
        orderDetails.addCell("#");
        orderDetails.addCell("Total");

        for (OrderDetail detail : order.getOrderDetails()) {
            orderDetails.addCell(detail.getBook().getTitle());
            orderDetails.addCell(detail.getBook().getPrice().toString());
```

---

[5] http://itextpdf.com/

```
            orderDetails.addCell(String.valueOf(detail.getQuantity()));
            orderDetails.addCell(detail.getPrice().toString());
        }

        document.add(orderDetails);

    }

}
```

Next let's add org.springframework.web.servlet.view.ContentNegotiatingViewResolver to our view configuration. We do this so that we can have our order page rendered in HTML or PDF, and we don't want to change our com.apress.prospringmvc.bookstore.web.controller.OrderController because that is already doing what we want, adding the selected order to the model. Listing 8-22 shows the changed com.apress.prospringmvc.bookstore.web.config.ViewConfiguration. This is also where we will start using our custom view resolver (see the discussion of implementing your own view resolver).

Listing 8-22. ViewConfiguration with ContentNegotiatingViewResolver

```
package com.apress.prospringmvc.bookstore.web.config;

// Other imports omitted
import org.springframework.web.servlet.view.ContentNegotiatingViewResolver;
import org.springframework.web.servlet.view.document.AbstractPdfView;

import com.apress.prospringmvc.bookstore.web.view.OrderPdfView;
import com.apress.prospringmvc.bookstore.web.view
    .SimpleConfigurableViewResolver;                    see PAGE 247

@Configuration
public class ViewConfiguration {

    @Bean
    public ContentNegotiatingViewResolver contentNegotiatingViewResolver() {
        ContentNegotiatingViewResolver viewResolver;
        viewResolver = new ContentNegotiatingViewResolver();
        List<ViewResolver> viewResolvers = new ArrayList<ViewResolver>();
        viewResolvers.add(pdfViewResolver());
        viewResolver.setViewResolvers(viewResolvers);
        return viewResolver;
    }

    @Bean
    public ViewResolver pdfViewResolver() {
        SimpleConfigurableViewResolver viewResolver;
        viewResolver = new SimpleConfigurableViewResolver();
        Map<String, AbstractPdfView> views;
        views = new HashMap<String, AbstractPdfView>();
        views.put("order", new OrderPdfView());
        viewResolver.setViews(views);
        return viewResolver;
    }
```

```
    // Other methods omitted, see Listing 8-13
}
```
on PAGE 250

The changed configuration contains our own view resolver, and we use it to resolve the com.apress .prospringmvc.bookstore.web.view.OrderPdfView. We do this because we also want to be able to resolve an order view for an Excel document (see the "Excel" section).

After these changes we need to redeploy our application, if we log in and navigate to our account page we can now click the PDF link and actually get a PDF instead of the HTML version. Figure 8-5 shows the result of clicking the PDF link.

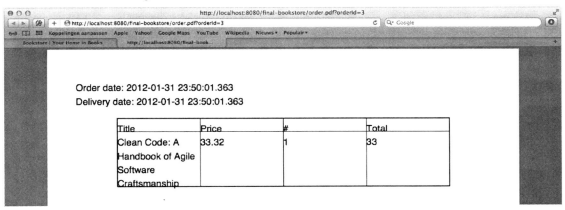

Figure 8-5. Generated PDF

Although this approach is very flexible, the drawback is that we would need to code the construction of PDFs for each PDF we want. If we have some complex PDF or need to apply a certain style, this will be quite cumbersome and hard to maintain. In such cases, it might be worthwhile to look at solutions like JasperReports (see the section "JasperReports").

Excel

Spring has two ways of rendering an Excel document. The first is by using the JExcel library,[6] and the other is using the Apache POI library.[7] Both approaches need us to implement a view (just as with a PDF); to do that, we extend either
org.springframework.web.servlet.view.document.AbstractJExcelView or
org.springframework.web.servlet.view.document.AbstractExcelView. They are respectively for JExcel and Apache POI. Both implementations hide the setup and allow for a template xls to be loaded and processed; we need to add the view-specific rendering. We need to implement the buildExcelDocument method for that. Listing 8-23 shows a JExcel example of an order as an Excel document.

---

[6] http://jexcelapi.sourceforge.net/
[7] http://poi.apache.org/

NOTE: EXAMPLE USE JEXCEL (NOT POI)

Listing 8-23. *OrderExcelView*

```
package com.apress.prospringmvc.bookstore.web.view;

// Other imports omitted
import jxl.write.DateTime;
import jxl.write.Label;
import jxl.write.WritableSheet;
import jxl.write.WritableWorkbook;

import org.springframework.web.servlet.view.document.AbstractJExcelView;

import com.apress.prospringmvc.bookstore.domain.Order;
import com.apress.prospringmvc.bookstore.domain.OrderDetail;

public class OrderExcelView extends AbstractJExcelView {


    @Override
    protected void buildExcelDocument(Map<String, Object> model,
                                      WritableWorkbook workbook,
                                      HttpServletRequest request,
                                      HttpServletResponse response)
    throws Exception {
        Order order = (Order) model.get("order");

        WritableSheet sheet = workbook.createSheet("Order", 0);
        sheet.addCell(new Label(1, 1, "Order :" + order.getId()));
        sheet.addCell(new Label(1, 2, "Order Date"));
        sheet.addCell(new DateTime(2, 2, order.getOrderDate()));
        sheet.addCell(new Label(1, 2, "Delivery Date"));
        sheet.addCell(new DateTime(2, 2, order.getDeliveryDate()));

        sheet.addCell(new Label(1, 4, "Title"));
        sheet.addCell(new Label(2, 4, "Price"));
        sheet.addCell(new Label(3, 4, "#"));
        sheet.addCell(new Label(4, 4, "Total"));

        int row = 4;
        for (OrderDetail detail : order.getOrderDetails()) {
            row++;
            sheet.addCell(new Label(1, row, detail.getBook().getTitle()));
            sheet.addCell(new jxl.write.Number(2, row, detail.getBook().getPrice()↩
.doubleValue()));
            sheet.addCell(new jxl.write.Number(3, row, detail.getQuantity()));
            sheet.addCell(new jxl.write.Number(2, row, detail.getPrice().doubleValue()));
        }
    }

}
```

Next to the view we need to add a view resolver. In our sample application we are going to add this, just like the PDF view, to our ViewConfiguration class. We are going to add another instance of our custom implementation (see Listing 8-24) and let the ContentNegotiatingViewResolver decide what to do.

Listing 8-24. *ViewConfiguration with OrderExcelView*

```
package com.apress.prospringmvc.bookstore.web.config;

//Other imports omitted, see Listing 8-22
import org.springframework.web.servlet.view.document.AbstractJExcelView;
import org.springframework.web.servlet.view.document.AbstractPdfView;

import com.apress.prospringmvc.bookstore.web.view.OrderExcelView;

@Configuration
public class ViewConfiguration {

    @Bean
    public ContentNegotiatingViewResolver contentNegotiatingViewResolver() {
        ContentNegotiatingViewResolver viewResolver;
        viewResolver = new ContentNegotiatingViewResolver();
        List<ViewResolver> viewResolvers = new ArrayList<ViewResolver>();
        viewResolvers.add(pdfViewResolver());
        viewResolvers.add(xlsViewResolver());
        viewResolver.setViewResolvers(viewResolvers);
        return viewResolver;
    }

    @Bean
    public ViewResolver xlsViewResolver() {
        SimpleConfigurableViewResolver viewResolver;
        viewResolver = new SimpleConfigurableViewResolver();
        Map<String, AbstractJExcelView> views;
        views = new HashMap<String, AbstractJExcelView>();
        views.put("order", new OrderExcelView());
        viewResolver.setViews(views);
        return viewResolver;
    }
    // Other methods omitted see Listing 8-22
}
```

But, wait, isn't our application going to break because we have multiple view implementations resolving to the order view name? The special view resolver ContentNegotiatingViewResolver is going to help us here. It will determine which of the resolved views best matches the content-type requested. So without changing our controller and by simply adding some configuration (and view implementations), we can differentiate which view is being served.

To test, click the xls link and an Excel document will be downloaded for you to view.

XML and JSON

Spring MVC has another way of serving XML or JSON to our clients. We can use the
ContentNegotiatingViewResolver to our advantage. Spring has two special view implementations to
convert objects to XML or JSON, respectively, org.springframework.web.servlet.view.xml
.MarshallingView and org.springframework.web.servlet.view.json.MappingJacksonJsonView. The XML-
based view uses the Spring XML support to marshall our model to XML. The JSON view uses the Jackson
library. We can quite easily configure our view resolver to also expose XML and/or JSON to our clients.
We simply can add a default view for XML and JSON (we can also add additional view resolvers, as we
did for the PDF and Excel documents). Listing 8-25 is the modified configuration (see the highlighted
parts).

Listing 8-25. ViewConfiguration for XML and JSON

```
package com.apress.prospringmvc.bookstore.web.config;

// Other imports omitted

import org.springframework.oxm.Marshaller;
import org.springframework.oxm.xstream.XStreamMarshaller;
import org.springframework.web.servlet.view.json.MappingJacksonJsonView;
import org.springframework.web.servlet.view.xml.MarshallingView;

import com.apress.prospringmvc.bookstore.web.view.OrderExcelView;
import com.apress.prospringmvc.bookstore.web.view.OrderPdfView;

@Configuration
public class ViewConfiguration {

    @Bean
    public ContentNegotiatingViewResolver contentNegotiatingViewResolver() {
        ContentNegotiatingViewResolver viewResolver;
        viewResolver = new ContentNegotiatingViewResolver();
        List<ViewResolver> viewResolvers = new ArrayList<ViewResolver>();
        viewResolvers.add(pdfViewResolver());
        viewResolvers.add(xlsViewResolver());
        viewResolver.setViewResolvers(viewResolvers);
        List<View> defaultViews = new ArrayList<View>();
        defaultViews.add(jsonOrderView());
        defaultViews.add(xmlOrderView());
        viewResolver.setDefaultViews(defaultViews);
        return viewResolver;
    }

    @Bean
    public MappingJacksonJsonView jsonOrderView() {
        MappingJacksonJsonView jsonView = new MappingJacksonJsonView();
        jsonView.setModelKey("order");
        return jsonView;
    }
```

```java
@Bean
public MarshallingView xmlOrderView() {
    MarshallingView xmlView = new MarshallingView(marshaller());
    xmlView.setModelKey("order");
    return xmlView;
}

@Bean
public Marshaller marshaller() {
    return new XStreamMarshaller();
}

// Other methods omitted, see listings 8-22 and 8-24
}
```

For XML to work, we also need to configure an org.springframework.oxm.Marshaller implementation. We choose here to use the XStream[8] library because that is quick and easy to use. To use another solution, simply configure the appropriate marshaller. More information on marshalling and XML can be found in the Spring Reference guide.

■ **Caution** When using these type of views together with an ORM implementation (like in our sample) one could get issues like lazy loading or loading half the database due to collections getting initialized.

If we now change the URL in the browser to end in either .json or .xml, we will get a JSON or XML representation of our order (Figure 8-6 is the JSON sample). We have now five different ways of viewing our order (HTML, PDF, Excel, JSON and XML) without touching our controller and by simply changing our configuration.

Figure 8-6. JSON Representation of our Order

---

[8] http://xstream.codehaus.org

JasperReports

Spring MVC provides support for the reporting engine called JasperReports.[9] This reporting engine uses report designs in XML and can output different formats based on that XML. There is a powerful report designer called iReport Designer which can be used to create the report designs. One could use an XML or text editor to create the designs, but that isn't recommended because the XML is very verbose.

Spring supports JasperReports with a view resolver and six different view implementations. The view resolver is, not surprisingly, the `org.springframework.web.servlet.view.jasperreports` `.JasperReportsViewResolver`. The view implementations can be found in the same package. They are

- `JasperReportsCsvView`

- `JasperReportsHtmlView`

- `JasperReportsPdfView`

- `JasperReportsXlsView`

- `ConfigurableJasperReportsView`

- `JasperReportsMultiFormatView`

The first four implementations produce a predefined format, either CSV, HTML, PDF, or Excel. For the fifth you can configure the format to export; it allows for setting the specific `net.sf.jasperreports.engine.JRExporter` implementation to use to generate a report. The last view implementation acts as a wrapper around the first four views or can be configured with specific implementations. It maps a format to a specific view implementation. Table 8-11 lists the defaults.

Table 8-11. JasperReportsMultiFormatView Default Mappings

Format	View
csv	JasperReportsCsvView
html	JasperReportsHtmlView
pdf	JasperReportsPdfView
xls	JasperReportsXlsView

To use one of the views, we need to add the view and configure the URL of the report design. This can be either an XML file (.jrxml file) or in a compiled form (.jasper file). Either way, internally a compiled version of the report is needed for performance reasons. It can be wise to precompile the reports for production usage. Listing 8-26 shows a sample configuration for a JasperReports-based PDF view of our order.

---

[9] http://jasperforge.org/projects/jasperreports

Listing 8-26. JasperReports View Configuration

```
package com.apress.prospringmvc.bookstore.web.config;

// Other imports omitted

import org.springframework.web.servlet.view.jasperreports
        .JasperReportsPdfView;


@Configuration
public class ViewConfiguration {

    @Bean
    public View jasperReportsView() {
        JasperReportsPdfView orderPdfView = new JasperReportsPdfView();
        orderPdfView.setUrl("/WEB-INF/jasper/order.jrxml");
        return orderPdfView;
    }
  // Other methods ommitted see listing 8-18
}
```

The special org.springframework.web.servlet.view.jasperreports.JasperReportsMultiFormatView needs the format to be rendered available in the model. By default there should be a key named format in the model that tells us which format to render. It is more flexible and less intrusive to use the ContentNegotiatingViewResolver to resolve the correct view implementation to use. This allows you to configure the views without modifying your controllers. The multi-format view needs our controller to be modified, and we need to put logic in there to determine what to render.

Filling the Report

Just as in the PDF and Excel examples earlier, it would be nice if there were something to show to our users. Like the other view implementations, the View implementations for Jasper Reports use the data from the model for rendering. However, Jasper does this a little differently than other view technologies.

If our model contains a single attribute and it is a net.sf.jasperreports.engine .JRDataSource, net.sf.jasperreports.engine.JRDataSourceProvider or javax.sql.DataSource, it will be used as is (in the case of a DataSource it expects a query in the report). If the attribute is a Collection or array, it will be converted into a usable JRDataSource implementation.

If our model contains multiple attributes, we need to specify which attribute we want to use. We do this by setting the reportDataKey property on the view. Failing to do so might lead to unexpected results, as the first JRDataSource, Collection or array detected is used to fill the report.

The net.sf.jasperreports.engine.JRDataSource is needed by the report to retrieve the data and render the report. There are several implementations available from JasperReports for different data sources, ranging from databases to Excel documents.

Summary

This chapter covered the view part of Spring MVC. We looked at view resolving by covering several general-purpose `ViewResolver` implementations. We also covered several view technologies supported by Spring MVC and explained how to configure Spring to use them. We started with JSPs and we briefly touched on JSF and how you can integrate Spring into a JSF application. Next we looked at several templating solutions; specifically, we covered Tiles, Velocity, and FreeMarker.

After the web-based views, we looked at different view technologies like how to create PDF and Excel without changing our controllers but by simply adding a `ContentNegotiatingViewResolver` and an appropriate `View` implementation.

In the previous chapter we covered JSON, and in this chapter we covered another way of exposing (part) of our model as JSON or XML. Finally we looked at JasperReports for creating reports based on a templating language.

One important thing to take away from this chapter is the separation of controller logic and view logic (which was demonstrated by the different representations of our order). This shows the power of applying separation of concerns and the flexibility it gives one.

We will probably never use all the technologies in a single application. It will probably be limited to two or three different technologies (for our pages and probably creating a PDF or Excel file). But it is nice to have the flexibility to change or simply add a new view layer to our application.

CHAPTER 9

Testing Spring MVC Applications

Testing is in most projects a bit of a struggle point. We all know testing is important, but we also know that testing takes time and writing good tests is difficult. Testing also requires adequate infrastructure in your code base.

Testing is also not very sexy. It doesn't involve producing flashy UIs with cool effects, and it doesn't require you to make brilliant designs either (don't get us wrong, testing requires *good* design, but it is mostly repetitive and not as engaging as production code can be). Maybe the biggest challenge is that your project doesn't seem to move forward when you are writing tests. It feels like you are wasting time while you could be building functionality instead. Because of this, testing is sometimes "forgotten," or promises are made to write tests later on.

While there are numerous books and even more references to be found on the Internet, we are not going to talk about methodologies and the like. In this chapter, we want to start by reminding you why tests are really so important, and we'll also try to define how we are going to approach testing throughout the chapter.

In the code examples, we will introduce you to a way of testing using Spring's test support that will be appealing and easy to handle. We will show different methods for testing your application and how to build those tests.

The title of this chapter is "Testing Spring MVC Applications," and this is meant in the broader sense, as we will discuss testing on every level of the application. We will start with the easy part, how to test our back-end modules: the repositories and services using Spring's test support. We'll also show you how and when to use mock objects. Later, we will discuss how to test MVC controllers and finally perform full-fledged browser tests of our pages.

Introducing Testing

Before we dive into the code, we want to make sure you are aware why writing tests is so beneficial. We will also look at some important things you can do to make (and keep) testing attractive within your project. When writing tests is a pain, you can be sure that the test quality is poor or even worse, no tests are written. To conclude our introduction we will look at the different kind of tests. We will explain the differences among them and look deeper into the kind of tests we will be covering in this chapter. So let's start by having a look why you should be investing your time in writing tests.

Why Should I Bother Writing Tests?

Testing should be a natural reflex that is part of your daily development process, just like writing functionality, delivering builds, fixing bugs, tracking issues and so on.

Testing takes time and we know that. Writing good test cases sometimes can be more complex than writing the code to implement the actual business case. Therefore you should do everything in your power to make testing within your project as smooth and easy as possible. This is the first requirement for having successful testing within a project. If it takes too much trouble to write a test, or a test is never automatically run, people will find excuses not to write them. A test should be considered a first-level citizen within your project.

We all know the feeling; after you changed some code, how can you be sure the code actually works? Some might argue that depending on your experience, background, and skills this fact alone does not require a test per se. That might be so, but what about the impact of your change? Your code might work fine, but do you know it doesn't break any other code depending on it? Also, have you thought about the people coming behind you who will need to change your code? They are looking for some guarantee that what they did is actually OK and did not break anything else.

Without testing, your implementation might look like Figure 9-1 before you even realize it:

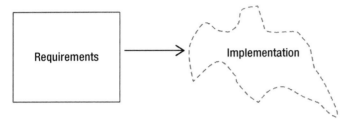

Figure 9-1. *Implementation deformation without tests*

This diagram represents the requirements to be implemented and the actual implementation. It is referred to as the "amoeba effect" in Jaroslav Tulach's book *Practical API Design*[1] – admittedly in a different context, but the idea is also applicable here. If we were all perfect developers, writing 100% correct code, the implementation would have the same rectangular shape as the requirements. Unfortunately, that is not the case, and the implementation will be deformed. You can also call it "buggy," or "not compliant" in terms of what has been asked for.

■ **Note** Here we consider the requirements as being the absolute truth, since they are drawn in straight lines forming a rectangular shape. In practice, this is also not true. The requirements will also contain a failure margin beyond to what is really been asked for. But from the developer's point of view the requirements are what they are, and the code should resemble them 100% (if not, the requirements should be changed first).

So, wouldn't it be great to have some kind of robot super developer that is integrated in the project, and that told you every time your implementation was going to deform, so you could have stopped this?

Deformation might sneak into your code in different ways. You might have caused it by simply refactoring something in the application, or after changing some functionality. After performing even the smallest change, you could call the robot developer for free and ask it to check all dependencies and analyze all impacts of your work. After a couple of seconds, the robot developer could say; "you did a

---

[1] Jaroslav Tulach, *Practical API Design: Confessions of a Java Framework Architect* (Apress 2008)

good job, I inspected all code and everything seems to be OK!" Or maybe the robot says: "Attention, you broke a business rule in that class at line x!" In both cases you will be very happy. In the first case you will be experiencing the "cozy warm feeling effect." In the second case you are thankful to the robot pointing out a potential bug. In that case you continue by changing your code (or your test) so it maintains the rectangular form as closely as possible.

That robot developer exists and is hidden in your tests. But you have to build it, bit by bit. Every time you can write a test case, you should. Every time you write a test case, you should make the best out of it and you should treat it as important as the code you are testing. Test cases are investments, and they safeguard the future of your project.

After you have a suitable test harness (a suite of tests), you can make sure that after every change your code still complies with the harness. The harness is formed after the requirements, which means that each test tests a part of the requirements. If you add up all the tests, you ideally have tested all the requirements of your project (see Figure 9-2).

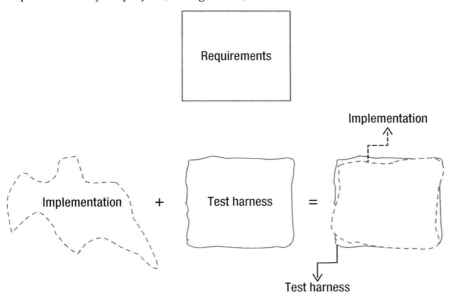

Figure 9-2. Adding a test harness to keep the code in line with the requirements

In this figure we added a test harness that attempts to map our testing to our requirements. As you can see, the test harness isn't a perfect rectangle either, but it is a lot closer than the badly deformed implementation. A test harness cannot be perfect, because it never truly tests everything and also can contain bugs itself. However, applying the harness on this deformed implementation will yield a lot of failures that you can fix until your implementation becomes more and more like your requirements. And above all, after fixing this code to map closely to the requirements, your test harness will act as a monitor for your code. Every time a new deformation occurs, you will be alerted so you can take proper action.

How you write your tests, before or after your actual production code is up to you. That discussion is beyond the scope of this chapter. But it can be said that if you write a test after writing the code, it's best to keep the interval as short as possible. In the model shown in Figure 9-2, the implementation that we are testing should be seen as a very small part of your project. It would represent a single class or even a single method, for which you write a unit test— as soon as possible after writing the code.

Promoting Testing Within Your Project

If it is too hard to write a test, or a lot of refactoring has to be done in your code to test a particular module, you can be sure that no single test is going to be written. Many developers see testing as an extra task that they have to fulfill. In this section we want to give some tips to promote testing within your project, so that writing tests becomes easier and more appealing. The project should be as supportive as possible to write tests for. This section is of course not exhaustive, but we hope it gives an idea about the more important aspects.

Goals: The first thing you can do within a project is setting a testing goal; for example, targeting a high percentage of production code covered by tests is a nice goal to strive for. EclEmma[2] is a very nice plug-in that will do that for you. We will show you its output after we have written our first test in the next section. There is also a plug-in for Gradle and Maven to run Emma[3] in an automated fashion. You could even set minimum goals of coverage before a build is considered successful. Code coverage can work psychologically to make developers have a target; to get the percentage of covered code as high as possible. This is a form of "gamification"; it helps motivating ourselves to do the best job possible in writing tests by engaging ourselves to obtain a high as possible coverage rate. However, beware that quantity is not more important than quality, so one should not lose sight of the quality aspect. Writing a test that gives 100% coverage is not very difficult, but that doesn't mean the code by itself is well tested. Code testing coverage is a minimum indicator to get a feel about the test quality.

Infrastructure: We are talking about frameworks and structure within your project. Without a good infrastructure, testing becomes painful. You should start building out a good platform to write your tests upon. As mentioned before, writing tests is an investment, and that investment should be well protected. Tests are like your car's comprehensive insurance. It costs money and it doesn't buy you anything. But if anything happens to your car it will pay for the costs, and oh boy, when this happens you are glad you paid for that insurance! The same is true with tests (only accidents will happen on a daily basis, and using your tests is free once you build them). They will start to pay off as soon as you start to refactor or change your application.

Importance of testing: Tests are sometimes more important than the code they test, because they are the proof that the code is working. Without a test the code doesn't mean anything, as its behavior is an unverifiable state. Even if you can really be sure that the code will work, you probably have no idea about the impact. Others are depending on your code and might suddenly notice a change in behavior breaking your project. If every component was adequately tested, this would immediately show up after running the tests.

Understanding: You should understand the different levels of testing and when to apply which type of test in which situation. You could test an entire application by using frontend testing, but that would be a bad idea. You should

---

[2] http://www.eclemma.org/
[3] http://docs.codehaus.org/display/GRADLE/Plugins#Plugins-Emmaplugin

also understand where testing should stop. You are not required to test Spring, or Hibernate, or whatever library you are using. They have their own test sets.

Environment: Your tests (both unit and integration) should run on a constant basis. You should have a dedicated machine just building your project on every commit. For a CI (Continuous Integration) system, we advise you to check out Jenkins[4] (which was called Hudson before they changed the name for legal reasons). It is extremely simple to set up and works very well. It will check out THE (?) code from your Version Control System (VCS) and build it. If your project can be built with a build tool (like Gradle, Ant, Maven, and so on) it will only take a few minutes to schedule an automated build. Also, because you will be using such tools to automate your build, your tests should be environment-agnostic. They should be able to run even on your Smartphone without requiring any resource or environment dependency. Tests should be able to run everywhere. Tests should also be easy to run, preferably with a single command without requiring any form of configuration or setup.

■ **Note** The best way to verify your project's test suite is to take a random device that is able to run Java, perform a checkout from your VCS, disable all network interfaces, and enter a single command that should perform a build and run your tests. There should be no failures, and your test coverage should clearly indicate that the major part of your project is tested. There is also a great tool called sonar[5] (open source) which does exactly that, checking out your code from VCS and applying all kinds of metrics to it, including test coverage. We would certainly advise you to try this, as it is very easy to set up and the advantages for safekeeping your code quality are major.

Different Types of Testing

Testing comes in different types. It is important that we decide which level of testing we are going to cover, and most of all give a clear definition of it. In this chapter we will look at unit, integration, and system testing. We will start by giving an overview of the different types of testing and a word of explanation. This list is not exhaustive, but it gives an idea of the level of testing we are going to cover.

- **Unit Testing:** The basic definition of a unit test is "a discrete test condition to check correctness of an isolated software module." A unit test functions at the lowest possible level of a software module, preferably a single method of a class, without having any dependencies (like resources). We will look into unit testing in more detail in the next sub section.

- **Integration Testing:** Unlike a unit test, integration tests have a larger scope that involves testing several layers of your application. We will look at integration testing in more detail in the "Integration Tests" section.

---

[4] http://jenkins-ci.org/
[5] http://www.sonarsource.com/

- **System Testing:** Like integration testing but using the real resources. The resources could be scaled-down versions of the actual production resources, but it is important that the environment setup and topology match as closely as possible. This will make sure that the transition of your project to other environments goes smoothly. The tests are also written without any internal knowledge of how the application is built; they treat the application to test as a black box. Front-end testing with a real browser is also a form of system testing.

- **User Acceptance Testing:** Acceptance testing is testing performed by users interacting with the interface of the application. It is a manual kind of testing that is performed whenever a piece of the software is implemented. It is a good thing to perform acceptance testing frequently and as early as possible; however, unit and integration tests should locate most of the issues before they ever reach the users. So acceptance testing should not be seen as a replacement for unit and integration testing.

- **Performance Testing:** Ideally performed on as close as possible a mirror of the production setup where the application will finally be deployed. By *setup* we mean everything—the hard- and software, but also the dependencies such as the databases (including data), external services, and so forth. Performance tests aim at detecting what the throughput of the application will be under normal load. For web applications it can be the average response time of requests with a predicted user load. The results of performance testing can verify whether the application will be able to comply with the proposed Service Level Agreements (SLAs).

- **Stress Testing:** Ideally requires the same setup as performance testing. However here we are putting the application under an abnormal amount of load (or stress). It aims at detecting weak spots such as transactions that start to break or other failures that do not appear under normal operation. In general it gives an idea about the stability and robustness of the entire setup when the borders of normal load are crossed.

As explained we will limit ourselves to discussing unit, integration, and system testing. For system testing we will limit ourselves to automated front-end testing. These three layers are the ones that should make up 90% or more of your entire (automatic) test set. They are the ones that will prove that your code is working and will remain working when features are added or code is refactored. These tests will be able to run automatically and everywhere. At this level Spring's test support will also prove itself to be the most useful. Let's continue by taking a closer look into unit tests.

Unit Tests

A unit test accompanies the code on its lowest level possible and is written at development time. It can take many forms, from a basic test that verifies the behavior of a domain object to a more compelling test that verifies the behavior of a business service. Most important, a unit test is system independent and does not depend on any resource whatsoever. If a piece of code depends on a resource, that resource is "simulated" one way or the other. We will discuss mock objects, or mocks (which are a form of simulators) in the coming sections, but for now it's enough to understand that a mock is a code replacement for a resource. The most important criteria a good unit test should comply with can be listed as follows. A good unit test should do all of the following:

- **Run fast:** A unit test must run extremely fast. If it needs to wait for database connections or external server processes, or to parse large files, its usefulness will quickly become limited. A test should provide an immediate response and instant gratification.

- **Have zero external configuration:** A unit test must not require any external configuration files, not even simple text files. The test's configurations must be provided and set by the test framework itself by calling code. The intent is to minimize both the runtime of the test and to eliminate external dependencies (which can change over time, becoming out of sync with the test). Test case conditions should be expressed in the test framework, creating more readable test conditions.

- **Run independent of other tests:** A unit test must be able to run in complete isolation. In other words, the unit test can't depend on some other test running before or after itself. Each test is a stand-alone unit. In fact, every test method inside a test should be stand-alone and not depend on another method or on the test methods being run in a certain order.

- **Depend on zero external resources:** A unit test must not depend on any outside resources, such as database connections or web services. Not only will these resources slow the test down, but they are outside the control of the test and thus aren't guaranteed to be in a correct state for testing.

- **Leave external state untouched:** A unit test must not leave any evidence that it ever ran. Unit tests are written to be repeatable, so they must clean up after themselves. Obviously, this is much easier when the test doesn't rely on external resources (which are often harder to clean up or restore).

- **Test smallest unit of code possible:** A unit test must test the smallest unit of code possible in order to isolate the code under test. In object-oriented programming, this unit is usually a method of an object or class. Writing unit tests such that a method is tested independently of other methods reduces the number of code lines that could contain a potential bug.

Integration Tests

An integration test accompanies the code and is written at development time, just like a unit test. However, unlike the unit test, an integration test spans multiple layers and tries to use as many resources as it possibly can. In our case integration tests are designed to never depend on "real" system resources in such a way that the test depends on a specific environment. Your tests should be able to run anywhere and anytime.

An example that breaks this rule might be a prepopulated external database. In that case you can only run the test in the environment where you can access the database. If the database is down or experiences problems, you will be unable to run your tests. Also, all users should have their proper database tables. Otherwise, multiple users will not be able to run the tests at the same time without interfering with each other. When you are developing remotely and don't have a VPN connection, you won't be able to connect to the database and thus won't be able to run the tests. All of this makes your life harder than it should be and may quickly demotivate you from writing good and complete tests.

Our integration tests will use in-memory equivalents of these resources: in-memory databases, in-memory directory servers, in-memory browsers, and so forth. They allow testing the "integration" of several layers of our application without being affected by the environment. If at a certain point it becomes impossible to fall back on such resources, mock objects are used in the same way as with unit testing.

An integration test is no replacement for system testing using the real resources. But it tries to simulate the target environment as closely as possible, reducing issues when performing the actual system or user acceptance testing. Real system testing is usually more resource-intensive and harder to automate. You will benefit in these latter testing stages if you have created a solid integration testing harness, because many problems will already have been detected and solved thanks to these integration tests.

The important thing to remember is that these tests are all accompanying the project. They are made at development time, by developers. They are run by developers in an automated fashion. If any test fails, your project is "broken." Also, don't forget that integration testing that isn't dependent on actual resources and users enables you to nail down a lot of fundamental problems in an efficient manner early in the project's lifecycle. This makes later system testing and user acceptance testing smoother and easier. It is always better to use a resource (which runs in memory or does not create a dependency) than to use a static simulator or a mock.

As a final word on in-memory resources: it could well be that your project uses special queries that only run on a specific DMBS, and hence there is no use in firing them at another database. It might also be the case that the statements in question are not even supported. In most cases these special queries only take up a very small amount (for an average project) of the code base. It is better to create resource-dependent (system) tests just for those specific cases than to make your entire test set dependent on real resources.

Also, if you are using DBMS-specific features or complex query logic that is impossible to simulate on another resource, are you sure that your Java code is the right place for it? Isn't a database object such as a (materialized) view, procedure or function a better solution? This point leads into an architectural discussion, but it is important to consider and can have impact not only on your overall architecture and reusability but also the testability of your (Java) project.

■ **Note** There is not always a clear separation between a unit and an integration test, although this discussion has emphasized the idea of a noticeable dividing line. Sometimes you just need to test that business algorithm without being bugged with "how to get the data." We would call that a unit test. In another situation, you want to make sure that an HQL or JPQL query translates to executable SQL and performs what you want. This is something we would execute against an in-memory database and hence call it an integration test.

Setting Up a Basic Unit Test

In this section we will explain how to set up a basic unit test using the JUnit framework[6] without any Spring involvement. We will address some specific JUnit features using annotations. If you are already familiar with JUnit,[6] feel free to skim this section quickly.

---

[6] http://www.junit.org/

■ **Note** From experience we know that most developers are at least familiar with JUnit. Since we want to explicitly show you the Spring testing framework, we opted to do this in combination with JUnit. However, we also advise you to take a look at TestNG.[7] While it is not source-compatible with JUnit, they look the same on the surface. If you know JUnit, using TestNG will be a breeze. However, TestNG has noticeably more features related to ordering tests, expressing dependencies, and managing greater amounts of tests. TestNG is also more flexible than JUnit. There is also an STS (Eclipse) plug-in (and build plug-in for Gradle and Maven). See this IBM[8] resource for a nice comparison between the two frameworks and see what suits you and your project best.

Our basic setup starts by creating a Java class (which will become our test) in the test class path (src/test/java). We will be using JUnit4, which uses annotations to denote specific functionality. We create a DummyDao class in the production classpath (src/main/java), which will serve as our class to test (see Listing 9-1). The DummyDao will execute operations on a virtual database, in our case a simple ArrayList. The DummyDao class has three operations: delete an entry from the database, add an entry to the database, and search for entries in the database that contain the given query word.

Listing 9-1. A simple class representing a DAO (Data Access Object) that we are going to unit-test

```
package com.apress.prospringmvc.bookstore.dao;

public class DummyDao {

    private List<String> database;

    public DummyDao(List<String> database) {
        this.database = database;
    }

    public void delete(String element) {
        database.remove(element);
    }

    public void add(String element) {
        database.add(element);
    }

    public List<String> find(String queryWord) {
        List<String> result = new ArrayList<String>();
        for (String element : database) {
            if (element.contains(queryWord)) {
                result.add(element);
            }
```

---

[7] http://testng.org/doc/index.html
[8] http://www.ibm.com/developerworks/java/library/j-cq08296/

```
        }
        return result;
    }
}
```

Next we add tests for each of the methods (see Listing 9-2).

Listing 9-2. The test case for DatabaseDao

```
package com.apress.prospringmvc.bookstore.basic;

import static junit.framework.Assert.assertEquals;
import static junit.framework.Assert.assertTrue;

import org.junit.Before;
import org.junit.Test;

import com.apress.prospringmvc.bookstore.dao.DummyDao;

public class BasicUnitTest {

    private List<String> database;
    private DummyDao dummyDao;

    @Before
    public void dataSetup() {
        database = new ArrayList<String>();
        for (int i = 0; i < 20; i++) {
            database.add("test" + i);
        }
        dummyDao = new DummyDao(database);
    }

    @Test
    public void testDeleteQuery() {
        assertEquals(1, dummyDao.find("test0").size());
        dummyDao.delete("test0");
        assertEquals(19, database.size());
        assertEquals(0, dummyDao.find("test0").size());
    }

    @Test
    public void testAddQuery() {
        assertEquals(0, dummyDao.find("test20").size());
        dummyDao.add("test20");
        assertEquals(21, database.size());
        assertEquals(1, dummyDao.find("test20").size());
    }

    @Test
    public void testFindQuery() {
        List<String> results = dummyDao.find("2");
```

```
assertEquals(2, results.size());
    for (String result : results) {
        assertTrue(result.equals("test2") || result.equals("test12"));
```

The `@Test` annotation denotes a method as a test method. This method will be picked up and executed by JUnit. Inside this test method you will write the code to test your actual production code. Other methods in the test class not carrying a specific annotation are left alone. The `@Before` annotation is run before every test method. It will make sure our database is populated with our initial data. If a `@Test` method changed the data, we will make sure the data is reset to its initial state. It is important that each method runs as an independent test. You should not make dependencies between `@Test` methods, as your test code becomes brittle and hard to understand very fast. Also, you have no control over the order in which the @Test methods are executed.

STS comes shipped with a JUnit plug-in out of the box. Once you have at least one `@Test` method, you can right-click on the class and select Run As. The extra run option JUnit Test will automatically appear. Click it to run the test.

The `assertTrue` and `assertEquals` methods were imported as static imports from the `junit.framework.Assert` class (as you can see at the top of Listing 9-2). These methods allow you to verify the behavior, and let the test stop if the behavior is not what you expect. This is just a bit of sugar syntax, as it makes your code more fluent to read. Mostly you don't need a lot of these methods. With `assertTrue` and `assertEquals`, you will already get far.

If we take the `testDeleteQuery` method as an example, we first execute the delete query to delete an entry in our database. Next we check to see whether the database indeed contains one entry less. When this is not the case, the `assertEquals` fails and that particular test method is marked as failed, as shown in Figure 9-3.

Figure 9-3. *A JUnit test failure*

If all tests succeed, you see a green bar like the one in Figure 9-4.

Figure 9-4. *A JUnit test success*

Besides the `@Before` method, there is also `@After`. The `@After` method is run after each test method, even if the method throws an exception or if one of the assertions fails. There are also the `@BeforeClass` and `@AfterClass`, which are executed once, before the first test method starts and after the last test method ends, respectively. You can see the order visualized in Figure 9-5.

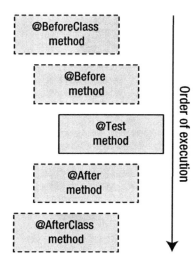

Figure 9-5. JUnit annotation execution order

The @BeforeClass, @Before, @After and @AfterClass are of course optional annotations (that's why they are shown in dashed rectangles). If you don't specify an @Before, for example, JUnit will immediately start with your test method, and then, if you specified it, execute the @After method. If you didn't specify it, the next test method will run. Don't forget that @Before and @After run before and after *every* test method. @BeforeClass and @AfterClass run only once, at the beginning of the test and at the end. JUnit has a few more extra features such as Suites and Categories, but they are outside the scope of this chapter. You can find more information on the JUnit website[9] and in the JavaDoc.[10]

This wraps up our quick introduction to JUnit and how to write a quick test. This will be sufficient for the remainder of this chapter.

Testing Code Coverage

Using the STS plug-in EclEmma, you can get an overview of the code that has been tested by your test. This is as easy as going to the Spring dashboard, clicking the extension tab on the bottom of the view, and typing **eclemma** in the search field, and installing the EclEmma plug-in (see Figure 9-6).

---

[9] http://www.junit.org/
[10] http://kentbeck.github.com/junit/javadoc/latest/

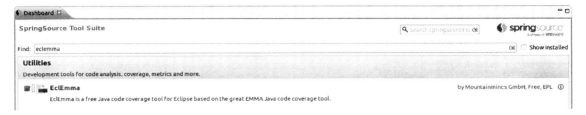

Figure 9-6. Installing EclEmma

After installing the plug-in you can right click on your test and select Coverage as ➤ JUnit test. The result will come in a separate panel, as shown in Figure 9-7. If this panel doesn't show up, you can open it manually by selecting Window in the STS menu bar, and then Show View ➤ Other. If you then type **coverage** in the text field that appears, one result will appear in the list: "Java" with "Coverage" underneath it. Select Coverage and then click OK.

Element	Coverage	Covered Instructions	Missed Instructions	Total Instructions
▸ 📖 bookstore-shared	0.0 %	0	2493	2493
▾ 📖 chapter9-bookstore	9.6 %	157	1479	1636
▾ 🗀 src/main/java	4.3 %	44	977	1021
▸ ⊞ com.apress.prospringmvc.bookstore.web.controller	0.0 %	0	313	313
▸ ⊞ com.apress.prospringmvc.bookstore.web.view	0.0 %	0	271	271
▸ ⊞ com.apress.prospringmvc.bookstore.web.config	0.0 %	0	173	173
▸ ⊞ com.apress.prospringmvc.bookstore.web	0.0 %	0	92	92
▸ ⊞ com.apress.prospringmvc.bookstore.web.method.support	0.0 %	0	74	74
▸ ⊞ com.apress.prospringmvc.bookstore.web.interceptor	0.0 %	0	39	39
▸ ⊞ com.apress.prospringmvc.bookstore.web.servlet	0.0 %	0	15	15
▾ ⊞ com.apress.prospringmvc.bookstore.dao	100.0 %	44	0	44
▾ 🗎 DummyDao.java	100.0 %	44	0	44
▾ ⊙ DummyDao	100.0 %	44	0	44
⚡ DummyDao(List<String>)	100.0 %	6	0	6
● add(String)	100.0 %	6	0	6
● delete(String)	100.0 %	6	0	6
● find(String)	100.0 %	26	0	26
▸ 🗀 src/test/java	18.4 %	113	502	615

Figure 9-7. Code coverage after running EclEmma

We can clearly see that our DummyDao class has been tested 100%, so every line of code has been touched by our test case. Depending on the type of class you test, it is not always possible to get 100% coverage, but this is the goal you should strive to for each test you create. Note that in some cases it is not feasible or simply not required to have 100% coverage. For example, if your object has multiple get/set methods (generated by your IDE), then testing those is a bit superfluous, even though it results in not getting 100% coverage. However, don't give up too soon, either. If you lose coverage because of code depending on resources, you can use in-memory resources or mocks as we will discuss in the next sections.

After performing the coverage, you can also double-click on the actual production class you have tested: DummyDao in our case. EclEmma will indicate the lines that have been (or have not been) tested. In this run everything will turn up green, since every line of code has been tested. We also performed a second run, removing all references in the test method to the find method of the DummyDao. We placed the results next to each other in Figure 9-8.

```
DummyDao.java ☒

 package com.apress.prospringmvc.bookstore.dao;          package com.apress.prospringmvc.bookstore.dao;

⊕import java.util.ArrayList;▯                           ⊕import java.util.ArrayList;

 public class DummyDao {                                  public class DummyDao {

     private List<String> database;                           private List<String> database;

     public DummyDao(List<String> database) {                 public DummyDao(List<String> database) {
         this.database = database;                                this.database = database;
     }                                                        }

     public void delete(String element) {                     public void delete(String element) {
         database.remove(element);                                database.remove(element);
     }                                                        }

     public void add(String element) {                        public void add(String element) {
         database.add(element);                                   database.add(element);
     }                                                        }

     public List<String> find(String queryWord) {            public List<String> find(String queryWord) {
         List<String> result = new ArrayList<String>();           List<String> result = new ArrayList<String>();
         for (String element : database) {                        for (String element : database) {
             if (element.contains(queryWord)) {                       if (element.contains(queryWord)) {
                 result.add(element);                                     result.add(element);
             }                                                        }
         }                                                        }
         return result;                                           return result;
     }                                                        }
 }                                                        }
```

Figure 9-8. EclEmma showing tested (green) and untested (red) lines of code

On the left you can see the 100% code coverage of our first run (all green). On the right you see the run where we removed every reference to the find method in our test. The find method will turn up in red, as it has not been touched by our test. The diamond icons on the left of some lines indicate whether the loop ran for each element in the list or not. For example, if we put a break statement after the if, the loop would only run once, and the first diamond would appear yellow and indicate that the branch was not completely covered. The same goes for the second diamond, which covers the if statement. If this statement was not executed, the diamond would also show up in orange.

Using Spring's Test Support

In the previous section you saw how we can create a basic unit test using JUnit. This was a very isolated test, not requiring any dependencies like Spring or other resources, as a unit test should be. In this section we will introduce Spring's test support to create integration tests that actually use these dependencies together in the test.

The Spring test support is all about integrating Spring within your tests. With a couple of annotations, you can load a Spring context and make it available to your unit test. This allows you to inject dependencies directly in the test using, for, example autowiring.

Setting Up Our Integration Test

Next we are going to setup an integration test that will test our com.apress.prospringmvc.bookstore .repository.JpaBookRepository. We start by creating a normal class in the test classpath (see Listing 9-3). Ideally you place your test in the same package as the class you are going to test, but on the test class path instead of the production classpath (which is src/main/java). So we will create a com.apress .prospringmvc.bookstore.repository.JpaBookRepositoryTest in the src/test/java classpath.

Listing 9-3. The start of our integration test testing JpaBookRepository, in src/test/java

```
package com.apress.prospringmvc.bookstore.repository;

public class JpaBookRepositoryTest {
}
```

To enable the Spring test context, we tell JUnit it has to bootstrap Spring, by adding the following annotation on top of the class, as shown in Listing 9-4.

Listing 9-4. Adding the runner to enable Spring's test support

```
package com.apress.prospringmvc.bookstore.repository;

import org.junit.runner.RunWith;
import org.springframework.test.context.junit4.SpringJUnit4ClassRunner;

@RunWith(SpringJUnit4ClassRunner.class)
public class JpaBookRepositoryTest {
}
```

SpringJUnit4ClassRunner is a Spring-specific integration class for JUnit. JUnit inspects those classes with the @RunWith annotation. When you indicate you want to run a class as a JUnit test, the test class is passed as a parameter to the JUnit runtime (in our case this is done by the IDE). JUnit will then scan for @RunWith annotations. In our case it will execute org.springframework.test.context.junit4 .SpringJUnit4ClassRunner. This class will start Spring's test support by using the Spring org.springframework.test.context.TestContextManager and org.springframework.test.context .TestContext. This will enable all Spring functionality, such as loading your application context (based upon the @ContextConfiguration, as we will see next), enabling autowiring, and executing implementations of org.springframework.test.context.TestExecutionListener. The latter are special listeners that can be executed before initialization of a test class, before running a test class, and before running a test method within a test class. They can be registered using the TestExecutionListener annotation. There are three listeners registered by default:

- `org.springframework.test.context.support`
  `.DependencyInjectionTestExecutionListener`

- `org.springframework.test.context.support`
  `.DirtiesContextTestExecutionListener`

- `org.springframework.test.context.transaction`
  `.TransactionalTestExecutionListener`

For our purposes here, only the last one is relevant as it will manage our transactions within our tests; we will discuss this later on.

Finally, we have to indicate which (test) context we want to load for our test class. At this point you have two options:

- One way is to load one or more production contexts. These are the contexts your application is actually using. If you want to differentiate between test runs and the actual application run, you can make use of Spring profiles.

- You can also opt for setting up specific contexts just for your test. This way you can specify exactly which resources you need.

Each of these approaches has its pros and cons, so you should weigh them based on your application and what you are going to test to determine which is best. The more modular your Spring configuration is (either in terms of annotated classes or XML configuration files), the easier it will become to mix both approaches. When you have a Spring configuration listing your repositories, but a separate configuration for the datasource, you could load the production configuration for the repositories in your test combined with a separate test context for the datasource (which will in that case point to an in-memory database).

When you have identified which contexts you want to load, you can use the @ContextConfiguration annotation on top of the class to specify them. Using this annotation you can either specify a context XML file, using the locations attribute (which takes an array of XML config files) or the classes attribute, which takes an array of @Configuration classes to load the context. You *cannot* use both. If you want to mix XML and classes, you have to load the one from the other. That means that if you want to work with XML, but also need to load @Configuration classes, you have to load them from one of the XML context files. If you are working with @Configuration classes, you have to use @ImportResource in one of these classes to load the desired XML config file.

We are going to use our production context classes, so we will use the classes attribute (see Listing 9-5).

Listing 9-5. Adding the context configuration for loading our Spring config

```java
package com.apress.prospringmvc.bookstore.repository;

import org.junit.runner.RunWith;
import org.springframework.test.context.junit4.SpringJUnit4ClassRunner;
import com.apress.prospringmvc.bookstore.config.↵
        InfrastructureContextConfiguration;
import com.apress.prospringmvc.bookstore.config.TestDataContextConfiguration;
import org.springframework.test.context.ContextConfiguration;
@RunWith(SpringJUnit4ClassRunner.class)
@ContextConfiguration(classes = { InfrastructureContextConfiguration.class,↵
 TestDataContextConfiguration.class })
public class JpaBookRepositoryTest {

}
```

That is all. When you run the test as a JUnit test, the Spring context will be booted thanks to the Spring test support (which is itself initially booted by the SpringJUnit4ClassRunner). In our case this means that all repositories and services are loaded into the context, and an in-memory database is started and prepopulated with data.

In this section we are only going to test the JpaBookstoreRepository. But there are plenty of other classes to test. We will create a matching test for each of them and apply the same annotations to load the context for each test class.

Note Instead of repeating the annotation configuration for each test class independently, we could have moved it to a common superclass from which each test could extend. This would have saved us repeating the same annotation configuration in each test class. The same goes for JUnit annotations, like the ones we saw before (@Before, @After, and so on). However, to make every class complete by itself we duplicated the configuration. Also, you should not create superclasses merely to avoid repeating annotation configuration. Only do that if the classes have something more in common. For example, to test your repositories you could set up a superclass that has the annotation configuration and sets up a minimal data set useful for all repository tests. Creating superclasses containing only annotation configuration can quickly result in the wild growth of those classes and make your code less clear.

Because this is a small project, the context almost loads instantly. For bigger projects, that might take some more time. To make sure the context is not loaded separately for each class independently, the Spring Test Framework provides consistent loading of Spring application contexts and caching of those contexts. Support for the caching of loaded contexts is important, because startup time can become an issue, not because of Spring itself, but because the objects instantiated by the Spring container take time to instantiate. For example, a project with many Hibernate mapping files might take several seconds to load because of the parse time required for each of the mapping files. If the context is only loaded once, an extra load time of 5 seconds won't be noticeable. But if it loaded for each test individually (and you have 200 tests, for example) then 5 seconds extra load time means that your test set runs 16 minutes longer without any good reason. If your tests run slowly, this starts to degrade your infrastructure, which could then result in excuses not to write tests "because they run so slow." It is important to keep your test set lean and mean, so that it costs as little time as possible to run the test set.

By default, once the configured ApplicationContext is loaded, it is reused for each test. Thus the setup cost is incurred only once (per test suite), and subsequent test execution is much faster. In this context, the term *test suite* means all tests run in the same JVM. However, when you run tests from STS one by one, this means the application context will be booted separately for each of them. The solution (using JUnit) is to build a suite, or run them using your build tool, in our case Gradle. In that case the application context will only be loaded once for all tests that are run. Building the chapter9 sample project with Gradle will automatically run the tests. You start the build by first going into the chapter9 sample directory, and then issue following Gradle command:

```
$ gradle build
```

The output will look similar to this:

```
:bookstore-shared:compileJava UP-TO-DATE
```

--further gradle output omitted for brevity--

```
:chapter9-bookstore:testClasses
:chapter9-bookstore:test
22:30:31.392 [Thread-15] INFO  o.s.c.s.GenericApplicationContext - Closing
org.springframework.context.support.GenericApplicationContext@39518cc: startup date [Thu Mar
29 22:30:28 CEST 2012]; root of context hierarchy
```

```
22:30:31.397 [Thread-15] INFO  o.s.b.f.s.DefaultListableBeanFactory - Destroyi
```

-- further gradle output omitted for brevity--

```
22:30:31.401 [Thread-15] INFO  o.s.o.j.LocalContainerEntityManagerFactoryBean - Closing JPA
EntityManagerFactory for persistence unit 'bookstore'
```

```
:chapter9-bookstore:check
:chapter9-bookstore:build
```

```
BUILD SUCCESSFUL
```

```
Total time: 17.033 secs
```

In the above example all tests were run by Gradle, and thus share a single application context instance. In the unlikely case that a test corrupts the application context (for example by modifying a bean definition or the state of an application object) and requires reloading, Spring's test support can be configured to reload the configuration and rebuild the application context before executing the next test. The latter can be accomplished by putting the @DirtiesContext annotation on the class, or even the test method, that is altering the application context. The next test class (or test method) will get a refreshed application context. You can also inject the ApplicationContext directly if that would be required (see Listing 9-6).

Listing 9-6. *If required, the application context can be autowired.*

```
@Autowired
Private ApplicationContext ApplicationContext
```

Because we enabled Spring's test support, we now enabled Spring for our test cases with the supplied configuration. All Spring features are now enabled from out tests. We can for example autowire any bean directly in our tests that is loaded in our Spring configuration. Our test class has now become fully Spring-aware.

Managing Transactions from Within the Test

Since we are going to write an integration test that will access our in-memory database (through the repository we are testing), we need to manage our transactions from within the test case. In our production code the transactions are managed by the services and not the repositories themselves. The repositories take part in the transaction started by the service. So in this case we need our test case to start the transaction, since we will be testing the repositories directly. We will do this by putting the @Transactional annotation on the test class, making each test method start a transaction first.

When such an annotation is found the automatically registered TransactionalTestExecutionListener will assure a transaction *rollback* by default when the test method ends. As mentioned earlier in the chapter, TransactionalTestExecutionListener is one of the default listeners that are registered by the Spring's test support. To give you a quick insight; these listeners (and all other possible registered TestExecutionListener's) are invoked before (and after) a test method is executed. This listener in question will automatically mark the transaction for rollback after the test method ended. Remember, this is something specific to Spring's test support. These listeners are not there when you boot your application context the normal way. So in a normal production scenario the transaction would commit when no exceptions occurred.

Rolling back is actually the behavior you want. It means that CUD operations (Create, Update and Delete) will not modify data in our database. Allowing them to do so would be the least desirable approach, since that might create data dependencies between tests. When tests are changed, or for some reason the order in which tests are run is altered, some tests suddenly might start to fail because they depend on data being added by another test that has not yet run. The best pattern here is to insert the data you need on the method level and let the transaction roll back. This way the data is not persisted in the database and no traces remain.

■ **Note** When testing a repository, you will probably need some default data setup that can be used for each test method. Instead of repeating the same data setup over again for each test method, you can safely create this data in an `@Before` annotated method. This method will automatically run before each test method. It will also run in the same transaction as the test method itself, and hence data inserted, modified, or deleted will be rolled back the same way as with the test method that is being executed.

This approach of automatically rolling back the transaction at the end of each test method also has a drawback. When using an ORM (Object Relational Mapping), rolling back works great for Read operations, since all queries have been sent to the database, giving you a complete coverage. However, when using an ORM like Hibernate (directly or via JPA), CUD operations might not be flushed. Hibernate does write-behind. It flushes statements to the database when it thinks the time has come or at least when the transaction commits. So while you called that method which triggered an update or insert statement, the statement might never be flushed to database when rolling back the transaction. In that case you never had the certainty the query was actually executed on the database. You have two options for handling this:

- Let the transaction commit anyway. You can do this by adding `@Rollback(false)` on the test method. You can then create a tear-down method (`@After`) which removes the data you inserted.

- Before the end of the test method, call `flush` on the `EntityManager` (in the case of JPA) to let it flush all outstanding statements to database. Remember that the transaction will roll back, so the changes will not remain persistent. But they have been received and verified by the database, so you are sure they will work.

Choosing one of the two approaches is a matter of preference; both will yield the same result. The first approach requires you to have some additional code in the teardown method. The second approach is more automatic, but requires some more understanding of the ORM you are using. For the second solution you could also put the `flush` in a `@After` method, perhaps inherited from a superclass.

As we mentioned before, the integration test doesn't give a 100% guarantee. For starters, we are working against a different RDMBS than your actual target environment. When rolling back transactions instead of committing them, you're increasing the possibility that something might go wrong when it actually commits. However, when applying any of the previously discussed strategies, it is very unlikely that this will happen. If you flush, all statements have been processed by the database, so there is normally no reason the commit will fail. Although in very specific scenarios there might still be something that goes wrong, chances of that are very small. The big advantage is that your tests remain independent and you will never have to figure out why suddenly 10 tests are starting to fail when you add another test that by itself is fully working. Your test set will also be resource-independent and run everywhere. It is clear that these are major advantages.

■ **Note** As you know, a big code base is hard to manage in terms of design, API, consistency and so on. Do not forget that your tests might even become a bigger code base than your actual production code. Take care of them and they will take care of you.

Testing the JpaBookRepository

We now have all the bits and pieces to start building our test. For the transaction strategy, we will choose the second option. That is, we depend on the infrastructure to start and roll back the transaction and we will manually call flush on test method that perform CUD operations.

Next, we continue to define a test method for each of the methods exposed by the BookRepository interface and test them. For the sample code we will restrict the test to two read methods and one create method of the BookRepository. The other methods are tested in the same fashion and would not show anything new. We will also create a setup method (annotated with @Before) which will load the common data used by each of the test methods. Let's first look at the test code in Listing 9-7.

Listing 9-7. *The complete test class in src/test/java*

```
package com.apress.prospringmvc.bookstore.repository;

import static junit.framework.Assert.assertEquals;

import javax.persistence.EntityManager;
import javax.persistence.PersistenceContext;

import org.junit.After;
import org.junit.Before;
import org.junit.Test;
import org.junit.runner.RunWith;
import org.springframework.beans.factory.annotation.Autowired;
import org.springframework.test.annotation.Rollback;
import org.springframework.test.context.ContextConfiguration;
import org.springframework.test.context.junit4.SpringJUnit4ClassRunner;
import org.springframework.transaction.annotation.Transactional;

import com.apress.prospringmvc.bookstore.config.
        InfrastructureContextConfiguration; ↵
import com.apress.prospringmvc.bookstore.config.TestDataContextConfiguration;
import com.apress.prospringmvc.bookstore.domain.Book;
import com.apress.prospringmvc.bookstore.domain.Category;
import com.apress.prospringmvc.bookstore.domain.support.BookBuilder;
import com.apress.prospringmvc.bookstore.domain.support.CategoryBuilder;
import com.apress.prospringmvc.bookstore.domain.support.EntityBuilder.
        EntityBuilderManager; ↵
```

```
@RunWith(SpringJUnit4ClassRunner.class)
@ContextConfiguration(classes = { InfrastructureContextConfiguration.class,
TestDataContextConfiguration.class })
@Transactional
public class JpaBookRepositoryTest {

    @Autowired
    private BookRepository bookRepository;
    @Autowired
    private BookBuilder bookBuilder;
    @Autowired
    private CategoryBuilder categoryBuilder;
    @PersistenceContext
    private EntityManager entityManager;

    private Book book;
    private Category category;

    @Before
    public void setupData() {
        category = categoryBuilder.name("Evolution").build();
        book = bookBuilder.description("Richard Dawkins' brilliant
                reformulation of the theory of natural selection")
                .author("Richard Dawkins").title("The Selfish Gene:↵
                        30th Anniversary Edition")
                .isbn("9780199291151")
                .category(category).build();
    }

    @Test
    public void testFindById() {
        Book book = bookRepository.findById(this.book.getId());
        assertEquals(this.book.getAuthor(), book.getAuthor());
        assertEquals(this.book.getDescription(), book.getDescription());
        assertEquals(this.book.getIsbn(), book.getIsbn());
    }

    @Test
    public void testFindByCategory() {
        List<Book> books = bookRepository.findByCategory(category);
        assertEquals(1, books.size());

        for (Book book : books) {
            assertEquals(this.book.getCategory().getId(), category.getId());
            assertEquals(this.book.getAuthor(), book.getAuthor());
            assertEquals(this.book.getDescription(), book.getDescription());
            assertEquals(this.book.getIsbn(), book.getIsbn());
        }
    }
}
```

```
    @Test
    public void testStoreBook() {
        Book book = bookBuilder.description("Something").author("JohnDoe").title("John Doe's↵
life")
                .isbn("1234567890123").category(category).build();
        bookRepository.storeBook(book);

        // Explicitly flush so any CUD query that is left behind is sent to the database
        // before rollback
        entityManager.flush();
    }
}
```

In this code we make our test transactional by default. For the read methods we insert additional data using the already discussed JUnit @Before method. We use the Builder pattern to build our data and it is by default inserted using an EntityManager instance injected in the builders. This data is also removed when the test method ends because of the transaction rollback.

▪ **Note** We said before that one should perform a flush in a test method testing functionality that performs CUD, to make sure all statements are flushed to database. While testing a read-only method, we first inserted data in the database using JPA. What about flushing these insert statements? Well, actually, we don't care. The ORM will flush them as it sees fit to make sure our read operations work on the latest data. It might hold back the insertion of the category and book, but from the moment it sees our query to select a book by ID, it will first flush the book and category to database. The point is that we are not testing any of our CUD operations. How the ORM manages the write-behind internally to make sure our read operations see the latest data is not our concern.

In our method that tests the creation of new book records, we explicitly flushed before the test method ends. This way we are sure that the insert statement (generated by the query in the storeBook method of our repository) was send to database (which is probably the only statement). After that, the test method ends and the transaction is rolled back.

Using Mock Objects

In this section we will introduce you to using mock objects. When creating a unit test, you want to make sure your test is as isolated as possible and does not depend on resources. In your integration tests, on the other hand, you try to use as many resources as you can, as long as you remain in control and they don't make your test dependent on a specific resource or environment. For those cases where you are not able to accomplish this, mock objects will help you. Let's start at looking what mock objects really are.

What Are Mock Objects?

As explained in the introduction, in some cases you want to isolate a certain algorithm to unit-test. That algorithm might depend on a repository feeding it data, and you don't want to fiddle with setting up data for testing the algorithm. You want to concentrate the test on the algorithm alone. A mock object is a good solution here, as it enables you to plug in a replacement of the real resource and preprogram it with data. Whenever the algorithm makes a call to the mock, it is able to return data that you programmed it with as part of the test setup.

Mocks also have other benefits. A mock is smart. For example, it can be designed to return data only if the parameter of the method call matches a certain value. A mock can also be verified. When the test is done, you can ask the mock to check if all methods you programmed it with were indeed called with the expected parameters. If not, it will let your test fail. Another use case for mock objects is for resources for which there are no easy in-memory alternatives; for example, you have a dependency on a legacy system.

Mock objects fall in the category of so called "test doubles." There are different kinds of test doubles, but only one of them is a real mock. In his article "Mocks Aren't Stubs,"[11] Martin Fowler distinguishes the different test doubles and names them appropriately. Let's have a look at them:

- **Dummy.** Dummies are mostly real implementations of a given interface. We could, for example, build a DummyBookRepository. The method bodies of dummies are mostly empty. If their signature requires them to return a value, it is mostly "null." Dummies are useful to build objects that you are going to test and have a mandatory dependency on the dummy. But the dependency in question is not used for testing the given functionality.

- **Fake.** A fake is a working replacement for a real resource, such as an in-memory database or an in-memory implementation of a web service. It is clear that in-memory fakes enjoy real advantages over any external dependency, since those would again break our rule that our tests should be able to run everywhere, while still supplying a high level of guarantee that your code will work against the real resource once the fake is replaced with the real resource.

- **Stub.** Stubs are replacement objects that are able to return preprogrammed values when their methods are called. They normally don't respond outside the values that they have been programmed with. The way they capture state is very basic, and the verification process mostly does not allow you to do behavior verification. These are sometimes also referred to as "simulators."

- **Mock.** Mocks add extra functionality in the training (setting up the preprogrammed data) and verification phase compared to a stub. A mock will allow you to verify not only that a given method was called on the mock, but also that it was called with the desired parameters. This is normally built in the mock framework and is not something you have to build yourself (unlike with stubs).

From our experience, all of these deserve a certain place in the project. While all test doubles can in fact also be replaced by mocks, you probably shouldn't do so. A mock object is something that is built on the fly in your test, is programmed with data, expects certain behavior, and is verified before the test

---

[11] http://martinfowler.com/articles/mocksArentStubs.html

ends. A dummy is a real class that sits in your project code. In addition to the `com.apress.prospringmvc.bookstore.repository.JpaBookRepository`, there could also be a "`DummyBookRepository`." It is not supposed to do anything, besides being there. The advantages are that you could use Spring profiles or selective context loading in your test to wire up the one or the other. This might keep your code base cleaner and tests easier to understand. Also, when using a mock where you really want a dummy, you will be sending out wrong signals to other developers reading your code. They will see a mock, which is not programmed and not verified, so they will think it is a developer error. Using a dummy, you clearly indicate that the dependency is not relevant in the scope of the test you are performing, but the object you are testing has a mandatory dependency on it and so you gave it a dummy implementation.

At certain points you want to build a real integration test. In the previous section we tested our `JpaBookRepository` against an in-memory database. Although we could have mocked the `EntityManager`, not doing so added an enormous value; it taught us that our JPQL queries were translated to SQL that was actually correct and could be executed by an RDBMS. Replacing this with a mock would cut critical things from our test and degrade its effectiveness.

Stubs are probably only useful in special integration testing when there is no in easy fake available for a given resource, for example for a legacy system. The stub could then be wired in as a "dummy with data."

As a final note, think carefully about which kind of testing double you will be using. When writing a unit test, think about using dummies first. If you really need state and behavior verification for the dependency, consider a mock. If you are integration testing, consider using in-memory fakes as much as you possibly can. If you are doing integration testing from another interface (front-end testing using an in-memory browser, for example) consider using stubs.

In this discussion we will limit ourselves to using and creating mocks for our unit tests. In the next section we will dive into the code and test our `AccountService`, while using a mock for its `AccountRepository` dependency.

Testing the AccountService

Our `com.apress.prospringmvc.bookstore.service.AccountService` has two methods: save, which saves a new `com.apress.prospringmvc.bookstore.domain.Account` to the database, and login, which takes a username and password as parameters and verifies the credentials. If the credentials are correct, it returns the `Account` that belongs to the given user. It does that by loading an `Account` from the database where the username matches. After that, it tries to verify passwords. The passwords are SHA-256 hashed. So the service first creates a hash from the password parameter and then compares it with the value retrieved from the database (where we store only the hashed values of the passwords).

We are writing a unit test that will test the login method. In order to do this, we will create a mock for `com.apress.prospringmvc.bookstore.repository.AccountRepository` (this is the repository used to load the `Account` from database based upon the username). We will create a test method that tests a successful login and another that performs a negative test, in which we intentionally supply bad credentials, which should lead produce an exception. Let's look at our first version of the test in Listing 9-8.

Listing 9-8. Setting up the AccountServiceTest in src/test/java

```java
package com.apress.prospringmvc.bookstore.service;

// Other imports omitted, see Listing 9-7

import static junit.framework.Assert.assertEquals;

import org.mockito.Mockito;
import org.springframework.context.annotation.Bean;
import org.springframework.context.annotation.Configuration;

import com.apress.prospringmvc.bookstore.domain.Account;
import com.apress.prospringmvc.bookstore.domain.support.AccountBuilder;
import com.apress.prospringmvc.bookstore.repository.AccountRepository;

@RunWith(SpringJUnit4ClassRunner.class)
@ContextConfiguration
public class AccountServiceTest {

    @Autowired
    private AccountService accountService;
    @Autowired
    private AccountRepository accountRepository;

    @Test(expected = AuthenticationException.class)
    public void testLoginFailure() throws AuthenticationException {
        accountService.login("john", "fail");
    }

    @Test()
    public void testLoginSuccess() throws AuthenticationException {
        Account account = accountService.login("john", "secret");
        assertEquals("John", account.getFirstName());
        assertEquals("Doe", account.getLastName());
    }

    @Configuration
    static class AccountServiceTestContextConfiguration {

        @Bean
        public AccountService accountService() {
            return new AccountServiceImpl();
        }

        @Bean
        public AccountRepository accountRepository() {
            return Mockito.mock(AccountRepository.class);
        }
    }
}
```

Mockito[12] is a state of the art mock framework that we will be using. It is flexible and has a very intuitive API. Throughout this section we will make you more familiar how you can use Mockito for all your mocking needs. The line in bold is all that is needed to create a mock using Mockito. You pass along an interface or class, and Mockito will return a mock object which is not yet programmed.

What further happens is that when adding the ContextConfiguration annotation, Spring will automatically scan for @Configuration classes within the scope of the class and find our AccountServiceTestContextConfiguration. Alternatively, you can also specify classes directly on the ContextConfiguration annotation using the classes attribute, or XML files with the locations attribute. In the AccountServiceTestContextConfiguration configuration class, we created two beans: the first one is the AuthenticationService, the second is the AccountRepository. For the second case we have used Mockito to create a mock. Spring will now auto-inject the AccountRepository into the AuthenticationService when creating the context (remember, Spring will be injecting our mocked version of the AccountRepository).

At this point the test will not run, since we have not yet programmed our mock. When the login method of the AuthenticationService calls a method on our AccountRepository mock, it will return null values. So the next thing to do is program our mock as can be seen in Listing 9-9.

▓ **Note** The testLoginFailure (being a so called "negative" test) uses a JUnit feature to verify that indeed an exception is thrown: @Test(expected = AuthenticationException.class). In this case we require that the AuthenticationException is actually thrown. If it isn't, the test fails.

Listing 9-9. Programming the mock

```
@Before
public void setup() {
    Account account = new AccountBuilder() {
        {
            address("Herve", "4650", "Rue de la gare", "1", null,↵
                    "Belgium");
            credentials("john", "secret");
            name("John", "Doe");
        }
    }.build(true);

    Mockito.when(accountRepository.findByUsername("john"))
            .thenReturn(account);
}
```

We first created the data that our mock will have to return. In our case it is an instance of an Account. The last line of code of Listing 9-9 programs the mock. Whenever the mock receives a call on method findByUsername with the parameter "john", it will return the account. If it receives calls with other parameters (or other methods that aren't programmed), null is returned. This logic is put in an @Before

---

[12] http://code.google.com/p/mockito/

method since we will reset our mock after every test method invocation. The mock will be reprogrammed before a new test execution starts.

Finally, in Listing 9-10, we have the @After method, which will verify the mock's state. It will check that the method we programmed the mock with was indeed called. Here we will strictly check that the method was called once (exactly once). After that we reset to mock so it forgets about its programmed data and verification state. It can then be reprogrammed (which will happen in the @Before method before the next method is executed).

Listing 9-10. Verifying the mock's state and resetting it

```
@After
public void verify() {
    Mockito.verify(accountRepository,
                   VerificationModeFactory.times(1))↵
               .findByUsername(Mockito.anyString());

    // This is allowed here: using container injected mocks
    Mockito.reset(accountRepository);
}
```

The first line verifies that the findByUsername method was called exactly once. If it hadn't been, the verify method would raise an error, letting our test fail. In the second line we reset the mock. You might notice the comment above the reset method. Resetting a mock is normally bad practice. Normally you create a mock in scope of a single test method. You create it, program it, verify it, and that's it. In the next test method you create a new instance of the mock. However, in our case the AccountRepository is autowired (by Spring) in the AccountService. When we create a new instance of the mock, we need to find a clean way to inject it in the AccountService. Yes, as an alternative we could have opted for an extra (AccountRepository) setter on the AccountService, so we could have set the AccountRepository using the setter. This is a matter of preference. In any case we are not violating any rules by resetting the mock this way. Just be sure you don't reset a mock in the middle of a test, for example. In that case you should probably have created two test methods instead.

▪ **Note** You can also use static imports for Mockito methods, just as we did with JUnit. It is in fact a recommended practice, as it keeps your code clean and readable. In the code examples, we deliberately left the classes visible to make it clear that it is a Mockito object rather than a JUnit object (which might not be obvious if you are new to Mockito or mocks in general).

Listing 9-11 shows the complete test case.

Listing 9-11. The complete test case

```
package com.apress.prospringmvc.bookstore.service;

// Other imports omitted, see Listing 9-7

import static junit.framework.Assert.assertEquals;
```

```
import org.mockito.Mockito;
import org.mockito.internal.verification.VerificationModeFactory;
import org.springframework.beans.factory.annotation.Autowired;
import org.springframework.context.annotation.Bean;
import org.springframework.context.annotation.Configuration;

@RunWith(SpringJUnit4ClassRunner.class)
@ContextConfiguration
public class AccountServiceTest {

    @Autowired
    private AccountService accountService;
    @Autowired
    private AccountRepository accountRepository;

    @Before
    public void setup() {
        Account account = new AccountBuilder() {
            {
                address("Herve", "4650", "Rue de la gare", "1", null,↵
                        "Belgium");
                credentials("john", "secret");
                name("John", "Doe");
            }
        }.build(true);
        Mockito.when(accountRepository.findByUsername("john"))
                .thenReturn(account);
    }

    @After
    public void verify() {
        Mockito.verify(accountRepository,↵
                        VerificationModeFactory.times(1))
                        .findByUsername(Mockito.anyString());
        // This is allowed here: using container injected mocks
        Mockito.reset(accountRepository);
    }

    @Test(expected = AuthenticationException.class)
    public void testLoginFailure() throws AuthenticationException {
        accountService.login("john", "fail");
    }

    @Test()
    public void testLoginSuccess() throws AuthenticationException {
        Account account = accountService.login("john", "secret");
        assertEquals("John", account.getFirstName());
        assertEquals("Doe", account.getLastName());
    }
```

```
@Configuration
static class AccountServiceTestContextConfiguration {

    @Bean
    public AccountService accountService() {
        return new AccountServiceImpl();
    }

    @Bean
    public AccountRepository accountRepository() {
        return Mockito.mock(AccountRepository.class);
    }
}
}
```

This concludes the testing of our AccountService using a mocked AccountRepository. We hope we have shown you how easy it is to set up and verify mocks using Mockito and how useful they are in isolating logic to be tested. There are plenty of other features that can help you set up the desired mocking environment. Those are out of scope for this chapter, so we invite you to take a look at the Mockito website for a good starting point.

Testing Your MVC Logic

As shown in Figure 9-9, Spring MVC consists of our view layer (JSPs), the controller (Spring internal code), our model, and our application controllers. It is important that we first decide which of these components we should actually test and which not.

To test JSPs, you need a running servlet container. This will be part of our system tests and we will test it later in this chapter in the section "Automated Front-End Testing." We don't need to test the controller, as this is Spring Framework internal code. We explained before how to test the domain using unit and integration tests, so these are already tested. The only things left to test are our application controllers.

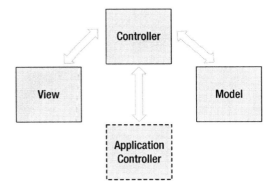

Figure 9-9. Components in an MVC architecture

com.apress.prospringmvc.bookstore.web.controller.LoginController is the application controller we are going to test, more specifically the handleLogin method. Our first advice is to keep the logic inside the application controllers as limited as possible. E.g., when you have extensive validation, put that code in separate classes. This way they become standalone components which are easy to test without requiring your application controller. If you apply this rule consistently, you will be able to test 90% (or more) of your code on the frontend using plain unit tests. This way the application controller will only remain a thin layer between the controller framework and these standalone (easy to test) classes and your model.

Using Spring Mock Objects

When the time has come to test your application controller, you can use the helpers from Spring: `org.springframework.test.web.ModelAndViewAssert` combined with `MockHttpServletRequest`, `MockHttpServletResponse`, and `MockHttpSession` (all found in `org.springframework.mock.web`). Although they are named "Mock" they are more like stubs by our definition of the terms. You can, for example, add attributes to the `MockHttpSession` via `MockHttpServletRequest` and retrieve them later on (`MockHttpServletRequest` uses `MockHttpSession` internally as its session stub). Depending on things you set or do, some `MockHttpServletRequest` methods might react differently when you call them (it also contains some inner logic to simulate the `HttpServletRequest` where possible). We will first show the handle login method, in Listing 9-12, so you can easily follow what we are testing.

Listing 9-12. The handleLogin method from the LoginController

```
@RequestMapping(method = RequestMethod.POST)
public String handleLogin(@RequestParam String username, @RequestParam String⏎
                          password, HttpSession session)⏎
                          throws AuthenticationException {
    Account account = this.accountService.login(username, password);
    session.setAttribute(ACCOUNT_ATTRIBUTE, account);
    String url = (String) session.getAttribute(REQUESTED_URL);
    session.removeAttribute(REQUESTED_URL); // Remove the attribute

    if (StringUtils.hasText(url) && !url.contains("login")) {⏎
        // Prevent loops for the login page.
        return "redirect:" + url;
    } else {
        return "redirect:/index.htm";
    }
}
```

The method in Listing 9-12 takes care of handling the login from the login page. It accepts a username and password submitted from the login form. It will then authenticate the user using the `AccountService` and put the result (an Account) on the HTTP session using the constant `ACCOUNT_ATTRIBUTE` as key. You can see the `SecurityHandlerInterceptor` defined in the Chapter 6 section "Implementing a HandlerInterceptor."

Next we show the test case (see Listing 9-13) and then discuss some specific code snippets.

Listing 9-13. The test for the LoginController handleLogin method

```
package com.apress.prospringmvc.bookstore.web.controller;

// Other imports omitted, see Listing 9-7
```

```java
import static junit.framework.Assert.assertEquals;
import static junit.framework.Assert.assertNotNull;
import static junit.framework.Assert.assertNull;

import org.mockito.Mockito;
import org.mockito.internal.verification.VerificationModeFactory;
import org.springframework.beans.factory.annotation.Autowired;
import org.springframework.context.annotation.Bean;
import org.springframework.context.annotation.Configuration;
import org.springframework.mock.web.MockHttpServletRequest;

import com.apress.prospringmvc.bookstore.service.AccountService;
import com.apress.prospringmvc.bookstore.service.AuthenticationException;
import com.apress.prospringmvc.bookstore.web.interceptor.↵
        SecurityHandlerInterceptor;

@RunWith(SpringJUnit4ClassRunner.class)
@ContextConfiguration
public class LoginControllerTest {

    @Autowired
    private LoginController loginController;
    @Autowired
    private AccountService accountService;

    @Before
    public void setup() throws AuthenticationException {
        Account account = new AccountBuilder() {
            {
                address("Herve", "4650", "Rue de la station", "1", null, ↵
                        "Belgium");
                credentials("john", "secret");
                name("John", "Doe");
            }
        }.build(true);

        Mockito.when(accountService.login("john", ↵
                "secret")).thenReturn(account);
    }

    @After
    public void verify() throws AuthenticationException {
        Mockito.verify(accountService,↵
         VerificationModeFactory.times(3)).login("john", "secret");
        Mockito.reset();
    }

    @Test
    public void testHandleLogin() throws AuthenticationException {
```

```
        MockHttpServletRequest mockHttpServletRequest = ↵
            new MockHttpServletRequest();
        mockHttpServletRequest.getSession().setAttribute(↵
            SecurityHandlerInterceptor.REQUESTED_URL, "someUrl");

        String view = loginController.handleLogin("john", "secret", ↵
            mockHttpServletRequest);

        Account account = (Account)↵
            mockHttpServletRequest.getSession().getAttribute(↵
            SecurityHandlerInterceptor.ACCOUNT_ATTRIBUTE);

        assertNotNull(account);
        assertEquals("John", account.getFirstName());
        assertEquals("Doe", account.getLastName());
        assertNull(mockHttpServletRequest.getSession()↵
                    .getAttribute(SecurityHandlerInterceptor.REQUESTED_URL));
        assertEquals("redirect:someUrl", view);

        // Test the different view selection choices
        mockHttpServletRequest = new MockHttpServletRequest();
        view = loginController.handleLogin("john", "secret", ↵
                mockHttpServletRequest);
        assertEquals("redirect:/index.htm", view);

        mockHttpServletRequest = new MockHttpServletRequest();
        mockHttpServletRequest.getSession().setAttribute(↵
            SecurityHandlerInterceptor.REQUESTED_URL, "abclogindef");
        view = loginController.handleLogin("john", "secret", ↵
            mockHttpServletRequest);
        assertEquals("redirect:/index.htm", view);
    }

    @Configuration
    static class LoginControllerTestConfiguration {

        @Bean
        public AccountService accountService() {
            return Mockito.mock(AccountService.class);
        }

        @Bean
        public LoginController loginController() {
            return new LoginController();
        }
    }
}
```

As you can see, we use mocking to mock out the AccountService the same way we mocked out the AccountRepository while testing the AccountService, so this should already be familiar to you. The only noticeable new element is the use of the MockHttpServletRequest. First we use the

MockHttpServletRequest to set a session attribute that our LoginController will use to decide on which view to redirect to:

```
mockHttpServletRequest.getSession().setAttribute(SecurityHandlerInterceptor.REQUESTED_URL,↩
  "someUrl");
```

This is actually the URL that was requested before the user was redirected to the login page. Thanks to the stub, the LoginController is able to retrieve this value from the MockHttpSession (via MockHttpServletRequest) and perform its logic, which we will validate later on using

```
assertEquals("redirect:someUrl", view);
```

When the user was authenticated successfully, the LoginController also puts an attribute on the session. This is the account attribute having the Account as value. Here we validate that this is indeed the case:

```
Account account = (Account) mockHttpServletRequest.getSession().getAttribute(↩
             SecurityHandlerInterceptor.ACCOUNT_ATTRIBUTE);
```

In the last two tests (below the comment: // Test the different view selection choices) we tested how the code reacts when we have no initial REQUESTED_URL set on the MockHttpServletRequest. The first test simply tests with no value at all. The last test tests with a value that contains login. In both cases we verify that the view rendered is the index (home) page.

Introducing Spring MVC Test

Another option for testing application controllers is using the brand-new Spring MVC test module.[13] At the time of writing it is not yet integrated with Spring, but it is scheduled to be included in Spring 3.2. There is, however, already a usable *snapshot* which is fairly stable (the 1.0.0 snapshot).

Before we proceed, we have to warn you that depending on snapshots (particularly when there isn't a prior release) implies some risks, as things still might change. Therefore we won't go into detail, but just cover the ideas and the basic setup. Things will probably change here and there, making in-depth coverage outdated before the module is released into Spring. However, the ideas that we are showing here should remain stable and should still be applicable in later versions.

Having said that, to be able to use this module we added the dependency in the build.gradle of our chapter9 sample:

```
testCompile 'org.springframework:spring-test-mvc:1.0.0.BUILD-SNAPSHOT'
```

Because this is a snapshot dependency, we also added the snapshot repository to the list of repositories in the dependency management configuration. We did this in build.gradle in the root of the sample directory:

```
repositories {
    mavenRepo url: 'http://maven.springframework.org/release'
    mavenRepo url: 'http://maven.springframework.org/snapshot'
    mavenCentral()
    mavenRepo url: 'http://maven.springframework.org/milestone'
    mavenRepo url: 'https://repository.jboss.org/nexus/content/repositories/releases/'↩
    mavenRepo url: 'http://download.java.net/maven/glassfish/org/glassfish/'
```

---

[13] https://github.com/SpringSource/spring-test-mvc

}

Spring MVC test aims at making your application controllers easier to test, extending the idea behind the MockHttpServletRequest, MockHttpServletResponse and MockHttpSession helpers, which we used in the previous section. It tries to simulate Spring MVC even better without having to boot an actual Servlet container. For example; with Spring MVC test you will be able to verify which JSPs were actually selected to render when using Tiles as the view resolver. This is something that was not possible until now, and could only be verified at runtime (possibly using front-end tests). The more we can test using unit or integration tests, the better.

The example we will create will show how to use the basics. The first step is to bootstrap an org.springframework.test.web.server.MockMvc. This object initializes the MVC infrastructure, and will be your main entry into the API. You can initialize it in different ways:

- From one or more MVC annotated configuration classes

- From one or more Spring XML files

- Using a WebApplicationContext

- Individual @Controller classes

The first three possibilities are managed modes. In these cases there is an application context started. Controllers that are required to process the request you fire at them are looked up from the application context. Also, the MVC environment will be configured as it will be at runtime, with the same view resolvers, resource handlers, interceptors, and so on, just as you have specified in the configuration.

The last possibility is the so called standalone mode. In this mode you supply the application controllers directly, and the minimum set of Spring MVC infrastructure components are instantiated— only those required for the processing of requests with the registered application controllers. The set of infrastructure components is very similar to that provided by the MVC namespace or the MVC Java configuration. Important to note is that the actual Spring MVC configuration will not be tested (because it was never loaded).

The desired method of initialization is the one where the entire Spring MVC configuration is loaded. However, if you instantiate the MockMvc for every test, it can become expensive. The preferred way is to use the third method using the WebApplicationContext, which will combine the best of both worlds. The WebApplicationContext is injected into the test. The configuration is loaded by Spring's test support as usual. For the configuration (supplied in the classes attribute) you will use your Spring MVC annotated configuration classes. It could be something like this:

```
@RunWith(SpringJUnit4ClassRunner.class)
@ContextConfiguration(classes = { ....})
public class ApplicationControllerTest {

    @Autowired
    private WebApplicationContext wac;
```

This will load the @Configuration classes you indicated with the classes attribute and boot up a WebApplicationContext. You will then be able to construct a MockMvc object from the injected WebApplicationContext, which will be inexpensive. Spring's test support will cache the initialization of the contexts that it loads, which are indicated via @ContextConfiguration, possibly loading only one instance for the entire test suite. At this time, however, the WebApplicationContext support is not yet available, though it will be starting in Spring 3.2.

After you initialized the MockMvc object (one way or the other), you can start throwing requests at it. It will process them using actual Spring MVC logic and invoke your controller. At the end you are able to verify the results. In Listing 9-14 we have rewritten the LoginControllerTest using Spring MVC test. To keep things simple we constructed the MockMvc object in standalone mode. Let's have a look at the code first.

Listing 9-14. Rewriting the LoginController test using Spring MVC test

```
package com.apress.prospringmvc.bookstore.web.controller;

// Other imports omitted, see Listings 9-7 and 9-13

import static org.springframework.test.web.server.request.↵
            MockMvcRequestBuilders.post;
import static org.springframework.test.web.server.result.↵
            MockMvcResultMatchers.redirectedUrl;
import static org.springframework.test.web.server.result.↵
            MockMvcResultMatchers.request;
import static org.springframework.test.web.server.result.↵
            MockMvcResultMatchers.status;

import org.springframework.test.web.server.MockMvc;
import org.springframework.test.web.server.setup.MockMvcBuilders;

@RunWith(SpringJUnit4ClassRunner.class)
@ContextConfiguration
public class SpringMvcTestLoginControllerTest {

    @Autowired
    private LoginController loginController;

    @Autowired
    private AccountService accountService;

    private Account account;

    @Before
    public void setup() throws Exception {
        account = new AccountBuilder() {
            {
                address("Herve", "4650", "Rue de la station", "1", null,↵
                        "Belgium");
                credentials("john", "secret");
                name("John", "Doe");
            }
        }.build(true);

        Mockito.when(accountService.login("john",↵
                "secret")).thenReturn(account);
    }
```

307

```java
@Test
public void testHandleLogin() throws Exception {
    MockMvc mockMvc = MockMvcBuilders.standaloneSetup(loginController)↵
                        .build();
    mockMvc.perform(post("/login")↵
            .param("username", "john")
            .param("password", "secret"))
            .andExpect(status().isOk())
            .andExpect(request().sessionAttribute(↵
                    SecurityHandlerInterceptor.ACCOUNT_ATTRIBUTE, account))
            .andExpect(redirectedUrl("/index.htm"));
}

@After
public void verify() throws AuthenticationException {
    Mockito.verify(accountService, VerificationModeFactory.times(1))↵
            .login("john", "secret");
    Mockito.reset();
}

@Configuration
static class LoginControllerTestConfiguration {

    @Bean
    public AccountService accountService() {
        return Mockito.mock(AccountService.class);
    }

    @Bean
    public LoginController loginController() {
        return new LoginController();
    }
}
}
```

The initial setup remains unaltered and is the same as in LoginControllerTest. For example; we are still using Mockito to mock the AccountService, and we are still injecting the LoginController using the local Spring configuration setup via the LoginControllerTestConfiguration class.

The first thing we did is construct the MockMvc object in standalone mode. We did that by supplying it our LoginController as a constructor argument:

```java
MockMvc mockMvc = MockMvcBuilders.standaloneSetup(loginController)↵
                        .build();
```

The LoginController is pretty straightforward to test, so all defaults loaded by the standalone mode are sufficient. You can, however, apply customizations before calling build if that would be required. For example, a custom view resolver would be set like this:

```java
MockMvc mockMvc = MockMvcBuilders
                .standaloneSetup(loginController)
                .setViewResolvers(viewResolver)
                .build();
```

When the context is initialized we can let it process a request. Our LoginController only accepts HTTP post requests, so we build a post request with two parameters:

```
mockMvc.perform(post("/login")
    .param("username", "john")
    .param("password", "secret"))
```

The methods such as post and param are included via static imports on top of the class (see Listing 9-14). In this case we left this on purpose to show you how compact the syntax becomes when applying this strategy. In the beginning however it takes some time to get used to the different methods that are available. Finally we verify the result. We check that the HTTP status code is 200 (isOk), that the account has been set on the session, and that we are being redirect to the index.htm page:

```
.andExpect(status().isOk())
.andExpect(request().sessionAttribute(↩
        SecurityHandlerInterceptor.ACCOUNT_ATTRIBUTE, account))
.andExpect(redirectedUrl("/index.htm"));
```

This looks pretty sweet. You don't have to create separate mock objects for request, response, and session, because this is all taken care of by the Spring MVC test module. If you compare this with our previous test case, LoginControllerTest, you will immediately see that this code looks a lot better, is more compact, and above all tests the complete controller including the Spring MVC annotations.

By the way, building a MockMvc in managed mode that actually loads the configuration based upon @Configuration classes is not much different and would look as follows:

```
MockMvc mockMvc = MockMvcBuilders
            .annotationConfigSetup(WebMvcContextConfiguration.class, ↩
                              InfrastructureContextConfiguration.class, ↩
                              TestDataContextConfiguration.class, ↩
                              LoginControllerTestConfiguration.class)
            .configureWebAppRootDir("src/main/webapp", false)
            .build();
```

This wraps up our short introduction to Spring MVC test. We hope that we have shown you something which will become a very powerful tool in testing your Spring MVC application controllers with a minimum of effort. We already look forward having this fully integrated in Spring!

Automated Front-End Testing

Automated front-end testing is the last piece in the unit testing puzzle. It helps us test our final untested component, our views. JSPs can be tested, just like all the other components, in an automated fashion. There are many forms of front-end testing. You can, for example, test your web application on different browser to check that the look and feel is similar. You can also test your application for performance, render times, and usability. All of these are tests which are probably applied in other testing phases possibly using external tools.

The testing that we are after here is to make sure that all our pages render, and that all functionality offered by them also works. Nothing more, nothing less. When you have done a good job testing all previous components, this should be a breeze. Be sure that you have:

- Set up a *good* infrastructure for front-end testing. This requires a running container, data setup, and possibly fakes or stubs for certain resources and functionality. The tests also need to run (like any unit test) automatically via your continuous integration system, meaning it should all be integrated in your build system.

This is not as easy as it seems, since you have one little problem: you need to start up a Servlet container that can run your application (see Figure 9-10). There are plug-ins for Gradle (and Maven) like Cargo,[14] which can start a container and deploy your application before these tests are run.

Figure 9-10. Running a front-end test against Tomcat

- Designed your views well. Normally you will have already tested your views by hand when you were designing them. So normally when every level is well-tested, there should be only minor faults coming out of your front-end testing.

The most important part is that they enforce your "test harness." Even when you forgot to test something in your services, it could well be tested be one of your frontend tests. Also, if someone refactors your views later on, you still have the test harness that ensures that your pages are still working.

To set up a front-end test we have chosen Selenium.[15] It can be run in two modes, using a real browser like Firefox, and using HtmlUnit, which is an in-memory browser.

HtmlUnit is capable of running JavaScript and handling AJAX. This can all run completely in memory and does not have any external dependency, that way it can be considered as an integration test.

Front-End Testing Using Selenium

The current version of Selenium, which we will be using, is Selenium 2.x (we will refer to Selenium 2.x as "Selenium" from now on). Selenium makes use of the so called WebDriver project. This enables Selenium to run tests against a browser of choice out of the box without having the need of additional software. With the previous version (Selenium 1.x) this was different. It required you to have a so called Selenium RC server running between the test case and the browser. You can see this in Figure 9-11. However, the Selenium RC server can still be used in combination with the current version of Selenium. To explain this, we will first look at how Selenium 1.x works.

---

[14] http://cargo.codehaus.org/
[15] http://seleniumhq.org/

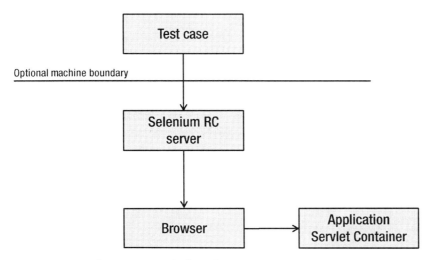

Figure 9-11. Selenium 1.x with the Selenium RC server setup

With Selenium 1.x the communication between the test case and the Selenium RC server goes over the network (your test commands are translated into HTTP requests being sent to the Selenium RC server). Potentially the Selenium RC server can be running on another machine than where the actual test is running. The Selenium RC server then translates the commands received over HTTP to JavaScript calls and injects them into the target browser. This is a nontrivial process, but it is shielded from the user. While this setup considered deprecated, it might still be interesting to see how it works. You can read more about it on the Selenium documentation page.[16]

Selenium now offers a different method, using WebDriver, which controls the browser directly using the browser's native API. So it no longer requires a complex (internal) setup as with Selenium RC that Selenium 1.x used. Using Selenium you can directly control the browser without having a need for the Selenium RC server. You simply select the appropriate driver via the API, depending on the browser you want to use.

However, you can still use the RC server. In that case the RC server will also use WebDriver. Instead of your test directly using WebDriver to control a browser on your local machine, you now instruct the RC server running on a different machine to communicate with a local browser using WebDriver. The main difference between the Selenium RC server setup and Selenium 1.x is that the Selenium RC server does much more than that; it also injects JavaScript and acts as proxy, which with WebDriver is no longer needed. It just functions as a "remote JVM," enabling you to control a browser on a remote machine.

---

[16] http://seleniumhq.org/docs/05_selenium_rc.html#selenium-rc-architecture

---

■ **Tip** Using Selenium RC server is especially interesting for those cases where you want to run the test on machine A but use machine B's browser. For example, you could run the test on your CI, which is a Unix-type machine. You want to run your front-end tests against IE 7, 8 and 9. To do so, you could set up three virtual machines, each installed with Windows and one of the three browsers, and running a Selenium RC server. You could then run the test suite three times. The first time you would use the IP address of the virtual machine running IE 7. The second time the IP address of the virtual machine running IE 8, and so forth. You could create Spring test profiles to dynamically inject another IP address depending on the profile with which the tests are run.

Writing a Selenium Test

Now that we have seen some theory about Selenium and its predecessor Selenium 1.x, let's have a look how we can actually use it. Before we can start we have to add its dependencies in build.gradle. We will add them in the gradle build file of chapter9-bookstore sample.

```
testCompile 'org.seleniumhq.selenium:selenium-java:2.20.0'
testCompile 'org.seleniumhq.selenium:selenium-firefox-driver:2.20.0'
testCompile 'org.seleniumhq.selenium:selenium-htmlunit-driver:2.20.0'
```

We added the core dependency (selenium-java) and a WebDriver dependency for Firefox and HtmlUnit. Other drivers[17] currently are selenium-android-driver, selenium-chrome-driver, selenium-ie-driver, selenium-iphone-driver, and selenium-remote-driver. Next let's look at the Selenium test for the LoginController in Listing 9-15.

Listing 9-15. *Testing the login sequence with Selenium*

```
package com.apress.prospringmvc.bookstore.web.frontend;

// Other imports omitted, see Listing 9-7

import static org.junit.Assert.assertEquals;

import org.openqa.selenium.By;
import org.openqa.selenium.WebDriver;
import org.openqa.selenium.firefox.FirefoxDriver;

public class SeleniumLoginFrontendTest {

    private WebDriver browser;

    @Before
    public void setup() {
```

---

[17] http://repo1.maven.org/maven2/org/seleniumhq/selenium/

```
        browser = new FirefoxDriver();
    }

    @Test
    public void startTest() {
        browser.get("http://localhost:8080/chapter9-bookstore/");

        browser.findElement(By.id("login")).click();

        // Will throw exception if elements not found
        browser.findElement(By.id("username")).sendKeys("jd");
        browser.findElement(By.id("password")).sendKeys("secret");

        browser.findElement(By.id("loginButton")).click();
        browser.findElement(By.id("account")).click();

        assertEquals("John", browser.findElement(↵
                            By.id("firstName")).getAttribute("value"));
    }

    @After
    public void tearDown() {
        browser.close();
    }
}
```

In the setup method we start our browser, which is the actual API to control the browser from within our test case. Here we are using Firefox via the FirefoxDriver:

```
browser = new FirefoxDriver();
```

If we want to switch to an in-memory browser (HtmlUnit) all code would remain the same. We just need to assign the HtmlUnitDriver instead of the FirefoxDriver:

```
browser = new HtmlUnitDriver();
```

Running this will run the tests against the in-memory browser. There will be no browser popping up when we run the tests like this. To get an idea of which browsers are supported and their specifics, the best resource is the Selenium documentation.[18]

---

[18] http://seleniumhq.org/docs/03_webdriver.html#introducing-webdriver-s-drivers

▓ **Note** if you want to use Selenium RC server with WebDriver, you can use `org.openqa.selenium.remote` `.RemoteWebDriver`. On the target machine you will have to run the Selenium RC server in order for this to work. You can use the `org.openqa.selenium.remote.DesiredCapabilities` class to further configure the driver. For example: `browser = new RemoteWebDriver(new URL("remoteHostRunningSeleniumRC:4444"),` `DesiredCapabilities.firefox());` This tells Selenium that we will be using `RemoteWebDriver`, and that it should connect to a Selenium RC server running on host `remoteHostRunningSeleniumRC` on port 4444. It also tells the remote instance that it should run the tests against Firefox (which will then be started on the remote machine).

To continue with the overview of the test class, we will now proceed to the actual test method `startTest`. The first line of the test method tells the browser to which URL to open:

```
browser.get("http://localhost:8080/chapter9-bookstore/");
```

The next lines of code take care of the navigation (clicking on links, entering text, and so forth). When we click on a link or a button we are using the ID. You can, however, use more advanced selectors, like CSS and XPath. You can find more about them in the Selenium reference guide.[19]

Using the Selenium IDE

When you look back at Listing 9-15, you will see that navigation with the browser requires you to look at the JSP source and check the identifiers of the elements you want to use. For example, to click a button you have to know its ID and then write this line of code:

```
browser.findElement(By.id("login")).click();
```

In this case we are clicking on a button with ID "login". Our scenario was a very short one, but for longer scenarios this can be become time-consuming and pretty boring. Fortunately there is a great tool called Selenium IDE which will be able to generate this code for you. It creates not only Java code, but also other languages as we will see. The Selenium IDE comes as a plug-in for Firefox. According to the Selenium website,[20] the Selenium IDE runs only in Firefox at this time. In order to download the Selenium IDE plug-in, go to the Selenium website[21] and follow the instructions. You basically click the Download link and Firefox will present you with a question to install the software as can be seen in Figure 9-12.

---

[19] http://seleniumhq.org/docs/03_webdriver.html#locating-ui-elements-webelements
[20] http://seleniumhq.org/about/platforms.html#browsers
[21] http://seleniumhq.org/download/

Figure 9-12. Installing Selenium IDE for Firefox

After clicking Allow, you will get a display like Figure 9-13, asking for your permission to install.

Figure 9-13. Installing selenium IDE for Firefox

After installation you have to restart Firefox. You can then open Selenium IDE by selecting it from the Tools menu. After that a separate window should appear, as in Figure 9-14.

Figure 9-14. The Selenium IDE main window

Selenium IDE will inspect the interactions you do on a page within Firefox and "record" all the events, such as clicking a button, entering text, and so forth. In order to set this up, you have to add the application for which you want to record in the Base URL text field (See Figure 9-15). Next you switch back to Firefox and navigate to the application you want to capture a scenario from. In our case we will navigate Firefox to `http://localhost:8080/chapter9-bookstore`. When you are on the home page of the chapter9-bookstore application, you switch back to the Selenium IDE window and click the Record button, which is the round red button on the right top, just below the Base URL input (it looks like an "indicator" but is actually a button you can click). After clicking it, Selenium will be in recording mode. You can now go back to your browser and perform a test scenario. We will perform the same actions as we did in the test. So we will click the Login link, enter username and password, click Login, and then click the Account link. After that, you can go back to the Selenium IDE window and you will see that lines have appeared in the Table tab, as shown in Figure 9-15.

Figure 9-15. Selenium recording a scenario

You can click the Record button again to disable recording. You can now export the captured interactions to Selenium commands for a specific language. Among the supported languages are Ruby, C#, Python, and of course Java. First we select the language to which we will export; we will choose JUnit 4 with WebDriver as shown in Figure 9-16.

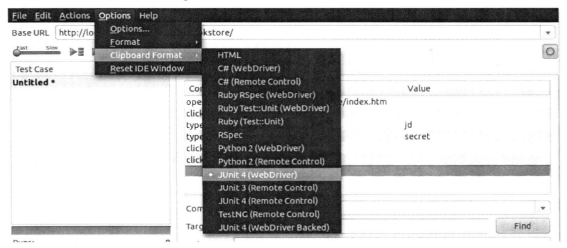

Figure 9-16. Selecting the language to export the scenario to

Now, copy all lines in the Table list, by selecting them, right-clicking, and selecting Copy, as can be seen in Figure 9-17.

Figure 9-17. Copying the scenario to the clipboard

After copying, you can paste this right in your test class file. The scenario will immediately be in the desired format, as you can see in Listing 9-16.

Listing 9-16. The scenario in Selenium WebDriver JUnit style generated by the Selenium IDE

```
driver.get(baseUrl + "/chapter9-bookstore/index.htm");
driver.findElement(By.id("login")).click();
driver.findElement(By.id("username")).clear();
driver.findElement(By.id("username")).sendKeys("jd");
driver.findElement(By.id("password")).clear();
driver.findElement(By.id("password")).sendKeys("secret");
driver.findElement(By.id("loginButton")).click();
driver.findElement(By.id("account")).click();
```

This is almost the same code as we came up with ourselves in the example. The only difference here is that Selenium also performs an explicit clear of the fields before adding text to them.

Besides using the plug-in to generate code from recorded scenarios, you can also replay scenarios using the plug-in. For more information we recommend visiting the Selenium IDE documentation page.[22]

Running the Front-End Tests via Gradle

Besides the normal unit and integration tests, we also want to run the front-end tests via our build tool. When we run the normal build using Gradle (with the command gradle build), the front-end tests are not run. We created a separate task called systemTest which can be run separately just to run the front-end tests. The systemTest command makes use of the Cargo plug-in to deploy the application to Tomcat. It will then run the tests that end in FrontendTest. The systemTest task looks as follows in our root build.gradle:

```
task systemTest(type: Test) {
    include '**/*FrontendTest.*
    dependsOn(war)
    doFirst {
        cargoStartLocal.execute()
    }
}
```

The systemTest tasks include every class that ends in FrontendTest. It also depends on the war task, which means that Gradle will first build a war of the project. Finally the task cargoStartLocal is executed, which is available because we enabled the Cargo plug-in. This task will start Tomcat and deploy the war file, which was previously generated by the war task.

In order to exclude these FrontendTests from the normal Gradle test lifecycle, we extended the test task to specifically exclude these files:

```
test {
    exclude '**/*FrontendTest.*'
}
```

Running FrontendTests is as easy as opening a command-line interface, navigating to the chapter 9 sample directory, and typing:

---

[22] http://seleniumhq.org/docs/02_selenium_ide.html

318

```
gradle systemTest
```

In order for the system tests to work, Firefox should be installed on your system. The tests will take some time as the application needs to get deployed on Tomcat. During the tests you will also see Firefox opening and closing, as this is the Selenium test at work. At the end you should get a "Build successful" confirmation and if you to go the build/reports/test directory in chapter 9 and open index.html, you can see the report (see Figure 9-18) that both tests have been run.

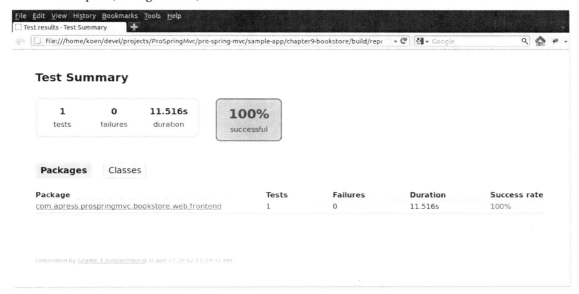

Figure 9-18. The test result report

■ **Note** There are problems reported with the current version of Selenium not being compatible with the latest version of Firefox (which is version 12 at the time of writing). The code was, however, developed and tested when Firefox was still at version 11. If you experience problems running the system tests, use Firefox 11 or check the Selenium website for newer versions that fix this issue (which are expected to become available anytime soon).

Summary

In this chapter we have seen that it is important to really think about how to handle testing in your project. It is clear that a project deserves adequate testing to be able to grow and to be maintainable. Your test should be considered as important as the actual production code. We have introduced some guidelines; making sure that you test at the right level, and how you can assure that testing remains attractive in your project, as that is one of the key elements to ensure that tests are actually written adequately.

We also explained the different levels of testing. We started with a basic unit test and continued by introducing Spring's test support, which we used to write an integration test, testing our repositories using an in-memory database. On the MVC side we showed how you can test an application controller using Spring's test support and the brand-new Spring MVC test. With these two tools at hand you are now capable of increasing your overall code coverage even further.

We wrapped up with a full-fledged front-end test, testing our view but also indirectly testing all the logic behind it. We showed you that it is possible to create a system test using a real browser with Selenium, but that you can also configure it to use an in-memory browser instead (HtmlUnit), making it an integration test.

We hope that the philosophy and techniques introduced here will help you write more and better tests. The only thing left to do is go out there and put these testing strategies into practice!

C H A P T E R 10

Spring Web Flow

Spring Web Flow 2 (which we will call Web Flow from now on) is an important piece of the puzzle when it comes down to building scalable, easy-to-develop-and-maintain web applications. In the upcoming three chapters, we will make you familiar with Web Flow and its strengths and weaknesses; we will also cover why, when, and, above all, how you should use it. In this chapter, we start off explaining what Web Flow is and what it can do for you. Later on, we will discuss some basic Web Flow elements that you need to understand before you can start building your first flow.

The common thread throughout the Web Flow chapters is the sample application, which we create as we go through these chapters. We will start in this chapter by illustrating how you can turn a plain MVC sample with a bit of configuration into a Web Flow-enabled application. Next, we will gradually enhance the bookstore sample application with Web Flow functionality, explaining each feature in detail along the way. We took special care to ensure that you don't need the sample application at hand when reading these chapters. All relevant code will be shown and explained accordingly.

In this chapter, we will limit ourselves to creating a single flow: the create (book) order flow. Chapters 11 and 12 will go more into detail about the application. In Chapter 11, we will expand the functionality of the sample application, and we will cover some more detailed configuration options. In Chapter 12, we will make you familiar with some more advanced aspects such as using AJAX, flow-managed persistence, and so forth.

If you already have some Web Flow experience, you might want to skim this chapter quickly and advance to the next chapter. If you are new to Web Flow, or want a refresher, then this is the right place to start!

Why Web Flow

In the Web Flow chapters, we will start by discussing the Web Flow 2.x family. We will always refer to version 1 of the tool as *Web Flow 1*. Otherwise, all features discussed relate to Web Flow 2.x (version 2.3.1 at the time of writing).

You may wonder why you should bother reading about Web Flow. You might especially be wondering why you should bother learning Yet Another Framework. Because let's be honest: the Java landscape is wide, and there is tremendous amount of choice available in web frameworks (you have clearly opted for Spring MVC—good!). However, within those frameworks, there are still extras that you can add to make your life easier.

Easier, we say? Well, yes. We really mean this. By the end of these three chapters, we will have convinced you that using Web Flow can make management of your web applications easier. Let's start with some theory first, so we can illustrate what Web Flow can do for you. Hopefully, this will get you interested enough to read through all three of the Web Flow chapters!

The Flow Concept

Despite the many features and advantages Web Flow has to offer, it all revolves around "the flow" (no wonder it is also called Web *Flow*). Before going any further, let's back up and cover what a flow is and what it is modeled after. This will help a lot in understanding what Web Flow is trying to accomplish and how it will help you.

A flow is something that occurs naturally in most applications (see Figure 10-1). The basic example is a wizard. Imagine a web shop order wizard that requires you to follow several steps to place your order. These steps form a flow. You start with Step 1, where you fill in some identification data, such as your first and last name, and then click the Next button. This takes you to Step 2, which asks you where to ship your order. Step 3, the last step, allows you to enter delivery options: the type of shipment, whether you would like your package to be sent before a certain date (it's possible there might be multiple shipments if the package wasn't complete by that date), and so forth. If the wizard is any good, it will allow you to navigate back and forward between steps, remembering the state (data) you entered for that specific step in the flow. Each step is small piece of the flow. They are linked together by a form of navigation. Sometimes you could also have the option to skip a step. At the end of the process, you can finalize your flow. In our example, this would process your order and make sure your products are delivered as soon as possible.

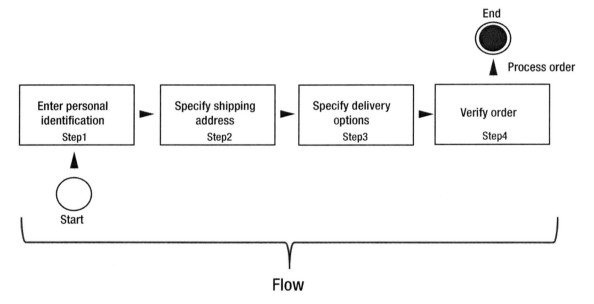

Figure 10-1. *A basic flow in an application*

Web Flow is all about creating these flows, which you accomplish by managing state between the different flow steps, expressing navigation, and so forth. So far we've discussed the core aspects of a flow; however, there are also some other nifty features associated with flows. We will discuss these next.

Fine-Grained Scoping

The first major strength of Web Flow is that it adds extra scopes. No doubt you already noticed that the servlet specification declares three scopes in which your application can retain state.

A scope is nothing more than a map in which you can store *key value pairs*, which are, depending on the scope type, stored for a determined amount of time. There are three scopes defined by the servlet specification: application, session, and request.

In Table 10-1, we will briefly summarize the different scopes and explain how you should use them. Although this is a very basic topic for anyone who has done Java web development before, we suggest you quickly skim it over, so as not to miss anything.

Table 10-1. Web Application Scopes and Their Usage

Scope	Usage
Application	Everything on application scope is visible for the entire web application. This scope should just contain general initialization stuff or read-only parameters that are shared for your web application. In 99% of cases, it should *not* be used to store any user-related state whatsoever. Most of the time, you will use it as a kind of system properties map, but one that is local to your web application. Where Java system properties are in fact visible for the entire JVM—and thus visible for every web application running inside that JVM instance—application scope is limited to the web application itself.
Session	The session scope is finer grained; for every client, a session is created and maintained. The session dies if explicitly requested by you, the developer, or the session timeout kicks in. Because of the stateless nature of the HTTP protocol, a client identifies the session with a so-called *session id* (handed out by the web container). Whenever a request is received, the container associates the request with the client's session based on that id. Information stored in the session is thus available during the lifetime of the client's session.
Request	The request scope is the lowest level scope and survives only one request-processing cycle. It is created by the web container from the moment it receives a new request and destroyed when the view has been rendered (and the rendered data is sent back to the client); in other words, it is destroyed when the container finishes processing the request. There is no request id because the request does not survive more than a single HTTP call: for each new call, a new request is created.

You might wonder what this has to do with Web Flow. Let's look at an example that uses our bookstore web application. Just as with any online store, we have an order and checkout process. In the first step of this process, the user is able to select a category. The category could be IT, Sci-Fi, Thriller, and so forth. In the next step, books can be selected from the previously chosen category. Finally, the user we will be able to select some options, such as the delivery details. However, each step is on a separate page. In this example, we would have three pages. When the user confirms the order, we will need to locate that information (which we gathered in the three previous pages) and create an order from it. We need to store this data somewhere in between these different steps; the question is where do we store this data? Let's look at some options:

- **Application scope:** Obviously, we don't want information from user x to be visible to user y. Not only is this unwanted, but it would also create security leaks, where sensitive data from one user might become visible to other users.

- **Request scope:** This is also a bad choice because you would not be able to store the data over multiple pages; the request scope is destroyed after every page render. You could piggyback data on your pages by adding hidden fields, but this is generally a bad idea. While this solution offloads data to the client (which might be considered a pro in some situations), it might also trigger security holes (what if you have an internal state that should not be made visible to the client, but is retained?), and you would have to manage this manually within your code. To put it simply, the lifecycle of the request scope is simply too short to gracefully fulfill our requirement.

- **Session scope:** Well, we have no other options! And while this scope is usually the best of these three options, it has some drawbacks. We will discuss these drawbacks in the upcoming paragraphs, to give you some background on the issues you will face when using this. Finally, we will examine how Web Flow can help you overcome the drawbacks of this scope.

The problems with storing such data on the session boil down to clean up and management. For example, consider what will happen with our data once the user finishes his order and does something else with the application. Will this data be sitting on the session needlessly until the session times out?

Yes, it will. There are a bunch of mechanisms to help you remove data from the session, but none is guaranteed to work. This might be a bold statement; however, remember that users can do what they want: hit the back button, jump out of your use case, manually type in another URL within your app, and so forth.

Also, how are you going to call your keys in the session map: myData? Are you sure no one else has used that key before? The session can be used by any component within your web application, so you would have to start namespacing your keys (e.g., page.x.data).

So, what do you store on the session? It must be good for something! Consider this example: after a user logs in, you probably want to maintain a security context containing data from the authenticated user. This information might be needed from anywhere in the application—it might even be required by *every* page. For example, you might want to put some personal information (such as the user's first and last name) in a header section that is automatically shown on every page. This kind of information deserves to live and die with the user's session; in this case, the session is clearly the right candidate for storing this kind of context data. *Context data* refers to data that is tightly coupled to the session or the application itself; it is data that spans a greater use than a single process or use case within the application.

But in this example, we are talking about plain user data (data captured via a form for a specific process within the application), which is inherently different from context data. The user walks through multiple screens and enters data in each one of them. You will need that user data, not only for the current view, but also for subsequent views.

Of course, you may be wondering why we are making a fuss about keeping data on the session longer than needed. Well, your session should be kept as small as possible; Table 10-2 lists some of the more important reasons for this (albeit others probably exist).

Table 10-2. Important Reasons for Keeping HTTP Sessions Small

Constraint	Reason
Memory usage	The session is kept in the memory of the web container. The more objects you have (the more data), the more memory the session will consume. Basically, bigger sessions mean that, for a given amount of memory, your server will be able to handle *fewer* clients.
Session replication	When you have multiple servers running in a cluster and your application is load balanced, the cluster might need to replicate the session state. User x might be on server instance 1 right now; but for the next request, user x might be directed to server instance 2 by the load balancer. At that time, the server must make sure the data user x created/used on server instance 1 is also available on server instance 2. The bigger the session, the more expensive this kind of synchronization becomes. Note: When using a cluster with a load balancer in front of it, by definition your sessions are not replicated. When configuring session affinity, requests for the same session are always redirected by the load balancer to the same cluster instance, thus making replication unnecessary.
Housekeeping	As with your house, you want a clean session. Remember, it's just a map. Items put on the session by controller x might be interesting for controller y. Still, controller y should not start using controller x's data simply because it can. Doing so might lead to an uncontrollable dependency between the two controllers and end up in a brittle design.
	Whenever you see something useful on the session, you should not need to track back where it's coming from. You should be able to rely on the fact that it is something useful for every component. Unfortunately, this is not possible with standard servlet scopes because you have no options other than putting use case specific data on the session and making it public for other components.

Thus far, we have seen that storing a state is not as easy as it seems. The scopes made available by the servlet specification don't give us much in the way of choices; and in most cases, this would cause us to overuse the session. This might become a problem later in the application's lifecycle as it continues to grow.

Web Flow offers a solution to this problem by introducing five new scopes: *conversation, flow, view, flash,* and *request* (see Figure 10-2).

We won't cover them into detail here; however, be aware that they are positioned between the session and request scopes. For example; something put on a flow scope would survive longer than request, but not as long as a session scope. Flash scope might survive longer than request, but not as long as a flow scope. Also, the content of these scopes is automatically managed for you with more guarantees than standard session housekeeping. We will discuss how this works in the upcoming chapters.

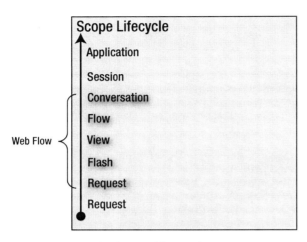

Figure 10-2. *Web Flow's additional scopes*

These extra scopes are stored on the session scope. However, the Web Flow machinery is specifically designed to make sure you don't have to worry about the creation and cleanup of these extra scopes. This is the point where you start to benefit from using Web Flow's automatic state management.

Automatic State Management

Whenever Web Flow executes an action within your flow, it will store the state you used on the different Web Flow scopes in a state snapshot. Although we haven't seen any introduction to Web Flow terminology yet, a flow is made up of different *actions*. For example, an action could be displaying a page or executing logic on an application controller. The data that is put on the different Web Flow scopes is automatically managed and versioned for you. Each time Web Flow returns from executing a requested action, it creates a snapshot of your data, including all its internal *state* information.

You can compare this process with that of taking pictures. Before returning to the browser, Web Flow takes a picture of the data and stores it, which means you can potentially refer back to it later, if required. For example, you can go back to a previous state by using the Back button of your browser. It is important to realize that this *snapshotting* feature is built into Web Flow and is automatically at your disposal. You can configure how many snapshots should be stored.

In addition to storing snapshots of all the data associated with a flow, Web Flow can also maintain multiple flows, or *executions*, at the same time (see Figure 10-3). Execution is a bit of an abstract term; the best way to think of it is as the runtime variant of a flow and all the elements that flow includes. In this case, flow refers to the definition itself (i.e., the XML that composes the flow); whereas execution refers to the in-memory representation of a flow once it has been started. This execution includes all the flow's states and, possibly, all subflows started by it (we will explain subflows in the next chapter). Web Flow retains different flow executions for you. For example, assume you start an execution involving flow x, followed by an execution involving flow y (i.e., after starting flow x, you abandon it at some point to start a completely separate flow y). You can still go back to execution of flow x simply by using your browser's Back button. Each flow execution will retain its own set of state snapshots. Similar to the way you can configure the maximum number of snapshots for a flow, you can also configure the maximum number of active executions. We will discuss both settings in more detail in Chapter 12.

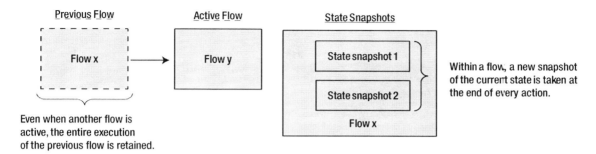

Figure 10-3. The Web Flow state-management mechanism

Request Synchronization

When designing web applications with Spring MVC (or any other request-driven web framework), sooner or later you are going to feel that you are missing some other important features. For instance, have you considered what would happen if a user were to click a Submit button on an order books form twice? In theory, there is no good reason why this would happen because clicking a button brings you instantly to the next page. In theory, that is. In practice, this can imply a certain delay, depending on how fast (or how slow) your application responds. Users tend to be impatient; if there isn't anything happening within a couple of seconds, the user might even doubt that the first click was successful (maybe he didn't click correctly?). So, before you know it, you will have to deal with a double submit coming from the same user and page.

What happens after the double submit depends mostly on sheer luck. Maybe your form submit was *idempotent*[1] in some way? In this case, being idempotent comes down to executing the operation multiple times without being impacted by any undesirable side effects from the business process point of view. Creating (and later on, delivering) the same order twice simply because the user double-clicked the Submit button is certainly an unwanted side effect. Although idempotence is mostly implied by read-only operations, sometimes form submits can be idempotent as well, depending on how you design them. For example, when creating an account, there will probably be some kind of unique or primary key constraint on the username column in your database table. If your form is submitted twice, the second submit will fail with a *duplicate key*, and no harm to your system will occur. Still, the user probably will probably see an error page. This is clearly something you want to avoid, but at least you don't end up creating any duplicate users in your database. In this example, you are saved by the uniqueness constraint on the table; but with a bit less luck, the opposite could be true, and it would be very easy to trigger undesirable side effects by submitting the form twice. This might ultimately lead to data corruption or other inconsistencies in your system.

Thus, you typically want to design your application so that submitting a form twice is not possible; or, at a minimum, that it results in no unwanted side effects. While a simple line of JavaScript might seem to solve this (i.e., you might disable a button after the first click), remember that this will only reduce the possibility of a submitting a form twice. Disabling the button is far from an ideal or complete solution. For example, the following scenarios would still be possible:

---

[1] http://en.wikipedia.org/wiki/Idempotence (Computer science meaning)

- After clicking the Submit button, the user presses F5; this will cause the form to be resubmitted. (The browser will warn the user about this, but it is still possible to submit that form twice.)

- A user can easily bypass your JavaScript by simulating multithreaded HTTP requests using something as trivial as cURL.[2] Or, the user can turn off JavaScript altogether in the browser; you don't need to be a professional developer to do that!

The point here is that you are looking for something mature that serializes access to a given form submission (for a given session, of course), so your application logic is relieved from handling a duplicate submission (i.e., you don't want to have to write specific code to deal with this).

Spring Web Flow solves this by serializing access to your flow executions. After you get the HTTP session id, you'll get a *flow execution key*. The flow execution key is to Web Flow as the HTTP session id is to your Web container. Each flow execution will get a unique id. Web Flow will use this id to identify the execution the user is currently participating in. But it will also use this id to serialize access to your flow execution (i.e., it will prevent two requests from operating on the same execution at the same time). But don't worry: this is also automatically managed for you, and you won't even notice it.

Whenever a form is submitted twice in your flow, Web Flow guarantees that only one of the two requests (for that flow execution within a given HTTP session) will be executed at a time. It does so by serializing the flow execution key. The second request is still pending because the flow execution was locked by the first request. It will eventually be executed after the first request is processed, unless the first request ends the flow. In that case, the second request will simply restart the flow, because the flow already ended (see Figure 10-4).

---

[2] http://curl.haxx.se/ A very neat and easy-to-use command line interface-based tool that transfers data with URL syntax (http, https, smtp, and so on).

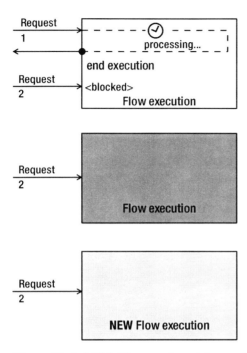

Figure 10-4. *A Web Flow synchronizing multiple requests to the same flow execution*

In Figure 10-4, the top rectangle represents the flow execution dealing with two requests (a double submission from the same browser session). Only one request is allowed through for processing (request1), while the second request (request2) is blocked by the flow execution (other requests would also be blocked). After processing request1 and before the request ends, it triggers an end state (which we will discuss later on). An end state ends the entire flow execution. In the middle rectangle, you can see the flow execution after the first request has been processed. The lock is freed, so the second request has a chance to enter the flow execution. However, the execution is already destroyed; at the bottom rectangle, you can see that a new flow execution is started instead. In other words, the second request will bring the user back to the entry point of the flow instead of re-executing the action.

This means that a double submission inside a flow execution is still possible. Web Flow serializes access to the flow execution, but as long as the flow hasn't ended (as illustrated in the previous paragraph), the second request still executes the exact same logic as the first request, and you still get a double submission. Normally, you would execute your process transaction just before you end the flow. In the book order process, we go over the different steps, with each step composing a part of the order. If the user double-clicks in this process, nothing bad happens (in the worst case, a book is added twice). But when the user finalizes the order, we perform our create order transaction and commit everything to the data store. When the first request returns, the flow will already have ended. This means the second request will not trigger a second create order transaction, but will merely restart the flow.

■ **Note** You may ask yourself whether synchronizing access based on a token (the flow execution key) has any performance impact. The answer to that is no. Synchronization happens within a flow execution that executes within an HTTP session. In other words, it serializes access for the operations sent out by a single client, to the same flow execution. For example, a client's double submission would be serialized because a double submission makes multiple requests in parallel within the same HTTP session and to the same flow execution. However, if two different clients (and thus two different sessions and different flow executions) were to push the same Submit button at the exact same time, nothing would get serialized, and everything would be executed in parallel.

Now let's return to the issue raised by that F5 (Refresh) button. Even if the user doesn't double-click, refreshing a submitted form accidently will trigger the same effect. It will not be detected as a double-click (there is only one request, sequentially after the first request). For this problem, Web Flow offers you a Post Redirect Get (PRG) pattern. This is a complicated name for a very easy-to-understand pattern that solves the "accidental" resubmit.

Post Redirect Get (PRG)

By applying PRG, Web Flow performs a two-stage processing of the request. In the first stage, the HTTP request is received from the browser. First, it triggers the invocation of the application logic (if any). Next, Web Flow issues a redirect to the browser before starting the second stage, which is renders and sends back the view. This makes the browser forget the form and issue an (idempotent) GET request to acquire the view. Hitting F5 after that just resends the last GET. Thus, it re-executes only the second stage, rendering and sending back the view (see Figure 10-5).

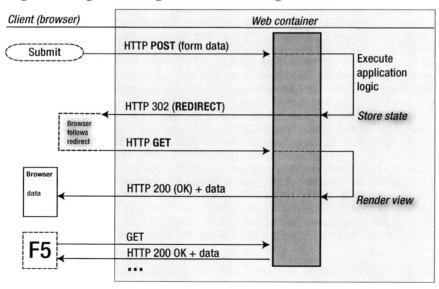

Figure 10-5. *The PRG (Post Redirect Get) pattern*

At first, you trigger a normal form submission. Remember: If you were to double submit, only one submit would be treated at a time thanks to Web Flow's serialization mechanism. The other submit would be processed after the first one completes. If case the first request ends the flow, the second simply restarts the flow.

When the request (an HTTP POST) enters the web container, it executes the requested logic. Instead of directly rendering the view and sending an HTTP 200 (+ view data), Web Flow will send a 302 REDIRECT to the client's browser. At this point, the flow execution is "paused" and the state is internally stored for you. The mechanism to store the state between requests is all handled by Web Flow.

The browser will follow the redirect and issue an HTTP GET to the web container. Here Web Flow picks up the request again and lets the view be rendered. The view is eventually sent back to the client's browser and displayed. Remember: The last action was not a POST, but a GET. If the user presses F5, the (idempotent) GET is executed without any side effects; it merely returns the last view without (double) processing the same logic again. Thus there is no chance of an accidental re-submit of a form. You get all that functionality for free. Cool!

Controlled Navigation

Until now, you primarily have used Spring MVC to take care of navigation in your app. For example, using an org.springframework.web.servlet.ModelAndView lets you indicate the next view to render. When working within a flow, Web Flow will take over the navigational control. It will literally be pulled out of your controllers and modeled within your flows. You will also be able to trigger actions on your application controllers or execute logic directly from within your flows.

When we are speaking about application controllers, do we still need application controllers when working with Web Flow at all? The answer to that depends on the scenario. Your flow has actually become the application controller. It controls navigation and can execute logic via an expression language. You can directly call a façade (or service, if you like) from within your flow. However, most of the time a plain-old-java-object (POJO) as application controller doesn't hurt. Java is still more readable than heavy expressions and XML. For trivial things that would have taken a single method with a single line of Java, your flow alone will do just fine. If you need more logic and feel the need to start writing code, then it is probably better to create a separate POJO application controller (annotate it with @Controller) and let your flow call methods on it.

░ **Note** You might wonder whether @Controller annotations are still required on your application controllers when working with Web Flow. What is important to know is that, when applying these annotations, the class in question becomes a Spring-managed bean. This means you can refer to the application controllers directly from within your flows. Annotation-wise, you can do that by using @Controller or @Component. An @Controller is just a specialization for a @Component. In other words, both do the same thing—@Controller just adds an extra indication that the class in question is an application controller (something that lives on the front end). It is probably a good idea to continue to use @Controller even if your application controllers are only used by your flow and perhaps not by Spring MVC. Ultimately, application controllers are an extension of your flow (which can also be considered an application controller).

When to Avoid Web Flow

As with everything, there are pros and cons when using Web Flow. We've already introduced you to some of the pros that Web Flow will deliver for your application. Now let's look at situations where it might be inappropriate to use Web Flow.

Fortunately, we can think of only three reasons to avoid using Web Flow. First, you'll (obviously) want to avoid using Web Flow when your web application framework has no support for it. We would suggest finding different solutions in that case. But since we are using Spring MVC, this is not an issue for us. (By the way, Web Flow also supports JSF and portlets, or JSR-168[3] environments.)

Second, Spring MVC already has some (primitive) support for building wizards (sequential views that share state), so one could say that the Spring MVC infrastructure can be used for simple, interdependent pages. On the other hand, introducing Web Flow is pretty easy (as we will see). Web Flow will add a great deal of functionality and other possibilities that won't bother you if you don't need them, but are there when you do. Web Flow is, like almost all Spring technology, non-intrusive.

Third, Web Flow is not very useful for places in your application where there are no flows. If everything is contained in a single page, then Web Flow will only cause overhead. This page could still be backed by normal Spring MVC controllers and remain Web Flow-unaware.

So, outside of these situations and the fact that it is yet another framework/concept to learn, we see little or no disadvantages to introducing Web Flow to your application. If you don't need it for some specific, very easy use cases and can get along with Spring MVC controllers, then do so. Our Web Flow setup will still allow you to use Spring MVC and Web Flow next to each other in the same application, allowing you to pick the right option for each situation.

■ **Note** The basic Spring MVC flow functionality we talked about is supported via a specific Spring MVC controller: `org.springframework.web.servlet.mvc.AbstractWizardFormController`. This class is now deprecated, and you should use the standard `@Controller` annotation instead. You can build a flow in combination with `@SessionAttributes` and `org.springframework.web.bind.support.SessionStatus` to end the flow when processing is over. While this is still a valid alternative, it is a bit cumbersome. Be aware that this way of working is very limited and in no way resembles the extra power that Web Flow gives you. Our advice is to use this approach only as a small helper in case you need to build very discrete and small bits of flow logic for a very small part of your application. For all other needs, save yourself the trouble and consider using Web Flow.

The Basic Ingredients of a Flow

In this section, we will look at the basic building blocks required for building a so-called flow. We will start off with a simple flow example, and then explain the different elements that this flow consists of. We will not go into detail about all the possible options of each element, but simply stick to the basics. In the next chapter, we will revise certain elements laid out here (as well as cover some new ones) and go more into more detail about how to use those elements. Therefore, don't panic if certain functionality is not described here—we will get there.

---

[3] http://jcp.org/aboutJava/communityprocess/final/jsr168/index.html

Flow

A flow is the main component that you will be interacting with. It is an XML document written by you and interpreted by Web Flow. A flow defines the possible steps in your application and defines the following things for each step:

- Which view should be rendered and the interaction between views

- Which actions are possible and whether to delegate execution to application controllers or execute expressions directly in your flow

Each flow definition is an XML document and should therefore comply with XML syntax standards. You start with the XML declaration, followed by the flow root element (see Listing 10-1).

Listing 10-1. *A Flow Root Element Declaration*

```
<flow xmlns=http://www.springframework.org/schema/webflow
      xmlns:xsi="http://www.w3.org/2001/XMLSchema-instance"
      xsi:schemaLocation="
        http://www.springframework.org/schema/webflow
        http://www.springframework.org/schema/webflow/spring-webflow-2.0.xsd">
```

There is an XML Schema for a flow definition that will tell you which elements/attributes are allowed at which location. This schema will also give you a short summary that covers what each (basic) element/attribute is good for.

In Figure 10-6, we can see the visualization of the flow definition XML schema.[4] This schema allows us to give an overview of the elements and attributes a flow definition can consist of.

■ **Note** Depending on how familiar you are with XML schemas, you might know that the schema visualization only resembles the top-level elements of a flow. Most of the elements have their own attributes, but these attributes are not listed here (you can see them when you drill down in the schema). When we discuss the elements in this or the next chapter, we will list and explain the attributes of these elements. Also, some of the elements can contain nested elements, but these nested elements cannot exist as top-level elements (and are therefore not listed here). For example, the `<set>` element can be nested in an `<on-start>` element, but it cannot be used as top-level element. As we discuss a given element, we will also cover the different possibilities enabled by that element.

---

[4] http://www.springframework.org/schema/webflow/spring-webflow-2.0.xsd

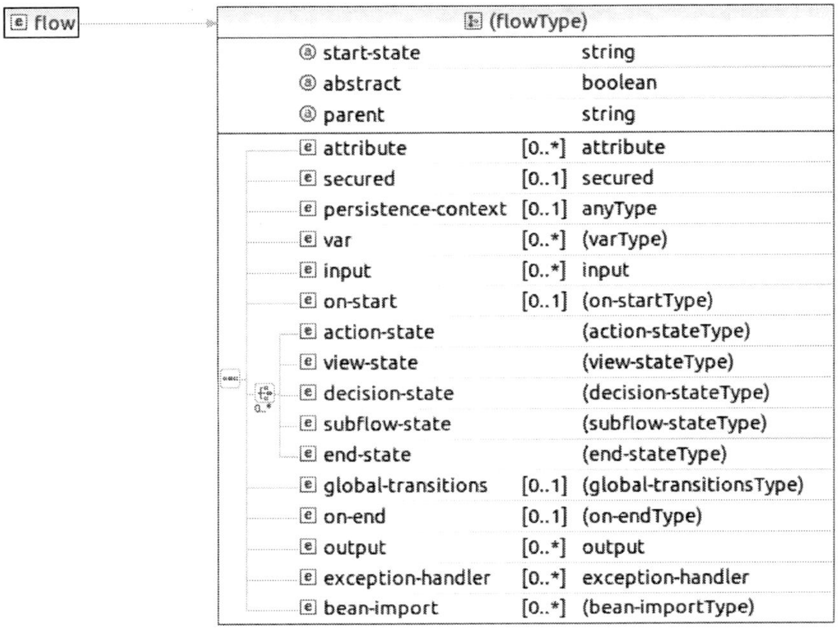

⑤ flow	ⓘ (flowType)		
	ⓐ start-state		string
	ⓐ abstract		boolean
	ⓐ parent		string
	⑤ attribute	[0..*]	attribute
	⑤ secured	[0..1]	secured
	⑤ persistence-context	[0..1]	anyType
	⑤ var	[0..*]	(varType)
	⑤ input	[0..*]	input
	⑤ on-start	[0..1]	(on-startType)
	⑤ action-state		(action-stateType)
	⑤ view-state		(view-stateType)
	⑤ decision-state		(decision-stateType)
	⑤ subflow-state		(subflow-stateType)
	⑤ end-state		(end-stateType)
	⑤ global-transitions	[0..1]	(global-transitionsType)
	⑤ on-end	[0..1]	(on-endType)
	⑤ output	[0..*]	output
	⑤ exception-handler	[0..*]	exception-handler
	⑤ bean-import	[0..*]	(bean-importType)

Figure 10-6. *The flow definition XML schema visualisation*

In Figure 10-6, the flow on the right is the top element. Each flow definition should start with the <flow> element. The top-level section (beginning with start-state) contains the three attributes that can be used inside the flow root element.

In the lower section (starting with attribute), you can see the elements that can be used inside the flow definition. Their order is important, and you should follow the order listed here. For example, you cannot place a <var> element after an <on-start> element.

▪ **Note** Only the five states are non-positional in the flow definition. This is because they are connected via the special choice structure. All other elements are positional and should appear in the order shown in Figure 10-6.

The middle column (e.g., [0..*]) displays the multiplicity of the element. It indicates how many times the element can exist in a single flow definition. The number on the left is the minimum, the number (or asterisk for unlimited) is the maximum. For example, [0..*] indicates that the element is optional and can appear an unlimited amount of times. Now look at the <var> element. Its multiplicity ([0..1]) means that the element is optional, but that it can only appear once for a given flow definition (e.g., the <on-start> element).

The different states (starting with <action-state> and ending with <end-state>) are connected by a choice. Typically, you can only have one element of the listed elements present within a choice. For example, typically you could only have one <view-state> or one <action-state>, but not both. However, if you look carefully at the choice icon, you will see the choice symbol has a multiplicity of (0..*). This means that a state is optional; however, it also indicates that every element of the choice can appear an unlimited number of times. Thus, there is no restriction on how many states you can define. Furthermore, because of the choice, the states are non-positional (probably the main reason for introducing this as a choice). For example, you can have a <view-state> (one or more times) followed by an <action-state> (one or more times)—or the other way around. Both approaches are valid.

If you look back at Listing 10-1, you will see that we declared Web Flow itself as the default namespace. This means we don't have to use prefixes for each element. Each element or attribute is automatically validated against the schema coupled to the default namespace. Finally, we also specify the schema location. The schema location is used by IDEs to load the schema and validate the XML and to give command-line completion. Notice that we are using the schema for Web Flow 2.0.

For the remainder of the Web Flow coverage, we will omit the flow root element and its namespace declarations in the code listings. This keeps everything compact and more readable. We will only show this information if there is any relevance to it, such as when we cover attributes that belong to the flow root element. Be aware that, even when the flow root element and its namespace declarations are not shown in a given listing, they are still at the beginning of every flow and are mandatory.

Now take a look at the flow definition in Listing 10-2.

Listing 10-2. *An Example of a Flow*

```
<flow xmlns="http://www.springframework.org/schema/webflow"
      xmlns:xsi="http://www.w3.org/2001/XMLSchema-instance"
      xsi:schemaLocation="
        http://www.springframework.org/schema/webflow
        http://www.springframework.org/schema/webflow/spring-webflow-2.0.xsd">

    <on-start>
        <evaluate ↵
            expression="orderController.initializeForm()"↵
            result="flowScope.orderForm"/>
        <evaluate ↵
            expression="orderController.initializeSelectableCategories()"↵
            result="flowScope.selectableCategories"/>
    </on-start>

    <view-state id="selectCategory" view="selectCategory" model="orderForm">
        <transition on="next" to="selectBooks" >
            <evaluate ↵
expression="orderController.initializeSelectableBooks(flowScope.orderForm)"↵
result="flowScope.selectableBooks" />
        </transition>

        <transition on="cancel" to="end" />
    </view-state>

    ...

    <end-state id="end" view="redirect:/index.htm"/>
</flow>
```

In this example, we created a simple flow definition. It is not a complete definition (hence the ellipsis (...) at the end); however, we want to give you a gentle introduction to what a flow definition looks like.

We would also like to point out that, when using STS, you have Web Flow support in your IDE. You can also display the flow XML graphically. Once you double-click the flow XML file, the content panel will open, typically showing the XML view. At the bottom of this panel, you will notice tabs. Next to the Source tab, you should also find flow and flow-graph tabs. The flow tab gives a list-based overview of the elements in your flow (see Figure 10-7).

Figure 10-7. *The flow tab, which provides an overview of the flow components*

The flow-graph tab graphically shows the elements and the different relations between them (see Figure 10-8). You can also use the palette on the left to add new elements and combine them.

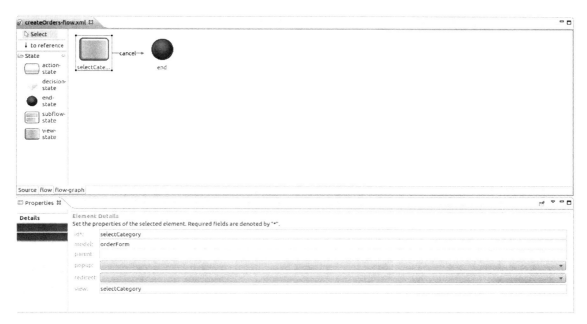

Figure 10-8. The flow-graph tab, which gives a graphical overview of the flow

All of the information in this palette is directly reflected in the source, and vice versa. If you add a component from the palette, the corresponding XML will be added to the source. If you add an element directly in the XML and go back to the flow-graph (or graph), the new element will also appear there.

For now, it's enough to understand that, when this flow is started, it will eventually enter the `selectCategory` view state. This view state will render the `selectCategory` view (which will be resolved by the Tiles[5] configuration) and use the form that is available under the `orderForm` key.

We use an on start action to instantiate the model and assign it to flow scope before we enter the view state. We will discuss the evaluate and on start actions in the following sections. For now, it is enough to know that the on start action is executed before Web Flow enters its first state, and that it will execute the `initializeForm` method on the `com.apress.prospringmvc.bookstore.web.controller.OrderController`. This will create an initialized model and return it. The model will then be put on flow scope. The model name can then be used in a `<spring:form modelAttribute="orderForm".../>` tag in your view. This will bind the fields in a form during submission to the specified form. Web Flow will take care of the parameter binding, as well as the conversion and form validation (as we will see later). Note that the `modelAttribute` must already be present on one of the Web Flow scopes.

---

[5] We introduced you to Tiles in Chapter 8, so we will assume that you already have a basic understanding about this templating framework. If you have skipped ahead to read this chapter on Web Flow, but have no idea how Tiles works, then we suggest that you read the introduction to Tiles before proceeding with the rest of this chapter.

■ **Note** The OrderController is just a Spring bean defined in the application context. In our case by using annotations; applying the @Controller annotation, doing so the class will be picked up by classpath scanning and become a Spring bean.

Also notable are the possible transitions that can be triggered within the view state. When the view is rendered, it is possible to execute a next or cancel transition. The next transition will execute a method on the controller, and then forward to the next state (this could be view state or any of the other states that Web Flow supports, as we will see later on). The cancel transition will navigate to the end state. We will cover the end state in detail in the next chapter; for now, it is sufficient to know that transitioning to the end state terminates the flow.

The flow definition root element (flow) allows you to specify some extra attributes, which are optional. It is fine to skip specifying them for a simple flow; however, these attributes might come in handy once you get a more complex flow layout or you want more customization (see Table 10-3). This root element allows you to override the default start-state, inherit from another existing flow, and mark your flow as abstract. We will cover the latter two cases in detail in Chapter 12 in the "Applying Inheritance" section.

Table 10-3. *Attributes of the Flow Root Element*

Attribute	Definition and Usage
start-state	When absent, the start-state (the state that will be entered first) of a flow is the first state that appears in the flow. This could be any of the five states.[6] In our example flow (see Listing 10-2), however, the first element is an on-start action, meaning that this action will be entered first. An on-start is not a state, which means that Web Flow will execute whatever action is specified inside the on-start and then proceed with the first actual state specified by the flow. In our case, this is the view state. Upon entering the view state, the flow is started. You can override this behavior by specifying the name of another state, using the start-state attribute. In that case, that given state will be executed first, no matter where this state appears in the flow definition. Note that if an on-start is present, it is always executed! It does not matter if you specify a start-state, nor does it matter which state you specify as start-state.

The View State

The <view-state> element is a basic element in each flow. As we will see, there are four other *-state elements. The view state is probably the most important of these elements, so we will describe this one first.

The view state models a view that is being rendered from the moment the view state is entered. A view state can be entered as a starting point by starting a flow or by a transition event from another state within that flow. When the view state renders the view, the execution is paused (at that time the user is

[6] We will discuss the view-state in detail next. The other states are decision state, action state, subflow state, and end state. We left them out here on purpose, since they are not required to build a basic flow.

looking at the view rendered on her browser). The user can then trigger a transition allowed within that view state to continue processing.

In Listing 10-2, there are two such transitions described: next and cancel. Whenever the user triggers such action (by clicking a button or a link on the page) the flow resumes and executes the given action.

The view state is identified with its id attribute. You use that attribute to refer to this view state from other states. The ids must be unique over all states in the same flow definition. The view attribute indicates which view this view-state will render. The model attribute identifies the name of an object that is present on any of the Web Flow scopes, which will be used to bind the received parameters on. These parameters are the request parameters part of the form submission. Table 10-4 lists the attributes with descriptions and their uses.

Table 10-4. *Attributes of the <view-state> element*

Attribute	Definition and Usage
id	Every view state must have an associated id. This id must be unique over all states within the same flow definition. It will identify the view state if you want to navigate to it from another state.
view	This is the name of the view that will be rendered. Depending on the configured Spring MVC org.springframework.web.servlet.ViewResolver, this can be one of the following: • An absolute path like /WEB-INF/view/selectCategory.jsp. • A relative view to the location where the flow XML is placed: selectCategory.jsp. In this situation, the flow must be placed in same directory as the view. • A logical view name that is interpreted by the ViewResolver and mapped to a physical file. In Listing 10-2, we used the third option: namely, a logical view name. You are also allowed to use expressions, as in this example: view="literal_text#{expression}"
model	When the user submits a form, and the model attribute is specified, Web Flow will bind the request parameters to that model. It will, by default, bind all request parameters that are part of the request. As explained before, you have to instantiate the model yourself (as we did using the on start), and make it available on one of the Web Flow scopes. Web Flow will check them to find an attribute with the key you specified in the model attribute.
redirect	This attribute indicates whether PRG (Post Redirect Get) should happen for this view state. Although the documentation specifies that the default value is false (i.e., no PRG), in practice it seems to be the other way. Whenever a view state is entered or an action is executed within the view state, a PRG occurs unless you specify redirect="false". We submitted a bug entry for this.[7]

---

[7] See https://jira.springsource.org/browse/SWF-1518 if you want more details.

There are some other attributes listed in Figure 10-9 that we will not discuss at this time because they are outside the scope of this basic chapter. They are also not required to build a basic flow. For your convenience, if you are reading this for reference or you want to jump ahead, the parent, popup, and history attributes are discussed in Chapter 12's "Inheritance," "Reworking the Orders Overview," and "Execution and Conversation Snapshots" sections, respectively.

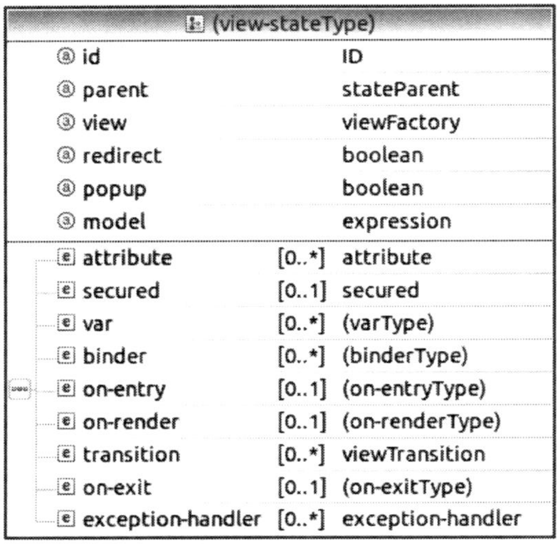

ⓔ (view-stateType)		
ⓐ id		ID
ⓐ parent		stateParent
ⓐ view		viewFactory
ⓐ redirect		boolean
ⓐ popup		boolean
ⓐ model		expression
ⓔ attribute	[0..*]	attribute
ⓔ secured	[0..1]	secured
ⓔ var	[0..*]	(varType)
ⓔ binder	[0..*]	(binderType)
ⓔ on-entry	[0..1]	(on-entryType)
ⓔ on-render	[0..1]	(on-renderType)
ⓔ transition	[0..*]	viewTransition
ⓔ on-exit	[0..1]	(on-exitType)
ⓔ exception-handler	[0..*]	exception-handler

Figure 10-9. The XML schema overview for the <view-state> element

The attribute element is common for each state, and it can also be applied on the flow root element. This is an element you will probably never use, but we will cover it here for the sake of completeness. The attribute element is used to supply metadata to tooling, for example.

■ **Note** You have an element with the name "attribute" when an attribute is also part of the XML syntax, such as the id or view attribute. All of this makes the name of this attribute name needlessly confusing!

Tooling that visualizes the flow can read these attribute elements and use their content to display additional information. The element has three attributes: name, value, and type. The name and value attributes can be anything. The type attribute is there to convert the value (which is otherwise treated as a String datatype) to a specific type, if required.

Of the remaining elements (see Figure 10-9), we will only discuss the <transition> element in this chapter. Please consult the Table of Contents or the Index to find explanations for the remaining elements, as they are scattered throughout the next several chapters.

State Transitions

A transition literally means a state transition from the current state to the same or to a different state within the flow. In some cases, the flow might execute an action before executing the actual transition. You can see this in the selectCategory view state in Listing 10-2, where there are two transitions. The transition is triggered by the literal defined in the on attribute. You basically supply a request parameter with a specific naming convention where the on literal is nested. You will see how to define this in your view when building your first pages in the upcoming "Selecting the Category" section.

■ **Note** Web Flow works internally with events. When you specify a literal in the on attribute, it will create a matching event from that. Whenever a request comes in to trigger a transition, it will match the event. This is not really important yet, as you will specify a literal in your view and in the on attribute. Chapter 11's "Form Validation Using the Application Controller" and "Working with Outcome Events" sections will cover how this correlates with events. In addition to literals, you can also use expressions in both the on and to attributes.

The target state can be any of the five possible state types, and you reference them with the to attribute. The value is the id of the other state you wish to transition to. Remember that you can also transition to the same state (or to the same view state in our case). Omitting the to attribute will yield the same effect, although it will not trigger a real transition. In that case, the view state is not explicitly reentered. This will become important when we discuss the on entry and on exit actions in the next chapter. For now, it is safe to assume that both alternatives will yield the same result; however, not specifying the to attribute is the most logical thing to do here. Notice that the cancel transition transitions to another state with the end id (i.e., the end state). This is one of the four other special states, as we will see later on.

Table 10-5 lists the various attributes for the transition element.

Table 10-5. *Attributes for the Transition Element*

Attribute	Definition and Usage
on	The literal that triggers this particular transition. Within a given state, you can only trigger transitions available in that state. In the example (see Listing 10-2), you can only trigger the next or cancel transitions while in the selectCategories view state. These transitions can use the to attribute on their turn to trigger other states within the same flow. You can also specify expressions and a wildcard (*) as the value. Specifying a wildcard has the same effect as omitting the on attribute. The matching rule is that the first matching transition (based on the on attribute's value) is executed. In the case of a wildcard, putting the transition with the first in a given state means that it will always be executed, no matter what. Remember that the literal is actually translated to an Event behind the scenes by Web Flow. We will see this in detail in Chapter 11 in the "Form Validation Using the Application Controller" and "Working with Outcome Events" sections.
to	An optional literal that references the id of the target state we are going to transition to. When omitted, the current state is re-executed, without actually exiting or entering the state.
bind	This optional attribute defaults to true and indicates that all request parameters should be bound to the model. If you don't want this, you can do one of the following: • Specify false; in that case, nothing will be bound. This might be handy for a "back" transition that goes to a previous state. In that case, there won't be any binding, nor will there be validation that might stop the user from going back. • When specifying a binder (see Chapter 12's "Explicit Form Binding" section), only those elements specified are bound, giving you fine-grained control over the binding process.
history	We already introduced you to the snapshot mechanism. Whenever you transition from one view state to another, you have the ability to go back. By default, you can do this by using the browser's Back button. You can also disable the snapshotting feature on a global scale (see Chapter 12's "Execution and Conversation Snapshots" section). If you want to disable this feature's fine-grained per view state, you can specify the history attribute with the preserve, discard, and invalidate values. The default value is preserve, and it enables you to go back. On the other hand, discard disables the ability to go back to the given view state (the view state where you define the transition with the history attribute), and invalidate completely disables the ability to go back to any previous view state your application has been through thus far.

The Evaluate Action

The evaluate action enables your flow to interact with other components such as the Spring MVC controllers (or any other Java classes, as long as they are Spring beans). The evaluate action takes an expression that is executed when the evaluation takes place. The evaluate action must be the child of another element, and it cannot exist on its own. It is executed as part of a certain *action* that is triggered within your flow. In the example, we nested the evaluate action in a transition inside the view state and in the on start action. As we will see, next to the transition and on start, you can use the evaluate action in combination with other elements.[8] No matter where the evaluate action is used, its goal remains the same: to evaluate an expression that executes a method, manipulate some object state, and potentially return a result.

When the expression returns a value, you can use the result attribute to bind the return value to a variable in a given scope. Attributes of the evaluate action are listed in Table 10-6.

Table 10-6. *Attributes of the Evaluate Action*

Attribute	Definition and usage
expression	An expression that is executed whenever the action in which this evaluate action is nested in is triggered.
result	This optional attribute determines where the result obtained from executing the expression should be bound to. Basically, it allows you to specify a scope or an object within a given scope to bind the result to. See the "Implicit Objects" section in Chapter 11 for the different possibilities. When omitted, the result (if any) is not stored in any scope.
result-type	This optional attribute makes it possible to convert the result to the specified type. When storing a result in a scope, you are basically storing it in a map that has an Object value type. In other words. the map is not typed and accepts any value. Sometimes you want to explicitly trigger a conversion to another type. In other scenarios, you would deduce from the field types that a conversion is required. For example, suppose you want to bind a received request parameter (in String format) to a form where the target field has the Integer type. It would be obvious that some conversion needs to be done first. In this case, there is no such indication because a scope just accepts Object. However, in your view, you could be expecting that the value is of a certain type other than the one returned by the method invoked by the expression. This attribute will allow you to explicitly trigger a conversion to the desired target type before storing the result value in the specified scope. This requires that there be a converter available able to do the conversion, whether it's a default converter or a custom converter you write (as you will see in the "Type Conversion" section in Chapter 11).

Expressions

After reading about the evaluate action and expressions, you will probably be thinking "expression"? Great. But which expression language is that? Unified EL? OGNL? SpEL? Something else. maybe? Well, it turns out that Spring's developers made it easy this time. By default, Web Flow uses Spring EL (SpEL) as its expression language. If you've used Spring before, you're probably familiar with SpEL and understand that this makes the whole more consistent. You can now use SpEL within Web Flow the same way you use it in your Spring applications.

If you are not familiar with SpEL, you can find a good overview of it in the Spring reference.[9] Only a very basic understanding of this expression language is necessary for the Web Flow chapters, and we will

---

[8] See Chapter 11: on start, on entry, on render, on exit, and on end are covered in the "Execution Actions Overview" section, and action state is covered in the "Action State" section.

[9] http://static.springsource.org/spring/docs/3.1.0.RELEASE/spring-framework-reference/htmlsingle/spring-framework-reference.html#new-feature-el

only use it to invoke methods and pass along parameters. We will quickly cover everything you need to know about SpEL to understand its usage in the Web Flow chapters.

To start off, SpEL is similar to the Unified EL, but it has some additional features like method invocation and string templating functions. With SpEL, we can manipulate our object graph at runtime. To access a property from a bean, we refer to that bean and simply specify the property we want to get. The expression is a string starting with #{ and ending with }. Spring will detect the expression and use it to resolve the value.

To access a property, we simply write #{bean.property}, which tells Spring to execute the getProperty() method on the bean called bean. The *dot* (.) is the separator between the first part that is used to find the object with name bean and the second part, which is the name of the attribute as specified by the JavaBeans specification (so you don't specify get or set).

In this case, the bean name is a key on any of the scopes available to Web Flow (we will discuss these in the "Different Web Flow Scopes" section in Chapter 11). Web Flow will by default scan all available scopes to find a bean with a matching key. If no match is found, the application context is tried next to resolve a bean with a matching bean identifier.

Note The application context (typically) stores your controllers, services, repositories, and so forth. These are types of objects that are stateless (and act as singletons). Your real state, such as a form containing user data, is stored on any of the available scopes, whether the ones that Web Flow offers or the actual Servlet-provided scopes.

Besides accessing properties, you can also call methods and pass along parameters. This works the same way. For example, take this expression in an evaluate action in Web Flow:

```
<evaluate expression = "someService.someMethod(someObject)"/>
```

This will execute the someMethod—a method of someService that passes along someObject as a parameter. Again, the expression parser will scan all scopes by default to find the service object and the parameter (including the application context). You will also be able to use implicit objects to denote scopes or other special objects that are made directly available to you. While these are not strictly related to the expression language, they can be considered as *aliases* that are always available. Again, we cover implicit objects in Chapter 11.

In the earlier example in Listing 10-2, we called the initializeForm() method of the orderController:

```
<on-start>
    <evaluate
        expression="orderController.initializeForm()"↵
        result="flowScope.orderForm"/>
    <evaluate
        expression="orderController.initializeSelectableCategories()"↵
        result="flowScope.selectableCategories"/>
</on-start>
```

When executing the expression, the orderController was found in the application context. The result returned from this method is the fully initialized model that we will use throughout the flow. The result is bound to the flow scope.

When looking at the preceding expressions, you might notice that we omitted the expression delimiter (#{}). The reason for placing the delimiter is to make clear to the infrastructure that you are defining an expression. Otherwise, how could it distinguish between a normal literal value and an expression? However, in the case of the evaluate action, there is an explicit `expression` attribute. We only expect an expression there, so there is no need to use the delimiters. It is even *prohibited* to use the expression delimiter in this case. We think that this is a bit bizarre, but that's how it is.

In cases where you are creating a template expression or using expressions in attributes that are destined for both literals and expressions (such as the `view` attribute of the view state, for example), you must use the delimiters to denote where your expression part is. For example, consider this snippet:

```
<view-state view="myView#{someVariable}"/>
```

Here we denote that #{someVariable} is the expression part. If we had put `myViewSomeVariable` instead, then the entire value would have been interpreted as a literal value.

Note It's possible you are a Web Flow 1 user, and you prefer OGNL (the default expression language for that version). It's also possible that you are upgrading from an earlier version of Web Flow 2, where Unified EL was the default expression language. In Chapter 12, we will illustrate how you can change the default expression language to Unified EL or OGNL. However, we encourage you to go with SpEL (the default) and only deviate from this option if there is a good reason to do so.

Configuration

Now that you have seen what a basic flow and its main elements look like, it is time for some action. The first thing we should do is configure our web application framework of choice (Spring MVC). Next we will configure Web Flow and explain how Web Flow integrates with Spring MVC.

In addition to Spring MVC, Web Flow has special integration support for the following:

- Spring Portlet MVC

- JSF2

These options are not discussed here, but it's important to inform you that Web Flow is not bound to Spring MVC only. This is a good thing because the knowledge you will gather here could be useful for projects using one of the other web technologies.

Note The pieces of configuration and sample code explained here can be found under the `chapter10-bookstore` samples section. In the beginning of this book, you will find extended information detailing how to import this project in the STS IDE or how to run it directly from the embedded web container. To understand the configuration, it is not required to know the ins and outs of the application we are building—that's why we discuss this setup first. Here we focus first on the generic Spring MVC/Web Flow configuration. As explained in the

---

"Welcome" section, we paid special attention to illustrating the code in this book as completely as possible, so that you wouldn't need access to the sample application to follow what is going on.

Dependencies

First, you should add Spring Web Flow to your build and deploy path. When using Gradle (as in our samples) it suffices to declare dependencies to the following artifacts in the `build.gradle`:

```
compile "org.springframework.webflow:spring-webflow:$springSwfVersion"
compile "org.springframework.webflow:spring-js:$springSwfVersion"
compile "org.springframework.webflow:spring-binding:$springSwfVersion"
```

You can find this code in the `build.gradle` file located in the `chapter10-bookstore` sample. The dependency is declared on project level (as opposed to the root, `build.gradle`). The reasoning behind this is that the previous sample projects in the book do not use Web Flow. Declaring the dependency in the root `build.gradle` file would implicitly mean that all these projects have an unnecessary Web Flow dependency. By declaring the Web Flow dependency specifically in the `build.gradle` of the Web Flow samples, we limited this dependency by introducing it only when we were ready to tackle the topic of Web Flow. The version variable is maintained in the `build.gradle` in the root of the `/samples` directory. This is a clean way to manage the versions of your core libraries. This works great for a monolithically structured project, where every subproject is supposed to use the same version of a given library.

This will provide all the dependencies (including transitive ones) required to get started using Web Flow. Of course, you will need the Spring and Spring MVC dependencies as laid out earlier in this book. At the time of writing, the latest Web Flow 2 version is 2.3.1. Check the SpringSource Web Flow[10] website to make sure there isn't a newer version available when you start working with Web Flow in your application.

Web Flow Configuration

Here we will start by explaining what you need for the Web Flow-specific configuration. It consists of the components that are required to bootstrap Web Flow. We will first describe what you need for Web Flow itself. For example, we will cover how to configure the flow executor and flow registry. The flow executor is the actual Web Flow engine that will run our flows, and the flow registry will look up and parse our flow definitions. We will also have a look at the flow builder services that can be used to customize the configuration. Finally, we need of a piece of separate configuration that will link the Web Flow configuration into the Spring MVC framework. This piece of "glue" configuration will be described in the "Spring MVC Glue Configuration" section.

Core Configuration

The core Web Flow configuration is simplified by making use of Spring's so-called *namespace configuration*. This means that you will use components in the Spring Web Flow namespace to configure Web Flow (see Listing 10-3). The machinery behind it will create all the beans necessary to bootstrap it.

---

[10] http://www.springsource.org/webflow

All of this is configured in a Spring XML configuration file. At this time, there are no annotation alternatives. The Spring configuration file looks standard; but in this case, we added an additional namespace that holds the Web Flow-specific configuration elements and attributes. Also, the namespace has the webflow prefix; we will use this prefix to address elements in the Web Flow configuration namespace.

Listing 10-3. The src/main/resources/spring/webflow-config.xml and Web Flow configuration namespaces

```
<beans xmlns=http://www.springframework.org/schema/beans
    xmlns:xsi="http://www.w3.org/2001/XMLSchema-instance"
    xmlns:webflow="http://www.springframework.org/schema/webflow-config"
    xsi:schemaLocation="http://www.springframework.org/schema/beans
        http://www.springframework.org/schema/beans/spring-beans-3.1.xsd
        http://www.springframework.org/schema/webflow-config
        http://www.springframework.org/schema/webflow-config/spring-webflow-config.xsd">
```

▪ **Note** At this time, there are no annotations for configuring Web Flow. However, the namespaces configuration approach makes configuration rather straightforward. With a couple lines of XML, you can set up your Web Flow configuration.

The two core components that let Web Flow do its work are the org.springframework.webflow .executor.FlowExecutor and the org.springframework.webflow.definition.registry .FlowDefinitionRegistry. The first component is the main entry point for the web application framework to drive the flow execution. Listing 10-4 shows how to configure the flow executor.

Listing 10-4. Configuring the Flow Executor

```
<webflow:flow-executor id="flowExecutor"/>
```

Optionally, you can specify the flow-registry attribute, which defaults to a bean with the id of flowRegistry. This means that, if you stick to that bean naming convention, you won't need to specify this attribute. If you name the FlowDefinitionRegistry something else (e.g., myFlowRegistry), you will have to specify it explicitly, as shown in Listing 10-5. There are only two reasons why you would want to do this:

- There is a bean with a conflicting name. In other words, there is already a bean which has flowRegistry as its identification.

- You are not using the namespaces configuration and instead created a custom flow registry bean, giving it a specific name. For example, you could create a flow registry that reads its flow from database and give it the id of databaseReadingFlowRegistry In this case, you could decide to give it a different name to make its intention clear.

We will go with the defaults in our sample code and not specify the flow-registry attribute.

Listing 10-5. Configuring a non-standard Flow Registry: myFlowRegistry

```
<webflow:flow-executor id="flowExecutor" flow-registry="myFlowRegistry"/>
```

The only notable subelement to be used within the flow executor is `<webflow:flow-execution-repository>`, which lets you customize the internals of the flow executor. We will discuss this in depth in Chapter 12's "Web Flow Configuration Customizations" section.

The `FlowDefinitionRegistry` is responsible for finding and reading the flows that you have created. Roughly, you have two options:

- Define each flow manually with the `<webflow:flow-location path="" id="">` subelement.

- Specify a pattern. Web Flow will automatically scan for flows and add them to the registry when it finds them.

In the sample, we have opted for the second option (see Listing 10-6).

Listing 10-6. Configuring the Flow Registry to Automatically Scan for Flow Definitions

```
<webflow:flow-registry base-path="/WEB-INF/view">
    <webflow:flow-location-pattern value="/**/*-flow.xml" />
</webflow:flow-registry>
```

Setting the base-path means that the registry will start to look for flows in `/WEB-INF/view` and all its subdirectories. We have opted to put the flows together with our views. However, you could change the value of `base-path` to another directory if you would like to store your flows separately.

The `base-path` helps in keeping your flow ids clean. The flow id (that's the id you will use to start a flow) is the location of the flow within your web application, followed by the filename (but minus the .xml). So a flow x.xml located in `/WEB-INF/view` would start like this: `http://host:port/contextRoot/x`. However, A flow y.xml located in `WEB-INF/view/`**subdir**`/y.xml` would be start with this URL: `http://host:port/contextRoot/`**subdir**.

■ **Note** The last URL was not a mistake; there is no "y" missing at the end. When a flow is not located in the root directory, Web Flow accumulates the subdirectories as part of the flow id and stops at the last subdirectory. The name of the flow itself is in that case *not* part of the flow id. For example, a flow in `WEB-INF/subdir1/subdir2/someFlow.xml` would start with this URL: `http://host:port/contextRoot/subdir1/subdir2`. While this might sound bizarre, Web Flow encourages you to create a unique subdirectory *per* flow. You are encouraged to put the flow together with your other artifacts, such as your pages. From that point of view, it does make sense.

We will store our flows together with the views. The option that allows you to store flows separately from your views will be discussed in Chapter 12's "Web Flow Configuration Customizations" section.

Flow Builder Services

With the flow builder services, you can further configure and customize the flow registry. (It is actually an attribute of the flow-registry, as you will see later in this chapter.) You only need to specify this when you want something other than the defaults. Since we have a special requirement—namely, that we are using Tiles as a templating framework—we need to configure a custom flow builder service (see Listing 10-7).

Listing 10-7. *Configuring Flow Builder Services*

```
<webflow:flow-builder-services id="flowBuilderServices" view-factory-↵
"creator="mvcViewFactoryCreator development="true"/>"

<bean id="mvcViewFactoryCreator" class="org.springframework.webflow.mvc↵
.builder.MvcViewFactoryCreator">
    <property name="viewResolvers">
        <list>
            <ref bean="tilesViewResolver"/>
        </list>
    </property>
</bean>
```

Let's look at the two attributes that are of importance at the moment (see Table 10-7). The first is the view-factory-creator and the second is development.

Table 10-7. *Attributes of the Flow Builder Service*

Attribute	Definition and Usage
view-factory-creator	Web Flow needs to be able to resolve the view names that you specify in the view attribute of the view state elements. The default implementation looks for views that are put alongside your flows and end with .jsp. In our case, this will not work. While we put our flows together with our views, and our views end with .jsp, we are using tiles to compose our views. Thus Web Flow needs to know about our TilesViewResolver. This resolver will look up the view definitions based on the literals you specified in your flow view states. The resolver is defined as part of the Spring MVC configuration in the WebMvcContextConfiguration class.
development	Set this to true to switch on flow development mode. Development mode switches on hot-reloading of flow definition changes, including changes to dependent flow resources such as message bundles. Basically, this means that the flow definitions are not cached, but reread from the file store when you access them. This happens every time you (re)start the flow. So if you change something to the flow definition XML, it is sufficient to restart the flow in your browser, so you can immediately see the changes. By enabling this feature, you avoid having to restart your web container each time you make changes to your flow definitions. For production, you should change this to false because this could impose a (very small, but still present) performance penalty or unnecessary file access appearing when doing file-system monitoring. You also could make this dynamic with a SpEL expression or by using Spring profiles.

After specifying the flow builder services, you can hook it up to the flow registry:

```
<webflow:flow-registry base-path="/WEB-INF/view" flow-builder-services="flowBuilderServices">
    <webflow:flow-location-pattern value="/**/*-flow.xml" />
</webflow:flow-registry>
```

The flow builder services can be used to customize other things, as well. For example, you can configure Web Flow to perform JSR 303 validation (AKA bean validation). This means that, if you annotate your model with annotations from the javax.constraints.validation package (e.g., @Min, @Max, and so on), then validation will take place and error messages will be created for that path within your model. Validation is discussed in more detail in the "Selecting Books and Delivery Options" section in Chapter 11.

After performing the validation, you can configure custom type conversion and formatting. These topics are discussed in Chapter 11's "Type Conversion" and "Type Formatting" sections, respectively.

Finally, the flow builder services also allow you to switch the expression parser. This is discussed in more detail in Chapter 12 in the "Web Flow Configuration Customizations" section.

Gluing Spring MVC and Spring Web Flow

Our Spring MVC configuration is the default setup. We have set it up just as we did in the previous chapters. There is also a basic com.apress.prospringmvc.bookstore.web.config .WebMvcContextConfiguration class that starts like this:

```
package com.apress.prospringmvc.bookstore.web.config;

import org.springframework.context.annotation.Configuration;
import org.springframework.web.servlet.config.annotation.EnableWebMvc;
import org.springframework.context.annotation.ComponentScan;
//Other imports omitted for brevity

@Configuration
@EnableWebMvc
@ComponentScan(basePackages = { "com.apress.prospringmvc.bookstore.web" })
public class WebMvcContextConfiguration extends WebMvcConfigurationSupport{
```

Inside the class, we added beans for the following:

- Localization (messagesource)

- Standard view resolver

- Tiles view resolver

We also have the com.apress.prospringmvc.bookstore.web.interceptor .CommonDataHandlerInterceptor to support our random book feature in the right pane. However, this is nothing new compared to the previous chapters (it is explained in Chapter 6's "Configuring Interceptors" section). On the same line, there is also the org.springframework.web.servlet.i18n .LocaleChangeInterceptor, which is used to dynamically switch languages on the pages (explained in Chapter 5's "LocaleChangeInterceptor" section). We will not discuss this class further because it is exactly the same as in the previous chapters.

Later in this chapter, we will configure Web Flow with the same Tiles view resolver that is defined for and used by Spring MVC. The point is that we will still be able to use Spring MVC as-is, without added

Web Flow functionality. In that case, Spring MVC will works as it normally does, and it should have the means to resolve its views.

Selecting between vanilla Spring MVC and Web Flow happens in the main Spring MVC entry point; the org.springframework.web.servlet.DispatcherServlet. Using org.springframework.web.servlet .HandlerAdapter mappings enables Spring MVC to forward the request either to one of its own HandlerAdapters or to Web Flow's org.springframework.webflow.mvc.servlet.FlowHandlerAdapter (see Figure 10-8).

This mechanism is specially built, so that the Spring MVC DispatcherServlet remains your single entry point. The distinction is made depending on the request, and the request is forwarded to either Web Flow or Spring MVC itself (which might then be a resource or even a call to your controller). In the case of Web Flow, there is an org.springframework.webflow.mvc.servlet.FlowHandlerMapping registered with the DispatcherServlet. This FlowHandlerMapping will detect whether the URL points to an existing flow id. If so, the request is treated as a Web Flow request; otherwise, the next org.springframework.web .servlet.HandlerMapping in line tries to identify the type of request.

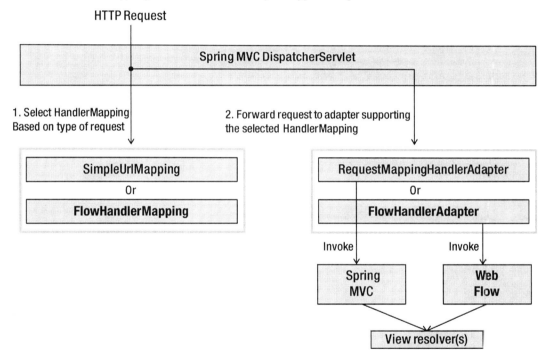

Figure 10-10. Spring MVC's configurable HandlerAdapter mechanism to forward requests

You can see that the DispatcherServlet uses HandlerAdapter and HandlerMapping to send a request to a specific part—to either Web Flow or Spring MVC in our case. These two components (i.e., the FlowHandlerMapping and FlowHandlerAdapter) need to be registered before Web Flow will be able to receive requests from the DispatcherServlet.

We declared these components in the com.apress.prospringmvc.bookstore.web.config .WebflowContextConfiguration. This class does two things:

- It imports the `webflow-config.xml` (as discussed in the previous section) into the ApplicationContext using the `@ImportResource("classpath:/spring/webflow-config.xml")` annotation.

- It defines and configures the two beans with the following ids: `flowHandlerAdapter` and `flowHandlerMapping`.

In the Listing 10-8, we show what the `WebflowContextConfiguration` looks like. This listing brings all these components together and effectively serves as the glue between Web Flow and Spring MVC.

Listing 10-8. *Adding the FlowHandlerAdapter and FlowHandlerMapping Beans*

```java
package com.apress.prospringmvc.bookstore.web.config;

import org.springframework.web.servlet.DispatcherServlet;
import org.springframework.web.servlet.i18n.LocaleChangeInterceptor;
import org.springframework.webflow.definition.registry.FlowDefinitionRegistry;
import org.springframework.webflow.executor.FlowExecutor;
import org.springframework.webflow.mvc.servlet.FlowHandlerAdapter;
import org.springframework.webflow.mvc.servlet.FlowHandlerMapping;
import com.apress.prospringmvc.bookstore.web.interceptor.↵
        CommonDataHandlerInterceptor;
//Ommited other imports for brevity

@Configuration
@ImportResource("classpath:/spring/webflow-config.xml")
public class WebflowContextConfiguration {

    @Autowired
    private FlowExecutor flowExecutor;
    @Autowired
    private FlowDefinitionRegistry flowRegistry;
    @Autowired
    private CommonDataHandlerInterceptor commonDataHandlerInterceptor;
    @Autowired
    private LocaleChangeInterceptor localeChangeInterceptor;

    @Bean
    public FlowHandlerAdapter flowHandlerAdapter() {
        FlowHandlerAdapter flowHandlerAdapter = new FlowHandlerAdapter();
        flowHandlerAdapter.setFlowExecutor(flowExecutor);
        return flowHandlerAdapter;
    }

    @Bean
    public FlowHandlerMapping flowHandlerMapping() {
        FlowHandlerMapping flowHandlerMapping = new FlowHandlerMapping();
        flowHandlerMapping.setInterceptors(new Object[] { commonDataHandlerInterceptor,↵
localeChangeInterceptor });
        flowHandlerMapping.setFlowRegistry(flowRegistry);
        return flowHandlerMapping;
    }
```

```
    }
}
```

■ **Note** When we discussed the `WebMvcContextConfiguration`, we said that it declares the two interceptors, just as it did in the previous Spring MVC chapters. These interceptors are `CommonDataHandlerInterceptor` for the random books, and `LocaleChangeInterceptor` for supporting dynamic language change. In the `WebflowContextConfiguration`, we repeat this mapping, passing the same interceptor references to the `FlowHandlerMapping`. This is because the two systems are separated from each other. Once Web Flow is handling the request, it doesn't know about interceptors added to Spring MVC handler mappings, and vice versa. If you did not add these interceptors here, changing the language or showing random books would no longer work from the moment you started a flow.

In the preceding sections, we covered the different configuration details for configuring Web Flow. We also investigated and explained how to integrate Web Flow with Spring MVC. In the next section, we will focus on building something workable using Web Flow.

Building Your First Flow

In this section and hereafter, we will build a small part of our bookstore sample application using Web Flow. We already have seen some of the important elements that make up a flow. Now we will use them to build an entire working flow. To make you familiar with the basic building blocks required to assemble our first flow, we will build it step by step describing each part into detail. Finally, we will show the complete assembled flow. The following sections will contain a lot of snippets, so you might want to peak to the complete flow as listed in the Overview section if you get lost in between.

We will implement the create order use case. This use case will allow a user to order books. The first screen shows a dropdown list for selecting a category, while the next screen allows a user to select books that belong to that selected category. One or more different books can be added to the list. Next, the user can enter order details such as the delivery date. When the user confirms, the order is made. The user is also able to cancel the process in each of the different stages. This flow consists of following actions/pages:

1. The user selects the link to buy books from the navigation bar.

2. A category must be selected (page1).

3. The books within that category must be shown (page2).

4. A user can select one or more different books and add them to the list of selected books.

5. The user can enter some order details, such as the date of delivery (page3).

6. The order is placed.

See the flow diagram for creating an order in Figure 10-11; Table 10-8 explains the flow steps.

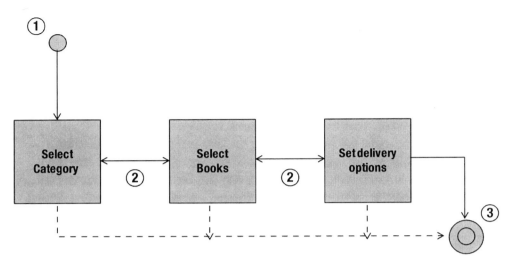

Figure 10-11. *The flow the sample application implements*

Table 10-8. *Explaining the Flow Steps*

Number	Explanation
1	On the left is the start of our flow with a single circle. The start of a flow does not have a special element; it can be either of the following: • The first state defined in the flow • The state indicated by the start-state attribute of the flow root element When there is no `<start-state>` attribute, the first state of the flow is automatically executed when the flow is started.
2	The arrow marks the direction of the navigation. In this case, the navigation is bidirectional, which means that you can go back and forth between these view states. This is offered to you by Web Flow, and you do not have to configure anything special for it. It will be offered by a Next/Previous button on the screen; however, you could also use your browser's Forward/Back button. You will see that the state of the previous step is retained and still visible in your browser, even when you go back from the last step to the first.
3	On the bottom right, the end of our flow is indicated with a double circle. Once the end is reached, our flow will be terminated. The end of a flow does have a special element: end state (which we cover in Chapter 11). It is one of the five state types Web Flow understands.

We can summarize things as follows:

- We don't perform any kind of authentication in this sample application. But because we need to link orders to a user, every user is authenticated automatically when entering the web application. This is done for you in the sample. We will not discuss this here because we are taking this part of the process out of your control for the moment. We will leave the explanation for this to the next chapter.

- After the order has been made, the user is sent back to the home page.

■ **Note** The approach we take with the Spring Web Flow sample for selecting books and creating the order is somewhat different than the previously discussed Spring MVC approach. We deliberately left out the shopping cart and transformed the book selection and order process to a more flow-based approach. This better suits our needs when explaining the different Web Flow elements.

Creating the Home Page

Before we proceed in building our flow, we first want to cover how a user gets into the application. In other words, we want to go over what the user sees when she enters the bookstore URL.

The first page shown is the so-called home page. It consists of the template with no content in the middle (the content area). This page will allow the user to select an action from the navigation menu. Let's take a quick look at how this is implemented.

The controller com.apress.prospringmvc.bookstore.web.controller.MainController is a normal Spring MVC controller defined as a Spring bean using the @Controller annotation. The goal of this controller is simply to render the home page, which is physically the main.jsp. The controller uses the @RequestMapping "index.htm" to do this. This controller is defined in Listing 10-9.

Listing 10-9. The Main Controller

```
package com.apress.prospringmvc.bookstore.web.controller;

import org.springframework.stereotype.Controller;
import org.springframework.web.bind.annotation.RequestMapping;
import org.springframework.web.servlet.ModelAndView;

@Controller
public class MainController {
    @RequestMapping("index.htm")
    public ModelAndView main() {
        ModelAndView mov = new ModelAndView();
        mov.setViewName("main");
        return mov;
    }
}
```

The view is rendered via Tiles. If you open tiles-configuration.xml located in /WEB-INF/tiles/tiles-configuration.xml, you will see that the main view extends the fullTemplate and sets main.jsp as the content pane (see Listing 10-10).

Listing 10-10. The Tiles Configuration

```
<definition name="main" extends="fullTemplate">
    <put-attribute name="content" value="/WEB-INF/view/main.jsp"/>
</definition>
```

To access the application and show this home page, you simply have to point your browser to `http://localhost:8080/chapter10-bookstore/`. Thanks to the `index.jsp`, which is automatically picked up as the web application's welcome file, the Welcome screen is shown. This `index.jsp` will internally be forwarded to the `index.htm` request mapping on which the `MainController` is listening and trigger the view-rendering process. Note that a welcome file must be a physical file. It cannot be the name of a fictional view (such as our `index.htm`) that is resolved by Spring MVC. To make this happen, we have an `index.jsp` file right under the `webapp` folder, as you can see in Listing 10-11. This folder is directly accessible by your browser. Tomcat (or tc Server) will be default place to look for the `index.jsp` welcome file. Remember that `index.jsp` is outside our `WEB-INF` directory (in the STS Java view, it is under the `/webapp` directory), so it will be directly accessible by external clients. This is unlike the JSPs of our other views, which are placed under `WEB-INF/view` and are not directly accessible by external clients.

Listing 10-11. The index.jsp Forwarded to the Internal Tiles-Composed Main View

```
<!DOCTYPE HTML>

<%@ page pageEncoding="UTF-8" contentType="text/html; charset=UTF-8"%>

<jsp:forward page="/index.htm" />
```

▓ **Note** You can check the welcome file defaults by first going to your workspace server home directory. The home directory can be found by double clicking the "Servers" project (while being in the Java or Java EE perspective) and then by double clicking on the server instance (which is named "VMware vFabric tc Server Developer Edition v2.6-config" by default). In there you can open the `web.xml`. The entries in this file are the defaults for each web application that will be deployed on this server instance. At the end of the file, you will find the `welcome-file-list`, which lists all the files (and their extensions) that are recognized as welcome files by default.

Implementing the Create Order Flow

To implement our flow according to the required use case, we will need three major elements:

- An `<on-start>` element to initialize our model and selectable categories
- Three view states, one for each page
  - Transitions in each view state to navigate back/cancel/forward
  - Some evaluation actions

- To prepare our list of selectable books

- To add a book to the list of selected books

- To clear the list of selected books

- To create our order in the last step

- An end state to terminate our flow

We decided to start building the sample page-by-page. In the upcoming sections, we will build the three pages (in the order as displayed in Figure 10-5) and the required flow components. Let's get started by building the page that lets users select the category.

Selecting the Category

We need to begin by initializing our model and retrieving the selectable categories that we will have to present to the user. The model is the `com.apress.prospringmvc.bookstore.web.controller.OrderForm`. We will use this model throughout the flow to gather the user's input. The categories are required for the first step of the flow, and these are displayed to the user in a dropdown list that the user can select from. These categories need to be retrieved from database first.

■ **Note** The flow we are building here is the `createOrders-flow.xml`, which is located in `WEB-INF/view/createOrders/`. This is also the location where we will put the pages that we are going to create, along with the flow.

Earlier in this chapter, we covered the `<on-start>` element, which allows you to execute logic when the flow is initially starting. This logic will execute before the flow enters any other state. The action should appear before any other state, and it can appear only once in the flow. This will be perfect for our initialization (see Listing 10-12).

Listing 10-12. The <on-start> Element of Our Create Order Flow

```
<on-start>
    <evaluate expression="orderController.initializeForm()"↵
        result="flowScope.orderForm" />
    <evaluate expression="orderController.initializeSelectableCategories()"↵
        result="flowScope.selectableCategories"/>
</on-start>
```

The first evaluate action will initialize our form and set some initial values (this code is executed on the `com.apress.prospringmvc.bookstore.web.controller.OrderController`). It calls the method shown in Listing 10-13. The initialized `OrderForm` is then set to the flow scope. `flowScope` is an implicit variable to access the flow scope. (Scoping is explained in the next chapter in the "Different Web Flow Scopes" section; similarly, you can learn about implicit variables in the next chapter's "Implicit Variables" section).

Listing 10-13. The Method to Initialize Our Form, Called from the <on-start> element

```
public OrderForm initializeForm() {
    OrderForm orderForm = new OrderForm();
    orderForm.setQuantity(1);
    orderForm.setOrderDate(simpleDateFormat.format(new Date()));
    return orderForm;
}
```

We can specify more than one evaluate action in an on start, and these actions will be executed in order. If one of the evaluate actions results in an exception, then the processing stops and no transition takes place. The second evaluate action will put a map of selectable categories (com.apress.prospringmvc.bookstore.domain.Category) on the flow scope. To keep things simple, we used a map with a key type of Long (the surrogate key of each category record) and a value type of String (the name of the Category) as can be seen in Listing 10-14. Later on we will see how we can use Category Objects directly instead of transforming them to String's first.

Listing 10-14. The Method to Initialize Categories, Called from the on-start

```
public Map<Long, String> initializeSelectableCategories() {
    Map<Long, String> selectableCategories = new HashMap<Long, String>();
    for (Category category : categoryService.findAll()) {
        selectableCategories.put(category.getId(), category.getName());
    }
    return selectableCategories;
}
```

■ **Note** We explicitly stored our categories separately from the OrderForm. We could have also saved this on the form itself, but we kept it separate, so as not to cause bloat on the form.

Next, we are going to create our view state, as shown in Listing 10-15.

Listing 10-15. The selectCategory View State

```
<view-state id="selectCategory" view="selectCategory" model="orderForm">
    <transition on="next" to="selectBooks">
    <evaluate expression="orderController.initializeSelectableBooks(flowScope.orderForm)"↵
  result="flowScope.selectableBooks"/>
    </transition>
    <transition on="cancel" to="end" />
</view-state>
```

This view state will render the selectCategory view. This is a definition entry in our tiles-configuration.xml that extends from the full template (see Listing 10-16).

Listing 10-16. The Tiles Configuration for the Select Categories View

```
<definition name="selectCategory" extends="fullTemplate">
    <put-attribute name="content" value="/WEB-↵
      INF/view/createOrders/selectCategory.jsp"/>
</definition>
```

The view state will use our `orderForm` (as indicated with the `model` attribute) that we initialized previously in the `<on-start>` element. Web Flow will automatically bind every request parameter to the specified form. As we will see in Chapter 11's "Explicit Binding" section, this can be overridden. Remember: We are keeping this sample as simple as possible; therefore, we left explicit binding, validation, and conversion out of the picture. We will address those things in the following chapters.

Our view will require some kind of control component that will trigger the `next` or `cancel` transition. The `next` transition will bring us to the next view state. We already named it `selectBooks`. However, before making the transition, we prepare the list of books that are available within the chosen category. We do this by calling a method on the `OrderController`. This method will use the selected category to load the books available for that category. The result is a map with the same structure as the categories; it is also set to the flow scope (see Listing 10-17).

Listing 10-17. The Initializer for Our List of Selectable Books

```
public Map<Long, String> initializeSelectableBooks(OrderForm orderForm) {
    orderForm.getSelectedBooks().clear();
    orderForm.resetSelectedBooks();

    Map<Long, String> selectableBooks = new HashMap<Long, String>();
    for (Book book : bookstoreService.findBooksByCategory(categoryService.findById↵
(orderForm.getCategoryId()))) {
        selectableBooks.put(book.getId(), book.getTitle());
    }
    return selectableBooks;
}
```

The page that will be shown to the user and drive the transition in the previously mentioned view state is located at `WEB-INF/view/createOrders/selectCategory.jsp` and shown in Listing 10-18.

Listing 10-18. The Actual Page for Our Select Categories

```
<form:form modelAttribute="orderForm" action="${flowExecutionUrl}">
    <table style="width: 100%">
        <tr>
            <td width="30%">
                <spring:message code="label.page.category"/></td>
            <td>
                <form:select path="categoryId" ↵
                    items="${selectableCategories}"/>
            </td>
        </tr>
    </table>
```

```
    <div align="right" style="margin-bottom: 20px; margin-top: 10px" >
        <button type="submit" id="return" name="_eventId_cancel">
            <spring:message code="button.cancel"/>
        </button>
        <button type="submit" id="continue" name="_eventId_next">
            <spring:message code="button.next"/>
        </button>
    </div>
</form:form>
```

Note that we are using a Spring MVC form. This is useful if we later want to bind our errors for the specific input fields. Our action (${flowExecutionUrl}) is a special implicit object that refers to the current flow execution. This is the current URL together with the flow execution key. You should think of this as the post back URL to the running flow. In your final rendered HTML, this could be translated like this in the following listing :

```
action="/chapter10-bookstore/createOrders?execution=e4s1"
```

The flow execution key will allow Web Flow to load the state again where it was saved before returning the response (i.e., before pausing the flow).

The `<form:select>` element is a basic Spring MVC tag library for rendering a HTML select list. It can work perfectly with a map; in that case, it will use the key as value for the HTML option element (which is the text that will be send as part of the form submission) and the value as the content of the HTML option (which is the text that will be shown in the list).

Finally, there are two buttons. These are the control components that will drive the transition. If you look at the name, you see that they end with the on value of our transitions and are prefixed with _eventId_. This is how Web Flow will identify which transition to execute. The name of the buttons are sent along with the request when submitting the form. The scheme is _eventId_*<on_transition>*.

Oh wait; there is one more thing to do. As can be seen on the home page in Figure 10-10, our idea is to initiate our flow with a Buy books link. We still need to configure this link in the navigation bar to start our flow.

To find the link, we have to open the header.jsp, which you can find in WEB-INF/templates/. Remember that we use Tiles for templating. A page consists of a header, content, and a footer panel. The menu is rendered as part of the header.jsp (see Listing 10-19).

***Listing 10-19** The Link in Our Navigation Bar to Start the Create Order Flow*

```
<li>
    <spring:url value="/createOrders" var="createOrder" />
    <a href="${createOrder}">Buy books</a>
</li>
```

In our case, the flow is located under (WEB-INF/view)/createOrders/createOrders-flow.xml, along with the pages that will be used in our flow. The URL created is simply appending "/createOrders" to the base URL. As we saw in the "Core Configuration" section, the flows under the WEB-INF/view directory are addressable directly via the directory structure they reside in.

■ **Note** You might wonder why we don't embed `<spring:url>` inside the `href` attribute directly, instead of working with a variable. We could have done this; while this notation is a bit more elaborate, it is also more readable. Let's just say it's a matter of personal style and taste.

At this point you should be able to test the application. Open your browser and point it to `http://localhost:8080/chapter10-bookstore/`. On the home page, you can now click the Buy books link. Doing so should display the view shown in Figure 10-12.

Figure 10-12. Our Select Categories Rendered in the Browser

Clicking the Next button will yield an error because we haven't implemented the next view state yet. However, clicking the Cancel button should bring us back to the home page. This is accomplished by transitioning to the end state. For now, it is enough to know that the end state will simply end the flow execution and perform a last redirect to a view we configure. As mentioned previously, we will examine the <end-state> element in detail in Chapter 11.

That rounds out how to select a category, so let's move onto selecting and adding books.

Selecting and Adding Books

Next, we need to build a page where the user is presented with a list of books for the previously selected category. The user should be able to add a selected book to an order list, and there should also be an input field to specify the number of books the user wants to add.

In our previous view state, before transitioning to the view state we are going to build here, we loaded the books on the flow scope under the selectableBooks key—so that part is already done. What remains is for us to specify the view state and define all available transitions to handle the part of the use case where the user selects a book and adds it to the list. In this section, we will continue by describing the functionality that we need to accomplish this. Next, we will place the actual transition underneath, so you can see what it looks like. Finally, we will give an overview of the entire view state.

Let's begin by implementing something that takes us back to the previous page (see Listing 10-20).

Listing 10-20. *Transitioningto the Previous View State*

```
<transition on="previous" to="selectCategory" />
```

The to attribute is the id of the previous view state. So, when a _eventId_previous comes in via the request parameters, Web Flow will automatically take us back to the previous view state. The previous view will then be shown, including its data.

We should be able to select a book from the available books list, and then add the book to our list of selected books that is stored on our form (see Listing 10-21).

Listing 10-21. *Transition to Add a Seleted Book to Our Selected Book List*

```
<transition on="add" >
    <evaluate expression="orderController.addBook(flowScope.orderForm)" />
</transition>
```

This preceding snippet will invoke the method in Listing 10-22 on the OrderController.

Listing 10-22. *Executing the Controller Code to Add a Book to Our Selected Book List*

```
public void addBook(OrderForm orderForm) {
    Book book = bookstoreService.findBook(orderForm.getBookId());
    if (orderForm.getSelectedBooks().containsKey(book)) {
        orderForm.getSelectedBooks().put(book, ↵
        orderForm.getSelectedBooks().get(book) + orderForm.getQuantity());
    } else {
        orderForm.getSelectedBooks().put(book, orderForm.getQuantity());
    }
}
```

We will use the OrderForm to retrieve the selected book id. This was bound by Web Flow on the form when the form was submitted (i.e., when executing the add transition). We retrieve the book and add it to the map of selected books with the specified amount.

Also, notice that this transition does not have a to attribute. As we have already seen, this attribute is optional. When left unspecified, the same view state is rendered again. This is exactly what we want; after adding a book; that is, we want to stay on the same page and show the user that the new book was added to the list.

Once some books are added to the list, the user might want to start over and thus clear the currently selected books. Listing 10-23 shows the transition, and Listing 10-24 shows the code that clears the list.

Listing 10-23. *The Transition to Clear Our List of Selected Books*

```
<transition on="reset" to="selectBooks">
    <evaluate expression="orderForm.resetSelectedBooks()" />
</transition>
```

Listing 10-24. *The Code that Actually Clears the List*

```
public void resetSelectedBooks() {
    selectedBooks.clear();
}
```

As in the previous view state, the user must be able to opt out of the current order process by clicking the Cancel button (see Listing10- 25).

Listing 10-25. *Canceling the current order and Proceeding to the end-state*

```
<transition on="cancel" to="end" />
```

The user should also be able to advance to the final page (see Listing 10-27).

Listing 10-26. *Proceeding to the Next View to Select Our Delivery Options*

```
<transition on="next" to="selectDeliveryOptions" />
```

Finally, Listing 10-28 shows how our view state will look.

Listing 10-27. *The selectBooks View State Overview*

```
<view-state id="selectBooks" view="selectBooks" model="orderForm">

    <transition on="previous" to="selectCategory"/>

    <transition on="add" >
        <evaluate expression="orderController.addBook(flowScope.orderForm)" />
    </transition>


    <transition on="next" to="selectDeliveryOptions" />
```

```
    <transition on="reset" to="selectBooks">
        <evaluate expression="orderForm.resetSelectedBooks()" />
    </transition>

    <transition on="cancel" to="end" />
</view-state>
```

In Listing 10-28, you can see the Tiles definition that corresponds to the selectBooks view.

Listing 10-28. The Tiles Definition for Our Select Books View

```
<definition name="selectBooks" extends="fullTemplate">
    <put-attribute name="content" value="/WEB-INF/view/createOrders/selectBooks.jsp"/><
/definition>
```

Next, we will create the page (see Listing 10-29), which will consist of three parts. You can find this page at /WEB-INF/view/createOrders/selectBooks.jsp. The first part allows you to select the book, enter the quantity, and add it to the list of selected books. You can also clear the list. You invoke this functionality by clicking the Add and Reset buttons, which will call the add and reset transitions, respectively. The second part of the page is the list itself; it shows the list of currently selected books and their quantity. Finally, the third part of the page displays the buttons to drive the remaining transitions: previous, cancel, and next.

Listing 10-29. The Page for Our Selected Books

```
<form:form modelAttribute="orderForm" action="${flowExecutionUrl}">
    <table style="width: 100%">
        <tr style="height: 10px;"/>
        <tr>
            <td>
                <spring:message code="label.page.books.select.book" />
            </td>
            <td>
                <form:select path="bookId" items="${selectableBooks}"/>
            </td>
        </tr>
        <tr>
            <td>
                <spring:message code="label.page.books.select.quantity"/>
            </td>
            <td>
                <form:input path="quantity" />
            </td>
        </tr>
        <tr height="10px"/>
        <tr align="right">
            <td colspan="2">
                <button type="submit" id="add" name="_eventId_add">
                    <spring:message code="label.page.books.add.book"/>
                </button>
                <button type="submit" id="cancel" name="_eventId_reset">
                    <spring:message code="button.reset"/>
```

```
                </button>
            </td>
        </tr>
    </table>
    <p/>
    <h3><spring:message code="label.page.books.selected.books"/></h3>
    <div style="margin-top: 10px; margin-bottom: 10px;">
        <table style="width: 100%;" rules="groups">
            <thead>
                <tr>
                    <th width="80%" align="left">
                        <spring:message code="label.page.books.book.name"/>
                    </th>
                    <th width="20%" align="left">
                    <spring:message code="label.page.books.book.quantity"/>
                    </th>
                </tr>
            </thead>
            <tbody>
                <tr height="10px"/>
                    <c:forEach items="${orderForm.selectedBooks}" var="book">
                        <tr>
                            <td>${book.key.title}</td>
                            <td>${book.value}</td>
                        </tr>
                    </c:forEach>
                <tr height="20px"/>
            </tbody>
        </table>
    </div>
    <div align="right" style="margin-bottom: 20px;" >
        <button type="submit" id="previous" name="_eventId_previous">
            <spring:message code="button.previous"/>
        </button>
        <button type="submit" id="previous" name="_eventId_cancel">
            <spring:message code="button.cancel"/>
        </button>
        <button type="submit" id="next" name="_eventId_next">
            <spring:message code="button.next"/>
        </button>
    </div>
</form:form>
```

There are a few key things to note about the preceding listing, particularly the parts in bold type:

- **${flowExecutionUrl}**: This will eventually render in the postback URL to point to our flow execution when the form submits.

- **<form:select path="bookId" items="${selectableBooks}"/>**: This will render our selectableBooks list as an HTML dropdown list.

- **eventId_add** and **eventId_reset**: When clicked, these will trigger the add and reset transitions, respectively.

- **`<c:forEach items="${orderForm.selectedBooks}" var="book">`**: This is a standard JSTL forEach that will look over our available books and render them in an HTML table.

- **`eventId_previous`, `eventId_cancel`**, and **`eventId_next`**: When clicked, these will trigger the previous, cancel, and next transitions, respectively.

After implementing Listing 10-30, we restart the flow, select the category, and click the Next button. If we were to add *Agile Software Development, Principles, Patterns, and Practices* 11 times, we would see the view shown in Figure 10-13.

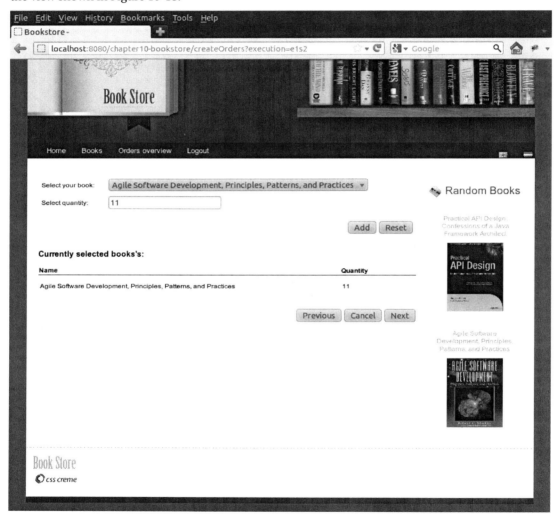

***Figure 10-13.** The browser-rendered view to select books*

Specifying the Order Details and Creating the Order

This brings us to the last part of implementing our flow. We will display the order date (which was set to the current date when we initialized our form); and below that, we will offer the user an input field to enter a desired delivery date. This is the final page of the three; at this point, the user should be able to go to the previous page, cancel the order, or finalize the order. When the user clicks the Order! button, we will create the order using the information stored in the form and then store the order in our database.

Listing 10-30 shows the code to implement our view state.

Listing 10-30. The View State for the Select Delivery Options

```
<view-state id="selectDeliveryOptions" view="selectDeliveryOptions"
    model="orderForm">
    <transition on="previous" to="selectBooks" />
    <transition on="finish" to="end">
        <evaluate expression="orderController.placeOrder(flowScope.orderForm,↩
            externalContext.sessionMap.authenticatedAccount)"/>
    </transition>

    <transition on="cancel" to="end" />
</view-state>
```

The first transition is nothing new; it takes us back to the previous view state. The second transition finalizes the order and transitions to the end state, which we will see in a moment. To create the order, we pass the com.apress.prospringmvc.bookstore.domain.Account (domain objects are part of the bookstore-shared module) and the OrderForm to the placeOrder method on our controller. The Account is nothing to worry about for now; just know that it was automatically set to the session scope when the user opened the web application. Remember that, for this sample, we kept everything as simple as possible, so the user was logged in automatically (always with the same hardcoded user). In the next chapter, we will implement the authentication ourselves, as a way of illustrating some new Web Flow concepts.

The Account identifies the user currently logged in and making the order. The orders will be added to that user. As you can see, we are using another implicit object, externalContext—this time to access the javax.servlet.Servlet session scope and retrieve the Account from there. The session scope is the ideal place to store information like authentication, which is really bound to the lifetime of the session.

The placeOrder method will use the com.apress.prospringmvc.bookstore.domain.support .OrderBuilder to start the creation of a new com.apress.prospringmvc.bookstore.domain.Order (see Listing 10-32). Next, it will loop over the selected books and add each one of them to our order. We use the book id to retrieve the com.apress.prospringmvc.bookstore.domain.Book object from database.

Listing 10-31. The Controller Method for Placing an Order

```
public void placeOrder(final OrderForm orderForm, final Account account) throws↩
 ParseException {
    OrderBuilder orderBuilder = new OrderBuilder() {
        {
            deliveryDate(simpleDateFormat.parse(orderForm.getDeliveryDate()));
            account(account);
            orderDate(simpleDateFormat.parse(orderForm.getOrderDate()));
        }
    };
```

```
    for (Entry<Book, Integer> selectedBook : orderForm.getSelectedBooks().entrySet()) {
        orderBuilder.addBook(selectedBook.getKey(), selectedBook.getValue());
    }

    bookstoreService.store(orderBuilder.build(true));
}
```

After the order is made, the flow transitions to the end state and all other states will be cleaned up. The user is then redirected to the home page. We will discuss the end state in the next chapter in detail. For now, it is enough to know that it will end our current flow and that it performs the entire cleanup (see Listing 10-33).

Listing 10-32. *Ending Our Flow and Redirecting to the Home Page*

```
<end-state id="end" view="redirect:/index.htm"/>
```

In Listing 10-34, we show the Tiles configuration that defines the selectDeliveryOptions view.

Listing 10-33. *The Tiles Definition for Our Select Delivery Options*

```
<definition name="selectDeliveryOptions" extends="fullTemplate">
    <put-attribute name="content" value="/WEB-INF/view/createOrders/↩
selectDeliveryOptions.jsp"/>
</definition>
```

Listing 10-35 shows the select delivery options page, which is located at /WEB-INF/view/createOrders/selectDeliveryOptions.jsp.

Listing 10-34. *The Select Delivery Options Page*

```
<form:form modelAttribute="orderForm" action="${flowExecutionUrl}">
    <table style="width: 100%">
        <tr>
            <td>
                <spring:message
                code="label.page.selectdeliveryoptions.select.order.date"/>
            </td>
            <td>
                <form:input path="orderDate" disabled="true" />
            </td>
        </tr>
        <tr>
            <td>
                <spring:message
                code="label.page.selectdeliveryoptions.select.delivery.date"/>
            </td>
            <td>
                <form:input path="deliveryDate" />

                <script type="text/javascript">
                    Spring.addDecoration(new Spring.ElementDecoration({
                    elementId : "deliveryDate",
```

```
                    widgetType : "dijit.form.DateTextBox",
                    widgetAttrs : { datePattern : "MM-dd-yyyy",
                    required : true }}));
                </script>
            </td>
        </tr>
    </table>

    <div align="right" style="margin-bottom: 20px; margin-top: 10px" >
        <button type="submit" id="previous" name="_eventId_previous">
            <spring:message code="button.previous"/>
        </button>
        <button type="submit" id="cancel" name="_eventId_cancel">
            <spring:message code="button.cancel"/>
        </button>

        <button type="submit" id="finish" name="_eventId_finish">
            <spring:message code="label.page.selectdeliveryoptions.order"/>
        </button>
    </div>
</form:form>
```

Note the code highlighted in bold. We used a bit of Spring JS (Spring JavaScript, based on DOJO) to render the date picker, as you can see on the view in Figure 10-14. The addDecoration decorates an existing HTML element—with id deliveryDate, in this case. We specify the type of widget (date picker) and supply it with some attributes such as the format that it is required. This is a form of client-side validation. In the next chapter, we will also add matching server side validation. We will also discuss some more JavaScript options in Chapter 12 when we talk about Ajax.

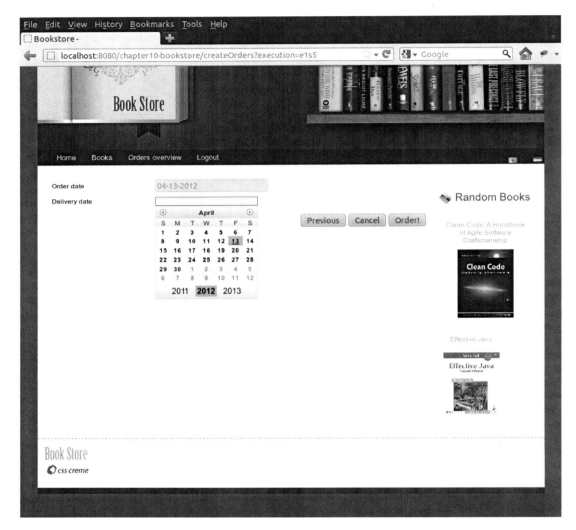

Figure 10-14. Selecting the delivery options—our delivery date

If you want to verify that the order has been made, you can click "Orders overview" link in the menu bar. You will see that there now is a sixth order, the order that we made throughout this process. Note that the other five were inserted automatically when the application started by the com.apress .prospringmvc.bookstore.domain.support.InitialDataSetup.

Note You will notice that clicking the "Order!" button without entering the (mandatory) delivery date will raise an ugly server side exception. In this flow, we did not apply validations or any of those features. The decoration (date picker) we applied on the field will indicate that it is mandatory; however, not filling in the delivery date won't prevent the user from clicking the Submit button, and thus submitting the form without the delivery date. In the upcoming chapters, we will examine how we can improve this, and show an appropriate validation message instead.

Overview

In the previous sections we went through the different steps of building our first flow. We introduced each part of the flow and also described the other elements which we needed, like the JSP page and the tiles configuration. Before we conclude, you can find a complete overview of the flow we have build so far in Listing 10-35.

Listing 10-35. Overview of our first flow: createOrders-flow.xml

```
<flow xmlns="http://www.springframework.org/schema/webflow"
    xmlns:xsi="http://www.w3.org/2001/XMLSchema-instance"
    xsi:schemaLocation=
        "http://www.springframework.org/schema/webflow
         http://www.springframework.org/schema/webflow/spring-webflow-2.0.xsd">

    <on-start>
        <evaluate expression="orderController.initializeForm()" result="flowScope.orderForm"/>
        <evaluate expression="orderController.initializeSelectableCategories()"
                        result="flowScope.selectableCategories"/>
    </on-start>

    <view-state id="selectCategory" view="selectCategory" model="orderForm">
        <transition on="next" to="selectBooks" >
            <evaluate expression="orderController.initializeSelectableBooks
(flowScope.orderForm)"                              result="flowScope.selectableBooks" />
        </transition>

        <transition on="cancel" to="end" />
    </view-state>

    <view-state id="selectBooks" view="selectBooks" model="orderForm" >
        <transition on="previous" to="selectCategory" />

        <transition on="add" >
            <evaluate expression="orderController.addBook(flowScope.orderForm)" />
        </transition>

        <transition on="next" to="selectDeliveryOptions" />
```

```
            <transition on="reset" to="selectBooks">
                <evaluate expression="orderForm.resetSelectedBooks()" />
            </transition>

            <transition on="cancel" to="end" />
    </view-state>

    <view-state id="selectDeliveryOptions" view="selectDeliveryOptions" model="orderForm">
        <transition on="previous" to="selectBooks" />

        <transition on="finish" to="end">
            <evaluate expression="orderController.placeOrder(flowScope.orderForm, ↵
                                  externalContext.sessionMap. authenticatedAccount)"/>
        </transition>

        <transition on="cancel" to="end" />
        </view-state>

    <end-state id="end" view="redirect:/index.htm"/>
</flow>
```

Summary

In this chapter, we started out with some theory about why and how Web Flow can ease your web application development. We also addressed some of Web Flow's more important features, such as its expanded scoping mechanism, automatic state saving, and how it can help protect the integrity of your web application state, using Post Redirect Get and request token synchronization.

Next, we learned how to configure Web Flow, including how to manage its specific configuration details. We also learned how you how glue together Web Flow and Spring MVC. We continued by touching on most of the Web Flow basics that you will need to get started implementing basic flows in your application. Finally, we showed off some of Web Flow's features with a live code example that builds a basic book order flow.

We are now ready to advance to the next chapter, where we will go deeper into some of the untouched features of Web Flow, using these features to transform our sample application into a real Web Flow application.

CHAPTER 11

Building Applications with Spring Web Flow

In the previous chapter on Spring Web Flow, we introduced you to Web Flow's main features and what it can do for you. We also covered what a basic Web Flow configuration looks like and how it can be integrated with Spring MVC. We saw some basic elements that are part of almost every flow, such as the view state and the evaluate action. And we ended by converting our Bookstore to a basic Web Flow-enabled application.

In this chapter, we will continue to look at more features of Web Flow. For example, we will see all the features required to turn the bookstore in a real-world application. We will be starting from the bookstore as we left it in the previous chapter, which we will be refactoring as we go along. The general approach of this chapter is a mix; we will introduce you to some new features first, explaining them in detail. Next, we will see how these concepts can be applied by refactoring the existing application or using these features to modify the bookstore.

We have chosen this approach, so that the table of contents can continue to be referenced. When working with Web Flow, you probably want to browse back to certain functionality and read about all its details. If we were to mix everything together, this would become difficult. We will tackle the sample in two stages, to make everything more digestible.

Important Web Flow Concepts

Now that you have seen some basic Web Flow coverage, we want to explain some specific new Web Flow concepts and terminology, as well as to expand on some concepts introduced in Chapter 10. Specifically, we will expand the definition of "flow" introduced in the Chapter 10. We will also take a closer look at scopes and how they work, and then introduce and define the implicit objects available for Web Flow expressions.

Flow Definition

In a flow definition, we can have five states, two of which we have already seen: the view state and the end state. The remaining states are the action state, decision state, and the subflow state. We will go over these in more detail in this chapter. However, in this section, we want to give a short introduction to subflows, since we will refer to them before covering them fully in the "Subflows" section. The concept of a subflow is pretty easy. For example, the structure and setup of a subflow is not too different from any other flow; it is defined in its own flow definition XML, and it has its own flow id.

Sometimes a given flow is started from another flow, rather than starting it at the top level by referring to it directly. We call such a flow a *subflow*. This process creates a parent/child relationship between the two flows. As we will see later, this relationship implies that the two flows can share state using the `conversation` scope, as well as map data from one flow to the other. It also serves as a modularization technique because it can help you build reusable components.

Another important element—one that drives your flow—is an *event*. The user signals an event by submitting the contents of a form to the URL that contains the flow id as a path and the flow execution key as one of the parameters. Other parameters can be values of input components, such as text fields, select boxes, check boxes, and so forth. Web Flow will use the flow id and execution key from the submission to resume the flow execution, and it will parse the event from the submitted parameters. Remember that, in our sample, the event is encapsulated in the name of the Submit button using this format: _eventId_event. After parsing the event, Web Flow will use it to invoke the transition, which has a matching on attribute for the event that we submitted. It will then be forwarded to the state indicated by the to attribute of the transition.

A transition takes the flow from one state to another state of that same flow. Before you can go back to a view, you must either transition to another view state (possibly going through other states) or transition to an end state. As we will see, an end state has also an option to specify a view. This view is rendered after the flow execution has terminated.

Different Web Flow Scopes

We already mentioned in the previous chapter that Web Flow adds a lot of different scopes into the picture (five to be exact): `conversation`, `flow`, `view`, `flash`, and `request` (see the "Fine-Grained Scoping" section in Chapter 10). Each of them has a well-defined lifecycle.

■ **Note** Every object you put on `conversation`, `flow`, `view` or `flash` scope should implement `java.io.Serializable` (for the `request` scope, this is not required). This is the case because Web Flow stores the state of these scopes between requests. The default implementation relies on Java serialization. Also note that this is recursive; every object your object refers to should be serializable, as well. If you do not want to retain certain objects, you can use the Java `transient` keyword on the field. This way, the field is exempted from being serialized. When the flow state is restored, these fields will resolve to `null`.

Next, we will explain each of the five scopes in detail, from the shortest life cycle to the longest. Let's start with the `request` scope.

Request Scope

Figure 11-1 shows two HTTP requests entering the view state: HTTP request 1 and HTTP request 2. While they are shown in the same figure, they should be interpreted sequentially. First, HTTP request 1 enters and gets processed, and the response is returned. Second, HTTP request 2 enters, and the cycle repeats for this request. When the first request enters, `request` scope 1 is started. It is possible that an event is triggered, and a transition is executed. Whatever is executed has access to that `request` scope. When the processing is done, `request` scope 1 is destroyed, and the response for HTTP request 1 returned. When the next request (HTTP request 2) comes in, a *new* request scope (request scope 2) is created.

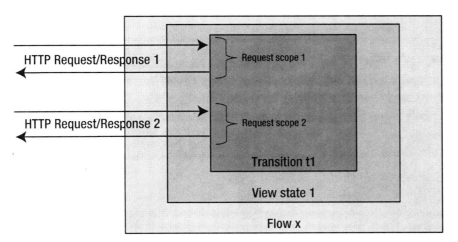

Figure 11-1. Illustrating the request scope

■ **Note** We want to point out that, from now on, a curly brace indicates the scope available at that moment in a "scope figure." The creation and cleanup of a certain scope is denoted by the curly brace itself; between the top and bottom of the brace, the scope is available to any execution trying to use it.

The request scope is tied at the level of a single request into the flow execution. Each and every request coming into the flow execution will start with a new and empty request scope.

It is important to realize that the request scope is not linked to a flow execution by itself. Consequently, a parent flow executing a subflow (or vice versa) always sees the same request scope. You can use the request scope to store objects that are only required while processing the current request. Objects that are cheap to create or load can also be put in the request scope because they can be recreated or reloaded every time they are needed.

For example, if you need to load a list of results, you could load them with an <on-render> action (as we will explain later on). The <on-render> is executed right before the view is rendered. The result could then be stored on the request scope for a very brief moment, until the view is rendered using that information and then cleared.

There is a great resemblance between the Servlet request scope and Web Flow request scope. The major difference is that the latter scope is local to Web Flow components. It is an internal artifact used within Web Flow, and it isn't exposed to external components (e.g., Servlets).

■ **Note** Including a `request` scope in Web Flow was a design decision to have an abstraction over the standard Servlet `request` scope. The designers targeted Web Flow for other platforms, as well (which may not have the notion of a `request` scope as the Servlet specification does). For you as a developer, there is no real difference apart from the fact that Web Flow's `request` scope is easier to reach from, for example, expressions inside your flow.

Flash Scope

You can think of the `flash` scope as a bigger `request` scope that survives two requests in a Post Redirect Get until the view finally gets rendered. Attributes with `flash` scope are persisted until the view is rendered and then cleared.

Storing objects in the `flash` scope is particularly useful for objects that are required in the view, but are not needed anywhere else. A good example of using `flash` scope is to store messages that are rendered on a view, like errors or warning messages. While an action executes, they can be put on `flash` scope by your application controller or by validation logic in your flow. The `request` scope is not sufficient because model validation occurs in the first request of the PRG. As a result, when the view gets rendered, the messages put on `request` scope will be gone. The `flash` scope provides an elegant solution for these kinds of use cases.

Figure 11-2 shows this by having a `flash` scope available that spans request 1 and 2 in transition t1. From the moment the view is rendered, the existing `flash` scope is cleared. This implies that, if you refresh the view, the messages will be gone, which is typically what you want for things like error and warning messages.

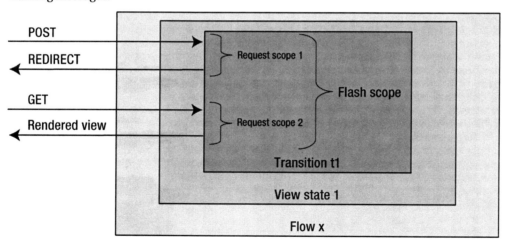

Figure 11-2. Showing the flash scope

Because flash scope is an extended request scope, it is also available to any subflow that is used. For example, when a transition within a view state delegates to a subflow which then renders the view, the flash scope will also be available to the execution that happens within the subflow. However, after the view has been rendered, any subsequent requests to that subflow will operate in their own flash scope.

View Scope

The view scope gets allocated when a view state enters, and it is destroyed when the view state exits. The view scope can only be referenced from within a view state. In Figure 11-3, you can see that, for each new view state, a new view scope is available.

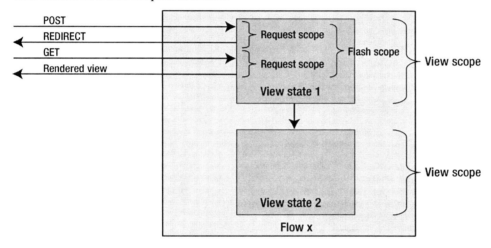

Figure 11-3. Showing the view scope

You could use view scope for storing data that is only required within the given view. For example, when you have a data table with pagination, you could load the results and put them in view scope. Using transitions within the view state (e.g., a next and previous transition), you could scroll through the list each time, showing a certain part of the result set. From the moment the view state is exited (e.g., after selecting a result in the data table), the view scope is destroyed, and the resources are released.

Flow Scope

The scope of the flow scope is a flow session. You can see this in Figure 11-4, where the execution of the parent flow has a flow scope, as does the flow session of the subflow (a subflow runs in the same flow execution as the parent flow but in a different flow session). This means that an attribute placed in a flow scope by a parent flow will not be accessible from the flow scope of a subflow.

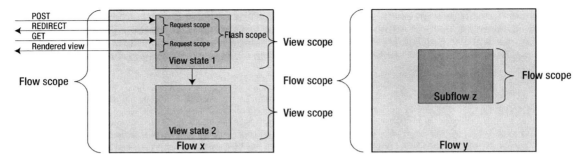

Figure 11-4. The flow scope

You can use the flow scope to store objects that should be available for the entire flow session, but which are only for that session and not other flow sessions started in the same flow execution (i.e., subflows).

Objects in the flow scope are mostly related to the application and the functionality it implements (e.g., domain object instances manipulated by the flow).

Conversation Scope

The conversation scope is scoped at the level of an entire conversation, or execution (see Figure 11-5). The term "conversation" is a bit misleading, but that is merely an implementation detail (especially in Web Flow 2) that is not important in this discussion. Although we are forced to use this term, you can think of conversation scope as a scope that maintains state over the entire flow execution. We think that "execution scope" would have been a better naming. Attributes in the conversation scope are available to every flow session contained within the conversation (or execution). The conversation scope is therefore also available to all subflows.

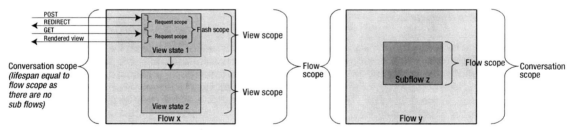

Figure 11-5. The conversation scope

Just like the flow scope, the conversation scope mostly stores application-related objects. Use the conversation scope if those objects should be available for every flow session (for that flow and/or its subflows), rather than for a single flow session. If your flow does not use subflows, the lifespan of conversation and flow scopes can be considered equal. Note that we are not saying that both scopes "become equal"; they remain two physically separated scopes, so setting something on flow scope will *not* become visible on conversation scope. But in this case, they will be "logically" equal because they have the same lifespan, and the lifespan is normally the attribute that makes one flow different from another.

Because their lifespan is the same, one could argue that it would be equal either to choose flow or conversation scope. However, by default it makes more sense to opt for flow scope and not conversation scope. This is because subflows could be introduced later on (i.e., when your flow gets extended), and subflows will automatically be able to access the data on the conversation scope. As we will see shortly when introducing subflows, the best practice is to think about which data the subflow needs and only expose the right amount of data.

In Figure 11-5, you can see that, for flow x, the conversation and flow scopes are equal because there is no subflow present. You can also see that there is a new conversation scope (and flow scope) created for flow y. Also, for flow y, there will be a different flow scope created for the subflow. However, the conversation scope remains accessible for both the parent and the subflows. As already explained, the flow scope visible for the subflow is a new one, and the subflow cannot access the flow scope of the parent flow.

■ **Caution** Be careful when storing large objects in flow or conversation scope. These scopes have relatively long life spans, which means that the data stored in them needs to be maintained for a long period of time. As an alternative to storing large objects in the flow or conversation scope, consider reloading those objects for every request and storing them in request scope.

Implicit Objects

Just as you have implicit objects in JSPs (scriptlets) and EL, you also have implicit objects defined by Web Flow. An implicit object is a shortcut to certain functionality that is frequently used (e.g., the HTTP request parameters). While you can access the request parameters through the javax.servlet.http.HttpServletRequest, both EL and Web Flow include a "shortcut" that gives direct access to the request parameter map. In EL, this implicit object is called param; in a Web Flow expression, you can use requestParameters.

In addition to data-related implicit objects, there are also references to key framework objects. For example, if you need the javax.servlet.ServletContext in a Web Flow expression, you can reference the implicit variable, externalContext, in the expression. The externalContext variable will indirectly expose the javax.servlet.ServletContext, as well as other context-related information. In this case, the expression would become as follows:

"#{externalContext.nativeContext}"

■ **Note** You can also use these implicit objects from EL in your views (JSP). These objects are bound by Web Flow to the Servlet request scope. For example, using something like #{flowExecutionUrl} will resolve to the flowExecutionUrl implicit object that is bound to the Servlet's request scope.

Table 11-1 outlines each implicit object that can be used in Web Flow expressions.

Table 11-1. Web Flow's Implicit Objects

Implicit objects	Usage
conversationScope, flowScope, viewScope, flashScope, requestScope	Allows you to access the scope in question. The function of each scope is explained in the preceding section.
requestParameters	Allows you to access the request parameters that are part of the ongoing client request.
currentEvent	Allows you to access the current org.springframework.webflow.execution .Event. It can be the event that triggered the state transition or a result Event from executing a method on an application controller. Events are further discussed in the "Working with Outcome Events" section.
currentUser	Returns a reference to the current authenticated Principal, delegating to org.springframework.webflow.context.ExternalContext.getCurrentUser, which eventually delegates to javax.servlet.http.HttpServletRequest .getUserPrincipal (when running in a Servlet environment, at least).
messageContext	Accesses a context for retrieving and creating flow execution messages, including error and success messages. See the org.springframework .binding.message.MessageContext for more information. Or, you can check the sample in createOrders-flow in the authenticate view state, where we pass along the messageContext to the application controller. This way, we can inject error messages from the controller: <evaluate expression= "authenticationController.authenticate(flowScope.authenticationForm, externalContext, messageContext)"/>
resourceBundle	Allows you to access a message resource. This delegates to Spring's org.springframework.context.ApplicationContext, which implements org.springframework.context.MessageSource. You can use the getMessage methods to resolve message. See the Javadoc for more information.
flowRequestContext	An org.springframework.webflow.execution.RequestContext object that provides a general entry point for manipulating or getting information about the current request into the flow execution. For example, it exposes the current active flow definition and the current transition (if any). Most of its remaining functionality is directly exposed via other implicit objects (e.g., messageContext, the different scopes, and so forth). See the JavaDoc for more details.
flowExecutionContext	An org.springframework.webflow.execution. FlowExecutionContext object that provides information about the current flow execution in general, such as its current state. For example, it can indicate that a flow started, is active, has ended, and so forth. See the JavaDoc for more details.

Implicit objects	Usage
flowExecutionUrl	The context-relative URL for the current flow execution that consists of the complete path that points to the flow id, as well as the flow execution key. When forwarding a user to another page (outside the flow and/or your application), you can pass this URL as a callback URL. Later, the URL can be used for going back to a given flow and restoring the latest view state.
externalContext	Accesses an instance of ExternalContext, which enables you to access the client environment where Web Flow is running. In our case (a Servlet container), it will return access to the javax.servlet.ServletContext, javax.servlet.http.HttpServletRequest and javax.servlet .http.HttpServletResponse, enabling us to access the session attributes and so forth. See the JavaDoc for more details on which properties you are able to call.

Enhancing the Bookstore

In the previous sections, we covered general Web Flow terminology in some detail. We needed to introduce these concepts prior to diving back into the code. Now that we have covered them, we are going to look at specific Web Flow features. We will do this by illustrating them with code and explaining them along the way.

In the previous chapter, we made our first pass at introducing a basic flow for ordering books. We did this with some basic web flow components that illustrated how easy it is to transform a given use case using Web Flow. Now we will continue adding functionality to and improving our sample application, illustrating and explaining various Web Flow features along the way. For example, the sample application as we left it in the previous chapter is not much of an application, yet. A lot of things are still missing, to name a few:

- *There is no validation*: It should not be possible to make an order when there is no book selected. The delivery date is also mandatory, and the site should trigger an exception when the user does not specify this date.

- *There is no conversion*: We mapped a Category and Book in our form as a Long using the identifier for each of these objects. It would be more elegant if we could map directly to a Category or Book from our domain.

In the following sections, we will address these and other shortcomings, gradually refactoring our sample application to show how you can use Web Flow to implement some real-world use cases. We will start from the very beginning, by revising our first step in the flow: selecting the book category.

Selecting the Category

To load our list of selectable categories, we used an on start action. This action loaded our categories into flow scope before entering the view state to render the selected category view. As we already explained in the "Different Web Flow Scopes" section, this is not the ideal place to store this information. The selectable categories are only required in the scope of the selected category view. We will see that a better alternative exists.

Also, we mapped the category using its id in our form instead of mapping it as a domain object. The next sections will show how we can change this.

On Start

We will still use the on start to initialize our OrderForm. Remember, the on start is executed automatically when the flow session starts. Even if you have a specific <start-state> attribute defined in your top-level flow element, Web Flow will always execute the actions defined in on-start when starting the flow, executing each action listed sequentially. Since we will not be loading our categories here, we deleted it, so that only the initialization of our form remains (see Listing 11-1).

Listing 11-1. The <on-start> Action that Initializes the Order Form

```
<on-start>
    <evaluate expression="orderController.initializeForm()"
              result="flowScope.orderForm"/>
</on-start>
```

The code initializing the form remains unaltered. There is one small detail worth noting: in the previous version of the com.apress.prospringmvc.bookstore.web.controller.OrderForm class, we deliberately kept all elements of the form simple. For example, the selected com.apress.prospringmvc .bookstore.domain.Book and com.apress.prospringmvc.bookstore.domain.Category Objects were not stored themselves, but we only stored their ids, and the order and delivery dates were stored as a java.lang.String type. From now on, we will use the normal data types and leave conversion and formatting to Web Flow and Spring MVC. Thus, we will change the delivery and order date to java.util.Date instead of java.lang.String. This changes our initialization of the OrderForm; and in Listing 11-2, you can see that we are now storing this information as a Date instead of a String.

Listing 11-2. Initializing an Instance of Our OrderForm with a Date Type

```
public OrderForm initializeForm() {
    OrderForm orderForm = new OrderForm();
    orderForm.setQuantity(1);
    orderForm.setOrderDate(new Date());
    return orderForm;
}
```

On Render

Now that we've removed the initialization of our categories (Category), we have to find another solution. The solution lies in the use of an on render action and using the request scope. It would be beneficial to load the categories right before our view gets rendered and remove them directly afterwards.

The on render action allows exactly that. Every action specified in the on render is executed right before the view state renders. Remember: When Web Flow uses PRG, the view state renders on the second request. The first request executes our controller and selects the view to render. When the second request comes in (the GET), our on render action executes. We then load the categories and put them on the request scope (see Figure 11-1 in the "Request Scope" section). Our view, which is rendered next, will be able to access the categories and render them (see Listing 11-3).

Listing 11-3. Loading the categories with on render

```
<view-state id="selectCategory" view="selectCategory" model="orderForm">
    <on-render>
        <evaluate
            expression="orderController.initializeSelectableCategories()"
            result="requestScope.selectableCategories"/>
    </on-render>
    <transition on="next" to="selectBooks" >
        <evaluate expression="orderController.↵
                            initializeSelectableBooks(flowScope.orderForm)"
                    result="flowScope.selectableBooks" />
    </transition>
    <transition on="cancel" to="end" />
</view-state>
```

Basically, we moved the evaluate expression from the on start action to the on render action and chose requestScope instead of flowScope.

The existing version of the code for retrieving the categories selects all categories and puts them in a map using the id as the key and the name as the value (see Listing 11-4).

Listing 11-4. The Existing Way of Loading the Categories

```
public Map<Long, String> initializeSelectableCategories() {
    Map<Long, String> selectableCategories = new HashMap<Long, String>();
    for (Category category : categoryService.findAll()) {
        selectableCategories.put(category.getId(), category.getName());
    }
    return selectableCategories;
}
```

We will now make this code more natural by simply returning a List holding types of our domain entity Category (see Listing 11-5). Later, we will look at how the conversion takes place.

Listing 11-5. The Category is Currently Loaded As-Is

```
public List<Category> initializeSelectableCategories() {
    return categoryService.findAll();
}
```

■ **Note** Our initialize method is refactored down to a single line of code; a good alternative would have been to simply call categoryService.findAll() directly from our flow.

In our page, we will no longer have a Map, but a list of Category objects. We need to change the <form:select>, so that the name is displayed as a label and the id as a value. We will still need the id (as the select value) to perform the conversion later on (see Listing 11-6).

Listing 11-6. The Form Select with an Extra itemLabel and itemValue

```
<form:select path="category" items="${selectableCategories}" itemLabel="name" itemValue="id"/>
```

■ **Note** Instances of categories and books are the ideal candidates for caching. However, instead of caching them on any of the Servlet or Web Flow scopes (which end up on the user's session and would duplicate the values for each user), we cache them in the back-end, using the ORM's 2nd level cache. As you will see, there are @Cacheable and @Cache annotations on both the Book and Category entities. When executing queries on them, we also explicitly cache these queries. The ORM is configured to use Ehcache as cache implementation. This offloads redundant objects from the user's session and keeps them cached in the back-end, usable for the entire application. If you enable Hibernate (our JPA implementation) debugging, you will see that, after a server startup, categories are only fetched from the database once. They won't be fetched again until the next server restart or the cache expires.

Type Conversion

Now we have a list of selectable categories, which are in fact domain entity objects. At binding time, the id of category needs to be converted to a Category because that is the type we specified on our OrderForm object.

Listing 11-7. The Category In The OrderForm Is Now Our Entity Class and No Longer a Long

```
private Category category;
```

To enable type conversion, we have to go back to our Web Flow configuration. We already specified a flow builder service. Remember that the flow builder service allows us to customize certain Web Flow behavior. We gave an introduction to the flow builder possibilities in the previous chapter under the "Web Flow Configuration" section. We will now see how we can use the flow builder services to specify a custom conversion service. Listing 11-8 shows our current configuration; this file can be found in src/main/resources/spring/webflow-config.xml.

Listing 11-8. The Current Flow Builder Services Configuration

```
<webflow:flow-builder-services id="flowBuilderServices" view-factory↵
-creator="mvcViewFactoryCreator" development="true"/>
```

The conversion service is a bit a pain to explain because we feel it is rather more complicated than it should be. The conversion service is able to perform type conversion. For example, if your model has a field of type java.lang.Integer, the code that performs the binding from the request parameter to your model has to perform a conversion. Request parameters are always received as String, so someone has to convert java.lang.String into java.lang.Integer. Fortunately, a lot of basic converters are already there, and you might not even notice that a conversion took place.

Until now, Web Flow has had its own type conversion mechanism. Spring MVC uses a very similar, but incompatible, type-conversion system, so a custom converter written for Spring MVC should theoretically be rewritten for Web Flow. Fortunately, there is now an adapter that allows you to plug your Spring MVC-specific converters into Web Flow.

Note Web Flow advises you to use the standard Spring MVC conversion mechanism and that you no longer write converters the "Web Flow way". You can recognize such converters based on their package. The converter machinery you should be using is the one from the `org.springframework.core.convert` package and *not* the one from the Web Flow `org.springframework.binding.convert` package. The latter is the one used solely by Web Flow, and it should be considered deprecated for writing new, customized converters.

In our case, we will have to write a converter that is able to convert from a `String` (representing a numerical value from the select list) to a `Category` object. Let's begin by configuring the conversion service (see Listing 11-9), which is found in `src/main/resources/spring/webflow-config.xml`.

Listing 11-9. Defining the Conversion Service

```
<bean id="conversionService"
 class="org.springframework.binding.convert.service.DefaultConversionService">
    <constructor-arg ref="mvcConversionService"/>
</bean>
```

This code basically creates a Web Flow `DefaultConversionService`. The default conversion service registers all default converters, and these are able to convert all primitive types, such as `Integer`, `Long`, and so on. However, it also includes types such as `java.math.BigDecimal` and `java.util.Date`. The conversion services also give you a hook to register your own converters or register another conversion service as a delegate conversion service. The hook provided to register a delegate is used to pass along the core Spring MVC conversion service. The `DefaultConversionService` has explicit support for the "new style" of delegate conversion services. Whenever the conversion service is asked to convert a given type, it will look to see whether it can deal with the conversion itself (possibly using existing Web Flow converters). If it cannot, it then checks the converters available in the Spring MVC supplied conversion service.

For the record, the Spring MVC conversion service (`org.springframework.format.support .DefaultFormattingConversionService`) is configured automatically for us by Spring; it is one of the beans created automatically when using the `@EnableWebMvc` annotation in `WebMvcContextConfiguration`. The created Spring bean has the id of `mvcConversionService`. Next, we can pass on the reference for our `conversionService` to the flow builder services (see Listing 11-10). You can find this service in `src/main/resources/spring/webflow-config.xml`. This concludes the integration regarding conversion and formatting between Web Flow and Spring MVC. The two sides are now joined and will act as one big conversion or formatting service.

Listing 11-10. The Flow Builder Services with the Custom Conversion Service

```
<webflow:flow-builder-services id="flowBuilderServices" view-factory↵
-creator="mvcViewFactoryCreator" conversion-service="conversionService" development="true"/>
```

Finally, we still have to register our custom converter. In Chapter 5 (see the "Configuring Type Conversion" section), we introduced the generic `com.apress.prospringmvc.bookstore.converter`

.StringToEntityConverter. We will reuse this converter, which will convert a java.lang.String (representing our id in this case) to a target entity, our Category domain object (see Listing 11-11). You can find this bean in com.apress.prospringmvc.bookstore.web.config.WebMvcContextConfiguration.

Listing 11-11. Defining the Category Converter

```
@Bean
public StringToEntityConverter categoryConverter() {
    return new StringToEntityConverter(Category.class);
}
```

As we have already seen, the MVC and Web Flow conversion/formatting services are linked. We will use the Spring core service for adding custom converters, which will then be available to Web Flow. In Listing 11-12, we will add our converter to Spring MVC's org.springframework.format .FormatterRegistry. The addFormatters method is called automatically by Spring, supplying the FormatterRegistry. This is explained in detail in Chapter 5's "Configuring Type Conversion" section.

Listing 11-12. Adding the Converter to the Registry in WebMvcContextConfiguration

```
@Override
protected void addFormatters(FormatterRegistry registry) {
    registry.addConverter(categoryConverter());
}
```

■ **Note** If you pay close attention, you will notice that we are adding a converter to a FormatterRegistry. As you will see, formatting is a specialization of conversion. The FormatterRegistry extends the org.springframework.core.convert.converter.ConverterRegistry, so you can add both converters and formatters to the registry. As a reminder, conversion and formatting is a part of core Spring MVC and is explained in detail in Chapter 5 (see the "Converters" and "Formatters" sections).

Type Formatting

A formatter is nothing more than the specialization of an org.springframework.core.convert.converter .Converter. Internally, formatters are transformed to an org.springframework.core.convert.converter .GenericConverter.[1] This makes sense if you think about it; a formatter is a one-way converter, where you define the rules for how a certain object is visualized when rendered in the view.

By enabling the conversion service in Web Flow and coupling it to the Spring conversion service, we implicitly enable formatting via the Spring MVC conversion service. Any formatter registered with the service will also be useable by Web Flow.

We will have to customize the formatting of our delivery and order date. We don't have to register a specific converter or formatter because date formatting is available by default. However, we want a

---

[1] You can see this in the addFormatterForFieldType method in the org.springframework .format.support.FormattingConversionService.

specific pattern, so we added the default Spring annotation for formatting dates and time to the definition of the fields in the OrderForm. This will steer the formatting process (see Listing 11-13).

Listing 11-13. Formatting the Delivery and Order Date in the OrderForm

```
@DateTimeFormat(pattern = "MM-dd-yyyy")
private Date deliveryDate;
@DateTimeFormat(pattern = "MM-dd-yyyy")
private Date orderDate;
```

Selecting Books and Delivery Options

We have to repeat the refactorings we performed in the previous part for our selecting books view state. In the previous chapter, we used an evaluate action in the next transition after transitioning to the selectBooks view state, as shown in Listing 11-14.

Listing 11-14. The Old Way: Initializing Books with an Evaluate Action

```
<transition on="next" to="selectBooks" >
    <evaluate
    expression="orderController.initializeSelectableBooks(flowScope.orderForm)"
    result="flowScope.selectableBooks" />
</transition>
```

We will remove the evaluate action just listed and replace it using the same on render mechanism (see Listing 11-15).

Listing 11-15. Using on render to Initialize Our Selectable Books

```
<view-state id="selectBooks" view="selectBooks" model="orderForm" >
    <on-render>
        <evaluate expression="orderController.↵
                              initializeSelectableBooks(flowScope.orderForm)" ↵
                result="flowScope.selectableBooks" />
    </on-render>
    <transition on="previous" to="selectCategory" />
    <transition on="add">
        <evaluate expression="orderController.addBook(flowScope.orderForm)" />
    </transition>
    <transition on="next" to="selectDeliveryOptions" />
    <transition on="reset" to="selectBooks">
        <evaluate expression="orderForm.resetSelectedBooks()" />
    </transition>
    <transition on="cancel" to="end" />
</view-state>
```

This makes the evaluate action in the on next transition of the previous selectCategory view state obsolete.

Likewise, we changed the select list, selectBooks.jsp, to render the title as item label and the id as item value because the objects stored for the selectable books will now be Book domain entities (see Listing 11-16). You can find the select books file in src/main/webapp/WEB-INF/view/createOrders /selectBooks.jsp.

Listing 11-16. Adding itemLabel and itemValue to the Book Form's Select

```
<form:select path="book items="${selectableBooks}" itemLabel="title" itemValue="id"/>
```

Finally, we also need to register a converter for the Book domain entity. This will be the exact same procedure as for the Category. Here we use the generic com.apress.prospringmvc.bookstore.converter .StringToEntityConverter. We just need to register the converter with the correct parameterization in our Spring MVC configuration class (located in com.apress.prospringmvc.bookstore.web.config .WebMvcContextConfiguration.java), as shown in Listing 11-17.

Listing 11-17. Defining the Book Converter

```
@Bean
public StringToEntityConverter bookConverter() {
    return new StringToEntityConverter(Book.class);
}
```

Next, we can continue with the specific refactorings for the select book and select delivery options of our application. This involves adding validation, so a user is notified when submitting a form with invalid or missing data. We will see that there are roughly three ways of performing validation: using the JSR 303 annotations, using validator methods in our form (or separate classes) that are recognized by Web Flow, and applying validation in our application controller itself.

Form Validation Using JSR 303 Annotations

You can configure Web Flow to perform JSR 303 validation (i.e., bean validation). For example, if you annotate your model with annotations from javax.constraints.validation (e.g., @Min or @Max), then validation will take place and error messages will be created for that path within your model. For this to work, you have to supply the flow builder services with an org.springframework.validation .beanvalidation.LocalValidatorFactoryBean.

Listing 11-18 defines the factory bean that will enable JSR-303 validation. You can find this bean in src/main/resources/spring/webflow-config.xml.

Listing 11-18. Defining the Bean Validator Factory Bean

```
<bean id="validator" class="org.springframework.validation.beanvalidation↵
.LocalValidatorFactoryBean" />
```

Next, we can complete our flow builder services configuration, as shown in Listing 11-19. You can find this configuration file in src/main/resources/spring/webflow-config.xml.

Listing 11-19. Enabling Bean Validation

```
<webflow:flow-builder-services id="flowBuilderServices" view-factory-creator=↵
"mvcViewFactoryCreator" conversion-service="conversionService" validator="validator"↵
 development="true" />
```

When this is all set, we can simply apply annotations on our form (see Listing 11-20), which is located in the com.apress.prospringmvc.bookstore.web.controller.OrderForm. For now, we will just use the validation for the quantity field. This is the field that a user can change when adding books to the order. The default value is 1, but the user can also add multiple books to the order directly.

Listing 11-20. Adding Validation Annotations

```
package com.apress.prospringmvc.bookstore.web.controller;

import javax.validation.constraints.Max;
import javax.validation.constraints.Min;
import javax.validation.constraints.NotNull;

@NotNull
@Min(1)
@Max(999)
private Integer quantity;
```

We could use bean validation for the other fields, as well. However, there are two reasons why this would be troublesome:

- First, the validation API is good at validating a single field, but we will also have to validate a combination of fields. For example, later on we will have to check that the entered delivery date is after the order date. The validation API has the group feature to validate fields in a group, but it is not possible to indicate a more complex relationship without writing a custom bean validator. Unfortunately, this is not something the bean validation supports out of the box. We will use one of the two other ways of validation (yet to be seen) to do this.

- Second, the problem with this validation setup is that the entire form gets validated as a whole, yet we only use a part of it for each step or our flow. Basically, this means that, when setting the Category on the first page, all of the other validation annotations would be triggered, as well. If we were to put a @NotNull annotation above the Book instance field, then we would get an error that no Book is selected when we select a Category. A solution could be to divide the form into multiple smaller forms. But for now, we will validate the other fields in a different way. Also, note that the quantity field does not suffer from this problem because we initialized its value to 1. So, when selecting a Category, the quantity field will be validated, but it will be found valid because its value is 1. Later, when the user can select the quantity in the select books page, the validator will trigger an error when the user specifies a value that is not allowed.

■ **Note** For JSR303 validations, you need the validation API (that contains the `javax.constraints.validation` annotations) on your compile classpath. But at runtime, we also need a provider. Tomcat does not ship with one, so we are using the Hibernate Validator (which is also the RI, Reference Implementation, for JSR 303).[2] We just have to put these validations on our classpath—but that's all we have to do because we previously configured Web Flow with the `LocalValidatorFactoryBean`. To define the dependency, we added it to the project's root gradle file (`build.gradle` in the samples root directory):

```
compile "org.hibernate:hibernate-validator:$hibernateValidatorVersion"
compile "javax.validation:validation-api:1.0.0.GA"
```

Form Validation Using the Web Flow Validator Method and Classes

The second way to perform validation is by implementing a method in the form of a "validate*State*" method in our model. This type of validation is detected by Web Flow purely by following naming conventions. The word "validate" is mandatory, while "*state*" is a placeholder that needs to be replaced by the id of state for which the validation should be applied to. Web Flow will execute the validation on post back to the defined state. So the validation is not executed the first time the view state is rendered, but when a postback is made (e.g., when a form is submitted).

In the example in Listing 11-21, the validation is triggered when we make a transition to the selectCategory state. We check that the event that triggered the transition is the next event. If the user were to click the cancel button, then we would not want to perform the validation. The `org.springframework.binding.validation.ValidationContext` is automatically injected by Web Flow. If we were to add an error code, then the code would be automatically resolved with the registered `org.springframework.context.MessageSource` (this code can be found inside the `com.apress` `.prospringmvc.bookstore.web.controller.OrderForm`).

Listing 11-21. Validating the Category

```
public void validateSelectCategory(ValidationContext context) {
    if (context.getUserEvent().equals("next")) {
        MessageContext messages = context.getMessageContext();
        if (category == null) {
            messages.addMessage(new ↵
            MessageBuilder().error().source("category")↵
            .code("error.page.category.required").build());
        }
    }
}
```

A variation on this is to store the validation logic separately from your model in a `validator` class (see Listing 11-22). To do so, you have to follow more naming conventions for classname and the

[2] `http://download.oracle.com/otndocs/jcp/bean_validation-1.0-fr-oth-JSpec/`

validation method. The class should be named modelnameValidator, while the method should be named validateState. In our case the classname would become OrderFormValidator, and the method would be the same one used previously in validateSelectShop. In the case of an external validator, you would also get the model as a parameter to the validate method and, optionally, the Spring MVC Errors object.

Listing 11-22. The Separate Validator Class

```
@Component
public class OrderModelValidator{
    public void validateSelectShop(OrderForm orderForm, ValidationContext context,↩
 Errors errors) {
```

The final requirement is that the bean should be registered as a Spring bean. In an annotation-driven model like this one, you can simply add the @Component above the class definition and make sure the class will be picked up by the component scan.

■ **Note** In the sample application, we have opted to store the validation together with the model, so you will not find an external OrderFormValidator. But feel free to experiment and try to move validation logic from the OrderForm to a separate validator.

Form Validation Using the Application Controller

The final validation method performs custom validation inside a controller method that is called by a Web Flow expression (see Listing 11-23). You can see an example of this in the validateDeliveryDate method of the com.apress.prospringmvc.bookstore.web.controller.OrderController, which is called right before finalizing the order on the select delivery options page (see Listing 11-24).

Listing 11-23. Calling the Validation Method on the Application Controller

```
<view-state id="selectDeliveryOptions" view="selectDeliveryOptions" model="orderForm">
    <transition on="previous" to="selectBooks" />
    <transition on="finish" to="end">
        <evaluate expression="orderController.validateDeliveryDate↩
            (flowScope.orderForm, messageContext)"/>
        <evaluate expression="orderController.placeOrder(flowScope.orderForm,
            externalContext.sessionMap.authenticatedAccount)"/>↩
    </transition>

    <transition on="cancel" to="end" />
</view-state>
```

Listing 11-24. The Validation Method on the OrderController

```
public Event validateDeliveryDate(OrderForm orderForm, MessageContext
    messageContext) {
    if (orderForm.getDeliveryDate() == null){
        MessageBuilder errorMessageBuilder = new MessageBuilder().error();
        errorMessageBuilder.source("deliveryDate");
            errorMessageBuilder.code("error.page.selectdeliveryoptions.↵
                deliverydate.required");
        messageContext.addMessage(errorMessageBuilder.build());
        return new EventFactorySupport().error(this);
    }

    if (orderForm.getDeliveryDate().before(
            DateUtils.truncate(orderForm.getOrderDate(), Calendar.DAY_OF_MONTH))){
        MessageBuilder errorMessageBuilder = new MessageBuilder().error();
        errorMessageBuilder.source("deliveryDate");
        errorMessageBuilder.code("error.page.selectdeliveryoptions.↵
                            deliverydate.in.past");
        messageContext.addMessage(errorMessageBuilder.build());
        return new EventFactorySupport().error(this);
    }
    return new EventFactorySupport().success(this);
}
```

The evaluate action for validating the delivery date is executed when a user clicks the finish button (triggering the finish transition) after entering the delivery options. The invocation occurs before the invocation to create the actual order. We pass along the form and messageContext (a Web Flow implicit object). Inside this, we use the message context to add a custom message when the validation fails, as you can see in the preceding code snippet.

You might have noticed that this method returns the org.springframework.webflow.execution.Event. This is in contrast to other methods we have called previously when using an evaluate expression. For example, the addBook method in the com.apress.prospringmvc.bookstore.web.controller.OrderController simply returns void.

When executing an expression, the result (if it isn't already an Event) is internally converted to an Event. These objects drive the transition, indicating whether the evaluation succeeded or failed (or any other java.lang.String based outcome). Also, these objects can optionally have objects as attributes associated with them.

When you do not need to trigger outcome conditions, there is no need to use an Event as a return value, and you can return the value as-is (or simply return void). Web Flow will do the conversion to a successful Event for you.

However, in this case we need to differentiate between a validation success and a validation failure. Both will render different results. In the first case, we want to proceed with the order-creation process; in the second case, we want to render the select delivery options page again to show the error message and let the user try again. We signal this explicitly with events. Note that we could have attached a result with the successful Event, which could then be bound using the result attribute of the evaluate action. We will discuss this later in this chapter's "Working with Outcome Events" section.

Showing Validation Messages

Finally, after adding validation messages with one of the three different approaches shown so far, we must still show them to the user. To do this, we can use the Spring MVC standard `<form:errors>` tag to do one of two things. First, we can render the messages for a specific path in our model. Alternatively, we can render all messages by specifying the wildcard for the `path` attribute.

It is important to realize that messages generated by all validation methods can be shown in this way. Whether a message is added by bean validation, Web Flow form validation, or using the `org.springframework.binding.message.MessageContext` in an application controller, a message will end up being shown with the `<form:errors>` tag. At this point, we are going to refactor all our input components within our pages to be followed with a `<form:errors path="<name of the form field>"/>`. This will enable us to show the validation message in case the validation fails for that field.

We will demonstrate this with the select delivery options page (see Listing 11-25) that can be found in the `src/main/webapp/WEB-INF/view/createOrders/selectDeliveryOptions.jsp` page. (The other two pages repeat the exact same process, so we won't bore you by showing those, as well.)

Listing 11-25. Refactoring the Select Delivery Options Page to Show Validation Messages

```
<form:form modelAttribute="orderForm" action="${flowExecutionUrl}">
    <table style="width: 100%">
        <tr>
            <td>
                <spring:message↵
code="label.page.selectdeliveryoptions.select.order.date"/>
            </td>
            <td>
                <form:input path="orderDate" disabled="true" />
            </td>
        </tr>
        <tr>
            <td>
                <spring:message↵
code="label.page.selectdeliveryoptions.select.delivery.date" />
            </td>
            <td>
                <form:input path="deliveryDate" />
                <span style="margin-left: 5px">
                    <form:errors path="deliveryDate" cssClass="error"/>
                </span>
        ...
```

If we were to proceed without selecting a delivery date, the error message would be shown next to the field (see Figure 11-6).

Figure 11-6. *Showing the Validation Message When the Delivery Date is Left Blank*

The localization part of our custom error message comes from the default resource bundle included in our application. This has been explained in the Spring MVC chapters. For example, the key of the message shown in Figure 11-6 is used in the `validateDeliverydate` method of the `OrderController` class. It is used as "error code" to be added to the error message that is created. To refresh our memory, let's look at a snippet from the method that builds the error message:

```
MessageBuilder errorMessageBuilder = new MessageBuilder().error();
errorMessageBuilder.source("deliveryDate");
errorMessageBuilder.code("error.page.selectdeliveryoptions.deliverydate.required");
```

The message code in bold is specified in the resource bundle with base name, `messages.properties`. The resource bundle has the code as the key and the translation (which you can see in Figure 11-6) as its value.

■ **Note** The resource bundles are physically located in the shared project bookstore-web-resources. There is one for the English language (`messages_en.properties`) and one for the Dutch language (`messages_nl.properties`). You can change the language dynamically by clicking the flags at the right end of the navigation bar.

In the case of bean validation messages, there is a standard resource bundle that is loaded by default. You can override these messages in your own resource bundle. The default resource bundle is part of the validation API's implementation. In our case, this is the RI (i.e., the Hibernate validator). If we were to open the Hibernate validator JAR file, we would see the message bundles (see Figure 11-7).

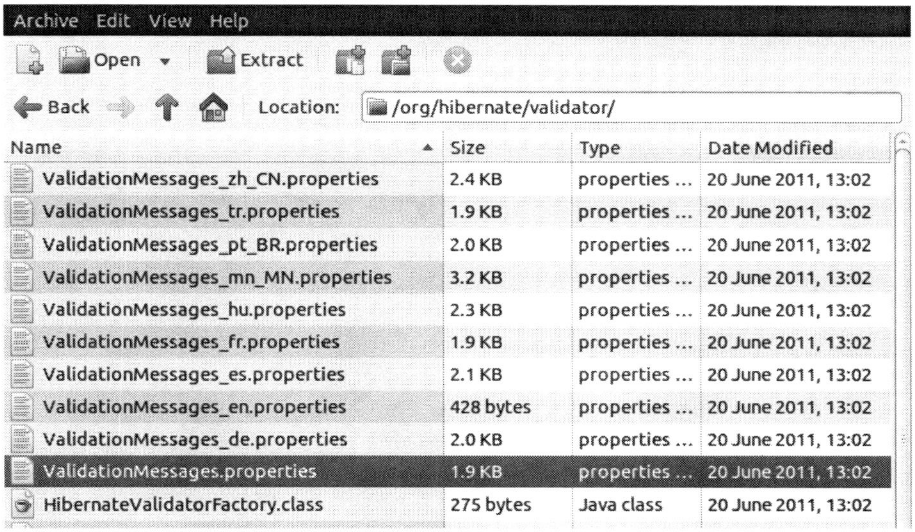

Figure 11-7. The hibernate validator jar containing the resource bundles

Opening the default message bundle, ValidationMessages.properties, would show the translations shown in Listing 11-26 for the @Min and @Max annotations (which we have used on the quantity property in our com.apress.prospringmvc.bookstore.web.controller.OrderForm).

Listing 11-26. The default validation API messages

```
javax.validation.constraints.Max.message= must be less than or equal to {value}
javax.validation.constraints.Min.message= must be greater than or equal to {value}
```

You can override these by specifying your own ValidationMessages.properties (with or without a language/country extension) in your application's classpath.

Overview

Before closing our first refactoring, we want to summarize the different things we have done so far. This will give you a complete code overview of our flow and the involved OrderController and OrderForm.

We started out by loading our categories and books using the <on-render> action. Next, we replaced the book and category references in our form with the real entity object. In order for this to work, we had to create and register two custom converters. Finally, we added validation to our flow, so that it is no longer possible to trigger application errors by not entering values for the mandatory fields. We also showed you that there are three ways for you to implement validation.

Listing 11-27 shows our createOrders-flow thus far; this can be found in src/main/webapp/WEB-INF/view/createOrders/createOrders-flow.xml.

Listing 11-27. *The createOrders-flow file After Our First Refactoring*

```
<on-start>
    <evaluate expression="orderController.initializeForm()"↵
     result="flowScope.orderForm"/>
</on-start>
<view-state id="selectCategory" view="selectCategory" model="orderForm">
    <on-render>
        <evaluate
            expression="orderController.initializeSelectableCategories()"↵
            result="requestScope.selectableCategories"/>
    </on-render>
    <transition on="next" to="selectBooks"/>
    <transition on="cancel" to="end" />
</view-state>
<view-state id="selectBooks" view="selectBooks" model="orderForm" >
    <on-render>
        <evaluate
            expression="orderController.initializeSelectableBooks↵
            (flowScope.orderForm)" result="requestScope.selectableBooks" />
    </on-render>
    <transition on="previous" to="selectCategory" />

    <transition on="add" >
        <evaluate expression="orderController.addBook(flowScope.orderForm)" />
    </transition>
    <transition on="next" to="selectDeliveryOptions" />
    <transition on="reset" to="selectBooks">
        <evaluate expression="orderForm.resetSelectedBooks()" />
    </transition>
    <transition on="cancel" to="end" />
</view-state>
<view-state id="selectDeliveryOptions" view="selectDeliveryOptions" model="orderForm">
    <transition on="previous" to="selectBooks" />
    <transition on="finish" to="end">
        <evaluate ↵
         expression="orderController.validateDeliveryDate(flowScope.orderForm, ↵
         messageContext)"/>
        <evaluate expression="orderController.placeOrder(flowScope.orderForm, ↵
         externalContext.sessionMap.authenticatedAccount)"/>
    </transition>
    <transition on="cancel" to="end" />
</view-state>
<end-state id="end" view="redirect:/index.htm"/>
```

Similarly, Listing 11-28 shows our OrderForm, which can be found in com.apress.prospringmvc
.bookstore.web.controller.OrderForm.

Listing 11-28. Our OrderForm after Our First Refactoring

```
package com.apress.prospringmvc.bookstore.web.controller;

import javax.validation.constraints.Max;
import javax.validation.constraints.Min;
import javax.validation.constraints.NotNull;

import org.springframework.binding.message.MessageBuilder;
import org.springframework.binding.message.MessageContext;
import org.springframework.binding.validation.ValidationContext;
import org.springframework.format.annotation.DateTimeFormat;

import com.apress.prospringmvc.bookstore.domain.Book;
import com.apress.prospringmvc.bookstore.domain.Category;
import com.apress.prospringmvc.bookstore.domain.Order;

public class OrderForm implements Serializable {
    private Map<Book, Integer> books = new HashMap<Book, Integer>();
    private Book book;

    @NotNull
    @Min(1)
    @Max(999)
    private Integer quantity;
    private Category category;
    @DateTimeFormat(pattern = "MM-dd-yyyy")
    private Date deliveryDate;
    @DateTimeFormat(pattern = "MM-dd-yyyy")
    private Date orderDate;
    // ---- Form validation methods triggered by webflow according to ⏎
            convention, see reference 5.10. Validating a model
    public void validateSelectCategory(ValidationContext context) {
        if (context.getUserEvent().equals("next")) {
            MessageContext messages = context.getMessageContext();
            if (category == null) {
                messages.addMessage(new ⏎
                MessageBuilder().error().source("category")⏎
                .code("error.page.category.required").build());
            }
        }
    }
    public void validateSelectBooks(ValidationContext context) {
        if (context.getUserEvent().equals("next")) {
            MessageContext messages = context.getMessageContext();
            if (books.isEmpty()) {
                messages.addMessage(new ⏎
                MessageBuilder().error().source("books")⏎
                .code("error.page.books.required").build());
            }
```

```
        }
    }
    public void resetSelectedBooks() {
        books.clear();
    }
…<omitted getters and setters for brevity>…
```

And Listing 11-29 shows our OrderController, which can be found in com.apress.prospringmvc .bookstore.web.controller.OrderController.

Listing 11-29. Our OrderController After Our First Refactoring

```
package com.apress.prospringmvc.bookstore.web.controller;

import javax.servlet.http.HttpSession;

import org.apache.commons.lang3.time.DateUtils;
import org.springframework.beans.factory.annotation.Autowired;
import org.springframework.binding.message.MessageBuilder;
import org.springframework.binding.message.MessageContext;
import org.springframework.stereotype.Controller;
import org.springframework.web.bind.annotation.RequestMapping;
import org.springframework.web.servlet.ModelAndView;
import org.springframework.webflow.action.EventFactorySupport;
import org.springframework.webflow.execution.Event;
import org.springframework.webflow.execution.RequestContextHolder;

import com.apress.prospringmvc.bookstore.domain.Account;
import com.apress.prospringmvc.bookstore.domain.Book;
import com.apress.prospringmvc.bookstore.domain.Category;
import com.apress.prospringmvc.bookstore.domain.Order;
import com.apress.prospringmvc.bookstore.domain.support.OrderBuilder;
import com.apress.prospringmvc.bookstore.service.BookstoreService;
import com.apress.prospringmvc.bookstore.service.CategoryService;

@Controller
public class OrderController {

    @Autowired
    private BookstoreService bookstoreService;

    @Autowired
    private CategoryService categoryService;

    @RequestMapping("ordersOverview.htm")
    public ModelAndView retrieveOrders(HttpSession httpSession) {
        List<Order> orders = bookstoreService.findOrdersForAccount((Account) ↵
            httpSession.getAttribute(↵
            AuthenticationController.AUTHENTICATED_ACCOUNT_KEY));

        ModelAndView mov = new ModelAndView();
        mov.setViewName("ordersOverview");
```

```java
        mov.getModel().put("orders", orders);

        return mov;
    }

    public OrderForm initializeForm() {
        OrderForm orderForm = new OrderForm();
        orderForm.setQuantity(1);
        orderForm.setOrderDate(new Date());
        return orderForm;
    }

    public List<Category> initializeSelectableCategories() {
        return categoryService.findAll();
    }

    public List<Book> initializeSelectableBooks(OrderForm orderForm) {
        return bookstoreService.findBooksByCategory(orderForm.getCategory());
    }

    public void addBook(OrderForm orderForm) {
        Book book = orderForm.getBook();
        if (orderForm.getBooks().containsKey(book)) {
            orderForm.getBooks().put(book, orderForm.getBooks().get(book) + ↵
            orderForm.getQuantity());
        } else {
            orderForm.getBooks().put(book, orderForm.getQuantity());
        }
    }

    public Long placeOrder(final Account account, final OrderForm orderForm) {
        Order order = new OrderBuilder() {
            {
                addBooks(orderForm.getBooks());
                deliveryDate(orderForm.getDeliveryDate());
                orderDate(orderForm.getOrderDate()).account(account);
            }

        }.build(true);

        return bookstoreService.store(order).getId();
    }

    public Event validateDeliveryDate(OrderForm orderForm, MessageContext ↵
                                                    messageContext) {
        if (orderForm.getDeliveryDate() == null) {
            MessageBuilder errorMessageBuilder = new MessageBuilder().error();
            errorMessageBuilder.source("deliveryDate");
            errorMessageBuilder.code("error.page.selectdeliveryoptions.↵
                                deliverydate.required");
            messageContext.addMessage(errorMessageBuilder.build());
            return new EventFactorySupport().error(this);
```

```
        }

        if (orderForm.getDeliveryDate().
                before(DateUtils.truncate(orderForm.getOrderDate(),↵
                Calendar.DAY_OF_MONTH))) {
            MessageBuilder errorMessageBuilder = new MessageBuilder().error();
            errorMessageBuilder.source("deliveryDate");
            errorMessageBuilder.code("error.page.selectdeliveryoptions.↵
                                      deliverydate.in.past");
            messageContext.addMessage(errorMessageBuilder.build());
            return new EventFactorySupport().error(this);
        }
        return new EventFactorySupport().success(this);
    }
}
```

Setting Variables and Accessing Scopes

Ok, we've completed our first refactoring. Before going any further we would first like to introduce you to some other Web Flow features. In this section we will cover how you use flow variables and access the different Web Flow scopes using the implicit objects.

A scope is treated as a `java.util.Map`, so you just pass along a key for reading values out of a scope, as well as a key plus value for setting something on a scope. The expression language makes reading the scope straightforward. For example, here's what you do if you want to read the value with the `myKey` key from the `flow` scope and pass this value to an application controller:

```
expression="myApplicationController.someMethod(flowscope.myKey)"
```

Setting variables can be done using the `<set>` element. This element is valid in all five states (which we will cover in the upcoming sections), except one: the decision state. This element can also be used within transitions. The example in Listing 11-30 sets a literal value, `someValue`, on a `flow` scope with the `myKey` key through a flow start action. We could have used other scopes to put the value on (e.g., `conversationScope` or `requestScope`); however, not every scope would make a lot of sense or would be allowed. For example, `view` scope would yield an error because we are not yet in a view state, so no `view` scope exists. Finally, if we specify a literal value, you are forced to put it between single quotes. The `value` attribute is expecting an expression by default, meaning that the value of `value` attribute is automatically interpreted as an expression. (i.e., it is not required that we place them between "#{}").

Listing 11-30. Setting a Value with a Literal Value on Flow Scope

```
<on-start>
    <set name="flowScope.myKey" value="'someValue'"/>
</on-start>
```

In addition to the `<set>` element, you can also set variables using the expression language in an evaluate action. Listing 11-31 shows how to store the result returned from executing an application controller method on `flow` scope. The expression contains the logic to be executed (in this case, it executes the `someMethod` method on the `myApplicationController` bean), passing the value retrieved from `flow` scope by using the `myKey` key as a parameter and storing the result in `flow` scope under the `someMethodResult` key.

Listing 11-31. Calling an Application Controller Method with a Parameter and Storing the Result on flow Scope

```
<evaluate expression="myApplicationController.someMethod(flowScope.myKey)"
 results="flowScope.someMethodResult"/>
```

Flow Variables

A flow may declare one or more instance variables. These variables are allocated when the flow starts, and they are destroyed when the flow ends. The syntax for declaring them looks like this:

```
<var name="orderForm" class="com.apress.prospringmvc.bookstore.web.OrderForm"/>
```

The name is the key under which the created instance will be available on flow scope, while the class attribute is the fully qualified class name of the class to be instantiated. Web Flow creates an instance using the default (or *parameterless*) constructor of the class.

Note that Web Flow will create a Spring-managed bean from the created instance. In doing so, Spring will fully initialize the instantiated class, applying all applicable BeanPostProcessors. The instance will eventually be registered as a Spring bean with the application context. This means that you can use for example @Autowired annotations in the class. During initialization, these dependencies will be injected by Spring.

■ **Note** The "Different Web Flow Scopes" section explains that the class you specify in the class attribute should implement java.io.Serializable because the object created is put on flow scope. This also counts for referenced objects not marked as transient. However, references to objects that hold no state (e g., services, facades, DAOs, and so on) should be declared as transient. Java's transient keyword excludes these objects from the Java serialization process. Such objects do not need to be serialized because they do not contain any state. If these instances are autowired beans (using @Autowired), then Spring will make sure they are rewired when the flow resumes.

The <var> element is primarily used to create instances of classes before the flow starts, and these classes are used in the scope of that flow execution. You can only use this element on top of the flow definition. In comparison, the <set> element is better suited for setting or moving values between already existing instances. For example, if you want put a given request parameter value on a search criteria object, you could use the <set> element. In the name attribute, you would refer to the key that represents the search criteria object. In the value attribute, you would refer to the requestParameters implicit object, which would then allow you to access the parameter with the desired name (e.g., requestParameters.myParam).

Accessing Scoped Variables from Views

As we have seen, there is an implicit object available for each of the Web Flow scopes that you can use to reference the scope from within expressions inside your flow. As we have already said, Web Flow uses Spring Expression Language (Spring EL). The Spring EL context is modified by Web Flow, so that these implicit objects are made available.

From the moment we enter our view (in our case, a JSP), we will be indirectly using Unified Expression Language (Unified EL). What happens next is that Web Flow will make these implicit objects available via the Servlet request scope. For example, in our JSP we can still use #{flowExecutionUrl}. The Unified EL will scan each Servlet scope and find the flowExecutionUrl key on the Servlet request scope. However, scope-related implicit objects (e.g., flowScope and flashScope) are not available. At this point, you might wonder how you can access information that you put on any of the Web Flow scopes from within your view.

What Web Flow does is put every object from every Web Flow scope directly onto the Servlet request scope before the view is rendered. This means two things:

- You can access any object from any of the Web Flow scopes in your flow directly from the Servlet request scope. For example, if you have an object under key x on flow scope within your flow, you can access that using the expression #{x} in your JSP (as noted previously, the Unified EL scans the different Servlet scopes and will resolve this from the Servlet request scope). Likewise, if you had a variable y on conversation scope, you would access it the same way because it is also put on Servlet request scope: #{y}.

- You have to be careful with the names of the keys. If you have a value with key x both on flow and conversation scope, only one of the two will be present in the Servlet request scope (one will be overwritten). Normally, this would not present a problem because having the same key on different scopes does not make much sense.

Programmatically Accessing Scopes

In addition to accessing scopes from expressions using implicit objects, we can also access each Web Flow scope using the org.springframework.webflow.execution.RequestContext object in our code. This object has a getter for each scope. Likewise, we can use the org.springframework.webflow.context .ExternalContext object for accessing Servlet scopes. We can obtain a reference to the RequestContext or ExternalContext object by injecting them using an expression. For example, flowRequestContext and externalContext are both implicit objects, referring to the RequestContext and ExternalContext interfaces, respectively.

If we have an evaluate action, we can use an expression like this:

```
<evaluate expression="myApplicationController.someMethod(flowRequestContext)"/>
```

The someMethod method accepts the RequestContext as a parameter (see Listing 11-32).

Listing 11-32. Injecting the RequestContext with an Expression

```
import org.springframework.webflow.execution.RequestContext;

public void someMethod(RequestContext requestContext) {
    requestContext.getConversationScope();
}
```

There are also two thread-bound holder classes that give you instant access to the RequestContext and ExternalContext:

- RequestContextHolder.getRequestContext()—see Listing 11-33

- ExternalContextHolder.getExternalContext()—see Listing 11-34

Listing 11-33. Accessing the Web Flow Scopes

```
import org.springframework.webflow.execution.RequestContext;
import org.springframework.webflow.execution.RequestContextHolder;

RequestContext requestContext = RequestContextHolder.getRequestContext();
requestContext.getFlowScope();
requestContext.getFlashScope();
...
```

Listing 11-34. Accessing the Servlet Scopes

```
import javax.servlet.http.HttpServletRequest;
import javax.servlet.http.HttpSession;

import org.springframework.webflow.context.ExternalContext;
import org.springframework.webflow.context.ExternalContextHolder;

ExternalContext externalContext = ExternalContextHolder.getExternalContext();

//Shortcut for respectively accessing Servlet session map and request map
externalContext.getSessionMap();
externalContext.getRequestMap();

//We can also retrieve the HttpServletRequestObject itself
HttpServletRequest httpServletRequest↵
  =(HttpServletRequest)externalContext.getNativeRequest();
```

Controlling Action Execution

We've already seen three ways of controlling the execution of Web Flow actions: on transition, on start, and on render. However, there are other ways to execute these actions, all of which have some specifics that govern when they execute their contained actions. These conditions are summed up with a detailed overview in the upcoming sections.

Each of these elements can also have three sub-elements; these are described in the "Controlling Action Execution: Sub-elements" section.

<on-start>

The <on-start> element executes one or more actions when the flow starts. The actions contained by this element will only be executed once. When multiple actions are specified, the execution of the next action will depend on the success of the previous action (if one action fails, the next is skipped and an error is thrown). Actions will be executed in the order they are defined in the flow.

There can be only one <on-start> for an entire flow. If a flow has one or more parent flows with <on-start> elements, the content is merged into one <on-start> in the merged flow (we will discuss flow inheritance further in Chapter 12).

This action is useful for executing the overall initialization of the flow execution/session. In our sample, we used it to initialize our form with some defaults.

<on-end>

The <on-end> element is the counterpart of <on-start>, and the same rules apply. The actions defined herein are the last ones executed before the flow ends. If the end state of a flow has an <on-entry> (see below), then that <on-entry> is executed before the <on-end> executes.

If a flow throws an error before reaching the end of the flow, <on-end> is not executed. Do not confuse <on-end> with a Java finally block. There is no guarantee that the <on-end> will be executed. For example, assume a given flow enters a certain view state and renders a view to the user's browser. At this point, the flow execution (i.e., the one living in the web container) is paused. The user can now decide to trigger a new event that continues to converse with that flow execution. However, the user can also decide to navigate to another page (or another flow), leaving the current flow execution as-is. When the maximum number of concurrent executions is reached, Web Flow will start to clean up the oldest flow execution. If our given flow execution is the oldest, it is cleaned up; but in that case, the <on-end> element will not be triggered. It is only triggered when the flow execution ends normally (after hitting an end state).

This element is especially useful in a flow with multiple end states where certain logic needs to be executed when the flow ends. Without this element, the logic needs to be repeated for each end state, but it can now be placed in a single on end. This will ensure that the required logic is executed, no matter which of the different end states terminated the flow.

<on-entry>

The <on-entry> element can be applied on all five states: view, action, decision, subflow, and end state. The action specified by the <on-entry> element is executed every time the state is entered.

However, this is only true when the state is *explicitly* entered. For example: when you omit the to attribute in a transition (nested in a view state), you remain in the same view state (i.e., the view state will be re-rendered). However, the <on-entry> will not be triggered in that case. There must be an explicit transition to a state in order to execute the <on-entry>.

In other words, you need the to attribute to be specified to trigger <on-entry> (or <on-exit>, as we will see in the next section). The state to which the to attribute refers is of no importance; this holds true whether it is the same state where the transition is defined or another state altogether. For example, in the case of a view state, if a transition returns to the same view state (explicitly specifying the to attribute), then the <on-entry> will be executed again.

If we were to place an <on-entry> in the selectBooks view state of the createOrders-flow (see Listing 11-15), then it would be executed every time we trigger the reset transition. However, it would *not* be executed when we trigger the add transition because it does not explicitly transition back to the selectBooks view state (it has no to in the transition).

<on-exit>

The <on-exit> element is executed whenever a state is exited. This element can be applied on the following states: view, action, decision, and subflow. However, it cannot be applied on the end state.

The action specified by the <on-exit> is executed every time the state is exited. This also applies when a transition occurs to the same state; in that case, the state is exited and entered again if the to attribute is specified (the same rules apply to the <on-exit> element that apply to the <on-entry> element). Now let's extend the <on-entry> example we gave before. If we were to add an <on-exit> in the selectBooks view state of the createOrders-flow (see Listing 11-15), then executing the reset transition would trigger the <on-exit>. In that case, we would exit the selectBooks view state to enter it again.

<on-render>

The <on-render> element is applicable on only one of the five states: the view state. As discussed in the Chapter 10, Web Flow uses a two-phase approach in processing requests (Post Redirect Get). An expression in a transition is executed in the POST phase. The <on-render> element is executed right before the view is rendered, in the GET phase.

When dealing with large result sets, we can benefit from this behavior by loading them into request scope right before the view renders. We already seen this in action in this chapter, when we covered the first phase of refactoring the sample application (see the "On Render" section earlier in this chapter).

Controlling Action Execution: Sub-elements

Each of the previously described elements supports three sub-elements:

- evaluate
- set
- render

You're already familiar with the evaluate action. It accepts a (by default SpEL) expression and executes it. Optionally, you can store the result on a scope with a certain key using the result attribute, and you can specify the result type if you require the result to be of a certain type (using the result-type attribute). If so, a conversion is attempted; and if no converter is applicable, a conversion exception is thrown. The expression can return the result object directly or wrap it in an org.springframework .webflow.execution.Event class to indicate different outcome states, as required. We discuss events further in the "Working with Outcome Events" section.

As explained in "Setting Variables and Accessing Scopes" section earlier in this chapter, the `<set>` element allows you to set something on a given scope. You can specify a name and value, which are respectively the key under which the variable will be known and the value bound to it. The value can be an expression. Optionally, you can require the result to be of a certain type. If the value is not of the required type, a conversion is attempted; and if no converter is applicable, then a conversion exception is thrown.

The render element is somewhat special. It supports a `fragments` attribute that takes the id of a *fragment* to be rendered. But what is a fragment? To make use of these features, you need Tiles. When configuring Tiles, you define the parts that fill up your template. A fragment refers to the name of such an attribute or definition. It allows you to partially render a part of the page composition. When a page consists of multiple parts (each identified by a `tiles` attribute), you can name the part in the fragment that you specifically want to re-render. All the other content of the page remains untouched. This allows for a partial page update in the browser. For this to work, it requires some special configuration on both the server and client sides. Also, it will only work for Ajax requests. When doing a normal request, specifying the `<render>` action will have no effect. We will further discuss this in the "Web Flow AJAX Support" section in Chapter 12.

Global Transitions

As we have seen, a transition may take the user to another view, or it may simply execute an action and re-render the current view. In the next chapter, we'll also see how a transition may request the rendering of parts of a view called "fragments" when handling an Ajax event. Until now, we have only seen transitions in states. These transitions are local to that specific state. To be able to trigger them, you have to be in that given state.

In addition to transitions defined in a particular state, a flow can also have *global transitions*. When an event occurs, if Web Flow cannot find any matching transitions in the current state of the flow, it will try to find a matching global transition. Global transitions have to be defined at the end of the flow. See the flow structure figure in Chapter 10 (see Figure 10-1) for its exact location within the flow.

You may find that some transitions are duplicated in several view states. With global transitions, you can now define them in one place. After that, each state will be able to execute that transition as if it were directly part of the given state. The most common example of this is a Cancel button that terminates the flow, but which might be present on each step of the flow.

To define a global transition, just take the transition out and nest it within the `<global-transitions>` element, as shown in Listing 11-35.

Listing 11-35. *Defining a Global Transition*

```
<global-transitions>
    <transition on="cancel" to="endCancel" />
</global-transitions>
```

Subflows

Subflows give you an alternative way to structure your flows. As it turns out, one of the strong points of Web Flow (which we haven't really discussed until now) is its support for composition and modularity.

Composition allows you to combine different flow definitions to build a more complete definition. To do this, you reuse existing definitions, which saves you code duplication. In the next chapter, which is on advanced Web Flow, you will see this in practice using inheritance.

If you design for *modularity*, you will be able to treat certain parts of your flow as separate modules. This also promotes reuse, as you will be able to refer to those modules from other parts in your application without having to duplicate code. In this section, we will look at subflows, a Web Flow technique that will help you in accomplishing such reuse.

As is true for any object-oriented language, you need some kind of design. The design will cost you a little extra effort, but this feature will be a (very) important aspect of your project. For example, it will dictate how manageable your application will be in the near future.

Whereas in Java we could write everything in a single class or even in a single method, we all know that this would turn into an unworkable project in less than a day. Therefore, we try to apply good design principles because we know we will benefit from doing so in the long run. It will make our project easier to test and our code easier to read. It will also improve the quality of our code and make it easier to extend without spending weeks of refactoring.

This principle also applies to flows. Flows don't contain real Java code, but they do replace (or accommodate) your application controllers, which are an important part of the logic inside your flows. A good design in your flows makes them easy to read, easy to refactor, and, above all, reusable.

■ **Note** Web Flow 1 included a feature called *inline flows*, which is a flow that is inline with, or embedded inside, another top-level flow. Such a flow does not need to be registered with Web Flow separately (you have to provide the flow id yourself inside the `<inline-flow>` flow element). The best way to compare an inline flow is to a private Java nested class (or a private inner class, if you like). Inline flows are no longer supported in Web Flow 2. If you must migrate such flows, the advised action is to simply move them to a top-level flow definition and register them with a flow id in the flow registry. The flow id should be equal to the id attribute of the `<inline-flow>` element. Or, you can use the flow definition update tool to do this for you. We will explain how to use this tool in the "Web Flow 1 Migration" section in Chapter 12.

A subflow is no different than a normal flow, which we've already covered. It is more like a concept. As we will see in the next section when we continue refactoring our sample application, calling a subflow requires a special state and some consideration about passing along state between the parent flow and the subflow. The flow that includes the subflow is referred to as the *parent* flow. The subflow is sometimes also referred to as the *child* flow.

In short: Subflows enable you to move parts of a flow contained in one flow (flow-x) to another top-level flow (flow-y). Next, you can point from flow-x to flow-y using the `<subflow-state>` element in flow-x; this enables you to execute the parts that you moved to flow-y. This refactoring does not influence the behavior of your flow (or your application altogether), but it has an impact on your flow design.

By doing this, you promote reuse. When you have a piece of flow logic that is required in multiple flows, you can extract that logic, place it in another top-level flow, and then delegate to that flow as a subflow in the other flows.

You can compare this feature to *delegation* in Java. When you have some logic in different classes that does the same thing, you extract it, put it in a separate class, and call that from within the classes you extracted the logic from. You can apply the same pattern with flows; simply extract the common parts and put them in a separate flow. When changes are required, you only need to make them once, instead of changing them separately in every flow.

As noted previously, it is important to understand that a subflow is no different than a normal flow. In fact, you don't create subflows per se; you just create a normal flow. You cannot determine by looking at a flow whether it is a subflow. A subflow should be registered as a normal flow, and the same rules apply.

In Figure 11-8, both flow-x and flow-y are normal flows. Both can be started like any normal flow. However, flow-y is also included as a subflow in flow-x. So, from the point of flow-x, flow-y is considered a subflow.

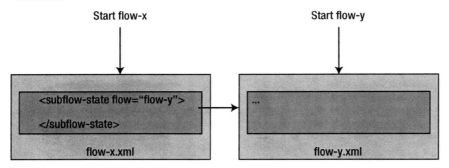

Figure 11-8. Flow-x starts as a top-level flow and calls another flow (flow-y), which becomes its subflow.

When you include a subflow in your flow, that flow can itself delegate to a subflow and so forth. There is no hard limit defined for how many levels of subflows can exist.

■ **Note** As we have seen, a subflow is defined as a normal top-level flow in its own flow definition XML. We speak about a flow being a subflow from the moment it is included in another flow. However, because it is a normal flow, you can still start it like any other normal top-level flow. However, in most cases you will design a flow specifically for use as a subflow; hence, starting it directly without the context of the parent flow would not make much sense. Nevertheless, there exist scenarios where it might make sense for a given flow to be started as a top-level flow from one part in your application, but also to be included as a subflow in another part.

Further Enhancing the Bookstore

We will continue our refactoring effort with the elements we have discussed in the previous sections. So far, we have not added any security to our application. In the previous chapter, we explained that, once you enter the application, you are automatically logged in. We did this to simplify things. However, we will now replace the login process with a traditional login page. We will also require that the user be logged in prior to making an order. And while we will dedicate a separate upcoming chapter to security (Chapter 13), in this section we'll take a first look at security by creating our own home-grown security mechanism. We will use this to illustrate several aspects of flows, including subflows and the remaining states that have not yet been covered.

Until now, a user was automatically logged in as "jd" when using the application; this happened behind the scenes using the com.apress.prospringmvc.bookstore.web.AuthenticationSessionListener. This is a javax.servlet.http.HttpSessionListener that will authenticate user "jd" programmatically from the moment a new javax.servlet.http.HttpSession is started. You can check out the implementation if you want, but it is of no importance to our explanation here. It was required in the previous sample to be able to add orders to a user (you must be logged in to be able to add an order and view existing orders).

In this chapter's sample, we've removed the listener because we will be implementing our own security mechanism. Let's review the altered flow shown in Figure 11-9. The numbered steps in the diagram are described in Table 11-2.

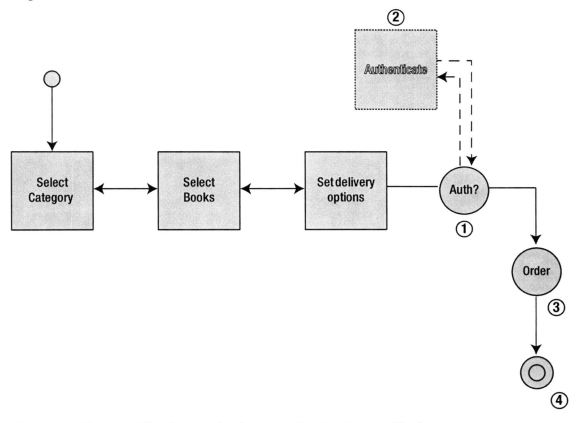

Figure 11-9. The revised flow from our book store application that we will refactor

Table 11-2. *The Sample Flow Refactoring Steps*

Number	Explanation
1	We must check whether the user is already authenticated. As we will see, the user has the option to log in via the login link in the navigation bar (using plain Spring MVC).
2	If the user is not authenticated, we call the authentication-flow as a subflow of our createOrders-flow. The authentication-flow will render the login screen and perform the authentication. When authentication is successful, control is returned back to the createOrders-flow.
3	Creating the order has been implemented using an evaluate expression in the finish transition. As we will see, a more elegant solution would be to use action states.
4	The <end-state> terminates the flow.

Implementing Authentication as a Subflow

Our first action is to implement a flow that is able to capture the username and password from a page and verify its authenticity. To do this, we need the following:

- A page and form to capture the username and password; our login page

- An application controller method to verify the username and password and mark our user as authenticated

- A flow which will manage the navigation and act as glue between the login page and our application controller. We will include this flow as a subflow. This flow must be able to

  - Render the login page after being started

  - Perform the authentication by calling the appropriate method on the application controller

  - Indicate that authentication has succeeded. If the authentication failed, we would remain inside the subflow, showing a message and offering the user another chance to enter the correct credentials

  - Indicate that we want to go back to the previous page, in case the user decided not to place the order at this time

We'll first start with the flow. Listing 11-36 shows the flow definition. We call our flow the authentication-flow.xml and place it in this directory: src/main/webapp/WEB-INF/view/authentication. We will see in a minute how we can include this flow as a subflow.

Listing 11-36. The authentication-flow

```
<on-start>
    <evaluate expression="authenticationController.initializeForm()"
        result="flowScope.authenticationForm" />
</on-start>
<view-state id="authenticate" view="login" model="authenticationForm">
    <transition on="authenticate" to="authenticationOk" >
        <evaluate
                expression="authenticationController.authenticate(↵
                flowScope.authenticationForm, externalContext, ↵
                messageContext)"/>
    </transition>
    <transition on="previous" to="previous" bind="false"/>
</view-state>
<end-state id="previous"/>
<end-state id="authenticationOk"/>
```

The subflow looks like any other flow. When it starts it will call `initializeForm` on our
`AuthenticationController` which will put a new instance of the
`com.apress.prospringmvc.bookstore.web.controller.AuthenticationForm` on flow scope. This form will
be used to capture the username and password submitted from the login page.

```
public AuthenticationForm initializeForm() {
    return new AuthenticationForm();
}
```

Next it will proceed by entering the view state, which eventually renders the login page.

When the authentication transition is executed, it will invoke the authenticate method on our
`com.apress.prospringmvc.bookstore.web.controller.AuthenticationController`. We will discuss this
method later on in this section.

Finally there are two end states to let the caller of the sublow differentiate between going back to the
previous screen or continuing processing because authentication succeeded. If authentication would
fail, we remain inside the subflow, show a message that indicates that the user provided bad credentials
and should try to login again after altering them.

Next, we build our login page (`login.jsp`) in the same folder as our flow; thus, it will be located in
`src/main/webapp/WEB-INF-view/authentication/login.jsp` (see Listing 11-37).

Listing 11-37. The Authentication Page Located in authentication/login.jsp

```
<spring:url value="/authenticate.htm" var="authenticate" />
<form:form modelAttribute="authenticationForm" action="${flowExecutionUrl != ↵
            null ? flowExecutionUrl  : 'authenticate.htm'}" method="POST">
    <table style="width: 100%">
        <tr>
            <td>
                <spring:message code="label.page.login.username" />
            </td>
            <td><form:input  path="username" disabled="false" />
                <form:errors cssClass="error" path="username"/>
            </td>
```

```
            <td>
                <spring:message code="label.page.login.password" />
            </td>
            <td>
                <form:password showPassword="false" path="password" />
                <form:errors cssClass="error" path="password"/>
            </td>
        </tr>
        <tr>
            <td colspan="4">
                <form:errors cssClass="error"/>
            </td>
        </tr>
    </table>
    <div align="right" style="margin-bottom: 20px; margin-top: 10px" >
        <button type="submit" id="previous" name="_eventId_previous">
            <spring:message code="label.page.login.previous"/>
        </button>
        <button type="submit" id="login" name="_eventId_authenticate">
            <spring:message code="label.page.login.login"/>
        </button>
    </div>
</form:form>
```

The first thing to notice is the value of the form's action attribute:

```
${flowExecutionUrl != null ? flowExecutionUrl  : 'authenticate.htm'}
```

We refer to the authentication page from two places in our application. The first reference occurs when clicking directly on the login link in the navigation bar. When clicking the login link in the navigation bar, we navigate to chapter11-bookstore/login.htm, which renders the webapp/view/authentication/login.jsp page (as can be seen in Listing 11-38). In that case, we don't start a flow, but navigate directly to the login page using plain Spring MVC. There is also no need for a flow because, in this scenario, the authentication process only consists of a single page. This is useful if the user wants to login directly from the main page.

Since there is no flow active, the else of our conditional operator is used for the form's action attribute: when clicking the Login button (after filling in username and password), the form will submit to authenticate.htm. In that case the first @RequestMapping will be executed of the AuthenticationController, as shown in Listing 11-38. Executing this application controller method will retrieve the submitted username and password bound to the AuthenticationForm and authenticate the user.

Listing 11-38. Using Spring MVC to Navigate and Perform the Authentication

```
// ----- Spring MVC logic

    public AuthenticationForm initializeForm() {
        return new AuthenticationForm();
    }

    @RequestMapping("login.htm")
    public ModelAndView authentication() {
        ModelAndView mov = new ModelAndView();
```

```
        mov.setViewName("login");
        mov.addObject("authenticationForm", initializeForm());
        return mov;
    }

    @RequestMapping(value = "authenticate.htm", method = RequestMethod.POST)
    public ModelAndView authentication(@ModelAttribute AuthenticationForm ↵
        authenticationForm, Errors errors, ModelAndView mov, ↵
        HttpSession httpSession) {
        try {
            authenticate(authenticationForm, httpSession);
            mov.addObject("authenticationOk", "true");
            mov.addObject("username", authenticationForm.getUsername());
            mov.setViewName("main");
        } catch (AuthenticationException authenticationException) {
            errors.reject(LOGIN_FAILED_KEY);
            mov.setViewName("login");
        }

        return mov;
    }
    @RequestMapping(value = "authenticate.htm", params = "_eventId_previous",↵
                    method = RequestMethod.POST)
    public ModelAndView previous(ModelAndView mov) {
        mov.setViewName("main");
        return mov;
    }
```

The second place from which we refer to the authentication page occurs in our authentication-flow, by executing the authenticate transition as we have already seen in Listing 11-36. As we will see in a minute, we include the authentication-flow as a subflow of our createOrders-flow. When the user wants to create an order, but is not yet authenticated, she is redirected to the login page first.

When performing the login being in an active flow, the then of our conditional operator is executed (as shown in Listing 11-37) and the action attribute of the form will redirect back to our authentication-flow using the flowExecutionUrl as a callback URL. To discover whether our authentication page was loaded directly from Spring MVC or from our authentication-flow, we check whether there is a flowExecutionUrl. If there is, then we know it is loaded from within the authentication-flow (so we post back to flowExecutionUrl); else, we know our authentication page was loaded directly from Spring MVC, and we post back to authenticate.htm.

The second thing to notice in Listing 11-38 is that there are the two input fields (username and password) being bound to the authenticationForm. As seen in Listing 11-39, we have <form:form modelAttribute="authenticationForm"…>, which indicates that the form we are using is the authenticationForm. Next, we declare the path within that form for each input text:

```
<form:input path="username"… >
```

The authenticationForm is used both from our AuthenticationController for Spring MVC, as well as from our authentication-flow. The latter can be seen in Listing 11-35 in the <view-state>:

```
<view-state id="authenticate" view="login" model="authenticationForm">
```

Finally, we also have two buttons: login and previous. The first button starts the authentication process, while the second returns the user to the previous page. When the login button is clicked, the form is simply submitted to the authentication method in case the page was loaded by Spring MVC. The method executed is the one with the annotation, as seen in Listing 11-38:

```
@RequestMapping(value = "authenticate.htm", method = RequestMethod.POST)
```

If the previous button is clicked, then the last request mapping in Listing 11-40 is executed:

```
@RequestMapping(value = "authenticate.htm", params = "_eventId_previous",↵
            method = RequestMethod.POST)
```

The distinction is made based on the presence of the _eventId_previous parameter. If present, the last @RequestMapping is invoked (because it has the params = "_eventId_previous" attribute), and the main page is rendered.

If the authentication page was loaded by Web Flow, the eventId present in the name of the button will determine which transition to execute. When the button with name _eventId_authenticate is clicked, then the authenticate transition will execute. If the button with name _eventId_previous is clicked, then the previous transition will execute. Listing 11-39 shows the authentication form located at com.apress.prospringmvc.bookstore.web.AuthenticationForm holds the username and password.

Listing 11-39. The AuthenticationForm

```
public class AuthenticationForm implements Serializable {
    private String username;
    private String password;

    public String getUsername() {
        return username;
    }
    public void setUsername(String username) {
        this.username = username;
    }
    public String getPassword() {
        return password;
    }
    public void setPassword(String password) {
        this.password = password;
    }
}
```

Because there is an entry point for Spring MVC to start the authentication process (i.e., the second @RequestMapping method in our AuthenticationController—see Listing 11-38), there is also a separate entry point for our authentication-flow. This method will be executed when the login button is clicked and the authenticate transition is executed. This transition is the first method seen in Listing 11-40. The second method is a shared method that is used from the Spring MVC entry point as the Web Flow entry point.

Listing 11-40. The authenticate Method for Web Flow in our AuthenticationController

```
// ---- POJO logic
public Event authenticate(AuthenticationForm authenticationForm,
                    MvcExternalContext externalContext,
```

```
                        MessageContext messageContext) {
    try {
        authenticate(authenticationForm, ((HttpServletRequest)
        externalContext.getNativeRequest()).getSession());
    } catch (AuthenticationException authenticationException) {
            messageContext.addMessage(new
            MessageBuilder().error().code(LOGIN_FAILED_KEY).build());
            return new EventFactorySupport().error(this);
    }
    return new EventFactorySupport().success(this);
}

// ---- Helpers
private void authenticate(AuthenticationForm authenticationForm, HttpSession
                        httpSession) throws AuthenticationException {
    Account account = accountService.login(authenticationForm.getUsername(),
                    authenticationForm.getPassword());
    httpSession.setAttribute(AUTHENTICATED_ACCOUNT_KEY, account);
}
```

As everything is set now, we can include our authentication flow as a subflow from our createOrders-flow. We can do that using the <subflow-state> element. Figure 11-10 shows the different attributes and elements that are possible for this element.

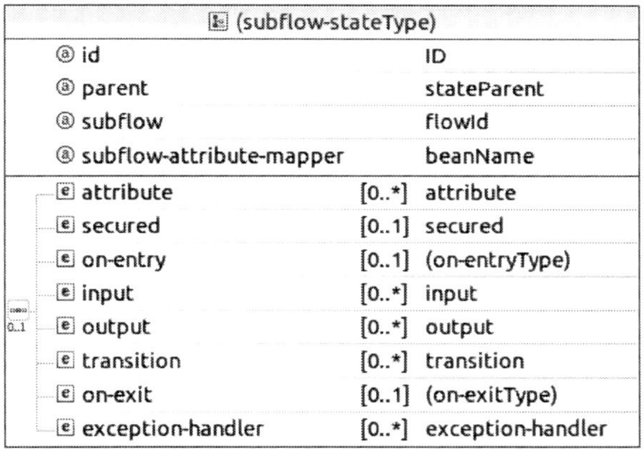

🔳 (subflow-stateType)		
ⓐ id	ID	
ⓐ parent	stateParent	
ⓐ subflow	flowId	
ⓐ subflow-attribute-mapper	beanName	
ⓔ attribute	[0..*]	attribute
ⓔ secured	[0..1]	secured
ⓔ on-entry	[0..1]	(on-entryType)
ⓔ input	[0..*]	input
ⓔ output	[0..*]	output
ⓔ transition	[0..*]	transition
ⓔ on-exit	[0..1]	(on-exitType)
ⓔ exception-handler	[0..*]	exception-handler

Figure 11-10. The different attributes and elements of the subflow state

You'll learn more about many of these elements in various places in this book. General elements such as <on-entry> and <on-exit> are discussed in the "Controlling Action Execution" section; <transition> has the same meaning as when it was introduced for the view state; <exception-handler> will be discussed in depth in Chapter 12; <secured> will be introduced in Chapter 13; input/output will be covered later in this chapter; the parent attribute will be covered in Chapter 12 when we discuss inheritance; and the subflow-attribute-mapper will be covered later in this chapter when we look at subflow input/output mapping.

The subflow state we declared for calling the authentication flow can be seen in Listing 11-41.

Listing 11-41. Declaring the subflow

```
<subflow-state id="authenticate" subflow="authentication">
    <transition on="authenticationOk" to="placeOrder"/>
    <transition on="previous" to="selectDeliveryOptions"/>
</subflow-state>
```

The subflow attribute refers to the id of a registered flow. As explained before, a subflow is a normal flow, so the id you specify there would be the id that you would use to launch a flow as a top-level flow within your application.

The transition on attribute of the <subflow-state> element should match one of the end state ids of the subflow. This way, the subflow can tell the parent flow which state to transition to, depending on which end state was executed on the subflow. If the subflow were to end with the end state that had the previous id, then the parent flow (our createOrders-flow) would transition back to selectDeliveryOptions. However, if our subflow were to end with an end state with the authenticationOk id, then we would continue to the placeOrder state.

We still don't have everything we need to be able to wire everything together. In our createOrders-flow, we need to decide whether we need to go to the subflow. If our user was already authenticated, then there is no need to execute the subflow. We need a decision state to help us out.

Decision State

A decision state can contain any number of if elements that define an if-then-else structure. The test attribute of the if element defines the condition, while the then and else attributes identify the target state. When the flow enters a decision state, the first matching if is used to transition to the next state. This means that all other if elements will not be processed. The decision state can also delegate the criteria for the decision to Java application code using expressions. You can see the different elements and attributes of the decision state (including their order) in Figure 11-11.

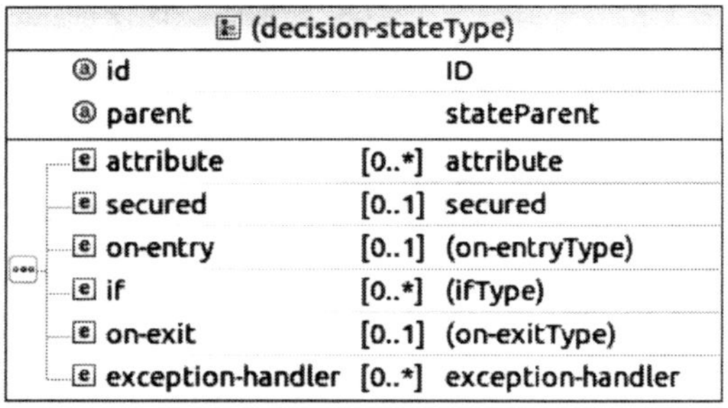

(decision-stateType)		
ⓐ id		ID
ⓐ parent		stateParent
ⓔ attribute	[0..*]	attribute
ⓔ secured	[0..1]	secured
ⓔ on-entry	[0..1]	(on-entryType)
ⓔ if	[0..*]	(ifType)
ⓔ on-exit	[0..1]	(on-exitType)
ⓔ exception-handler	[0..*]	exception-handler

Figure 11-11. Different attributes and elements of the decision state

In our sample, we will use a decision state in the createOrders-flow to check whether the user is authenticated. If the user is not authenticated, then we will proceed to the authentication subflow, which will render the login screen. If the user was previously authenticated, we can immediately proceed with creating the order.

■ **Note** Remember that the authentication mechanism is a self-invented, session-based model. Web Flow has security integration with Spring security, as we will see in Chapter 13. There is usually no need to build such a model yourself. However, we opted not to distract you by introducing Spring security because right now we want you to focus on the core Web Flow items being discussed in this chapter. When authenticated, the model simply places a token on the session scope.

You can see the implementation of the decision state in Listing 11-42.

Listing 11-42. *The Login Decision State*

```
<decision-state id="loginCheck">
    <if test="externalContext.sessionMap.contains('authenticatedCustomer') == ↵
            true" then="placeOrder" else="authenticate"/>
</decision-state>
```

If multiple if conditions are supplied, then they are evaluated one by one. If none of the conditions evaluates to true, then an org.springframework.webflow.engine.NoMatchingTransitionException is thrown. You can implement a chain of if conditions; however, be aware that any if condition that defines an else clause will, by definition, evaluate to true. This means that none of the remaining if conditions will be evaluated. For this reason, if you have multiple if elements, it only makes sense for the last if element to have an else. If one of the previous ifs had an else, then the subsequent if elements would never be evaluated. This makes sense if you think about it; if an if has also an else condition, either the then or the else is executed. Hence, all if elements that are defined below an if condition are skipped.

Before we show you an overview of what we have done in this chapter, we want to perform one last refactoring—for the create order process. This process is now embedded as an evaluate action of the finish transition. We are going to replace this with an action state.

Action State

An action state executes an action as its activity. Figure 11-12 shows its various attributes and elements. In an XML flow definition, an action state is defined using the <action-state> element, and the action to execute is defined using a nested <evaluate> element. Action states are typically used to interact with back-end services, either directly or via controllers. Action states execute automatically and do not pause the flow execution. A view state pauses the flow execution (the view gets rendered, and the user spends time working with the view), but an action state signals events that leads to transitioning to another state.

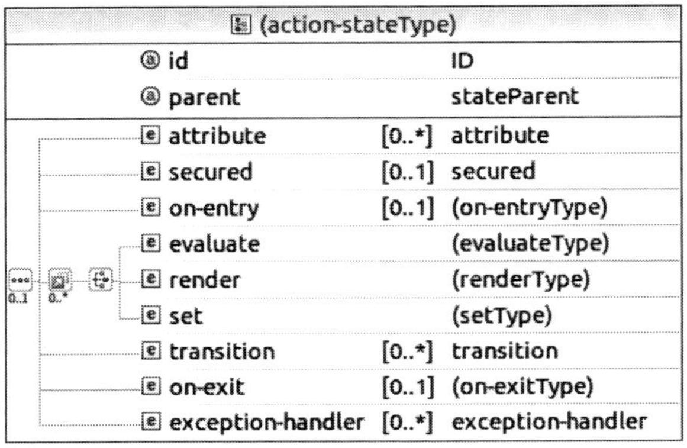

Figure 11-12. Different attributes and elements of the action state

In the example that follows, we transition to the end state when an order is successfully made. We could also react to on "error" events and transition to an error page instead.

■ **Note** There is no single rule for determining whether you need an action state. You should probably be using an action state if there are multiple outcomes that you could react upon or in cases where processing is more complex (e.g., when executing multiple actions).

To refactor this, we simply move the evaluation expression to an <action-state> and adjust the transitions accordingly. The code shown in Listing 11-43 becomes the code for the action state shown in Listing 11-44. This code can be found in src/main/webapp/WEB-INF/view/createOrders/createOrders-flow.xml.

Listing 11-43. Refactoring the Evaluate Action to an Action State

```
<transition on="finish" to="end">
    <evaluate expression="orderController.placeOrder(flowScope.orderForm,
      externalContext.sessionMap.authenticatedAccount)"/>
</transition>
```

Listing 11-44. The Action State for Placing an Order

```
<action-state id="placeOrder">
    <evaluate expression="orderController.placeOrder(externalContext.↵
                    sessionMap.authenticatedAccount, ↵
                    flowScope.orderForm)"
            result="flowScope.orderId"/>
    <transition on="success" to="end"/>
</action-state>
```

The `authenticatedAccount` variable is looked up from `session` scope. It was placed there when the user logged in using the `AuthenticationController`. You can see this in the last method of Listing 11-40. The `OrderForm` was created in the beginning of the `createOrder-flow` in the on start element. It was placed on flow scope. We don't need to specify a scope per se because the expression language will look in all Web Flow scopes automatically (i.e., specifying `orderForm` without the implicit `flowScope` object would also be correct and yield the same result).

Working with Outcome Events

As we have seen, we can use our evaluate action to invoke methods on application controllers. When called from action states or decision states, these method return values can be used to drive state transitions. Since transitions are triggered by events, a method return value must first be mapped to an Event object.

For example, in the `AuthenticationController`'s authenticate method, we created so-called events that were returned by the application controller directly:

```
return new EventFactorySupport().error(this);
return new EventFactorySupport().success(this);
```

In this case, the action's result event becomes the primary basis for the transition decision. When combined with a controller or POJO action, this allows you to call a method in application code that returns a single value that can be used as the basis for a routing decision.

If you do not return an `org.springframework.webflow.execution.Event`, Web Flow will automatically adapt the method return value to an appropriate result event according to a set of rules. The rules are simple and identified in Table 11-3.

Table 11-3. Event Mapping

Method return type	Mapped event identifier expression
`java.lang.String`	The String value
`java.lang.Boolean`	yes (for true), no (for false)
`java.lang.Enum`	The Enum name
`any other type`	success

In our action state, the `placeOrder()` method returned an object of type `Long`. This resulted in Web Flow creating an event with the `success` id—hence, our transition of `on="success"`.

Whenever you return a value, whether an explicit event with an attribute or any other object (for which Web Flow creates an Event for you), you can bind that value using the `result` attribute (see Listing 11-43 for an example) of the evaluation expression. If the id of the event does not match any transition of the action state, then a `NoMatchingTransitionException` is thrown.

If you however have a evaluate action nested in a transition instead, you can only decide whether the transition is allowed to continue or abort. You can do this by returning a success or error event, either directly or by letting Web Flow map it for you.

If you do not return an explicit success or error event, then Web Flow will map your return value to an Event, as described in Table 11-3. In case of a `String`, `Enum`, or `Boolean`, the value must be success, yes, or true to be interpreted as a success Event. In all other cases, the transition is aborted and the last view state is re-rendered.

■ **Note** In the `AuthenticationController`, we have chosen to generate the Event in the application code itself to illustrate how such events can be created. In that particular case (where the outcome is either OK or not OK (i.e., the authentication is either a success or failure), using a `Boolean` would have definitely been a good choice, as well.

Overview

With all the previous refactorings applied, Listing 11-45 shows what our `createOrders-flow` now looks like. You can find this file in `src/main/webapp/WEB-INF/view/createOrders/createOrders-flow.xml`.

Listing 11-45. The createOrders-flow After Our Final Refactoring

```
<on-start>
    <evaluate expression="orderController.initializeForm()"
        result="flowScope.orderForm" />
</on-start>
<view-state id="selectCategory" view="selectCategory" model="orderForm">
    <on-render>
        <evaluate⤶
          expression="orderController.initializeSelectableCategories()"⤶
          result="requestScope.selectableCategories" />
    </on-render>
    <transition on="next" to="selectBooks" />
    <transition on="cancel" to="end" />
</view-state>
<view-state id="selectBooks" view="selectBooks" model="orderForm">
    <on-render>
        <evaluate expression="orderController.⤶
                initializeSelectableBooks(flowScope.orderForm)"⤶
                result="flowScope.selectableBooks" />
    </on-render>
    <transition on="previous" to="selectCategory" />
    <transition on="add">
        <evaluate expression="orderController.addBook(flowScope.orderForm)" />
    </transition>
    <transition on="next" to="selectDeliveryOptions" />
    <transition on="reset" to="selectBooks">
        <evaluate expression="orderForm.resetSelectedBooks()" />
    </transition>
    <transition on="cancel" to="end" />
</view-state>
<view-state id="selectDeliveryOptions" view="selectDeliveryOptions" model="orderForm">
    <transition on="previous" to="selectBooks" />
```

```
    <transition on="finish" to="loginCheck">
        <evaluate ↵
        expression="orderController.validateDeliveryDate(flowScope.orderForm,↵
        messageContext)"/>
    </transition>

    <transition on="cancel" to="end" />
</view-state>
<decision-state id="loginCheck">
    <if test="externalContext.sessionMap.contains('authenticatedAccount')↵
            == true" then="placeOrder" else="authenticate" />
</decision-state>
<subflow-state id="authenticate" subflow="authentication-flow">
    <transition on="authenticationOk" to="placeOrder" />
    <transition on="previous" to="selectDeliveryOptions" />
</subflow-state>
<action-state id="placeOrder">
    <evaluate expression="orderController.placeOrder(externalContext.sessionMap↵
.authenticatedAccount, flowScope.orderForm)"↵
     result="flowScope.orderId"/>
    <transition on="success" to="endOrderOk"/>
</action-state>
<end-state id="end" view="redirect:/index.htm" />
```

Subflow Input/Output Mapping

As we have seen in the "Different Web Flow Scopes" section, every flow session has its own flow scope. We also illustrated that this is the case for subflows. On scope level, subflows are no different than ordinary flows, and they work in their own flow session—hence, they have their own flow scope. Only conversation scope is shared between multiple flow sessions. So, what should you do if you need to access data from the parent flow when within a subflow? Sure, you could put it on conversation scope, but that has some drawbacks.

A subflow is best seen is a black box with a specific input and output contract. Putting everything on conversation scope merely to make data access easy violates encapsulation and might lead to brittle flow design. A better option would be to bring the data over to the subflow's flow scope—but only the data that the subflow is demanding. Web Flow supplies some special functionality to define an input and output contract for subflows. That way, you exactly know what data it takes as input and what data is gives back.

You can define the input contract of a flow by adding an *input mapping* to your flow. Input mapping is responsible for mapping all input provided to the flow when it is launched into its flow scope. You can also define the output contract via an *output mapping*. The output mapping defines the values that are to be expected as a result of executing the flow, and they can be mapped back into to flow scope of the parent flow.

Before we continue, you should understand how Web Flow treats input and output attributes. It dedicates a separate map for input and output. This map is standalone and will merely be created to form the transition between the attributes coming from the parent flow and going to the flow scope of the subflow. When a flow starts, it gathers information to put into the input map. This information might come from the URL or an input from a <subflow-state>. You can access the input map with the <input> element in the starting subflow.

Here flow-x exposes an attribute with name of varX to the subflow, flow-y. It does that by specifying the input element in the subflow state. This enables Web Flow to fetch the key, varX, from the flow scope of flow-x and then place the key/value on the input map. When flow-y starts, it will look in the input map for a varX attribute and place it on the flow scope of flow-y.

In Figure 11-13, you also see that the input map is populated with values coming from the URL. That is the second option you have. In addition to passing values using the <input> element of a <subflow-state>, Web Flow reads your URL and puts any request parameter available in the input map. The reason for this behavior is that it allows you to easily use a flow as a standalone flow and as a subflow.

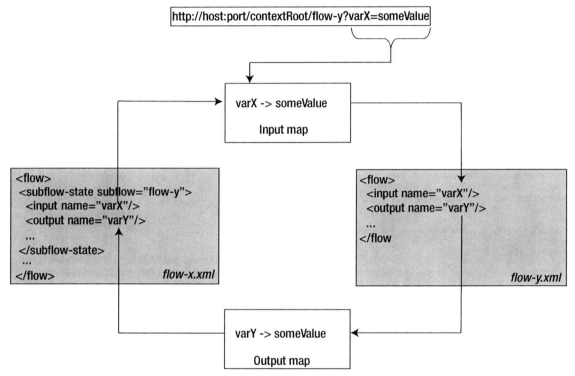

Figure 11-13. *Subflow input/output mapping*

■ **Note** The output mapping mirrors the input mapping, the same principles and rules apply. However, instead of two <input> elements we now have two <output> elements. One in the <subflow-state> of the parent flow and one in the subflow itself. There is also an output map, which maps values from the subflow back to the parent flow (as you can see in Figure 11-13).

In addition to using the `<input>` and `<output>` elements, you can also specify a custom subflow-attribute-mapper. This is an attribute of the `<subflow-state>` element. It enables custom mapping using a Java class rather than performing the mapping inside the flow. This attribute takes a bean reference to an implementation of the `org.springframework.webflow.engine.SubflowAttributeMapper` interface. This class has two methods:

```
public MutableAttributeMap createSubflowInput(RequestContext context);
public void mapSubflowOutput(AttributeMap output, RequestContext context);
```

When using this approach, you can specify the mapping yourself inside your custom implementation of a SubflowAttributeMapper. This is pretty exotic; normally, the standard input and output elements should be sufficient to map whatever you need. However, if you need some resource access while mapping data, this will help you accomplish that because you will have full control over the mapping process.

Creating the Order Process as a Subflow

So far, we've created a subflow for performing the authentication. Next, we will further refactor the createOrders-flow and extract the part that actually *places* the order into a subflow. Remember that we previously refactored this to an action state in the createOrders-flow (see Listing 11-46).

Listing 11-46. Recapping the Action State for Placing an Order

```
<action-state id="placeOrder">
    <evaluate
      expression="orderController.placeOrder(↵
      externalContext.sessionMap.authenticatedAccount, flowScope.orderForm)"↵
      result="flowScope.orderId"/>
    <transition on="success" to="endOrderOk"/>
</action-state>
```

Next, we are going to move the action state into a subflow called the placeOrders-flow.xml. This flow will be placed in this directory: src/main/webapp/WEB-INF/view/placeOrders/. In order for the action state to work in the subflow, we need to pass along our order form. The order form is stored on flow scope of the parent flow; and, as we have already seen, the subflow will have its own flow scope. Thus, we need to map the order form from the parent's flow scope to the subflow's flow scope. The account is not required to be mapped because we put the account on the Servlet session scope. This scope is reachable from our entire flow (and even beyond Web Flow such as in Servlets or JSPs because it is a JEE scope). We will also need to send back the order id to the parent flow once the subflow completes. Our subflow will look like Listing 11-47; this code can be found in placeOrders/placeOrders-flow.xml.

Listing 11-47. Creating the Flow

```
<input name="orderForm" required="true" ↵
       type="com.apress.prospringmvc.bookstore.web.OrderForm"/>

<action-state id="placeOrder">
    <evaluate expression="orderController.placeOrder(externalContext↵
.sessionMap.authenticatedAccount, orderForm)"
      result="flowScope.orderId"/>
```

```
    <transition on="success" to="endOrderOk"/>
</action-state>

<end-state id="endOrderOk">
    <output name="orderId" />
</end-state>
```

First, we map the orderForm from the input map to the flow scope of the subflow. We also declare the input to be mandatory and declare it to be of a specific type. Both the required and type attributes are optional. The type is just an extra check to ensure that the input is of the correct type. When the input is not of the indicated type, a type conversion will be attempted. If that fails, an exception is raised. If a mandatory input is absent, an exception (FlowInputMappingException) is raised when the subflow is started.

In the end state, we use the output element to map the result (in this case, the id of the order) back to the parent flow. If you have multiple end states and all of them output the same result back to the parent flow, then you can also remove the output element from each of the end states and put the output element below the latest end state. This way, you don't have to repeat the output element for each end state. The output is then mapped, no matter which end state terminated the subflow. Listing 11-48 shows how to declare a single output element that maps the declared variable to the parent flow when any of the end states terminate the subflow.

Listing 11-48. *Declaring a Single Output Element*

```
<end-state id="endstateOne"/>
<end-state id="endstateTwo"/>
<output name="varX"/>
```

Finally, Listing 11-49 shows the subflow-state in our parent flow; this will declare which subflow to execute and is indicated by the subflow attribute. The value is the id by which the flow we want to run as a subflow is mapped in Web Flow. This is nothing new—we covered this previously in the "Implementing Authentication as a Subflow" section.

Listing 11-49. *The subflow-state in the Parent Flow*

```
<subflow-state id="placeOrder" subflow="placeOrders">
    <input name="orderForm"/>
    <output name="orderId"/>

    <transition on="endOrderOk" to="endOrderOk"/>
</subflow-state>
```

Inside the subflow state, we can see the input mapping. This is the value we will be making available to the subflow. Here, we refer to the orderForm variable.

The output mapping is the inverse of the input mapping; in other words, this is the value returned by the subflow that we will be binding to a variable within our parent flow. For the output mapping, we chose the variable name, orderId, which will be put on flow scope by default. The output value (the order id) will be used by our end state, which will use it to pass on the target URL that will be rendered when the flow ends (we will discuss the end state in the next section). The transition is also nothing new—we covered this in the "Implementing Authentication as a Subflow" section. When the subflow terminates, it will trigger this transition because the on attribute matches the end state id of the subflow and brings us to the end state of the parent flow.

■ **Caution** You cannot specify a scope in either the input or output element. For example, specifying input name="flowScope.orderForm" will yield an exception. By default, the values you refer to in the input element are resolved from flow scope, and values are put back on flow scope with the name you specify in the output element. It is arguable whether this is a valid limitation. The fact is, flow scope is the only logical scope to use for input/output mapping because the conversation, flash, and request scopes are shared with the subflow. Note that view scope is not shared, but it clears anyway, as soon as your flow leaves the view state.

■ **Note** It might seem bizarre that an element (<input>) occurs in both the <subflow-state> and the subflow itself. The best way to understand this is that, in the <subflow-state> element, you define which keys from a given value/expression you want to map *to* the *input* map. In the <input> element of the flow started as a subflow, the <input> element says which keys *from* the *input* map you want to put into the flow scope of the subflow (the same story goes for the <output> element, which maps to an output map).

End State

An end state terminates the active flow session. Figure 11-14 shows the attributes and elements for this state.

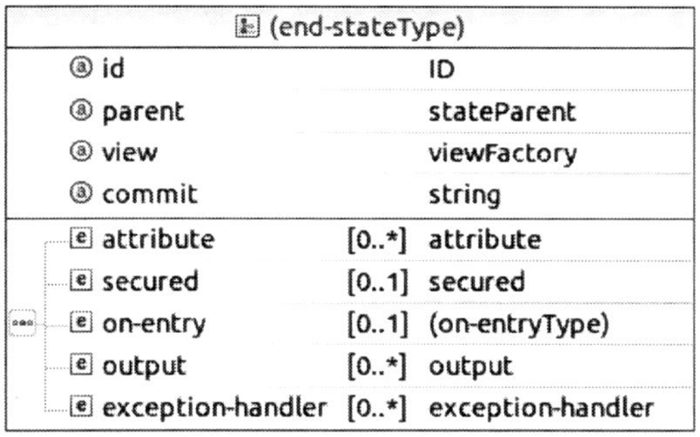

⊞ (end-stateType)		
ⓐ id		ID
ⓐ parent		stateParent
ⓐ view		viewFactory
ⓐ commit		string
ⓔ attribute	[0..*]	attribute
ⓔ secured	[0..1]	secured
ⓔ on-entry	[0..1]	(on-entryType)
ⓔ output	[0..*]	output
ⓔ exception-handler	[0..*]	exception-handler

Figure 11-14. Different attributes and elements of the end state

Listing 11-50 shows an example of an end state terminating the active flow session. You can find this code in the src/main/webapp/WEB-INF/view/createOrders/createOrders-flow.xml. If the terminated flow session is the root flow session of the ongoing flow execution, then the entire flow execution will end. When the session is a subflow session, then processing will resume in the parent flow.

Listing 11-50. An End State Terminating the Active Flow Session

```
<end-state id="endOrderOk" view="redirect:/ordersOverview.htm?orderOk=↵
true&amp;orderId={orderId}"/>
<end-state id="end" view="redirect:/index.htm"/>
```

■ **Note** In Listing 11-50, we are using an XML entity (&) to escape the & character. This is mandatory because several characters (e.g. " < > and &) are not allowed directly in XML because they have a special meaning and therefore need to be escaped.

A flow can have any number of end states. And it is not uncommon for a flow to have no end states, such as when you have a repetitive process like searching (where you typically have a Search Again button). Having multiple end states is also common—one for each logical outcome of the flow. As shown in the sample code, we have an end state in case the user wants to cancel the order flow. If this happens, we redirect the user to the home page. We also have an end state that redirects the user to the order overview page once an order has been successfully created.

An end state can optionally reference a view. Such a view can be used to confirm that flow processing ended successfully; this is typically called a *confirmation view*. The view referenced by an end state will only be rendered when that end state terminates the entire flow execution. If the end state ends a subflow session, view selection becomes the responsibility of the resuming parent flow.

In the "Subflows" section, we also saw that an end state can have an output element. This allows the end state to map data back to the parent flow. You can see this in action in Listing 11-47.

■ **Caution** We have seen that Web Flow uses PRG. However, the end state is a bit of an exception. When an end state is triggered, Web Flow will terminate the flow execution after handling the first request in the PRG idiom (the POST request). It will also render and send back the view after processing the first request—however, it will not send a redirect, as it normally does. If a normal redirect is issued, the second request in the PRG idiom (the GET) triggers a flow execution restart because the flow execution was already terminated after handling the first request (again, the POST). This means that, if you refresh the page after hitting an end state, you will be restarting the flow. To avoid this, it is better to let the end state redirect to a *stable* (possibly external) URL. The sample code accomplishes this with some `redirect` syntax. For an external redirect, outside of the application's context, you could use the `externalRedirect` attribute. In this case, there will be no more incoming requests to the flow execution because the newly rendered URL has nothing more to do with the flow.

Summary

After finishing this chapter, you should have a solid understanding about most Web Flow features and how to apply them. You should be able to start using Web Flow in your own applications, referring back to this chapter and Chapter 10 whenever you are in doubt or need to refresh your memory on the specifics of Web Flow's behavior.

In this chapter, we showed how you can solve real-world use cases using Web Flow. These use cases included conversion, formatting, and validation. Along the way, you learned in detail how you can choose among the different types of validation. This chapter also addressed subflows, which allow you to build more maintainable and reusable flows. For example, we covered all of the different scopes, as well as how to use them. We also reviewed all of the action states and covered how to use them in our use sample application.

You are now ready to proceed to the next and final Web Flow chapter, where you will explore some of the more advanced functionality that Web Flow has to offer.

CHAPTER 12

Advanced Spring Web Flow

Welcome to the final chapter on Spring Web Flow. In the couple previous chapters, we made you familiar with the Web Flow basics, such as how to configure Web Flow, glue it together with Spring MVC, and set up a basic flow. We also explained the different elements, such as action states, model binding, validation, application controllers (and how to call them), expressions, and so forth.

Our approach for the previous chapters was to gradually introduce you to the concepts contained therein and to build on those concepts as the chapters went on. In Chapter 10, we started with a basic high level view of Web Flow, introduced a simple use case, and then built that out as a sample application to illustrate the different aspects of using Web Flow.

In Chapter 11, we extended that by further refactoring and building out the sample application with new Web Flow functionality.

This chapter will continue to build on those topics covered previously; however the topics in this chapter are less coupled. Every topic should be more or less seen as an individual topic that discusses its own Web Flow feature.

We will continue with the sample application as we left it in the previous chapter, and we are going to make modifications to support the features we discuss here. A feature can be something completely new or an extension to something we saw in a previous chapter. We intentionally divided the chapters this way to keep the previous chapter as digestible as possible, but also so that you can start in this chapter with the required Web Flow knowledge to jump right into a given feature.

After reading this final chapter on Web Flow, you should have a thorough understanding of nearly all the most important Web Flow features, including how and when to use them in practice.

Inheritance

In the previous chapter, we introduced you to subflows, which will help you in structuring and reusing your flows. But there is another Web Flow feature that can help you with this structure and reuse: *inheritance*. Web Flow offers two forms of inheritance:

- Flow inheritance
- State inheritance

In the previous chapter, we also saw there is a special attribute on the flow root element that you can use to declare flow inheritance (the parent attribute). In this chapter, we will demonstrate that functionality. In addition to the flow, inheritance can also be applied to the five different states individually (i.e., the view, action, decision, subflow, and end states). In the following sections, we will discuss each of these modularity features in detail. And again, we will build these examples on top of the sample application constructed in the previous couple of chapters.

Flow Inheritance

You can enable a flow to inherit elements defined by another flow or set of flows. You declare the inheritance by using the parent attribute to mark each flow that has elements you want your flow to inherit from. A common use case is for a parent flow to define global transitions and exception handlers. The flow should be seen as merger between the parent and the current (child) flow. Unlike with Java, you *can* inherit from multiple parent flows. You simply separate each flow with a comma; the order is of no importance (see Listing 12-1).

Listing 12-1. *Flow Inheritance Allows a Flow to Have Multiple Parents*

```
<flow parent="global-initialization-flow, global-actions-flow"/>
```

■ **Tip** Suppose you have several flows that share a lot of common functionality. In that case, you can move the common functionality out of the individual flows and into a *parent flow*. You can then let each of the individual flows inherit from that parent flow. However, if you define it as such, the parent flow will be a normal flow like any other flow (it needs to have an id, be registered with Web Flow, and so forth). This also means that you will be able to start the parent flow because it is a separate flow. However, doing so doesn't make sense in this case because the parent flow must always be combined with one of the child flows. It is the child flows that should be started, not the parent flow they have in common. Note that you can declare the parent flow to be abstract. This will tell Web Flow to disallow starting flow executions (either top level or via subflows) for that flow. However, if extend from such a flow, the child flow can be started normally as a top-level flow or subflow. You can do this by setting the abstract attribute to true on the flow root element.

Web Flow will create a *merged* flow from the child flow and all its parent flows. The rules for duplicate elements are split into *mergeable* and *non-mergeable* elements. Mergeable elements will always attempt to merge together if the elements are similar. Non-mergeable elements in a parent or child flow will always be retained intact in the resulting flow; they will not be modified as part of the merge process.

Mergeable elements are identified as mergeable when the following conditions are met:

- Their key attributes match: If they don't match, they fall into the non-mergeable category and are taken as-is in the resulting merged flow. The key attribute is an element's attribute that is identified by Web Flow as the one used for mergeability matches. In other words, when the same element type exists in both the parent and child flows, and the value of this attribute matches, then the element is considered mergeable.

- They are marked as merge always (see Table 12-1): In that case, the mergeable elements are always merged, no matter what. In that case, there is no *key* attribute that should match first.

For example, Listing 12-2 shows an invented flow with a single view state that has two transitions. Focusing on the inheritance aspect, it doesn't matter which view the view state renders, nor is it important to which states each of the transitions transition.

Listing 12-2. A Flow That Has a Single view State with Two Transitions

```
<flow xmlns="http://www.springframework.org/schema/webflow"
    xmlns:xsi="http://www.w3.org/2001/XMLSchema-instance"
    xsi:schemaLocation="http://www.springframework.org/schema/webflow
      http://www.springframework.org/schema/webflow/spring-webflow-2.0.xsd">

    <view-state id="someViewState" view="someView" >
        <transition on="x" to="someState"/>
        <transition on="y" to="someOtherState"/>
    </view-state>
</flow>
```

If we were to divide this over two flows, such as a parent and child flow, it would look like what is shown in Listings 12-3 and 12-4.

Listing 12-3. The Parent Flow, which Contains One of the Two Transitions

```
<flow xmlns="http://www.springframework.org/schema/webflow"
    xmlns:xsi="http://www.w3.org/2001/XMLSchema-instance"
    xsi:schemaLocation="http://www.springframework.org/schema/webflow
      http://www.springframework.org/schema/webflow/spring-webflow-2.0.xsd"↵
    abstract="true">

    <view-state id="someViewState" view="someView" >
        <transition on="x" to="someState"/>
    </view-state>
</flow>
```

Listing 12-4. The Child Flow, which Contains the Other Transition and Inherits from the Parent Flow

```
<flow xmlns="http://www.springframework.org/schema/webflow"
    xmlns:xsi="http://www.w3.org/2001/XMLSchema-instance"
    xsi:schemaLocation="http://www.springframework.org/schema/webflow
      http://www.springframework.org/schema/webflow/spring-webflow-2.0.xsd"↵
    parent="parent-flow">

    <view-state id="someViewState" view="someView" >
        <transition on="y" to="someOtherState"/>
    </view-state>
</flow>
```

The parent flow listed in Listing 12-3 cannot be started directly because it is declared to be abstract. The child flow listed in Listing 12-4 can be started directly. Because the child flow inherits from a parent flow, Web Flow will scan for mergeable elements. It will find that, in both the parent and child flows, a view state with the id of someViewState exists. It will now merge the view state, combining all elements inside. This results in a merged flow (see Listing 12-5) that looks like the original flow.

431

Listing 12-5. The Merged Flow

```
<flow xmlns="http://www.springframework.org/schema/webflow"
    xmlns:xsi="http://www.w3.org/2001/XMLSchema-instance"
    xsi:schemaLocation="http://www.springframework.org/schema/webflow
      http://www.springframework.org/schema/webflow/spring-webflow-2.0.xsd">

    <view-state id="someViewState" view="myView" >
        <transition on="x" to="someState"/>
        <transition on="y" to="someOtherState"/>
    </view-state>
</flow>
```

This merged flow doesn't exist physically; rather, it is generated in memory when Web Flow starts and scans your flow definitions. Physically, you only have the parent and child flows. In this case, the view state was a mergeable element because it had the same id, which is the key attribute for a view state on which Web Flow decides to merge the element. If the id value were different, then Web Flow would have taken the element from the parent flow as-is and copied and pasted it into the merged flow.

In Table 12-1, you can see the different elements and their key attributes. If there is an element in both the child and the parent flow that has the same key attribute, then the element will be marked for merging. Otherwise, the element is taken completely as-is into the merged flow. If an element has Always merged as a key attribute, it means that no specific attribute must match, and elements of the same type between parent and child are always merged.

Table 12-1. The Merging Strategy for the Different Web Flow

Element	Merged when matches key attribute
action-state	Attribute "id"
attribute	Attribute "name"
decision-state	Attribute "id"
end-state	Attribute "id"
flow	Always merged
If	Attribute "test"
on-end	Always merged
on-entry	Always merged
on-exit	Always merged
on-render	Always merged
on-start	Always merged
input	Attribute "name"
output	Attribute "name"
secured	Attributes

subflow-state	Attribute "id"
transition	Attributes "on" and "on-exception"
view-state	Attribute "id

The following are non-mergeable elements: bean-import, evaluate, exception-handler, persistence-context, render, set, and var. As explained before, they become part of the merged flow as-is, and they are copied and pasted as a whole from the parent flow(s) into the merged flow.

Attributes on elements that are not marked as key attributes in Table 12-1, and that are specified on the element in both the parent and the child flows, will be overwritten by the child flow. For example, consider the view attribute of a <view-state> element. When the parent contains a <view-state id="x" view="a"> and the child contains a <view-state id="x" view="b">, then the element is eligible for merging because the view state ids match. So, every sub-element will be inherited from the parent; but in this case, the view attribute is defined both in the parent and child flows with a different value. The resulting merged flow will navigate to view "b" when the flow is rendered.

The same goes for non-mergeable elements that are specified in both parent and child flows with the same identifiers: the child flow values take precedence. For example, the parent flow has the following var element: <var name="x" value="com.apress.prospringmvc.bookstore.ClassX"/>. The child flow has also a var element with the exact same name, but a different value: <var name="x" value="com.apress.prospringmvc.bookstore.ClassY "/>. The general overwrite rule applies, and the variable with the name of x will have as a value an object of type com.apress.prospringmvc.bookstore .ClassY, which is that of the child flow. If we were to remove the <var> element from the child flow, then there would be only one var element with the name of x left (the one in the parent flow). In that case, the variable x will become an object of type ClassX.

■ **Warning** Paths to external resources in the parent flow should be absolute. Relative paths will break when the two flows are merged unless the parent and child flow are in the same directory. Once merged, all relative paths in the parent flow will become relative to the child flow. In our samples, this is not much of a problem because we are not dealing with resources directly. Our views are literals, which match up with definition names in the Tiles configuration. However, if you are not using Tiles, and you are referring to the JSPs directly from within your flows, then you could have something like this (imaginary example) of a parent-flow flow that is in WEB-INF\views\parent\parent-flow.xml and has a single view state:

```
<view-state id="someViewState" view="thePage.jsp"/>
```

In this case, thePage.jsp is in the same location as the flow (WEB-INF\views\parent\thePage.jsp). Hence, it is a relative pointer to the resource. If a child flow in another directory (e.g., WEB-INF\views\child\child-flow.xml) were to now inherit from this flow, then the thePage.jsp resource from the view state of someViewState would now try to resolve from the location of the child flow's WEB-INF\views\child \thePage.jsp—which, of course, does not exist. In such a case, you should make the path to the resource absolute by specifying the full path. Instead of specifying view="thePage.jsp" in the parent flow, you should instead specify this path:

```
view="WEB-INF\views\parent\thePage.jsp"
```

State Inheritance

In addition to specifying a parent attribute on the flow element, you can also specify a parent attribute on the individual states. This could be useful if you want more fine-grained control over which elements from the parent flow are actually inherited. This only makes sense if you did not apply inheritance on the flow level; in other words, it makes sense only if you did not specify the parent attribute on the flow element, but instead specified it only on those states for which you want to have inheritance:

- Unlike with flow inheritance, you can only inherit from a single state.

- The parent state you're inheriting from should be of the same type. For example, a view state cannot inherit from an action state.

- Basically, the same rules that apply for flow inheritance also apply here. The only difference is that the granularity level is less coarse-grained because you can now indicate which elements need to be inherited. The only notable difference is that the state is always merged with the indicated parent state. With flow inheritance, it matters if the element has the same key attribute, so it can be merged or taken as-is. Since we are specifying the state directly here, it is always merged, no matter what.

- You have to specify the flow in which the state you want to inherit from is defined. The format looks like this: parent="parent-flow#parent-state"

■ **Note** You might wonder what happens if there is a view state with the same name in both parent and child flows and there is state inheritance applied on them. For example, in the child flow, assume there is a view state like this: <view-state id="viewStateX" view="someView" parent="parent#viewStateX">. Meanwhile, the parent also has a view state of viewStateX. As stated before, it doesn't matter. The states are always merged. In this case, every attribute and element of the viewStateX defined in the parent is merged with the viewStateX in the child. If both the parent and the child provide the same attributes or elements with the same identifier, then the child version is the one that is retained.

Web Flow Configuration Customizations

In the first chapter, we introduced you to the core Web Flow configuration. Next, we will see how we can make some adjustments to this configuration that could be important for your application's performance and/or how your flows are managed within your application.

We also saw that Web Flow uses SpEL by default, but it doesn't have to be this way. The second customization we are going to discuss explains how you can change the default expression language to something else.

Execution and Conversation Snapshots

We've already configured the `org.springframework.webflow.executor.FlowExecutor` without any specific options. The out-of-the-box configuration was fine for our basic setup:

```
<webflow:flow-executor id="flowExecutor"/>
```

The only notable sub-element used within `flow-executor` is **`<webflow:flow-execution-repository>`**, which lets you customize the internals of the flow executor. It has two interesting attributes: namely, `max-execution-snapshots` and `max-executions`. We will illustrate how you define them in Listing 12-6 and then describe them in the next paragraph.

***Listing 12-6.** Customizing the Flow Registry Configuration*

```
<webflow:flow-executor id="flowExecutor" flow-registry="flowRegistry" >
    <webflow:flow-execution-repository max-execution-snapshots="30"↵
                                       max-executions="5"/>
</webflow:flow-executor>
```

The `max-execution-snapshots` and `max-executions` attributes allow you to fine-tune how far back you can go in "the past." In the preceding code sample, we have set them to their default values. Thus, specifying 30 for `max-execution-snapshots` and 5 for `max-executions` has the same effect as not specifying them at all because these are the default values when no other values are in place. We entered these values in the code snippet to illustrate how to use these attributes, as well as to highlight their default values.

In Chapter 10, we mentioned that each request into a flow execution creates a snapshot of its state before the response is returned (see Chapter 10's Figure 10-2 and its depiction of the Web Flow state management mechanism). The `max-execution-snapshots` attribute maps to how many of these snapshots within a flow execution can be stored. If we set this value to 0, then it will not be possible to go to a previous state within a flow execution. In fact, your Back button will look like it doesn't work. A value of -1 means "unlimited"—you would probably never want to use this value because you want to keep the size of the user's session within limits.

The `max-executions` attribute maps to how many concurrent flow executions can be active within a given session. Whenever you start a new flow execution (and you don't end the previous one explicitly), you can still go back to the previous one—it remains stored together with all it states, depending on the value of the `max-execution-snapshots` attribute. So, the configuration in Listing 12-3 means that you can go back five previous flow executions; and within each flow, you can browse the last 30 view states. Again, a value of 0 disables this feature completely, while -1 sets the amount to infinite (remember: you probably don't want to use that value).

For both the `max-execution-snapshots` and the `max-executions` attributes, whenever the configured maximum value is reached, Web Flow will respectively remove the oldest snapshot or the oldest execution. So, if we were to set `max-executions` to 2, then, after starting the third execution, Web Flow would simply clean up and remove the first started execution. The same principle goes for the `max-execution-snapshots`.

▪ **Note** These settings are always applicable for a user's session, but not for the entire application. So, if we set `max-conversations` to 5, that would mean that each user (and thus each session) could have a maximum of five conversations active at the same time (if a sixth conversation is started, the oldest is cleaned up and removed by Web Flow).

▪ **Caution** We are telling you right here and now that you should think about these defaults. You probably want to tweak them to fit your needs, especially if you have lots of `view` states in your flows and you store lots of state in your flows—in such a case, these defaults would start to hog memory very fast (hence, you would probably want to bring these numbers down). For a memory-heavy application (or a memory-poor environment), setting `max-execution-snapshots` to 5 and `max-executions` to 1 is a perfectly sound setting. Also, most applications don't need to be able to go back more than five states or more than one previous flow execution. If you don't need this state "save/restore" snapshot functionality at all, then set both values to 0 to disable it.

Changing the Expression Parser

In the previous chapter, we saw how we could use the `<webflow:flow-builder-services>` to customize behavior. A feature we haven't discussed yet is the `expression-parser` attribute. This attribute will allow you to plug in another parser that supports other types of expression language.

By default, Web Flow uses SpEL as its expression language. Depending on your background or preferences, you might want to switch the expression language to something else.

Another good reason to change your expression parser might be that you are migrating from Web Flow 1. In the next section, you will see that there is a tool to help you migrate your Web Flow 1 flows to Web Flow 2 syntax. However, this migration will not change your expressions. Setting OGNL as the default expression language could help you in upgrading Web Flow step-by-step.

As it turns out, switching the expression language is just a matter of configuring the correct class in the `expression-parser` attribute (see Listing 12-7).

Listing 12-7. Changing the Expression Parser

```
<webflow:flow-builder-services id="flowBuilderServices" view-factory-
creator="mvcViewFactoryCreator" conversion-service="conversionService" validator="validator"
development="true" expression-parser=""/>
```

In Listing 12-7, we left the `expression-parser` attribute empty. For example, specifying the following class, `org.springframework.webflow.expression.el.WebFlowELExpressionParser`, will enable you to use the unified expression language (EL) as it is used, for example, in JSF. If you use the `org.springframework.webflow.expression.WebFlowOgnlExpressionParser` class instead, then OGNL will be enabled as the expression language (this is the default in Web Flow 1).

Web Flow 1 Migration

This section may not be of interest to you if you didn't use Web Flow 1, or you're not involved in a Web Flow 1 project. However, we wanted to make sure that you are aware of the possibilities of migrating, in case you do happen to be a Web Flow 1 user, or in case you come across a project using Web Flow 1 that you want to migrate. Even if it doesn't apply to you, you can quickly skim this section because it is very short and might be of help in the future.

Although there was a lot of rework in Web Flow 2, conceptually from a user's point of view, it remains very much like Web Flow 1 (which is a good thing). That said, it does add some new stuff, refactor some quirks, and implement some internal optimizations. Web Flow 2's flow-definition syntax also very much resembles that of Web Flow 1; however, it is *not* backward compatible. An <inline-flow> element is an example of this. This feature was simply removed in Web Flow 2, and there is no replacement. Fortunately, Web Flow 2 does offer you a tool that will convert your Web Flow 1 flows, so they can be used in Web Flow 2 (this tool comes bundled with Web Flow 2).

Suppose you have the Web Flow 1 flow shown in Listing 12-8 and that you want to migrate this flow to Web Flow 2, which no longer supports <inline-flow>.

Listing 12-8. *A Web Flow 1 Flow to Be Converted to a Web Flow 2 Flow*

```
<?xml version="1.0" encoding="UTF-8"?>
<flow xmlns="http://www.springframework.org/schema/webflow"
    xmlns:xsi="http://www.w3.org/2001/XMLSchema-instance"
    xsi:schemaLocation="
      http://www.springframework.org/schema/webflow
      http://www.springframework.org/schema/webflow/spring-webflow-1.0.xsd">

    <var name="someVar" scope="flow"/>

    <start-state idref="loadDetail"/>

    <action-state id="loadDetail"/>

    <inline-flow id="testInlineFlow">
        <flow/>
    </inline-flow>
</flow>
```

To run the flow definition updater tool, you will need the following jars on its classpath: the main Web Flow jar, which is named org.springframework.webflow-2.3.0.RELEASE.jar if you downloaded it manually; the Spring core jar, which is named org.springframework.core-3.1.0.RELEASE.jar if you downloaded it manually; and an XSLT processor. When running Java6 or later, the XSLT processor that comes shipped by default as part of the JRE will be sufficient, so you won't need any additional jar(s). If you do encounter any problems, it is advised that you download Saxon (the home edition). In that case, you just have to put the jar file (saxon9he.jar at the time of writing) in the same directory where you are putting the Spring core and Spring Web Flow jar files.

As described previously, you put the Spring core and Web Flow dependencies together with the flow from Listing 12-8 in a single directory; in this case, that directory is /tmp/convert. If you do a directory listing, it should look like this:

```
/tmp/convert$ ls -l
org.springframework.core-3.1.1.RELEASE.jar
org.springframework.webflow-2.3.0.RELEASE.jar
web-flow-1-flow.xml
```

Next, fire up the converter:

```
java -cp *: org.springframework.webflow.upgrade.WebFlowUpgrader web-flow-1-flow.xml
```

The output is shown on the console and not stored in a file. You can use your console tooling to *pipe* the output to a file, if desired. The output generated with the preceding command is an equivalent flow definition converted to Web Flow 2 flow syntax (see Listing 12-9)

***Listing 12-9.** The Web Flow 2 Converted Flow*

```xml
<?xml version="1.0" encoding="UTF-8"?>
<flow xmlns="http://www.springframework.org/schema/webflow
    xmlns:xsi=http://www.w3.org/2001/XMLSchema-instance
    xsi:schemaLocation="
        http://www.springframework.org/schema/webflow
        http://www.springframework.org/schema/webflow/spring-webflow-2.0.xsd"
    start-state="loadDetail">

    <var name="someVar"/>
    <action-state id="loadDetail"/>

    <inline-flow>
    <!-- WARNING: inline-flow is no longer supported.  Create a new top level
        flow.
     -->
      <flow xsi:schemaLocation="http://www.springframework.org/schema/webflow
      http://www.springframework.org/schema/webflow/spring-webflow-2.0.xsd">
      </flow>
    </inline-flow>
</flow>
```

In the preceding snippet, you can see that the <start-state> element has been moved to the top-level flow element as an attribute. The <start-state> element does not exist anymore as a separate element in Web Flow 2. Also, the <inline-flow> element is extracted as a separate flow with a warning that you should add it as a top-level flow.

■ **Note** While this tool will help you convert your Web Flow 1 flows, be aware that the definitions around scoping (especially for flash scope) has been altered in Web Flow 2. Also, the conversion requires changes to other aspects, such as the flow execution listener API (these changes are covered in following sections). A migration from Web Flow 1 to Web Flow 2 is not as easy as just running this tool. You will still need to go through the flows and a portion of your code to check whether additional modifications are required. However, this tool will at least put you on the right track. Finally, depending on how many Web Flow 1 flows you have, and assuming your Web

Flow 1 flows are using OGNL (chances are high because that was the default), it might be a good idea to switch your expression language in Web Flow 2 to OGNL, as well. This way, you are at least relieved from having to change every expression in your flows.

Exception Handling

There are three major ways in which you can deal with exception handling while using Web Flow. We have already (indirectly) seen the first of these. In that case, we let the application controller handle the exception. In the com.apress.prospringmvc.bookstore.web.controller.AuthenticationCortroller authenticate method, you can see that we return another event type (of type error) in case the authentication fails after adding a message to the message context (see Listing 12-10).

Listing 12-10. The Authenticate Method of the AuthenticationController

```
public Event authenticate(AuthenticationForm authenticationForm,
                          MvcExternalContext externalContext,
                          MessageContext messageContext) {
    try {
        authenticate(authenticationForm, ((HttpServletRequest)
        externalContext.getNativeRequest()).getSession());
    } catch (AuthenticationException authenticationException) {
        messageContext.addMessage(new
        MessageBuilder().error().code(LOGIN_FAILED_KEY).build());
        return new EventFactorySupport().error(this);
    }
}
```

The flow can react to this event type. In the case of an error event, the flow will do something else (e.g., render the same view again, so that error messages are shown) instead of continuing, which would be the case if the event was a successful event. Capturing exceptions in your application controller and steering the outcome using specific events is the preferred way of dealing with exceptions. To some extent, this might be a matter of personal preference; however, when working with an application controller, this approach makes it more visible if the exception handling is also performed inside the method itself, rather than delegating it to the flow.

However, there are two other mechanisms you can use to handle exceptions, both of which involve handling the exceptions within the flow:

- The on exception transition attribute
- A custom exception handler via the <exception-handler> element

The On Exception Transition

If you work with the on exception transition, you can specify the fully qualified exception class as the attribute's value. The transition will automatically be triggered if one of the other executions in that state triggers the exception or any of its subclasses. You can only specify on or on-exception for a given transition, not both. For example, in the authentication flow, you could have added an on exception transition like the one in Listing 12-11.

Listing 12-11. A view State with an On Exception Transition

```
<view-state id="authenticate" view="login" model="authenticationForm">
    <transition on="authenticate" to="authenticationOk">
        <evaluate expression="authenticationController.authenticate↵
                            (flowScope.authenticationForm, ↵
                             externalContext, messageContext)"/>
    </transition>

    <transition on="previous" to="previous"/>

    <transition on-exception="com.apress.prospringmvc.bookstore.↵
                            service.AuthenticationException"↵
                            to="authenticate"/>
</view-state>
```

When dealing with the exception inside the flow using the on exception transition, we need to rethrow the com.apress.prospringmvc.bookstore.AuthenticationException in the AuthenticationController instead of catching it and returning an error event. In that case, the return value of the method is void.

If no exception occurred, then the execution of the application controller method completes normally, without a result value. This would automatically be translated into a successful event by Web Flow, and the execution would continue as normal. If the AuthenticationException error is thrown, then the on exception transition is executed. In this case, the to attribute transitions to the same view state and renders the same view. This allows us to display the error messages added by the application controller's authenticate method.

Custom Exception Handler

Flow execution exception handlers can be attached to either a flow or a state using the <exception-handler bean=""> element. When an exception occurs in a flow execution, Spring Web Flow will first try the exception handlers attached to the current state of the flow. If none handles the exception, the exception handlers attached to the flow itself will be tried. If the exception is not handled by any of the available exception handlers, it will be rethrown.

The bean attribute of this element identifies an org.springframework.webflow.engine .FlowExecutionExceptionHandler bean available in the Spring application context (see Listing 12-12). You can attach any number of exception handlers to the flow or any of its states.

Listing 12-12. The FlowExcecutionExceptionHandler Interface

```
package org.springframework.webflow.engine;

import org.springframework.webflow.engine.support.
        TransitionExecutingFlowExecutionExceptionHandler;
import org.springframework.webflow.execution.FlowExecutionException;

public interface FlowExecutionExceptionHandler {

    public boolean canHandle(FlowExecutionException exception);
    public void handle(FlowExecutionException exception, RequestControlContext↵
    context);
```

```
}
```

The first method has an `org.springframework.webflow.execution.FlowExecutionException` as its parameter. Web Flow wraps an exception that was thrown in the flow execution inside a `FlowExecutionException`. You can access the original thrown exception by calling the `getCause` method on it. It is also possible that the actual type is one of the different subclasses of a more specific Web Flow exception (e.g., an `org.springframework.webflow.execution.ActionExecutionException`, which is a subclass of `FlowExecutionException`). In this `canHandle` method, you can determine if you want the exception handler to be invoked for the type of exception. If the `canHandle` method returns true for a given exception type, then the second method, `handle`, is called to let you handle the exception. However, if you look at the return type of the `handle` method, you will see that there is more difficulty involved than just handling the exception and returning void.

Where an on exception transition just delegates navigation to Web Flow (i.e., upon a certain exception, it navigates to a given state), a custom exception handler is expected to drive the navigation itself, after dealing with the exception.

If implemented incorrectly, a `FlowExecutionExceptionHandler` can leave a flow execution in an invalid state, which can render the flow execution unusable or its future use undefined. For example, you define a `FlowExecutionExceptionHandler` on flow level. When an exception gets thrown at flow session startup (e.g., in an `<on-start>` element) the exception gets routed to the exception handler. The exception handler must transition the flow to its start state after dealing with the exception. The handler should not simply return—thereby leaving the flow with no current state set—because that would leave the flow execution in an undetermined state. This extra complexity is the tradeoff you have to make when deciding to use the `FlowExecutionExceptionHandler` over the on exception attribute. The former gives you more control over the exception-handling process, but it also confers more complexity. The latter does everything for you, but you don't have any programmatic control over the exception-handling process.

■ **Tip** When using custom exception handlers, it is advised to use the support class, `org.springframework.webflow.engine.support` `.TransitionExecutingFlowExecutionExceptionHandler`. When using this support class, you can be sure that navigation is handled as it should be after handling the exception. This class can be configured with a map of exceptions to handle and a matching target state that should be executed after dealing with the exception. By default, this class also exposes the exception on `flash` scope. You can override the `handle` method to perform custom exception handling. In that case, it is advised that you call `super.handle` at the end of the method, so that the exception is still exposed on `flash` scope, and the transition to the target state is executed.

You configure a `TransitionExecutingFlowExecutionExceptionHandler` with one or more mappings that consist of an exception class as the key and a target state id as the value. These two values become the exception mapping. Whenever an exception is thrown within the scope of the handler, the `TransitionExecutingFlowExecutionExceptionHandler` will check whether it has a mapping for the given exception by comparing the exception class of the thrown exception with those in its initially configured mapping. If a mapping exists, the `exposeException()` method is called, and finally, the flow will transition to the target state you indicated with that particular mapping.

When looking up exceptions, the TransitionExecutingFlowExecutionExceptionHandler will not only consider the FlowExecutionException (or any of it subclasses), but also its cause chain. An exception from the cause chain will also match with a mapping for one of its superclasses. For example, a FlowExecutionException instance wrapping a java.io.FileNotFoundException will match with a mapping for java.io.IOException because that is a superclass of FileNotFoundException.

A TransitionExecutingFlowExecutionExceptionHandler can be configured as a normal Spring bean, as shown in Listing 12-13.

Listing 12-13. Configuring a TransitionExecutingFlowExecutionExceptionHandler

```
@Bean
public TransitionExecutingFlowExecutionExceptionHandler
                                    ioFlowExecutionExceptionHandler() {
    TransitionExecutingFlowExecutionExceptionHandler
    handler = new TransitionExecutingFlowExecutionExceptionHandler();

    handler.add(IOException.class, "targetState");
    return handler;
}
```

The ioFlowExecutionExceptionHandler can then be configured as the bean attribute of the `<exception-handler>` element:

```
<exception-handler attribute="ioFlowExecutionExceptionHandler"/>
```

We have seen that Web Flow gives us three ways of dealing with exceptions:

- Inside the application controller. We do so by catching the exception and adding the appropriate message to the Messagecontext.

- Inside the flow by specifying the on exception attribute of a transition.

- Inside the flow by specifying an `<exception-handler>` element that uses a FlowExecutionExceptionHandler. This element can either be declared in a fine-grained manner inside one of the five states, or in a coarse-grained manner for the entire flow (in that case, the `<exception-handler>` element is a direct sibling of the flow element).

The question is this: when is it most appropriate to use each of these techniques? When working with application controllers in combination with your flow, the first approach is probably the most natural. It gives you direct control over the exception-handling process, and it remains coupled to the code.

However, if you execute services or facades directly from within your flow (not using any application controller), then you can only react to exceptions using flow functionality. In that case, using the second approach (i.e., using the on exception attribute) would be the preferred way to deal with application exceptions.

The last approach, using a FlowExecutionExceptionHandler, is more applicable for overall exception behavior. For example, assume you want to log whenever an exception arises. You could handle that by declaring a FlowExecutionExceptionHandler on flow level.

Explicit Form Binding

In Chapter 11, we saw that when a model is specified, the request parameters submitted with the form are bound to the model. This happens automatically when you specify a model, and you don't explicitly turn off binding for a given transition.

After binding, the model gets validated when it contains validation methods or a custom validator exists, as we have seen in the validation section of the preceding chapter.

Sometimes, this automatic binding can be too coarse-grained. If you want more control over the request parameters that get bound, you can specify a binder, as shown in Listing 12-14. For example, suppose that not every property on your model is used on your page. You could have properties that are private to the application and are never rendered on the view (e.g., helper methods for exploiting the model). Because Web Flow automatically tries to map every request parameter, a user could abuse this by submitting a value for these properties (by manipulating the request URL and parameters). Chances are pretty small that this will be exploited because the user must to know the name of the property, and this property's name is used nowhere in these pages. But still, it could be a potential hole in your security. If you have a model that contains "application private" properties that should never be populated with request parameters, then you can use a binder that explicitly lists only those properties that are allowed to be bound with incoming request parameters.

Listing 12-14. Specifying a Per-Property Based Binding

```
<view-state id="authenticate" view="login" model="authenticationForm">
    <binder>
        <binding property="username" required="true"/>
        <binding property="password" required="true"/>
    </binder>

    <transition on="authenticate" to="authenticationOk" >
        <evaluate expression="authenticationController.authenticate(↩
            flowScope.authenticationForm, externalContext, messageContext)"/>
</transition>

    <transition on="previous" to="previous" bind="false"/>
</view-state>
```

In the preceding code, we explicitly bound the username and password from the request parameters to the model. We also marked them as required; when the value is absent, an error message will be added. We will discuss how these messages are localized in a moment.

There is also a third attribute: converter. You can use this to point to a named converter. This works with the older Spring Web Flow conversion mechanism, but it should no longer be used.

In Chapter 11, we explained that we create converters from the org.springframework.**core**.convert.converter package and not from the org.springframework.**binding**.convert.converter package. The Spring core conversion service does not support named converters. Hence, using a named converter would mean that you need to explicitly register it with the Web Flow custom conversion service, but it cannot be used as such (via naming) in Spring MVC. This way of working is discouraged.

The preferred approach is to create an org.springframework.core.convert.converter.Converter, and then register it as a Spring bean and with an org.springframework.format.support .FormattingConversionServiceFactoryBean for Spring Web Flow. This will cause the right converter to be chosen automatically.

Finally, notice that we specified bind="false" on the previous transition. The previous transition is triggered via a normal submit button in the form. The only difference is the event id. Without explicitly disabling binding, we can require that the username and password be filled in to go back.

▪ **Caution** You might recall from Chapter 11 that we had a Previous button in the sample application, as well. In that example, we tackled this issue programmatically by checking the state in the model validation method:

```
if (context.getUserEvent().equals("next")) {
...
```

In this case, the better solution is to indicate that binding="false". If you rename a transition in your flow, the code in the model will break. So, for simple cases, it is better to set the flow binding attribute to false. Nevertheless, the programmatic solution might be convenient in some cases where certain validations need to be conditionally performed, depending on the state.

We marked both username and password as required, but how are they localized to an error message? In order for the required message to show up, we must declare the message keys. Web Flow follows a predefined structure in trying to find the key that belongs to a field that is missing:

- required
- *<fieldname>*.required
- *<modelname>*.*<fieldname>*.required

In our message bundle (messages_xx.properties), we used the third option:

```
authenticationForm.password.required=Password is required
authenticationForm.username.required=Username is required
```

Another possibility is to use required and a place holder. The first placeholder contains the field name:

```
required= {0}: is required
```

Finally, you need to declare a standard <form:errors> in your JSP with the path of the field to show the error for the different fields:

```
<form:errors cssClass="error" path="password"/>
<form:errors cssClass="error" path="password"/>
```

Note In addition to the `required` error type, there are also others you can use, such as `typeMismatch`. When an adequate type conversion cannot be executed, an error of this type is added. You can find other error types by looking at implementations of `org.springframework.binding.mapping`
`.MappingResult`. The implementation's `getCode()` method returns the error type. The following error types exist and might be raised: `required`, `propertyNotFound`, `evaluationException`, and `typeMismatch`. You can define messages for these errors in the same manner as just discussed.

Web Flow AJAX Support

Web Flow has support for AJAX on both the server and client sides. The server side supports selective partial rendering via the `<render>` element, on which one or more fragments can be specified that need to be rendered.

On the client side, there is a JavaScript library available that will automatically interpret the partial responses and execute the partial page refreshes.

The JavaScript part is based on the Dojo framework and is branded Spring JS (Spring JavaScript). It is packaged as part of Web Flow, but as a separate artifact. This means you have to put a separate dependency in your build system to obtain this dependency because it does not come directly with the main Web Flow dependency. In our sample project, `build.gradle`, we explicitly defined this dependency (see Listing 12-15).

Listing 12-15. Defining the Extra Dependency via Gradle on Spring JS

```
compile "org.springframework.webflow:spring-js:$springSwfVersion"
```

This dependency contains the AJAX `ViewResolver` and the AJAX Tiles view. You will also get JS resources as a transient dependency. This dependency contains the JavaScript dependencies. The convention is to put them under `META-INF/web-resources` (see Figure 12-1).

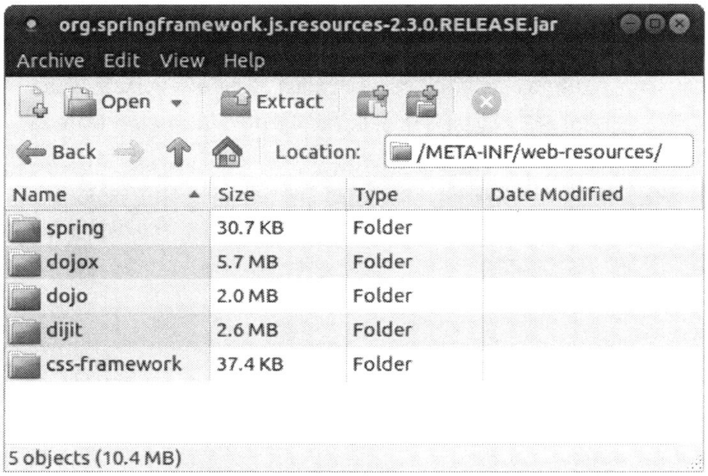

Figure 12-1. *The directory structure of the Spring JS resources, which shows a central web-resources folder under which all artifacts are packaged*

The same convention is followed in our sample application. This relaxes the number of places where resources can be found, and it lets us get away with a single resource handler definition in our Spring MVC configuration, `com.apress.prospringmvc.bookstore.web.config` `.WebMvcContextConfiguration`:

```
public void addResourceHandlers(ResourceHandlerRegistry registry) {
  registry.addResourceHandler("/resources/**/*")↵
        .addResourceLocations("classpath:/META-INF/web-resources/");
}
```

Before we can use that AJAX functionality, we need to set up different elements. This section will summarize those elements, providing an overview of what we will need to address for the sample application to support AJAX partial rendering:

- We need to enable the special AJAX `ViewResolver` with the AJAX Tiles view. This `ViewResolver` has special support built-in for detecting AJAX requests.

- We need to rework a page, so that we can rerender a part of it via an AJAX call. We also need to adjust the `tiles-config.xml` with the separate fragment that we will rerender.

- We need to adjust the flow with the `<render>` element and specify the fragment to render.

- Finally, we need to use the Spring JS in our page to start an AJAX request and let it partially refresh the part of that page that matches the fragment.

446

Configuring Web Flow for AJAX

Let's begin by replacing the standard `UrlBasedViewResolver` with the AJAX decorated `org`
`.springframework.js.ajax.AjaxUrlBasedViewResolver` in the `WebMvcContextConfiguration` class (see
Listing 12-16). The `org.springframework.web.servlet.view.tiles2.TilesView` is also replaced with the
`org.springframework.webflow.mvc.view.FlowAjaxTilesView`.

Listing 12-16. Configuring the AjaxUrlBasedViewResolver for Ajax support in
WebMvcContextConfiguration

```
@Bean
public ViewResolver tilesViewResolver() {
    UrlBasedViewResolver urlBasedViewResolver = new AjaxUrlBasedViewResolver();
    urlBasedViewResolver.setOrder(1);
    urlBasedViewResolver.setViewClass(FlowAjaxTilesView.class);
    return urlBasedViewResolver;
}
```

In the preceding example, we simply replace the existing view resolver with the Ajax decorated one.
When a non-AJAX view is detected, the behavior is the same as for a normal URL-based view resolver.

Preparing the View

Now that we have configured Web Flow for AJAX, we will change our view by partially rerendering a part
using an AJAX call (as opposed to triggering a complete page refresh). In this section, we'll see what
modifications we have to make to support this.

We will also have to modify the Tiles configuration, but we'll tackle that in a separate section to keep
things separated and to make them easier to understand.

We will start in our `selectBooks.jsp` view, where there is a form that allows us to add books to the
order. Once the books are added, they are immediately shown in the table below the selected book. This
will be a good candidate for partial rendering, as seen this in Figure 12-2. We added three different books
to the table: *Effective Java, Refactoring: Improving the Design of Existing Code*, and *Practical API Design:*
Confessions of a Java Framework Architect.

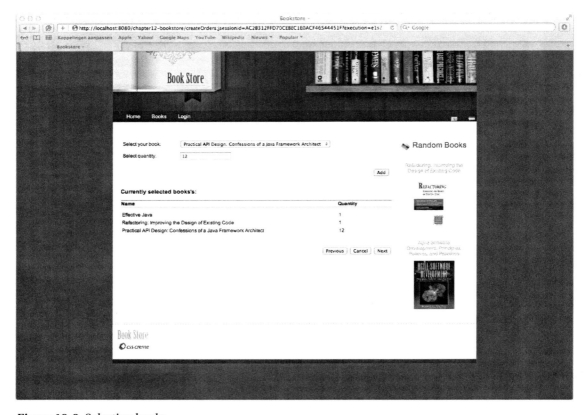

Figure 12-2. Selecting books

What we will do is extract the table part from the selectBooks.jsp view and put it in a separate view named showSelectedBooks.jsp, which is located at WEB-INF/view/createOrders/showSelectedBooks.jsp (see Listing 12-17).

Listing 12-17. The showSelectedBooks.jsp view

```jsp
<%@ taglib prefix="c" uri="http://java.sun.com/jsp/jstl/core"%>
<%@ taglib prefix="spring" uri="http://www.springframework.org/tags"%>
<%@ taglib prefix="form" uri="http://www.springframework.org/tags/form"%>
<%@ taglib prefix="fn" uri="http://java.sun.com/jsp/jstl/functions"%>

<div id="selectedBooks" style="margin-top: 10px; margin-bottom: 10px;">
    <table style="width: 100%;" rules="groups">
        <thead>
            <tr>
                <th width="80%" align="left">
                    <spring:message code="label.page.books.book.name"/>
                </th>
```

```
            <th width="20%" align="left">
                <spring:message code="label.page.books.book.quantity"/>
            </th>
        </tr>
    </thead>
    <tbody>
        <tr height="10px" />
            <c:forEach items="${orderForm.books}" var="book">
                <tr>
                    <td>${book.key.title}</td>
                    <td>${book.value}</td>
                </tr>
            </c:forEach>
        <tr height="20px" />
    </tbody>
</table>
</div>
```

■ **Note** We should point out that we explicitly named the top-level `<div>` element with an `id` attribute. In our case, we named it `selectedBooks`. In the following sections, we will see that it is used to identify the part of the page that should be replaced by the incoming AJAX response. The AJAX response will contain the rendered partial `showSelectedBooks.jsp`, as shown in Listing 12-17. By inspecting the first element, Spring JS knows which piece of HTML to replace on the actual page. In this case, it will look up the `<div>` with `id` `selectedBooks` and replace it with the version that came in via the AJAX response.

Next, in the `selectBooks.jsp` view, we are going to add a Tiles placeholder to insert the content from `showSelectBooks.jsp` (see Listing 12-18). To this point, we are still just playing with Tiles, and we have not done anything special that is Web Flow AJAX related. Thus far, this example could be a normal refactoring where we want to extract a part into a separate view (e.g., for readability, easier maintenance, or reuse).

Listing 12-18. The Tiles attribute in createOrders/selectBooks.jsp

```
<h3>
    <spring:message code="label.page.books.selected.books"/>
</h3>
<tiles:insertAttribute name="selectedBooks"/>
```

Where the `<tiles:insertAttribute>` is now located, we previously had the JSP code that has been moved to `showSelectedBooks.jsp`. Before Tiles will replace this with the real content, we must tell it about this new attribute.

We also explicitly gave the form an `id` attribute of `selectBookForm`; we will need this later when applying AJAX. For the sake of convenience, we'll provide the modified `WEB-INF/view/createOrders/selectBooks.jsp` page in Listing 12-19, with these changes applied.

Listing 12-19: The selectBooks.jsp after our modifications

```jsp
<%@ taglib prefix="c" uri="http://java.sun.com/jsp/jstl/core"%>
<%@ taglib prefix="spring" uri="http://www.springframework.org/tags" %>
<%@ taglib prefix="form" uri="http://www.springframework.org/tags/form" %>
<%@ taglib prefix="fn" uri="http://java.sun.com/jsp/jstl/functions" %>
<%@ taglib prefix="tiles" uri="http://tiles.apache.org/tags-tiles" %>

<form:form id="selectBookForm" modelAttribute="orderForm" action="${flowExecutionUrl}">
    <table style="width: 100%">
        <tr>
            <td colspan="2">
                <form:errors path="books" cssClass="error"/>
            </td>
        </tr>
        <tr style="height: 10px;"/>
            <tr>
                <td>
                    <spring:message code="label.page.books.select.book" />
                </td>
                <td>
                    <form:select path="book" items="${selectableBooks}"
                                 itemLabel="title" itemValue="id"/>
                </td>
            </tr>
            <tr>
                <td>
                    <spring:message code="label.page.books.select.quantity"/>
                </td>
                <td>
                    <form:input path="quantity" />
                    <span style="margin-left: 5px">
                        <form:errors path="quantity" cssClass="error"/>
                    </span>
                </td>
            </tr>
            <tr height="10px"/>
            <tr align="right">
            <td colspan="2">
                <button type="submit" id="add" name="_eventId_add">
                    <spring:message code="label.page.books.add.book"/>
                </button>
            </td>
        </tr>
    </table>

    <p/>
    <h3>
        <spring:message code="label.page.books.selected.books"/>
    </h3>
```

```
<tiles:insertAttribute name="selectedBooks"/>

<div align="right" style="margin-bottom: 20px;" >
    <button type="submit" id="previous" name="_eventId_previous">
        <spring:message code="button.previous"/>
    </button>
    <button type="submit" id="previous" name="_eventId_cancel">
        <spring:message code="button.cancel"/>
    </button>
    <button type="submit" id="next" name="_eventId_next">
        <spring:message code="button.next"/>
    </button>
</div>
</form:form>
```

Configuring Tiles

For the selectBooks view, we simply used the configuration shown in Listing 12-20.

Listing 12-20. The current Tiles configuration for selectBooks.jsp

```
<definition name="selectBooks" extends="fullTemplate">
    <put-attribute name="content" ↵
            value="/WEB-INF/view/createOrders/selectBooks.jsp"/>
</definition>
```

This snippet tells Tiles that it should render the full template, replacing the content of the Tiles placeholder with the selectBooks.jsp view. What we want now is to extend this because selectBooks is also a template at this point.

Let's begin by creating a new template that identifies selectBooks as a template. This template will be included in the original selectBooks definition. To illustrate this, we will give it an *internal* name: show.selected.books. As you can see in Listing 12-21, this has the selectBooks view as a template, and instructs it to replace the selectedBooks Tiles placeholder with the newly created view, /WEB-INF/view/createOrders/showSelectedBooks.jsp.

Listing 12-21. The new Tiles definition for the showSelectedBooks.jsp with selectBooks.jsp as a template

```
<definition name="show.selected.books"↵
template="/WEB-INF/view/createOrders/selectBooks.jsp">
    <put-attribute name="selectedBooks"↵
     value="/WEB-INF/view/createOrders/showSelectedBooks.jsp"/>
</definition>
```

Finally, we need to link this template with the content attribute of the main template. This is actually the same as the original configuration we had; but instead of pointing to the actual view, we point to the definition we just created: show.selected.books (see Listing 12-22).

Listing 12-22. The adapted selectBooks Tiles definition using the previously defined show.selected.books as content

```
<definition name="selectBooks" extends="fullTemplate">
    <put-attribute name="content" value="show.selected.books"/>
</definition>
```

Figure 12-3 shows our new layered design. Until now, we've had the main template (fullTemplate), which filled its content directly with a page (e.g., WEB-INF/view/createOrders/selectBooks.jsp). However, in that page, we've also included a Tiles placeholder. With the configuration we've just created, we can also make a second template that renders selectBooks.jsp, but replaces its content attribute with the showSelectedBooks.jsp page.

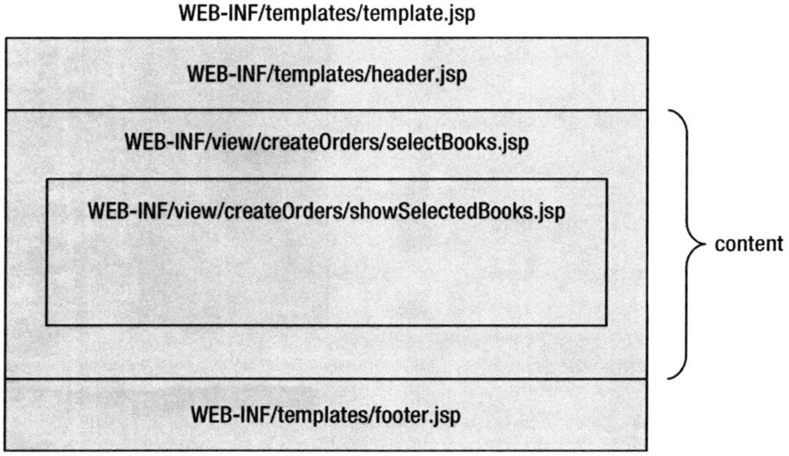

WEB-INF/templates/template.jsp

Figure 12-3. The selectBooks page as it will be finally rendered, including all compositions

Let's summarize what we've done so far: these two Tiles definitions together form our new configuration. If The selectBooks view is rendered, the template fullTemplate will be used, and the tiles content placeholder will be replaced with show.select.books. The latter refers to another Tiles definition which in turn renders /WEB-INF/view/createOrders/selectBooks.jsp and replaces the Tiles selectedBooks placeholder with the /WEB-INF/view/createOrders/showSelectedBooks.jsp view.

■ **Note** The show.selected.books definition is part of a composition, and we will never render this directly because we will still need to include it in a definition that extends from the fullTemplate (in our case, the selectBooks definition). If we were to render show.selected.books directly, we would see the selectBooks.jsp page with the included showSelectedBooks.jsp; however, we would still be missing the header and footer because these have not yet been inserted into the main template. Since the top-level definition we are rendering is still called selectBooks (we just changed its internal composition), nothing must be changed in our controllers or flows, and the view name remains unaltered. By the way, there is also a shorter notation for defining this composition that uses an inline form. This will yield the same result, but is syntactically a bit more elegant. We will illustrate this when we refactor the Tiles configuration in the "Flow Managed Persistence Context" section later in this chapter.

With this code in place, we can already test the refactored application. It should yield the exact same results that it did before we changed the composition by moving the "show selected books" result table into a different view; in other words, the merged view that is being rendered should be same as the view rendered before.

Adjusting the Flow

As discussed previously, we have to indicate which parts need to be rerendered explicitly. We can do this with the <render> element, which takes a fragments attribute (see Listing 12-23). This attribute will point to the Tiles attribute to render. We can also specify multiple fragments by separating them with a comma, and we are also allowed to use expressions (that must evaluate to Tiles attribute names, just as their literal equivalents do).

If we take the createOrders-flow, we can add the render element in the add transition. The render element only makes sense for transitions that rerender the same view, so we can mark the Tiles attribute, selectedBooks, for rendering. This means that the <put-attribute name="selectedBooks" value="/WEB-INF/view/showSelectedBooks.jsp"/> will be rerendered when the partial render is triggered.

Listing 12-23. Rendering fragments in the createOders/createOrders-flow.xml

```
<view-state id="selectBooks" view="selectBooks" model="orderForm" >
    <on-render>
        <evaluate expression="orderController.↵
                initializeSelectableBooks(orderForm)"
                result="flashScope.selectableBooks" />↵
    </on-render>

    <transition on="add" >
        <evaluate expression="orderController.addBook(flowScope.orderForm)" />
        <render fragments="selectedBooks"/>
    </transition>

    <transition on="next" to="selectDeliveryOptions" />

    <transition on="reset" to="selectBooks">
        <evaluate expression="orderForm.resetSelectedBooks()" />
    </transition>

    <transition on="previous" to="selectCategory" />

    <transition on="cancel" to="end" />

</view-state>
```

Adding AJAX to the View with Spring JS and JQuery

Finally, we need to physically invoke an asynchronous call from our browser. Doing this will request a partial page update, causing that specific piece of our DOM to be updated. Unfortunately, the XMLHttpRequest API (the browser API leveraging asynchronous support) is a bit problematic to use because of the nonstandard support for this feature over different browsers.

Fortunately, we have been blessed by some very good JavaScript frameworks that hide all those dirty details for us as application developers. We will discuss two options. The first uses Spring JS, which we already have because we are depending on it. The second relies on JQuery, which we will need to download a separate library for. Let's begin by demonstrating how to implement the client-side AJAX using Spring JS.

Using Spring JS

In this example, we will use Spring JS to make an AJAX call when a user pushes the Add button (see Listing 12-24). The Add button is a normal HTML submit button, and it will remain untouched.

Listing 12-24. The submit button that remains unchanged

```
<button type="submit" id="add" name="_eventId_add">
    <spring:message code="label.page.books.add.book"/>
</button>
```

A central concept in Spring JS is the notion of applying decorations to existing DOM nodes. This technique is used to progressively enhance a web page so that it will still be functional in a browser that has JavaScript disabled or simply has problems with JavaScript itself. The addDecoration method is used to apply these decorations, and we will use this method to add an Ajax decoration to the already existing submit button with the id of add.

In order to be able to use the AJAX libraries, we have to include references to them in our pages. Because we are using templates, this is pretty easy; these references are simply added in the HTML head section of our template. We can see this in the sample application when opening template.jsp (see Listing 12-25).

Listing 12-25: The extra JavaScript imports required to enable Ajax

```
<spring:url value="/resources/dojo/dojo.js" var="dojo"/>
<script type="text/javascript" src="${dojo}"></script>
<spring:url value="/resources/spring/Spring.js" var="springJs"/>
<script type="text/javascript" src="${springJs}"></script>
<spring:url value="/resources/spring/Spring-Dojo.js" var="springDojo"/>
<script type="text/javascript" src="${springDojo}"></script>
```

■ **Note** The script element is assumed to be non-empty. If you close such an element with the (normally syntax equivalent) "/>", the scripts are not loaded. That's why they are explicitly closed with </script>. This has nothing to do with Spring JS; rather, it is an HTML peculiarity.

Next, we have to decorate the button with the AJAX handler. We can do this by adding the script in Listing 12-26 to the selectBooks view, which is added at the bottom of WEB-INF/view/createOders/selectBooks.jsp.

Listing 12-26. The JavaScript decoration, which will enable AJAX on the add button

```
<script type="text/javascript">
    dojo.addOnLoad(function() {
        Spring.addDecoration(new Spring.AjaxEventDecoration({
        elementId : "add",
        event : "onclick",
        formId: "selectBookForm"
        }));
    });
</script>
```

Several key things are worth noting about the preceding listing:

- The elementId is the id of the HTML element to which the decoration should be applied. In our case, it is the submit button with the id of add.

- The event is the trigger event of the HTML element, which invokes the decoration. In our case, it is add button's onclick event.

- The formId must match the form that contains all the information that is required to be submitted along with the Ajax request. We added this id to the form element in Listing 12-19.

- The dojo.addOnLoad() method will make sure the decoration is added after all elements are loaded. This method may not be required for this type of decoration, but it is considered a best practice to use it unless you have good reasons not to. By the way, it does not matter where you place the <script> element. We chose to put it at the bottom, but it could have appeared anywhere in the file.

The decoration will submit the form, causing all input to be transmitted to the server. Because of the AJAX decoration, this happens in an asynchronous fashion. It will take the name from the button as the event id to be triggered (which is also transmitted with the parameters). The request is actually a normal form submission. Figure 12-4 shows what you'll see if you inspect the request with Firebug.

Figure 12-4. Firebug's capture of the request and showing of the request parameters

On the server side, the request is identified as an AJAX request by the AjaxUrlBasedViewResolver. When the flow resumes, it finds out that we wanted to execute the add transition, based upon the event id in the request parameters. It also knows that there is a render element specified in the flow definition. With this information, it has enough to continue selecting the view part that should be rendered.

■ **Note** if you look carefully at Figure 12-4, you will see that there is an ajaxSource POST parameter listed in bold under the Parameters column (it is the second parameter). This is noteworthy because there is no such component defined in our view. This parameter is added by Spring JS. It allows Web Flow to identify the request as an AJAX request. You can see that in org.springframework.js.ajax .SpringJavascriptAjaxHandler:

```
protected boolean isAjaxRequestInternal(HttpServletRequest request, HttpServletResponse ↵
response) {
String acceptHeader = request.getHeader("Accept");
String ajaxParam = request.getParameter(AJAX_SOURCE_PARAM);
if (AJAX_ACCEPT_CONTENT_TYPE.equals(acceptHeader) || StringUtils.hasText(ajaxParam)) {
    return true;
} else {
    return false;
    }
}
```

The response received by the browser once Web Flow has finished executing the request is a partial response that contains data only from the showSelectBook view. We can use Firebug to verify that this is indeed the case (see Figure 12-5).

Figure 12-5. *Firebug capturing the partially rendered response*

As you can see, the result contains only a portion of the entire page; namely, just the part defined in the showSelectedBooks.jsp. The JavaScript that receives the partial view update will now try to match an element with the same type and id as in the update (that is why we explicitly named the id of the <div> element selectBooks). It will then replace that content with the received update.

That's it! If you now click the Add button, you'll notice that the browser no longer performs an ordinary form submission or page refresh. For example, in Safari you will no longer see the submit form progress bar in the browser's status bar, which pops up when you click the add button. Now the view update that occurs when pushing the add button will give a smoother impression because only the table containing the selected books is updated, not the entire page.

Using JQuery

Instead of using Spring JS, the client part can also easily be replaced by other JavaScript libraries. For example, you might be more familiar with JQuery (or ProtoType or another library). These libraries will yield the same effect, as long as the mandatory extra request parameters _eventId_xxx and ajaxSource are present. These parameters were automatically added by Spring JS, but they need to be added manually when using other JavaScript libraries.

For example, if you replace the Spring JS script with the JQuery script in Listing 12-27, you will see that this also works without any problem. To create that script, we need to download the latest version of JQuery (version 1.7.1 at the time of writing) and add it to the HTML head section.

Listing 12-27. *The extra JQuery imports in WEB-INF/templates/header.jsp*

```
<spring:url value="/resources/jquery/jquery-1.7.1.min.js" var="jquery" />
<script type="text/javascript" src="${jquery}"></script>
```

Next, we can replace the Spring JS with a JQuery equivalent in `WEB-INF/view/createOrders` `/selectBooks.jsp`, as shown in Listing 12-28.

Listing 12-28. *The Spring JS JavaScript replaced by JQuery*

```
<script type="text/javascript">

    $(function () {
        var submit = $('#add');

            submit.click(function() {
                var form = $('#selectBookForm');
                var event = submit.attr('name');
                var data = form.serialize()+ '&amp;' + event + '=' + event +↵
                        '&amp;ajaxSource=' + submit.attr('id');

                $.ajax({
                    type: "POST",
                    dataType: 'text',
                    url: form.attr( 'action' ),
                    data: data,
                    success : function(result) {
                        $('#selectedBooks').replaceWith(result);
                    }
                });
            return false;
        }):
    });
</script>
```

As you can see, the JQuery alternative requires more code. We could probably make it a bit shorter, but Spring JS has the advantage of being optimized specifically for this job. However, if you're used to JQuery, you might find this to be a better alternative.

The script builds every step manually. We start by adding a click event listener to the add button, which is our submit button for adding new books. The event listener is bound when everything is loaded.

You can also see that, when we compose the request data in the `data` variable, we serialize the form for adding all input elements, and we manually add the parameters `ajaxSource` and `_eventId_xxx`.

> **Note** $(#xxx) is a JQuery selector that finds objects in the DOM based on their id. $(function () {}) is a shorthand for $(document).ready(function(){}). It has the same function as dojo.addOnLoad(function(){}.

Next, we assemble the request, and we identify the submit button and the form. We serialize the form, and we manually append the required parameters. These parameters are based on the name and id of the submit button. The URL to submit to is taken from the form, as well. With this URL, we can now perform the POST Ajax call, and the URL and parameters are the same as those sent out by the Spring JS. As a response, we get the partially rendered view back from the server. The only thing left to do is replace the entire target object with the HTML response content.

It must be said: when using JQuery, you should also take care that you handle errors that come back from the server. When working with the Spring JS, you get automatic support for error detection: errors are nicely shown in a popup window. Also, it is possible to show the rendered content directly in a popup window.

Flow Execution Listeners

When executing a flow, Web Flow will go through different steps before it actually performs a transition or executes a method on your application controller. For example, we have already seen that the flow execution is paused after the view has been rendered and sent back to the client. Likewise, when a new request comes in for an existing flow execution, the flow execution needs to be resumed. Pausing and resuming a flow execution are just two of the steps that Web Flow will be performing, but there are many more. We say that these steps are part of the Web Flow *lifecycle*, which consists of the (noteworthy) steps that Web Flow goes through when executing a request. Web Flow will allow us to configure an implementation of an org.springframework.webflow.execution.FlowExecutionListener that will receive callbacks when any of those special lifecycle steps take place.

Getting a callback from these lifecycle steps is typically useful only for more infrastructure-related code (e.g., crosscutting concerns). For example, you could use the FlowExecutionListener to apply special security checks. Or, you could use it to log access. The functionality offered by a FlowExecutionListener looks a lot like that offered by Aspects in that sense that it is transparent to the actual target, regardless of whether any of those callbacks happened.

The FlowExecutionListener is in no way a replacement for Aspects, which remain more powerful. However, Aspects are also more complex. You should evaluate whether the flow execution listener approach is sufficient to do the job you want to do. If not, you can still revert to AOP.

In the following sections, we will cover how we can write our custom FlowExecutionListener. Finally, we will walk through all of the methods in the FlowExecutionListener and give a detailed explanation about each of them.

Writing Flow Execution Listeners

Writing a flow execution listener is as simple as implementing the FlowExecutionListener interface. This interface defines a lot of callback methods that will be invoked when certain things happen in the course of a flow execution life cycle. Spring Web Flow also provides an org.springframework.webflow.execution.FlowExecutionListenerAdapter as a convenience class, which implements all of the methods defined by the FlowExecutionListener interface using empty method bodies. You can also subclass FlowExecutionListenerAdapter and override only those methods that you require at a given time.

■ **Note** The flow execution listener is by no means using AOP or any byte-code manipulation. It is a hook built into the Web Flow subsystem to give you callbacks for certain events during the flow execution. This is comparable to a web container that calls back on a registered HttpSessionListener to inform you about a session creation or destruction.

Flow execution listeners are declared via the flow executor (see Listing 12-29). Their order is important; if more than one flow execution listener is defined, their callback methods will be called in the order in which the listeners are defined in the <webflow:flow-execution-listeners> element. The flow execution listener defined on top is called first; the listener immediately that one is called next; and so forth.

Listing 12-29. Configuring the flow execution listener

```
<webflow:flow-executor id="flowExecutor" flow-registry="flowRegistry">
    <webflow:flow-execution-listeners>
        <webflow:listener ref="loggerListener" />
        <webflow:listener ref="securityListener" />
    </webflow:flow-execution-listeners>
</webflow:flow-executor>
```

You can also specify the criteria attribute on the <webflow:listener> with a comma separated list of flow ids. This will enable a given listener only for the given flows. If you leave it empty, the listener is enabled for all flows. This is the equivalent of specifying an asterisk (*), which is the default value for the criteria attribute if you don't specify it. Flow ids and the asterisks are the only allowed values for this attribute (see Listing 12-30).

Listing 12-30. Configuring the flow execution listener only for a specific flow id

```
<webflow:flow-executor id="flowExecutor" flow-registry="flowRegistry">
    <webflow:flow-execution-listeners>
        <webflow:listener ref="loggerListener" criteria="myFlowId" />
        <webflow:listener ref="securityListener" />
    </webflow:flow-execution-listeners>
</webflow:flow-executor>
```

Flow Execution Listener Methods

The FlowExecutionListener interface defines a lot of methods that can inform you when Web Flow is executing (or is about to execute) different steps in processing your flow execution request. For example, you can get callbacks when resuming or pausing an execution, triggering events, executing actions, and so on. Such callback methods become unpleasant when there are too many of them and they are badly documented. They can also be unpleasant to use if you have too few of them, and you cannot use the listener to capture what you need. In this subsection, you will find a complete explanation of each of the callbacks methods, so that you are prepared to make the right choice for a given job.

We don't suggest trying to remembering all of these; it is better to quickly skim over them, so you know what the possibilities are. When you need such functionality, you can return to this section and verify which callback suits your requirements best. The thing to keep in mind is this: some execution listener methods are very similar, but also sneakily different. You should always make sure you test properly and don't assume that a given listener method does what you think it will do.

Let's look at the methods defined by the `FlowExecutionListener` interface. (Note that we left out the return type for better readability, it is always `void`.) A flow execution listener method cannot return anything; if it changes something, it should do so with the parameters supplied to the callback method in question.

requestSubmitted(RequestContext context)
requestProcessed(RequestContext context)

`requestSubmitted` is invoked at the beginning, and `requestProcessed` is invoked at the end of a request entering a flow execution. `requestSubmitted` is the first method that is called of all the `FlowExecutionListener` callback methods, while `requestProcessed` is the last method called. You can use these callbacks if you want to perform something upfront in the processing lifecycle that has an impact over the entire request execution. Note that, when a new flow execution is started, the `requestSubmitted` callback is called *before* the flow execution is actually started (there will be no active flow yet at that time). The equivalent is also true with `requestProcessed`: when a flow execution terminates (because it hits an end state), the flow will already be terminated when `requestProcessed` is invoked. You can test whether the flow execution is active by using `context.getFlowExecutionContext().isActive()`.

sessionCreating(RequestContext context, FlowDefinition definition)

`sessionCreating` is called to indicate that a new flow execution is about to be created. An exception may be thrown from this method to veto the creation of a new flow execution by throwing any kind of runtime exception.

sessionStarting(RequestContext context, FlowSession session, MutableAttributeMap input)

`sessionStarting` is called after a new flow execution is created, but before that new flow execution actually starts. In the case of launching a subflow, the flow execution has not yet been started, so the parent flow execution is still active. The input parameter is the input map that will be passed to the spawning flow, as prepared by the subflow state `<input>` mapping or as provided externally. The listener is also allowed to manipulate the input. A listener could veto the start of the newly starting flow execution session by throwing any kind of runtime exception.

sessionStarted(RequestContext context, FlowSession session)

`sessionStarted` is called after the new flow execution has been initialized and started processing. Startup behavior has already been performed (e.g., a flow `<on-start>` or the `<on-entry>` of the first state that is executed). This callback is useful if you want to do something every time a flow session has been started and initialized successfully.

eventSignaled(RequestContext context, Event event)

`eventSignaled` is invoked every time an event is signaled in the flow execution. The event could be an event signaled externally by the user or an event signaled internally (e.g., by an application controller). This method is called prior to the transition actually taking place.

transitionExecuting(RequestContext context, TransitionDefinition transition)

`transitionExecuting` is called when a transition is matched, but before the transition occurs. It is interesting to compare this method to `eventSignaled`; in this case, the transition is further along. At this stage, you already know the source and (what will be) the target of the transition, whereas in `eventSignaled`, you simply know "something" is going to happen.

stateEntering(RequestContext context, StateDefinition state) throws EnterStateVetoException

stateEntering indicates that the flow execution is about to enter a given state. This method will be called after the transition matched, but before the state has been entered (e.g., no entry actions are executed at this point). Note that the listener can veto entering the state by throwing an org.springframework
.webflow.execution.EnterStateVetoException.

stateEntered(RequestContext context, StateDefinition previousState, StateDefinition state)

stateEntered informs the listener that the flow has successfully transitioned from one state to the next. All entry logic of the given state has now been executed, and the state is fully initialized.

viewRendering(RequestContext context, View view, StateDefinition viewState)

viewRendering is called when a view selection has already occurred, and the information has been retrieved from the triggered view state. This happens before any render actions are executed.

viewRendered(RequestContext context, View view, StateDefinition viewState);

viewRendered is called after the view has been fully rendered, and it is ready to be sent back to the client.

paused(RequestContext context)

paused will be called after the active flow session has been paused, and the view has been rendered. Note that it will not be called if the flow execution ends (i.e., it passes through an end state). In that case, sessionEnding and sessionEnded will be called instead.

resuming(RequestContext context)

The resuming callback informs the listener that a paused flow execution has been restored and is going to resume.

sessionEnding(RequestContext context, FlowSession session, String outcome, MutableAttributeMap output)

sessionEnding is called when a flow hits an end state and is going to end the flow execution. At the point this callback method is invoked, the flow execution is still active. Possible <on-entry> actions (e.g., those that appeared on the end state) have already executed. If the flow is a subflow and has mapped out anything using the <output> mapping, it is also available via the *output* parameter. This allows the listener to inspect or manipulate the output returned to the parent flow. The *outcome* parameter matches the outcome reached by the ending session; this will be the id of the terminating <end-state>.

sessionEnded(RequestContext context, FlowSession session, String outcome, AttributeMap output)

sessionEnded is called after sessionEnding, when the flow execution has completely ended. When this method is invoked, the flow execution is no longer active. If the flow in question was a subflow and it mapped data back to the parent, then the flow output map can no longer be manipulated at this point. Also, if the parent flow has already been reactivated, but is not yet resuming. then session.isRoot() will indicate whether the session ended for a subflow (in that case, isRoot will be false) or for a parent flow (isRoot will be true).

exceptionThrown(RequestContext context, FlowExecutionException exception)

The exceptionThrown callback method will be called whenever an exception occurs during the processing of a request in an active flow execution. If there are flow exception handlers configured, they will be invoked after this method has been called.

Flow Managed Persistence Context

With this section, we come to the last feature of Web Flow that we'll be covering. This feature allows you to extend a JPA persistence context into your presentation layer, while making it persistent for the duration of an entire flow execution.

While this is a simple feature when seen from the Web Flow side, fully understanding when or why to use it is a bit more complicated. In this section, we will look in detail at what it actually can do for you, explaining and then illustrating how it works by using parts of the sample application.

This feature is not a solely Web Flow or web application-related feature. All the other things we have seen in the Web Flow chapters are related to how we do something in the presentation layer. However, this feature starts all the way back in the backend data access layer (DAL).

As you are aware from Chapter 1, we use an ORM to manage our persistence. To be vendor neutral, we opted to use JPA as the ORM API. Hibernate is used as provider for JPA. In doing this, we could let the application run with other JPA providers, as well (e.g., EclipseLink). You can distinguish this in the Repositories by the imports; we use classes from the javax.persistence package, which is the Java Persistence API part of the Java APIs.

JPA can be used either inside or outside a JEE managed context. We are using it outside a JEE managed context, which requires some manual intervention when it comes down to transaction management and other configuration. Thanks to Spring, we can simulate a managed environment, so that there is in fact little difference from using JPA within a managed environment.

> **Note** While we are running in a managed environment (Tomcat), we actually mean a fully managed/compliant JEE application server with or without the EJB profile. For example, Tomcat only implements a partial web profile of a JEE server, and it cannot be considered to be a managed environment from the JPA point of view. In Tomcat, at least from the JPA point of view, your application would have to deal with the transaction management itself, and JPA would be configured as in a normal SE environment.

From Database to View

Let's begin by explaining how the data access is handled in the sample application to this point. As explained in Chapter 1, we configured Spring to use JPA, and we use Hibernate as the ORM implementation. Our application follows a typical, simple three-layered approach: we have a presentation layer, a business (logic) layer, and a data access layer. Whenever our application controllers need something, they talk to a service. The service uses the domain model and repositories to retrieve data from a relational database.

The objects retrieved from database are called *entities*. An entity is part of the domain model and reflects data backed by the database. Such an entity is managed by JPA; or more precisely, by a persistence context. One of the features an ORM may offer is *lazy loading*. This feature allows you to retrieve only a small amount of data and (automatically) fetch additional data when you ask for it. For example, when retrieving an Order, we could lazily load the Customer. If we don't need the Customer in our processing, no Customer data is loaded. The less data we load, the better.

However, this feature only works when an entity is managed by the persistence context. Normally, the persistence context is closed when the transaction ends. Outside the transaction, the entity becomes *detached*. Calling a method to load additional data that was not loaded while the transaction was active will result in an exception being thrown (in case of Hibernate, you will see the famous org.hibernate .LazyInitializationException).

However, in our sample application, we have been using the org.springframework.orm.jpa.support .OpenEntityManagerInViewFilter. This means our business transaction is committed (or rolled back), but the persistence context is kept open. This also means that our entities remain managed, and we can still let them load data from our presentation layer (and thus, from within our views). However, we should be careful not to perform changes or create operations in the presentation layer because there is no longer a spanning transaction when using the entities. Each interaction will operate in its own transaction; this is unlike our business logic layer, where the entire service method call happens in one big transaction.

You can see this illustrated in Figure 12-6. We simulate a method call originating from the presentation layer that goes into the business logic layer, starting a transaction on its way. In the business logic layer, we are allowed to make modifications because all modifications we make are covered by the global transaction. The transaction is ended when the result is returned back to the presentation layer, either committing or rolling back the transaction. We can see that the entity is in a managed state in all layers. Outside of the business logic layer, however, there is no more transaction. Nevertheless, the persistence context is kept open for read operations during the render view phase, thanks to the OpenEntityManagerInViewFilter.

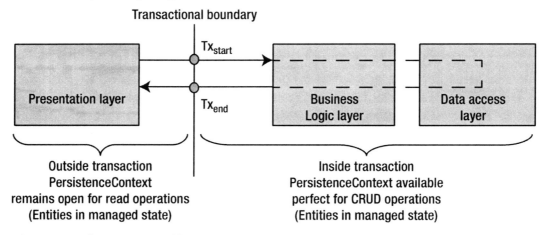

Figure 12-6. The transactional boundary lies on the business services

While this works great, the problem is that, once the view has been rendered, the OpenEntityManagerInViewFilter will close the persistence context before returning the view back to the browser. This means that, if you put an entity on (for example) flow scope, it will become detached. This becomes a problem if you need to load associations using that entity over multiple requests because that will again trigger a LazyInitializationException.

To explain this better, let's assume we show an order on the user's screen. In order to do this, we load the Order entity from database using our service. The Order entity is stored on flow scope and retrieved when the view is rendered to show the actual content of an order. Potentially, we also show some information about the account of the user, which requires an extra query to be performed from within the view to retrieve the `Account` entity. This is all good because everything is happening in the same request—our persistence context is still open, and our entity is still managed. After the view is rendered, the flow session is paused and the view is sent to the browser. But before the view was sent back, the `OpenEntityManagerInViewFilter` closed the persistence context. Until now, that was just fine because our view was rendered, anyway. However, suppose the order view allows the user to click an order that will show the details of the order (e.g., the products contained by the order). In that case, after the user clicks the detail button, a new request comes in and the flow session is resumed. When the view tries to get the `OrderDetail` entities from the `Order` entity (which is retrieved from flow scope), it will receive a `LazyInitializationException`. This is strange because the `OpenEntityManagerInViewFilter` opened a new persistence context when the request came in. While that is true, it will not reattach the entities that were detached when the previous request ended.

What this basically means is that, while the persistence context is extended into the presentation layer, it does not survive multiple requests. Once a request has been processed (and the view has been rendered), the persistence context is closed. When entities are stored on a given scope, they will be in a detached state when the next request comes in and tries to work with them.

Prolonging the Persistence Context

Web Flow allows you to prolong the continuity of the persistence context over multiple requests. This is known as the Flow Managed Persistence Context (FMPC) pattern. It is an extension to the Open EntityManager In View Pattern (OEMIV) which we have already been using (it is implemented by the `OpenEntityManagerInViewFilter`). As we explained in the previous section, the persistence context is opened when the request comes in, but is destroyed after rendering the view. In the OEMIV pattern, the persistence context is not retained across multiple requests; in the FMPC pattern, the persistence context is stored for the next request in the flow session.

The good thing about this pattern is that we can just touch whatever we need in our presentation layer because we still have an active persistence context during the entire execution of our flow.

When using the FMPC pattern, we also no longer need to denote an explicit business transaction. In our flow, there is only one place where we need a transaction, and that is in the last step: when we place the actual order. In the intermediate steps, we just perform read access, which actually requires no transaction; or at most, a read-only transaction if we retrieve different types of entities, and we want to keep a certain amount of consistency.

In Figure 12-7, we can see how Web Flow will ensure that the persistence context is bound and unbound from flow scope before starting or resuming a flow session. This will ensure that we are able to access the database from the different steps in our flow from the presentation layer, even on entities that are retrieved from flow scope.

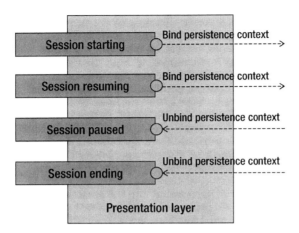

Figure 12-7. Automatic binding and unbinding of the persistence context by Web Flow

In this approach, the persistence context is opened when the flow session starts and remains open until the session ends. The pattern should be used with read-only operations and ended in a single create/update transaction when the flow ends, as we will illustrate later on.

When you make a call that requires data (e.g., a lazy initialization of a collection or property), a separate transaction is spawned, and the data is retrieved. This means that you don't need any @Transactional annotation on the services. If you need read consistency, you are allowed to do this; however, you are advised to make the transactions read-only. Any modifications you might make are not flushed until the update transaction is executed at the end of the flow.

Applying Flow Managed Persistence Context

We will rework our createOrders-flow to take advantage of the managed-persistence context. Let's begin by enabling the prolonged persistence context on a per-flow basis. We'll do so by using the `<persistence-context/>` element at the beginning of our createOrders-flow flow.

We need to enable a special flow execution listener (see Listing 12-31). This listener will bind and unbind the persistence context as a flow is starting, ending, pausing, or resuming (at least for each flow for which we've enabled the `<persistence-context/>` element).

Listing 12-31. Registering the flow execution listener that will handle the flow managed-persistence context

```
<webflow:flow-executor id="flowExecutor" flow-registry="flowRegistry">
    <webflow:flow-execution-repository max-executions="3" max-execution-snapshots="10" />
        <webflow:flow-execution-listeners>
            <webflow:listener ref="jpaFlowExecutionListener"/>
        </webflow:flow-execution-listeners>
    </webflow:flow-executor>

<bean id="jpaFlowExecutionListener" ↵
        class="org.springframework.webflow.persistence.JpaFlowExecutionListener">
    <constructor-arg ref="entityManagerFactory" />
```

```
        <constructor-arg ref="transactionManager" />
</bean>
```

The listener requires access to the javax.persistence.EntityManagerFactory (which will create the javax.persistence.EntityManager, also called the persistence context) and the transaction manager. The transaction manager is used to create a transaction when the flow ends. At that moment, the entity manager is joined with the transaction, so that your modifications can be flushed to the database in an all-succeed or all-fail fashion. You can see this in Listing 12-32, which is taken from the JpaFlowExecutionListener.

Listing 12-32. The JpaFlowExecutionListener, which joins the EntityManager with a transaction when ending the flow session

```
public void sessionEnding(RequestContext context, FlowSession session, ↵
                          String outcome, MutableAttributeMap output) {↵
    if (isParentPersistenceContext(session)) {
        return;
    }

    if (isPersistenceContext(session.getDefinition())) {
        final EntityManager em = getEntityManager(session);
        Boolean commitStatus = ↵
            session.getState().getAttributes().getBoolean("commit");

        if (Boolean.TRUE.equals(commitStatus)) {
            transactionTemplate.execute(↵
                new TransactionCallbackWithoutResult() {
                    protected void doInTransactionWithoutResult(↵
                                        TransactionStatus status) {
                        em.joinTransaction();
                    }
            });
        }
     unbind(em);
     em.close();
    }
}
```

The listener will also detect subflows, so that no transaction is executed when a subflow ends. The create/update transaction is only executed when the top-level flow ends.

Next, we need to indicate which end state will trigger the commit (see Listing 12-33).

Listing 12-33. The end state that triggers the commit

```
<end-state id="endOrderOk" ↵
view="redirect:/ordersOverview.html?orderOk=true&amp;orderId={orderId}" commit="true"/>
```

There is one thing left to do. Thus far, we've used the org.springframework.orm.jpa.support .OpenEntityManagerInViewFilter, which was configured in our com.apress.prospringmvc.bookstore.web .config.BookstoreWebApplicationInitializer. OpenEntityManagerInViewFilter and JpaFlowExecutionListener don't play nicely together. This makes sense if you think about it because they both try to extend the persistence context; however, only our JpaFlowExecutionListener will extend it a bit longer. Therefore, we need to disable the OpenEntityManagerInViewFilter. In Listing 12-34, you can see that we have put this in comments, so that it will not be loaded. We will now fully depend on the JpaFlowExecutionListener for extending the persistence context.

Listing 12-34. Disabling OpenEntityManagerInViewFilter in BookstoreWebApplicationInitializer

```
@Override
public void onStartup(ServletContext servletContext) throws ServletException {
    registerListener(servletContext);
    registerDispatcherServlet(servletContext);
    // We are using JpaFlowExecutionListener instead
    //registerOpenEntityManagerInViewFilter(servletContext);
}
```

That is all we need to do. What is happening now is that, during our flow execution, our entities remain managed. When the flow ends, we indicated that Web Flow should commit. This means that it will start a transaction and let the EntityManager join that transaction, so it can flush the modification operations (i.e., creates, updates, and deletes) to the database. This basically means that the createOrder method on our service does not require an @Transactional annotation anymore because the transaction is now managed by Web Flow.

■ **Note** When using disconnected transactions in the same flow (e.g., several read transactions in each step of the flow, followed by a modification transaction at the end), it is advised that we configure optimistic locking. In our case, this is not that important because we are inserting new data. However, this becomes very important if we want to update data that was previously read in a previous step of the flow (and thus belongs to a different transaction) because that data might be updated by the time we perform our modification transaction. Without optimistic locking, we could end up overwriting the changes of other users without knowing it.

Reworking the Orders Overview

The preceding section illustrated that we can use Web Flow to manage our transaction. and that it can create a committing transaction at the end of a flow that pushes out all changes to the database when the flow ends.

Finally, we want to illustrate that the persistence context is also available in our view for entities that are stored in a scope. Normally this would not be possible because the persistence context would no longer available after a request ended.

The Orders Overview page shows the orders a customer made. We will add an additional popup window that shows the details of the order. In the domain model, we have an Order that has a list of zero or more OrderDetails. At the moment, the orders overview is backed by a Spring MVC controller, and it is not governed by a flow. In Listing 12-35, we will begin building a flow for the orders overview. You can find this code at WEB-INF/view/ordersOverview/ordersOverview-flow.xml.

■ **Note** In Listing 12-35, we are building a flow for something that is not really a "flow"; rather, it is just an overview page with a detail. We created a flow purely in terms of the sample application, so we could demonstrate the flow-managed persistence context. In a real-world app, this would probably not benefit from being modeled as a flow.

Listing 12-35. The newly created ordersOverview-flow

```
<persistence-context/>

<view-state id="ordersOverview" view="ordersOverview">
    <on-render>
        <evaluate expression="orderController.retrieveOrders(
                externalContext.sessionMap.authenticatedAccount)" ↵
                result="viewScope.orders" />↵
    </on-render>
    <transition on="showOrderDetail" to="orderDetail">
        <set name="flashScope.order" ↵
             value="orders[requestParameters.index]">
        </set>
    </transition>
</view-state>

<view-state id="orderDetail" view="orderDetail" popup="true">
    <on-render>
        <render fragments="content"></render>
    </on-render>
</view-state>
```

The following aspects of the preceding listing are noteworthy:

- We have added the <persistence-context/>, which will enable the flow-managed persistence context for this flow (we did the same thing for our createOrders-flow).

- We also set the selected Order on flash scope using a <set> action. The index of the selected order is retrieved from the request parameters: orders[requestParameters.index].

- The first view state renders the ordersOverview view, which renders the ordersOverview.jsp.

- The second view state renders the orderDetail view, but will only partially render it. Because the popup attribute is set to true, this will, in conjunction with Spring's client-side JavaScript, render the content in a popup window.

In Listing 12-36, you can see the orderDetail.jsp, which is just a fragment of a complete page because it will be rendered as a popup.

Listing 12-36. The orderDetail.jsp, which will render the order details

```
<%@ taglib prefix="c" uri="http://java.sun.com/jsp/jstl/core"%>

<h2>Order detail</h2>
<div style="width: 550px; height: 100px; margin-top: 15px;">
    <table style="width: 100%;">
        <thead>
            <tr>
                <th align="left">Book title</th>
                <th align="left">Book description</th>
                <th width="60px" align="left">Book price</th>
            </tr>
        </thead>
        <tbody>
            <tr height="10px" />
            <c:forEach items="${order.orderDetails}" var="orderDetail" varStatus="status">
                <tr>
                    <td>${orderDetail.book.title}</td>
                    <td>${orderDetail.book.description}</td>
                    <td>${orderDetail.book.price}</td>
                </tr>
            </c:forEach>
            <tr height="20px" />
        </tbody>
    </table>
</div>
```

The Tiles configuration for this for is straightforward (see Listing 12-37).

Listing 12-37. The Tiles definition for orderDetail.jsp

```
<definition name="orderDetail" extends="contentOnlyTemplate">
    <put-attribute name="content" value="/WEB-INF/view/ordersOverview/orderDetail.jsp"/>
</definition>
```

In the preceding listing, we extend from the contentOnlyTemplate because the content will be rendered in a popup, so we don't need the header and footer, which are part of the fullTemplate.

In the ordersOverview.jsp, we still need to add the link that will make the Ajax call and open the popup window (see Listing 12-38). It is important that this link be nested in a form. We will also submit the index (which we retrieve from the JSTL supplied by a varStatus object) through a hidden field. This will allow us to determine which order we want to see the details from (as we have seen in the flow, it uses the index request parameter to determine the selected Order object in the list).

Listing 12-38. The link in the ordersOverview.jsp that will trigger the order

```
<c:forEach items="${orders}" var="order" varStatus="status">
    <tr>
        <td>${order.id}</td>
        <td>${fn:length(order.orderDetails)}</td>
        <td><spring:eval expression="order.orderDate" /></td>
        <td>${order.totalOrderPrice}</td>
```

```
<td>
    <form:form id="orderDetailForm_${status.index}" ↵
            action="${flowExecutionUrl}">
        <input type="hidden" name="index" value="${status.index}" />
        <a name="_eventId_showOrderDetail" ↵
            id="orderDetailLink_${status.index}" href="#">View</a>
    </form:form>
</td>
</tr>
</c:forEach>
```

We'll conclude by decorating the link with an Ajax decoration. Because we need both the link and the form— and because there are multiple versions of each—we use dojo to query all links where the id starts with orderDetailLink_. From that, we can parse out the index. With this information, we can also compose the id of the anchor to bind to, as well as the form. We also enable the popup functionality, so Spring JS knows to render the response inside a popup window. All of this is accomplished in Listing 12-39.

Note To enable the form to be shown as a popup window, we enabled the popup attribute on the view state that renders the popup content.

Listing 12-39. The JavaScript that will decorate the button and trigger an AJAX request to display the order details that will be shown in a popup window

```
dojo.query("[id^='orderDetailLink_']").forEach(function(element) {
    var index = element.id.substr(element.id.lastIndexOf('_')+1,element.id.length);
    Spring.addDecoration(new Spring.AjaxEventDecoration({
        elementId : element.id,
        event : "onclick",
        formId : "orderDetailForm_"+index,
        popup : "true"
    }));
});
```

With the final modification in place, we can run the application and go to the Orders overview page. We do this by clicking Orders overview in the navigation bar. Figure 12-8 shows the orders for our customer with the user id of jd.

Figure 12-8. *The new Orders overview page, which shows the orders and a link to view the details*

In the preceding code, the Order entity is stored on view scope. The Book entities of the OrderDetails page (which we will need in the details view) are not yet initialized. Finally, when a user clicks the View link, the details will open in a popup window (see Figure 12-9).

Figure 12-9. *Clicking the view link brings up a popup window that shows an order's details*

Web Flow placed the selected Order entity from view scope in flash scope. Next, we instructed Web Flow to render our view state of orderDetail. This view state shows information about the Book entity. In a normal situation, we would now receive a LazyInitializationException because the Book entity still has to be loaded. However, thanks to our flow-managed persistence context, the entities are still managed, and the extra data is loaded. We get the details without any exceptions being thrown.

To illustrate that this is really working, we switched back to the OpenEntityManagerInViewFilter and disabled the JpaFlowExecutionListener. We also disabled the CommonDataHandlerInterceptor in both the WebMvcContextConfiguration and WebflowContextConfiguration. The CommonDataHandlerInterceptor is responsible for loading the random books. When enabled, it will silently load books in our persistence context, and we will not be performing an objective test. Finally, we also have to mark the Book @ManyToOne association in the OrderDetail entity as lazy:

```
@ManyToOne(optional = false, fetch=FetchType.LAZY)
private Book book;
```

This is required because JPA (by default) loads many-to-one associations eagerly. If we don't explicitly tell JPA to load the association lazily, the Book entity will already be loaded when we load the overview page. The overview page indirectly loads the OrderDetail collection because it shows the number of books as part of the order. This is accomplished by calling the size method on the Collection of OrderDetails; therefore, this association must be initialized. This will implicitly trigger loading of the Book entity because it is eagerly fetched when the OrderDetail association is loaded. After making the Book association explicitly lazy, we can click a view link to see the details. As can be seen in Figure 12-9, we get an exception instead.

Figure 12-10. *An exception is triggered when loading the book details if you are not using the flow-managed persistence context.*

If we scroll further down in the stack trace, we will see that it was actually caused by a LazyInitializationException (see Figure 12-11).

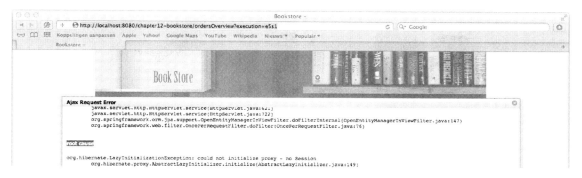

Figure 12-11. *The cause of the exception is a* `LazyInitializationException`

Summary

And that concludes the final chapter on Web Flow. We have now covered all the noteworthy features that Web Flow has to offer and even shown you how to use them.

In this chapter, we took a more advanced and in-depth look at some of the functionality that was introduced in the previous couple of chapters. For example, we showed you how to apply flow inheritance by implementing an extension on flow composition and modularity. We also showed how it is possible to perform explicit form binding and to deal with exceptions in the flow (instead of dealing with them in your application controllers).

And then we dove still deeper into executing Web Flow actions. For example, we discussed some powerful new features such as flow execution listeners, handling Ajax requests with Web Flow, and finally, the flow-managed persistence context.

There is one important thing that we did not discuss in these Web Flow chapters: security. Web Flow plugs seamlessly into Spring Security. We decided that it would be better to cover the topic of security in its own, standalone chapter. Our next (and final) chapter will cover Spring security for Spring MVC (this will be our starting point); and along the way, we'll show you how Web Flow fits into this security setup.

CHAPTER 13

Spring Security

As we all know, security is important for any application. This is especially true for web applications, which are exposed to the Internet. Exposure to outside threats is obvious, and dealing with it will be a major part of your effort to develop secure solutions. However, the challenges that confront a developer are not only external threats.

Because security doesn't add functionality, it is often underemphasized and sometimes even hard to justify in terms of time and resources. It often ends up being forgotten or implemented badly under the pressure of tight deadlines and the demands for fulfilling all functional requirements. Of course, it is a mistake to look at security in terms of "functionality."

Security should be looked at from the same perspective as writing tests or refactoring code. Testing doesn't add direct value in terms of new functionality, but it does improve existing functionality and enable future additions or bug fixes to be made without destabilizing your project. The same goes for refactoring. As a good developer, you refactor code on a daily basis, no matter how small the changes, to improve the application's performance and stability. Security should be considered even more important. Even though you may not be specifically asked for security, you should be aware of the threats to your application and make sure that what you deliver is as secure as possible.

On the other hand, do not forget that the entire "security" process is not entirely in your hands. Security crosses many layers. If you secure your application at application level, but the infrastructure team runs your app on a four-year-old web container without any patches applied, and a comparable operating system, you will probably get unwanted visitors no matter how secure your application is. It is important for organizations to understand the importance of security and everything that affects it.

From the organization's standpoint, the issue is not only a technical one. Awareness and perception also are very important. With even the slightest anomaly that can be exploited, customers or other users may consider an application insecure. Depending on the level of visibility your application enjoys, discovery of such anomaly (no matter how trivial) might trigger a storm of protest and give the organization bad publicity. This might even be worse than the damage an attacker is able to do with the attack itself!

In this chapter we will show you how to fulfill your duties as an application developer and make your application as secure as possible on the application level. We will do this by introducing you to Spring Security, which is a state-of-the-art, Spring 3.1-ready, security extension. In this chapter we will show you how to secure your application in a couple of hours! We will start off from a basic security configuration that secures your app with a couple lines of XML. Continuing from there, we will show how to use the database as storage for your users and credentials. We will also investigate how you can integrate security with Spring Web Flow. Finally, we'll discuss the different options for applying authorization checks with Spring MVC in our JSP pages and application controllers.

Introducing Security

Before we start talking about what Spring Security can do for you and how we are going to apply it to secure our application, we first need to provide some introduction to security. It is important that we first set the context in which Spring Security will operate. In the first part of this section, we will give an overview of application security, which is the type of security we are going to handle. Next we will look at some general security principles and terminology that will be important for a good understanding of the remainder of the chapter.

Finally, we give a more detailed summary of the topics we will cover in this chapter, so you'll know exactly what to expect. To be complete as possible, we will touch on different aspects of Spring Security;

What Is Application Security?

From a high-level view, application security is all about controlling access to your application's functionality. In our bookstore, for example, every user should be able to view the books we are selling. But not every user should be able to create an order without fulfilling some conditions (such as creating an account and being logged in). If we decided to further extend the bookstore with some CMS-like features, say editing or adding new books to the system, we would then want only a select set of users to be able to make modifications. With application-level security you will be able to specify which resources in your application are restricted, and which are publicly available. For the restricted resources you will be able to make further distinctions; a user who is able to access restricted functionality A would therefore not be allowed to access restricted functionality B.

Depending on your application's context, this set of rules might vary from very complex to nonexistent. In the first case you could be requiring detailed roles, complicated authentication mechanisms, and so on, while in the latter case you could be building a web site that has only read only content that is public for everyone, and so application security is probably not of your concern.

░ **Note** As explained in the introduction to this chapter, security crosses many layers, and not just your application layer. So that's why the topic here is explicitly "application security." No matter what level of application security your application demands, the environment surrounding your application needs to be secure. You should not be afraid to ask your network or infrastructure team what they are doing to keep the environment secure where your application will reside. An expression you probably are already familiar with summarize this very nicely: "your security is only as strong as its weakest point."

General Security Principles

We will start off covering some general security principles that will become important once you start securing your application:

- **Identification:** Identifies a user based upon a certain identity; such as a username, token or certificate.

- **Authentication:** The process of verifying the presented identity. In case of a username it is as simple as checking the supplied password.

- **Authorization:** The process of identifying the functionality an authenticated user is allowed to use.

If you need to provide application security, you will first have to think about how to *identify* your users. Identification will allow you to recognize a user who wants access to a protected resource. This is the first process in applying security. Identification can be simple, such as a username. It can also be a token, or even an x.509 certificate issued to a person or organization.

Next you will have to verify the identity that the user provides. This process of verifying the identity is called *authentication:* checking the identification for its authenticity.

In the case of a username, authenticity might be verified by asking for a password and comparing the entry with the password stored for that user.

Finally, if a user's identity is authenticated, the user is allowed access to the restricted zone of your application. At that point you might want to make distinctions among your authenticated users. In other words, you want to give certain privileges to authenticated users. Suppose you have a web store. Before ordering something, a user must be authenticated, because you want to know who made which order, you need access to the delivery/contact addresses, or maybe to stored payment credentials like a credit card number. However, it is clear that a normal customer who is authenticated as a user of your application should not be allowed to add or change products. Allowing or disallowing an authenticated user certain functionality is called *authorization.*

Spring Security will especially concentrate on the authentication and authorization parts. Also note that the method of authentication is in a certain way related to the type of identification your users will have to supply.

What We Will Cover

Spring Security, (formerly known as Acegi Security), has become a very important piece in the puzzle if you want to secure your application. Spring Security will especially help to secure your application by offering authentication and authorization schemes. It will help you provide integration with many authentication systems, such as a simple database, directory services (offering an LDAP interface, for accessing, for example, open LDAP or Active Directory). But it will also help you manage authorization. This chapter will cover how you can instruct Spring Security to take care of both the authentication and the authorization parts.

▨ **Note** Spring Security has generally seen a low intrusion level. This allows us to add security in the more final stages of our application implementation. Although some refactoring will be required, it will normally be very minimal. This is one of the reasons we kept this chapter as last.

We will start by making you familiar with the basic security configuration. We will configure Spring Security so that every request that goes into our application passes the security configuration. We will see that this configuration is based on a filter mechanism through which a request has to pass before it is received by the requested resource. We will also show you how easy it is to define which resources need to be protected and which can still be left publicly available (our login page, resources such as images, and so on).

For the authentication part we will be using username and password. We will use a login form, which will include the typical username and password fields. Besides creating the page (containing the login form) itself, we will see that we only need some XML configuration to let Spring Security handle this. (By contrast, in the previous chapters we coded our own authentication mechanism.) To keep things simple, the authentication will at this point be backed by a basic in-memory data store. Later we will see how can easily change this to a database store.

In applications using Web Flow, it's likely that a lot of your application controller logic and view selection has been moved into flows. Web Flow has support for securing flows directly. We will see how we can plug Web Flow into the security mechanism so that your application is secure from top to bottom.

After we configure the authentication, we will see how we can further secure the login and order process. Until we do that, all data is transmitted over plain HTTP. We will see that adding transport security is just a matter of configuration.

Next we will also look at localization. Spring Security supports localization of exception messages, which are by default in the English language. We will see what you should configure in order to support other locales.

We will also extend the security by implementing a role-based access model. This will grant rights to your users that you can later use to check authorization when requiring access to a given resource.

Authorization with Spring Security can be applied programmatically, by means of code, or declaratively. The declarative method will allow you to assert authorization using metadata in the form of annotations, expressions, or XML. We will cover how Spring Security's authorization can be applied in the following elements:

- Views, to be able to show which component is visible or for a given user

- Controllers

- Web Flow flows

- Service layer

We will cover both declarative security (using annotations) and programmatic security and show in detail how to apply them both in your views, application controllers, and flows. Finally we will introduce using the Spring Security Tag libraries in your JSP pages.

■ **Note** For your information, Spring Security can also be applied in the same declarative way on your back-end (mostly on the services) as it is for your application controllers. However, Spring Security in the back-end will not be covered in this chapter.

Preparing the Example Application

We are going to reuse the latest and greatest version of our example, from Chapter 12. This application includes Spring MVC functionality, flows, application controllers, and a service layer. It will be the ideal candidate for applying security.

In the current version, we have already applied a self-invented security mechanism. A user can enter the site and browse books without any restriction. Books can also be added to the shopping cart without restrictions. A user who is not authenticated, however, cannot do a final checkout and cannot view his or her orders. Before this is possible a user has to log in, by means of username and password.

To support this, we have a login form which takes the credentials and compares them to the information stored in our database. Once a user is authenticated, we put a token (the

`com.apress.prospringmvc.bookstore`
`.domain.Account` domain object) on the user's session to indicate that authentication was successful. (To refresh your memory, you can see this happening in the Chapter 11 section "Implementing Authentication as a Subflow"; Listing 11-39 demonstrates authentication via Spring MVC, and Listing 11-41 shows authentication via Web Flow.) As you will see, we can do all of this just by means of configuration using Spring Security instead of creating the security setup ourselves.

While our self-invented setup helped us to avoid some extra complexity at the time, and it apparently seems to do its job, there are still some serious flaws to be discovered if we look closer.

First, there is no security applied on controllers or flows. For example, let's go back to the previous example (Chapter 12) where we are still using our home-grown security implementation. Without being authenticated, try to start the orders overview flow directly by typing this URL in your browser to open the page shown in Figure 13-1:

`http://localhost:8080/chapter12-bookstore/ordersOverview`

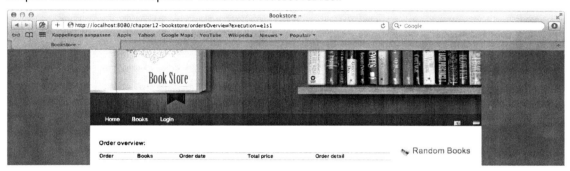

Figure 13-1. *Directly starting a flow bypasses security.*

You can see that we are not logged in, as the Orders overview is not available in the navigation bar. So even though this link is not available for an unauthenticated user, one can simply start it by copy/pasting the name of the flow in the browser's address bar, and the page will load. Talk about security flaws…

In this particular case no harm is done, and there is no even an exception being thrown. We are in luck; the only thing that happens is an empty order page. The service/repository will try to load the orders from account "null", which results in an empty list, so nothing is shown. However, it could have turned out otherwise. If we had developed the repository with less care, we might have omitted the criteria "user" when it was null; in that case it would result in retrieving *all* orders for *all* customers!

It is clear that this is a serious vulnerability, so we have to make sure that our security is, well, real security and cannot be longer circumvented by simply typing the correct URL in the browser address bar.

Second, there is also no way to make a distinction among authenticated users, and thus there is no way to limit access. Once a user is authenticated, he or she gets access to all restricted functionality, an approach that is in most cases too coarse-grained (most applications support different levels of authorization).

We brought this up just to show you that rolling out your own Security is not something to take lightly. Thankfully, Spring Security will solve these issues for us.

In our first attempt we will try to introduce you to the Spring Security basics and show you how easy it is to set up a basic security scheme that will already look very professional. It will:

- Make sure that no restricted functionality is accessible if the user is not authenticated, no matter what they try.

    - So the cheap URL trick will have no longer any effect.

    - Even a user who is authenticated will not be able to access pages or flows for which no explicit access rules are defined.

- Use form-based authentication, which will show the user a login page on which credentials can be entered using a username and password field.

- Redirect users to the login page automatically whenever they try to access a secured resource directly, and redirect them back to that resource after authentication was successful.

- Use Spring Security to do the authentication part instead of writing this kind of code ourselves.

We will explain some of the Spring Security architecture and internals as we go along securing the application. Later, in the following sections, we will extend this basic scheme and discuss more about authorization and how to apply it in our application. We will extend the application by adding functionality to add categories and books, which will only be available to a selection of authenticated users.

Securing Our Bookstore

To demonstrate the basic security scheme, we will apply it to our sample application. In this first section, we will show you how to

- Configure Spring Security to act as a giant wrapper for our application, so that every request that comes in passes via Spring Security

- Configure our login page

- Mark certain resources as available only for authenticated users

- Enable auto-redirection when a secured resources is accessed without being authenticated, and then redirect them back once authenticated

- Use Spring Security's out-of-the-box in-memory data store for users

- Store passwords securely with salted hashes

Adding the Right Dependencies

Before you can use Spring Security you have to declare the correct set of dependencies. Like Web Flow or Spring MVC, Spring Security is a module on which you must declare a specific dependency in order to use it. Conveniently, Spring Security itself is further divided into submodules. This is convenient because your project can depend on the modules it actually needs; no more, no fewer. This helps to keep your dependency tree clean, as no unused modules (which again have dependencies) are pulled into your project. The modules we will be using (and the ones you will probably always use to secure a web application) are listed in Table 13-1.

Table 13-1. *The Spring Dependency Modules Used in Our Example*

Module	Usage
spring-security-core	The Spring Security core library
spring-security-web	Web support, enabling Spring Security for the web tier
spring-security-config	Namespace Configuration Module, which allows easy and concentrated configuration within Spring
spring-security-taglibs	A set of JSP taglibs that will enable us to apply authorization constraints in our views

In the sample project, you will find these modules translated to dependency entries in the build.gradle (see Listing 13-1).

Listing 13-1. *Dependencies in gradle*

```
compile "org.springframework.security:spring-security-core:$springSecurityVersion"
compile "org.springframework.security:spring-security-web:$springSecurityVersion'
compile "org.springframework.security:spring-security-config:$springSecurityVersion"
compile "org.springframework.security:spring-security-taglibs:$springSecurityVersion"
```

Since Spring Security is a core dependency, we used a variable to indicate its version, $springSecurityVersion. The value of this variable can be found in the root Gradle file. (At the time of writing, it is 3.1.0.RELEASE.)

░ **Note** You've seen that Spring Security is divided into several modules. The modules we are depending on, as can be seen in Listing 13-1, are only a subset of these, since we will not be using every functionality Spring Security has to offer. In case you require other functionality (LDAP, for example) you have to include it as an extra module in your dependency list. A list of these modules can be found in the Spring Security reference under the dependency section[1]. Here you will see each module listed together with its own dependencies. The dependencies of the module itself are only there as information; they will be pulled in automatically by your build tool/dependency management system from the moment you add a dependency to one of the Spring Security modules.

---

[1] http://static.springsource.org/spring-security/site/docs/3.1.x/reference/appendix-dependencies.html

Enabling Spring Security

Before we can secure anything, we need to enable Spring Security. The core concept is that it will capture every request coming in to our system and decide if the request can go through or not. The mechanism to support this begins with a standard JEE Servlet filter.

Spring Security uses the Spring Core `org.springframework.web.filter.DelegatingFilterProxy` (which is an implementation of a standard `javax.servlet.Filter`), which will be configured to intercept every request. This filter will serve as a hook to delegate the captured requests to Spring Security. The configuration of the filter is done the same way as with the Spring MVC dispatcher servlet, in our `com.apress.prospringmvc.bookstore.web.BookstoreWebApplicationInitializer`. We can make use of the JEE dynamic servlet API to add this filter, as shown in Listing 13-2.

Listing 13-2. *Registering the Spring Security Filter in BookstoreWebApplicationInitializer*

```
private void registerSpringSecurityFilterChain(ServletContext servletContext){
    FilterRegistration.Dynamic springSecurityFilterChain = ↵
      servletContext.addFilter(BeanIds.SPRING_SECURITY_FILTER_CHAIN, new ↵
      DelegatingFilterProxy());
    springSecurityFilterChain.addMappingForUrlPatterns(null, false, "/*");
}
```

The first argument of `addFilter` is the name we will be giving to the filter. In this case the name of the filter we are adding is `springSecurityFilterChain`. We didn't choose a random name, but in fact referred to a Spring class containing these predefined names as constants (so the constant `org.springframework.security.config.BeanIds.SPRING_SECURITY_FILTER_CHAIN` has the value `springSecurityFilterChain`). When we cover the Spring side in a moment, we will explain why this filter's name is of importance. The second argument is the filter instance itself.

Also note that the filter `DelegatingFilterProxy` is a "catch-all" filter. Looking at the filter pattern "/*" it will capture ANY request (see Figure 13-2)! So there is no request that can go into our application without being captured by this filter.

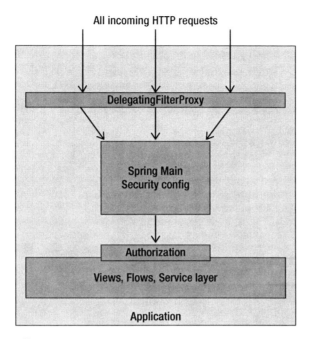

All incoming HTTP requests

DelegatingFilterProxy

Spring Main
Security config

Authorization

Views, Flows, Service layer

Application

Figure 13-2. Filter catches all requests.

The first parameter of addMappingForUrlPatterns (dispatcherTypes) indicates when the filter should be invoked. The default (when supplying null) is to invoke it for all requests coming from "outside" the Servlet container. You can also specify, for example, that the filter should be invoked when a resource is accessed by an internal include or forward statement. In that case you must supply a java.util.EnumSet with one or more enumerations of type javax.servlet.DispatcherType. Leaving this value as null is sufficient, since your resources are protected from the outside, and even when making includes or forwards you will be checking authorization on your pages using security tags (which we will cover later). However, in some situations it can be desirable to go through the security filter chain again when performing such operations.

The second parameter of the addMappingForUrlPatterns (namely isMatchAfter) declares the order if multiple filters match the same URL pattern (or the same Servlet); its value can be true or false. In that case filters are normally applied in the order they appear in the web.xml or when working via the API (as we do) in the order in which they are added in the code. If you supply true for isMatchAfter, the filter will be invoked last in the chain of filters that match for that given URL pattern (or Servlet). If multiple filters match for that same URL pattern (or Servlet) and also have set this flag to true, the order in which they are defined is used (but they will still match after all other filters). If this flag is set to false, the inverse happens, and the filter will be invoked before invoking other filters that map to the same URL (or Servlet). Since we are in control of all filters we register, we can change the order ourselves simply by altering the order in which we register them. So there is no need to think about this attribute, and we choose a value (false in this case) which we use for every other filter registration. In this case the order in which they are defined will determine the order in which they are invoked.

> ■ **Note** There seems to be an issue with Tomcat (7.0.26 at the time of writing), where this flag seems to be interpreted the other way around. So if you declare a `Filter` to be `isMatchAfter` equal to true, it will match before all other filters for the same URL pattern (or Servlet). We have posted a message on the Apache Tomcat development mailing list[2] for this.

Now that we have seen how all requests are captured by a filter, we will see how the requests end up in the Spring Security machinery. As the class name of the configured filter (**Delegating**FilterProxy) implies, it is clear that it will delegate incoming requests to somewhere. That "somewhere" is the core of Spring Security and is configured in our Spring configuration.

We created a separate spring configuration file for this, called `spring-security.xml`, located in `src/main/resources/spring/`. This piece of configuration will configure the "Spring Main Security Configuration" as illustrated in Figure 13-2.

To do this we first need to configure the Spring Security namespace that will contain all the artifacts we need to set up the main configuration (see Listing 13-3).

Listing 13-3. The xml header of the Spring security configuration file

```
<?xml version="1.0" encoding="UTF-8"?>
<beans xmlns="http://www.springframework.org/schema/beans"
       xmlns:xsi="http://www.w3.org/2001/XMLSchema-instance"
       xmlns:security="http://www.springframework.org/schema/security"
       xsi:schemaLocation="
         http://www.springframework.org/schema/beans
         http://www.springframework.org/schema/beans/spring-beans-3.1.xsd
         http://www.springframework.org/schema/security
         http://www.springframework.org/schema/security/spring-security-↵
         3.1.xsd">
```

Every security feature will use the namespace prefix "security."

> ■ **Note** You can also make the Spring Security namespace the default namespace. Here we have chosen to use the default namespace for the core Spring beans functionality, which is the default in all our other Spring configuration files as well. However, it would also work to switch them in this case, since this is a configuration file dedicated to Spring Security, where you will be using more of the Spring Security elements than from the bean namespace. In that case, you could drop the "security" prefix, as all security elements will be accessible in the default namespace, without any prefix. When there is a lot of security configuration, it can make your XML look less cluttered.

---

[2] http://markmail.org/message/5q7gpipxdiqxsu6p?q=+list:org.apache.tomcat.dev

Next, we need to define the "delegate" to which our DelegatingFilterProxy will delegate. This is done with the <security:http> element, as shown in Listing 13-4.

Listing 13-4: The Spring Security namespaced filter chain configuration

```
<security:http>
    <security:form-login login-page="/public/authentication/login.htm" default-target-↵
url="/public/main.htm"/>
</security:http>
```

What this element does is create a filter chain and registers it in the application context with the default bean ID springSecurityFilterChain. The DelegatingFilterProxy will use the name of the filter to look up this bean, and delegate control to it. If you name the filter someFilter, it will look up the filter chain with bean ID someFilter, which results in no bean being found. Before we continue we need to explain what the Spring Security filter chain is and what it will do for us.

The filter chain is the core component in capturing requests and dealing with what has to be done. Almost everything in the main Spring Security configuration is handled by a filter in the filter chain. You can plug in or remove filters at will, and every filter will have a specific job (see Figure 13-3).

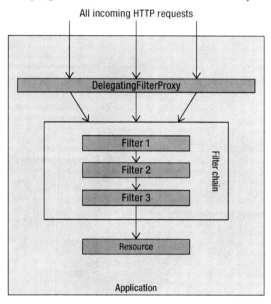

Figure 13-3. Filter delegates to the configured application filter chain

In Listing 13-4, we implicitly configured an element that will send the user to the login.htm (specified by the login-page attribute) page if accessing a secured resource without being authenticated. When the user logs in, the filter will automatically redirect the user back to the requested secured resource. Or, the user might be redirected to main.htm, which renders the home page (defined by the default-target-url attribute) if there was no previously requested secure page but the user logged in directly via the login page. In that case we also send a parameter, indicating that authentication was successful. The main page in question will detect this and show a message that the authentication process succeeded. This element will result in a filter being added to the filter chain to take care of this.

While you will be able to plug in your own custom filters, many existing filters are already at your disposal. It is beyond the scope of this book to discuss them all, but in the Spring Security reference manual[3] you will find more information about them.

For your convenience we have included the complete list here in Table 13-2. It will give you an idea of what is already available for you to use. The bean alias will be important to refer to the filter if you defined such. For example, if you add your own custom filters, you will be able to position them in the chain. Custom filters can be defined using the `<security:custom-filter />` element, for example `<security:custom-filter ref="myCustomFilter"/>`. By explicitly referencing these filters you can position them before or after a specific filter. For example, if you want to position `myCustomFilter` after the `FORM_LOGIN_FILTER`, you could define it as

```
<security:custom-filter ref="myCustomFilter" after="FORM_LOGIN_FILTER"/>
```

The namespace element or attribute is the configuration element that triggers the addition of the filter in the chain. The filters are listed in the table in the order they would be in the chain if you define them.

Table 13-2. *The Link Between the Created Filter and the Namespace Element or Attribute*

Bean alias	Filter class	Namespace element or attribute
CHANNEL_FILTER	ChannelProcessingFilter	http/intercept-url@requires-channel
CONCURRENT_SESSION_FILTER	ConcurrentSessionFilter	session-management/concurrency-control
SECURITY_CONTEXT_FILTER	SecurityContextPersistenceFilter	http
LOGOUT_FILTER	LogoutFilter	http/logout
X509_FILTER	X509AuthenticationFilter	http/x509
PRE_AUTH_FILTER	AstractPreAuthenticatedProcessingFilter Subclasses	N/A
CAS_FILTER	CasAuthenticationFilter	N/A

---

[3] http://static.springsource.org/spring-security/site/docs/3.1.x/reference/springsecurity-single.html#filter-stack

FORM_LOGIN_FILTER	UsernamePasswordAuthenticationFilter	http/form-login
BASIC_AUTH_FILTER	BasicAuthenticationFilter	http/http-basic
SERVLET_API_SUPPORT_FILTER	SecurityContextHolderAwareFilter	http/@servlet-api-provision
JAAS_API_SUPPORT_FILTER	JaasApiIntegrationFilter	http/@jaas-api-provision
REMEMBER_ME_FILTER	RememberMeAuthenticationFilter	http/remember-me
ANONYMOUS_FILTER	AnonymousAuthenticationFilter	http/anonymous
SESSION_MANAGEMENT_FILTER	SessionManagementFilter	session-management
EXCEPTION_TRANSLATION_FILTER	ExceptionTranslationFilter	http
FILTER_SECURITY_INTERCEPTOR	FilterSecurityInterceptor	http
SWITCH_USER_FILTER	SwitchUserFilter	N/A

As it turns out, we already configured a filter in Listing 13-4, by adding:

```
<security:form-login login-page="/public/authentication/login.htm" default-target-↵
url="/public/main.htm"/>
```

If you take a look at the Table 13-2, you will see that the http/form-login configured the UsernamePasswordAuthenticationFilter. This filter will leverage the previously described functionality of redirecting the user to the login page or the index page. As the name implies, it also covers other functionality, as we will discuss later.

Defining Which Resources to Secure

Next we must tell Spring Security which resource should be secured. This is again done by implicitly adding a filter to the filter chain. We don't declare a new filter, but instead use an existing one provided by Spring Security. We will use an element from the security namespace: <security:intercept-url>. If you look at Table 13-2, you will see that this element (intercept-url) matches the ChannelProcessingFilter and will be a child element of the http element. This is the filter that Spring Security will add automatically to the chain when we specify <security:intercept-url>. The filter will perform the authentication check if the resource you entered in the pattern matches with the resource requested.

At this point we have a mixture of flows and pages, the latter being controlled directly by a Spring MVC controller. We will list them here for completeness. For each we will indicate whether it should be available publicly or privately (authenticated access only). Let's start with the flows, in Table 13-3.

Table 13-3. *The Flows within the Application and the Level of Authentication Required*

Flow	Access	Description
`createOrders-flow`	Public	Allows a customer to select a book and enter all order details.
`placeOrders-flow`	Authenticated	Without being authenticated, you cannot place an order.
`ordersOverview-flow`	Authenticated	The orders are linked with a customer. If a customer is not logged in, it would be impossible to retrieve the orders.

Next, in Table 13-4 we will list the URLs for which there is an `@RequestMapping` in a Spring MVC controller. We again define if they should be available publicly or only after authentication.

Table 13-4. *The URLs within the Application and the Level of Authentication Required*

URL	Access	Description
`authentication/login.htm`	Public	The login page presenting username and password fields to enable the user to login to the application.
`main.htm`	Public	The homepage, showing an empty body with on top the menu and at right the random book image.
`index.jsp`	Public	Redirects to `main.htm`. Used when hitting the context root of the application. In that case the application server will automatically look for a welcome file and will find `index.jsp`.
`/resources`	Public	These are resources such as our JavaScript, CSS, and images, which are located under `/resources` via the configured resource handler.

To organize the pages that require public or authenticated access, we are going to group them under `WEB-INF/view/public` and `WEB-INF/view/secured`.

Configuring Access to Resources

Listing 13-5 shows the preceding access rules converted to our XML configuration and added to the base configuration we already put together in Listing 13-4.

Listing 13-5. Adding the intercept-url rules based on the request URIs we explicitly want to configure

```
<security:http use-expressions="true" >
    <security:form-login login-page="/public/authentication/login.htm" ↵
    default-target-url="/public/main.htm"↵
    authentication-failure-url="/public/authentication/login.htm"  />

    <security:intercept-url pattern="/index.jsp" access="permitAll" />

    <security:intercept-url pattern="/public/**" access="permitAll" />
    <security:intercept-url pattern="/secured/**" access="fullyAuthenticated"/>

    <security:intercept-url pattern="/**" access="denyAll" />
</security:http>
```

This listing should be read from top to bottom. This means that you should specify the more specific rules first, followed by the more general rules. If a resource matches a pattern, either directly or by wildcards specified in the pattern, the level of authentication specified by the access attribute will be required. If that condition is met, access is granted; otherwise it is denied.

First we declared that index.jsp (our welcome) file is accessible for everyone. Next we defined the /secured/** and /public/** matching patterns. By default ant[4] style matching patterns are used. Every URL beginning with /secured requires the user to be fully authenticated before access is granted. URLs beginning with /public are able to be accessed by any one. We will discuss the access attribute and where those values are coming from in a minute.

As you recall, our flows are placed together with our pages. To start ordersOverviewflow you need to be fully authenticated, since the path for this flow is secured/ordersOverview. Because of this we do not need to specify extra rules, since access to anything under /secured will be captured by our /secured/** rule.

If you store your flows in a separate location, however, for example under WEB-INF/flows, and you made WEB-INF/flows your base path using the base-path attribute of the <webflow:flow-registry>, you will have to follow the same convention. That is, you will have to put secured flows under flows/secured and public flows under flows/public. If you don't, for example if you put all flows under /flows, you will have to add separate <security:intercept-url> rules for each flow.

If we request access to the /createOrders-flow we don't need to be authenticated to get access. If we try to access the /placeOrders-flow, however, we will need to be authenticated first. If we are not authenticated, we are redirected to the login page. After the login succeeds, Spring Security takes us back to the secured resources we asked for in the first place (/placeOrders-flow in this case).

You might also have noticed that we added an attribute in the <security:http> element called use-expressions with value true. We also have to explain where the fullyAuthenticated, permitAll and denyAll values suddenly come from. Before we can do that we have to explain a bit more about how Spring Security works.

Whenever a <security:intercept-url> matches an incoming request URL, Spring Security needs to know which conditions should be checked to grant or deny access. These conditions are checked by a so called org.springframework.security.access.AccessDecisionManager. An AccessDecisionManager has in turn one or more instances of org.springframework.security.access.AccessDecisionVoter. Each voter will evaluate if access is granted, abstained, or denied. This is indicated by the return value of the vote

---

[4] http://static.springsource.org/spring/docs/3.1.0.RELEASE/javadoc-api/org/springframework/util/AntPathMatcher.html

method of the `AccessDecisionVoter`. This return value is a primitive `int`, which can be one of the following constants: `AccessDecisionVoter.ACCESS_ABSTAIN`, `AccessDecisionVoter.ACCESS_DENIED`, or `AccessDecisionVoter.ACCESS_GRANTED`

There are three implementations of the `AccessDecisionManager` interface. We will be using `org.springframework.security.access.vote.AffirmativeBased`. This `AccessDecisionManager` will allow access if at least one of its voters returns `ACCESS_GRANTED`. The other two are `org.springframework` `.security.access.vote.ConsensusBased`[5] and `org.springframework.security.access.vote` `.UnanimousBased`.[6] See their respective JavaDoc for more details.

The access-decision-manager-ref attribute of the `http` element is the way to reference an `AccessDecisionManager`. However, when defining the use-expressions attribute, an `AffirmativeBased` `AccessDecisionManager` will be added for us automatically. So there is no need to configure an `AccessDecisionManager` ourselves, and thus we can leave the access-decision-manager-ref attribute absent. The `AccessDecisionVoter` that is used is `org.springframework.security.web.access` `.expression.WebExpressionVoter`, which will help resolving the (SpEL) expressions you will be able to use in the access attribute.

At this stage we have configured Spring Security so that it will intercept each request and scan our list of `<security:intercept-url>` entries. If the request resource matches any of the listed entries, either directly or by wildcard matching, the access attribute is checked to see what has to be done. If the access attribute is `permitAll`, access is always granted. If the access attribute is `fullyAuthenticated`, the user must be authenticated to be allowed access. If that is not the case, the user is redirected to the login page automatically. After login, the user will be redirected back to the secured resource.

Finally, if the requested resource does not match any entry, access is denied by default by using the `denyAll` access attribute. By default this will render the server's default "403 access denied" page. So accessing a random URL will bring up this page. Even after the user has logged in, accessing a random URL will still trigger the "access denied" page, because there was no previous rule that explicitly *granted* access. All resources that are not explicitly listed are now by default shielded from any user access.

■ **Tip** When configuring access to resources, it is always wise to close up with a deny all rule. If the access requirements for the requested resource aren't listed, access is simply denied. When the user accesses a resource other than the ones we listed, a "403 access denied" page will be shown on the user's browser. This makes sure that resources which are not explicitly configured cannot be accessed by accident.

■ **Note** In the list of resources, we mentioned that access to resources should be public. To do this, we changed the mapping in the resource holder defined in `WebMvcContextConfiguration`. We prefixed the URL with `/public` in order to make our resources publicly available without requiring authentication:

```
public void addResourceHandlers(ResourceHandlerRegistry registry) {
registry.addResourceHandler("/public/resources/**/*").
    addResourceLocations("classpath:/META-INF/web-resources/");
}
```

---

[5] http://static.springsource.org/spring-security/site/docs/3.1.x/apidocs/org/springframework/security/access/vote/ConsensusBased.html

We refactored all URL mapping in the pages accordingly to be prefixed with /public.

Overview of Expression Methods and Literals

We still need to explain where the permitAll, fullyAuthenticated and denyAll come from. These are all Spring EL expressions that are evaluated with a special Spring Security-aware context. In a normal Spring EL environment, evaluating denyAll would trigger an exception. However, in this scope, extra methods and properties are implicitly available for your expressions.

Although we cannot cover all possibilities here, Table 13-5 provides a quick overview of the methods you can use in the access attribute when using expressions, and Table 13-6 summarizes the properties).

Table 13-5. SpringEL Security Method Expressions

Method expressions	Description
hasRole([role])	Returns true if the current principal has the specified role.
hasAnyRole([role1,role2])	Returns true if the current principal has any of the supplied roles (given as a comma-separated list of strings).
isAnonymous()	Returns true if the current principal is an anonymous user.
isRememberMe()	Returns true if the current principal is a remember-me user.
isAuthenticated()	Returns true if the user is not anonymous.
isFullyAuthenticated()	Returns true if the user is not an anonymous or a remember-me user.
hasIpAddress(ipAddress)	Returns true if the IP address of the incoming request matches the IP address passed as literal. Optionally you can specify a range by supplying the netmask in the CIDR (Classless Inter- Domain Routing[6]) notation (ipaddress/mask).

■ **Note** These methods can be found in the super class org.springframework.security.access.expression .SecurityExpressionRoot and its subclass org.springframework.security.web.access.expression .WebSecurityExpressionRoot. You will see that in the super class there are additional methods not covered in Table 13-5. We didn't include them, because they are aliases; for example, hasAuthority and hasAnyAuthority

---

[6] http://en.wikipedia.org/wiki/CIDR_notation

are aliases for respectively `hasRole` and `hasAnyRole`. We also omitted the `hasPermission` methods, which are specifically for method-based security in combination with post- and pre filtering.

The methods in Table 13-6 can also be accessed as properties. They provide access to a getter method that returns an `Object`, such as the `principal`. The principal is just an `Object`. Most of the time this is an instance of the `org.springframework.security.core.UserDetails` interface, as we will discuss later. Or they provide a shortcut for a getter method that returns a boolean (those properties start with `is` rather than `get`). For example, the method `boolean isFullyAuthenticated()` can be called directly as the property `isFullyAuthenticated`. The result is exactly the same as the method syntax, but saves you the effort of typing the parentheses.

Table 13-6. SpringEL Security Property Expressions

Property expressions	Description
principal	Allows direct access to the principal object representing the current user.
authentication	Allows direct access to the current Authentication object obtained from the SecurityContext.
permitAll	Always evaluates to true.
denyAll	Always evaluates to false.
anonymous	See isAnonymous() in Table 13.5.
authenticated	See isAuthenticated() in Table 13.5.
rememberMe	See isRememberMe () in Table 13.5.
fullyAuthenticated	See isFullyAuthenticated() in Table 13.5.

Remember that the expressions, whether you are using methods or properties, are Spring EL expressions. You will be able to use logical operators such as and, or etc. For example
`access="hasRole('ROLE_X') `**`and`**` hasRole('ROLE_Y')`

Configuring Authentication

When users are redirected to the login page, the application asks them to enter a username and password combination in order to proceed. Spring Security will receive this information but needs to verify that the user exists and that the password supplied matches for that user.

In order to do this we need some kind of user store to hold the users (and passwords) that are able to access the application. To keep things simple for now, we will use an in-memory data store, which we will fill with users and passwords entirely specified in the configuration. Later we will see how to replace this with a database store.

We need to configure an `org.springframework.security.authentication.AuthenticationManager` to do this. Spring Security offers a namespacing construct (`<security:authentication-manager>`) that, unlike the `org.springframework.security.access.AccessDecisionManager,` will keep the coding required short and easy. Using this construct we don't have to wire this authentication manager explicitly; it will be auto detected by Spring.

In order for the authentication manager to do its job, it needs a reference to an authentication provider. This is the bridge to the store that contains the user details. In this case we won't reference an external provider but use the in-memory user-service, which is declared as `<security:user-service>` and takes a list of `<security:user>` elements, each representing a user in our system (see Listing 13-6). A user has a username (abbreviated `name` in this case), a password, and a comma-separated list of authorities. The authorities are of no importance for the moment. Later we will show how we can use them.

Listing 13-6. The authentication manager configuration with in-memory user-data store

```
<security:authentication-manager>
    <security:authentication-provider>
        <security:user-service >
            <security:user name="jd"
                password="5238377ba2eac049901b54004ee9e03db62c0ab0b48133a4a162ab3aedfc809f" ↵
                authorities="ROLE_CUSTOMER"/>
        </security:user-service>
    </security:authentication-provider>
</security:authentication-manager>
```

What is important is that this code is not yet complete. As you can see, we have a strange and long password. This is called a *one-way hashed password*. A one way hash is a cryptographic function that takes plain text as input and generates another, weird-looking, string as output, called a hash (or digest). The general idea is that the hash cannot (without taking decades of computing time) be reverse-engineered to the original plain-text form. In order to compare these passwords, one takes the password as entered by the user, hashes it with the hash function and then compares the output with the hash stored in the data store. If the hashes match, the password is the same.

In this case we used the SHA2 hashing algorithm with an output size of 256-bit (so SHA-256). The only problem is that Spring now expects the user to enter the hash

`"5238377ba2eac049901b54004ee9e03db62c0ab0b48133a4a162ab3aedfc809f"`

as the password, instead of the readable password. Because Spring does not know that what we stored is actually a hash, it thinks that this long string is the actual password that the user has to enter.

What is left to do is configure Spring to take the real plain-text password by the user, hash it using the selected hashing algorithm, and then compare the output hash with the hash value we supplied in the password field. In Listing 13-7, we do this by specifying the `<security:password-encoder>`. There is not much to configure. We just say we are using SHA-256 bit (which is actually SHA version 2). There is also a weird sub element, which we will discuss in a minute. With this password encoder, Spring Security knows that our passwords are hashed, and that it should hash the user's entered password first before comparing the value with the one in our data store.

Listing 13-7. Adding the password encoder

```
<security:authentication-manager>
    <security:authentication-provider>
        <security:password-encoder hash="sha-256">
            <security:salt-source user-property="username"/>
        </security:password-encoder>
```

```
        <security:user-service >
            <security:user name="jd" ↵
                password="5238377ba2eac049901b54004ee9e03db62c0ab0b48133a4a162ab3aedfc809f" ↵
                authorities="ROLE_CUSTOMER"/>
        </security:user-service>
    </security:authentication-provider>
</security:authentication-manager>
```

▪ **Note** Why did we make things more complex by introducing a hashed password rather than a plain text one, when we are creating just the basic setup? We did this for a good reason. Never, ever, store a password in plain text. Not even in a temporary (or basic) solution. A wise man once told us "in practice, a temporary solution is the equivalent of a production ready solution that will stay there forever." Ask yourself; how many times have you developed something temporary that is still out there? Also, when working with Spring Security or Java, there is no good reason not to hash your passwords. With the Apache Commons Codec,[7] you can create a hash with a single line of code. Never store plain-text passwords! Also, if someone performs an audit and sees that passwords are in plain text, you will be in trouble. This is the first step of any secure application.

You might wonder, how did we generate the hash in the first place? We could have written a small Java tool which does that for us, using the Apache Commons Codec:

```
String hashedPassword = ↵
org.apache.commons.codec.digest.DigestUtils.sha256Hex(plainTextPassword);
```

Or, we could have Googled an online site to do that. There are also plenty of free tools out there that can generate any kind of hash. Just one note, be careful using online generators, as you will be passing around real passwords. For testing purposes this will do fine, but for real case scenarios, think about writing a tool yourself or downloading a well-known tool[8] instead.

The password we hashed is "secret". If you would verify this you'll notice that the hashes don't quite match. In this case we are using a "salted hash" which is nothing more than the password suffixed with extra data that can be found when authenticating the user. For example, it could be the first name of the user. In this case we have chosen the easiest element; the username.

The goal of the salt is to make the digests more unique. If two users use the same password, the same hash will be generated. When using a salt, the hashes will differ, as they are calculated using another suffix (in this case their username).

Having the same hash doesn't hurt, as they (practically) cannot be reverse engineered. However, you are giving away a free hint: someone looking at the hashes might note that multiple users have the same hash, and thereby implicitly know that they also have the same password. By adding the salt you are taking away that last hint, and you are also making the passwords longer. The longer the password, the more resistant the hash will be against attacks.

---

[7] http://commons.apache.org/codec/
[8] http://www.slavasoft.com/hashcalc/ (Windows only - freeware)
 http://sourceforge.net/projects/hash-calculator/files/hash-calculator/ (Java - open source)

Spring calculates the salted hash by using this scheme:

```
plaint_text_password{salt}
```

In our case we have to calculate the hash as secret{jd}, where jd is the username of our user. If you now try to regenerate the hash with this input string, you'll notice that it will match with the hash shown above. We will configure this as shown in Listing 13-8.

Listing 13-8. *The password encoder using a property as salt*

```
<security:password-encoder hash="sha-256">
        <security:salt-source user-property="username"/>
</security:password-encoder>
```

We have now configured the password encoder with a type of hash. Internally, we supplied it with a salt source that has a user-property with the value "username". Let's look in more detail at how Spring Security will handle this:

1. Before applying the hash function, first resolve our salt. The salt is retrieved from the UserDetails object (which we will introduce later). The property that should be used from this Object is indicated by the value of the user-property attribute ("username"). The value from the username property is retrieved from the UserDetails Object. That value will be our salt. The salt is then added at the end of the password between braces. So, when our password is secret and the username property of the UserDetails object is jd, our password string will now be secret{jd}.

2. Hash the password string secret{jd} using SHA 256bit.

3. Finally, compare the result from the hash function with the one retrieved from the users data store.

Putting It All Together

Before we can test our application, we still have to make some modifications to our pages. In the previous application our pages were adapted for the custom authentication scheme that we created ourselves. In particular, the login and landing page need some modifications to work together with Spring Security.

First we will take care of the login page. Spring Security will perform authentication, based on the username and password that we will supply. We will do this by our login page, which has username and password fields. But Spring needs to know about these items, so we are going see how to handle that. We will also see how we can show error messages that the login might have produced.

Next we will make a small modification to our home page to indicate whether the authentication was successful. Previously, if a user logged in using the login link, he or she could only infer that the login must have succeeded since there was no error. We will enhance this a bit with a message saying that the authentication succeeded.

Finally, we will change the logout so it is handled by Spring Security as well.

Changing the Login Page

As we explained previously, we implicitly configured a filter (UsernamePasswordAuthenticationFilter) that will perform redirection to the login page and landing page. Besides this, this filter will also listen to a preconfigured URL and look for preconfigured request parameters for username and password. These default key values are as follows:

- Username request parameter name: j_username

- Password request parameter name: j_password

- Request URL: /j_spring_security_check

■ **Note** You can change all three of these values on the `<security:form-login>` element by specifying the attributes: *username-parameter*, *password-parameter,* and *login-processing-url*. We mention this option because it might be worth considering in your own Spring projects, although we will leave the values at their defaults for the duration of the chapter. The request URL will be in the action of the HTML form. Anyone inspecting your HTML source will know you are using Spring Security. While "security through obscurity" might by itself give a false sense of security, if applied in a well-controlled and secured environment (as we are building here) it is considered a plus, since you are removing one more hint. In this case, it is the version or software product you are using to secure your application.

The login.jsp now looks like Listing 13-9.

Listing 13-9. The WEB-INF/view/public/authentication/login.jsp adapted to integrate with the Spring Security form based login filter.

```
<%@ taglib prefix="c" uri="http://java.sun.com/jsp/jstl/core"%>
<%@ taglib prefix="spring" uri="http://www.springframework.org/tags"%>
<%@ taglib prefix="form" uri="http://www.springframework.org/tags/form"%>

    <spring:url value="/j_spring_security_check" var="login" />
        <form action="${login}" method="POST">
            <table style="width: 100%">
                <tr>
                    <td>
                        <spring:message code="label.page.login.username" />
                    </td>
                    <td>
                        <input type="text" name="j_username"/>
                    </td>
                    <td>
                        <spring:message code="label.page.login.password" />
                    </td>
                    <td>
                        <input type="password" name="j_password" />
                    </td>
                </tr>
                <tr>
                    <td colspan="4">

                        <c:if test="${not empty param.authenticationNok}">
```

```
                            <font color="red">
                                    <spring:message code="label.login.failed" ↵
                    arguments="${SPRING_SECURITY_LAST_EXCEPTION.message}" />
                            </font>
                        </c:if>
                    </td>
                </tr>
            </table>

            <div align="right" style="margin-bottom: 20px;
                margin-top: 10px" >
                <button type="submit" id="login">
                    <spring:message code="label.page.login.login"/>
                </button>
            </div>
        </form>
</jsp:root>
```

As you can see, we have made sure the input fields for password and username have the requested name, so that the parameter will be picked up by Spring. We are also submitting our form to the default Spring Security URL for authentication.

What you might also notice is that we added a section to display login errors:

```
<c:if test="${not empty param.authenticationNok}">
    <font color="red">
        <spring:message code="label.login.failed"↵
            arguments="${SPRING_SECURITY_LAST_EXCEPTION.message}" />
    </font>
</c:if>
```

When a user supplies bad credentials, Spring Security makes the exception available on the session with the key SPRING_SECURITY_LAST_EXCEPTION. The only thing we have to do is display it. The message can be localized and can also be changed. We will discuss this further in the "Localization" section of this chapter. To detect that a new login failure occurred, we check for the presence of the parameter authenticationNok.

This parameter is added by us. When Spring Security detects a login failure, it can direct to a specified URL. Doing so you can pass along additional parameters. To do this redirection we need to modify the <security:form-login> as shown in Listing 13-10.

Listing 13-10. Forwarding when authentication fails using a parameter

```
<security:form-login login-page="/public/authentication/login.htm" ↵
    authentication-failure-url="/public/authentication/login.htm?↵
                                authenticationNok=1"
</security:form-login>
```

On authentication failure we redirect back to the login page, but this time we append the parameter authenticationNok, which will make the message appear. We are supplying a value 1 for the parameter, just to let it have a value so we can easily test if this parameter is present. The value is of no real importance, however. This rounds up the modifications to the login page; now we will move on to the home page.

■ **Note** We also removed the `authentication-flow.xml` from the previous example, as login is now handled by Spring Security infrastructure. This also means we changed the anchor in `header.jsp` to go to `/public/authentication/login.htm` instead of launching the (no longer existing) authentication flow.

Changing the Home Page

When authentication is successful we redirect to the home page. In this case we want to show a message that authentication was successful. In order to do this, we will add a parameter to the URL specified in the `default-target-url` attribute (see Listing 13-11).

Listing 13-11. Configuring the default-target-url, with an extra parameter, which Spring Security will redirect the user to after successful authentiction

```
<security:form-login login-page="/public/authentication/login.htm" default-target-↵
url="/public/main.htm?authenticationOk=1" authentication-failure-↵
url="/public/authentication/login.htm?authenticationNok=1"  />
```

In Listing 13-12 we show the relevant portion of the home page (`main.jsp`, located in WEB-INF/view/public/), which will display the message to the user when login was successful. The code that displays the message is indicated in bold.

Listing 13-12. Adapting the home page to show the appropriate message when login was successful

```
<%@ taglib prefix="c" uri="http://java.sun.com/jsp/jstl/core"%>
<%@ taglib prefix="spring" uri="http://www.springframework.org/tags"%>
<%@ taglib prefix="form" uri="http://www.springframework.org/tags/form"%>
<%@ taglib prefix="fn" uri="http://java.sun.com/jsp/jstl/functions"%>
<%@ taglib prefix="sec"↵
        uri="http://www.springframework.org/security/tags"%>
```

```
<sec:authorize access="fullyAuthenticated">
    <c:if test="${not empty param.authenticationOk}">
        <div id="authenticationOk"↵
            style="color: green; display: block; margin-left: 15px;
            margin-bottom: 10px;">
            <table>
                <tr>
                    <td>
                        <ul style="list-style-type: disc">
                            <li>
                                <h3>
                                    <sec:authentication
                                     property="principal.username"↵
                                     var="username" scope="request"/>↵

                                    <spring:message
                                     code="label.page.main.authentication.ok"↵
                                     arguments="${username}" />↵
                                </h3>
                            </li>
                        </ul>
                    </td>
                </tr>
            </table>
        </div>
    </c:if>
</sec:authorize>

<script>
    dojo.addOnLoad(function(){
        function fadeIt() {
            if(dojo.byId("authenticationOk")){
                dojo.style("authenticationOk", "opacity", "1");
                var fadeOutArgs = {node: "authenticationOk", duration: 15000};
                dojo.fadeOut(fadeOutArgs).play();
            }
        }
    fadeIt();
    });
</script
```

If someone were to append this parameter (authenticationOk=1) manually, this would have no side effects, and the message would also not be shown. On the home page there is an authentication check around the code that shows the message using the security tag library (<sec:authorize access="fullyAuthenticated">).

We only check for the authenticationOk parameter if the user is already authenticated. If we then see that this parameter is present, we display a message so the user knows authentication was successful. This authentication strategy ensures that the message is shown only once. If the authenticated user were to return to the welcome page using the "home" link, or any other way, we have ensured that the message is not shown a second time.

We will discuss the Spring Security taglibs in detail later in the "Authorizing Access" section.

501

Logging Out

The logout functionality was until now implemented in our `com.apress.prospringmvc.bookstore` `.web.controller.AuthenticationController`. Let's repeat the code snippet to refresh our memory.

```
@RequestMapping(value = "/logout", method = RequestMethod.GET)
public String logout(HttpSession session) {
    session.invalidate();
    return "redirect:/index.htm";
}
```

When the user clicks the logout link, it will direct to /logout, which will invoke the controller method `logout`, and call `invalidate` on the HTTP session. After that the user is redirected to the homepage. Although this is not very complex, it should no longer be part of our application code. Spring Security can take care of this as well. We can safely remove the code in the `AuthenticationController`.

After that we will configure Spring Security to take over the task. We will do this by configuring the `LogoutFilter`. In Table 13-2 earlier, we gave an overview of the possible filters; the `LogoutFilter` is one of them. This filter had the following entry in the table:

Table 13-2.

Bean alias	Filter class	Namespace element or attribute
LOGOUT_FILTER	LogoutFilter	http/logout

This filter can be declared as an element (`<security:logout>`) within the `http` element. The code for this configuration is shown in Listing 13-13.

Listing 13-13. Configuring the logout functionality in our src/main/resources/spring/spring-security.xml

```
<security:logout logout-success-url="/public/main.htm" logout-url="/logout" invalidate-↵
session="true"/>
```

The `logout-success-url` attribute indicates the page to which Spring Security should redirect when the logout was successful. In our case this is the home page. The second attribute, `logout-url`, indicates the URL where the filter should listen. In our case this is /logout. Whenever a call is made to /logout, the `LogoutFilter` will be invoked and the user logged out. The last attribute indicates whether the HTTP session should be invalidated as well. If you specify `false`, only the `org.springframework.security.core` `.context.SecurityContext` will be cleared, and no invalidation occurs on the HTTP session. We will cover this class in a minute; for now it is enough to know that from the moment you are authenticated, the authentication information will be accessible via `org.springframework.security.core` `.context.SecurityContext`. Optionally you can also indicate to clear the entire HTTP session. While it is not mandatory, it is in nearly all cases the safest to clear the session as well. Invalidating the session is the default behavior if you don't specify the `invalidate-session` attribute. We specified it here explicitly so anyone reading our security configuration understands that the session is cleared for sure (not that we doubt the default value is working, but to give a clear indication, not everyone is aware of the defaults).

The logout link itself in our `header.jsp` remains unaltered, as you can see in Listing 13-14.

Listing 13-14. The logout link in our WEB-INF/templates/header.jsp

```
<spring:url value="/logout" var="logout" />
<a href="${logout}">
    <spring:message code="nav.logout"/>
</a>
```

This link now directs to /logout. The only thing missing is that this link should only appear when the user is actually logged in. We will see how to handle this when we introduce the authorization tag. Our logout control is now fully operational.

The Complete Security Configuration

In Listing 13-15 you will find the complete security configuration that we build for this part of the chapter (located in src/main/resources/spring/spring-security.xml). Although we have included a lot of functionality, the configuration part is still pretty digestible, as you will see.

Listing 13-15. A complete overview of the basic security setup

```
<security:http use-expressions="true" >
    <security:form-login login-page="/public/authentication/login.htm"    ↵
        default-target-url="/public/main.htm?authenticationOk=1" ↵
        authentication-failure-url="/public/authentication/login.htm↵
                            ?authenticationNok=1"/>

    <security:intercept-url pattern="/index.jsp" access="permitAll" />

    <security:intercept-url pattern="/public/**" access="permitAll" />
    <security:intercept-url pattern="/secured/**"
    access="fullyAuthenticated"/>

    <security:intercept-url pattern="/**" access="denyAll" />
    <security:logout logout-success-url="/public/main.htm" ↵
            logout-url="/logout" invalidate-session="true"/>
</security:http>

<security:authentication-manager>
    <security:authentication-provider>
        <security:password-encoder hash="sha-256">
            <security:salt-source user-property="username"/>
        </security:password-encoder>
    <security:user-service >
        <security:user name="jd" ↵
password="5238377ba2eac049901b54004ee9e03db62c0ab0b48133a4a162ab3aedfc809f"↵
            authorities="ROLE_CUSTOMER"/>
        </security:user-service>
    </security:authentication-provider>
</security:authentication-manager>
```

Together with the login and home page modification explained in the previous two sections, this secures our entire application. We are now able to log in via a form login. The authentication is handled securely via Spring Security. All our resources are now secured; some require authentication before a user can access them, and others are publicly accessible. Resources that are not explicitly listed are denied access by default.

Let's continue and see what else we can do!

Going to the Database

Up until now we have stored our user information in the configuration itself. By making use of the `<security:user-service>`, Spring Security created an in-memory data store which would be populated with the data we specified there. In our current application, users are actually stored in the database and modeled as instances of `org.springframework.security.authentication.dao.Account`. It would be better to adapt our configuration so that we can load the user's account from the existing database tables. As it turns out, this is a very easy step to take.

By defining the `<security:authentication-provider>` Spring registered a `org.springframework.security.authentication.dao.DaoAuthenticationProvider`. This class will deal with all low-level plumbing. What is important for us is that this class delegates to a so-called `org.springframework.security.core.userdetails.UserDetailsService` class, which will be responsible for loading the user information from wherever suitable. In our previous implementation this was loaded from the in-memory data store. Now we will provide our own implementation. This is a very easy interface to implement, as it only has one method:

```
UserDetails loadUserByUsername(String username) throws UsernameNotFoundException;
```

■ **Note** The UserDetailsService is not responsible for authentication. That is the job of the authentication provider. In our case this will be the `DaoAuthenticationProvider` from Spring Security. The goal of the `UserDetailsService` is to access the data store (database, directory server, or possibly a file) that contains the user information and possibly credentials. It should map this information from that data store's internal structure to predefined standard object (`org.springframework.security.core.userdetails.UserDetails`) and return it to the provider so it can continue to do its work.

Basically, the implementation should load the user information from wherever its configuration determines and convert that information to a `UserDetails` object. As we will see later, a `UserDetails` object is the main object you will be using when asking for security information. The implementation is shown in Listing 13-16.

Listing 13-16. Implementing a custom UserDetailsService

```
package com.apress.prospringmvc.bookstore.web.security;

import org.apache.commons.lang3.StringUtils;
import org.springframework.beans.factory.annotation.Autowired;
import org.springframework.security.core.GrantedAuthority;
import org.springframework.security.core.authority.SimpleGrantedAuthority;
import org.springframework.security.core.userdetails.UserDetails;
import org.springframework.security.core.userdetails.UserDetailsService;
import org.springframework.security.core.userdetails.UsernameNotFoundException;
import org.springframework.stereotype.Component;
```

```
import com.apress.prospringmvc.bookstore.domain.Account;
import com.apress.prospringmvc.bookstore.domain.Permission;
import com.apress.prospringmvc.bookstore.domain.Role;
import com.apress.prospringmvc.bookstore.service.AccountService;

@Component
public class BookstoreUserDetailsService implements UserDetailsService {

@Autowired
private CustomerService customerService;

    @Override
    public UserDetails loadUserByUsername(String username) throws UsernameNotFoundException {
        return new BookstoreUserDetails(customerService.getCustomer(username));
    }
}
```

We use our CustomerService to load the Customer and pass it along to our custom UserDetails object. This object is implemented as shown in Listing 13-17.

Listing 13-17. Implementing a custom UserDetails

```
package com.apress.prospringmvc.bookstore.web.security;

// Imports omitted, see Listing 13-16

public class BookstoreUserDetails implements UserDetails {

    private Customer customer;
    private List<GrantedAuthority> authorities = new ↵
        ArrayList<GrantedAuthority>();

    public BookstoreUserDetails(Customer customer) {
        this.customer = customer;
    }

    //Omitting getter and setter methods for class instance variables
}
```

There are getters for the username, password and our Customer object. At the moment we return an empty list with for the GrantedAuthority property. We will later see how this will fit into our application. All the other methods are features for the UserDetails, such as account expiry and so on. We won't be using these features, so true is returned for all of them. Once a user has been authenticated, the information about that user is stored in an implementation of org.springframework.security.core.context.SecurityContext. The org.springframework.security.core.context.SecurityContextHolder class which is a java.lang.ThreadLocal,[9] will give access to the SecurityContext. The SecurityContext itself has only a getter (and setter) for an org.springframework.security.core.Authentication Object. This means you will be able to access the Authentication Object anywhere in your web application by calling

---

[9] http://docs.oracle.com/javase/6/docs/api/java/lang/ThreadLocal.html

```
SecurityContextHolder.getContext().getAuthentication();
```

On the Authentication object, we are especially interested in the getPrincipal method. This returns details about the user currently authenticated. In the previous section, we introduced you to the UserDetails, well this is what the getPrincipal returns, a UserDetails implementation. In our case it will be the a custom UserDetails, namely our BookstoreUserDetails.

■ **Note** If you look at the API, you will see that getPrincipal returns Object. So it can also return other types besides a UserDetails implementation. If you define your own custom org.springframework.security .authentication.AuthenticationProvider, you are free to construct your own authentication objects. In that case the return value from getPrincipal can be whatever type you want the principal to be.

Securing Our Flows, the Right Way

The setup we've put in place until now still secures our flows as normal request mappings. While this might seem to work, it actually doesn't. It only works for requests coming from outside to access a flow. If a flow wants to start a subflow, the request is already behind the Security filters and will not be picked up (see Figure 13-4).

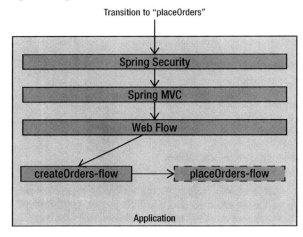

Figure 13-4. *Securing flows as request URI using the filter chain is not enough. Starting a sub flow from a parent flow would bypass this mechanism.*

If you remember from the request mappings, the placeOrders-flow (located in WEB-INF/view/secured/placeOrders/) can only be accessed by authenticated user. The createOrders-flow (located in WEB-INF/view/public/createOrders/) is publicly available. What happens here is that no authentication is triggered when the request comes in to transition to placeOrder (as it is still for createOrders-flow). The placeOrder is a subflow state within createOrders-flow. To refresh our memory you can see the code snippet below from the `createOrders-flow` which starts the sub flow from the moment the flow transitions to `placeOrder`:

```
<subflow-state id="placeOrder" subflow="secured/placeOrders">
    <input name="orderForm"/>

    <output name="orderId"/>
        <transition on="endOrderOk" to="endOrderOk"/>
</subflow-state>
```

When Web Flow makes the internal state transition to the sub-flow, it will actually execute without redirecting the user to the login page. What we really want is Web Flow integration with Spring Security, so that Spring Security is involved when Web Flow executes flows.

Adding Access Attributes to Your Flows

Here we will see what you have to do in order to invoke Spring Security for Web Flow. When you do so, your inter flow communication will also be secured.

In order to secure your flows, you can add the following element on top of your flow definitions:

```
<secured attributes="…"/>
```

The usage of the `attributes` attribute is the same as the `access` attribute in the `<security:intercept-url>` of the spring security configuration. You can use it to place the expressions you want to be valid before this flow can execute.

If you return to the "Configuring Which Resources to Secure" section, you will see that the following two flows required authentication:

- `placeOrders-flow`

- `ordersOverview-flow`

The third flow, `createOrders-flow` (located in `WEB-INF/view/public/createOrders/`, was public and did not require any authentication to be executed. We add the `fullyAuthenticated` condition to `placeOrders-flow.xml`(located in `WEB-INF/view/secured/placeOrders/`) and `ordersOverview-flow.xml` (located in `secured/ordersOverview/`), as shown in Listings 13-18 and 13-19.

Listing 13-18. Adding the fullyAuthenticated authorization check as top element in ordersOverview-flow.xml and placeOrders-flow.xml

```
<flow xmlns="http://www.springframework.org/schema/webflow"
      xmlns:xsi="http://www.w3.org/2001/XMLSchema-instance"
      xsi:schemaLocation="http://www.springframework.org/schema/webflow
                          http://www.springframework.org/schema/webflow/
                          spring-webflow-2.0.xsd">

<secured attributes="fullyAuthenticated" />
...
```

Listing 13-19. Adding the permitAll check as top element in createOrders-flow.xml

```
<flow xmlns="http://www.springframework.org/schema/webflow"
      xmlns:xsi="http://www.w3.org/2001/XMLSchema-instance"
      xsi:schemaLocation="http://www.springframework.org/schema/webflow
                          http://www.springframework.org/schema/webflow/
                          spring-webflow-2.0.xsd">

<secured attributes="permitAll" />
...
```

The `<secured>` element also has a second attribute, called `match`. This attribute is of no importance when using SpEL. But without using SpEL you are much more limited. For example, it is not possible to define an "or" or "and" relation. Later on we will introduce the concept of roles, but you should know that you can allow or deny a flow to be executed depending on one or more roles being present. With SpEL you would simply use the and operator if you only want the flow to execute when both roles are present, or the or operator if one suffices. When not using SpEL you must use the `match` attribute, which will let you switch between any; if one of the roles requested are present, the flow will execute, or all; meaning that all of the roles in the `attributes` attribute must be present before the flow is executed.

■ **Note** The flow security configuration on `createOrders-flow` and `ordersOverview-flow` is a bit superfluous, since they are both top-level flows. The `<security:intercept-url pattern="/public/**"` `access="permitAll" />` and `<security:intercept-url pattern="/secured/**"` `access="fullyAuthenticated"/>` have already checked that we had the proper authentication before letting us even go any further. However, the `<secured>` element in the flow could be used to perform finer-grained access control or authorization. While the filter configuration could allow the user to go through (the user was authenticated successfully for example) you could still check that access would only be granted if the user has a certain role; for example, `<secured attribute="hasRole(ROLE_SOMEROLE)"/>`. Roles will be discussed in the "Role-Based Access Control" section.

Configuring the SecurityFlowExecutionListener

The `org.springframework.webflow.security.SecurityFlowExecutionListener` class will enable the integration between Web Flow and Spring Security. It is required in order for the `<security>` element we discussed previously to do anything. This class is an implementation of the Web Flow `org.springframework.webflow.execution.FlowExecutionListener` that we saw in Chapter 12.

Normally this would have been a two-paragraph section, since you ordinarily just define a bean (the `SecurityFlowExecutionListener`) and bind it to the flow executor using the `<webflow:flow-execution-listeners>` element in `webflow-config.xml`. As it turns out, there is currently a problem with the `SecurityFlowExecutionListener` when using SpEL-enabled security expressions with Spring Security. It might well be that this problem is resolved by the time you read this; and if so then you can continue as normal (simply configuring the SecurityFlowExecutionListener as we will see in Listing 13-21). If the issue[10] has not been resolved, however, you have two options:

- Use the SecurityFlowExecutionListener as-is, but in that case you cannot use SpEL in your flow <security> elements. You would have to fall back to mainly using roles.

- Use our custom com.apress.prospringmvc.bookstore.web.security.BookstoreSecurityFlowExecutionListener, which should do the trick as a workaround. With this approach you will still be able to use SpEL.

For the sake of consistency we went with the second solution for the examples.

To configure the BookstoreSecurityFlowExecutionListener we open src/main/resources/spring/webflow-config.xml and define a Spring bean, as shown in Listing 13-20.

Listing 13-20. Defining the SecurityFlowExecutionListener

```
<bean id="securityFlowExecutionListener" ↵
class="com.apress.prospringmvc.bookstore.web.security.BookstoreSecurityFlowExecutionListener↵
"/>
```

Next we configure the listener with the flow executor (see Listing 13-21).

Listing 13-21: Integrating the SecurityFlowExecutionListener with the flow executor

```
<webflow:flow-executor id="flowExecutor" flow-registry="flowRegistry" >
    <webflow:flow-execution-repository max-executions="3" max-execution-snapshots="10" />
    <webflow:flow-execution-listeners>
        <webflow:listener ref="securityFlowExecutionListener"/>
    </webflow:flow-execution-listeners>
</webflow:flow-executor>
```

That's it! If you want to configure the default SecurityFlowExecutionListener, it is done in exactly the same way, except that the class of bean securityFlowExecutionListener would be org.springframework .webflow.security.SecurityFlowExecutionListener instead of com.apress.prospringmvc.bookstore .web.security.BookstoreSecurityFlowExecutionListener.

─────

▨ **Note** We did not add the BookstoreSecurityFlowExecutionListener code into this section, since that would take us too far. If you come to a point where you need this, and it isn't fixed, we suggest you read the issue (see the link in the footnote) and look at the source code at the same time. This will be the best way to understand the fix we applied.

─────

───────────────

[10] https://jira.springsource.org/browse/SWF-1508

Transport Security

At the moment we still have one major security hole in our security setup. When our users log in they supply username and password credentials, which will be authenticated by Spring Security. These credentials are, however, sent via the browser to the web server using HTTP, which is a plain-text protocol. Anyone capturing data will be able to see the username and password in clear text. To illustrate this we started up Wireshark[11] and let it listen on the loopback adapter. Next we performed a login in our application, and Figure 13-5 shows the results.

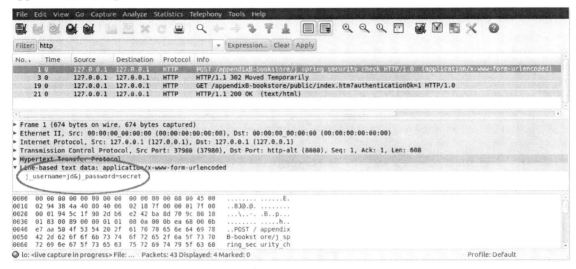

Figure 13-5. *Network capture of an HTTP session showing plain credentials when logging in via the form*

This seems very unsecure. To change this behavior we are going to switch to SSL (Secure Socket Layer, which is now called TLS, or Transport Layer Security, its successor, but for consistency we'll call it SSL), whenever a user logs in. From that point everything will be served using SSL.

Before we proceed, you must prepare your tomcat or tomcat STS instance to add an extra SSL connector. It is beyond the scope of this book to go deeper into the internals of the SSL protocol or the PKI(Public Key Infrastructure), but for this to work you need to supply tomcat with a keystore, which contains a private/public key pair and a certificate for that public key. Normally the certificate part is generated by a third-party Certificate Authority (CA). Fortunately, you can self-sign such a certificate which is ideal for tests or closed production setups.

As a small intermezzo we wanted to share something about self-signed certificates, since there is sometimes a misunderstanding about them. Using PKI with self-signed certificates has exactly the same encryption level as using an official CA signed certificate. So your SSL will not be less safe; the encryption strength, the procedures, and everything that depends on them offers the exact same guarantees.

---

[11] http://www.wireshark.org/

The difference lies in the trust. With a self-signed certificate your users will have to explicitly accept the certificate, and the browser will give them a warning that the identity cannot be verified. How this is presented is browser dependent, but with Safari they will get the page as shown in Figure 13-6.

Figure 13-6. Browser confirmation for trusting our self signed certificate

In order to trust the certificate for the current session only, you can click "Continue". If you want to trust the certificate for future sessions, you have to click "Show Certificate". Doing so will present the dialog box shown in Figure 13-7. If you then check "always trust Bookstore when connecting to localhost" the certificate will be stored.

Figure 13-7. Accepting the self signed certificate

After you click Continue, the certificate will be trusted (for this session only or for future sessions depending if you clicked the checkbox in Figure 13-7) and you will be able to continue over SSL. It is clear that this trusting is only a good idea for internal testing.

With a real CA signed certificate, the CA has asked the certificate holder for credentials before actually issuing the certificate. For example, we would never get a server certificate for google.com from an authorized CA, since we cannot proof that we own the domain or have any authorization over it.

A client's browser truststore (which contains a list of authorized root CAs) will also not trust our self-signed certificate by default, since it cannot be verified by any of the known and trusted CAs. I will explicitly have to accept its trust.

So for a production website a self-signed certificate would be a bad idea, since users cannot verify that the identity behind the certificate is really what it claims to be (your server); there is no third party that verified the identity and gave any approval. However, if you are sending data among a limited set of users (closed production), and each party trusts the others, it is perfectly viable to send a self-signed certificate to each party. Each party knows that your identity (you gave it personally on a USB stick, or emailed it from your personal account) is the one that is coupled to that certificate (the identity could be a person, server, domain, or whatever). This way, you can easily save the costs of signing your public keys by a CA.

To generate a self-signed certificate we can use a Java tool called keytool. To use it, take the following steps:

1. Open a command line prompt and enter the following command (make sure the JDK is available on your path):

```
keytool -genkey -alias tomcat -keystore keystore.jks
```

2. Enter **tomcat** as the password and again when prompted to re-enter it:

```
Enter keystore password:
Re-enter new password:
```

3. Complete the prompts as follows:

```
What is your first and last name?
  [Unknown]:  Bookstore
What is the name of your organizational unit?
  [Unknown]:  Bookstore
What is the name of your organization?
  [Unknown]:  Bookstore
What is the name of your City or Locality?
  [Unknown]:  Brussels
What is the name of your State or Province?
  [Unknown]:  Brussels
What is the two-letter country code for this unit?
  [Unknown]:  BE
Is CN=Bookstore, OU=Bookstore, O=Bookstore, L=Brussels, ST=Brussels, C=BE correct?
[no]:  yes
```

4. Press Enter without typing anything. The prompt will return, and your self-signed key is ready in the keystore.

```
Enter key password for <tomcat>
        (RETURN if same as keystore password):
```

Place the keystore under your tomcat home directory /conf, which is spring-insight-instance/conf/ if you are using STS.

Next open the server.xml (spring-insight-instance/conf/server.xml) and configure the SSL connector, as shown in Listing 13-22.If you want a full explanation of the configuration shown here, see the Tomcat howto[12], in the section "Edit The Tomcat Configuration File."

---

[12] http://tomcat.apache.org/tomcat-7.0-doc/ssl-howto.html

Listing 13-22. *Adding an SSL connector to tomcat's server.xml*

```
<Connector executor="tomcatThreadPool" port="${bio.https.port}" ↵
protocol="org.apache.coyote.http11.Http11Protocol"↵
connectionTimeout="20000" redirectPort="${bio.https.port}" acceptCount="100" ↵
maxKeepAliveRequests="15"↵
keystoreFile="${catalina.base}/conf/keystore.jks" keystorePass="tomcat" keyAlias="tomcat"↵
SSLEnabled="true" scheme="https" secure="true"/>
```

In this example we are depending on the STS instance. The variables, like `${bio.https.port}`, are already predefined. If you are using Tomcat you can replace them with 8443, which will be our default SSL port.

After that you can start Tomcat. Do not forget to clean the server in STS before starting. After modifying anything in the server configuration you have to "clean" in order for the latest files to be copied over (right-click on the server instance in the server view and click Clean).

At this time verify that your server starts and that no errors are thrown. If there is anything wrong with the configuration, Tomcat will show errors almost directly after starting up.

The final thing to do is to tell Spring Security which mappings we would like to use SSL for (see Listing 13-23). We will use SSL for

- Our login page

- The buy books flow

Listing 13-23. *Configuring secured transfer for specific request URIs*

```
<security:intercept-url pattern="/index.jsp" access="permitAll" />
<security:intercept-url pattern="/public/authentication/**" access="permitAll" requires-↵
channel="https" />
<security:intercept-url pattern="/public/createOrders/**" access="permitAll" requires-↵
channel="https" />

<security:intercept-url pattern="/public/**" access="permitAll" />

<security:intercept-url pattern="/secured/**" access="fullyAuthenticated" requires-↵
channel="https" />

<security:intercept-url pattern="/**" access="denyAll" />
```

The `requires-channel` will automatically change our protocol from HTTP to HTTPS (which is HTTP over SSL). To illustrate this we are going to our home page (see Figure 13-8).

Figure 13-8. *Before login, we are still on HTTP.*

Next, we click the Login link in the navigation bar, which results in the page shown in Figure 13-9.

Figure 13-9. *After clicking on the Login navigation link, we automatically switch to HTTPS.*

When we log in now, our credentials are transmitted securely. If we take a look at the certificate, we will see the data we entered when generating it with keytool. We will also see that there is no trust, as it is not generated by a trusted CA stored in our browser's truststore. Figure 13-10 shows the self-signed certificate we created earlier. It is not trusted by our browser, in this case Safari.

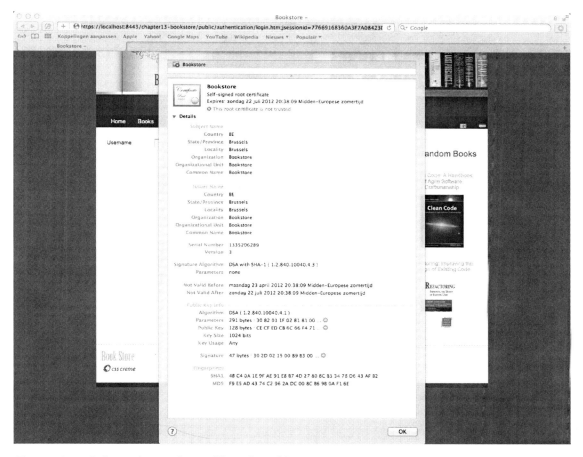

Figure 13-10. Information on the certificate issued by tomcat

■ **Note** When you run the sample application for the first time, going to the login page will automatically trigger the switch to SSL. In this case you will get warning of the self-signed certificate as shown in Figure 13-6 and Figure 13-7. So you will first have to accept the self-signed certificate before your browser will proceed over SSL to the login page.

When we inspect what's on the wire now, after configuring SSL, we will see that the initial request is a plain HTTP get to the login page. Spring Security will, however, send a redirect (HTTP 302) back to the browser indicating a protocol change. You can see that in the two highlighted lines in Figure 13-11. The first line is the HTTP 302 redirect. The second is the body content of the reply, in which you can see it is requesting our browser to `https://localhost....` What follows next is no longer plain HTTP, but SSL. In

Wireshark it is marked as TCP. The content of the packets are encrypted, and the password can no longer be intercepted by looking at the packets.

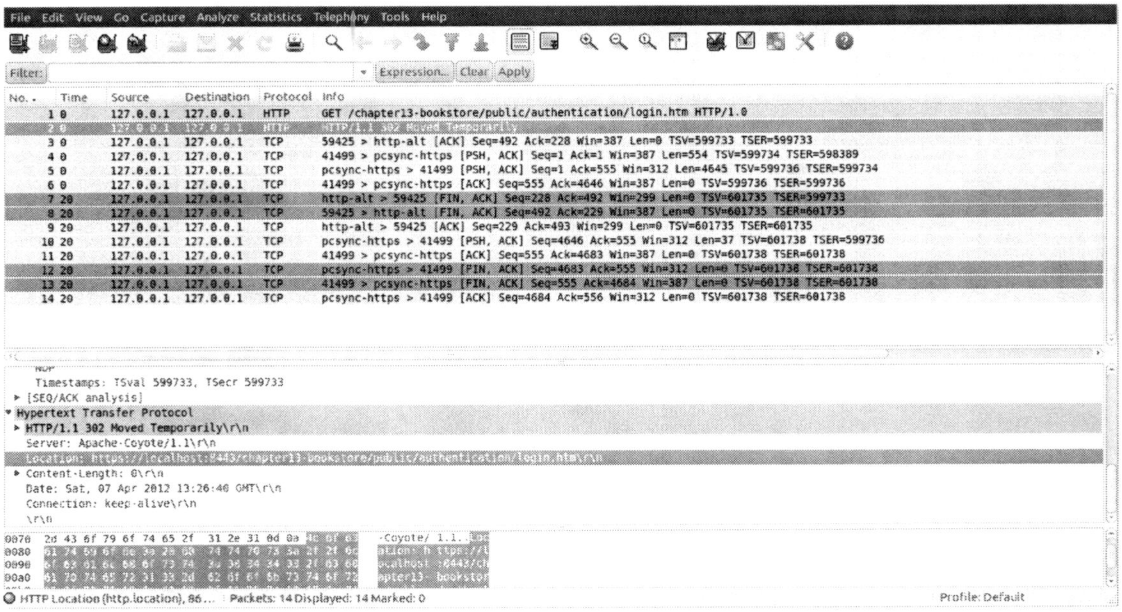

Figure 13-11. *All information submitted is now encrypted by SSL*

This concludes our discussion of Transport layer security. You have seen how we can switch from HTTP to HTTPS, just by altering the Spring Security configuration.

Localization

Spring Security supports localization of exception messages. If your application is designed for English-speaking users, you don't need to do anything as by default since all Security messages are in English.

If you need to support other locales, you should know that all exception messages can be localized, including messages related to authentication failures and access being denied (authorization failures). Exceptions and logging messages for developers or system deployers (including incorrect attributes, interface contract violations, using incorrect constructors, startup time validation, debug-level logging) are not localized and instead are hard-coded in English within Spring Security's code.

The resource bundle is located under `org/springframework/security/` with the base name `messages.properties` and can be configured in our `WebMvcContextConfiguration` (see Listing 13-24). We already have an `org.springframework.context.MessageSource` configured for our local resource bundle (`messages.properties`); here we will extend the configuration and pass along a second resource bundle, which is identified with the location in package format (`org.springframework.security.messages`) followed by the basename, which is the name of the file without country or language suffixed and without a "properties" extension.

Listing 13-24. Adding extra bundles for localizing Spring Security messages

```
@Bean
public MessageSource messageSource() {
    ResourceBundleMessageSource messageSource = new ↵
        ResourceBundleMessageSource();
    messageSource.setBasenames(new String[] { "messages", ↵
        "org.springframework.security.messages" });
    messageSource.setUseCodeAsDefaultMessage(true);
    return messageSource;
}
```

Spring Security relies on Spring's localization support to look up the appropriate message. In order for this to work, you have to make sure that the locale from the incoming request is stored in Spring's `org.springframework.context.i18n.LocaleContextHolder`. Spring MVC's `org.springframework.web.servlet.DispatcherServlet` does this for your application automatically, but since Spring Security's filters are invoked before the `DispatcherServlet`, the `LocaleContextHolder` needs to be set up to contain the correct locale before Spring Security is invoked. We do this by configuring a Spring `javax.servlet.ServletContextListener` implementation, namely `org.springframework.web.context.request.RequestContextListener`. This listener will be called before any filter is invoked.

The `RequestContextListener` is configured in the `BookstoreWebApplicationInitializer`, as you can see in Listing 13-25.

Listing 13-25: Code from the BookstoreWebApplicationInitializer configuring the RequestContextListener

```
@Override
public void onStartup(ServletContext servletContext) throws ServletException {
    registerListener(servletContext);
    registerDispatcherServlet(servletContext);
    // We are using JpaFlowExecutionListener instead, but we enable it for
    // Spring MVC served pages
    registerSpringSecurityFilterChain(servletContext);
    registerOpenEntityManagerInViewFilter(servletContext);
}

private void registerListener(ServletContext servletContext) {
    AnnotationConfigWebApplicationContext rootContext = ↵
        createContext(configurationClasses);
    servletContext.addListener(new ContextLoaderListener(rootContext));
    servletContext.addListener(new RequestContextListener());
}
```

Role-Based Access Control

Role-based access control (RBAC) is a beneficial access control model for organizations with many users and a high degree of diversity in the functions they are playing in their daily job. RBAC was modeled especially to support this kind of structure. Your role in RBAC is actually comparable with the role you would play in your organization; most likely that will have something to do with development. The permissions are the rights that have been granted to someone with that role.

While this level of detail mostly makes sense only for larger organizations, its basic implementation is not very difficult. As we will see, we can extend our domain model easily to support basic RBAC with a minimum of effort.

But to set the record straight, for something as simple our bookstore this is certainly overkill. Even if it were to become a popular store, the diversity of users will be very low; they will all be doing pretty much the same things. Hence we will not really benefit from an RBAC system. But we will demonstrate it just to show what is possible with Spring Security.

The model we are going to support comes down to the relationships shown in Figure 13-12.

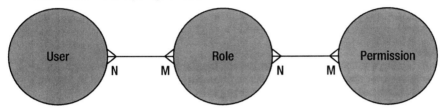

Figure 13-12. *The RBAC model*

A user (in our domain called "Account") has one or more roles. A role can have one or more permissions. The roles we define will depend on what's important for our application. A role can be thought of as a globalization of a set of permissions.

In our bookstore a role might be "customer" or "administrator," and a permission might be "create order" or "add books." Permissions are normally finer-grained than roles.

We decided to load both roles and permissions in the Security context. Checking on the role might be meaningful for a coarse-grained check. For example; should this navigation link be shown? This probably depends on the fact that a given user possesses a given role. However, going deeper, it could be that there are two different roles giving access to that same functionality. But within the functionality, only certain operations are allowed, depending on specific permissions. So here it would benefit us to check for the presence of a specific permission. As we will see, with Spring Security we can easily check on both.

For example, suppose that a company has a page that shows various benefits an employee enjoys. This could contain information about the medical plan, the meal vouchers, or group promotions. Accessing this information is allowed for internal employees only; contractors and other types of outside employees don't benefit from this and should be excluded from accessing this information.

For this reason we could opt to do a coarse-grained check on roles first. This will prevent the contractors from even seeing a link to this information. However, within the page itself we want to differentiate between normal employees, who can only read/query the information, and administrators, who will be able to modify the information. Here we will continue by checking the actual permissions. As employees, we will only have the permission to read the extra benefits, while administrators (also being employees) will have the extra *permission* to modify the information as well.

This whole story is not so interesting for Spring Security. It just wants to know a list of "strings" that you will use to check presence upon. That this list contains roles, permissions, or aliens, doesn't really matter. The role and permission division is just for the people administrating the application, so that access can be dealt with flexibly, without having to change the code of the application.

Roles or permissions will be transformed to Spring Security GrantedAuthorities. Our domain model has specific entities to support this. First is the familiar Account entity, which is shown in Listing 13-26. In bold you will see the many-to-many association it has with Order. The Role entity shown in Listing 13-27, along with its many-to-many association with Permission, is indicated in bold. Finally we have the Permission entity shown in Listing 13-28.

Listing 13-26. The Account, which has a many-to-many association with Role

```java
package com.apress.prospringmvc.bookstore.domain;

import java.io.Serializable;

import javax.persistence.CascadeType;
import javax.persistence.Embedded;
import javax.persistence.Entity;
import javax.persistence.GeneratedValue;
import javax.persistence.GenerationType;
import javax.persistence.Id;
import javax.persistence.ManyToMany;
import javax.validation.Valid;

import org.hibernate.validator.constraints.Email;
import org.hibernate.validator.constraints.NotEmpty;

@Entity
public class Account implements Serializable {

    @Id
    @GeneratedValue(strategy = GenerationType.AUTO)
    private Long id;

    private String firstName;
    private String lastName;

    private Date dateOfBirth;

    @Embedded
    @Valid
    private Address address = new Address();

    @NotEmpty
    @Email
    private String emailAddress;
    @NotEmpty
    private String username;
    @NotEmpty
    private String password;

    @ManyToMany(cascade = CascadeType.ALL)
    private List<Role> roles = new ArrayList<Role>();

    //Omitting getter and setter methods for class instance variables
}
```

Listing 13-27. The Role entity, which has in turn a many-to-many association with Permission

```
package com.apress.prospringmvc.bookstore.domain;

import java.io.Serializable;
import java.util.ArrayList;
import java.util.List;

import javax.persistence.CascadeType;
import javax.persistence.Entity;
import javax.persistence.GeneratedValue;
import javax.persistence.GenerationType;
import javax.persistence.Id;
import javax.persistence.ManyToMany;
import javax.persistence.Table;
import javax.persistence.UniqueConstraint;

@Entity
@Table(uniqueConstraints = { @UniqueConstraint(columnNames = { "role" }) })
public class Role implements Serializable {

    @Id
    @GeneratedValue(strategy = GenerationType.AUTO)
    private Long id;

    private String role;

    @ManyToMany(cascade = CascadeType.ALL)
    private List<Permission> permissions = new ArrayList<Permission>();

    Role() {
        // For ORM
    }

    public Role(String role) {
        this.role = role;
    }

    //Omitting getter and setter methods for class instance variables
}
```

Listing 13-28. The Permission entity

```
package com.apress.prospringmvc.bookstore.domain;

import java.io.Serializable;

import javax.persistence.Entity;
import javax.persistence.GeneratedValue;
import javax.persistence.GenerationType;
import javax.persistence.Id;
```

```
import javax.persistence.Table;
import javax.persistence.UniqueConstraint;

@Entity
@Table(uniqueConstraints = { @UniqueConstraint(columnNames = { "permission" }) })
public class Permission implements Serializable {

    @Id
    @GeneratedValue(strategy = GenerationType.AUTO)
    private Long id;

    private String permission;

    Permission() {
        // Form ORM
    }

    public Permission(String permission) {
        this.permission = permission;
    }

    //Omitting getter and setter methods for class instance variables
}
```

This setup is pretty straightforward. An Account has a number of roles, and each role has a number of permissions. As we've stated: an `Account` can have multiple Roles and a Role can have multiple Permissions.

Finally we need to populate our security principal with these roles and permissions. As you remember, we created a custom implementation of a Spring Security `UserDetailsService` (`com.apress.prospringmvc.bookstore.web.security.BookstoreUserDetailsService`). We will extend this now to load the list of granted authorities, as shown in Listing 13-29.

Listing 13-29. Extending the BookstoreUserDetailsService functionality to load the roles and permissions into granted authorities

```
package com.apress.prospringmvc.bookstore.web.security;

import org.apache.commons.lang3.StringUtils;
import org.springframework.beans.factory.annotation.Autowired;
import org.springframework.security.core.GrantedAuthority;
import org.springframework.security.core.authority.SimpleGrantedAuthority;
import org.springframework.security.core.userdetails.UserDetails;
import org.springframework.security.core.userdetails.UserDetailsService;
import org.springframework.security.core.userdetails.UsernameNotFoundException;
import org.springframework.stereotype.Component;

import com.apress.prospringmvc.bookstore.domain.Account;
import com.apress.prospringmvc.bookstore.domain.Permission;
import com.apress.prospringmvc.bookstore.domain.Role;

@Component
public class BookstoreUserDetailsService implements UserDetailsService {
```

```
@Autowired
private AccountService accountService;

@Override
public UserDetails loadUserByUsername(String username) throws
    UsernameNotFoundException {
    if (StringUtils.isBlank(username)) {
        throw new UsernameNotFoundException("Username was empty");
    }

    Account account = accountService.getAccount(username);

    if (account == null) {
        throw new UsernameNotFoundException("Username not found");
    }

    List<GrantedAuthority> grantedAuthorities = new ↵
        ArrayList<GrantedAuthority>();

    for (Role role : account.getRoles()) {
        grantedAuthorities.add(new    ↵
            SimpleGrantedAuthority(role.getRole()));
        for (Permission permission : role.getPermissions()) {
            grantedAuthorities.add(new ↵
                SimpleGrantedAuthority(permission.getPermission()));
        }
    }
    return new BookstoreUserDetails(accountService.getAccount(username), ↵
        grantedAuthorities);
    }
}
```

First we check that the username is not null or blank. If it is, we throw a org.springframework .security.core.userdetails.UsernameNotFoundException. Next we retrieve the Account for the given username. When no matching Account can be found for that username, we again throw a UsernameNotFoundException. Finally we will create a union of all the Roles that are linked to the Account, and all the Permissions linked to each Role and add them to a list of type GrantedAuthority. We wrap each Role or each Permission in a SimpleGrantedAuthority, which is an implementation of the interface GrantedAuthority. The class just takes a String as constructor value and offers a getter for retrieving it later on. You can see this here (we omitted the equals, hashCode and toString implementation for brevity):

```
package org.springframework.security.core.authority;

import org.springframework.security.core.GrantedAuthority;
import org.springframework.security.core.SpringSecurityCoreVersion;
import org.springframework.util.Assert;

public final class SimpleGrantedAuthority implements GrantedAuthority {
```

```
    public SimpleGrantedAuthority(String role) {
        Assert.hasText(role, "A granted authority textual representation is ↵
            required");
        this.role = role;
    }

    public String getAuthority() {
        return role;
    }
}
```

Our principal (`BookstoreUserDetails`) is now populated with a list of `GrantedAuthority`, in which each item represents a role or a permission. In the next section we will see how you can limit access based upon these authorities.

Authorizing Access

So far you have seen how we can secure our application by making all resources accessible for authenticated users only, unless specified otherwise. you saw how we can identify our users by requiring them to enter a username and password on the login page. We also showed how to configure Spring Security so it can authenticate the given credentials. In the previous section we introduced you to RBAC, which led to populating our `com.apress.prospringmvc.bookstore.web.security` `.BookstoreUserDetails` roles and permissions coupled to the user's `Account`.

Our security setup is now almost ready, as all the bits and pieces are in place. The only thing left to perform is authorization based on the information that we now have in our `org.springframework` `.security.core.context.SecurityContext` for an authenticated user. Or better said, we need to indicate which functionality the user is allowed to use based on the roles and permissions coupled to the user's `Account`.

In the following sections we will see how we can control authorization in our pages. We will see that Spring Security comes with its own tag library that offers special tags to disable or enable functionality directly in our JSP pages, based on the presence of certain roles or permissions.

Using Tag Libraries in Our Pages

Spring Security comes with a dedicated tag library you can use to conditionally render certain page components. The use case is always the same: determining whether a certain component or part of the page should be shown to the currently logged-in user based upon the set of authorities.

In order to use the tags, we have to declare the corresponding tag library in our pages. We do this by adding an extra JSP declaration:

```
<%@ taglib prefix="spring" uri="http://www.springframework.org/tags"%>.
```

In the following sections we will illustrate the most important tags and how you can use them.

The authorize Tag

This tag is used to determine whether its contents should be evaluated or not, based on one or more authorization checks. In our case we will use it in exactly the same way as the flow security attribute, or the access attribute of the intercept URL. Using a SpEL expression we will verify if the current authenticated user has the given role in order to let the content be evaluated.

In the first code snippet we will only show the content when the authenticated user has the role ROLE_AUTHOR. In the second snippet the content will only be shown if the authenticated user has the role PERM_ADD_BOOK.

```
<sec:authorize access="hasRole('ROLE_AUTHOR')">
…content…
</sec:authorize>
```

Or

```
<sec:authorize access="hasRole('PERM_ADD_BOOK')">
…content…
</sec:authorize>
```

To illustrate the use of this important tag, we created a separate page, manageBooks.jsp (located in WEB-IN/view/secured/manageBooks). This page will allow a user to add new books to the system, and new categories. In order to use this functionality, the user must be authenticated and have the role ADMIN or AUTHOR. However, for the two functions, adding new categories and books, two separate permissions are required. To add books you should have PERM_ADD_BOOKS and to add a new category you should have PERM_ADD_CATEGORIES.

To demonstrate this page we created two new users in our com.apress.prospringmvc.bookstore .domain.support.InitialDataSetup class, as shown in Listing 13-30.

Listing 13-30: Adding additional users to our initial data setup

```
private Permission permissionAddCategories = new Permission("PERM_ADD_↩
                                        CATEGORIES");
private Permission permissionAddBooks = new Permission("PERM_ADD_BOOKS");
private Permission permissionCreateOrders = new Permission("PERM_CREATE_↩
                                        ORDER");

private Role roleCustomer = new Role("ROLE_CUSTOMER");
private Role roleAdmin = new Role("ROLE_ADMIN");
private Role roleAuthor = new Role("ROLE_AUTHOR");

InitialDataSetup.this.johnDoe = new AccountBuilder() {
    {
        address("Brussels", "1000", "Nieuwstraat", "1", "A", "BE");
        email("foo@test.com");
        credentials("jd", "secret");
        name("John", "Doe");
        roleWithPermissions(InitialDataSetup.this.roleCustomer, ↩
                        InitialDataSetup.this.permissionCreateOrders);
    }
}.build();
```

```
new AccountBuilder() {
    {
        address("Antwerp", "2000", "Meir", "1", "A", "BE");
        email("bar@test.com");
        credentials("admin", "secret");
        name("Super", "User");
        roleWithPermissions(InitialDataSetup.this.roleAdmin,↵
                            InitialDataSetup.this.permissionAddBooks,↵
                            InitialDataSetup.this.permissionAddCategories);
    }
}.build();

new AccountBuilder() {
    {
        address("Gent", "9000", "Abdijlaan", "1", "A", "BE");
        email("baz@test.com");
        credentials("author", "secret");
        name("Some", "Author");
        roleWithPermissions(InitialDataSetup.this.roleAuthor,↵
                            InitialDataSetup.this.permissionAddBooks);
    }
}.build();
```

To summarize, we have the user admin with the role ROLE_ADMIN and the permissions PERM_ADD_BOOKS and PERM_ADD_CATEGORIES. Next we have the user author, who has the role ROLE_AUTHOR and the single permission PERM_ADD_BOOKS. The author user is only able to add books to existing categories, but is not allowed to make new ones (only the admin user is).

Next, in Listing 13-31, we add a new link in our navigation menu, and apply the right security settings using the authorize tag. Notice that we allow both ROLE_ADMIN and ROLE_AUTHOR to access the functionality. Users from both roles should be able to manage books, but inside the page we will further restrict access based on their permissions. We will see this next.

Listing 13-31. Using the authorize tag in our navigation bar to display only the Manage Books link to users with role ROLE_ADMIN or ROLE_AUTHOR

```
<sec:authorize access="hasRole('ROLE_ADMIN') or hasRole('ROLE_AUTHOR') ">
    <li>
        <spring:url value="/secured/manageBooks/manageBooks.htm" ↵
                    var="manageBooks" />
        <a href="${manageBooks}">
            <spring:message code="nav.manageBooks"/>
        </a>
    </li>
</sec:authorize>
```

It is clear that a normal customer (like our user jd) will not be able to see the Manage Books link at all. Only authors and administrators will.

Next we will modify the manage books functionality in the /WEB-INF/view/secured/manageBooks/manageBooks.jsp page (see Listing 13-32). Here we will further control authorization based on the specific permissions.

Listing 13-32. The finer-grained permission checks

```
<%@ taglib prefix="c" uri="http://java.sun.com/jsp/jstl/core"%>
<%@ taglib prefix="spring" uri="http://www.springframework.org/tags" %>
<%@ taglib prefix="form" uri="http://www.springframework.org/tags/form" %>
<%@ taglib prefix="fn" uri="http://java.sun.com/jsp/jstl/functions" %>
<%@ taglib prefix="tiles" uri="http://tiles.apache.org/tags-tiles" %>
<%@ taglib prefix="sec" uri="http://www.springframework.org/security/tags" %>

<c:if test="${not empty actionSuccess}">
    <div id="actionSuccess" style="color: green; display:
            block; margin-bottom: 10px;">
        <table>
            <tr>
                <td>
                    <ul style="list-style-type: disc">
                        <li>
                            <h3>
                                <spring:message code="label.page.managebooks.↵
                                                ${actionSuccess}.added"/>
                            </h3>
                        </li>
                    </ul>
                </td>
            </tr>
        </table>
    </div>
</c:if>


<sec:authorize access="hasRole('PERM_ADD_CATEGORIES')">
    <spring:url value="/secured/addCategory.htm" var="addCategory"/>
    <form:form  action="${addCategory}" commandName="manageCategoryForm">
        <table style="width: 100%">
            <tr>
                <td width="30%">
                    <spring:message code="label.page.managebooks.↵
                                    category.add"/>
                </td>
                <td>
                    <input type="text" name="category" path="category"/>
                    <form:errors path="category" cssClass="error"/>
                    <form:errors/>
                </td>
            </tr>
        </table>
        <div align="right" style="margin-bottom: 20px; margin-top: 10px" >
            <button type="submit" id="add">
                <spring:message code="label.page.managebooks.add.category"/>
            </button>
            <button type="reset" id="clear">
                <spring:message code="label.page.managebooks.clear.category"/>
```

```
            </button>
        </div>
    </form:form>
</sec:authorize>

<sec:authorize access="hasRole('PERM_ADD_BOOKS')">
    <spring:url value="/secured/addBooks.htm" var="addBook"/>
    <form:form modelAttribute="manageBookForm" action="${addBook}"
            method="POST">
        <table style="width: 100%">
            <tr>
                <td width="30%">
                    <spring:message code="label.page.managebooks.↵
                                    book.category"/>
                </td>
                <td>
                    <form:select path="category" items="${manageBookForm.↵
                                selectableCategories}" itemLabel="name" ↵
                                itemValue="id"/>
                    <form:errors path="category" cssClass="error"/>
                </td>
            </tr>

            <%--Omitting remainder of the rows for brevity--%>

        </table>
        <div align="right" style="margin-bottom: 20px; margin-top: 10px" >
            <button type="submit" id="add">
                <spring:message code="label.page.managebooks.book.add"/>
            </button>
            <button type="reset" id="clear">
                <spring:message code="label.page.managebooks.book.clear"/>
            </button>
        </div>
    </form:form>
</sec:authorize>

<script>
    dojo.addOnLoad(function(){
        function fadeIt() {
            if(dojo.byId("actionSuccess")){
                dojo.style("actionSuccess", "opacity", "1");
                var fadeOutArgs = {node: "actionSuccess", duration: 15000};
                dojo.fadeOut(fadeOutArgs).play();
            }
        }
    fadeIt();
    });
</script>
```

The first if block and the last JavaScript block are used to display a message whenever a Category or Book is added successfully. This JavaScript code is the same as we used to show a message when the user has logged or when an order is made. In the latter case the user is redirected to the ordersOverview page and a message pops up up with the username and the order ID of the newly placed order. In all cases the JavaScript will let the displayed message slowly disappear.

The first authorize tag (in bold) ensures that you must have the permission to add categories (PERM_ADD_CATEGORIES). In our case the author will not be able to do this. This "add category" section will not be shown to users with a role that does have the proper authorization; in our case the user author will not see this section.

The second authorize tag requires the permission to add books (PERM_ADD_BOOKS). Both authors and admins will be able to do this. To illustrate this, when we login with user "jd" the menu option to manage books will not even be shown, as you can see in Figure 13-13.

Figure 13-13. *Logging in with user "jd" does not display the Manage Books menu option.*

When we log in as an author, the menu option Manage Books is shown. When we click on it we will see that we only can add books, as shown in Figure 13-14.

Figure 13-14. *Logging in with user "author" displays the Manage Books menu option, but only allows us to add books.*

Finally, when we login as admin, the Manage Books link is shown in the navigation bar as well, but now we are allowed to add categories and books, as can be seen in Figure 13-15.

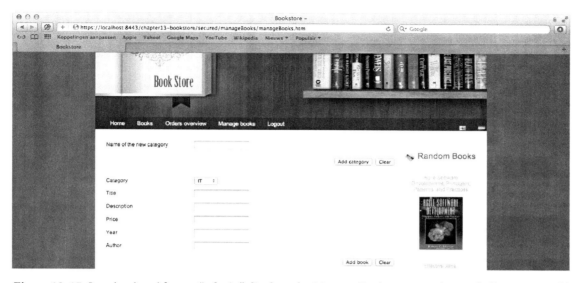

***Figure 13-15.** Logging in with user "admin" displays the Manage Book menu option and allows us to add books and categories.*

Before we wrap up this section, there is one last thing we want to show. In the earlier section "Logging Out," we said that we still need to make an additional change. The Logout button in the menu should only to be shown when the user has already logged in, and the Login button should be hidden (it should only be shown when the user is not authenticated yet). Now that we have seen the authorize tag, this is just a matter of adding another one in the header.jsp. In Listing 13-33 we show an excerpt from the header.jsp applying this tag around the Logout and Login menu links (shown in bold).

***Listing 13-33.** Adding the authorization tag for the login and logout link in WEB-INF/templates/header.jsp*

```
<ul>

    <%--Omitting other navigation bar links for brevity--%>

    <sec:authorize access="! authenticated">
        <li>
            <spring:url value="/public/authentication/login.htm" var="login"          />
            <a href="${login}">
                <spring:message code="nav.login"/>
            </a>
        </li>
    </sec:authorize>
    <sec:authorize access="hasRole('ROLE_ADMIN') or hasRole('ROLE_AUTHOR') ">
        <li>
            <spring:url value="/secured/manageBooks/manageBooks.htm" ↵
                    var="manageBooks" />
            <a href="${manageBooks}">
                <spring:message code="nav.manageBooks"/>
```

```
        </a>
    </li>
</sec:authorize>
<sec:authorize access="fullyAuthenticated">
    <li>
        <spring:url value="/logout" var="logout" />
        <a href="${logout}">
            <spring:message code="nav.logout"/>
        </a>
    </li>
</sec:authorize>
<ul>
```

The first authorize tag in bold will only render its contents (the Login link) when we are not authenticated yet. The second authorize tag in bold will only render its content (the Logout link) when we are authorized.

The authentication Tag

This tag allows access to the current org.springframework.security.core.Authentication object stored in the security context. It can render any property of the object directly in the JSP. You can use it, for example, to display information from the principal, which is in our case the BookstoreUserDetails object (see Listing 13-34).

Listing 13-34. The authentication tag rendering the username

```
<sec:authentication property="principal.username"/>
```

This will display the username of the user currently logged in.

We applied this code to our homepage, located in WEB-INF/view/public/main.jsp, as can be seen in Listing 13-12 earlier. We have configured Spring Security to forward us to the home page when login was successful. We also added a special parameter (authenticationOk) to indicate that. The home page will display a message that the login was successful, including the username. We have extracted that snippet from Listing 13-12 and repeated it in Listing 13-35 for your convenience. Here we use the var and scope attributes to bind the result (from the property indicated in the property attribute) with the given variable name (username) to the indicated scope (Servlet request scope)

Listing 13-35. The authentication tag storing the username in request scope

```
<h3>
    <sec:authentication property="principal.username" var="username" ↵
                        scope="request"/>

    <spring:message code="label.page.main.authentication.ok" ↵
                    arguments="${username}" />
</h3>
```

You can see the result in Figure 13-16, where we logged in as user jd. The JavaScript on the bottom is there to let the message slowly fade away as we have done elsewhere when showing notification messages.

Figure 13-16. *The message shown after logging in*

Using Annotations in Our Code

Securing your pages using the authorization tag is not sufficient, as we will see. Hiding a link (which is the main task of the authorization tag) won't do the trick if the user knows or guesses the direct link. In that case the user still will get access (assuming you didn't place a specific `intercept-url` for that page with proper authorization checks).

In this section we will see that you can also secure your application controller methods and back-end services using annotations. This way you are sure that if a user escapes the front-end security, the user will be blocked on the next level. Applying security in your back-end services can also be useful if you have different frontend layers using the same back-end.

Until now we have seen three places where we can put specific authorization check points:

- On the requested resource, using `intercept-url`

- On your flows

- For a more fine grained approach, in the pages themselves using the authorize tag

This leaves us with a gap. With our last example in mind, we added specific permission checks on the `manageBooks.jsp` page. Only users with the `PERM_ADD_BOOKS` permission are able to add books, and only users with the `PERM_ADD_CATEGORIES` are able to add categories. But what would happen if a user with the author role (who cannot add categories) were to simulate an http POST request adding a new category?

This is still a potential weakness in our system. While the authorization tag on the page only hides a component, the controller listening for the request is still there. So anyone who knows the correct URL and the request parameters can still invoke the controller directly.

Besides adding a `intercept-url` with fine grained authorization control (specifying roles and or permissions) for each of the pages, you can also use method-specific annotations as shown in Listing 13-36.

Listing 13-36. *Using method security in the application controller*

```
@RequestMapping("secured/addCategory.htm")
@PreAuthorize("hasRole('PERM_ADD_CATEGORIES')")
public ModelAndView addCategory(
```

By adding the annotation org.springframework.security.access.prepost.PreAuthorize on the controller request mapping to add books, we implemented an additional check. Try it out for yourself— put the <sec:authorize access="hasRole('PERM_ADD_CATEGORIES')"> in comments in the manageBooks.jsp and log in using the user author. Because the tag is commented out, the component to add categories is shown. If you try to add one, you'll get the famous "403 access denied" page.

Before Spring Security will process these annotations you need to enable method security. We did this in src/main/resources/spring-security.xml, as you can see in Listing 13-37.

Listing 13-37. Enabling method-level security

```
<security:global-method-security pre-post-annotations="enabled"/>
```

Next we will also secure the addBooks method, as we did for the addCategory method, in Listing 13-38.

Listing 13-38. Using method security in the application controller

```
@RequestMapping("secured/addBooks.htm")
@PreAuthorize("hasRole('PERM_ADD_BOOKS')")
public ModelAndView addBooks(
```

To make the entire chain secure, you can also add these annotations on your service layer. Once you do this there is no way that someone can bypass your security and invoke a function that is not allowed for the current principal.

To conclude, we want to say a few words about Security exceptions. Normally your users should not run against such exceptions as part of normal navigation throughout your application. We shielded all links in the pages using the authorization tag; so in other words, if a user does not have access to a certain link (or button) it will simply not be shown. However, if a user starts to fiddle with the URLs, it might still be possible to access a forbidden URL. In that case the user will hit the security annotations on your application controllers or back-end, and a 403 access denied message will be shown. If you want customize this behavior, you have two options:

- You can use the JEE Servlet <error-page> in a web.xml to forward to a certain page upon an <error-code> (in this case 403).

- You can use Spring Security org.springframework.security.web.access .ExceptionTranslationFilter, which can handle both org.springframework .security.access.AccessDeniedException and org.springframework.security .core.AuthenticationException. Its main purpose is to forward the user to a login page if not authenticated yet, or to a predefined error page if the current user lacks sufficient rights. For your convenience this filter was already registered by using the Spring Security namespace configuration (<security:http>). In fact one of the http element's direct attributes is access-denied-page="…", which allow you to specify a page to forward to whenever such a security-related exception occurs. This attribute will directly be given to the ExceptionTranslationFilter when the entire Spring Security configuration is built.

Summary

Security in general is a very complex and broad domain. However, we have shown you in this chapter that basic security for an average web application does not have to be complex. On the contrary, we have shown with a small bit of XML and a filter configuration how you can make your pages secure, so that only those pages explicitly listed can be accessed.

Later we showed that customization using a custom `UserDetailsService` is also not very complex, but it allows you to adapt your user store to any existing database structure you might have. Finally, we showed how to perform authorization based upon the permissions granted to a principal in your pages, your flows and controllers.

To conclude, we hope that you learned that with minimal effort your application can be secured. With such a great tool as Spring Security available, there should no longer be a reason not to build in basic security in your applications.

This chapter was written to give you an overview of the possibilities and get you started quickly. Your environment might have specific security requirements. In that case we hope that this chapter has warmed you up to go and read more detailed material about Spring Security and what it can do to suit specific requirements.

APPENDIX A

Cloud Foundry: Deploying to the Cloud

In this appendix, we will discuss what it takes to get our application to run on a different environment than what we have been running it on so far. Instead of running on any boring old Tomcat instance, we'll run it in the *cloud*. But before we get down to it, we'll talk just a little bit about what the cloud means.

Cloud Computing

You probably haven't been able to avoid the onslaught of cloud computing in the specialized media. But you may still not have an idea of what cloud computing entails. We'll try to give a short overview of what cloud computing is about.

It's hard to give a single definition of what cloud computing is, as it tends to mean different things to different people. One broader definition goes like this:

> *Cloud Computing is a distributed computing model consisting of three tiers— infrastructure, platform, and services—that enables ubiquitous, convenient, on-demand network access to a shared pool of configurable computing resources (e.g., networks, servers, storage, applications, and services).*

Consider Amazon S3,[1] for example: Amazon allows you to store data on its servers using web-based APIs. You pay Amazon for the bandwidth you use in uploading or downloading that data. At no point in time do you ever need to have your own storage infrastructure.

There are several kinds of cloud service models in use:

- *Infrastructure as a service (IaaS)*: Delivers computing infrastructure as a service. Examples of such infrastructure include virtual computers, storage, network infrastructure, and so forth. This is more the realm of sysadmins than developers. Amazon and Rackspace are two of the best-known IaaS providers.

---

[1] http://aws.amazon.com/es/s3/

- *Platform as a service (PaaS)*: Offers services beyond the infrastructure. Here, the emphasis is on the development environment, application services, and application-deployment mechanisms. The control over the actual infrastructure itself is mostly handed by the service provider. Good examples of a PaaS approach are Google App Engine and Cloud Foundry.

- *Software as a service (SaaS)*: Provides the delivery of a full solution as a service, eliminating the need to install and run the application on the customer's own computers and simplifying maintenance and support. Contrast this with the traditional delivery model for software, where end users install software on every desktop, manage the upgrades themselves, and so on. In this model, the user just visits a website and begins using the application online. Google Docs is a good example of a SaaS.

Cloud Foundry

In this appendix, we'll use Cloud Foundry as our PaaS of choice to deploy our bookstore application to. But what is Cloud Foundry and why would we want to use it?

Cloud Foundry describes itself like this:

> *[Cloud Foundry is] an open platform as a service, providing a choice of clouds, developer frameworks and application services. Initiated by VMware, with broad industry support, Cloud Foundry makes it faster and easier to build, test, deploy and scale applications. It is an open source project and is available through a variety of private cloud distributions and public cloud instances, including CloudFoundry.com.[2]*

Now what does this mean? It means that Cloud Foundry is not a proprietary, vendor-specific PaaS, but a truly open platform that is being developed by several individuals and organizations. For example, ActiveState offers Stackato,[3] an expansion of Cloud Foundry that offers Python, PHP, and Perl support. Ubuntu is also working on supporting Cloud Foundry under their Ubuntu Cloud[4] banner.

It also means that we have to define some things more explicitly:

- *Cloud Foundry* is the name of the open source project. You can find the code for this on github;[5] its website is at `www.cloudfoundry.org`.

- *Cloudfoundry.com* is a VMWare–hosted instance of Cloud Foundry that lets you deploy your application on VMWare–owned infrastructure.

In the course of this appendix, we don't differentiate between Cloud Foundry the platform and CloudFoundry.com the hosted service.

---

[2] `http://www.cloudfoundry.com`
[3] `http://www.activestate.com/stackato`
[4] `http://cloud.ubuntu.com`
[5] `https://github.com/cloudfoundry/`

Now that we've seen what Cloud Foundry is, why should we as Java/Spring developers care? Why should we use it over any other PaaS? One reason: The fact that Cloud Foundry is an open, multi-vendor platform is very nice because it helps us avoid the dangers of vendor-locking and the related costs.

Another reason: It also has multi-language support, including Ruby, Java, Scala, and NodeJs; and it offers many services, from relational stores such as MySQL and PostgreSQL, to queues like RabbitMQ, to NoSQL storage like MongoDB and Redis. Another big advantage is that it integrates very nicely with Spring. These things combined make Cloud Foundry a very interesting platform.

CloudFoundry.com, the VMWare–hosted version of Cloud Foundry, is still in beta at the time of writing. Nevertheless, you can sign up for it by going to https://my.cloudfoundry.com/signup and entering an e-mail address. After reading and agreeing with the Terms of Service, you can click the Request Invite button. You'll get an e-mail confirming your signup request. Later (it can take a few hours or even a day), you'll receive an e-mail with the credentials you need to actually deploy on CloudFoundry.com. That's all you need to do to register.

Deploying Our Application

In this section, we are going to describe how we can deploy the sample application on Cloud Foundry. We will describe each step in detail and also explain the modifications we must do to make everything work as expected. If you want to perform the actions described here yourself, we will assume that you have read the initial chapter on how to set up your environment. We are also assuming you have either STS or an Eclipse instance with the STS plug-in installed.

Installing the Cloud Foundry Plug-in

Although Cloud Foundry offers several tools to get your application deployed, the fastest way to get started when you first dive in is to use the Eclipse plug-in. The alternative is using the VMC command-line application, which is implemented as a Ruby gem. An advanced user can't escape using the VMC command-line; but for the scope of this appendix, we'll use the Eclipse plug-in.

Note RubyGems[6] is the package manager for Ruby. It is comparable to apt-get for Ubuntu or yum for Red Hat. A *gem* is a packaged Ruby application or library. You can find more info on the VMC install at http://start.cloudfoundry.com/tools/vmc/installing-vmc.html. If you have Ubuntu, you can also directly install the command-line client using apt-get install cloudfoundry-client.

We'll start by installing the Cloud Foundry Eclipse plug-in. Go to the STS plug-in Dashboard (it can be found under Menu ➤ Help ➤ Dashboard), click the Extensions tab found on the bottom of the window, and search for *cloud foundry* in the search bar. Check the found extension, and then click the Install button on the bottom right, as seen in Figure A-1.

---

[6] http://rubygems.org

Figure A-1. Finding the Cloud Foundry plug-in

You'll get the normal plug-in installation windows that ask you to accept or reject the license agreement. Click the Next and OK buttons until you get a dialog asking you to restart Eclipse, and then choose to restart it by clicking Restart now.

Now that we've installed the plug-in, we can proceed to the next step: deploying our application on Cloud Foundry.

Making Some Adjustments

The teams behind Spring and Cloud Foundry have worked at making it very easy to deploy Spring apps on Cloud Foundry. It is an explicit goal to make Spring applications deployable without changing one line of configuration or code in most cases.

Unfortunately, this is not entirely true for our application because it will not get deployed without us making some changes. The main reason is that Cloud Foundry, at the time of writing, only provides a Tomcat 6 instance (support for Tomcat 7 is on the road map). The other driver for change is the way SSL is set up in Cloud Foundry, which has some impact on the way we configure Spring Security.

Switching to Tomcat 6

Tomcat 6 is a Java EE5 servlet container, so it does not implement the Servlet 3 API. The local server instance we have been using so far is Tomcat 7, which is Java EE 6 compliant. Our sample applications have an explicit dependency on Java EE 6—and the Servlet 3 API in particular.

Until now, we've been bootstrapping the Spring application context in BookstoreWebApplicationInitializer, which is an implementation of org.springframework.web .WebApplicationInitializer. The WebApplicationInitializer mechanism is what allowed us to get by without using a web.xml file for so long; however, it depends on a Servlet 3 implementation to work.

Because of Cloud Foundry's use of Tomcat 6, we have to revert to a Servlet 2.5 environment, and we'll need to create a web.xml file in which we'll re-create what we're doing in the BookstoreWebApplicationInitializer. To do this, we need an ApplicationContext, a DispatcherServlet, an OpenEntityManagerInViewFilter, and the filter that configures Spring security.

By adding a ContextLoaderListener, we can make sure that an ApplicationContext will get booted (see Listing A-1).

Listing A-1. Adding a ContextLoaderListener in the web.xml File

```
<!-
    tells the ContextLoaderListener where to look for applicationContext
    xml files
-->
<context-param>
    <param-name>contextConfigLocation</param-name>
    <param-value>classpath:/spring/context.xml</param-value>
</context-param>

<!-- the Listener will be called by the servlet container,
    which will then boot a Spring ApplicationContext for us -->
<listener>
    <listener-class>
        org.springframework.web.context.ContextLoaderListener
    </listener-class>
</listener>
```

We also need to declare a DispatcherServlet by using the servlet tag, as shown in Listing A-2.

Listing A-2. Adding a DispatcherServlet in the web.xml File

```
<servlet>
  <servlet-name>dispatcher</servlet-name>
  <servlet-class>
    org.springframework.web.servlet.DispatcherServlet
  </servlet-class>
  <init-param>
    <param-name>contextClass</param-name>
    <!-- note that we're specifying the type of ApplicationContext here.
        We're using an AnnotationConfigWebApplicationContext and configure it
        to use the classes we specified in  contextConfigLocation as
        configuration classes.
      -->
    <param-value>
```

```
        org.springframework.web.context.support.
AnnotationConfigWebApplicationContext
      </param-value>
    </init-param>
    <init-param>
      <param-name>contextConfigLocation</param-name>
        <param-value>
        com.apress.prospringmvc.bookstore.web.config.WebflowContextConfiguration
        com.apress.prospringmvc.bookstore.web.config.WebMvcContextConfiguration
        </param-value>
    </init-param>
    <load-on-startup>1</load-on-startup>
</servlet>

<servlet-mapping>
    <servlet-name>dispatcher</servlet-name>
    <url-pattern>/</url-pattern>
</servlet-mapping>
```

We are creating two application contexts, splitting the back-end configuration (e.g., datasources, services, repositories, and so on) from the front-end configuration (e.g., Spring MVC, Spring Web Flow, the @Controllers, and so forth).

The ContextLoaderListener will be responsible for bootstrapping the back end–application context. The DispatcherServlet will bootstrap its own context for the front end. While the DispatcherServlet is booting its own context, it will find the back-end ApplicationContext we've booted using the ContextLoaderListener. It will set this context as a parent context for its own application context. The fact that we now have two application contexts instead of one doesn't have a real impact on us. You just need to be aware that the root context (which was booted by the ContextLoaderListener) will have no access to beans booted by the dispatcher servlet application context because a child context can access beans in the parent context, but not vice versa.

We are also using two types of application context classes now. For the back end, we are using the XmlWebApplicationContext, which will start from a standard XML application context file. The use of the XmlWebApplicationContext is not explicitly mentioned in the web.xml because the ContextLoaderListener uses this class by default. In that context file, we import the spring-security.xml and load the @Configuration-annotated classes using <context:annotation-config/> and <context:component-scan/>.

For the DispatcherServlet, however, we directly use the AnnotationConfigWebApplicationContext and feed it with the @Configuration-annotated configuration classes for the front end.

You might wonder why we didn't use AnnotationConfigWebApplicationContext in both cases. For example, we could have loaded the spring-security.xml from within an @Configuration class using the @ImportResource annotation in the same way we are using it with the webflow-config.xml in WebflowContextConfiguration:

```
@ImportResource("classpath:/spring/webflow-config.xml")
```

The reason: During deployment, Cloud Foundry will inspect our web.xml and add its own Spring context XML file to be loaded by the ContextLoaderListener at the end of our contextConfigLocation file. The Cloud Foundry Spring config will do some magic, such as automatically replacing our datasource with the internal Cloud Foundry one, which we will discuss later. The problem is that, when using AnnotationConfigWebApplicationContext, we cannot mix annotations and XML files in the contextConfigLocation. So, when using AnnotationConfigWebApplicationContext for the root context, our @Configuration classes would have been loaded, but the spring XML file (which will be added later by Cloud Foundry) would be ignored. Hopefully, this limitation will disappear in the future, so that we'll be able to use any type of application context implementation we want.

Finally, we need to configure the filters, as shown in Listing A-3.

Listing A-3. Adding the Filters to the web.xml File

```
<filter>
    <filter-name>openEntityManagerInViewFilter</filter-name>
    <filter-class>
        org.springframework.orm.jpa.support.OpenEntityManagerInViewFilter
    </filter-class>
</filter>

<filter-mapping>
    <filter-name>openEntityManagerInViewFilter</filter-name>
    <url-pattern>/*</url-pattern>
</filter-mapping>

<filter>
    <filter-name>springSecurityFilterChain</filter-name>
    <filter-class>
        org.springframework.web.filter.DelegatingFilterProxy
    </filter-class>
</filter>

<filter-mapping>
    <filter-name>springSecurityFilterChain</filter-name>
    <url-pattern>/*</url-pattern>
</filter-mapping>
```

We can see the `spring/context.xml` we've specified in the `contextConfigLocation` in Listing A-4.

Listing A-4. The context.xml File

```
<?xml version="1.0" encoding="UTF-8"?>
<beans xmlns="http://www.springframework.org/schema/beans"
       xmlns:xsi="http://www.w3.org/2001/XMLSchema-instance"
       xmlns:context="http://www.springframework.org/schema/context"
       xsi:schemaLocation="
         http://www.springframework.org/schema/beans
         http://www.springframework.org/schema/beans/spring-beans-3.1.xsd
         http://www.springframework.org/schema/context
         http://www.springframework.org/schema/context/spring-context-3.1.xsd">

    <context:annotation-config/>
    <context:component-scan
        base-package="com.apress.prospringmvc.bookstore.config,
        com.apress.prospringmvc.bookstore.web.security"/>
    <import resource="classpath:/spring/spring-security.xml"/>
</beans>
```

In this context file, we're telling Spring to enable the annotation configuration and to look for components in the `com.apress.prospringmvc.bookstore.config` and `com.apress.prospringmvc` `.bookstore.web.security` packages. Because @Configuration classes are also @Components, they will also get picked up.

We're now done with all the changes we need to do to prepare our application for running under Tomcat 6. Next, we'll look at the changes needed for Spring Security.

■ **Note** Chances are the changes just discussed will no longer be necessary by the time you're reading this. Tomcat 7 support is on the roadmap, and it might be implemented by the time you read this. This also demonstrates one of the disadvantages of running on a PaaS: you don't have control over the underlying infrastructure. For example, what if you needed to run on Tomcat 7 right now?

Spring Security Configuration

We are not yet done with our changes. As a consequence of enabling SSL in Spring Security in Chapter 13, Spring Security will now redirect us to an HTTPS connection if it detects we're connecting over HTTP. Cloud Foundry supports SSL, but there is a proxy standing in front of our application. This proxy will terminate the SSL connection. However, the connection between the proxy and the Cloud Foundry Tomcat instance running our application is plain HTTP. Figure A-2 is a bit of a simplification, but it comes close enough to illustrating how things look from a developer's point of view.

Figure A-2. Our application behind the proxy

Before going to our application, the proxy adds some headers that are the result of dealing with the SSL connection. It will tell us which cipher was used, as well as the client certificate if performing mutual (or two-way) SSL. If we just use "normal" SSL without a client certificate, this last header will also be present, but it will have "no value" as its value.

However, Spring Security detects an SSL connection by calling `isSecure()` on the `(Http)ServletRequest`. This will yield `false` because the connection type between the proxy and the application is HTTP. Spring Security will then send out a redirect to the browser, asking to switch over to SSL, which will result in an endless loop.

The work around is to wrap the `(Http)ServletRequest` using a custom filter. We will override the `isSecure()` method to also inspect the HTTP headers when considering whether a connection is secure. If the original implementation decides a connection is not secure, then we'll check for the presence of these specific SSL headers added by the Cloud Foundry proxy before we make a final decision. Listing A-5 shows the filter code, which does nothing more than call `chain.doFilter` using the wrapped `(Http)ServletRequest`. The more interesting part for us is the contained `CloudFoundryHttpServletRequestWrapper` static class, which acts as our wrapper.

What it will do first is call isSecure() from the superclass. If the default behavior says our request is secure, then we leave everything untouched and return the value (true) as-is. When the super implementation returns false, we try to retrieve the sslclientcipher and sslclientcertstatus headers from the HttpServletRequest. If both are present and have a non-empty value, we will consider the request as being a secured request (at least, we will assume that the user's browser used SSL up until the Cloud Foundry proxy), and we will return true instead.

Listing A-5. The Filter that Wraps the HttpRequest

```
public class CloudFoundryHttpServletRequestWrappingFilter extends GenericFilterBean {

    @Override
    public void doFilter(ServletRequest request, ServletResponse response,
                    FilterChain chain) throws IOException, ServletException {
        chain.doFilter(new CloudFoundryHttpServletRequestWrapper((HttpServletRequest)↵
    request), response);
    }

    static class CloudFoundryHttpServletRequestWrapper extends HttpServletRequestWrapper {

        private static final String[] TLS_HEADERS = new String[]
        {"sslclientcipher", "sslclientcertstatus"};

        public CloudFoundryHttpServletRequestWrapper(HttpServletRequest httpServletRequest) {
            super(httpServletRequest);
        }

        @Override
        public boolean isSecure() {
            boolean isSecure = super.isSecure();
            if (!isSecure) {
                boolean isActuallySecure = true;
                for (String header : TLS_HEADERS) {
                    isActuallySecure = isActuallySecure && StringUtils.isNotBlank↵
(getHeader(header));
                }
                isSecure = isActuallySecure;
            }
            return isSecure;
        }
    }
}
```

Overriding the isSecure() method might seem a bit of a drastic measure. However, the Javadoc indicates that it should return true if the connection is considered secure. It is not bound to a specific protocol, so one should never make the assumption that, when isSecure returns true, the protocol is HTTPS by definition. It could also be any other protocol that gives "security" guarantees. Also, given that this implementation is the least intrusive and is the least likely to break when upgrading Spring or Spring

Security, we prefer this solution. Cloud Foundry is also working on better SSL support in the near future, possibly allowing SSL going all the way up to our server.[7]

We'll also have to tell Spring Security to use our extra filter in /spring/spring-security.xml (see Listing A-6).

Listing A-6. *Adding the Filter to the spring-security.xml File*

```
<security:http use-expressions="true" >
    <security:custom-filter
      ref="cloudFoundryHttpServletRequestWrappingFilter"
      before="FIRST"/>

    <security:form-login login-page="/public/authentication/login.htm"
        default-target-url="/public/main.htm?authenticationOk=1"
        authentication-failure-url="/public/authentication/login.htm?authenticationNok=1"  />

    <security:intercept-url pattern="/index.jsp" access="permitAll" />
    <security:intercept-url pattern="/public/authentication/**"
                            access="permitAll" requires-channel="https" />
    <security:intercept-url pattern="/public/createOrders/**"
                            access="permitAll" requires-channel="https" />
    <security:intercept-url pattern="/public/**" access="permitAll" />

    <security:intercept-url pattern="/secured/**"
                            access="fullyAuthenticated"
                            requires-channel="https" />

    <security:intercept-url pattern="/**" access="denyAll" />
</security:http>

<bean id="cloudFoundryHttpServletRequestWrappingFilter"
      class="com.apress.prospringmvc.bookstore.web.security.↵
CloudFoundryHttpServletRequestWrappingFilter"/>
```

Now that we have all this in place, we should be able to deploy our application on Tomcat 6—and hence, on Cloud Foundry—so let's now try to do just that.

Deploying

Deploying to Cloud Foundry with the plug-in follows a process very similar to deploying to a Tomcat instance. Follow these steps to create a server to deploy to:

1.   In the Servers panel, right-click and choose New ➤ Server (see Figure A-3).

---

[7] http://support.cloudfoundry.com/entries/20672161-ssl-support-to-server-instance

Figure A-3. Creating a new server

2. Choose Cloud Foundry, which is found under the VMWare node. You can leave all other options as their defaults.

3. Click Next and you'll get a dialog requesting that you enter the account information that you used when signing up for Cloud Foundry (see Figure A-4). If you haven't done that yet, you can still click the CloudFoundry.com Signup button, which will take you to the website.

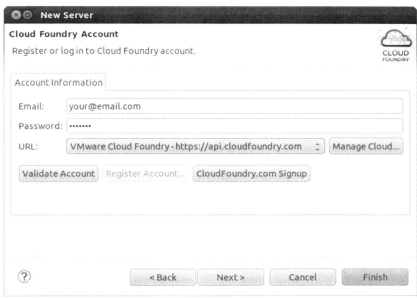

Figure A-4. Configuring your CloudFoundry.com account

4. At this point, it doesn't hurt to be a bit skeptical and click the Validate Account button. It will check that you can connect to Cloud Foundry and that your credentials are OK. Click Finish and the next dialog will ask you which applications you want to deploy.

5. In the left list (Available resources), you can select appendixA-bookstore and then click the Add ➤ button. This will move the application to the Configured resources list and mark it as ready for deployment (this is just like marking your application for deployment on an ordinary Tomcat instance). Next, click Finish.

6. This will take you to the Application Details dialog, which asks you what kind of app you're deploying. Choose Spring, as shown in Figure A-5, and click Finish.

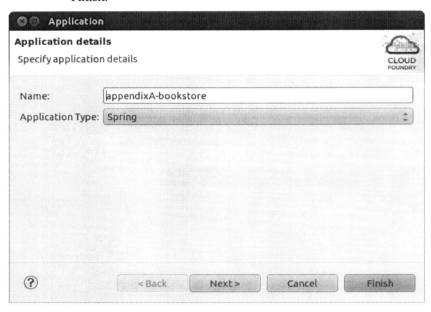

Figure A-5. Choosing the application type and name

7. You get one more dialog asking you for an URL to deploy your application under (see Figure A-6). By default, the URL will be *name-of-the-app*.cloudfoundry.com. You'll need to pick another URL because appendixA-bookstore will already be reserved. You also can choose the amount of memory you want to give to your application by changing the value for Memory Reservation.

Figure A-6. Choosing the URL for our application

8. Now click Finish. We kept the "Start application on deployment" check box selected, so the application will start deploying and booting. (You can also start the application later by manually clicking the Start button in the Cloud Foundry panel on the Applications tab.)

After it finishes deploying, you can point your browser to the URL you configured earlier (`http://appendixa-bookstore.cloudfoundry.com` in our case, but `http://the-name-you-just-chose.cloudfoundry.com` for yours), and see your app running on the cloud (see Figure A-7)!

Figure A-7. Our application running on the cloud

Configuring the Services

We may now have our application running, but there is still something missing: the application is still using its embedded H2 instance, so anytime we restart the app, the data will be gone again. So let's use one of the persistence options that Cloud Foundry offers us. We are using JPA for persistence, so our choice will be limited to the relational databases, MySQL and PostgreSQL:

1. Double-click the VMWare Cloud Foundry server in the Servers panel. You'll see the Overview panel where you can change your account details (see Figure A-8).

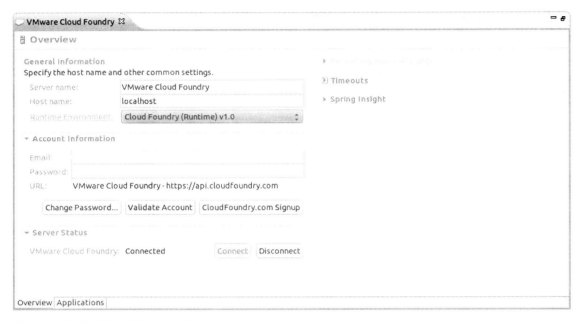

Figure A-8. *The Cloud Foundry Overview panel*

2. Click the Applications tab on the bottom, and you'll see the actual applications you've deployed, as shown in Figure A-9. Click the Add Service button next to the Services panel.

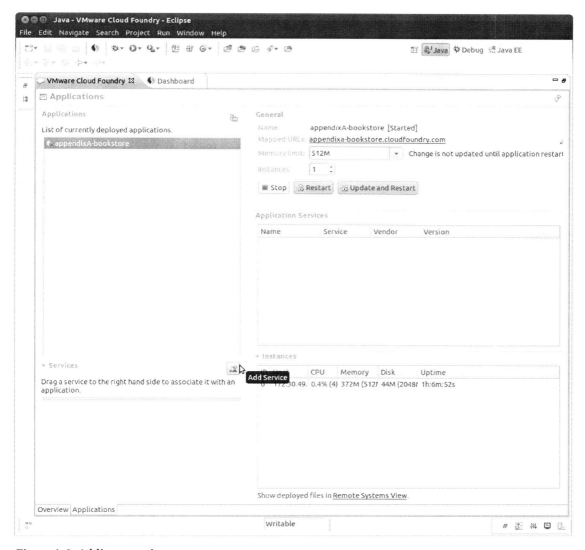

Figure A-9. Adding a service

3. Choose a MySQL database service and give it a name (see Figure A-10).

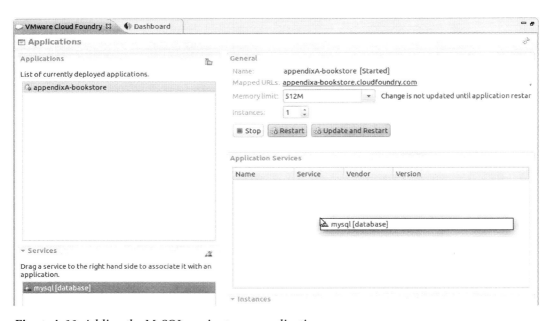

Figure A-10. *Adding a MySQL service*

4. Click Finish, and you'll be taken back to the Applications tab, where you'll see that MySQL is now an available service. (Note that, at the moment of writing, there's a bug in the plug-in that causes the Services panel not to show a service after just adding it. Restarting Eclipse will work around that.)

5. Now select your deployed application and drag the MySQL service from the Services panel to the Application Services panel (see Figure A-11).

■ **Note** You can see the available services (and their version) using the vmc services command.

Figure A-11. *Adding the MySQL service to our application*

That's all it takes to configure the MySQL database. Now click the Update and Restart button, and then navigate to the application with your browser. Orders you make should now survive the restart.

How Does It Work?

You may wonder how it is possible that we're able to save our data in a MySQL database, since we never did configure another datasource in our application. In fact, all we did was tell Cloud Foundry that we wanted to use MySQL as an application service. We never changed our datasource configuration in the `com.apress.prospringmvc.bookstore.config.InfrastructureContextConfiguration` class, and yet we still seem to be able to connect to MySQL on Cloud Foundry.

The magic behind this is explained by what Spring calls *auto-reconfiguration* (see the blog post at the Spring blog[8] for more information).

Remember how we had a choice of application type when deploying? We chose Spring and that enabled Cloud Foundry and Spring to do their magic. What happens is that, during the deployment process, additional configuration is added to your `web.xml` that registers some extra Spring beans into your `ApplicationContext`. (This was exactly the reason why we needed to use XML config, as explained previously.) One of those beans is an `org.cloudfoundry.reconfiguration.CloudAutoStagingBeanFactoryPostProcessor`[9] that will look for beans representing services (e.g., instances of `javax.sql.DataSource`, `org.springframework.data.mongodb.MongoDBFactory`, and so forth) that can be replaced by other cloud-aware beans that know about the application services that are bound to your application.

But what about the Hibernate dialect? Before we were using H2, and now we're using MySQL—yet we didn't have to tell Hibernate anything about this. As it turns out, recent Hibernate versions have a handy feature that can detect the type of database from an actual connection, so there is no longer a need to explicitly configure the dialect to use.

⬚ **Note** This has its disadvantages: if your database isn't up or reachable up while your application is booting, Hibernate will fail at runtime.

Other Configuration Options

Auto-reconfiguration isn't the only way to have your application configured. One of the other, more explicit possibilities is to use the cloud configuration namespace. Using that namespace, we could have configured a datasource in XML, as shown in Listing A-7.

---

[8] http://blog.springsource.org/2011/11/04/using-cloud-foundry-services-with-spring-part-2-auto-reconfiguration/
[9] https://github.com/cloudfoundry/vcap-java/tree/master/auto-reconfiguration/src/main/java/org/cloudfoundry/reconfiguration

Listing A-7. *Using the cloud namespace*

```xml
<?xml version="1.0" encoding="UTF-8"?>
<beans xmlns="http://www.springframework.org/schema/beans"
       xmlns:xsi="http://www.w3.org/2001/XMLSchema-instance"
       xmlns:context="http://www.springframework.org/schema/context"
       xmlns:cloud="http://schema.cloudfoundry.org/spring"
       xsi:schemaLocation="http://www.springframework.org/schema/beans
         http://www.springframework.org/schema/beans/spring-beans-3.1.xsd
         http://www.springframework.org/schema/context
         http://www.springframework.org/schema/context/spring-context-3.1.xsd
         http://schema.cloudfoundry.org/spring
         http://schema.cloudfoundry.org/spring/cloudfoundry-spring-0.8.xsd"
profile="cloud">

    <cloud:data-source id="dataSource" />
</beans>
```

Setting the `profile="cloud"` attribute on the beans element means that the beans defined within the element will only be used if the "cloud" profile is active. The `cloud:datasource` element is a "normal" datasource that represents the relational database application service that was bound to this application.

Combine this with the fact that Cloud Foundry automatically sets *cloud* as the active application profile, and we can have cloud-specific configuration using that profile. This type of explicit configuration is even required if we want to use more than one cloud service of the same type (e.g., a MySQL and PostgreSQL service) at the same time.

If we don't want Spring to use auto-reconfiguration, we can always use the *war* application type. Our application will not get touched in any way if we deploy using that type.

Deploying Locally

So far, we've deployed to the actual cloud infrastructure on cloudfoundry.com, hosted by VMWare. But CloudFoundry.com offers another solution, one that doesn't require us to always connect to a remote system. It's called *MicroCloud,* and it is distributed as a virtual machine (a VMWare image) that we can run locally (such as on the free VMWare player).

You can download MicroCloud from `https://my.cloudfoundry.com/micro` (a valid CloudFoundry.com account is required to download it). On the same site, you can also find instructions on how to configure your MicroCloud. Once that is done, the deployment process is exactly the same as deploying on CloudFoundry.com; you only use a different target.

Debugging with Cloud Foundry

Things don't always go as planned, and there will be times when you will need to debug your application.

While you can always debug your application when deploying on your own Tomcat instance, MicroCloud also supports connecting with a Java debugger. To do so, you can start your application using the Debug button instead your Start button. Once the application is started in debug mode, you can debug it just like any other application started locally.

Another way to find out what's going on while running in the cloud is to take advantage of the log files. You can access them in STS using the Remote Systems view, which you can find using Window ➤ Show View ➤ Other... and then searching for remote systems. You can navigate the remote directory structure and download log files to look at their contents (see Figure A-12).

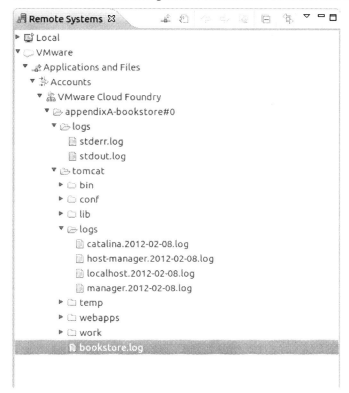

Figure A-12. The remote systems view

If you want remote access to your services (e.g., you want to inspect the current data), Cloud Foundry provides the Caldecott gem that allows you to create a tunnel[10] to them. For example, you can use a command like `vmc tunnel mysql --port 12345` to tunnel to your remote MySQL on local port 12345. Now it's only a matter of pointing your MySQL or JDBC client to that port to get to the data. You can find more info on Caldecott at `http://blog.cloudfoundry.com/post/12928974099/now-you-can-tunnel-into-any-cloud-foundry-data-service`.

---

[10] `http://bit.ly/akrcc1`

Summary

This appendix covered Cloud Foundry and how you can deploy your application on it.

There are a few things that separate Cloud Foundry from competing PaaS providers: one is the open source nature of Cloud Foundry, and another is its excellent integration with the Spring framework. While Cloud Foundry promises a seamless deployment model for most apps, which allows you to deploy your application as-is, you had to make some adjustments in the case of the bookstore application. These adjustments were required mostly because you are using a newer Tomcat version than the one you currently get with Cloud Foundry.

Cloud Foundry is currently still in beta, so it is rapidly evolving, with new features and services still being added. And while you may still run into some rough edges now and then, it is definitely worth keeping an eye on it to see how it evolves in the future.

Index

A

AccountRepository, 296, 298, 299
Acegi security. *See* Spring security
Action execution control
    <on-end> element, 404
    <on-entry> element, 404–405
    <on-exit> element, 405
    <on-render> element, 405
    <on-start> element, 404
    sub-elements, 405–406
Annotation-based controllers
    book detail page, 136
        BookDetailController, 134–135
        detail.jsp, 135
        modified search page, 134
        URL mapping, 135
    book search page
        BookSearchController alternate version,
          133
        BookSearchController with
          BookSearchCriteria, 131–133
        criteria method argument, 133
        data binding, 133
        form code, 130
        RequestParam, 133
        search results, 132
        search.jsp file, 130
    DefaultAnnotationHandlerMapping, 110
    HandlerMapping, 110
    IndexController, 110
    login controller
        AuthenticationException, 128
        handleLogin method, 128
        HttpServletRequest, 128
        initial LoginController, 126–127
        login page, 127
        login.jsp, 125–126
        modified LoginController, 127–128
        RedirectAttributes, 129–130
        RequestParam, 128–129
        username and password parameters, 128
    ModelAndView, 110
    RequestMapping annotation, 110
AnnotationFormatterFactory, 154
Application security, 478
Application testing
    amoeba effect, 274
    automated front-end testing
        infrastructure set up, 310
        minor faults, 310
        performance, render times, and usability,
          309
        Selenium *(see* Selenium)
        Servlet container, 310
        test harness, 310
        Tomcat, 310
    code coverage, 284–286
    environment, 277
    front-end tests via Gradle, 318–319
    goals, 276
    implementation deformation without tests,
        274
    importance, 276
    infrastructure, 276
    integration testing *(see* Integration tests)
    mock objects *(see* Mock objects)
    performance testing, 278
    robot developer, 274, 275
    Spring's test support
        integration test *(see* Integration tests)
        JpaBookRepository, 292–294
    stress testing, 278
    system testing, 278
    test harness, 275
    understanding, 276
    unit testing, 278–279
    user acceptance testing, 278
    VCS, 277
assertEquals method, 283
assertTrue method, 283
Asynchronous JavaScript (AJAX)

AJAX (*cont.*)
    Account Page PUT Ajax Form Submit, 227
    graceful degradation, 227
    HTML, 221–222
    JSON
        BookSearch Controller, 222
        org.springframework.web.bind.annotatio
            n.ResponseBody, 223
        search.jsp file., 223, 224
        sending and receiving, 224–226
    progressive enhancement., 227
    PUT request, 226
    template.jsp file, 220
authenticatedAccount variable, 419
Authentication process, 478, 479
AuthenticationController, 411–413, 420
AuthenticationException, 128
Authorization, 479

B

BookId, 135
BookRepository interface, 292
Bookstore enhancement
    action state, 417–419
    authentication
        action attribute, 412
        attributes and elements, 415
        AuthenticationController, 411, 414–415
        authentication-flow, 411, 413
        authenticationForm, 413, 414
        eventId, 414
        flowExecutionUrl, 413
        implementation procedure, 410
        initializeForm, 411
        page, 411–412
        @RequestMapping, 412
        Spring MVC, 412–413
        subflow attribute, 416
    books selection and delivery options, 387–
        388
    category selection
        on render, 382–384
        on start, 382
        type conversion, 384–386
        type formatting, 386–387
    createOrders-flow, 420–421
    decision state, 416–417
    form validation
        Application Controller, 391–392

        createOrders-flow file, 396
        JSR 303 annotations, 388–390
        messages, 393–395
        OrderController, 395, 398–400
        OrderForm, 395, 397–398
        Web Flow Validator Method and Classes,
            390–391
    javax.servlet.http.HttpSession, 408
    no conversion, 381
    no validation, 381
    outcome events, 419–420
    revised flow, 409
    sample flow refactoring steps, 410
    security mechanism, 408

C

CategoryConverter configuration, 157
Certificate authority (CA), 510, 511
Child flow, 407
Cloud computing, 535, 536
Cloud foundry
    debugging, 552–553
    deploying
        Add Service button, 548
        application details dialog, 546
        auto-reconfiguration, 551
        CloudFoundry.com account
            configuration, 545
        MicroCloud, 552
        MySQL database service, 549, 550
        namespace, 551, 552
        new server creation, 545
        overview panel, 547, 548
        plug-in, 537–538
        spring security configuration (*see* Spring
            security,configuration)
        Tomcat 6(*see* Tomcat 6)
        URL, 546
Collection-based tags, 146
ConditionalGenericConverter API, 152
ConfigurableWebBindingInitializer, 137–139
Confirmation view, 426
@ContextConfiguration, 306
Continuous integration (CI) system, 277
Controllers
    annotation-based controllers (*see*
        Annotation-based controllers)
    configuring view controllers, 111–112
    data binding (*see* Data binding)

definition, 107
implementations, 109–110
interface-based controllers, 108
internationalization (*see*
    Internationalization)
request-handling methods (*see* Request-
    handling methods)
Conversation scope, 378
ConversionService API, 152
ConverterFactory API, 151
CookieValue annotation, 123
CreateOrders-flow, 416

D

Data access object (DAO), 281–282
Data binding, 133
    BookSearchCriteria JavaBean, 136–137
    global customization, 137–139
    ModelAttribute
        form tag library (*see* Form tag library)
        on method arguments, 142–143
        on methods, 141–142
        SessionAttributes, 143–144
        spring tag library, 144
    nested binding, 137
    per controller customization, 139–141
    setCategory method, 137
    setTitle method, 137
    type conversion (*see* Type conversion)
    validation, model attributes
        AccountValidator implementation, 164–
            165
        bind errors, 163
        error codes, field errors, 165
        JSR-303, 167–170
        MessageSource configuration, 163–164
        registration page with error codes, 167
        RegistrationController, 166
        requiredFields, 165
        supports method, 163
        validator interface, 163
DateFormatAnnotationFormatterFactory, 154–
    155
DateFormatter, 153–154
DefaultHandlerExceptionResolver, 200
DispatcherServlet
    Bootstrapping
        ServletContainerInitializer, 76–77
        The Servlet 3.0 specification, 74

web.xml, 75–76
WebApplicationInitializer 77–78
web-fragment.xml configuration, 76
configuration
    application context, 80–83
    component resolution, 83–85
    default configuration, 85–86
    properties, 78–80
    Spring @MVC Defaults, 86–87
DummyDao class, 285–286

E

EclEmma, 284–286
EntityManager, 291
Event, 374
Execution scope, 378
ExternalRedirect attribute, 426

F

File uploads
    configuration
        Apache, 230–231
        exception handling, 235
        request handling method (*see* Request
            handling method)
        Servlet 3.0, 228–230
    controller modification, 228
    implementations, 228
    registration, 228
Flash attributes, 118
Flash scope, 376–377
Flow scope, 377–379
Flow variables, 401
flowExecutionUrl implicit object, 379
FlowInputMappingException, 424
Form tag library, 145
    order JSP, 147
    path attribute, 146
    search page with category, 148
    shared form tag attributes, 146
    title field, 147
Formatter API, 152–153
FormatterRegistry interface, 155–156

G

GenericConverter API, 151–152
Global transitions, 406

H

Handlelogin method, 128, 301–304
HandlerExceptionResolver, 198
Handlerexecution chain
    determination, 68, 69
    exception handling, 71
    execution, 69–71
Hibernate validator JAR file, 394, 395
Home page, 500–501
HTTP protocol
    HiddenHttpMethodFilter
        Account.jsp Heading, 219
        AccountController Update Method, 219
        BookstoreWebApplicationInitializer, 218
    methods of, 216
    URL points, 217
HttpPutFormContentFilter, 226, 227

I

Init-binder method, 141
Inline flows, 407
Integration tests, 277, 279–280
    annotation configuration, 289
    ApplicationContext, 289, 290
    architecture and reusability, 280
    @Configuration classes, 288
    context configuration addition, 288
    @ContextConfiguration annotation, 288
    @DirtiesContext annotation, 290
    DMBS, 280
    Gradle command, 289–290
    HQL/JPQL query, 280
    in-memory equivalents, 279
    JpaBookRepository, in src/test/java, 287
    listeners, 287
    "real" system resources, 279
    runner addition, 287
    Spring configuration, 288
    SpringJUnit4ClassRunner, 287
    test suite, 289
    testability, 280
    TestExecutionListener annotation, 287
    transaction management, 290–292
Interceptors
    callbacks, 186
    HandlerInterceptor
        AccountController, 196–197
        configuration, 196

        403 error page, 197
        interface, 187
        SecurityHandlerInterceptor, 195
    HandlerMapping configuration, 188
    interceptorregistry, 189–191
    WebRequestInterceptor
        CommonDataInterceptor, 192, 193
        postHandle method, 193
        Random Books section, 193–195
        welcome page, 192
    WebRequestInterceptor Interface, 187
Interface-based controllers, 108
Internationalization
    LocaleChangeInterceptor
        book search page in Dutch, 176
        book search page in English, 175
        book search page with message tag, 174–175
        configuration, 173
    LocaleResolver, 172
    message source, 170–172
Inversion of Control (IoC), 29

J, K

java.io.Serializable, 401
Java's transient, 401
javax.servlet.http.HttpServletRequest, 379

L

LocaleChangeInterceptor
    book search page in Dutch, 176
    book search page in English, 175
    book search page with message tag, 174–175
    configuration, 173
LocalValidatorFactoryBean, 390
Login page, 498–500
LoginController, 302–304
LoginControllerTest, 307–309

M

Match attribute, 508
Mock objects
    AccountService
        @After method, 299
        @Before method, 299
        AuthenticationService, 298
        complete test case, 299–301

ContextConfiguration annotation, 298
findByUsername method, 298, 299
login method, 296
Mockito methods, 299
programming, 298
save method, 296
src/test/java, 297
testLoginFailure, 298
verification, 299
dummy, 295, 296
fake, 295
JpaBookRepository, 296
MVC logic
handleLogin method, 302–304
MockHttpServletRequest, 304–305
RDBMS, 296
stubs, 295, 296
test doubles, 295
verification phase, 295
MockHttpServletRequest, 304–306
MockHttpServletResponse, 306
MockHttpSession, 306
Model View Controller (MVC), 51
crosscutting concerns
exception handling, 197–201
SimpleMappingExceptionResolver, 201–204
components, 301
DispatcherServlet (*see* DispatcherServlet)
FlashMapManager, 104, 105
HandlerAdapter
AnnotationMethodHandlerAdapter, 96
HandlerAdapter API, 94
HttpRequestHandlerAdapter, 95
implementations, 95
RequestMappingHandlerAdapter, 96
SimpleControllerHandlerAdapter, 95
SimpleServletHandlerAdapter, 96
HandlerExceptionResolver
API, 101
implementations, 102
ViewResolver, 103, 104
HandlerMapping
BeanNameUrlHandlerMapping, 90–91
ControllerBeanNameHandlerMapping, 92
ControllerClassNameHandlerMapping, 92–93
DefaultAnnotationHandlerMapping, 93–94
HandlerMapping API, 88

implementations, 89
RequestMappingHandlerMapping, 93–94
SimpleUrlHandlerMapping, 91–92
URL mapping, 90
JSPs, 301
LocaleResolver
AcceptHeaderLocaleResolve, 99
API, 98
CookieLocaleResolver, 99
FixedLocaleResolver, 99
implementations, 98
SessionLocaleResolver, 99
MultipartResolver
API, 96–97
implementations, 97
library, 97
StandardServletMultipartResolver, 97
org.springframework.web.servlet
afterCompletion method, 72, 73
Handlerexecution chain (*see*
Handlerexecution chain.)
request processing flow, 67–68
request processing summary, 73–74
request processing workflow, 66
view rendering process, 71–72
RequestDataValueProcessor, 212–213
RequestMappingHandlerAdapter
account page, 212
accountcontroller, 211
HandlerMethodArgumentResolver, 207
HandlerMethodReturnValueHandler, 207
Modified WebMvcContextConfiguration, 210–211
SessionAttribute Annotation, 208
SessionAttributeProcessor, 209, 210
RequestMappingHandlerMapping, 205–206
scopes
Add to Cart Link, 180–182
annotation property, 178
CartController Bean, 180
CheckoutController, 183–185
session, 178, 179
singleton scope, 178
Spring mock objects
handleLogin method, 302–304
MockHttpServletRequest, 304–305
Spring MVC test
@Configuration classes, 306
build.gradle, 305
configuration, 306
LoginControllerTest, 307–309

MVC, Spring MVC test (*cont.*)
    MVC infrastructure, 306
    snapshot, 305
    WebApplicationContext, 306
    ThemeResolver
        API, 100
        CookieThemeResolver, 101
        FixedThemeResolver, 101
        implementations, 100
        SessionThemeResolver, 101
    ViewNameTranslator, 102–103
ModelAndView, 108
ModelAttribute annotation, 120, 122, 124
    form tag library, 145
        order JSP, 147
        path attribute, 146
        search page with category, 148
        shared form tag attributes, 146
        title field, 147
    on method arguments, 142–143
    on methods, 141–142
    request-handling methods, 122
    spring tag library, 144
ModelnameValidator class, 391

N

NoMatchingTransitionException, 419

O

Object relational mapping (ORM), 291, 294
OrderController class, 392, 394
OrderFormValidator class, 391
org.springframework.validation.BindingResult
    attribute, 160
org.springframework.webflow.execution.Reques
    tContext object, 402

P, Q

Param, 379
ParameterizableViewController, 111
Parent flow, 407
PathVariable annotation, 122
Performance testing, 278
PlaceOrder() method, 419
Post Redirect Get (PRG) idiom, 426

R

RedirectAttributes, 118
RegistrationController, 158–160
Representational state transfer (REST)
    HTTP protocol (*see* HTTP protocol)
    PUT request, 226
    resources identification, 215–216
Request scope, 374–376
RequestBody annotation, 121
Request-handling methods
    account page, 231
    attributes, 113–114
    coarse-grained mapping, 113
    Multipart File, 232
    MultipartHttpServletRequest, 233
    sample file upload output, 232
    sample mappings, 114–115
    Servlet 3.0, 234
    supported method argument annotations,
        119
        CookieValue, 123
        HandlerMethodArgumentResolver
          interface, 119–120
        ModelAttribute annotation, 120, 122
        PathVariable, 122
        RequestBody, 121
        RequestHeader, 121
        RequestParam, 120
        RequestPart, 121–122
    supported method argument types, 115–117
        RedirectAttributes, 118
        UriComponentsBuilder, 118
    supported method return values, 123–125
    UploadOrderForm, 233–234
RequestHeader annotation, 121
RequestParam annotation, 120
RequestParameters implicit object, 401
RequestPart annotation, 121–122
ResponseStatusExceptionResolver, 200, 201
Role-based access control (RBAC)
    Account, 518, 521
    BookstoreUserDetailsService, 521, 522
    domain model, 518
    functionality, 518
    GrantedAuthority, 522
    information access, 518
    many-to-many association with permission,
        520
    many-to-many association with role, 519

permission entity, 520

S

Secure socket layer (SSL), 510
Security process, 477
SecurityHandlerInterceptor, 302
Selenium
   IDE
      copying to clipboard, 317
      for Firefox, 314–315
      JSP source, 314
      language selection, 317
      login, 314
      main window, 316
      scenario recording, 316
      WebDriver JUnit style, 318
   RC server, 310–312
   test writing, 312–314
   WebDriver project, 310
Servlet request scope, 379, 402
SessionAttributes, 143–144
<set> element, 401
Shared form tag attributes, 146
SimpleMappingExceptionResolver
   AnnotationMethodHandlerExceptionResolver, 204
   configuration, 201, 202
   ExceptionHandlerExceptionResolver, 204
   Improved Login Controller, 202–203
   Login page, 203
Snippet, 172
Spring development environment
   prerequisites
      integrated development environment, 2
      Java Development Kit, 2
      Servlet Container, 2
      software versions and download sites, 1
   sample application
      bookstore, 3–4
      deployment, 8–9
      ../gradlew build, 7–8
      gradlew script, 6–7
      STS (see SpringSource Tool Suite)
Spring expression language (Spring EL), 402
Spring framework
   application contexts
      configuration file, 36
      default configuration options, 35
      hierarchy, 38

MoneyTransferSpring class, 29–30
   org.springframework.web.context.WebApplicationContext interface, 34, 35
aspect-oriented programming, 45–47
component-scanning, 40–41
dependency injection
   annotation-based dependency injection, 33
   constructor-based dependency injection, 31
   contextualized lookup, 30 31
   hardcoded dependencies, 29–30
   IoC, 29
   setter-based dependency injection, 32
enabling features, 44–45
module dependency, 26–28
profiles, 41–44
resource loading, 38–40
scopes, 41
web applications, 47–50
Spring security, 477
   access authorization
      "add category", 528
      admin user, log in, 529
      authentication tag, 530–531
      authorize tag, navigation bar, 525
      code annotations, 531–532
      finer-grained permission checks, 526–527
      information, 523
      initial data setup, 524, 525
      JavaScript code, 527
      login and logout, 529
      manage books menu option, 528
      manageBooks.jsp page, 524
      tag library, pages, 523
   authentication and authorization schemes, 479
   basic security scheme, 481, 482
   bookstore
      access configuration, resource, 490–492
      addMappingForUrlPatterns, 485
      application filter chain configuration, 487
      authentication manager, 495
      complete security configuration, 503, 504
      core concept, 484
      expression methods and literals, 493–494
      filter, 484
      home page, 500–501
      logging out, 502–503
      login page, 498–500
      multiple filters, 485

Spring security, bookstore (*cont.*)
  namespace element/attribute, 488, 489
  namespaced filter chain configuration, 487
  one-way hashed password, 495
  password encoder, 496, 497
  resource, 489, 490
  right dependency, 482–483
  salted hash, 496, 497
  Spring class, constants, 484
  xml header, 486
configuration, 479
  chain.doFilter, 542, 543
  (Http)ServletRequest, 542
  isSecure(), 542
  spring-security.xml File, 544
database
  getPrincipal method, 506
  in-memory data store, 504
  SecurityContext, 505
  UserDetails object, 504, 505
declarative method, 480
flow bypass security, 481
flow security
  attributes addition, 507–508
  request mappings, 506
  SecurityFlowExecutionListener, 508–509
  URI, filter chain, 506
localization, 516–517
message localization, 480
RBAC (*see* Role-based access control)
Spring MVC, 480
transport security
  browser confirmation, 511
  CA, 510, 511
  HTTP, 510, 513, 514
  HTTPS, 514
  information encryption, 515, 516
  keytool, 512
  self signed certificate, 511
  SSL connector, 510, 513
  tomcat certificate, 514, 515
  URI, 513
Web Flow, 480
Spring Web Flow
  accessing scopes
    externalContext, 402
    flowRequestContext, 402
    RequestContext, 403
    Servlet request scopes, 402, 403
    Spring EL, 402

Unified EL, 402
action execution control
  <on-end> element, 404
  <on-entry> element, 404–405
  <on-exit> element, 405
  <on-render> element, 405
  <on-start> element, 404
  sub-elements, 405–406
bookstore enhancement (*see* Bookstore enhancement)
end state, 425–426
flow definition, 373–374
flow variables, 401
global transitions, 406
implicit objects, 379–381
java.util.Map, 400
scopes
  conversation, 378–379
  flash, 376–377
  flow, 377–378, 400, 401
  Java transient, 374
  java.io.Serializable, 374
  request, 374–376
  types, 374
  view, 377
subflows
  child flow, 407
  composition, 406
  inline flows, 407
  input/output mapping, 421–423
  modularity, 407
  vs. normal flow, 407
  normal top-level flow, 408
  order process, 423–425
  parent flow, 407
value attribute, 400
SpringSource tool suite (STS)
  dependency management, 5
  Extensions tab, 10
  gradle search results, 11
  index.jsp, 21
  IndexController code, 19, 20
  Install dialog box, 12
  Model Attribute, 20, 21
  sample importing, 12–16
  SpringSource vFabric tc Server, 17–19
  web page updation, 21, 22
Stress testing, 278
StringToEntityConverter, 156–157
Subflow, 373
  child flow, 407

composition, 406
inline flows, 407
input/output mapping, 421–423
modularity, 407
vs. normal flow, 407
normal top-level flow, 408
order process, 423–425
parent flow, 407
System testing, 278

T

@Test method, 283
TestNG, 281
Tomcat 6
    AnnotationConfigWebApplicationContext,
        540
    context.xml File, 541
    ContextLoaderListener, 539
    DispatcherServlet, 539
    filters configuration, 541
    XmlWebApplicationContext, 540
@Transactional annotation, 290
TransactionalTestExecutionListener, 290
Transport layer security (TSL). *See* Secure Socket
        Layer (SSL)
Type conversion
    account registration page, 161
    account registration page with error, 162
    configuration
        CategoryConverter configuration, 157
        FormatterRegistry interface, 155–156
        StringToEntityConverter, 156–157
    converters
        ConditionalGenericConverter API, 152
        ConversionService API, 152
        ConverterFactory API, 151
        GenericConverter API, 151–152
        interfaces, 150
    formatters
        AnnotationFormatterFactory, 154
        DateFormatAnnotationFormatterFactory,
            154–155
        Formatter API, 152–153
        sample DateFormatter, 153–154
    org.springframework.validation.BindingResu
        lt attribute, 160
    property editors, 149–150
    register.jsp file, 158
    registration page, 158

RegistrationController, 158–160
String instances, 148

U

Unified Expression Language (Unified EL), 402
Unit tests
    criteria, 278–279
    definition, 277
    JUnit
        @After method, 284
        annotation execution order, 284
        assertTrue and assertEquals methods, 283
        @Before annotation, 283
        DAO, 281–282
        DatabaseDao, 282–283
        test failure, 283
        test success, 283
        TestNG, 281
        @Test annotation, 283
        @Test method, 283
UriComponentsBuilder, 118
User acceptance testing, 278

V

ValidateDeliverydate method, 391, 394
ValidateSelectShop, 391
ValidationMessages.properties, 395
<var> element, 401
Version control system (VCS), 277
View resolvers
    BeanNameViewResolver, 239–240
    ContentNegotiatingViewResolver, 246–247
    getContentType method, 238
    hierarchy, 238, 239
    implementation, 247
    InternalResourceViewResolver, 245
    org.springframework.web.servlet, 238
    render method, 238
    ResourceBundleViewResolver, 241–243
    UrlBasedViewResolver, 243–245
    view rendering process, 237
    XmlViewResolver, 240–241
    XsltViewResolver, 245
View scope, 377
View technology
    excel
        OrderExcelView, 265–266
        ViewConfiguration class, 267

View technology (*cont.*)
    freemarker
        configuration, 257
        configurer property, 256
        Macros, 261, 262
        template language, 259–260
        templateLoaderPath, 256
        WEB-INF/freemarker/index.ftl, 258
    hierarchy, 248
    JasperReports
        configuration, 271
        multiformatview default mappings, 270
        report filling, 271
    Java Server Pages, 249
    JavaServer Faces, 249–250
    PDF
        configuration,
           ContentNegotiatingViewResolve, 264–265
        creation, 263–264
        generated PDF, 265
    tiles
        configuration, 250–251
        definitions files, 252
        Index JSP, 254
        template JSP, 252–253
        welcome page, 254
    velocity
        configuration, 257
        configurer property, 255
        dates and numbers, 262
        macros, 261, 262
        resourceLoaderPath, 256
        templating language, 259–260
        WEB-INF/velocity/index.vm, 258
    XML and JSON, 268–269

■ W, X, Y, Z

Web application architecture
    application layering, 53–55
    data access layer, 61–63
    domain layer, 56–57
    MVC Pattern, 51–53
    separation of concerns, 56
    user interface layer, 57–58
    web layer, 58–59
Web flow
    AJAX support
        Add button, Spring JS, 454
        addDecoration method, Spring JS, 454
        books selection, 448
        configuration, 447
        createOrders/selectBooks.jsp, 449
        extra dependency via gradle on Spring JS, 445
        Firebug's capture, 455–457
        JavaScript decoration, Spring JS, 455
        JavaScript dependency, 445
        JQuery, 457–459
        selectBooks.jsp after modification, 449–451
        showSelectedBooks.jsp view, 448
        tiles configuration, 451–453
    avoidance, 332
    bookstore sample application
        account, 367
        actual page, 359
        bold type, 365
        browser-rendered view, 366
        Buy books link, 360
        Controller Code execution, 362
        Controller Method, 367
        Delivery Options selection, 363
        delivery options—our delivery date, 370
        eventId<*on_transition*>, 360
        flow steps explanation, 354
        <form:select> element, 360
        header.jsp, 360
        Home Page creation, 355–356, 368
        http://localhost:8080/chapter10-bookstore/., 361
        implemention, 356
        <on-start> Element, 357, 358
        overview, 371–372
        page creation, 364–365
        Previous View State, 362
        Select Delivery Options Page, 368
        selectable books, 359, 362
        selectCategory View State, 358
        String, 358
        Tiles Configuration, 359
        Tiles Definition, 364
        View State, select delivery option, 367
    configuration
        .apress.prospringmvc.bookstore.web.config, 350
        automatically scan for flow definitions, 348
        dependency, 346
        flow builder services, 349–350

flow executor, 347
flow registry, 348
FlowHandlerAdapter and
   FlowHandlerMapping Beans, 351, 352
.prospringmvc.bookstore.web.interceptor
   , 350
src/main/resources/spring/webflow-
   config.xml and Web Flow configuration
   namespaces, 347
controlled navigation, 331
exception handling
   authenticationcontroller, 439
   Custom Exception Handler, 440–442
   On Exception Transition, 439
explicit form binding
   converter package, 443
   message keys, 444
   per-property based binding, 443
   preferred approach, 443
fine-grained scoping, 323
   automatic state management, 326–327
   bookstore web application, 323
   Context data, 324
   HTTP Sessions, 325
   myData, 324
   usage, 323
flow concept, 322
flow execution listeners
   configuration, 460
   eventSignaled, 461
   exceptionThrown, 463
   FlowExecutionListener interface, 459
   paused, 462
   requestSubmitted(RequestContext
      context, 461
   resuming, 462
   sessionCreating, 461
   sessionEnding, 462
   sessionStarting, 461
   stateEntering, 462
   transitionExecuting, 461
   viewRendering, 462
flow inheritance
   child flow, 431

mergeable and non-mergeable elements,
   430
merged flow, 432
parent attribute, 430
parent flow, 431
single view state, 431
flow managed persistence context
   binding and unbinding, 456
   database to view, 463–465
   end state, 467
   JpaFlowExecutionListener,, 467
   LazyInitializationException, 475
   new Orders overview page, 472
   OpenEntityManagerInViewFilter, 468
   orderDetail.jsp, 469
   registration, 466
   tiles definition, 470
   view link, 473
ingredients of
   apress.prospringmvc.bookstore.web.cont
      roller, 337
   cancel transition, 338
   choice, 334
   element multiplicity, 334
   evaluate action, 342–343
   flow and flow-graph tabs, 336
   flow definition, 335
   flow root element, 333
   namespace, 335
   selectCategory, 337
   state transitions, 341–342
   view state, 338–340
   XML Schema, 333–334
bookstore sample application, 363
PRG, 330, 331
request synchronization
   double submission, 329
   duplicate key, 327
   flow execution key, 328
   idempotent, 327
state inheritance, 434
Web Flow 1 migration, 437–439
WebApplicationContext, 306
WebDataBinder, 139–140
WebMvcContext, 171

CPSIA information can be obtained at www.ICGtesting.com
Printed in the USA
BVOW021836240612

293520BV00003B/17/P